Select Proceedings of the European Society of International Law

This book continues the series Select Proceedings of the European Society of International Law, containing the proceedings of the Fourth Biennial Conference organised by ESIL and the University of Cambridge in 2010. The title of the conference was 'International Law 1989–2010: A Performance Appraisal'. The highlights, selected for publication in this volume, cover a wide spectrum of topics in international law.

Select Proceedings of the European Society of International Law

Third Volume

International Law 1989–2010: A Performance Appraisal

Cambridge, 2–4 September 2010

Edited by

James Crawford and Sarah Nouwen

OXFORD AND PORTLAND, OREGON

2012

Hart Publishing, 16C Worcester Place, OX1 2JW
Telephone: +44 (0)1865 517530 Fax: +44 (0)1865 510710
E-mail: mail@hartpub.co.uk
Website: http://www.hartpub.co.uk

Published in North America (US and Canada) by
Hart Publishing
c/o International Specialized Book Services
920 NE 58th Avenue, Suite 300
Portland, OR 97213-3786
USA
Tel: +1 503 287 3093 or toll-free: (1) 800 944 6190
Fax: +1 503 280 8832
E-mail: orders@isbs.com
Website: www.isbs.com

British Library Cataloguing in Publication Data
Data Available

ISBN: 978-1-84946-202-0

Typeset by Criteria International

Printed and bound in Great Britain by
CPI Goup (UK) Ltd, Croydon, CRO 4YY

Foreword

HÉLÈNE RUIZ FABRI* AND ANNE PETERS**

LA QUATRIÈME CONFÉRENCE biennale de la Société européenne de droit international, tenue à l'invitation du Professeur James Crawford et de son équipe du Lauterpacht Centre for International Law, et dont le présent ouvrage rend disponibles la plupart des meilleures communications qui y ont été faites, a été un très grand succès. Tous les ingrédients étaient réunis à cette fin : un thème général stimulant décliné en de multiples sujets permettant de capturer les aspects les plus actuels de l'évolution du droit international, un auditoire nombreux mêlant toutes les générations, les spécialités, les nationalités, dans un lieu prestigieux empreint d'histoire et à l'avant-garde de la réflexion sur le droit international. Comme on pouvait s'y attendre et comme cet ouvrage en porte témoignage, une réflexion et une évaluation d'ensemble portant sur l'évolution du droit international au cours des deux dernières décennies a autant soulevé de questions qu'apporté de réponses. Elles ont, en toute hypothèse, donné l'occasion d'un vaste partage d'idées et de l'expression d'une belle diversité.

Cela correspond précisément à la vocation de la Société européenne qui puise dans chacun de ces événements et dans les publications auxquelles ils donnent lieu un dynamisme renouvelé. Nous souhaitons à cet ouvrage un destin éditorial à l'image du succès qu'a été la Conférence de Cambridge. Nous souhaitons qu'il donne envie à ceux qui ne le sont pas encore de devenir membres de la Société Européenne de Droit International et de participer à ses activités.

Enfin, nous exprimons notre très grande et chaleureuse gratitude au Professeur James Crawford et à son équipe non seulement pour avoir organisé la Conférence mais aussi en rendre aussi rapidement les résultats disponibles au plus grand nombre.

* Présidente de la SEDI, 2006–2010.
** Présidente de la SEDI, 2010–2014.

Foreword

SIR ELIHU LAUTERPACHT*

THE FOURTH BIENNIAL conference of the European Society of International Law demonstrated the extent to which international law has become a subject of ever-growing and now widespread attention. These conference proceedings demonstrate how, during the years 1989–2010, international law has expanded in range, substance, depth and technique. There are, for instance, new techniques for treaty making and for dispute settlement, none of which were dreamt of in the first decades of the last century. The great international lawyers of those days would surely be both surprised and pleased to see the vibrancy of their subject. The proceedings here recorded will no doubt keep the debates at ESIL 2010 alive for many years.

* Founder of the Lauterpacht Centre for International Law at the University of Cambridge.

Table of Contents

Introduction

JAMES CRAWFORD* AND SARAH NOUWEN**

'DON'T BE AFRAID of the Performance Appraisal', we wrote in the programme of the fourth biennial conference of the European Society of International Law that took place in Cambridge, UK, from 2 to 4 September 2010. There appeared to be little fear: our invited speakers jumped at the idea of assessing the performance of international law between 1989 and 2010. So did more than four hundred lawyers from across the globe who submitted abstracts in response to the questions of how international law, international institutions and international lawyers had fared in the 21 years since the fall of the Berlin Wall. This third volume of the Select Proceedings of the European Society of International Law contains a selection of the invited and selected speakers' answers to these questions.

Representing a multitude of views, this book employs keynote speaker Andrew Hurrell's 'eyes of many people' in order to guard against parochialism. Assessing the performance of the international system in the opening chapter, Hurrell observes how international society faces classical Westphalian challenges in a post-Westphalian context. In her response to Hurrell, Judge Xue Hanqin emphasises what has remained the same, while Daniel Bethlehem, FCO Legal Adviser, focuses on what must change. Bethlehem advocates a post-Westphalian discourse and warns against equating the performance of the international system with that of the international *legal* system. In their respective chapters, Tibor Varády and Randall Lesaffer take these issues further, Varády analysing changes in the discourse and Lesaffer assessing the importance of 1989 in international law. Jean d'Aspremont and Georg Nolte's chapters on democracy and change conclude the book's opening part on 'The World and International Law'.

Part II is devoted to developments in Legalisation and Law-making between 1989 and 2010. Alain Pellet and André Nollkaemper assess the meaning of the increase in international law, in Pellet's case an assessment notably pessimistic. Anne-Thida Norodom, Jörg Kammerhofer and Marjan Ajevski scrutinise the role of the Security Council, scholars and international criminal judges, respectively, in international law-making. George Galindo and Antonios Tzanakopoulos discuss the ever more important role of the domestic judge in applying international law.

Parts III, IV and V review post-Cold-War developments of specific international actors: the state, international institutions and regional organisations. In Part III, Anne Peters and Boldizsár Nagy shed new light on international law's classic protagonist, the state; while international-relations scholar Tarak Barkawi comments acerbically on their chapters. Taken together, these chapters reveal fundamental disagreements on the use

* Whewell Professor of International Law, University of Cambridge.
** Mayer Brown Research Fellow in Public International Law, University of Cambridge.

of history in law and underline Hurrell's point of the need for a discourse transcending disciplinary parishes.

Part IV turns to international institutions. Jan Klabbers discusses how to guard the guardians and Pierre Klein examines ways in which practice has answered this question. Yuval Shany measures the effectiveness of international courts from the perspective of compliance with their decisions. Stefan Talmon reveals how the Security Council has both dispensed, and dispensed with, international law in its burgeoning post-1989 practice. Edward Guntrip and Martins Paparinskis focus on international investment law.

In Part V, Lucie Delabie, Alberta Fabbricotti, Geert de Baere and Isabelle van Damme put legal regionalism at the centre of the discussion.

Part VI queries whether international law as it stands in 2010 is ready for the challenges we face. Matthew Gillett and Christine Larssen look at the relationship between law, individual citizens and the environment, Michael Waibel illuminates the dark area of international financial law and Sundhya Pahuja excoriates the 'poverty of development and the development of poverty' in international law.

In Part VII, five rapporteurs provide answers to the one conference question that appeared to have instilled some fear: how have we as international lawyers performed? With the conference as a case study, Guglielmo Verdirame, Jochen von Bernstorff, Anne Lagerwall, Thomas Skouteris and Amanda Perreau-Saussine point out the paradoxes, taboos and unquestioned agreements of our field. Joining the other contributors, they set the profession an agenda: clarity of language, engagement with policy, and development of ideas as to what a 'transformed' international law might actually entail.

Identifying the human heart as one more area in need of urgent attention, Roger O'Keefe's epilogue notes that whether or not there are silences in the law, international lawyers are never silent. At the conference, O'Keefe's observations remedied the observed problem: the audience was speechless with laughter. It was a brilliant and pointed coda to the proceedings.

* * *

The fourth ESIL Conference was organised by the Lauterpacht Centre of International Law. Thanks are due to Anita Rutherford, the Centre's Administrator, to Tara Grant for design, website management and much else, to Jean-Baptiste Fourcade, Karen Fachechi and many others. Alexis Glazer assisted in the copy editing of these Proceedings.

Lauterpacht Centre for International Law
Cambridge, December 2010

Part I:

1989–2010: The World and International Law

1

International Law 1989–2010: A Performance Appraisal

ANDREW HURRELL*

THE IDEA OF appraising the performance of international law across the post-Cold War years clearly represents a daunting challenge. It is daunting in terms of the range of possible criteria that might be used to evaluate performance—Justice? Legitimacy? Effectiveness? Survival? It is daunting in terms of the politics of place. All theories and evaluative schema are bounded by place and draw their relevance from the particular contexts in which they are developed and deployed. Indeed this is a central part of the intellectual challenge involved in studying global governance or global order. This necessarily presses us to imagine what patterns of order and governance look like—analytically and normatively—when we stand back from the parochial preoccupations of Washington, or Berlin, or Beijing, or New Delhi.

And it is daunting in terms of the politics of time. Trying to appraise and evaluate international law in the post-Cold War period must necessarily involve some view of how the period fits within broader narratives of historical change. On one side, as I will suggest, this means revising our views of how the Cold War and post-Cold War periods are linked and questioning the claim that the end of the Cold War represents quite such a decisive break in patterns of global politics as is often claimed. It also involves taking a position on where we might now be standing. On this question, we can, I believe, get a sense of the post-Cold War period as one that is now moving towards an end.

The tectonic plates are indeed shifting. Both the international political system and the structures of global capitalism are in a state of flux and uncertainty. Power is shifting in global politics from the old G7 to a new group of emerging powers. The global system is increasingly characterised by a diffusion of power, including to emerging and regional powers; by a diffusion of preferences with many more voices demanding to be heard both globally and within states as a result of globalisation and democratisation; and by a diffusion of ideas and values, with a reopening of the big questions of social, economic and political organisation that were supposedly brought to an end with the end of the Cold War and the liberal ascendancy. There is a strong argument that we are witnessing the most powerful set of challenges yet to the global order that the United States sought to construct within its own camp during the Cold War and to globalise in the post-

* Montague Burton Professor of International Relations and a Fellow of Balliol College, Oxford.

Cold War period. Many of these challenges also raise questions about the longer-term position of the Anglo-American and European global order that rose to dominance in the middle of the nineteenth century and around which so many conceptions and practices of power-political order, international legal construction and global economic governance have since been constructed.

It is for international lawyers themselves to discuss and debate the detailed and technical evolution of the international legal order itself. I am going to avoid any direct assault on the assembled mass ranks of the international legal community and, instead, probe down the flanks. In the first part of this lecture, I will say a little about the evolution of global politics in the post-Cold War period and consider some of the complex and contradictory ways in which this evolution has shaped debates about the legal order and about how international law might be appraised. In the second part of these remarks I will turn to arguments about global justice, again looking for connections between the performance of international law on the one hand and its normative aspirations and imaginative possibilities on the other.

I.

In the 1990s global order was widely understood through the lens of liberal internationalism or liberal solidarism.[1] Globalisation was rendering obsolete the old Westphalian world of Great Power rivalries, balance of power politics and an old-fashioned international law built around state sovereignty and strict rules of non-intervention. Bumpy as it might be, the road seemed to be leading away from Westphalia—with an expanded role for formal and informal multilateral institutions; a huge increase in the scope, density and intrusiveness of rules and norms made at the international level but affecting how domestic societies are organised; the ever-greater involvement of new actors in global governance; the moves towards the coercive enforcement of global rules; and fundamental changes in political, legal and moral understandings of state sovereignty and of the relationship between the state, the citizen and the international community.

In addition to an expansion of inter-state modes of governance, increased attention was being paid to the world of complex governance beyond the state. Such governance was characterised by the complexity of global rule-making; the role of private market actors and civil society groups in articulating values which are then assimilated in inter-state institutions; and the increased range of informal, yet norm-governed, governance mechanisms often built around complex networks, both transnational and trans-governmental, and the inter-penetration of international and municipal law and of national administrative systems. From this perspective the state was losing its place as the privileged sovereign institution and instead becomes one of many actors and one participant in a broader and more complex social and legal process.

Such developments were central both to the evolving practice of international law and to those who sought to chart and map its changing character—as, for example, Joseph Weiler's geological metaphor of four different layers of law and of law-making—from predominantly bi-lateral, contractual treaties, to a much greater emphasis on multilateral

[1] I examine these trends in more detail in Andrew Hurrell, *On Global Order. Power, Values and the Constitution of International Society* (Oxford, Oxford University Press, 2007) especially Ch 3.

agreements, to important constitutional treaties (such as the UN Charter), to an ever-thickening layer of administrative and regulatory rules.[2]

These developments posed great analytical and practical challenges for international law. A vast amount of normatively framed regulatory practice and global administration was emerging that did not at all easily fit within the standard model of law between states. Such rule-making and regulatory practice is hard to square with traditional doctrinal ideas of sources, of state voluntarism, of even delegated consent. The optimists did not seem to worry overmuch: they saw great potential in the disaggregated state, in fluid and flexible networks of experts, and in the claims that dynamic experimental rule making can be both efficient and deliberatively inclusive.[3] Skeptics worried about precisely these same features—the dangers posed by the often hidden rule by experts and embedded orthodoxy, the marginalisation of meaningful politics, and the perils of de-formalisation and of the deepening fragmentation of the legal 'system'.[4]

John Rawls famously observed that 'the correct regulative principle for a thing depends on the nature of that thing'.[5] The post-1989 period may indeed have been a period of intensive legalisation. Law may indeed have become ever more central—both functionally but also as a broadly appealed-to source of normative judgement. But, in the case of the international legal order, the nature of the 'thing' is extraordinarily difficult to pin down, identify and categorise. For example, it seems clear that many innovations in governance and many developments in international law have shifted or eroded our understandings of public and private and of the boundaries between them. If so, it follows that finding adequate regulative principles must involve broadening our understandings about what constitutes public power at the international or global level; that we can no longer see states as the only subjects of political legitimacy; and that we should instead concern ourselves with all those forms of power that constrain the autonomy or welfare of those subject to them. Others have sought to use notions of publicness and principles derived from public law as a basis for understanding legal normativity within the global administrative spaces that have become such an important element of global governance and for preserving the distinctively legal character of law in the face of rampant instrumentalism.[6] Much of the debate on the character of the legal order has been framed in terms of a set of choices: reassert the old doctrinal practices and boundaries; move forward to some variety of global constitutionalism; or try to navigate the messy byways of the new legal pluralism.[7]

[2] Joseph Weiler, 'The Geology of International Law: Governance, Democracy, and Legitimacy' (2004) *Heidelberg Journal of International Law* 624.

[3] See, for example, Anne-Marie Slaughter, *A New World Order* (Princeton, Princeton University Press, 2004); and Charles Sabel and Jonathan Zeitlin (eds), *Experimentalist Governance in the European Union* (Oxford, Oxford University Press, 2010).

[4] See, for example, Martti Koskenniemi, 'Miserable Comforters: International Relations as New Natural Law' (2009) 15 *European Journal of International Law* 395.

[5] John Rawls, *A Theory of Justice*, revised edn (Cambridge, Mass, Harvard University Press, 1999) 25.

[6] See Benedict Kingsbury, 'The Concept of "Law" in Global Administrative Law' (2009) 20 *European Journal of International Law* 23.

[7] Nico Krisch, *Beyond Constitutionalism. The Pluralist Structure of Postnational Law* (Oxford, Oxford University Press, 2010).

How to Explain What Was Going on?

Academics, especially in Europe and the United States, told three kinds of liberal stories. Some stressed institutions and the cooperative logic of institutions. Institutions are needed to deal with the ever more complex dilemmas of collective action that emerge in a globalised world. The complexity of the governance challenges meant that international law and international regimes would necessarily increase in number, scope and variety. It also meant that as large states, including large developing states, expanded their range of interests and integrated more fully into the global economy and world society—as they 'joined the world' in the idiom of the 1990s—they would be naturally drawn by the functional benefits provided by institutions and pressed towards more cooperative and 'responsible' patterns of behaviour. The process would not necessarily be easy or automatic; but, on this view, the broad direction of travel is clear.

Others stressed the Kantian idea of the gradual but progressive diffusion of liberal values, partly as a result of liberal economics and increased economic interdependence, partly as a liberal legal order comes to sustain the autonomy of a global civil society, and partly as a result of the successful example set by the multifaceted liberal capitalist system of states.

A third group told a more US-centred story. The US was indeed the centre of a unipolar world. But, true both to its own values and its rational self-interest, Washington had a continued incentive to bind itself within the institutions that it had created in the Cold War era in order to reassure smaller states and to prevent balancing against US power. A rational hegemon in an age of globalisation would understand the importance and utility of soft power. In return for this self-binding and the procedural legitimacy it would create, and in return for US-supplied global public goods and the output legitimacy that they would create, other states would acquiesce and accept the role of the United States as the owner and operator of the system.[8]

The challenge of the Second World had been seen off. Through a mix of these three processes those states of the old Third World that had previously challenged the western order would now become increasingly enmeshed, socialised and integrated. The nature and dynamics of power were changing. Soft power would outstrip hard coercive power in importance and concentrations of liberal power would attract rather than repel or threaten. Just as the example of a liberal and successful EU had created powerful incentives on the part of weaker and neighbouring states towards emulation and a desire for membership, so, on a larger scale and over a longer period, a similar pattern would be observed in the case of the liberal, developed world as a whole. A new *raison de système* would emerge that would alter and ultimately displace old-fashioned notions of *raison d'état*.

The 1990s, then, were marked by a clear sense of the liberal ascendancy; a clear assumption that the US had the right and power to decide what the 'liberal global order' was all about; and a clear belief that the western order worked and that it had the answers. Yes, of course there would be isolated rogues and radical rejectionists. But they were on the 'wrong side of history' as President Clinton confidently proclaimed.

[8] For the elaboration of this logic see G John Ikenberry, *After Victory: Institutions, Strategic Restraint, and the Rebuilding of Order after Major Wars* (Princeton, Princeton University Press, 2001).

Two other points should be noted here.

First, this was a period in which an enormous normative ambition ran together with relatively weak institutionalisation. Through the 1990s the normative ambition of the international legal order continued to expand dramatically. But these expansive and expanding goals were to be achieved on the back of very thin institutional structures—lots of networks, lots of market mechanisms, lots of private or hybrid governance; but rather little in the way of serious multilateralism or institutional renewal or reform. A comparison with the world order debates of the late 1940s is instructive. Looking back it is hard to avoid the conclusion that much of the talk of global governance was a rhetorical façade. The real heavy lifting was to be done by the apparently effective centralisation of power around the United States and a liberal Greater West.

Second, this was a period of striking and far-reaching legal and normative revisionism. It is often simply assumed that the dominant state or group of states in terms of power can be associated with the status quo. It is emerging states or rising powers that seek to challenge the 'basic norms of the system' or to revise its 'foundational principles'.[9] However, any status quo has at least two dimensions, the first focused more or less directly on the distribution of material power; the second on the character of the international order and its dominant norms. From the perspective of the dominant norms of the system, the United States has rarely been a status quo power and, as its power has grown so too has the revisionist character of its foreign policy. Since the end of the Cold War it has been in many ways a strongly revisionist power, sometimes a revolutionary power: in the 1990s in terms of pressing for new norms on intervention and for the opening of markets and for the embedding of particular sets of liberal values within international institutions; in the early years of this century, in terms of its attempt to recast norms on regime change, on the use of force, and on the conditionality of sovereignty more generally.[10] Hence, for example, the states of the Global South have not faced the United States within a stable notion of a 'Westphalian order'. Quite the contrary. Just as countries such as China had come to accept and to stress many of the core principles of the old pluralist system (non-intervention, hard sovereignty, hierarchy based on power), the dominant western states were insisting that many of the most important norms of the system ought to change, above all in ways that threatened greater interventionism and sought to mould the ways in which societies were to be ordered domestically. Nor is this simply a story of a traditional sovereignty-obsessed South seeking to remain in its comfort zone. In the case of climate change, it has been the South that has sought to protect the globalist commitments of Kyoto against the revisionism of the United States and some of its allies. Understanding the contested character of notions of 'status quo' and 'revisionism' and the political construction of ideas about 'responsible behaviour' is fundamental to understanding the ways in which changes in the distribution of power may be affecting the international legal order.

[9] On this debate see Steve Chan, 'Can't Get No Satisfaction? The Recognition of Revisionist States' (2004) 4 *International Journal of Asia-Pacific* 207.

[10] This brief summary should not imply that the sources of US revisionism run as a continuous thread through the post-Cold War period. Whilst there are important continuities both before and after the second Bush administration, there are major differences. In particular, the neo-conservative self-description of themselves as 'hard Wilsonians' should not disguise the extent to which the Bush administration was, in Drolet's words, 'ferociously predatory on liberal values'. See Jean-Francois Drolet, 'A Liberalism Betrayed? American Neo-Conservatism and the Theory of International Relations' (2010) 15 *Journal of Political Ideologies* 89.

II.

However, even before we get to the Bush Administration and to September 11, and certainly well before the financial crisis, it was clear that these sorts of liberal narratives represented only one part of the picture. Much of the academic analysis of international law and international order in the post-Cold War period took the form of critique—drawing out the many flaws of the liberal image of the 1990s and giving far greater weight to inequality, hierarchy and coercion.

Although analytically beguiling, liberal writing on global governance tended to skirt far too easily over the problem of managing power, especially unequal power, and the difficulties of mediating between conflicting values. Debates on governance focused on the identification of collective action problems and on the question of how global public goods are to be provided. The alternative view was sidelined, namely seeing governance as concerned with the ordering and preservation of power and with answers to the question of who exercises power. On whose behalf? And to whose detriment? Equally, liberal interest-driven accounts of the problems of global governance all too often disguised or evaded the deep conflict over values, underlying purposes and ways of seeing the world. Normatively, debates on governance were often dominated by issues of efficiency and effectiveness, rather than questions of moral worth, of whether a particular arrangement is good or bad, right or wrong.

Academic debates on global order were dominated by a dual liberal hegemony: a historicist hegemony that has too easily assumed that history is moving down a one-way street; and an analytical liberal hegemony that has tended to work with a narrow notion of agency; with too little room for the historical analysis of the structures within which supposedly a-historical logics of rational choice and collective action play out; and still less room for understanding their temporal and geographical rootedness.

It is here, of course, that we can place the upsurge in work that sought to analyze the links between international law on the one side and hegemony and empire on the other. It is here, too, that we can place the critical work that has been done on the pathologies of humanitarianism, on the dark side of human rights, as well as the worsening position of those such as refugees and the displaced who have never been very securely protected within the so-called liberal order even at the level of normative aspiration—and whose position continued to worsen through the period.

This work is of great importance. But, as a persistent sceptic about US empire, I think that we need to focus more on the long list of other developments that were gathering pace through the period and which, cumulatively, have been taking us towards a rather different destination.

These include (1) the renewed salience of security, the re-valorisation of national security as a value that can and—for a dispiritingly large number of people—should trump ideas of universal human rights, and a renewed preoccupation with war-fighting and counter-insurgency; (2) the continued or renewed power of nationalism, no longer potentially containable politically or analytically in a box marked 'ethnic conflict' but manifest in the identity politics and foreign policy actions of the major states in the system; (3) the renewed importance of nuclear weapons as central to major power relations, to the structure of regional security complexes, and in the construction of great power hierarchies and the distribution of seats at top tables; (4) the national and transnational power of religion (both aspects matter); and (5) the quiet return of balance of power as both a motivation for state policy (as with US policies in Asia) and as an element in the foreign policy of all second-tier states—not hard balancing and the building up of hard power; but soft balancing either in the form of attempts explicitly to de-legitimise US hegemony, to argue for alternative conceptions of legitimacy, and to reflect demands for status and recognition.[11]

Still more important, as the 1990s progressed so economic globalisation fed back into the structures and dynamics of a Westphalian state system rather than pointing towards its transcendence. The state as an economic actor proved resilient in seeking to control economic flows and to police borders; and in seeking to exploit and develop state-based and mercantilist modes of managing economic problems, especially in relation to resource competition and energy geopolitics. Most significant, the very dynamism and successes of liberal globalisation were having a vital impact on the distribution of inter-state political power—above all towards the East and parts of the South. If the debate over power shifts in the 1990s concentrated on the shift of power from states to firms and non-state actors, the 'power shift' of the past decade has focused on rising and emerging powers, on state-directed economic activity, and on the mismatch between existing global economic governance arrangements and the distribution of power amongst those with the actual power of effective economic decision.

The global financial crisis fed into these changes. In part this has been the result of the degree to which emerging economies have been relatively less directly affected. But in part it has followed from less direct impacts. For many influential figures in the emerging powers it is historically extremely significant that the financial crisis broke out and most seriously damaged both the economies but also the technical and moral authority of the centre of the global capitalist system. The crisis has also shifted the balance of arguments back to those who stress the advantages of large, continentally sized or regionally dominant states—states that are able to depend on large domestic markets, to politicise market relations globally and regionally, and to engage in effective economic mercantilism and resource competition.

It is of course possible to see these developments simply as international relations returning once more to its 'Westphalian norm'—the return of history and the end of dreams, as Kagan would have it.[12] But it is more accurate and more helpful to face up to the complex, hybrid and contested character of international society—a society that faces a range of classical Westphalian challenges (especially to do with power transition and the rise of new powers) but one that faces these challenges in a context marked by strong post-Westphalian characteristics (in terms of the material conditions of globalisation, the changed character of legitimacy, and the changed balance between the international and the domestic, even in large, introspective societies). My core argument is that it is this mixed, hybrid and contested character of the international political order that poses the most serious challenges to international law.

It is post-Westphalian, first of all, because of the structural changes in the nature of the foreign policy and governance challenges faced both by individual states and by international society collectively. Dealing with these challenges—climate change,

[11] On the idea of soft balancing see Stephen G Brooks and William C Wohlforth, *World Out of Balance. International Relations and the Challenge of American Primacy* (Princeton, Princeton University Press, 2008); and Andrew Hurrell, 'Hegemony, Liberalism and Global Order: What Space for Would-be Great Powers?' (2006) 82 *International Affairs* 1.

[12] Robert Kagan, *The Return of History and the End of Dreams* (New York, Vintage, 2009).

stable trade rules, flu pandemics, a credible system of global finance—will continue to involve the sustaining of rules that shape how societies are organised domestically; that are structurally tied to transnational processes, that go beyond entrenched notions of territoriality and sovereignty, that depend on the active and effective participation of a wide range of actors, and that necessitate many varied forms of governance, international law and international political organisation. For all the revived importance of Westphalian-style power-politics, this is a structural and probably irreversible change.

It is post-Westphalian, second, because of the changing problem of legitimacy.[13] All states and social orders need to gain the authority and legitimacy that the possession of crude power can never on its own secure. All major powers face the imperative of trying to turn a capacity for crude coercion into legitimate authority. The Bush years marked the bankruptcy of hegemonic or top-down modes of governance. The financial crisis has exacerbated the already evident decline in the idea that the legitimacy of international institutions could be grounded in claims to superior economic or technological knowledge. The inherited institutions of the western-led international order have proved manifestly dysfunctional and neither leading market actors nor technical specialists have ready ideas and answers. Legitimacy based on effective outputs and on technical knowledge is therefore likely to be in short supply and likely to strengthen demands for institutions to expand their membership in order to increase their legitimacy and representative authority.

But, whatever the short-term fixes (such as revising the voting structure of the international financial institutions or reforming membership of the UN Security Council) the deeper and far more fundamental issue concerns the meaning of global democracy in the 21st century. It has become ever harder to avoid discussion of the proper scope of democratic ideas beyond the state and how the values of democracy should be applied to global governance and to the global social choices that will inevitably shape the life chances of individuals and communities in the 21st century. Pressed by emerging powers and new social forces, the notion that the current distribution of decision-making power can be defended in democratic terms is likely to come under increasing attack. Indeed such arguments may well come to play the sort of critical role in the 21st century that the idea of national self-determination played in the 20th century.

The third element of post-Westphalian context has to do with what one might call the 'provincialising of Westphalia' and the shift in power away from the core western industrialised world—historically first built around Europe and the European colonial order and then around the United States and the Greater West. It is increasingly difficult to see the western state-based order either as a universal model or as the stable core of a successful global system.

It is here that we need to historicise the post-Cold War period. Instead of a Kojevian Hegelianism pointing to the end of history, it is important to see just how closely the dynamics of emerging powers today pick up on historically deep-rooted trends. We can, for example, think back to the 1970s—and to the debates about the rise of the Third World and the challenges to the western order; to the way in which North/South cleavages were shaping the politics of new global issues such as the environment, resource scarcity and nuclear non-proliferation; to the tensions within the capitalist core as the Keynesian orthodoxy unravelled in the face of social conflict, low growth and high inflation; and to the debates

[13] On the changing character of legal legitimacy see Jutta Brunnée and Stephen Toope, *Legitimacy and Legality in International Law: An Interactional Account* (Cambridge, Cambridge University Press, 2010).

surrounding the hegemonic decline of the United States. From the perspective of today's emerging powers we need to ask how far ideas and policies, maybe even identities, shaped within that earlier period were actually displaced by the adjustments to market-liberal globalisation in the 1990s and how much has persisted.

From the perspective of the core powers, we need to ask how far the solutions to the challenges of the 1970s helped to create the conditions for the diffusion of power today. One major response was to foster, encourage and enforce an aggressive phase of liberal globalisation, especially of financial globalisation. And yet it was precisely the particular character of economic globalisation and the debt-fuelled growth that helped to create the conditions both for the successful emerging economies of today and for the current challenges to US and western power and authority. The other central feature of the US policy in the 1970s was to revive a policy of active and aggressive interventionism in the South as part of the Second Cold War. Again, whilst this may have been a successful element in the victory of the West in the Cold War, it also helped to foster, or deepen, or shift the character of many of the conflicts that are proving so intractable to Washington today, especially in relation to the Islamic world. Seen in terms of both these responses the long 1970s become more important in understanding where we are today; and the end of the Cold War rather less so. As Arne Westad has suggested, such a conclusion appears more evident when we look back at the Cold War from a global rather than US or superpower-centric perspective.[14] Thus, as we reassess the 1970s we might also profitably view the power transitions currently underway not in terms of some a-historical process by which Great Powers rise and fall, but rather in terms of the gradual provincialising or de-centering of a western-dominated legal, political and economic order that developed in the second half of the 19th century.

Critical and post-colonial scholarship has challenged both the easy dichotomy between the 'West' and the 'Non-West' and also the confident and complacent, image of a global international society created via the universalisation of essentially European institutions for the maintenance of order and the pursuit of justice. The 'West' was itself formed through its long (and extremely bloody) engagement with the non-western world. And, as Dipesh Chakrabarty has argued, European thought itself and the categories of western international law and relations are a potential snare. They are both indispensable for understanding non-European political modernity and deeply flawed because of the way in which the categories of European thought are themselves implicated in the production of a world of hierarchy and domination.[15] But, however problematic the language that we may be forced to use, the challenge posed by contemporary power shifts to a western dominated legal order remains one of the most important features of our contemporary world.

Let me briefly draw out three sets of implications from this picture of a mixed or hybrid order, the first in terms of institutions, the second in terms of actors, and the third in terms of domestic politics.

Much of the early work on cooperation in International Relations sought to explain the general conditions under which cooperation might occur. Subsequent work focused on the features of particular institutions and on the factors that explain the 'rational design' of

[14] Odd Arne Westad, *The Global Cold War and the Making of Our Times* (Cambridge, CUP, 2006).

[15] Dipesh Chakrabarty, *Provincializing Europe: Post-Colonial Thought and Historical Difference* (Princeton, Princeton University Press, 2000).

institutions. More recently attention has shifted to discussion of 'regime complexity'—the presence of nested, partially overlapping, and parallel international regimes that are not hierarchically ordered.[16] There are clearly important linkages between these discussions of regime complexity within International Relations and the international legal concern with fragmentation.[17]

There are many factors and forces that lie behind the complex and fragmented structure of governance that exists in most issue areas. Many have to do with the complex dynamics of globalisation and with the way in which the range and variety of regimes can be viewed as a market-like response to complex challenges. But other factors are powerfully connected to the hybrid character of the global order that I discussed earlier. Alongside formal multilateral institutions and complex governance beyond the state, the post-1990 period witnessed a steadily increasing emphasis on different sorts of informal groupings, clubs, concerts and coalitions. And, as times become more troubled, one possible route is to try and return to a far more Great Power-centred order—both to get greater consensus and effectiveness in tackling the new and complex challenges such as climate change, terrorism and global economic governance but also as a direct response to the shifting distribution of power and the rise of new emerging powers.

Pressure to move in this direction also comes from the perception in Washington that the US must reduce the range of its burdens. This is reinforced by the view in Washington and elsewhere that, whilst formal multilateralism might be legitimate, it is also a bad way to reach agreements (clearly demonstrated for many by the climate change negotiations in Copenhagen) as well as ineffective when it comes to enforcement (as illustrated for many by the problems of enforcing sanctions against Iran). Thus ideological scepticism towards multilateralism has given way to a more pragmatic scepticism. But, whilst the particular emphasis has varied, the bottom line is clear: revising and reforming global order is about re-arranging the seats around the table to include those with the power and the relevant interests, as well as in some cases expanding the size of the table—as in the move from the G7/8 to the G20. The chairs around the table would be re-arranged and the table probably expanded. There would be a good deal of 'global à la cartism'—a mosaic of different groupings and a great deal of 'messy multilateralism'.[18]

It is certainly the case that much of this thinking picks up on the need for 'better' global governance. In part, new groupings and concerts would be functional and be formed according to the needs of the problem in hand. But issue-specific interests, functional problem-solving, and the provision of global public goods would be only one part of the story. The really important thing about such groupings is that their logic would be power-centred—both in terms of negotiating bargains quite narrowly around the core interests of the major powers and in terms of the forums being essentially hierarchical and exclusionary.

It is clearly difficult to move very far towards this kind of more power-centred order without coming into conflict or tension with important elements of the global liberal order that the US has espoused, especially since the end of the Cold War. For example,

[16] See Karen J Alter and Sophie Meunier, 'The Politics of International Regime Complexity' (2009) 7 *Perspectives on Politics* 13.

[17] Eyal Benvenisti and George Downs, 'The Empire's New Clothes: Political Economy and the Fragmentation of International Law' (2007) 60 *Stanford Law Review* 595; M Koskenniemi and P Leino, 'Fragmentation of International Law? Postmodern Anxieties' (2002) 15 *Leiden Journal of International Law* 553.

[18] Richard Haas, 'The Case for Messy Multilateralism', *Financial Times*, 5 January 2010.

accommodating the regional interests of other players by accepting claims for regional predominance cannot be easily compatible with expansive notions of democratisation and human rights. And it is perhaps harder still to move in this direction without coming into tension with even weak liberal notions of constitutionalism and the global rule of law, with their emphasis on such important procedural virtues as reason-giving, consultation and giving voice, transparency and accountability, and epistemic and moral openness. Even if ad hoc groupings and coalitions of major powers are supposed to act according to agreed international principles, where are such principles themselves supposed to come from? And by what principles other than effective power are the groupings themselves to be formed?

This leads to the question of actors. Multilateralism worked for much of the post-1945 period because it was not very multilateral. It was centred around a core of western developed states and many of the major institutions were dominated either by the US alone or by a small group of western and industrialised states. It excluded the Soviet bloc and the Soviet threat was essential to managing the geo-economic challenge posed by the economic rise of Japan, South Korean and the other Asian NICs (newly industrialising countries) from the middle of the 1960s on. The Third World played only a marginal role and, where it was engaged, its interests were limited and overwhelmingly defensive (very clearly illustrated by developing country participation in the GATT).

Today the situation is very different. Today's new emerging and regional powers are indispensable members of any viable global order. From a power-centred perspective such states are seen as central to the dynamics of the balance of power in the 21st century, as well as to the possible emergence of new concert-style groupings of major powers. From an institutionalist perspective such states are also crucial. Their detachment or opposition to current institutions is correctly seen as one of the most important weaknesses of existing institutions—think of the move away from the World Bank and IMF on the part of major emerging economies, or the opposition to developed country preferences in the WTO led by Brazil and India, or the effective breakdown of the global aid regime in the face of the new aid donors such as China and India. Such countries are clearly substantively critical to the management of major global issues such as climate change or nuclear proliferation. But they are also procedurally critical if international institutions are to re-establish legitimacy and a degree of representativeness, for example through reform of the United Nations Security Council or of the international financial institutions.

One obvious consequence of these changes is a greater heterogeneity of interests. From this perspective it is important that China, India and Brazil are large developing countries and that they will remain relatively poor in per capita terms. This has shaped—and will continue to shape—their conception of interests; it has forced a heavy priority on domestic development; it has tended to engender resistance to those external norms and institutions which are seen as either limits to their development or attempts to freeze the status quo; and it reduces their willingness to contribute to global public goods. They are also very large states and we should not underestimate the commonality of attitudes towards international law and sovereignty that go with sheer size, with the political introspection that this brings, and with the exceptionalism of their international identities. Within the company of great powers and centres of power, Europe is the outlier—and risks being the outsider—despite the EU's self-perception as the generator and exporter of ideas on governance and global governance.

Finally, we should also note the shifting role of domestic politics. This arises almost automatically in relation to the United States—not as a contingent matter of Obama's limited domestic space to manoeuvre but stemming rather from the persistent difficulty of meshing the external bargains that are inevitably involved in the on-going negotiation of hegemony with the complexity and relatively closed character of US domestic politics. But, and this is the critical point, something similar can be said about today's large, complex and fast-developing emerging powers. India's domestic constraints on climate change are every bit as complicated and contested as those in the US.

Is this new? In broad terms probably not. Think of the often stark domestic tensions produced by rapid economic change in the course of the rise of the United States, Germany and Japan, and the consequences that these tensions had for the foreign policy of these states and for their search for an international role commensurate with their rising power and their sense of themselves. But what is new—or at least harder to avoid—is the degree to which the substance of major power relations necessarily involves a wide range of issues that reach deep within the structure of domestic society. Here one might focus less on the BRICs as a group; and more on the intellectual and policy 'bricolage'—to use Mary Douglas's term—that has been taking place within each of the emerging states and through which old and new ideas and policies are melded together in ways that will work against these states becoming simply absorbable within some expanded version of a liberal Greater West.[19]

The socialisation and enmeshment stories of the 1990s have mostly been proved wrong. Being an active member of global multilateral bodies is perfectly compatible with a willingness to challenge the status quo, to reject US-favoured positions, and to favour new forms of global governance. Challenges to the US and the Greater West do not come only from non-democratic governments but from liberal and democratic states in the developing world whose liberal agenda speaks to a different range of interests, traditions and values. There is no solid or obvious basis for assuming that giving institutional priority or privileges to anything like a league of democratic states will produce greater cohesion or agreement than exists within the international bodies that we now have.

III.

Let me now turn to some remarks about global justice and to the ways which changing ideas and practices of global justice have interacted with the aspirations and achievements of international law.

Again, let us consider this historically and see how the global justice debate evolved as we move into and through our period. Looking back, it is clear that the Cold War was a very tough time for global justice. Nevertheless many saw the emergence of the Third World in the 1970s as raising important issues about justice—not just global distributive justice, but justice in relation to the emerging issues of the time such as global environment, nuclear proliferation, the reform of international institutions and energy scarcity. Third World states were commonly viewed as both carriers and catalysts for justice.

[19] Mary Douglas, *How Institutions Think* (Syracuse, Syracuse University Press, 1986).

All this changed in the course of the 1980s. The reformist rhetoric of the NIEO (New International Economic Order) had been both defeated and deflated. Power-centred accounts of North-South relations stressed the existence of a 'structural conflict' reducible to contending sets of power and interest—however encrusted within the empty rhetoric of justice. The powerful neo-liberal critique of rent-seeking southern elites cut deep into progressive third-worldism. On the left, post-colonial writers viewed the post-colonial state with deep disdain, whilst critical political economists argued that, to the extent that developing countries 'emerged', it would be as the result of structural changes in patterns of capitalist global production and would be built around transnational and class-based coalitions between Third World elites and the managers of the global capitalist economy.

The justice debate within the West shifted, and moved through the post Cold War years in two broad directions.

First, liberal theorists reacted strongly against the notion of state-based claims for distributive justice and against the so-called 'morality of states'.[20] Cosmopolitanism was clearly about achieving justice for individuals; it was about what 'we' in the rich world owed distant strangers. More broadly, the re-constitution of the hegemony of the so-called liberal 'Great West' set the agenda of much normative debate: the opening of space to intervention, apparently freed from the power-political and ideological distortions of the Cold War years and with the potential to serve a much broader range of liberal purposes; the focus on accountability and the need to find ways of holding the obvious power-holders of the day to account; the extent to which the apparent triumph of liberal democracy, combined with the deepening of globalisation, made global democracy and the application of western liberal political principles on a global scale an obviously important focus for normative analysis. Within academia there was an enormous growth of work on distributive justice, especially on the part of those who sought to deploy Rawlsian approaches to the global level.

Most of the western liberal work on global justice saw the post-Cold War dominance of the US and the West not as a problem but as an opportunity to be exploited. If this involved interventionism, paternalism, even renewed empire on the part of the rich and powerful then so be it—so long as social justice was being promoted. As one part of the rediscovery of empire Anthony Padgen usefully noted the close historical relationship between European cosmopolitan ideas and the spread of empire.[21] But, for much of the post-Cold War period such objections made little headway. Rather little work on global justice made reference to the self-understandings of the 'objects' of justice in the non-western world. There was very little sympathy with the view that post-colonial nationalism might have a value different from other forms of communitarianism. There was little apparent concern that emancipation into global liberal order might not be so emancipatory if the terms of entry involved a denial of agency and autonomy.[22] And it was rather easy to leave compliance problems, whether legal or moral, to one side when the direction of history seemed to be clear and when structural power appeared so clearly weighted on the side of the global liberal order.

[20] See, in particular, Charles R Beitz, *Political Theory and International Relations* (Princeton, Princeton University Press, 1979).

[21] Anthony Pagden, 'Stoicism, Cosmopolitanism, and the Legacy of European Imperialism' (2000) 7 *Constellations: An International Journal of Critical and Democratic Theory*.

[22] For an incisive critique see Rahul Rao, *Third World Protest: Between Home and the World* (Oxford, Oxford University Press, 2010).

The other major development was to shift normative attention away from Southern states and towards social movements and civil society groups within the Global South: the World Social Forum (WSF), anti-globalisation groups, and post-Seattle protest movements. The idea that the WSF represented the 'New Bandung' precisely captured this shift away from states and towards different forms of social movements.[23] In part anti-globalisation movements were seen as exercising effective political agency and the most viable means of developing countervailing power in the face of market-driven globalisation. But they also became central to a new generation of deliberative democratic theorists interested in bottom up approaches to the problems of unequal globalisation and in the need for greater global democracy. Far-reaching claims came to be made about the normative potentiality of global civil society as an arena of politics that is able to transcend the inside-outside character of traditional politics, and to fashion and provide space for new forms of political community, solidarity, and identity.[24]

But as with liberal cosmopolitanism, the enthusiasts for transnational deliberation had to—but often did not—confront serious problems and challenges: who was representing whom at gatherings like the WSF? Where did power lie within transnational civil society? On what basis could Northern activists justifiably criticise their Southern collaborators for 'not yet being able to look beyond the state'? Moreover, in contrast to progressive movements within domestic society, diffusing and developing new norms and values cannot be enough if there is only limited access to the institutions within which powerful states and other actors control the global economy.

If we ask about how the international legal order and the agenda of global justice might be connected, we therefore find two contrasting positions: one is top-down, trying to convince the powerful to act in the interests of greater global justice; the other is resolutely bottom-up: agency and activism must come from below; the politics that matters is the politics of the people.

But as power diffuses away from the western, liberal developed core and as the intractability of the international system to liberal prescriptions becomes more evident, so the character of writing on global justice changes. Global liberalism over the past decade has clearly entered far harder times. Two recent examples are emblematic of this shift.

For Charles Beitz it is not helpful for philosophers to try and tell us what human rights 'really are'. Instead we should seek to locate and build upon what Beitz calls a 'practical conception' of human rights: 'A practical conception takes the doctrine and practice of human rights in international political life as the source materials for constructing a conception of human rights'.[25] The embedded practices of international society occupy a central role in our theorising. 'We want to understand how these objects called "human rights" operate in the normative discourse of global political life. Whether we should accept claims about human rights as sources of reasons for action *for us* is a further question. But we cannot think clearly about this further question without first understanding the practice in which these claims are made and responded to'.[26]

[23] Michael Hardt, 'Today's Bandung?'(2002) 14 *New Left Review*.

[24] The literature is enormous but see especially: on transnational deliberative democracy James Bohman, *Democracy across Borders: From Demos to Demoi* (Cambridge, MIT Press, 2007); and on the democratic roles of NGOs, Terry Macdonald, *Global Stakeholder Democracy: Power and Representation Beyond Liberal States* (Oxford, OUP, 2008).

[25] Charles R Beitz, *The Idea of Human Rights* (Oxford, Oxford University Press, 2009)102.

[26] ibid, 105.

For Amartya Sen we should resist attempts to find universal principles for perfectly just social arrangements or to identify transcendental principles of global justice.[27] Instead we should concentrate on 'our shared sense of injustice' and on the possibility of agreement on realisation-focused strategies to mitigate some of the worst and most pressing forms of injustice. Just as important, we should see value pluralism both as an inescapable reality and as an opportunity. Hence the importance, as I will discuss below, of non-parochialism and of deploying the 'the eyes of many people'.

So if the empirical story is moving, as I have suggested, in a far more plural and far more strongly 'global' direction, what might follow for our thinking about global justice and the international legal order? Four strands can be identified, although it remains very hard to discern in which direction they might develop and how they may be related to each other.

In the first place, the combination of a shifting distribution of power and the intrinsic character of contemporary governance challenges makes it ever harder to escape from justice. If one trend in the post-Cold War period was the moralisation of politics, another was the attempt to evade overt discussion of justice and to stress the primacy of functional effectiveness. Take the example of climate change. For many, it was, and remains, intellectually clear and normatively proper that stressing effectiveness, efficiency and incentive-compatibility is the best way to design a regime for climate change. Let's work on the shared goal; let's build on what we know works; let's avoid contested arguments about what global justice might demand. But particular assumptions about the constraints of place and politics quickly creep in: carbon trading is needed because it can generate resources for the South but without financial flows having going through formal multilateral institutions in a way that that US political and public opinion would never accept. All of this is extremely cogent. But so too is the position of those in the developing world who believe that a forward-looking, incentive-based, sunk-costs view of the climate change regime means abandoning the legal and moral principles embedded in the Kyoto framework, especially those that maintain some residual notion of historic responsibility on the part of the North and the idea of common but differentiated responsibilities.

A second set of issues concerns agency and the power to hold to account. Cosmopolitan liberal theory has been strangely silent on the question of agency. Post-Cold War liberal discourses on global justice often appear to be discourses about what the rich and powerful owe to the poor, weak and oppressed. The weak and oppressed appear mostly as the passive objects of (potential) benevolence. Their voices, visions, and understandings of the world are seldom heard or seldom deliberated upon. To counter this tendency we might look to more strongly republican modes of liberal thinking with their emphasis on the importance of states as agents, with their powerful ideal of non-domination, and with their central concern with minimising alien control. Deliberation is never enough if the political terms of deliberation are insufficient or lacking. As Pettit suggests, the most serious danger posed by international institutions is not that they themselves will exercise alien domination but that they will fail to prevent different forms of inter-state domination. The legitimacy of international institutions will be seriously weakened to the degree that inter-state inequalities generate asymmetrical bargaining and involve the domination of weaker parties.[28] It is also important to underscore the

[27] Amartya Sen, *The Idea of Justice* (Cambridge, Belknap Press, 2009).

[28] Philip Pettit, 'Legitimate International Institutions: A Neo-Republican Perspective' (2009) Princeton Law and Public Affairs Paper Series, paper No. 08.012.

extent to which liberal principles of political legitimacy are sustained by a combination of moral and strategic purposes. It is of course true that liberal political principles—such as 'transparency', 'accountability' and 'participation'—are underpinned in part by purely moral values, such as the values of individual autonomy and equality. But they are devised also to serve the *strategic* function of constraining—as effectively as possible—abuses and misuses of power by those who wield it without regard for these liberal moral values. Principles of political legitimacy must articulate not only underlying moral values, but also the kinds of strategic mechanisms that are required to protect these values from real threats arising from prospective abuses of power.

It is within this context that emerging powers that claim to speak for the South and that have helped to lead more effective coalitions of weaker states become potentially normatively important. Of course one valid set of questions involves asking how the US-led western liberal order has been challenged by an 'autocratic and illiberal revival' and by the 'return of history' in the challenges from powerful but clearly illiberal states such as Russia or China. But another crucial dimension of the debate is to recognise that there are many versions of liberalism and that leading democratic emerging powers such as Brazil and India have a valid claim to shape the character of what global liberalism and a 'global liberal order' mean in the 21st century.

One of the most important questions concerning today's emerging powers is the impact that their rise may be having on the concepts of the Third World and the Global South and on the very idea of North-South relations as a structuring feature of the international system. Do the rise and increasingly influence of major developing states bring North-South relations back to the centre-stage of international relations, and with it the potential for a new debate on the scope and nature of global justice? Or does the appearance of countries such as India and Brazil around the top table of global governance simply add one more argument to the essential irrelevance of the South or Third World as meaningful categories of political action and academic analysis, and one more piece of evidence for the recurring power-political logic of the rise and fall of Great Powers?

If this latter trend is indeed visible in the new concerts of power and governance arrangements that may be forming, then the normative debate needs to recover older notions of global justice, in particular those focused around the idea of major power responsibility. This is the third strand of the emerging normative picture. In a world where value conflicts over the nature of global justice are rife, where institutions remain fragile, and where the dangers of over power-political confrontation can never be discounted, Great Powers have a special responsibility to uphold international order—by negotiating with other major powers ground-rules as to what constitutes legitimate foreign policy behaviour; by agreeing who are the major players in the system and finding ways, individually and collectively, to manage the entry of new members into the club; by managing global problems, especially in such cases as nuclear proliferation where their collective self-interest in preventing new entrants can be said to coincide with a more general system interest; and, finally, by managing weaker states and by providing a hierarchical order within the regions or on the issues in which they have dominance.

This is in many ways an unattractive way of thinking about global justice and one that has certainly involved many morally problematic trade-offs and compromises. But the return of significant elements of Westphalia makes it impossible to avoid. Hence we need to foster renewed debate as to how far the tools of classical major power management (such as arms control, spheres of influence, and concert diplomacy) can accommodate both the material changes of globalisation and the moral claims that have become so much more densely incorporated into the institutional fabric of international law and society. In some crucial areas, the absence of even debate about what the guiding principles of such an accommodation ought to be is striking and extremely dangerous. Nuclear non-proliferation is perhaps the most obvious and the most problematic case in point.

The final set of questions picks up on the issue of non-parochialism. As in much of his previous work, Amartya Sen takes Adam Smith as his guide and mentor:

> We can never survey our own sentiments and motives, we can never form any judgement concerning them; unless we remove ourselves, as it were, from our natural station, and endeavour to view them as at a certain distance from us. But we can do this in no other way than by endeavouring to view them with the eyes of other people, or as other people are likely to view them.[29]

Although abstract human reason can assist in the search for impartial and generalisable principles of justice, it is 'the eyes of other people' and the inherited wisdom of different cultural traditions that are central. Non-parochialism becomes an essential requirement of justice in a global and interdependent world. My own appraisal of international law in the post-Cold War years would lay particular weight on this issue. Many of the traditional means by which pluralist international law had previously sought to mediate difference and to live with pluralism were being undermined. But they were being replaced with practices, institutions and ideas that were neither securely related to the changing structures of power nor that recognised the crucial importance of both epistemic openness and non-parochialism.

[29] Adam Smith, *The Theory of Moral Sentiments*, quoted in Sen, *The Idea of Justice*, 125.

Comments on Hurrell: The End of Geography?

DANIEL BETHLEHEM QC*

IT IS A GREAT pleasure to be here, to see old friends and colleagues and to be able to participate in this meeting. I have had fewer opportunities than I would have liked in recent years to be able to join in such discussions. It is a particular pleasure to come back to Cambridge and to this meeting organised by the Lauterpacht Centre for International Law. It is also a pleasure to have this opportunity to participate in the discussion on Andrew Hurrell's thought-provoking chapter. I had the opportunity of reading it in draft over the past days and it commends itself to careful review for its considered and nuanced appreciation of the state of the international system and the challenges that lie ahead. I agree with what I take to be Andrew's central thesis—that international society faces a range of classical Westphalian challenges but that it does so in a context marked by strong post-Westphalian characteristics. Indeed, there is little to disagree with in his analysis, even if one may want to question, for example, the proposition of the renewed importance of nuclear weapons as central to major power relations or to scrutinise more closely the proposition of the thinness of international structures. And, the image of simply re-arranging the seats around the table, or, in some cases, expanding the size of the table, in order better to address new challenges, should spur us on to greater critical scrutiny of whether the legal cloth that covers and warms and protects the changing international society about which Andrew is commenting is adequate enough.

It is this last thought that I take as the theme for my brief remarks—the adequacy of the legal cloth. Andrew reflected on the state of the international *system*. With a nod here and there to extra-state or post-Westphalian developments—such as climate change—his focus was almost exclusively on the Westphalian structure of the state and how it is doing in the face of contemporary challenges. His observation, in respect of the BRIC countries, that we should not underestimate the commonality of attitudes towards international law and sovereignty that go with sheer size, is very important. It could apply equally, though for different reasons, to many other states and groupings of states, such as developing countries, which see sovereignty as a bulwark against interventionism, both economic and of harder form. But Andrew's focus, wide ranging as it was, was on the Westphalian state

* Sir Daniel Bethlehem QC is Legal Adviser, UK Foreign & Commonwealth Office.

and the Westphalian state system and how it is adapting to post-Westphalian challenges. He did not, by design, talk about the international *legal* system, and its adequacy and the particular challenges that the law may face. And to this, my opening question is whether a performance appraisal of the international *system* is synonymous with a performance appraisal of international *law* or of the international *legal* system. In the end, I do not think it is. While the system and its legal framework are obviously closely related, the edifice of contemporary international law—with its central pivots of *territorial* sovereignty, *territorial* jurisdiction, *territorial* regulation, *territorial* accountability—faces important conceptual and practical challenges that are not quite the same as those faced by the system more generally. The international system looks very different when one looks at it through the lens of the Geneva institutions and the Specialised Agencies than it does when one views it through the lens of the UN General Assembly and Security Council, the IMF and World Bank, the G8 and the G20. The websites of the World Health Organisation and the Food and Agriculture Organisation, of the International Civil Aviation Organisation and the International Maritime Organisation, of the World Trade Organisation and the International Telecommunications Union, of the UN High Commissioner for Refugees and the International Organisation for Migration, paint a very different image of the international system, and of the challenges faced by international law, than that which we get when we look at the issues through a Westphalian prism. What one sees depends on one's vantage point and the direction one is facing. The question I have, therefore, in response to Andrew's paper, even if I agree, as I have said, with his analysis of classical Westphalian challenges marked by a context of strong post-Westphalian characteristics, is whether our analysis does sufficient justice to his injunction against parochialism.

Let me give you a few random statistics. In the period under review, since 1989, the world's population grew by about 1.5 billion people, about 82 per cent of whom were born into the developing world. In the next 40 years, my play it forward time frame, the current population of 6.8 billion is set to grow by a further 2.4 billion, to reach about 9.2 billion, 2.35 billion of whom will be born into the developing world.[1]

As we sit here today, about 43.3 million people have been forcibly displaced; 15.2 million are refugees; 27.1 million are internally displaced. There are about 214 million migrants worldwide. Their remittances back to their home countries amount to some $414 billion. This migration is set to increase over the next 40 years, with the countries of the highest projected net immigration being the United States, Canada, the UK, Spain, Italy, Germany, Australia and France; and the countries of the highest projected net emigration being Mexico, China, India, the Philippines, Pakistan, Indonesia and Bangladesh.[2]

There were 31 million foreign trips from the UK in 1989, up to 69 million in 2008.[3] ICAO records 750 million *international* air passenger movements through just the top 25 international airports in 2008, via 6 million international aircraft journeys.[4] According to the IMO, *international* commercial maritime trade volume went up from 4.3 billion tonnes in 1990 to 8.2 billion tonnes in 2008.[5]

[1] For population projections and statistics, see: esa.un.org/unpd/wpp2008/pdf/WPP2008_Highlights.pdf.

[2] For migration, refugee and IDP statistics, see, in addition to the document at note 3, www.unhcr.org/4c11f0be9.html and www.iom.int/jahia/jsp/index.jsp.

[3] See www.statistics.gov.uk/downloads/theme_transport/travel-trends09.pdf.

[4] See www.icao.int/icaonet/dcs/9921/9921_en.pdf.

[5] See www.imo.org/includes/blastDataOnly.asp/data_id%3D28127/InternationalShippingandWorldTrade-factsandfiguresoct2009rev1___tmp65768b41.pdf.

And then we come to the global health scares, of which the H5N1 (avian flu) and H1N1 (swine flu) pandemic risks are only the most recent and the most visible. Given the very high levels of migratory bird movements, and of human travel and migration, these risks have preoccupied the WHO and the FAO, as well as others.[6] The challenges not only to human health, but also to animal and plant health, and to global food security, are considerable. And in all this, one of the most interesting issues from the perspective of the international lawyer is the challenge of crafting an international legal framework that better addresses these issues from the perspective of potentially vulnerable communities—rather than simply from the perspective of a classical Westphalian model of states which, even in the BRIC format, would entrench notions of sovereignty and territoriality.

On a visit to Geneva recently, I heard from the WHO of the considerable and worrying challenges faced by the world health community in attempting to plan for and address the risks of global flu pandemics. I wonder how many in this hall are aware of the events around 2007 when Indonesia refused to share the strains of the human H5N1 avian flu virus that it had gathered, following the significant outbreak there, with the network of WHO linked laboratories on the Global Influenza Surveillance Network (GISN).[7] This Network collects and analyses flu viruses, selects the strains to be included in vaccines and provides them to manufacturers. Given the frequent mutations of the DNA of flu viruses, the international sharing of samples is crucial to keeping track of those mutations and to selecting the best strains for purposes of the manufacture of vaccines. Without this sharing of viruses, there can be no vaccines. And Indonesia refused to share its virus strains, potentially the most important in the network, given the scale of the Indonesian outbreak, because it wanted to patent those viruses and address issues of sharing in the context of discussions about financial recompense and questions about vaccine availability in developing countries.

The subsequent discussions in the WHO have been deadlocked, and are still on-going, with a greater realisation of shared vulnerabilities coming in the wake of the H1N1 (swine flu) outbreak in Mexico earlier this year and the appreciation that international cooperation is critical to the management and mitigation of risks.

My purpose in highlighting this issue is not to make a judgement on the matter—which engages other complex considerations that I have not touched upon—but only to highlight the significant risks and challenges associated with it and to observe, first, that this is not a challenge which is well or easily suited to Westphalian solutions, and, second, that there is already a very considerable technocratic post-Westphalian world out there which is largely invisible to most of us. Our question to ourselves, therefore, should be whether we are seeing the world in sufficiently non-parochial terms to allow us to take comfort that we are seeing the challenges sufficiently clearly, or indeed at all. Against this

[6] See, for example: www.who.int/ith/en/, www.who.int/mediacentre/factsheets/avian_influenza/en/index.html, www.who.int/csr/disease/swineflu/frequently_asked_questions/about_disease/en/index.html, www.fao.org/avianflu/en/index.html,www.fao.org/AG/AGAInfo/programmes/en/empres/AH1N1/Background.html, www.fao.org/foodchain/prevention-and-early-warning/en/.

[7] This issue is discussed by David P Fidler in 'Negotiating Equitable Access to Influenza Vaccines: Global Health Diplomacy and the Controversies Surrounding Avian Influenza H5N1 and Pandemic H1N1', 7(5) *PLoS Medicine* May 2010 (www.plosmedicine.org). See also Resolution WHA60.28 of the World Health Assembly, 102 ff on apps.who.int/gb/ebwha/pdf_files/WHASSA_WHA60-Rec1/E/reso-60-en.pdf, the 18 May 2009 Report of the WHO Director General on 'Pandemic influenza preparedness: sharing of influenza viruses and access to vaccines and other benefits', at apps.who.int/gb/ebwha/pdf_files/A62/A62_5Add1-en.pdf, and other associated documents at apps.who.int/gb/pip/.

backdrop, I wonder whether we should be reformulating Andrew's analytical framework a little to put it in terms of the complex, hybrid and contested character of international society which is increasingly, and perhaps in many respects predominantly, post-Westphalian in character but which remains rooted and bound by a classical Westphalian view of itself and is facing some key traditional Westphalian challenges.

In emailing with James Crawford about the shape of my remarks, I provisionally entitled them 'The End of Geography?'. The end of geography proposition is of course a caricature, and is not so much intended as a snipe at Francis Fukuyama's *The End of History* as it is inclined to take Thomas Friedman's *The World is Flat* onto the terrain of the looming challenges to the international legal system.[8] But, even though it is a caricature, it is intended to pose a serious question, which, as I look through the conference programme for these few days, seems to be everywhere in our discussions. From our vantage point deeply imbedded in a Westphalian discourse, are we seeing the world sufficiently clearly and is the system of international law with which we are so familiar, rooted at every turn in notions of territoriality—sovereignty, jurisdiction, regulation, accountability—adequate to the challenges that will face us over the coming 40 years?

My answer to this question is that there is a risk that our inquiry is akin to that of a passenger sitting on a train travelling at considerable speed such as to blur his or her vision of the landscape as they look out of the window. In this environment, in attempting to describe the landscape across which we are travelling, we resort to images drawn from the last station at which we stopped, and we project to the next point at which we hope to draw breath by reference to the views and atmospheric conditions of the last. There is a real danger that as we take stock of, as we appraise, the international legal system of the past 20 years it will have already moved decisively past us and we will be caught in a constant cycle of catching up.

From my perspective, as we look to the future and consider the shape of the international legal system, and its adequacy to meet new challenges, we should have in mind five areas of challenge:

(a) the international environment, shared spaces, the atmosphere and global commons;
(b) the movement of people, both forcibly displaced and voluntarily migrant, and the economic and financial flows, and the challenges of civic and social integration, that goes with them;
(c) the challenges to human, animal and plant life and health, and to global food security, that come from a growing and already massively interdependent world and the migratory movements of both people and animals;
(d) the enormous and increasing growth in global trade and financial flows and the symbiotic interconnectedness, and potential for systemic vulnerability, of the global economic system; and
(e) the dramatic increase in the global use of the electromagnetic sphere and the practical challenges and risks, and opportunities, that this presents, including for regulation and in the areas of the internet, including of an economic nature, and issues of security, ranging from cyber systems security to child prostitution and more widely.[9]

[8] Francis Fukuyama, *The End of History and the Last Man* (New York, Avon Books,1992); Thomas L Friedman, *The World is Flat—The Globalized World in the Twenty-First Century* (New York, Picador, 2007).
[9] For ITU work on this issue, see www.itu.int/cybersecurity/.

This is a pretty formidable array of challenges, which in many respects, and certainly in scale, go fundamentally beyond Westphalian conceptions of society and Westphalian concepts of international law. While states will continue to be key instruments of international interaction, organisation and law-making for a considerable time to come, and notions of sovereignty, jurisdiction and territoriality will continue to inform our approach to new challenges, we will have to move decisively beyond notions of Westphalia, including temperamentally, if we are to engage successfully with the challenges to come. International law is not the international system. It is the cloth that covers and warms it and enables its development. We, the international legal community, need to have a clear vision of international society. But we also need to have a vision of the role that the law can and should play in shaping that society in ways that will be most conducive to its peaceful and productive development.

Comments on Hurrell

XUE HANQIN*

PROFESSOR HURRELL'S SPEECH is an insightful, powerful, and thought-provoking analysis of international legal development since the end of the Cold War. I agree with most of what he has evaluated of the performance of international law in the last two decades. For the sake of our discussion, I would like to make a few critical comments from a non-western perspective in my capacity as the current President of the Asian Society of International Law rather than a new member of the International Court of Justice.

In his paper, Hurrell states three basic facts: first, the current political, economic and legal order is primarily western dominant; secondly, international law as the basis of international legal order is oriented by the preferences of the western world; thirdly, the legal order mainly reflects western liberal values. This is particularly true in the last two decades. In his view, the global system at the moment is characterised by three 'diffusions': a diffusion of power, a diffusion of preferences, a diffusion of ideas and values. This phenomenon tells us at least two things: in the past two decades, the internal structure of western society as a whole has fundamentally changed and is still changing, which has exerted great impact on international relations. Secondly, given the world changes, western domination in international relations is being seriously challenged for its legitimacy and justice. The issue is often not what the law says, but what it does, and what interests it serves in practice.

The oft-asked question whether we have moved from the Westphalian system to the post-Westphalian system, in my opinion, is not a real issue, as the concept of Westphalia has long gone away from its original notion. If, however, what Westphalia means is a western-centric legal order, I would cautiously say that such a legal order can no longer sustain the on-going changes of international relations. If democracy and democratisation sincerely mean anything in international affairs, the current challenges should be deemed as part of a natural course of events.

Scholars tend to examine the system change basically by emphasizing two principles: sovereignty and non-intervention. They question whether these two principles are still valid and pertinent in the contemporary parlance of international law and to what extent they have changed and to what extent such changes have affected international legal order. Basically these questions boil down to three factors: State, power and order.

* Judge Xue Hanqin is a Member of the International Court of Justice.

On the first factor, in the legal debate State is often juxtaposed to individual and to the international community, thus state versus individuals, state versus international community, domestic affairs versus international affairs and national law versus international law. In all these matrixes, we recognise that the status and role of the State is no longer the same as before. However, this process has been going on ever since the emergence of international law, not just over the past twenty years. The only difference lies in the degree and intensity of the change. Against the backdrop of the changes as described by Professor Hurrell, what we should ask is whether the ongoing changes are so fundamental and profound that they have transformed the basic structure and character of international relations.

Personally I think despite what has happened the State remains the major and decisive player for the direction of international law development, as pursuit of national interests, either in the form of unilateral action or by collective coalition, is still one of the driving forces for international law-making. There are increasing communal interests shared by all States, such as environmental protection, human rights promotion and protection and the fight against international crimes, but to realise these goals, States are the crucial actors at both national and international levels. In the last two decades, we have learnt the hard way that States' failure to protect human rights was often not on account of the State's being too strong for democracy, but because the State was too weak to uphold it. Any weakening of the status and role of the State, as demonstrated in many a case, could only mean more misery and sufferings for individuals, particularly when a constitutional system and democracy are yet to develop. The fact that we place emphasis on the State does not mean we bear any particular preference or liking for the 'Westphalian order', it only reminds us that the character of the international legal system has not fundamentally changed. In this context, we frequently confuse a few concepts: when we talk about the State, the notion is not necessarily identical with that of government; global governance does not mean global government. In addressing civil society, non-state entities, for instance NGOs, we are inclined to ignore two aspects: one is their representation and the other their accountability. According to the statistics issued in the Yearbook of International Organizations, over 70 per cent of all NGOs come from the Trans-Atlantic world. Could we perceive it as another Western-centric pattern? Who can hold such legal entities accountable at the international level, how and to whom?

The return of Westphalian norms, if ever, should not be deemed simply a result of mismanagement of State power after the Cold War, but a practical test on the new assertions on international law. Hurrell's analysis on the points of the post-Westphalian trend, namely, deeper intervention in domestic affairs, legitimate authority, provincialising of Westphalia, reveals the emergence of a new type of power balance, but not a new legal order that transcends national distinctions and priorities.

With respect to the factor of power, the liberal internationalism of the 1990s is in essence the outcome of imbalance of power. With the American declaration of its victory over the Cold War came the liberal solidarism, a solidarism that predominantly reflects western values and ideas over the world order and a solidarism that has made it possible for the West to export such values and ideas to the rest of the world.

International law from its inception was not, is not, and has never been, made through a democratic process, but is largely based on a balance of power. Its fundamental principles that uphold equality, justice and fairness are in reality often tainted by the power politics of the strong. Therefore, intervention is often the case where the strong intervenes into the domestic affairs of the weak rather than the other way around, albeit often in the name of the international community. That is why double standards, as a virus, jeopardise the general confidence and trust in the legal order. When political, economic, financial and technological powers are changing and shifting, the legal construct would respond. This has been true among Western powers throughout history since the Westphalian days.

The emerging powers with new economies in particular will have an impact on the existing legal order, which will hopefully be different from previous changes. As China asserts, the peaceful rise of the new players will be most likely a long and gradual process through their economic and social progress and through dialogue and cooperation with the existing powers with the aim of common development and lasting peace. It still remains to be seen whether the current transformation will eventually affect the existing legal order. Ultimately it will depend on the substantial growth of the new strength in international relations. It will depend on interactions between the existing powers and the rising third world. It will depend on what order States wish to build up in the new century.

Lastly, the third factor is order. For the first time in history, the international political landscape is being drastically changed without large-scale warfare among major powers. Instead, interdependency leads to cooperation and dialogue. In a way the proliferation of international law in the last twenty years has strengthened the rule of law in international affairs, contributing to the peaceful development of international relations on the whole. Nonetheless, legitimacy arguments cannot avoid the questions of political democracy in decision-making, equal opportunity for economic development for all and free choice of social formation and progress by all forms of civilisation.

If the Westphalian system is to be reformed, changed or abandoned, it is not merely about whether the notion of sovereignty or non-intervention should go away, but the whole legal order should be examined and reviewed. Legal pluralism as thus manifested is just part of the story, plural participation should first of all get the developing countries involved and accounted. The term 'provincialising of Westphalia' has a positive connotation, but may have the condescending implication that the poor and weak are at last allowed to enter the club. There is still a core above.

The new order is a new page but not a new book; the Western world still carries important responsibility in promoting world peace and security and in pursuit of common prosperity of mankind. The question whether we should take a top-down or bottom-up approach is not an optional issue. The two approaches should always go hand in hand, complementary to each other. Whether developed or developing, all states now have to take an international perspective in their decision-making, even on a purely domestic affair. Civil participation as a positive development of international relations should be encouraged in a way that strengthens rather than undermines the state's role and responsibility. In the final analysis, the State should be the one that is held answerable and responsible both internally and internationally.

The last five points raised by Hurrell, namely, justice, agency, power to hold to account, major power responsibility and non-parochialism, are all related to the future order, indeed to European perspectives on the world order. Europe is the stronghold of international law. This discussion is timely and important for the world. As the President of the Asian Society of International Law, I warmly welcome European scholars to the Beijing conference of the Asian Society next year to join us and continue this enlightening intellectual exploration.

2

The Impact of the East-West Divide on International Law: Patterns of Discourse and the Waves of 1989

TIBOR VÁRADY*

I. INTRODUCTION

IN ONE OF his letters from the Birmingham Jail, Martin Luther King writes: 'Injustice anywhere is a threat to justice everywhere. We are caught in an inescapable network of mutuality, tied in a single garment of destiny. Whatever affects one directly, affects all indirectly'.[1] The inspiration for these sentences may not stem from the domain of international law, but it is a striking caption of the reality (or of the predicament) of international law. Mutuality is, indeed, an inescapable element of the very existence of international law—particularly since the relevant arena has become global.

The focus of this paper is on a specific segment of history in which mutuality (or the absence of it) played an important role. The East-West divide was for several decades the single most important confrontation; steps taken and choices made were classified (and were labelled) according to their position in the light of this divide. It is not quite unequivocal what was 'East' and what was 'West'. According to the most common (and most relevant) understanding, the Soviet Union and other European socialist countries represented the 'East', while Western Europe and the United States were the 'West'. It is in the context of this understanding that 1989—marked by the fall of the Berlin Wall—is the historic turning-point marking the end of the divide.

This divide certainly had an important impact on international law. Both the rift itself, as well as endeavours to prevail over it, yielded much inspiration and motivation. International law has less inherent power than national law, and therefore it is more dependent on motivation. It is important to note that not only cooperation, but confrontation and competition might also craft motivation and synergies. The question arises how international law coped with this confrontation—and how the end of the confrontation influenced international law. One may also ask whether some patterns of

* University Professor at the Central European University, Budapest, Tenured Professor at Emory University School of Law.

[1] Martin Luther King Jr, Letter from Birmingham Jail, 16 April 1963.

thoughts and arguments which lost ground with the collapse of communism managed to find refuge in different environments and contexts. Of course, these issues deserve serious and detailed study—and some important studies have, indeed, been devoted to these questions. What I would like to submit are some observations, some of them made from angles that are not mainstream.

II. THE EAST-WEST DIVIDE AS A DETERRENT AND AS AN INSPIRATION

A. Competition and Confrontation

The title of this forum (An Era of International Law? The Years 1989–2010 in Perspective) suggests—although with a question mark—that 1989 was a year marking a consequential turning point (in the 'East', in particular), and that it might have introduced an era of international law. It is, indeed, quite clear that 1989 contributed to the importance of legal norms, and also brought about better observance of international law in the 'East'. In a newly acquired perspective, the question also arises how the divide was conceptualised in the sphere of international law. A further question is whether the pre-1989 divide left a mark on perceptions of international law in the 'West'.

Since I would like to make some observations about competition (which may be perceived as one dimension of confrontation), let me mention that competition is certainly not a new phenomenon in the domain of law. Going back in history, a quite striking parallel can be found as early as in the Iliad. Homer described competition for reward given for the best judgment in a dispute. As is written in Book XVIII:

> Meanwhile the people were gathered in assembly, for there was a quarrel, and two men were wrangling about the blood-money for a man who had been killed, the one saying before the people that he had paid damages in full, and the other that he had not been paid. Each was trying to make his own case good, and the people took sides, each man backing the side that he had taken; but the heralds kept them back, and the elders sat on their seats of stone in a solemn circle, holding the staves which the heralds had put into their hands. Then they rose and each in his turn gave judgment, and there were two talents laid down, to be given to him whose judgment should be deemed the fairest.[2]

How did the 'East' and the 'West' compete for the epithet of the fairest? Juxtaposing 'East' and 'West', one generally comes to the conclusion that there was a continuous pressure from the 'West' endeavouring to persuade the 'East' to follow international law. This conclusion reflects the truth, but not the whole truth. Influence was exerted in both directions, and some attitudes on both sides were shaped by competition. In his book *Soviet Legal Innovation and the Law of the Western World,*[3] John Quigley submits that the Bolshevik revolution brought a quite considerable number of new ideas that represented a challenge to the West. These ideas included the equality of sexes, abolishing the distinction between legitimate and illegitimate children and social welfare rights. All these ideas became legal norms in the USSR—and some of them became reality. The communist State also took important initiatives within the field of international law,

[2] Homer, Iliad, Book XVIII.

[3] John Quigley, *Soviet Legal Innovation and the Law of the Western World* (Cambridge, Cambridge University Press, 2007).

including, for example, a radical condemnation of colonialism. According to Quigley, in order to blunt a competitive edge in the making, Western societies went through a process of accommodation, adopting—or partially adopting—a certain number of ideas, which were first phrased as legal rules in communist Russia. According to Quigley's book, the Soviet model (or rather fear of the Soviet model) was an important factor in what the author calls 'accommodation in the West'. Speaking of the establishment of the International Labour Organization (ILO), for example, Quigley quotes Henkin, who states that 'improvement in the conditions of labour' and the ILO were 'capitalism's defense against the spectre of spreading socialism which has just established itself in the largest country of Europe [Russia]'.[4] The fact that fear was one of the inspirations that brought about the creation of the ILO has also left a mark in its Preamble, which states: 'Conditions of labour exist, involving such injustice, hardship and privation to large numbers of people as to produce unrest so great that the peace and harmony of the world are imperilled'.[5]

At this point, one could make the observation that ideological principles—including some truly progressive ones, but also some disastrous ones—had a shortcut towards legal norms in the USSR, a State in which the legislators had to heed the party line rather than the opinion of their voters. But this does not disprove, but only explains, the point Quigley is making. The Soviet legislator accepted some rules before Western societies were ready to accept them—and probably before Soviet citizens would have accepted them as a result of a democratic process.

At any rate, the most consequential rivalry during the second half of the twentieth century yielded some noteworthy adaptations—just as it yielded fierce competition.

B. Rhetoric Expressions of Competition and Confrontation—and a Side Note on Titles

It is important to take note of the fact that throughout a considerable part of its history, the USSR was an agitated society, and this left an imprint on the style of its legal norms and legal thinking. Titles of legislative acts were particularly combative and ideologically loaded. Of course, in the USSR—like everywhere—titles are important, because they catch the eye of even those legislators who may not take time to read the text and consider the content; titles are also more likely to reach the public, and possibly the headlines. Let me give an example: following a then fresh revolutionary fervour, on 11 November 1917, the new Soviet Russia adopted an act entitled: 'On the Fight with the Bourgeoisie and its Agents who are Disrupting the Supply of the Army with Food, and Who are Obstructing the Achievement of Peace'.[6] What is remarkable in such titles (and often in the content following such titles) is not just zeal in legal norms. What we have here is actually an abuse of the space of norms. The authority and dignity of the space of legal norms is ruthlessly abused when political messages, incantations and slogans are pushed into it, like junk mail pushed into the space

[4] Louis Henkin, *International Law: Politics, Values and Functions,* Recueil des Cours (Hague Academy of International Law, 1989 part 4) 216, quoted in Quigley, *Soviet Legal Innovation* 77.

[5] Constitution of the International Labour Organization, Preamble, cited in Quigley, *Soviet Legal Innovation* 78.

[6] "*О БОРЬБЕ СЪ БУРЖУАЗІЕЙ И ЕЯ АГЕНТАМИ, САБОТИРУЮЩИМИ ДЕЛО ПРОДОВОЛЬСТВІЯ АРМІИ И ПРЕПЯТСТВУЮЩИМИ ЗАКЛЮЧЕНІЮ МИРА*".

of our mailboxes. Cardozo warned about the danger of infecting the space of legal scholarship. In his words: '[M]agic words and incantations are as fatal to our science as they are to any other'.[7] The detriment is even more serious if not only legal science, but the space of the legal norms themselves is infected.

Agitated societies tend to plant magic, slogans, and incantations, into the space of legal norms—and into titles of legislative acts in particular. This is unfortunately not restricted to communist agitation, and to threats from the 'agents of bourgeoisie' who are obstructing the achievement of peace, and at the same time disrupting the supply of food. Other agitations in different societies—and outside the East-West divide—might bring about the same mindset. Prompted by 9/11, the US legislature crafted an act with the following title: 'Uniting and Strengthening America by Providing Appropriate Tools Required to Intercept and Obstruct Terrorism Act of 2001'. As is well known, this title contains an added rhetoric construct (not without some trace of strain and sweat of those who construed it). The first letters add up to supplementary magic and incantation: 'USA Patriot Act'.

C. Rivalry Targeting the Aura of International Law

One of the disciplines of East-West competition was a fight for the aura of international law. This was facilitated by the vast manoeuvring room left to rhetoric. International law became a strong symbol with inherent power and positive connotations, with which all players wished to associate themselves. Heeding this fact, the 'East' found it important to posit itself on the side of international law. We have witnessed a constantly positive and affirmative language relating to international law in the USSR, and in East-European countries in which Soviet political influence was present (along with the Soviet Army). In sum, one may note that the East-West divide did not yield fundamental differences regarding expressions of respect towards international law. It is a different matter, of course, to what extent norms of international law were truly observed.

At any rate, the authority of international law, which acquired solid ground in the Western World, was never challenged in the East—on the contrary, it received enthusiastic rhetorical support. The Soviet Union was heralded as a hero of the struggle for peace, for international legality, and for international law; and in this context, peace, international legality, and international law were understandably treated as uppermost values. In the words of Wolfgang Friedmann, '[S]oviet theorists maintained and developed a need to recognize the existing structure of international law, and to use it to the advantage of the Soviet Union'.[8] International law was posited as a discipline in which the 'socialist bloc' had a comparative advantage. Grigorij Tunkin, a leading Soviet scholar (who cites in his treatises about the same Western authors who are also cited in Western treatises published in the same period) states that the October Revolution shaped critically important ideas in the field of international law. Tunkin identifies three such ideas: socialist internationalism; the principles of equality and self-determination of nations (which imply rejection of colonialism and of oppression); and the principle of peaceful cooperation of States with different social systems.[9]

[7] Benjamin Cardozo, *The Growth of the Law* (Yale University Press, March, 1924) 66.
[8] Wolfgang Friedmann, *The Changing Structure of International Law* (London, Stevens & Sons, 1964) 328.
[9] Grigorij Tunkin, *Teorija mezhdunarodnogo prava*, 2nd edn (Moscow 1970) 4.

The same approach and rhetoric was adopted in other European socialist countries (with the exception of Yugoslavia, which espoused similar values, but demonstrated more self-reliance in shaping principles and arguments). In order to give a further illustration of this approach, I shall cite a few sentences from the standard Hungarian treatise on international law, first published in 1954, at the peak of the communist regime that prompted the 1956 Hungarian Revolution. According to Búza and Hajdú:

> We definitely have to reject the short-sighted and defeatist view according to which international law is just a collection of wishes devoid of substance, because a considerable part of States does not obey its rules, while others are not in the possession of instruments with which they could bring about the rule of law. Those who take such positions leave out of consideration that nowadays, already one third of mankind lives in socialist systems and—in the words of the Second Moscow Declaration—'the most distinctive feature of our epoch is that the socialist world order is becoming the decisive factor in the development of human society'. This socialist world order is fighting for the realization of international legality, since it secures peace.[10]

In the same spirit, various constitutions of the USSR gave ample emphasis to peace (tying it to Lenin) and to international cooperation. According to the last (1977) Constitution of the USSR: 'The USSR steadfastly pursues a Leninist policy of peace and stands for strengthening of the security of nations and broad international co-operation'.[11]

The difficult question arises whether such rhetoric may contribute towards a positive image and better observance of international law. It is certainly true that international law needs motivation—more so than various fields of internal law. The still imperfect system of sanctions needs substitutes. According to the classic sentences of Grotius, '[la]w, even though without a sanction, is not entirely void of effect. For justice brings peace of conscience, while injustice causes torments and anguish ... Justice is approved, and injustice condemned, by the common agreement of good men'.[12] Strong rhetorical support favouring international law may, in principle, yield positive motivation, and may foster observance. This chemistry may only work, however, if slogans are not completely out of touch, if they remain within some human range of realities. In some periods and with regard to some issues (like affirmation of social rights or rejection of colonialism), Soviet rhetoric and Soviet actions were within the same range. In this setting, strong wording and repeated emphasis may have contributed to motivation—and Soviet attitudes contributed to mutuality.

But this was not always the case. Some pledges of allegiance towards international law and incantations were capable only of engendering cynicism rather than motivation. To give an example, on October 31, 1956, a week after outbreak of the 1956 Hungarian Revolution—and four days before the brutal Soviet intervention—the Soviet Government issued a 'Declaration regarding the Bases of the Development and Further Strengthening of the Friendship and Cooperation between the Soviet Union and other States'.[13] The same principles (including the 'further strengthening of friendship') were asserted during the 1968 intervention in Czechoslovakia as well.

[10] Búza László—Hajdú Gyula, *Nemzetközi Jog*, 3rd edn (Budapest 1961) 454 (translated from the Hungarian original by the Author).

[11] Art 28(1) of the Constitution of the Union of Soviet Socialist Republics, Adopted at the Seventh (Special) Session of the Supreme Soviet of the USSR, Ninth Convocation, on 7 October 1977.

[12] Grotius, *On the Law of War and Peace (De Iure Belli ac Pacis), Prolegomena*—in 'Grotius Reader', (T.M.C. Asser Instituut, The Hague 1983) 234.

[13] See Friedmann, *Changing Structure*, 332.

Rivalry targeting the aura of international law had different facets. One way of competing was shifting emphasis to areas where the rival was more vulnerable; or, looking from another angle, where the 'East' (or the 'West') was able to assert loyalty without jeopardizing its interests. Instead of competing, for example, in the area of freedom of speech, politicians and scholars in the USSR opted to put emphasis on other (also commendable) values, such as decolonisation. Before the Soviet Revolution, Lenin extended his criticism of colonialism to (tsarist) Russia as well, and stated that 'if Morocco would declare war to France, India to England, Persia or China to Russia, these would be just wars'.[14] After the Soviet Revolution, these ideas were repeatedly stressed by Soviet scholars and diplomats. The Soviet Union had an important role in the adoption of the 1960 UN resolution entitled 'Granting Independence to Colonial Countries and Peoples'.[15] What we have here may be qualified as a ploy with the aim of moving to a playing field that provides advantages, but the fact remains that most of the arguments and steps taken by the USSR with regard to colonialism were progressive.

Of course, anti-colonialism had ardent advocates in the West as well. One can go back to Grotius who stated:

> Victoria then is right in saying that the Spaniards have no more legal right over the East Indians because of their religion, than the East Indians would have had over the Spaniards if they had happened to be the first foreigners to come to Spain. Nor are the East Indians stupid and unthinking; on the contrary they are intelligent and shrewd, so that a pretext for subduing them on the ground of their character could not be sustained. Such a pretext on its very face is an injustice. Plutarch said long ago that it was greed that furnished the pretext for conquering barbarous countries, and it is not unsuspected that greedy longing for the property of another often hid itself behind a pretext of civilizing barbarians.[16]

This is the logic and moral height which Lenin tried to claim, and where the USSR tried to posit itself. The principles espoused by Grotius remained, however, a challenge—both before and after 1989—when applied to the present environment. The critical question is whether one would recognise the 'greed under the pretext of civilization' pattern in new contexts—such as the context of armed intervention for the purpose of 'safeguarding socialist democracy' or for the purpose of 'establishing democracy'.

Still in connection with competition for a place under the aura of international law, I would like to take note, very briefly, of another technique. Just as there has been manoeuvring for the purpose of making comfortable things relevant, there has also been manoeuvring with the aim of making uncomfortable things irrelevant. In recent times, we have seen two techniques of displacing bothersome things, of pushing them beyond the realm of relevance. One is territorial displacement (one can take the example of Guantánamo). The other approach is logical displacement—placing vexing incidents outside the scheme of mutuality and consistency ('Kosovo is not a precedent').

[14] The citation is from the text 'Socialism and War', written in July/August 1915, cited from a Hungarian collection of Lenin's writings, Lenin a kommunista erkölcsröl (Lenin on Communist Morality) (Budapest 1970) 82.

[15] See Quigley, *Soviet Legal Innovation,* 143.

[16] Grotius Reader, 65.

III. THE YIELDS OF 1989

A. A Consequential Change of Style

There are several ways to characterise the yields of the fall of the Berlin Wall. One critically important change is the shift from rhetoric to reality. I am not going to suggest that there are no longer slogans or rhetorical manipulations in the 'East' (or in the 'West'), but there is a remarkable difference. Let us consider, for example, constitutional provisions. Prior to 1989, the constitutions of the 'East' had a combative tone. The Project (draft) of the first Soviet Constitution was introduced by Stalin at the Congress of Soviets, on 26 November, 1936. In his speech Stalin stressed that unlike bourgeois constitutions, the Project of the Soviet Constitution was 'deeply international' and started from the assumption that 'no difference in colour of skin, language, level of culture, level of development of the State, or any other difference between races and nations can justify inequality'.[17] Stalin stressed that the new Soviet Constitution would be a 'document evidencing that what millions of honest men were dreaming about and are still dreaming about in capitalist countries—is already implemented in the USSR'; and added that the 'new USSR Constitution will be an indictment against fascism'.[18] Many provisions of the first Soviet Constitution were imbued with this rhetoric. In later versions and modifications this combative tone subsided, but it did not disappear. The last (1977) Soviet Constitution had the following provisions dealing with international law:

> Chapter 4 'Foreign Policy':
>
> Article 28
>
> The USSR steadfastly pursues a Leninist policy of peace and stands for strengthening of the security of nations and broad international co-operation.
> The foreign policy of the USSR is aimed at ensuring international conditions favourable for building communism in the USSR, safeguarding the state interests of the Soviet Union, consolidating the positions of world socialism, supporting the struggle of peoples for national liberation and social progress, preventing wars of aggression, achieving universal and complete disarmament, and consistently implementing the principle of the peaceful coexistence of states with different social systems.
> In the USSR war propaganda is banned.
>
> Article 29
>
> The USSR's relations with other states are based on observance of the following principles: sovereign equality; mutual renunciation of the use or threat of force; inviolability of frontiers; territorial integrity of states; peaceful settlement of disputes; non-intervention in internal affairs; respect for human rights and fundamental freedoms; the equal rights of peoples and their right to decide their own destiny; co-operation among states; and fulfilment in good faith of obligations arising from the generally recognised principles and rules of international law, and from the international treaties signed by the USSR.
>
> Article 30
>
> The USSR, as part of the world system of socialism and of the socialist community, promotes and strengthens friendship, co-operation, and comradely mutual assistance with other socialist

[17] J V Stalin, Pitanja lenjinizma (Questions of Leninism) (Belgrade, 1946) 518.
[18] Stalin, Pitanja lenjinizma, 534.

countries on the basis of the principle of socialist internationalism, and takes an active part in socialist economic integration and the socialist international division of labour.

It is pertinent that the provisions relevant for international law have found place in the chapter entitled 'Foreign Policy'. The context is a consistently activist one. Definitions and delimitations have been replaced with drive and announcement of trends. The phrases posited into operative position are: 'steadfastly pursues', 'aimed at ensuring', 'based on observance', or 'promotes and strengthens'. The text comes closer to a straight normative commitment in Article 29, which refers in connection with international treaties to 'fulfilment in good faith of obligations arising from the generally recognised principles and rules of international law, and from the international treaties signed by the USSR'. But even here, the Constitution does not simply say that treaties will be observed. The context is that 'relations with other states are based on' the principle of fulfilment of international obligations. Critically important legal questions like that pertaining to the relationship between treaties and domestic law were not raised, let alone answered.

The year 1989 brought a radical change with regard to style and approach. Enthusiasm for international law ceded place to international law itself. Very shortly after 1989, some scholarly articles were published in the USSR suggesting a different discourse. In the well-known Soviet law journal *Sovetskoe Gosudarstvo I Pravo*, three Soviet authors proposed in 1990 a constitutional reform that would specify the place and authority of international law, including a provision giving priority to treaties over Soviet legislation.[19] The change came within a few years.

Let us take a look at the wording of some constitutions that replaced the Soviet era constitutions. According to the present (1993) Russian Constitution:[20]

Article 15, Part 4:

4. The universally-recognised norms of international law and international treaties and agreements of the Russian Federation shall be a component part of its legal system. If an international treaty or agreement of the Russian Federation fixes other rules than those envisaged by law, the rules of the international agreement shall be applied.

In a similar vein, the 1996 Ukrainian Constitution[21] states:

Article 9

International treaties in force, consented by the Verkhovna Rada of Ukraine as binding, shall be an integral part of the national legislation of Ukraine.
Conclusion of international treaties, contravening the Constitution of Ukraine, shall be possible only after introducing relevant amendments to the Constitution of Ukraine.

To give a further example, according to the 1997 Polish Constitution:[22]

Article 9

The Republic of Poland shall respect international law binding upon it.

[19] A S Vereshchetin, G M Danilenko, R A Mullerson, *Конституционная реформа в СССР и международное право* (Constitutional Reform in the USSR and International Law) Sovetskoe Gosudarstvo i Pravo, 1990, 13.

[20] Constitution of the Russian Federation, adopted at National Voting in December 1993, in force since December 25, 1993.

[21] Constitution of the Republic of Ukraine, adopted at the Fifth Session of the Verkhovna Rada of Ukraine, on 28 June 1996.

[22] Constitution of the Republic of Poland, adopted on 2 April 1997.

Article 87 Part 1

1. The sources of universally binding law of the Republic of Poland shall be: the Constitution, statutes, ratified international agreements, and regulations.

Article 91

1. After promulgation thereof in the Journal of Laws of the Republic of Poland (*Dziennik Ustaw*), a ratified international agreement shall constitute part of the domestic legal order and shall be applied directly, unless its application depends on the enactment of a statute.
2. An international agreement ratified upon prior consent granted by statute shall have precedence over statutes if such an agreement cannot be reconciled with the provisions of such statutes.
3. If an agreement, ratified by the Republic of Poland, establishing an international organization so provides, the laws established by it shall be applied directly and have precedence in the event of a conflict of laws.

All these (and other) post-1989 constitutional provisions have defined the position of international law within the (domestic) legal system. The Russian and the Polish constitutions have also recognised the supremacy of international law, stating that ratified international agreements shall have precedence over domestic statutes. The Ukrainian Constitution does not take an unequivocal position in this respect; it just states that ratified international treaties shall be part of the national legislation of the Ukraine. The constitutions of the Republic of Georgia,[23] Estonia,[24] and the Slovak Republic[25] have also granted priority to ratified treaties over domestic legislation. The Hungarian Constitution guarantees conformity between domestic law and accepted international obligations.[26]

A rule-based (rather than slogan-based) approach has positioned international law within an environment of legal norms. Of course, real norms need not be ideal norms. In the new setting we have witnessed debates and controversies regarding the exact meaning and range of norms of international law, as well as regarding the specific import of norms dealing with international law. In this setting some traditional dilemmas have re-emerged, and some new ramifications of legal questions have come to the fore. Newly established constitutional courts in former socialist countries have played a significant role in bringing about more clarity, and in confirming the authority of international law.

One could easily cite a significant number of consequential decisions of various constitutional courts. In order to demonstrate the emergence of new problem patterns (and of a new thinking) I shall refer to just one example—an early decision of the Constitutional Court of the Republic of Lithuania. Soon after 1989, Lithuania enacted a special statute on international treaties.[27] This Statute preceded the 1992 Lithuanian Constitution. Art 12 of the Statute provided that international treaties of the Republic of Lithuania 'shall have the force of law'. This Statute envisaged several ways of confirming treaties (which shall have the force of law): by ratification, confirmation by the Government, or confirmation by the Ministry of Foreign Affairs. Accession was

[23] Adopted on 24 August 1995, with amendments as of 27 December 2006—see Art 6.
[24] Adopted on 28 June 1992—see Art 123.
[25] In force since 1 October 1992, with amendments as of 2002—see Arts 7 and 154c.
[26] The 1949 Constitution of the Republic of Hungary, as amended through 25 May 2010—see Paragraph 7.
[27] Law on International Treaties of the Republic of Lithuania, Official Gazette (Valstybes Žinios) No 16-415, 1991.

identified as an additional method. On 19 June 1995, the Government of the Republic of Lithuania requested the Constitutional Court to take a position with regard to the constitutionality of this provision. The key issue was whether the provision of Article 12 of the 1991 Statute may endow with force of law all international treaties adopted by Lithuania, or only those that have been ratified by the Seimas (the Lithuanian Parliament). According to Article 138 of the Lithuanian Constitution 'International treaties ratified by the Seimas of the Republic of Lithuania shall be constituent parts of the legal system of the Republic of Lithuania'. The Government also pointed out that according to Article 7 of the Constitution 'Any law or other statute which contradicts the Constitution shall be invalid'. In the opinion of the Government, the status of treaties accepted by Lithuania but not ratified by the Seimas, had become 'indeterminate'. After a careful analysis (devoting considerable attention to the norms of the 1969 Vienna Convention on the Law of Treaties), the Constitutional Court came to the following conclusions:

> Pursuant to the Constitution only the legislator by the way of ratification may decide which statute of international law shall be the constituent part of the legal system of the Republic of Lithuania having the force of law. The Seimas shall have the right of legislation and the legislation shall not be delegated to any other institution of the State power. Upon recognizing that non-ratified international treaties have the force of law, the prerogative of the Seimas to pass laws would be negated. It is also important that the treaties which must be ratified have the essential significance to the further creation of the legal system. Therefore, the provision of Article 12 of the Law in dispute that 'international treaties of the Republic of Lithuania', i.e. also the international treaties which are not ratified by the Seimas have the force of law, unfoundedly extends their juridical force in the system of sources of law of the Republic of Lithuania. From this standpoint the provision of Article 12 of the disputable Law that international treaties of the Republic of Lithuania 'shall have the force of law' contradicts Part 3 of Article 138 of the Constitution.

Facing the issue of the supposedly 'indeterminate' nature of treaties not ratified by the Seimas, the Constitutional Court found the following solution:

> The Constitutional Court also points out that after the Constitution coming into force, the legal force of the concluded and enforced but non-ratified international treaties of the Republic of Lithuania does not remain indeterminate, as it is stated in the petition of the Government. They have force which is obligatory for entities of legal relations and which is characteristic of every legal act. However, their juridical force differs from ratified treaties in such fact, that they must be in compliance not only with the Constitution but also with the laws.[28]

B. Coping with Doubt

The shift towards a matter-of-fact approach in the 'East' has turned mutuality into a much more realistic goal. Results, steps towards compliance (or steps towards non-compliance) have become measurable by the same instruments and criteria. International institutions have become—more than before—a common arena, and their authority is nowadays more broadly respected. The 'East' joined the Council of Europe and the ECHR (European Convention for the Protection of Human Rights and Fundamental Freedoms) and its

[28] Decision of the Constitutional Court of the Republic of Lithuania of 17 October 1995. Full text of the decision is available in English at: www.lrkt.lt/dokumentai/1995/n5a1017a.htm.

additional protocols. Consequential disputes involving States and other actors from both the 'East' and the 'West' have been submitted to the European Court of Human Rights, decisions have been rendered—and heeded. The CSCE (Conference on Security and Cooperation in Europe—later OSCE, Organization for Security and Cooperation in Europe) has become an important actor.[29] The ICTY (International Criminal Tribunal for the Former Yugoslavia) and the ICTR (International Criminal Tribunal for Rwanda) have brought about major advances in the fight against impunity on the international arena. One hopes that the same will apply to the ICC (International Criminal Court).

Of course, 1989 did not eliminate all imperfections, and did not do away with doubt whether international law can be really efficient when important personalities or state interests are at stake. As a matter of fact, when in May 1999 the ICTY indicted Slobodan Milošević, charging him with crimes against humanity and violations of the laws and customs of war during the Kosovo conflict, this indictment did not have much more effect than the 21 September 2000 Judgment of the Belgrade District Court condemning—as was stated in the Judgment—William Clinton aka Bill Clinton, Madeline Albright, Anthony Blair, Jacques Chirac, Gerhard Schröder, Javier Solana, Wesley Clark and others, to 20 year of prison each, for their role in the same Kosovo conflict. Things changed after 5 October 2000 when Milošević was ousted. But—staying with the example of Serbia—doubts in the effectiveness of international law, along with doubts in the veracity of mutuality persisted, and reasons for doubt were further generated even after the end of the Milošević rule. It was not easy to supersede ethnic perceptions of 'just causes' in any of the successor countries of the former Yugoslavia.[30] There were also situations that raised doubts in the minds of those as well who had consistently opposed ethnic leaders and ethnic narrow-mindedness. The transfer of Milošević to The Hague posed great challenges, and yielded true controversies. The international obligation of the FRY existed, but the Constitution of the FRY (enacted in 1992) stated in Article 17 that a citizen of Yugoslavia cannot be extradited to another country. The Yugoslav Code of Criminal Procedure made this prohibition even more explicit. In this situation, Professor Grubač, then Minister of Justice of the Federal Republic of Yugoslavia (Serbia and Montenegro), proposed a federal legislative act that would supersede (or bypass) the Code of Criminal Procedure, and draw a distinction between extradition to a foreign country and transfer to an international tribunal. The draft was prepared as a matter of priority, but it became soon clear that the Montenegrin representatives in the Parliament would probably block it. The frustration mounted—and so did the temptation to disregard the Constitution (and the Code of Civil Procedure) for the sake of international reward. In this situation, the draft legislative act prepared by Minister Grubač was practically copied and submitted to the Federal Government in the form of a government decree. There was no force in the Federal Government that could have blocked the adoption of the decree. (It was, of course, very much questionable whether a government decree could replace a legislative act aiming to supersede the Code of Criminal Procedure.) The decree was adopted by the Government, but it was successfully challenged before the Constitutional

[29] This has come to the expression in the 6 December 1994 Budapest Summit Declaration and Decisions (Reprinted in 34 ILM 764—1995).

[30] See interesting reflections on this issues in Dan Saxon (from the ICTY Prosecution) 'Exporting Justice: Perception of the ICTY Among the Serbian, Croatian and Muslim Communities in the Former Yugoslavia', (2005) *Journal of Human Rights* 559; on perceptions in Serbia see also M Grubač, Hag očima Beograda (*The Hague in the Eyes of Belgrade)* Glasnik Advokatske komore Vojvodine, 9-10/2001, 439.

Court of Yugoslavia. Before rendering a final decision, the Constitutional Court issued an interim measure prohibiting the transfer of Milošević under the Government Decree. In the meantime international pressure mounted, and it became clear that sorely needed international financial aid would depend on extradition. The Serbian Government opted to transfer Milošević to The Hague, just a few days before an international donor-conference.[31] The situation was a difficult one, and it is not easy to tell whether waiting would have been the better approach. It was certainly in line with justice—and also in line with the international obligations of Serbia—that Milošević was delivered to The Hague. It is distressing that under the circumstances this was not a clear triumph of the rule of law.

Faith in international law and mutuality were exposed to new trials when diplomats visiting countries of the former Yugoslavia requested the arrest of war criminals who were still at large, and at the same time asked these countries to sign a statement that they would not extradite US indictees to the ICC.

Doubts are often tied to a perceived lack of mutuality. This perception is particularly typical in less powerful countries. In various countries, (certainly including those qualified as 'superpowers') time and again, the question has also emerged as to whether international law can (and should) supersede some 'more important' values and principles. Doubts have often been spurred by agitation—and this is not a phenomenon restricted to communism. Agitated societies (or leaders) often lose a sense for balance; they are blinded by one priority, and forget the well-established need for heeding more values at the same time. The words of John Bolton, US Ambassador to the UN, under the Bush Administration, represent a stunning example of such thinking:

> It is a big mistake for us to grant any validity to international law even when it may seem in our short-term interest to do so—because, over the long term, the goal of those who think that international law really means anything are those who want to constrict the United States.[32]

Bolton's position was shared by a number of influential authors and decision-makers.[33] At the same time, consequential arguments were advanced against this position. An analysis of arguments and counter-arguments would take me way beyond the limits of these observations. I would just like to refer—among other possible sources—to an important study of M Scharf, devoted to the influence of international law in the formation of American foreign policy, relying on empirical data supplied by former State Department Legal Advisers.[34] In the closing sentences of his article, Scharf reaches the conclusion that '[i]n the final analysis, the qualitative empirical data has shown that international law is real because it plays a real role in shaping the conduct of States (even a superpower in times of crisis)'.[35]

[31] See a more detailed description of this sequence of events in Grubač, ibid.

[32] See M Scharf, 'International Law in Crisis: A Qualitative Empirical Contribution to the Compliance Debate' (2009) 31 *Cardozo Law Review* 47, 56—quoting Samantha Power, Boltonism, *New Yorker*, March 21, 2005.

[33] See, among others, J Goldsmith and E Posner, *The Limits of International Law* (Oxford, Oxford University Press, 2005); M Paulsen, 'The Constitutional Power to Interpret International Law' (2009) 118 *Yale Law Journal* 1762. Paulsen's article found prompt criticism in R Ahdieh's 'The Fog of Certainty' (2009) *The Yale Law Journal Online* 41.

[34] M Scharf, International Law in Crisis.

[35] Ibid, 97.

The debate will certainly continue. 1989 is not the end of history, and it did not bring us to an end of trials awaiting international law. It is next to impossible to keep count of the predictions that heralded an end of history, the end of some intrinsic problem, or the arrival of the 'era of peace'. (One may incidentally take note of the fact that 'Peace of God' was proclaimed exactly one thousand years ago, by Robert II of France in 1010.) Doubts linked to international law will certainly continue, just as international law will continue to exist. Looking back at the situation prior to 1989, we can nevertheless say that a step forward was indeed taken. Instead of discarding doubt (which was the Soviet style solution), we have now gained an opportunity to face its causes. And as a matter of fact, it is easier to cope with doubt than with slogans of exuberant loyalty.

3

The End of the Cold War: An Epochal Event in the History of International Law?

RANDALL LESAFFER*

I. PERIODISATION IN THE HISTORY OF INTERNATIONAL LAW

PERIODISATION IS AT the best of times an occupational hazard of the historian. It is an exercise in generalisation and forces the historian to make stark choices. The historian has to single out these trends and events that sustain claims to the internal consistency of the historical epoch; he or she has to underplay those that contradict that consistency. Furthermore, the historian has to highlight the discontinuities with the epochs before and after. Often, the temptation is there to elevate a single event to an epochal event, a historical caesura that marks the beginning and end of an epoch. Each of these choices lays the historian open to criticism of subjectivity, of being driven by ideological motives that are rooted rather in the historian than in history. But it is exactly this subjectivity that makes periodisation an interesting object for historical study itself. If it does not have much to offer in terms of reconstructing the past, it says a lot about the basic assumptions that move the authors of the reconstructions and about the place they attribute themselves in the chain of history.

The difficulties inherent to historical periodisation are compounded when one is dealing with contemporary history, with an epoch that has not ended yet. While many accept that the end of the Cold War heralded the beginnings of a new era in international relations and international law, no one would claim that this epoch has come to an end by 2010. In that sense, the post-Cold-War years do not constitute a historical epoch yet, but can at best be considered the beginnings of a new epoch. It is not clear what this 'epoch' will lead to and what will follow. While this diminishes the danger of reducing the epoch to an era of transition from one epoch to another, it enhances the danger of seeing it as the logical accomplishment of a long historical evolution, as the end of at least one 'history', as Francis Fukuyama has so famously done in his historical rendering of the end of the Cold War.[1] The years since the end of the Cold War can only be assessed for the break they made or not with the previous period, and for the place they take at the end of existing grand narratives of the history of international law. Whereas assessment

* Professor of Legal History at Tillburg University and the Catholic University of Leuven.

[1] Francis Fukuyama, *The End of History and the Last Man* (London, Harper, 1992).

of past epochs can be both backwards and forwards looking, this assessment can only be the former.

In the introduction to his monumental survey of the history of international law since the Late Middle Ages, the German scholar and diplomat Wilhelm Grewe complained that little or no consensus exists on periodisation in the historiography of international law.[2] Whereas that is true on the level of detailed subdivisions of international law's history since the Late Middle Ages, most periodisations are based on a very few foundational assumptions that are shared among historians of international law and international lawyers alike. In all, one can discern three main types of periodisation in the historiography of international law since the Late Middle Ages. These are not mutually exclusive and can be combined in a single narrative.

The first type, the 'hegemonic approach,' is the one proposed by Grewe. It has been adopted by several other leading German historians of international law including Stephan Verosta, Wolfgang Preiser and Karl-Heinz Ziegler.[3] For Grewe and his followers, the determinant factor for each period is the predominant power of that day and age. Grewe considers this the best way to write a history that connects international relations with law and legal theory with state practice as he holds that 'both are forms of expression of the same power, which characterise the political style of an epoch just as much as its social, economic and legal organisation'.[4] As such, he hopes to overcome the biases of a historiography that he finds one-sidedly focused on the historical jurisprudence of international law and do not take enough account of state practice and the political context of international law. The period since the end of the Middle Ages is subdivided in the Spanish Age (1494–1648), the French Age (1648–1815), the British Age (1815–1919), the Age of the Anglo-American condominium (1919–1944) and the Age of American-Soviet rivalry (1945–1989). To the English translation of the book, published in 2000, Grewe and Byers added an epilogue on the years after 1989.

The second type, the 'Eurocentric approach', is based on the assumption that modern international law originated from Europe and then expanded over the world to become a universal system of law. Recently, another German historian of international law, Heinhard Steiger, proposed a periodisation on the basis of this idea. Steiger subdivides the history of international law since the Late Middle Ages in the Ages of Christianity (1300–1800), of Civilised Nations (19th century–1918) and of Mankind (since 1919). He tentatively indicates that we are currently moving towards the Age of the World Citizen. According to Steiger, modern international law originated in Christian Europe. Until the end of the 18th century, Christianity formed the 'major intellectual foundation of legal order'. The French Revolution disrupted the connection between the legal and religious orders but international law remained very much a European or Western affair. It was the legal order of the civilised nations, organised in states, to the exclusion of uncivilised peoples who did not know that level and form of political organisation. Only after World

[2] Wilhelm G Grewe, *Epochen der Völkerrechtsgeschichte* (Baden-Baden, Nomos, 1984) 19 (first written between 1939 and 1944) translated by Michael Byers as *The Epochs of International Law* (Berlin etc, De Gruyter, 2000).

[3] Wolfgang Preiser, 'Völkerrechtsgeschichte' in Karl Strupp and Hans-Jürgen Schlochauer (eds), *Wörterbuch des Völkerrechts* 2nd edn (Berlin, De Gruyter, 1962) vol 3, 680; idem, 'Völkerrechtsgeschichte' in Hermann Kunst, Roman Herzog and Wilhelm Schneemelcher (eds), *Evangelisches Staatslexikon* (Stuttgart, Kreuz, 1975) 2823; Stephan Verosta, 'Die Geschichte des Völkerrechts' in Alfred Verdroß, *Völkerrecht*, 5th edn (Vienna, Springer, 1964) 31; Karl-Heinz Ziegler, *Völkerrechtsgeschichte. Ein Studienbuch*, 2nd edn (Munich, Beck, 2007).

[4] Grewe, *Epochs of International Law*, 6.

War I, and then even more so after World War II, did a global legal order based on the idea of unity of all mankind emerge.[5] Grewe's writings show the hegemonic and the Eurocentric approaches not to be mutually exclusive. He acknowledges a scarlet thread of the expansion of the European law of nations into a global international law through the history of international law.[6]

Since the 1960s the notion of the European origin of modern international law has come under attack from several angles. On the basis of his studies of treaty practice between European and non-European powers during the Early Modern Age, Charles H Alexandrowicz has argued that the law of nations of that age was not exclusively European but 'universal' and that only during the 19th century international law became more exclusively European.[7] More recently, Antony Anghie has claimed that the colonial encounter played a central role in the formation of modern international law and of state sovereignty.[8] I acknowledge that although both these lines of argument have merit, it can hardly be contested that between the 16th and 19th centuries European powers had by far the greatest impact on the formation of international law, whether they did so in relation to one another, non-European powers or both.[9]

The third type of periodisation, the state-centric, is the most foundational. It underlies the vast majority of grand narratives of the history of international law, either because it is consciously used, because it is implicit or because it is contested. Most historians of international law, as well as most international lawyers, accept that modern international law is the result of a continuous historical evolution that started with the emergence of the sovereign state in Europe. Before the end of the 19th century, the origins of modern international law were commonly traced back to the 17th century, to the works of Hugo Grotius (1583–1645) and the Peace Treaties of Westphalia (1648). Since the beginning of the 20th century, the historical narrative of modern international law has come to include the so-called precursors of Grotius of the 16th century or even the Late Middle Ages (as of 1300).[10] This approach has been criticised for being reductionist and for ignoring the historical existence of types of international law that are not based on state sovereignty.[11]

[5] Heinhard Steiger, 'From the International Law of Christianity to the International Law of the World Citizen—Reflections on the Formation of the Epochs of the History of International Law' (2001) 3 *Journal of the History of International Law* 180.

[6] Wilhelm G Grewe, 'Vom europäischen zum universellen Völkerrecht. Zur Frage der Revision des "europazentrischen" Bildes der Völkerrechtsgeschichte' (1982) 42 *Zeitschrift für ausländisches öffentliches Recht und Völkerrecht* 449.

[7] Charles H Alexandrowicz, 'Treaty and Diplomatic Relations Between European and South Asian Powers in the Seventeenth and Eighteenth Centuries' (1960) 100 *Recueil des Cours de l'Académie de Droit International* 207; idem, 'The Afro-Asian World and the Law of Nations (Historical Aspects)', (1968) 123 *Recueil des Cours de l'Académie de Droit International* 117; idem, *An Introduction to the History of the Law of Nations in the East Indies, 16th, 17th and 18th centuries* (Oxford, Clarendon, 1967); idem, *The European-African Confrontation: A Study in Treaty Making* (Leyden, Sijthoff, 1973). Some even reject the European origins for the 19th century, Alexander Orakhelashvili, 'The Idea of European International Law' (2006) 17 *European Journal of International Law* 315.

[8] Antony Anghie, *Imperialism, Sovereignty and the Making of International Law* (Cambridge, Cambridge University Press, 2005). See also Yasuaka Onuma, 'When was the Law of International Society Born?' (2000) 2 *Journal of the History of International Law* 1.

[9] Grewe, 'Vom europäischen zum universellen Völkerrecht' (1982); Martti Koskenniemi, 'International Law in Europe: Between Tradition and Renewal' (2005) 16 *European Journal of International Law* 113.

[10] Wilhelm G Grewe, 'Vom europäischen zum universellen Völkerrecht' (1982) 449; idem, 'Was ist klassisches, was ist modernes Völkerrecht?' in Alexander Böhm, Klaus Lüdersen and Karl-Heinz Ziegler (eds), *Idee und Realität des Rechts in der Entwicklung internationaler Beziehungen. Festgabe für Wolfgang Preiser* (Baden Baden, Nomos, 1983) 111.

[11] Steiger, 'From the International Law of Christianity', 180.

Some historians, among whom Preiser and Ziegler stand out, have argued that several basic ideas of international law can be traced back way beyond the Middle Ages to classical and even pre-classical Antiquity.[12]

But these criticisms have not overcome the dominance of the assumption that the history of the discipline becomes only truly relevant to the understanding of current international law from the time the sovereign state first began to emerge: somewhere between the 14th and 16th centuries in Europe. This assumption has left its traces on almost all attempts at subdividing the history of modern international law in different historical epochs. Underlying most periodisations of the history of international law from the Late Middle Ages onwards is the story of the emergence (14th–18th century), heyday (19th century) and decline (20th and 21st centuries) of modern international law as a system premised on state sovereignty. This narrative is also highly Eurocentric in the sense that it goes hand in hand with a more general historical narrative of the rise, heyday and decline of Modern Europe, living its heyday in the 19th century.

In this narrative, the 14th to 18th centuries constitute the formative period of an international legal order based on state sovereignty. First accomplished in the 'classical law of nations' or the 'public law of Europe' of the dynastic states of Europe after Westphalia (1648–1815) the legal order then evolved into the 'international law' of the 19th-century nation-state and its colonial empires, through which it was spread over the globe. The end of World War I with the Peace Treaty of Versailles (1919) and the foundation of the League of Nations constitutes a fundamental turning point towards a new age in which the state, while still forming the foundational stone of the international legal order, starts to lose its monopoly as the sole subject, author and enforcer of international law and increasingly has to give way to other players, from individual human beings to private organisations and public international organisations.[13] This basic outline is also present underneath the narratives and periodisations of the first two types, such as those of Grewe and Steiger.[14] It forms a more foundational framework that brings relief to, for instance, Grewe's periodisation. Underneath the five epochs he discerns between the 15th and the 20th centuries actually lies the threefold division of the formation (Spanish and French Ages), the heyday (British Age) and decline (Anglo-American and American-Soviet Age) of the sovereign state system and its international law. Although Grewe considered these two latter periods to be self-standing epochs, he also acknowledged 'a certain conceptual continuity' and did not oppose the idea that the 20th century marked a gradual shift away from state-centric international law.[15]

[12] David Bederman, *International Law in Antiquity* (Cambridge, Cambridge University Press, 2001) 1; Wolfgang Preiser, 'Über die Ursprünge des modernen Völkerrechts', in Erik Brül (ed), *Internationalrechtliche und staatsrechtliche Abhandlungen. Festschrift für Walter Schätzel zum 70. Geburtstag* (Düsseldorf, Hermes, 1960) 373; Karl-Heinz Ziegler, 'Die römische Grundlagen des europäischen Völkerrechts' (1972) 4 *Ius Commune* 1.

[13] Randall Lesaffer, 'The Grotian Tradition Revisited: Change and Continuity in the History of International Law (2002) 73 *British Yearbook of International Law* 103.

[14] Grewe, 'Was ist klassisches, was ist modernes Völkerrecht' 117; Steiger, 'From the International Law of Christianity', 190.

[15] Grewe, *Epochs of International Law*, 639.

II. THE END OF THE COLD WAR AND THE HEGEMONIC APPROACH

One expects the end of the Cold War and the collapse of the Soviet Empire to stand out as epochal events in Grewe's hegemonic approach to the history of international law. In the German edition of his survey of the historical of international law, which appeared in 1984, Grewe defined the four decades since the end of World War II as the Age of American-Soviet rivalry and the rise of the Third World.[16]

Since 1494, each of the five epochs Grewe discerns in the history of international law starts at the end of a war that marks the decline of the dominant power of the previous age and the emergence of the new power. Each period also starts with a new peace ordering and the articulation of a new international legal order. The post-1945 epoch is unique in the sense that it is not dominated by one power or a 'condominium' of powers, but by the rivalry between the two leading powers, the United States and the Soviet Union. This rivalry put significant brakes on their power to mould international legal order and prevented the United Nations from truly embodying world legal order. It also left room for the newly independent Third World countries to make their mark on the international legal scene.[17]

The demise of the Soviet Empire in Central and Eastern Europe and in Central Asia (1989–1991) ended the bipolarity of world order that had existed since the late 1940s. Hence, of necessity it marked the end of the epoch which, for Grewe, had started in 1945. In the logic of Grewe's thought, it was now the time for the American Age to begin. But interestingly, in the epilogue on the English translation to Grewe's book, Grewe and Byers refrain from this conclusion. While they acknowledge it to be undeniably true that the United States is the sole superpower today and has by far the greatest influence of all states in and on the international legal order, Grewe and Byers state that the impact on the international order of the United States cannot be compared to that of Spain, France and Britain in their respective ages.[18] They attribute this to two factors. First, they hold that power has no longer the relevance it had before. Military power has lost much of its use, both because of the devastating power of nuclear weapons and because of legal constraints. But also in the economic or cultural fields, American power does not go uncontested. Second, American dominance also finds itself in a dynamic tension with what the authors describe as a 'new communitarian approach' or 'growing trends towards a stronger international community'. Although the authors warn against excessively elevated expectations, they see this 'communitarian approach' as a real brake on the freedom of action of states, including the predominant one. But this assessment does not bring Grewe yet to the point of breaking with his own hegemonic approach as far as the post-Cold-War Age is concerned. In his own words, '[i]t remains to be seen which trend will prevail,' American predominance or the communitarian approach.[19]

[16] The relevant Chapter in the *Epochen des Völkerrechtsgeschichte* was largely based on a paper dating from 1981, Wilhelm G Grewe, 'Über den Gesamtcharacter der jüngsten Epoche der Völkerrechtsgeschichte', in Ingo van Münch (ed), *Staatsrecht—Völkerrecht—Europarecht. Festschrift für Hans-Jürgen Schlochauer zum 75. Geburtstag am 28. März 1981* (Berlin, De Gruyter, 1981) 301.

[17] Grewe, *Epochs of International Law,* 639. See also: Antonio Cassese, *International Law* (Oxford, Oxford University Press, 2001) 35.

[18] I find this claim about the extent of Spanish, French of British relative position in their 'Age' strongly exaggerated and would rather hold that American relative power, notwithstanding many qualifications which need to be made (see below), is rather greater than theirs was.

[19] Grewe, *Epochs of International Law,* 703. See for the debate on American hegemony, Michael Byers and Georg Nolte (eds), *United States Hegemony and the Foundations of International Law* (Cambridge,

Regardless of Grewe's own qualms with the hegemonic approach for the post-Cold-War Age, it remains an interesting perspective to look at the end of the Cold War itself. This is certainly true from a contemporary point of view; that is contemporary to the 'epochal' years 1989–1991 themselves. President George H W Bush is often quoted in relation to the end of the Cold War for his reference to a 'new world order' which he most famously made in a speech on 11 September 1990 at a joint session of the US Congress. Moreover, he has frequently been upbraided for having achieved little in bringing about that new world order.[20] But this is at least a partial injustice to the president who presided over the victorious and peaceful ending of the Cold War.

The Cold War ended where it had begun, in Europe. The events that led to its end were the successful breaking away of Moscow's central and eastern European allies from the communist bloc (1989), the unification of Germany (1990) and the collapse of the communist regime in Moscow and of the Soviet Union itself (1991). Even if to almost all witnesses, from policy makers to policy watchers to the wider public, these events appeared sudden and unexpected, American political leaders were quick to assess these events as a victory of the West over the communist world, and to act accordingly. The potential power vacuum the communist empire threatened to leave was readily filled, not by the formation of a new international system but by the absorption of the former communist countries of Europe, and even Russia, into the pre-existing Western part of the formerly bipolar international legal order. The most dramatic example of this American and Western victory was German unification. After having entertained some vague thoughts about a confederation between the two Germanies, the architect of the unification process, Chancellor Helmut Kohl, with the full support of President Bush, absorbed the East German territories into the Federal Republic of Germany, even making use of a provision in the Federal Republic's Fundamental Law to that extent (Article 23). In order to achieve the acquiescence of Moscow and Paris to German unification, Kohl did not have to make any compromise on the extent of Western victory. To the contrary, his main concession—to France—was rendering full support to the strengthening of one of the linchpins of the Western fabric from the Cold War, Western European integration, by speeding up the transformation of the European Communities into the European Union and the introduction of a single European currency.[21] Later, the former European allies of the Soviet Union, and the three Baltic republics which after the Russian invasion of 1939 had become part of the Soviet Union, joined the main Western regional organisations, NATO and the European Union. As far as Europe, the main battlefield of the Cold War, was concerned, the unification of east and west that followed the collapse of communism was not a merger between two partners, nor the birth of a new legal order but the expansion of the Western legal order to the former communist bloc. That this was the successful outcome of a consequential strategy on the part of the dominant power's leaders is a matter of debate, but that it was the desired outcome is certain. Rather than Bush's new world order quote, the more relevant one is the remark Secretary

Cambridge University Press, 2003) esp Edward Kwakwa, 'The international community, international law, and the United States: three in one, two against one, one and the same?' 25.

[20] *Public Papers of the Presidents of the United States: George Bush,* 1990 (Washington, 1991) vol 2, 1218.

[21] For a good survey of the end of the Cold War in Europe: Mary Elise Sarotte, *1989. The Struggle to create Post-Cold War Europe* (Princeton and Oxford, Princeton University Press, 2009); also see volume 3 in Melvyn P Leffler and Odd Arne Westad (eds), *The Cambridge History of the Cold War* (Cambridge, Cambridge University Press, 2010).

of State James Baker dotted down in 1989 and which found its way into a speech Bush gave at Mainz on 31 May 1989: 'Something we wanted for 40 years * Eur[ope] that's whole and free'.[22]

With the expansion of the regional institutional framework of the West over Central and Eastern Europe came the export of its interpretation, conceptions, rules and foundational values of international order and international law. In the Charter of Paris for a New Europe of 21 November 1991, the expanding West defined the new legal order of Europe, and thus itself. The Charter laid down democracy, the rule of law, economic liberty and the respect for human rights as the fundaments of the international legal order of Europe.[23] A year later, the European Community made the recognition of new States in the broader European area, including the Soviet Union, conditional upon, among others, their acceptance of these values as expressed in the UN Charter, the Final Act of the Helsinki Conference on Security and Co-operation in Europe (1975) and the Charter of Paris as well as respect for minority rights.[24] Successful implementation of the European Community's guidelines was largely limited to the territories west of the Caucasus, and even then, hardly any attempts were made at promoting these guidelines into rules of general international law.

In parts of the Former Yugoslavia, the Caucasus and at several places outside Europe, the vacuum the fall of the Soviet Empire left was not filled in by the West—or at least not immediately— but by reviving nationalist or religious forces that had been on the ground before but now got the opportunity to rise. These had little direct influence on the international legal order as yet but were rather marginalised by it.

Under the hegemonic approach, the end of the Cold War only partly constituted an epochal event. The bipolar system of power of the Cold War disappeared and, at least as far as the Atlantic and European subsystems of international law are concerned, bipolarity made place for American dominated unipolarity. But the caesura of 1989 was different from that of 1648, 1815, 1919 or 1945 in that no new international legal order was created. What happened was that the international system of the victorious pole expanded to the other pole.

III. THE POST-COLD-WAR AGE AND THE HEGEMONIC AND EUROCENTRIC APPROACH[25]

In the historical narrative of international law under the Eurocentric approach, the 20th century is marked by the transition from a European to a universal legal order. Through the decolonisation of the 1940s to 1970s and the accession of the former European colonies in Asia and Africa to the United Nations, that transition was completed before the end of the Cold War. In this respect, the Eurocentric narrative has little to add to

[22] See usa.usembassy.de/etexts/ga6-890531.htm.

[23] See www.osce.org/documents/mcs/1990/11/4045_en.pdf.

[24] EC Guidelines on the Recognition of New States in Eastern Europe and in the Soviet Union of 16 December 1991, published in (1991) 62 *British Yearbook of International Law* 559. See James Crawford, *The Recognition of States in International Law,* 2nd edn (Oxford, Oxford University Press, 2006) 396.

[25] Some good surveys on recent developments in international law are to be found in the series of 'Centennial Essays' which appeared in (2006) 100 *American Journal of International Law*. For this and the next paragraph, I base myself largely on these, the 'Epilogue' in Grewe, *Epochs of International Law,* 701; Malcolm Shaw, *International Law,* 6th edn (Cambridge, Cambridge University Press, 2010) and works footnoted hereafter.

the question whether the end of the Cold War constitutes an epochal event. But there is another dimension to the Eurocentric historical narrative for the 20th century: that of the extent of the impact of the European and Western powers on international law.

In this perspective, the hegemonic and the Eurocentric narratives approach one another in their rendering of the history of international law in the 20th century. The question of the European or Western character of 20th-century international law becomes that of the extent of the dominance of the Western powers, in particular the United States after 1945.

The end of the Cold War saw the demise of the United States' competitor to world domination and left the United States the most powerful state on earth. But that leaves the question that Grewe raised open: to what extent could the United States and its Western allies dominate and mould world order? In 2000, Grewe spoke of a tension between American dominance and a new communitarian approach but left it unresolved which of the two trends would prove the stronger. Can we now, yet another decade later, add something more to the debate? For that, we need to address three questions.

First, did the Western model at the end of the Cold War expand outside Europe to encompass the whole world? In other words, did the end of the Cold War make the Western tenets of international order—democracy, rule of law, respect for human and minority rights and free trade—into the hallmarks of a 'new world order' as many hoped and expected in the early 1990s? Although reality could never live up to Fukuyama's idealism, the 1990s had a certain momentum towards the spreading of the Western order, or elements of it, over new parts of the world. In the early 1990s, democracy made headway in Central and Eastern Europe, Latin America and some African and Asian countries. In Africa, a regional system of human rights protection was set up, culminating in the foundation of the African Court of Human and Peoples' Rights (2006). In 1994, the Council of the Arab League adopted the Arab Charter on Human Rights. In Africa, the Americas and Asia, regional cooperation was enhanced through the foundation of the African Union (2001), the different American free trade zones and the strengthening of ASEAN. But maybe the West's biggest success lay in the founding of the World Trade Organisation (1995) with its institutions for dispute settlement. Through this organisation, free trade—with all its qualifications—has certainly gained a lot of ground towards becoming a real tenet of world legal order. But important though these steps were, they do not allow for the conclusion that the Western order became truly and effectively universal. Today, many regimes persist that are not democratic, in name or reality, and where respect for human rights and the rule of law are flimsy or non-existent. Europe's attempt at making respect for Western values a condition for state recognition was never carried through outside Europe, or even in the margins of Europe. The end of bipolarity did not make the order of the remaining pole in all its aspects into the new world order.

Second, is 'unipolar' after 20 years still a good qualification for world order? The end of the Cold War left the United States the sole superpower, giving the world a 'unipolar moment'. But did this last? The relative economic, military and cultural power of the US was and still is by far the greatest of any leading power ever. But the impediments to using that power effectively to dominate the world are also greater than ever before in history. Today, the interdependency between states is far greater, not only in the sphere of the economy, but also of culture, the environment and of the international dimension to ordinary people's lives. Even a rising world power such as China is as much a partner and objective ally to the US to address crucial problems as it is a competitor. The devastating potential of today's military arsenal hampers its full use, while even regional wars against minor powers or non-state actors are enormously costly in terms of money as well as diplomatic and political credit. Moreover, over the last decade, and particularly since the financial crisis of 2008, the relative economic power of the US has declined. Against this relative decline in power, stands the rise of new economic great powers outside the Western world such as China, India, South Korea, Indonesia or Brazil. The US's traditional allies, Western Europe and Japan, which in the 1980s and 1990s were still considered its main potential challengers, are also in decline. The gradual rearrangement of positions has found its clearest expression in the rise of the G20 (first convened in 1999). Whereas in the 1990s, it still seemed to suffice to expand the G7 into a G8 by adding Russia, now a growing part of the debate needs to be transferred from this 'Western' club (including Japan) to the global G20. In conclusion, we can say that over the last twenty years, the world has commenced to move away from the 'unipolar moment' of the early 1990s. Whether this will lead to a multipolar world or a new bipolarity opposing the two leading powers and their allies, is a matter for the future.

Third, to what extent does the United States dominate the actual workings of international law, its formation and its enforcement? In the context of this chapter, I will not try to address this question in a comprehensive way but will limit myself to one aspect of international law and the world's legal order. Because the relative preponderance of the United States is nowhere as great as it is in relation to military power, I will focus on use of force.

When President Bush spoke in September 1990 about a 'new world order' he did so in the context of the Kuwait Crisis. Bush called the Iraqi aggression on Kuwait 'the first assault on the new world that we seek' but also 'a rare opportunity toward an historic period of cooperation'.[26] The First Gulf War indeed became a joint effort of a large part of the international community to stop the aggression of one sovereign state against another and it put, for the first time since the Korean War, the United Nations Security Council centre-stage in a big military conflict.

During the Cold War, the security organ of the organised world community had been prevented of playing any significant role in the management of important conflicts because of superpower rivalry and the almost systematic use of the veto in the Security Council by the superpowers—and particularly the Soviet Union—to protect themselves and their allies against majority votes. Now, with the end of the Cold War, it was felt and hoped that the Security Council would finally be able to assume a bigger role. The Kuwait Crisis seemed to prove these expectations right. The attempt at revitalising the Security Council was an effort to revitalise a mechanism that the United States and its main Western allies had desired back in 1944–1945 and that the Cold War adversary had prevented from functioning properly; it fitted the pattern of expanding the Western order.

As of the early 1990s, the United Nations Security Council has come to play a vastly greater role in the management of armed conflicts than before, in three different ways. *Primo*, the Security Council expanded its factual competencies from international conflicts to a much wider range of armed conflicts such as internal conflicts and conflicts

[26] *Public Papers of the Presidents of the United States: George Bush*, 1990 (Washington, 1991) vol 2, 1218, 1219.

involving non-state actors. *Secundo*, a far greater number of peacekeeping operations was mounted since 1990 than in the four decades before. Moreover, over the years, the mandate of UN peacekeepers has grown both in terms of ambition but also of the right to use force. *Tertio*, beginning with the Kuwait Crisis, the Security Council has started to make more use of its powers under Chapter VII, including the imposition of sanctions under Article 41 of the UN Charter and the authorisation of the use of force under Article 42. The Kuwait Crisis was the first instance of authorisation of the use of force in an important armed conflict since the Korean War (1950) but it was followed by several more such as for Somalia, Bosnia-Herzegovina and Haiti. The purposes of these authorisations of the use of force extended from the stopping of aggression and the protection of human rights to the restoration of a democratic regime.

The Council's authorisation to use force against Iraq gave international sanction to the US-led military coalition to liberate Kuwait. But it also provoked a debate about the implementation of Article 43 of the UN Charter and to provide the Council with designated armed forces.[27] This was not to be; today the 'international community' can still act militarily only through the armed forces of states willing to contribute. This, together with its veto power and its relative political, economic and military preponderance, put the US safely with the foot on the pedals, including the brakes, of the newly invigorated world organisation. Over the last two decades, acting through the Security Council, the international community has met with success as well as disaster in the management of international conflicts, but in almost all important cases, the role of the United States has been determining.

On the other hand, since the end of the Cold War, the United States has shown a remarkably great preparedness to use force. In fact, this is the strengthening of a trend that already started in the 1980s when the United States got itself involved in several internal conflicts in Third World countries and started to make use of military force to repress state-sponsored terrorism. Whereas in the 1980s the involvement in Latin-American or African countries was motivated in terms of Cold War battlefields, it now became a matter of safeguarding or restoring international stability, protecting American citizens, human rights, democracy or, since 9/11, fighting international terrorism. Over the past two decades, different American administrations have shown smaller or greater willingness to work with and through the Security Council, regional organisations such as NATO or act alone or with particular allies. In most cases where a Council mandate was lacking, the US did not have to face condemnation because it was protected by its veto and the reluctance of other states to take the US head on by condemning its actions too clearly. All in all, the US has not had to use its veto much to protect itself or its allies, but the use of it or even the constant threat comes with rising costs. Whereas during the Cold War, the use of a veto against the majority had the effect of strengthening the coalition because it was used to protect one's block against the other, now it comes at the price of isolation because it is used to protect a particular interest. In short, over the last two decades, the US has not been seriously hampered in using force as it wanted, but it has become increasingly isolated by doing so. The US can lead the world community in the safeguarding of international peace and security where it wants to go, but it cannot change its direction single-handedly.

[27] 'An Agenda for Peace. Preventive diplomacy, peacemaking and peacekeeping,' Report of the Secretary-General of the United Nations, 17 June 1992, www.un.org/documents/ga/res/47/a47r120.htm.

Finally, a scholarly debate has been raging over the question whether the administration of President George W Bush (2001–2009) has tried, in the context of its 'war on terror', to change the law on the use of force by extending the interpretation of the right to self-defence, and whether it has been successful at that. More in particular, it is alleged that the US tried to extend the concept of self-defence to the use of force against states that only harbour terrorists and to include preventive self-defence against a non-imminent threat. Whereas President Bush and other American officials have certainly made such claims, the US have by and large refrained from arguing particular cases under these headings and only a very few states have adopted them. In general, one can say that these claims have not given rise to a consistent American state practice along these lines and that they found no general acceptance with the vast majority of states, or the International Court of Justice for that matter.[28] The changes the US was able to achieve in relation to use of force law are altogether more modest. The interpretation that state support to terrorist non-state actors constitutes an 'armed attack' under Article 51 of the UN Charter is now more generally and clearly accepted than it was before, but whether harbouring is enough is unclear.[29] Remarkably, in 2004, the UN High-Level Panel constituted to make recommendations on the revision of the Charter conceded anticipatory self-defence against an imminent attack to fall within the confines of Article 51, thereby taking a surprisingly clear stance in an old and unresolved debate.[30] But this remark has not met with much reaction of the world community either way so that even on the question whether Article 51 condones anticipatory self-defence against imminent threats, the jury is still out.

In the grand narrative of the transition away from a European and towards a universal international legal order, the post-Cold War Era marks another gradual step in the decline of Western domination. The third quarter of 20th century, with the decolonisation and the formation of a truly global world organisation, already saw the achievement of a global world order, but under the domination of two superpowers. The collapse of the Soviet Union created a 'unipolar moment' in which the United States and its Western allies might have hoped to impose their vision of world order on the whole globe. At this, they proved only partially successful. The rise of new, non-Western economic powers and the growing interdependency of the world foretell that the Western impact on the world's legal order will further decline. In this light, the post-Cold-War Age is at best a third transitional sub-period in the Age of Universal International Law. Whether this

[28] Protests against claims of preventive defence have been particularly loud and general. Claims regarding states which harbour terrorists have been met with more silence or even acquiescence, but certainly not enough to state that it has become an accepted customary interpretation of Article 51. The International Court of Justice in the *Wall Opinion* in 2004 and in *Armed Activities on the Territory of the Congo (DRC v Uganda)* in 2005 has refrained from answering that question. ICJ Reports (2004) 136 para 139 and (2005) 168, para 147.

[29] Christine Gray, *International Law and the Use of Force,* 3rd edn (Cambridge, Cambridge University Press, 2008) 193; Christian Henderson, *The Persistent Advocate and the Use of Force: The Impact of the United States upon the* Jus ad Bellum *in the Post-Cold War Era,* The Ashgate International Law Series (Farnham and Burlington, Ashgate, 2010); Marcelo G Kohen, 'The use of force by the United States after the end of the Cold War and its impact on international law' in Byers et al (eds), *United States Hegemony* (Cambridge, Cambridge University Press, 2003) 197; Heiko Meiertöns, *The Doctrines of US Security Policy. An Evaluation under International Law* (Cambridge, Cambridge University Press, 2010) 179; John F Murphy, 'Contemporary Practice of the United States Relating to International Law' (2002) 96 *American Journal of International Law* 237; idem, *United States and the Rule of Law in International Affairs* (Cambridge, Cambridge University Press, 2004) 142; Michael Reisman and Andrea Armstrong, 'The Past and Future of the Claim of Preemptive Self-Defense' (2006) 100 *American Journal of International Law* 525.

will be a transition towards a truly universal order without a single dominant power or civilisation but with a single, shared value system, or a divided—bipolar?—world order remains to be seen.

IV. THE POST-COLD-WAR AGE UNDER THE STATE-CENTRIC APPROACH

In the state-centric narrative of the history of international law, the end of World War I forms a watershed, a revolutionary moment. Whereas some authors are more nuanced than others, what often appears is a dialectical opposition between the 19th century as the heyday of the sovereign state and the 20th century as the age of its decline. Whereas this shift away from the sovereign state certainly has a foot in reality, one should be careful not to take this opposition too far. First, the 'revolution' of 1919 did not fall from a blue sky. As Koskenniemi and Steiger have stated, the ground for the changes of the early 20th century was already prepared during the late 19th century.[31] Second, all too often, the ages of the formation and heyday of state sovereignty are depicted one-sidedly in terms of the ascendancy of the sovereign state and its accommodation through the weakening of the law. In fact, also in the 17th, 18th and 19th centuries, there were 'communitarian' trends in the international legal order that stood in a dynamic tension with the sovereign state, even if these were much weaker than those of the 20th century. The classical law of nations and 19th-century international law were as much attempts at limiting state sovereignty as at accommodating it. Both the pre-1919 and post-1919 legal order were dualistic in the sense that state sovereignty and international community were competing, leading principles. The difference in the balance between the two may have shifted, but still it is historically more correct to consider that shift gradual rather than revolutionary.[32]

In the more radical interpretations of the sovereign state system and its international law the state is the sole subject, author and enforcer of international law. The sovereign state is the sole significant subject of international law. Individuals do not hold any rights or obligations under international law. There is a strict dualism between the intra- and the inter-state legal orders preventing the invocation of international law by individuals in any municipal or international forum. Consensualism and voluntarism reflect the monopoly of the state in the making of international law. States are bound only by rules of international law they have voluntarily consented to, either expressly (treaty law) or tacitly (international customary law). In the absence of any supranational enforcement mechanisms of international law, states are thrown back on their own devices to enforce their rights or protect their interests. For this, they hold the right to resort to force.

At no point in history did reality completely match this stark portrait of the sovereign state system, but still it offers a handy conceptual framework to catch the changes that the 20th century and the post-Cold War Age brought. First, the main evolutions of the 20th century up to 1989 are summarised; then, the main evolutions of the years since 1989 are sketched.

[30] 'A More Secure World: Our Shared Responsibility, Report of the High-Level Panel on Threats, Challenges and Change', UN Doc. A/59/565 (2004), 54, para 188.

[31] Martti Koskenniemi, *The Gentle Civilizer of Nations: The Rise and Fall of International Law 1870–1960* (Cambridge, Cambridge University Press, 2001) 19 and Heinhard Steiger, 'From the International Law of Christianity' (2001) 3 *Journal of the History of International Law* 190.

[32] See for examples of this state centric-narrative and my comments on it, Lesaffer, 'Grotian Tradition', 2002.

During the 20th century, the sovereign state lost its monopoly on all three points. First, apart from the states, individuals, multinational companies and non-governmental and governmental international organisations became bearers of rights and obligations under international law. In many countries, dualism made place for monism. International human rights treaties bestowed rights upon individuals which in many jurisdictions could be invoked before domestic courts. Some treaties, like the European Convention on Human Rights and Fundamental Freedoms (entry into force in 1953) or the American Convention on Human Rights (entry into force in 1978) granted remedies at the international level. The Versailles Peace Treaty (1919) provided for the international prosecution of the former German Emperor Wilhelm II (1888–1918) for having broken the peace as well as for the prosecution of war criminals. After World War II, political and military leaders from the defeated Axis-powers were tried before international tribunals at Nuremberg and Tokyo.

Second, although the doctrines of consensualism and voluntarism were not abandoned, they were dented through the emergence of the concepts of *ius cogens* and *obligationes erga omnes*. Whereas conceptually the codification of international law in multilateral conventions does not detract from the condition of consent for a rule to be binding upon a state, in reality the actual impact of individual states on the formation of rules they are bound by is far smaller than with bilateral treaties. The now generally accepted role of conventions in the constitution or interpretation of general international customarily law puts further brakes on the freedom of states. By the end of the Cold War, important parts of traditional international law, such as the laws of war, diplomatic law, the law of treaties and the law of the sea had been codified. Moreover, some international institutions, such as the United Nations Security Council and more significantly, the institutions of the European Community, obtained supranational powers in the sense that they could impose majority decisions upon all member states.

Third, the emergence of international institutions for adjudication and international arbitration provided alternatives to self-help. Between the Hague Peace Conferences of 1899/1907 and the adoption of the UN Charter in 1945, the right to use force has been dramatically limited, at least in black-letter law. The divisions of the Cold War severely hampered the Security Council in playing a significant role in the management of international armed conflicts, either through the condemnation of use of force or through the active intervention under Chapter VII of the Charter, and allowed states to reclaim much of the territory they had lost in the Kellogg-Briand Pact (1928) and the Charter. Over the Cold War, the interpretation of the right to self-defence was widened so that several other kinds of forcible measures short of war up to defensive warfare seemed to have become encompassed by it, or at least that states felt in a position to claim so without risking clear condemnation from the organs of the United Nations and their main allies.[33]

Each of these trends was continued and confirmed after the end of the Cold War. First, in the context of human rights protection, since 1998, the European Convention system allows citizens directly to appeal to the European Court of Human Rights in Strasbourg, whereas before they had to pass through the European Commission of Human Rights. The African system now provides the same remedy for the African Court. The main evolution

[33] Stephen C Neff, *War and the Law of Nations: A General History* (Cambridge, Cambridge University Press, 2005) 326.

with respect to the position of individuals as subjects of international law is in the field of international criminal jurisdiction and individual accountability for war crimes and crimes against humanity. After World War II, the Nuremberg and Tokyo tribunals had inspired hope that a permanent system of international prosecution of war crimes would be set up. The divisions of the Cold War prevented this. In the 1990s, the international community—in part through the Security Council—took up the thread by setting up The Hague and Arusha courts for the conflicts in the Former Yugoslavia and Rwanda. In 1998 in Rome, the Statute of the International Criminal Court was adopted, leading to the foundation of a permanent International Criminal Court in The Hague. By now, individual criminal responsibility for crimes of war and crimes against humanity both in the context of international and internal armed conflicts has been established, even if some of the most powerful states have not acceded to the Statute. Moreover, some states have made far reaching claims as regards universal jurisdiction for international crimes and adapted their national legislation to this effect. Furthermore, non-governmental organisations have come to play a significant role in the preparation of new multilateral conventions such as the Ottawa Convention against antipersonnel landmines (1996) and the Kyoto Treaty on climate change (1997). Transnational companies also have their voice increasingly heard, among others by influencing governments in the negotiation of bilateral and multilateral treaties of an economic nature, such as investment treaties. These private corporations also make their influence felt in the process of dispute settlement within the World Trade Organisation and are direct players on the international legal plane through the increasing use they make of international arbitration.

Second, the acceptance of the existence of *ius cogens* and *obligationes erga omnes* has certainly grown since the end of the Cold War. In the field of codification, the 1990s and the first decade of the 21st century have seen somewhat less progress than the 1960s to 1980s. Most progress has been made in the sphere of international criminal law, international humanitarian law, environmental law and economic law. In the European Union, majority decisions play a much bigger role than they did in the European Community from before the Treaty of Maastricht (1992). In the 1990s, the Security Council in some instances, like in the setting up of the Arusha Court, voted on resolutions which actually introduced new rules of international law.

Third, as said above, after the Cold War the Security Council started to play a much more active role in the management of armed conflicts, and extended its activities from international to internal armed conflicts. Although vetoes have been rare since the end of the Cold War, the permanent threat that radiates from the mere existence of veto power combined with the dominant position of the United States has certainly hampered the Council in stemming the relaxation of the prohibition to use force through widening the notion of self-defence. Although the United States has not been able to have all its interpretations accepted or even acquiesced to by a significant number of states, the Council has proved powerless to manage the use of force by the United States or its main allies.

V. CONCLUSION

The three types of historical periodisation hold some relevance for assessing whether the end of the Cold War heralded a new epoch in the history of international law. Of the three, the hegemonic approach is the least relevant and the state-centric the most. The fall of the Soviet Empire left the United States the sole superpower. But contrary to what was the case for previous epochal 'wars', the end of the Cold War did not lead to the constitution of a new international order. Rather, when and where the fall of communism left a vacuum, this was filled by expanding the Western order or by reviving religious or nationalist ideas. In the early 1990s, the United States and the West were at least perceived to have a momentum to mould the world order, but as the main representative of the hegemonic narrative himself concedes, they were only very partially successful. By 2010 the momentum has dwindled and the relative dominance of the West is in decline. Moreover, the growing interdependency of the world makes traditional power less relevant than it was before.

The most accurate assessment of the post-Cold-War years appears to be that of yet another gradual step in the decline of Western domination and, even more importantly, of yet another gradual step away from a system premised on the sovereign state. The balance between state sovereignty and international community is slowly shifting further away from the former. But it is still a dualistic order inasmuch as state sovereignty remains a foundational stone of the international legal order, among others in relation to the use of force. The years after the end of the Cold War certainly did not see an achievement of a paradigm shift from a state-based to a community-based system but just another move of the pendulum in the balance between the two.

Under the Eurocentric and state-centric perspectives, it does not seem justified to call the end of the Cold War 'epochal' but rather sub-epochal. Just like the year 1945, the year 1989 heralded in a new sub-epoch, a new evolution in an epoch that most historians would agree started at the end of World War I. Consequently, the year does not constitute a caesura of the magnitude of 1648, 1815 or 1919, but should, to take the example of the epoch between 1648 and 1815 rather be set on a par with intermediate marking points such as 1678/79 (Nijmegen), 1697 (Ryswick), 1713 (Utrecht) or 1748 (Aachen) that historians use to indicate different phases in the development of the 'classical law of nations'. This does not serve to underplay the significance of the changes of the past two decades such as the relative decline of the West or the strong showing of non-state actors, but only to put them in a wider historical perspective and thus to underline the fact that they are part and parcel of a long evolution. It also does not contradict that these changes might prove to be preparatory for a true epochal caesura that is yet to come and lead to a new paradigm of world order. But this remains in the dark.

The post-Cold-War Age—if one wants to consider an 'age' that has not ended yet just that—can best be called a third sub-period in the 'Age of Mankind', the 'Age of Universal International Law' or the 'Age of the International Community' after the Interbellum and the Cold-War Age. Is this a consequence of the end of bipolarity, or is it just a continuation of an evolution that would have happened regardless? Rather than indulging myself with a bit of counterfactual history, I prefer to conclude by raising another question. To what extent is the demise of the Soviet Union and of bipolarity itself an effect of the rise of international community and the growing interdependency of the world which had already begun before 1989?

4

1989–2010: *The Rise and Fall of Democratic Governance in International Law*

JEAN D'ASPREMONT*

PROMPTLY CELEBRATED IN the aftermath of the end of the Cold War by a group of American scholars,[1] the rise of the so-called principle of democratic legitimacy came to be seen as one of the major changes brought about by the fall of the Berlin Wall. While non-American international legal scholars proved more cautious as to the existence of an international legal obligation regarding the form of political regime of states, they incrementally accepted—although to a much more modest extent than their American counterparts—that the international legal order had grown more amenable to the principle of democracy.[2] Even though the scope of these rules as well as their conceptualisation have continued to be the object of much scholarly disagreement, the idea that contemporary international law enshrines some requirements as to the *democratic origin* of power at the domestic level gained currency.

This chapter concurs with the contention that the prescriptions as to *how* power must be exercised at the domestic level (by virtue of major international human rights conventions) and the prohibition of certain political regimes (for instance apartheid and fascist regimes[3]) already enshrined in international law before the end of the Cold War were subsequently supplemented by a new democratic rule. Indeed, the author of these lines believes, as is explained in the following paragraphs, that the practice since the end of the Cold War—and the accounts thereof in the legal scholarship—witnessed—and gave form to—a consolidation of a principle of democratic legitimacy. This development constituted a remarkable phenomenon, for it came to limit the classical constitutional autonomy of each state. In that sense, the years 1989–2010 can be hailed as an unprecedented epoch of international law during which domestic governance—understood here in a traditional way as the use of public authority at the domestic level through a central governmental authority—has been regulated by international law to an unprecedented extent, the latter going as far as to prescribe a given type of procedure to accede to power at the domestic level.

* Associate Professor of International Law, Amsterdam Center for International Law (ACIL), University of Amsterdam. An expanded version of this chapter can be found in the *European Journal of International Law*, volume 22 (2011).

[1] See n 12 below.

[2] See n 13 below.

[3] See n 7 and n 8 below.

This chapter submits, however, that the rapid rise of non-democratic super-powers, growing security concerns at the international level, the 2007–2010 economic crisis as well as the inevitable instrumentalisation of democratisation policies of Western countries[4] are currently cutting short the consolidation of such a principle of democratic legitimacy in international law. Contemporary practice shows signs of a return to realist and non-ideological foreign policies, threatening the centrality of democracy promotion in the foreign policies of most democratic states and the nascent consensus over the existence of international obligations about the democratic origin of power at the domestic level.

The following paragraphs start by exposing the possible rise (1) and fall (2) of the principle of democratic legitimacy in the practice of international law and the accounts thereof in the legal scholarship from 1989 to 2010 before seeking critically to appraise the lessons learnt from that period, especially regarding the ability of international law to regulate domestic governance (3).

I. 1989–2010: FROM HUMAN RIGHTS TO A REQUIREMENT OF DEMOCRATIC ORIGIN (THE RISE?)

It is commonly accepted that the determination of those entitled to act and speak on behalf of states is not based on a formal certifying operation and is inextricably left to the unconstrained discretion of states, although sometimes acting in the framework of international organisations. This abiding and inevitable absence of formal certification of governments has, before the fall of the Berlin Wall, been accompanied by a lack of rules affecting domestic governance. In particular, the form of the political regime of each state was considered to be an 'internal affair'[5] and the choice thereof was considered to be unconstrained by international law.[6] Apart from the prohibition of apartheid[7] and, to a lesser extent, of the fascist political system,[8] the only prescriptions related to domestic governance were found in human rights law—and especially the obligations pertaining to political and civil rights—which enshrines limitations as to *how* the power can be exercised by governments. Before the end of the Cold War, human rights law thus constituted the backbone of the international regulation of domestic governance.

The end of the Cold War impinged significantly on how domestic governance is regulated. International legal scholars promptly recognised that the post-Cold War international legal order had become more amenable to the prominent role of democracy.

[4] On the use of the concept of 'Western States', see the remarks by J Vidmar, 'Multiple Democracy: International and European Human Rights Law Perspectives (2010) 23 *Leiden Journal of International Law* 207.

[5] For a classical account, see L Oppenheim, *International Law*, vol I, 6th edn (Longmans, New York, 1912) 425.

[6] ICJ, *Case Concerning Military and Paramilitary Activities in and against Nicaragua*, ICJ Rep, 1986, para 261.

[7] See International Convention on the Suppression and Punishment of the Crime of Apartheid (1973), 1015 UN Treaty Ser 243 (1976); International Convention on the Elimination of All Forms of Racial Discrimination (1965), Art 3, 660 UN Treaty Ser 195 (1969). See also Security Council Res No 288, UN Doc S/RES/288 (1970); Security Council Res No 277, UN Doc S/RES/277 (1970); Security Council Res No 253, UN Doc S/RES/253 (1968); Security Council Res No 232, UN Doc S/RES/232 (1966); Security Council Res No 216, UN Doc S/RES/216 (1965); Security Council Res No 217, UN Doc S/RES/217 (1965); General Assembly Res No 1791, UN Doc A/RES/1791 (1962); General Assembly Res No 1598, UN Doc A/RES/1598 (1961); Security Council Res No 221, UN Doc S/RES/221 (1961).

[8] In particular, see General Assembly Res No 36/162, UN Doc A/RES/36/162 (Dec 16, 1981).

In what has been perceived as an intra-disciplinary truce,[9] some American scholars in particular—ie those that have subsequently been seen as forming the 'democratic entitlement school'[10]—have—albeit to various degrees[11]—enthusiastically supported the idea that democracy today plays a crucial role in the international legal order and have swiftly provided various optimistic accounts of the extent of the legal changes brought about by democracy.[12] European scholars, although they had usually voiced greater scepticism and refrained from embracing the whole array of consequences that the abovementioned American scholars attached to a lack of democracy, growingly came to recognise that democracy—at least in its procedural and electoral dimension—bears upon the rules and the functioning of the international legal order.[13]

Even if one does not agree with all the legal consequences that some American scholars have sometimes associated with the emergence of democracy in the international legal order,[14] living up to some democratic standards, in the view of the author of these lines, increasingly turned to correspond with an international customary obligation.[15] Indeed,

[9] E MacDonald, 'International Law, Democratic Governance and September the 11th' (2002) 3 *German Law Journal*, available at www.germanlawjournal.com.

[10] Because many of them were affiliated to New York University, these scholars were subsequently dubbed by David Kennedy as members of the 'Manhattan School'. See D Kennedy, 'Tom Franck and the Manhattan School' (2003) 35 *NYU Journal of International Law and Politics* 397, 432.

[11] G Simpson, 'Two Liberalisms' (2001) 12 *European Journal of International Law* 537.

[12] The most radical liberal view on this question is probably offered by F R Tesón, 'The Kantian Theory of International Law' (1992) 92 *Columbia Law Review* 53, 54–55. For milder forms of the democratic entitlement theory, see T M Franck, 'The Emerging Right to Democratic Governance' (1992) 86 *American Journal of International Law* 46, 46; C M Cerna, 'Universal Democracy: An International Legal Right or the Pipe Dream of the West?' (1994–1995) 27 *NYU Journal of International Law and Politics* 289, 329. For an overview of how participatory rights emerged in international law, see generally G H Fox, 'The Right to Political Participation in International Law' (1992) 17 *Yale Journal of International Law* 539. For a basic account of the arguments for and against the democratic entitlement theory, see generally G H Fox and B R Roth, 'Introduction: The Spread of Liberal Democracy and Its Implications for International Law' in G H Fox and B R Roth (eds), *Democratic Governance and International Law* (Cambridge University Press, Cambridge 2000) 1, 11. Many of the abovementioned works are reproduced in G H Fox and B R Roth (eds), *Democratic Governance and International Law* (Cambridge University Press, Cambridge 2000). For a critical appraisal of that literature, see S. Marks, *The Riddle of All Constitutions* (Oxford University Press, Oxford, 2003).

[13] J Crawford, 'Democracy and International Law' (1993) 64 *British Yearbook of International Law* 113; J Roldán Barbero, *Democracia y Derecho Internacional* (Civitas, Madrid, 1994); B Bauer, *Der volkerrechtliche Anspruch auf Demokratie* (Lang, Frankfurt am Main 1998); D Schindler, 'Völkerrecht und Demokratie' in G Hafner et al (eds), *Liber Amicorum Professor Seidl-Hohenveldern* (Kluwer Law International, The Hague, 1998) 611; L A Sicilianos, *L'ONU et la démocratisation de l'état; systèmes régionaux et ordre juridique universel* (Pedone, Paris, 2000); L A Sicilianos, 'Les Nations unies et la démocratisation de l'Etat: nouvelles tendances' in R Mehdi (ed) *La contribution des Nations unies à la démocratisation de l'Etat* (Pedone, Paris, 2002) 13; J d'Aspremont, *L'Etat non démocratique en droit international. Etude critique du droit international positif et de la pratique contemporaine* (Paris, Pedone 2008); A Peters, 'Dual Democracy' in J Klabbers, A Peters, G Ulfstein (eds), *The Constitutionalization of International Law* (Oxford University Press, Oxford, 2009) 273; S Wheatley, 'Democracy in International Law: A European Perspective' (2002) 51 *International and Comparative Law Quarterly* 225; C Pippan, 'International Law, Domestic Political Orders, and the 'Democratic Imperative': Has Democracy Finally Emerged as a Global Legal Entitlement?' (2010) *Jean Monnet Working Paper 02/10*, available at www.jeanmonnetprogram.org, 7 (who argues that such an entitlement can be said to have emerged only if we equate democracy and elections); P Klein, 'Le droit aux élections libres en droit international: Mythes et réalités' in Olivier Corten et al (eds), *A la recherche du nouvel ordre mondial* (Eds Complexe, Brussels, 1993) 93, 95; R Ben Achour, 'Le Droit International de la Démocratie' (2000) 4 *Cursos Euromediterráneos Bancaja de Derecho Internacional* 327. See contra N Petersen, *Demokratie als teleologisches Prinzip. Zur Legitimität von Staatsgewalt im Völkerrecht* (Springer Berlin, Heidelberg, New York, 2009) 139 and 220. See also N Petersen, 'The Principle of Democratic Teleology in International Law' (2008–2009) 34 *Brooklyn Journal of International Law* 33.

[14] For one criticism of the liberal theories of democracy, see J d'Aspremont, *L'Etat non democratique en droit international.*

[15] ibid, 291.

I contend that the post-1989 practice contains strong indications that, to a large degree, states consider the adoption of the main characteristics of a democratic regime to amount to an international obligation and act accordingly toward non-democratic states. For instance, entities which have reached statehood in the last few years thanks to the support or the involvement of the international community have been induced to adopt democratic institutions.[16] Likewise, each experience of international administration of territory has led to the creation of democratic states, as illustrated by the cases of East Timor and, irrespective of its final status, Kosovo.[17] Because the determination of subjects of international law and that of those who represent them are not carried out through a formal certification, democracy has never directly impinged on the legal existence of states or that their governments. Yet, practice has shown that, in the policies of recognition, the democratic character of domestic institutions often offsets the lack of *effectivité* of an entity.[18]

While new and restored states have been endowed with democratic institutions, violent changes of government have been deterred by a large array of sanction devices: coups, especially those that lead to the overthrow of a democratic government, are systematically the object of condemnations and sanctions, their authors being usually denied any external legitimacy.[19] These sanctions usually are eased once the authors of the coups pledge to organise free and fair elections. This systematic condemnation of coups against democratic governments surely buttresses the strong commitment of the international community to democracy—or at least the idea of a requirement of standstill[20] constraining existing democracies.[21] We have also witnessed the resort to peace-enforcement missions to restore overthrown democratic governments, as illustrated by the intervention in Sierra Leone.[22]

[16] See eg *Guidelines on the Recognition of New States in Eastern Europe and in the Soviet Union* (1991) 62 *British Yearbook of International Law* 559; *Declaration on Yugoslavia* (1991) 62 *British Yearbook of International Law* 559, 560.

[17] On this topic, see E de Brabandere, *Post-Conflict Administrations In International Law: International Territorial Administration, Transitional Authority and Foreign Occupation In Theory* (Martinus Nijhoff, The Hague, 2009); C Stahn, *The Law and Practice of International Territorial Administration: Versailles to Iraq and Beyond* (Cambridge University Press, Cambridge, 2008); J d'Aspremont, 'Post-Conflict Administrations as Democracy-Building Instruments' (2008) 9 *Chicago Journal of International Law* 1; J d'Aspremont, 'La création international d'Etats démocratiques' (2005) 109 *Revue générale de droit international public* 889. This tendency to install democracies through the international administration of territories has occurred even with the veiled support of non-democratic states, as if these states acknowledge that democracy is the only admissible political regime. See eg S.C. Res. 1546, U.N. Doc. S/RES/1546 (June 8, 2004) (unanimously adopted resolution addressing the question of the future democratic government of Iraq). But see S.C. Res. 1244, U.N. Doc. S/RES/1244 (June 10, 1999) (China abstaining from voting on the question of Kosovo).

[18] J d'Aspremont, *L'Etat non démocratique*, 57.

[19] See generally J d'Aspremont, 'Responsibility for Coups in International Law' (2010) 18 *Tulane Journal of International and Comparative Law* 451. See also J d'Aspremont, 'La licéité des coups d'Etat en droit international' in *Travaux de la Société française pour le droit international. L'Etat de droit en droit international* (Pedone, Paris, 2009) 117.

[20] J d'Aspremont, *L'Etat non démocratique*, 338.

[21] N Petersen, Demokratie als teleologisches Prinzip. Zur Legitimität von Staatsgewalt im Völkerrecht, 89 (this is what he calls the principle of Democratic Teleology). See also N Petersen, 'The Principle of Democratic Teleology in International Law', 33.

[22] See generally K Nowrot and E W Schebacker, 'The Use of Force to Restore Democracy: International Legal Implications of the ECOWAS Intervention in Sierra Leone' (1998) 14 *American University International Law Review* 388. It is noteworthy that some of these missions were led by non-democratic states as if non-democratic states themselves are coming to terms with the ascendancy of democracy over any other kind of political regimes. See eg B Nowrojee, 'Joining Forces: United Nations and Regional Peacekeeping—Lessons from Liberia' (1995) 8 *Harvard. Human Rights Journal* 133. See generally M Byers and S Chesterman, 'You

In the same vein, there is little doubt today that democracy has become a prominent yardstick with which to assess the legitimacy of governments.[23] This explains why complex and multi-layered election monitoring mechanisms have been put at the disposal of states, many of them regularly making use of such possibility to buoy the legitimacy which their government can earn from democratic elections.[24] This is not to say that a non-democratic government will never be deemed legitimate, especially if that government has been in power for a long time.[25] The non-democratic character of a government is sometimes disregarded because of overriding geopolitical and strategic motives.[26] But, leaving these situations aside, it can reasonably be argued that, since the end of the Cold War, democracy has become 'the touchstone of legitimacy'[27] for any new government.[28] All-in-all, these few examples—already much discussed in the literature[29]—suffice to demonstrate the far-reaching structural changes that international society has undergone after 1989 with respect to the form of governments.[30]

It is of particular relevance that many non-democratic states do not oppose the principle of democracy, and even claim that they are themselves in the midst of progress towards the establishment of democracy.[31] In that sense, non-democratic states, with a view to strengthening the legitimacy of their government, try to portray their political regime in a democratic fashion rather than choosing to dispute the role that democracy plays in the international order.

the People': Pro-Democratic Intervention in International Law' in G H Fox and B Roth (eds), *Democratic Governance and International Law* (Cambridge UP, Cambridge, 2000) 259.

[23] E Stein, 'International Integration and Democracy: No Love at First Sight' (2001) 95 *American Journal of International Law* 489, 494; Franck, 'The Emerging Right', 46.

[24] On international election monitoring, see C Binder, 'International Election Observation by the OSCE and the Human Right to Political Participation'. See also C Binder and C Pippan, 'Election Monitoring, International' in R Wolfrum (ed), *Encyclopedia of Public International Law* (Oxford University Press, Oxford, 2008) available at www.mpepil.com/.

[25] In the same vein, G H Fox, 'Election Monitoring: The International Legal Setting' (2001) 19 *Wisconsin International Law Journal* 295, 312. C Pippan, 'International Law, Domestic Political Orders, and the "Democratic Imperative"', 34. This finding has led some authors to contend that there exist 'double standards' in that regard. See M G Kohen, 'La création d'Etats en droit international contemporain' (2002) 6 *Cours euro-méditerranéens Bancaja de droit international*, 619.

[26] The most obvious example is the government of the People's Republic of China which is seen as legitimate by almost all countries in the world although it does not rest on any free and fair electoral process.

[27] On legitimacy, see the general observation of D Bodansky, 'The Legitimacy of International Governance: A Coming Challenge for International Environmental Law?' (1999) 93 *American Journal of International Law* 596, 599. See also J d'Aspremont and E de Brabandere, 'The Complementary Faces of Legitimacy in International Law: the Legitimacy of Origin and the Legitimacy of Exercise' (2010) 34 *Fordham Journal of International Law* 101.

[28] See generally J d'Aspremont, 'Legitimacy of Governments in the Age of Democracy' (2006) 38 *NYU Journal of International Law and Politics* 877; see also B Roth, *Governmental Illegitimacy*, 212, 413 and 415.

[29] See generally G Fox and B Roth (eds), *Democratic Governance and International Law*. See also J d'Aspremont, *L'Etat non démocratique*.

[30] This led some scholars to claim that we had reached the end of 'History'. On this use of such a terminology, see S Marks, 'International Law, Democracy and the End of History' in G H Fox and B Roth, *Democratic Governance and International Law*, 535.

[31] For one example, consider the 2007 events in Pakistan. In particular, see the interview of President Musharraf on November 11, 2007, C Gall, D Rohde, and J Perlez, 'Rebuffing US, Musharraf Calls Crackdown Crucial to a Fair Vote', *New York Times*, 14 November 2007, at A1. Musharraf has since stepped down from military leadership, see, for example, D Rohde and C Gall, 'In Musharraf's Shadow, a New Hope for Pakistan Rises', *New York Times*, 7 January 2008, at A3. Also relevant are the developments in Myanmar. On this issue, see, for example, S Mydans, 'Myanmar Claims Step to Democracy, but Junta Still Grips to Power', *International Herald Tribune*, 4 September 2007, 3.

The possible obligation[32] to be democratic to the emergence of which the abovementioned practice has contributed has been conceptualised by scholars in many different ways. Some authors have espoused a *human right-based conceptualisation* by defending the existence of a right to political participation,[33] the right to democratic governance,[34] the right to free and fair elections.[35] Other scholars have captured the emergence of requirements of democratic governance through the lens of *internal self-determination*, thereby arguing that self-determination expands beyond decolonisation.[36] Others—including the author of these lines—have, more simply, put forward the existence of an *international customary obligation* to be democratic without such an obligation taking the form of a human right or an expansion of the principle of self-determination beyond self-determination.[37] Eventually, there are scholars who simultaneously drew on all of these conceptualisations to buttress the existence of a requirement of democratic origin of governments in international law,[38] a path also arguably followed by the Human Rights Committee.[39]

However it is eventually conceptualised, this legal obligation to adopt a democratic regime must surely not be exaggerated. First, the scope *ratione materiae* of the principle of democracy in international law is limited, as the obligation only rests on an *electoral* and *procedural* understanding of democracy.[40] Although the free and fair character of the elections inevitably requires respect for some of the elementary political and civil rights,[41] states are only customarily obliged to abide by democracy to the sole extent that their effective leaders (or the parliamentary body that oversees their executive mandate) are chosen through free and fair elections. Indeed, by the account made here, the practice has only conveyed a restrictive and procedural definition of democracy,[42]

[32] In the same vein, see C Pippan, 'International Law, Domestic Political Orders, and the 'Democratic Imperative'', 7. See *contra* B Roth, *Governmental Illegitimacy,* 417.

[33] G H Fox, 'The Right to Political Participation in International Law' (1992) 17 *Yale Journal of International Law* 539. See also C Binder, 'International Election Observation by the OSCE and the Human Right to Political Participation', 134.

[34] Franck's right to democratic governance is itself very much ground in participatory rights of human rights treaties as well as the right to self-determination. See Franck, 'The Emerging Right'. In the same vein, see also J I Ibegbu, The *Right to Democracy in International Law* (Edwin Mellen Press, Lewiston 2003).

[35] C M Cerna 'Universal Democracy', 329.

[36] P Thornberry, 'The Democratic or Internal Aspect of Self-Determination with some Remarks on Federalism' in C Tomuschat (ed) *Modern Law of Self-Determination* (Brill, Dordrecht, 1993) 101, 134; A Rosas, 'Internal Self-Determination' in C Tomuschat (ed) *Modern Law of Self-Determination* (Brill, Dordrecht, 1993) 225, 241; A Cassese, *Self-Determination of Peoples. A Legal Reappraisal* (Oxford University Press, Oxford, 1995) 311. For a criticism of that approach, see Petersen, Demokratie als teleologisches Prinzip. Zur Legitimität von Staatsgewalt im Völkerrecht, 89. See also J d'Aspremont, *L'Etat non démocratique*, 271.

[37] Franck's right to democratic governance is primarily grounded in self-determination. See: Franck, 'The Emerging Right'. For a criticism of this understanding of self-determination, see J Vidmar, 'The Right of Self-Determination and Multiparty Democracy: Two Sides of the Same Coin?' (2010) 10 *Human Rights Law Review* 239.

[38] A Peters, 'Dual Democracy', 274, 277. For a criticism of the link between the right of political participation and self-determination, see J Vidmar, 'The Right of Self-Determination and Multiparty Democracy'.

[39] HRC General Comment 25, Right to participate in public affairs, voting rights and the right of equal access to public service, 12 July 1996, CCPR/C/21/Rev.1/Add.7.

[40] G H Fox, 'The Right to Political Participation in International Law' in Fox and Roth (eds), *Democratic Governance and International Law* 49.

[41] J d'Aspremont, *L'Etat non démocratique* 15. On the specific criteria that ought to be met for an election to be free and fair, see C Binder, 'International Election Observation by the OSCE and the Human Right to Political Participation'.

[42] This finding is also made (and subsequently discussed) by Susan Marks. See S Marks, *The Riddle of All Constitutions*, 50 et seq. See also C Pippan, 'International Law, Domestic Political Orders, and the "Democratic Imperative"'.

however defective such a conception may be from a conceptual and theoretical point of view.[43] Likewise, the ambit of that requirement should also not be overblown. While this customary obligation, whatever its conceptualisation, probably constitutes an *erga omnes* obligation,[44] it certainly is not of a *ius cogens* character, as it is underscored by the existence of numerous persistent objectors to that customary rule.[45]

As was already alluded to above, it would also be a mistake to consider the obligation to be democratic utterly groundbreaking. The development of a customary norm in this area is unsurprising, given that international law has long regulated some aspects of states' political regimes. Through human rights law, the international community has regulated the way in which power is exercised and has prohibited some types of political regimes—for example, apartheid[46] and, to a lesser extent, fascism.[47] Moreover, the obligation to organise free and fair elections is not entirely new in the international legal order, as a similar obligation[48] is already embedded in the International Covenant on Civil and Political Rights,[49] which has been ratified by 167 states.[50] It must be pointed out, however, that even if the international legal order enshrines a principle of *procedural* democracy applicable to the political regime of states, there is no corresponding requirement of democracy applicable to the structure and the functioning of the international legal system as a whole.[51] This is not totally astonishing, given the inapplicability of the classical domestic blueprints of governance to the international system.[52] Yet, the abovementioned practice has been interpreted by a very important part of scholarship as the manifestation of an existing international obligation to ensure the democratic origin of governments.

[43] See the famous criticism of this 'minimalistic' understanding of democracy by S Marks, *The Riddle of All Constitutions*, 52. In the same vein see B Gills, J Rocamora, and R Wilson, 'Low Intensity Democracy' in B Gills, J Rocamora and R Wilson (eds), *Low Intensity Democracy: Political Power in the New World Order* (Pluto, London, 1993) 3, 21; R Burchill, 'Book Review of The Developing International Law of Democracy' (2001) 64 *Modern Law Review* 123, 128; R A Miller, 'Self-Determination in International Law and the Demise of Democracy' (2003) 41 *Columbia Journal of Transnational Law* 601, 603–05, M Koskenniemi, 'Whose Intolerance, Which Democracy?' in G Fox and B Roth, *Democratic Governance and International Law*, 438. See also B Roth, 'Evaluating democratic progress' in G H Fox and B Roth (eds), *Democratic Governance and International Law*, 493 et seq; C Binder and C Pippan, 'Election Monitoring, International'; C Pippan, 'International Law, Domestic Political Orders, and the "Democratic Imperative"'.

[44] J d'Aspremont, *L'Etat non démocratique*, 291.

[45] The People's Republic of China and several states in the Middle East can probably be considered persistent objectors to that rule. See, for example, A J Nathan, 'The Tianammen Papers' (2001) 80 *Foreign Affairs* 2. I have defended this idea of persistent objector elsewhere. See J d'Aspremont, *L'Etat non démocratique,* 290. For a criticism of that idea, see C Pippan, 'International Law, Domestic Political Orders, and the "Democratic Imperative"' 27. See also C Pippan, 'Review of Jean d'Aspremont L'Etat Non Démocratique en Droit International' (2009) 20 *European Journal of International* Law 1276.

[46] See n 7 above.

[47] See n 8 above.

[48] See however J. Vidmar for whom the ICCPR obligation does not entail an obligation to organise multi-party elections. See J Vidmar, 'Multiparty Democracy', 209–240, esp at 222.

[49] International Covenant on Civil and Political Rights, General Assembly Res 2200A, UN Doc A/6316 (1966) ('ICCPR'). On the ICCPR and democracy, see generally A Mavrommatis, 'The International Covenant on Civil and Political Rights and Its Role in Promoting Democracy' in K Koufa (ed), *Human Rights and Democracy for the 21st Century* (Sakkoulas, Athens, 2000) 255.

[50] See Status of Ratification of the Principal International Human Rights Treaties, available online at treaties.un.org/Pages/ViewDetails.aspx?src=TREATY&mtdsg_no=IV-4&chapter=4&lang=en. On the possible ratification of the ICCPR by the People's Republic of China, see K Lee, 'China and the International Covenant on Civil and Political Rights: Prospects and Challenges' (2007) 6 *Chinese Journal of International Law* 445.

[51] On this debate, see generally A Peters, 'Dual Democracy', 263.

[52] See generally J H H Weiler, 'The Geology of International Law: Governance, Democracy and Legitimacy' (2004) 64 *Heidelberg Journal of International* Law 547.

While the requirement of democratic origin of governments, in the view of this author, has gained currency in the post-Cold War practice and legal scholarship, it would be untrue to say that this acceptance of a requirement of democratic origin of governments has been unchallenged. The above-mentioned scholarly enthusiasm for the principle of democracy has aroused some severe criticisms with respect to its imperialistic or neo-colonialist overtones[53] and the correlative reminiscence of the 19th century distinction between civilised and barbarian states.[54] It has also been said that a principle of democratic legitimacy can help secure systematic inequalities among states and even within states.[55] Because of the impossibility clearly to define democracy, others have contended that any obligation pertaining to the democratic origin of governments is not normative and cannot yield a normative directive towards states.[56] Even though it cannot be denied that the principle of democratic legitimacy stirs inevitable controversy as to its imperialist, neocolonialist character or its ability to produce any meaningful command towards international law addressees, it is not the aim of this chapter to discuss them.[57] Rather, the following section turns to the setbacks encountered by the legal requirement of the democratic origin of government in recent international practice.

II. BEYOND THE POST-COLD WAR PERIOD: THE RETREAT FROM A REQUIREMENT OF DEMOCRATIC ORIGIN AND THE RETURN TO CLASSICAL HUMAN RIGHTS (THE FALL?)

It is argued here that contemporary practice is jeopardising the consolidation of the abovementioned practice in favour of a requirement of democratic origin of governments. Indeed, subject to the important exception of regional regimes,[58] contemporary practice weathers an incremental de-emphasising of the democratic origin of governments and a growing emphasis on the requirements of transparency and the absence of corruption (good governance)[59] and the respect for human rights.[60] After almost two decades of

[53] M Koskenniemi, 'Intolerant Democracies: A Reaction' (1996) 37 *Harvard International Law Journal* 231. While recognising that such a criticism is not ill-founded Susan Marks puts forward an alternative reading of democracy to overcome such an object. See S Marks, *The Riddle of All Constitutions*, 101 et seq. For some historical underpinnings to the idea that democracy is primarily a Western idea, see D Held, *Democracy and the Global Order* (Polity Press, Cambridge, 1995), 282 et seq. For an attempted reconciliation see N Petersen, 'International Law, Cultural Diversity, and Democratic Rule: Beyond the Divide between Universalism and Relativism' (2010) 1 *Asian Journal of International Law* (forthcoming). See more generally on the question of global values, J d'Aspremont. 'The Foundations of the International Legal Order' (2007) 18 *Finnish Yearbook of International Law* 219.

[54] See eg E Nys, *Droit international, Les principes, les théories, les faits*, Tome I (Alfred Castaigne Brussels, 1904) 116 et seq; J Westlake, *International Law*, 2nd ed (Cambridge University Press, Cambridge, 1910) 40; J Kent, *Commentary on International Law* (Deighton, Bell, and Co, Cambridge, 1878); R Phillimore, *Commentaries upon International Law* (Butterworths, London, 1879–89); H Wheaton, *Elements of International Law* (Stevens & Sons, London, 1880).

[55] S Marks, *The Riddle of All Constitutions*, 101.

[56] H Steiner, 'Political Participation as a Human Right' (1988) 1 *Harvard Human Rights Yearbook* 77, 89. See also the remarks of G H Fox, 'Democracy, Right to, International Protection' in R Wolfrum (ed), *Encyclopedia of Public International Law*, para 6. On this understanding of normativity, see J d'Aspremont, 'Softness in International Law' (2008) 19 *European Journal of International Law* 1075.

[57] Many of them have been insightfully examined by S Marks, *The Riddle of All Constitutions*.

[58] For an outline of the mechanisms geared towards the promotion or the enforcement of democracy at the regional level, see G H Fox, 'Democracy, Right to, International Protection'. For an account of the European regional model, see S Wheatley, 'Democracy in International Law: A European Perspective', 225.

[59] J F Burns and A Cowell, 'Brown Issues Karzai a Stern Warning', *International Herald Tribune*, 7–8

care for the democratic origin of governments, it seems that we are witnessing a return to foreign policies centred on the manner in which governments exercise power. In that sense, the emphasis is less and less on governments originating in free and fair elections but rather on their respect for elementary political and civil rights as well as standards of good governance which have become the central features of foreign policies of states. This is exemplified by the great attention to what I have called elsewhere the *legitimacy of exercise* in the practice pertaining to recognition, accreditation or intervention by invitation, that is the idea that the manner in which power is exercised matters more than the origin of that power.[61]

Against the backdrop of this growing de-emphasising of free and fair elections, it is not surprising that the non-democratic origin of a government, while likely to provoke some temporary diplomatic isolation or unease, proves more often insufficient to trigger non-recognition of the new government, particularly if the latter is being re-elected.[62] Likewise, states are nowadays living up to a *principled engagement with non-democratic regimes*.[63] In the same vein, diplomatic relations seem less affected nowadays than during the years following the Cold War by the dubious democratic origin of one of the partners. Indeed, the non-democratic origin does not prevent such relations,[64] although diplomatic relations are occasionally downgraded at a lower level to manifest some discontent as to the absence of free and fair elections.[65] But even coups do not always lead to a suspension of diplomatic relations.[66]

The same can be said as far as various types of inter-state cooperation are concerned. Indeed, international cooperation among states in a wide variety of fields is increasingly unaffected by the lack of democratic virtue of one of the partners,[67] especially when it comes to security[68] or economy.[69] By the same token, cooperation policies based on

November 2009, 3. See the 2010 *US National Security Strategy*, 38, available at www.whitehouse.gov/sites/default/files/rss_viewer/national_security_strategy.pdf.

[60] E Sciolino, 'Rocky Time for Qaddafi During Visit to France', *International Herald Tribune*, 14 December 2007, 3.

[61] On the oscillations between democracy of origin and democracy of exercise, see generally J d'Aspremont, 'Legitimacy of Governments'. See more recently, J d'Aspremont and E de Brabandere, 'The Complementary Faces of Legitimacy in International Law'.

[62] See M Simons, 'Sudan Leader Can't Bypass Wall of Diplomatic Isolation', *International Herald Tribune*, 3 May 2010, 5; T Berthemet, 'Omar el-Béchir réélu sans péril président du Soudan', *Le Figaro*, 27 April 2010, 6.

[63] See for instance the *2010 US National Security Strategy*, 38, available at www.whitehouse.gov/sites/default/files/rss_viewer/national_security_strategy.pdf.

[64] M Slackman, 'Libya Seeks Greater U.S. Reward for Renouncing Weapons Projects', *International Herald Tribune*, 11 March 2009, 5; E Sciolino, 'Rocky Time for Qaddafi During Visit to France', *International Herald Tribune*, 14 December 2007, 3; see also the report that the US President would meet the prime minister of Myanmar on the occasions of a meeting with the 10 leaders of the Association of Southeast Asian Nations, *International Herald Tribune*, 9 November 2009, 8.

[65] M Lander and M Mazzeti, 'A Valuable Peek at North Korea', *International Herald Tribune*, 20 August 2009, 2; C Duhigg and C Dougherty, 'Gambling on the Global Economy', *International Herald Tribune*, 3 November 2008, 1.

[66] *International Herald Tribune*, 11–12 July 2009, 4.

[67] See S Mydans, '20 Uighurs, $1 billion and a clear signal', *International Herald Tribune*, 23 December 2009, 5.

[68] D E Sanger and E Schmitt, 'A Threat not Dwelled on: Pakistan', *International Herald Tribune*, 3 December 2009, 7; L Polgreen, 'France May Intervene to Back Chad's Leader', *International Herald Tribune*, 6 February 2008, 4; Associated Press, 'France Admits it Delivered Libyan Munitions to Chad', *International Herald Tribune*, 15 February 2008, 3.

[69] M Slackman, 'Libya Seeks Greater U.S. Reward for Renouncing Weapons Projects', *International Herald Tribune*, 11 March 2009, 5.

mechanisms of democratic conditionality are increasingly challenged by non-western states. It is not to say that after the Cold War all cooperation policies were systematically made conditional upon compliance with some democratic standards. It simply is that it is nowadays less so than it used to be. As is illustrated by the unprecedented challenge of the European Union famous democratic conditionality[70] by African states,[71] practice indicates that democratic conditionality is turning more controversial, which in turn may bring about its abandonment in some areas.[72]

Although it is too early to gauge the extent of these changes, these few examples suffice to show that contemporary practice manifests a return to *RealPolitik* after almost two decades of ideological foreign policies centred on the democratisation of foreign regimes through a requirement of democratic origin of governments. This change has been particularly noticeable in the foreign policy of the United States[73] and confirmed by the 2010 *National Security Strategy of the United States*.[74] As a result of this de-emphasising of the democratic origin of governments, the fall of the Berlin Wall has increasingly been seen in the recent scholarship as a culmination rather than a departure.[75] Interestingly, the international legal scholarship—which had until recently most of the time voiced an upbeat tone—has itself turned more sceptical as to the existence of a requirement (or the extent thereof) pertaining to the democratic origin of governments.[76]

Should future practice confirm these developments, this would underpin the idea that the emphasis put on the democratic origin of governments during the 1989–2010 is ebbing away and that, in the foreign policies of many states, the democratic origin of foreign partners has been demoted to a secondary issue. Because contemporary practice shows that the democratisation of foreign governments has taken the back seat and has given way to foreign policies prioritising other objectives, the classical

[70] J Verhoeven, 'La Communauté européenne et la sanction international de la démocratie et des droits de l'homme' in E Yakpo and T Boumedra (eds), *Liber amicorum Judge Mohammed Bedjaoui* (Kluwer, The Hague, 1999) 771; D Perrot (ed) *Les relations ACP/UE après le modèle de Lomé : quel partenariat?* (Bruylant, Brussels, 2007); see generally O Babarinde and G Faber (eds), *The European Union and the Developing Countries: The Cotonou Agreement, The Trade and Development Policy of the European Union* (Martinus Nijhoff, Leiden, 2005); L Bartels, 'The Trade and Development Policy of the European Union' (2007) 18 *European Journal of International Law* 715; P Leino, 'European Universalism?: the EU and Human Rights Conditionality' (2006) 24 *Yearbook of European Law* 329.

[71] See the reactions on the occasion of the Lisbon Summit. See eg para 52 of the 2007 Lisbon Africa-EU Strategic Partnership, available at www.africa-eu-partnership.org/pdf/eas2007_joint_strategy_en.pdf. Interestingly the Final Declaration of the 2007 Lisbon Summit between Europe and Africa mentions only good governance and human rights and fails to refer to the democratic origin of governments (available at www.africa-eu-partnership.org/pdf/eas2007_lisbon_declaration_en.pdf).

[72] See generally T Carothers, 'The Backlash against Democracy Promotion' (2006) 85 *Foreign Affairs* 55.

[73] See eg K Roth, 'Empty Promises? Obama's Hesitant Embrace of Human Rights, Foreign Affairs', March-April 2010; K Roth, 'Obama's hesitant embrace of human rights', *International Herald Tribune*, 24 February 2010, 8. In the same vein, J Traub, 'Keeping score on Obama's engagement' policy', *International Herald Tribune*, 21 December 2009, 4; B Knowlton, 'US Waiver Allows Aid to Nations with Child Soldiers', *International Herald Tribune*, 29 October 2010, 5; T Carothers, 'Repairing Democracy Promotion', *The Washington Post*, 14 September 2007. Some early signs were already flagged by T Carothers, 'Promoting Democracy and Fighting Terror' (2003) 82 *Foreign Affairs* 84.

[74] 2010 National Security Strategy of the United States, available at www.whitehouse.gov/sites/default/files/rss_viewer/national_security_strategy.pdf, 10 and 37.

[75] K Weisbrode, 'The false promise of 1989', *International Herald Tribune*, 7–8 November 2009, 8.

[76] See N Petersen, *Demokratie als teleologisches Prinzip. Zur Legitimität von Staatsgewalt im Völkerrecht*, 139 and 220. See also N Petersen, 'The Principle of Democratic Teleology in International Law', 33; G H Fox, 'Democracy, Right to, International Protection'; J Vidmar, 'Multiple Democracy', 209; J Vidmar 'The Right of Self-Determination and Multiparty Democracy'; see however C Pippan, 'International Law, Domestic Political Orders, and the 'Democratic Imperative': Has Democracy Finally Emerged as a Global Legal Entitlement?'.

motives for supporting policies in favour of democratic legitimacy must be briefly recalled.

The requirements pertaining to the democratic origins of governments had classically been promoted and enforced by states and international organisations because of their common—but very disputable—belief that democracy bolsters peace[77] and prosperity,[78] strengthens the respect for human rights[79] and even quells terrorism.[80] Recent practice seems to indicate that these avowed driving-forces of democratisation policies of the post-Cold War period have been outweighed by other political objectives which seem to indicate that, for many states, the 21st century imperatives can no longer accommodate democratisation policies and the requirements of democratic origin of governments that go with them. It probably is not the place to appraise the reasons underlying this retreat of democracy in recent practice. This is a task left to international relations and political sciences specialists whose expertise is much more adequate to take on such an examination. It suffices here to pinpoint four reasons underpinning the abovementioned return to less ideological and more pragmatic and realist foreign policies. First, it will not come as a surprise that the current economic crisis has made democratisation policies more of a luxury. Fewer and fewer countries have been able to afford trade policies conditioned on respect for some requirements as to the democratic origin of the partner. The same is true with the security agenda. The multilateralisation of the security agenda of the 21st century has elevated security in the overarching objective of states' national and international policies[81] thereby making it more clearly and more systematically trump democratisation policies. Third, the overt instrumentalisation to which democracy has been subjected in the past 20 years and the imperialistic policies which have been carried out under its banner have further curtailed the credibility and authority of such policies, democracy promotion being increasingly demoted to

[77] UN Secretary General, *Supplement to Reports on Democratization*, 1996, UN Doc A/51/761, para 3. In the scholarship, this has proved a widely discussed and controversial idea. See eg the neo-Kantian Liberal and democratic peace theories contained in M W Doyle, 'Kant, Liberal Legacies, and Foreign Affairs' (1983) 12 *Philosophy and Public Affairs* 205, 206; J Norton Moore, 'Beyond the Democratic Peace: Solving the War Puzzle' (2004) 44 *Virginia Journal of International Law* 341; J M Owen IV, *Liberal Peace, Liberal War: American Politics and International Security* (Cornell University Press, New York, 1997); W M Reisman, 'Humanitarian Intervention and Fledgling Democracies' (1995) 18 *Fordham International Law Journal* 794, 796; K A Schultz, 'Do Democratic Institutions Constrain or Inform? Contrasting Two Institutional Perspectives on Democracy and War' (1999) 53 *International Organizations* 233; A M Slaughter, International Law in a World of Liberal States (1995) 6 *European Journal of International Law* 503. This thesis has been severely criticised. See eg B Roth, *Governmental Illegitimacy*, 424 et seq.; J Vasquez, 'Ethics, Foreign Policy and Liberal Wars (2005) 6 *International Studies Perspectives* 307; B Jahn, 'Kant, Mill and Illiberal Legacies in International Affairs' (2005) 59 *International Organization*, 177; S Marks, *The Riddle of All Constitutions* at 42 et seq. For a recent discussion, see A Peters, 'Dual Democracy', 281.

[78] G.A. Res. 46/151, Annex II, para 13, U.N. Doc. A/RES/46/151 (Dec. 18, 1991). *But see* World Conference on Human Rights, Preparatory Comm., Fourth Session, *Statement to the World Conference on Human Rights on Behalf of the Committee on Economic Social, and Cultural Rights*, Annex I, para 9, U.N. doc. A/CONF. 157/PC/62/Add. 5 (Mar. 26, 1993).

[79] UN Secretary General, *Supplement to Reports on Democratization*, 1996, UN Doc A/51/761, para 3.

[80] See UN Secretary General, *A More Secure World: Our Shared Responsibility, Report of the High Level Panel on threats, Challenges, and Change*, para 148, *follow-up to the outcome of the Millennium Summit*, U.N. Doc. A/59/565 (Dec. 2, 2004), *available at* www.un.org/secureworld/report.pdf. See also President George W Bush, President Addresses the Nation (Sept. 7, 2003), available at www.whitehouse.gov. For some criticisms of this aspect of the global war on terror, see T Carothers, 'Promoting Democracy and Fighting Terror'.

[81] T Carothers, 'Promoting Democracy and Fighting Terror'; T Carothers, 'Repairing Democracy Promotion. See also E MacDonald, 'International Law, Democratic Governance and September the 11th'.

a mere code word for 'regime change'.[82] This also is an aspect which Susan Marks has long tried to unravel.[83] Eventually, the rise of the People's Republic of China as the first superpower—and its avowed rejection of any democratic standards regarding the origin of power[84]—has enticed many emerging democracies to prefer the ideologically free cooperation offered by this new global power to the cooperation of Western countries and international organisations which is classically made conditional upon the respect for democratic standards.[85]

III. LESSONS FROM AN INTERLUDE: THE POSSIBLE LIMITS OF INTERNATIONAL LAW IN REGULATION OF DOMESTIC GOVERNANCE

Some of the changes brought about by the end of the Cold War in terms of the regulation of domestic governance—which have been described in section I—are probably too well ingrained in positive international law to be subject to the fluctuations—described in section II. In that sense, the possible retreat of the requirement of democratic origin of governments mentioned here is certainly not comprehensive. If the practice reported above were to be confirmed, there is no doubt that some of the changes experienced in the international legal system in the aftermath of the Cold War would outlive this return to—more realist—policies centred on classical human rights and good governance rather than the democratic origin of governments. In particular, democracy would most probably remain a standard to assess the legitimacy of governments[86] and governments in quest for greater legitimacy would continue to seek an improvement of their democratic standards.[87] In the same vein, coups, especially those that lead to the overthrow of a democratic government, would certainly remain systematically condemned, and sanctions usually eased once the authors of the coups pledge to organise free and fair elections.[88]

Despite the inevitable persistence of some requirements pertaining to the democratic origin of governments, it cannot be excluded that, in the light of the practice reported above, the years 1989–2010 could someday constitute more an *interlude* than a sustainable change in the regulation of governance in international law. Indeed, 20th century

[82] On this point, see T Carothers, 'The Backlash Against Democracy Promotion', 64. See also T Carothers, 'Repairing Democracy Promotion'. See also E MacDonald, 'International Law, Democratic Governance and September the 11th'.

[83] See generally S Marks, *The Riddle of All Constitutions*.

[84] If the requirement of democratic origin of governments is considered as a customary obligation, China could be considered a persistent objector. See J d'Aspremont, *L'Etat non démocratique*, 290. For a criticism of that idea, see n 45 above.

[85] This is a change to which I had already alluded in my previous work. See J d'Aspremont, *L'Etat non démocratique*, 316.

[86] See the reactions following the 2010 coup in Kyrgyzstan: A E Kramer, 'U.S. signals backing of new Kyrgyz leadership', *International Herald Tribune*, 15 April 2010, 4; see also A E Kramer, 'Deposed leader leaves Kyrgyzstan', *International Herald Tribune*, 16 April 2010, 3.

[87] See S Mydans, 'Rulers of Myanmar shed uniforms for civilian skins', *International Herald Tribune*, 3 May 2010, 2. See T Fuller, 'Junta in Myanmar raises promise of 2010 election', *International Herald Tribune*, 11 February 2008, 2.

[88] See the reactions following the coup in Niger in February 2010. See A Nossiter, 'Niger Junta Names Chief after Coup Oust Leader', *International Herald Tribune*, 20–21 February 2010, 4. On the practice pertaining to the 2009 coup in Honduras, see News Reports, 'Ousted Honduran leader vows to return', *International Herald Tribune*, 1 July 2009, 5.

international law, especially in its second half, had come to regulate domestic governance through political and civil rights. As was indicated above, the end of the Cold War spawned the hope that international law could expand its grip on domestic governance beyond classical political and civil rights and could enshrine some requirements as to the origin of governments. Although not embracing the all-out—and somewhat naïve—enthusiasm of some American counterparts, I have myself defended a prudent and circumspect understanding of the obligation for states to ensure that their governments be of democratic origin.[89] Whilst I still believe that international law regulates the way in which power is gained at the domestic level, I argue that the last years of that period have shown that even this minimalist customary obligation may be fading away. In that sense, these years could one day be perceived as being nothing more than an *experiment* for regulation of governance through international law returning to a more classical set of requirements centred on the exercise of power in the form of civil and political human rights. Yet, a rebound cannot be entirely excluded. Indeed, it may be that we are only witnessing a temporary lull in the consolidation of legal requirements pertaining to the democratic origin of governments. However, the current economic and socio-political configuration of the global order seems to point to a move away from democratic legitimacy centred on the origin of power. Should such an enfeeblement of the principle of democratic legitimacy be confirmed in future practice, this could indicate that international law is not the appropriate normative instrument to regulate the origin of governments.

It is probably too early to infer any definite lessons from the abovementioned practice. Many of the observations made here are speculative in nature. Accordingly, it is of great import that the principle of democratic legitimacy, even though the odds are rather ominous as to its consolidations, remains on the research agenda of international legal scholarship.[90] If future research were to demonstrate that the years 1989–2010 have constituted a unique experience in the history of international law from the standpoint of regulating governance, legal scholars would have to come to terms with the possibility that international law is not the adequate normative instrument to regulate such an aspect of domestic governance. Rather than vainly trying to re-animate the rules pertaining to the democratic origin of governments once witnessed between 1989 and 2010 or creating soft conceptualisation of democracy in the international legal order, they should then make clear to those actually involved in international norm-making that other avenues need to be pursued if one wants to require governments to be of a democratic origin. This would surely not be idiosyncratic. Indeed, it seems to the present author that domestic governance may simultaneously be regulated through other normative systems. In particular, it cannot be excluded that non-legal norms, political or moral directives may also enshrine some instructions as to the origin of domestic governance.[91] From the vantage point of compliance, these instructions may sometime carry more weight

[89] See n 15 above.

[90] According to C Pippan, democratic governance remains a topic that has not lost its attraction and continues to inspire scholars of international law. See C Pippan, 'International Law, Domestic Political Orders, and the "Democratic Imperative"' 5.

[91] These norms are often referred to by legal scholars as constituting soft legal norms. For a criticism of the concept of soft law, see J d'Aspremont, 'Softness in International Law: A Self-Serving Quest for New Legal Materials'.

than legal rules.[92] Here it suffices to say that contemporary practice shows that international law could be falling short of extending its grip on domestic governance well beyond the imposition of legal requirements as to *how* the power is exercised at the domestic level. This must entice international lawyers to re-think the efficacy of international law as a tool to regulate accession to power at the domestic level.

[92] For a survey of the recent developments in the study of compliance in both international relations and international law scholarship, see K Raustiala and A M Slaughter, 'International Law, International Relations and Compliance' in W Carlnaes, T Risse and B Simmons (eds), *The Handbook of International Relations* (Sage Publications, London, 2002) 538. For an insightful account of various compliance theories, see A T Guzman, 'A Compliance-Based Theory of International Law' (2002) 90 *California Law Review* 1823.

5

Persisting and Developing between Hope and Threat: International Law during the Past Two Decades and Beyond

GEORG NOLTE*

After shedding the shackles of the Cold War's containment policies, international law was free to serve as an instrument of change. But have social groups and political and judicial actors perceived international law any differently since the end of the Cold War? Have they used international law as a transformative force and, if so, how?
(Introductory query by the conference organisers)

'AFTER SHEDDING the shackles of the Cold War's containment policies, international law was free to serve as an instrument of change'. This proposition, although it appears to state the obvious, is really rather questionable. It is true that international law 'shed the shackles of the Cold War containment policies', but its primary role immediately after the fall of the Berlin Wall was not so much to serve as an 'instrument for change', but to be a beacon of hope and a promise for the realisation of the, as yet unrealised, programme of the UN Charter. International law was not immediately seen as an 'instrument of change', to be used by different actors. Indeed the success of international law after 1989 depended on the perception that it embodied the hopes of almost everybody.

The nineties were a decade of hope. Despite and even because of the eruption of another type of violent conflict—ethnically motivated civil war—the rules and ideas of the UN Charter could be unfolded. The nineties saw unprecedented Security Council activities, in particular all sorts of peace operations, as well as the establishment of international criminal courts. Many new treaties were concluded, institutions established, forms of cooperation enhanced. Commentators identified a move away from the inter-state paradigm of international law towards a world in which the individual takes centre-stage, and in which non-governmental actors and civil society play an ever more important role. Human rights, democracy, and just war theories were on the rise. State sovereignty as the building block of international law was in the process of factual and normative transformation. Despite debates over the universality or cultural relativity

* Georg Nolte is Professor of International Law at Humboldt University Berlin since 2008 and a member of the International Law Commission since 2007.

of human rights, a self-confident liberal conception of international law was the lodestar of the decade.

The nineties were a window of opportunity and a period of advancement of western values, as far as they are embodied in the UN Charter and other documents. This process of the unfolding of international law in a liberal spirit slowed down considerably at around the turn of the century. The turn was not immediately visible, and some even mistakenly assumed that the trend had accelerated. Indeed, certain events in 1999 could be interpreted as a translation of the general trend of the nineties into a substantially recalibrated international legal system. The Kosovo intervention could be interpreted as a sign that the protection of core human rights took precedence over a Cold-War-inspired, broad interpretation, of the prohibition of the use of force. The Pinochet decision of the British House of Lords could be interpreted as a sign that the sanctioning of grave and systematic human rights violations was beginning to take precedence over formal protections of state sovereignty. And the 'Battle of Seattle' could be interpreted as a sign that an international civil society was beginning to take shape which instilled a first dose of more immediate democratic participation in international decision-making.

It turned out, however, that these cases were not easily digested by the international community. Even though most NATO states had not even claimed a new right of unilateral humanitarian intervention, and the House of Lords had not asserted a broad new human rights exception to the rule of state immunity, and although the 'Battle in Seattle' had not been the main cause for the stalling of the further development of the WTO, these—and other—cases nevertheless had a catalytic effect on the perception of international law in general. Resistance formed against an alleged new right of unilateral humanitarian intervention, and the ensuing debate was uneasily contained in the process of developing a responsibility to protect. The impulse of the Pinochet decision was not amplified by the European Court of Human Rights or by the International Court of Justice, as some had expected. And the 'Battle in Seattle' did not turn out to be a precursor of politically more significant movements—although the issues of participation and transparency remain on the table and civil society is now an established factor in many treaty negotiations.

Why was the unfolding of a liberal international law arrested ten years ago? It is probably too early to give a definitive answer. But one possibility is that incidents like Kosovo, Pinochet and Seattle were not anymore generally perceived as signs of an unfolding of the shared expectations for international law, but that they were rather perceived as efforts to use international law as an instrument for change in the interest of particular states or groups. The Kosovo intervention was perceived by some as an effort by western states to change a basic rule. The idea behind the Pinochet decision was thought selectively to undermine the sovereignty and legitimacy of certain states. And civil society movements were more critically observed as to whether they represented only the particular interests or world views of certain groups. These three cases involved claims which could not easily fit the, until then, shared understanding of international law. Thus, international law itself contributed towards the—correct or mistaken—identification of certain claims as being driven by special interests. In this sense, international law, as traditionally understood, proved rather resilient against hopes to transform it into an instrument of change.

But the capacity of international law to contain larger historical trends should not be overestimated. Perhaps the development of the nineties was bound to reach a limit. The 'unilateralism' of the United States was discussed even before the terror attacks of '9/11', and the assumption that the 'last remaining superpower' was reconciling its own interests with the general interest of the international community at large was increasingly being questioned.

After 9/11 the paradigm of hope for the unfolding of a liberal international law under a benign US supervision finally turned into a widely-held perception of the US as posing a threat to international law by behaving as a wounded and an assertive great power. The Bush doctrine and the attack against Iraq, Guantanamo and waterboarding, all stood for the calling into question of the most basic rules of international law. Certainly, the United States did not dispute the existence of the basic rules of international law on the use of force and for the humane treatment of persons, but it attempted to interpret and apply those rules in such a novel and obviously self-interested way that its credibility suffered substantially. The past decade also saw the rise of other phenomena which could be perceived as threats to international law and which were more indirectly connected to the role of the United States. Suffice it to mention the expansion and concentration of decision-making power in the Security Council, the prime example being the listing procedures, and the possible disconnections which were discussed under the rubric of the 'fragmentation' of international law.

Interestingly, those real and imagined threats to international law of the past decade have been countered not so much by traditional inter-governmental exchanges, but rather by 'social groups and political and judicial actors'. It was not so much governments who strongly resisted the excesses of the US reaction to 9/11, but advocacy groups, world public opinion and, after a while, national and international courts and other legal bodies. The same is true for the efforts to repair the one-sidedness of the Security Council's listing procedures. And concern about the blindness of expertocratic overbearing against rights and interests outside the respective institutional context was often most effectively articulated by independent non-governmental and judicial actors.

So, all in all, international law has remained rather stable between the hopes of the nineties and the threats of the past decade. In the nineties, 'social groups and political and judicial actors' contributed to the progressive realisation of certain unfulfilled aspects of international law. But they did so in the context of a permissive inter-governmental environment. During the past decade, 'social groups and political and judicial actors' have assumed a more important function, but they have not been so much motors of change, but rather defenders of rights and other public interests against the one-sided evolution of special—inter-governmental—regimes. NGOs defend the environment against the logic of international economic regimes, and courts protect terrorist suspects and national sovereignty against the Security Council and the European Union.

So, 'have social groups and political and judicial actors perceived international law any differently since the end of the Cold War' and 'have they used it as a transformative force'? Probably all these actors have taken international law more seriously than before, and many of them, including courts, have *tried* to use it as a transformative force. There are even examples where advocacy groups and courts have provided decisive impulses for the development of particular aspects of international law, in particular in the humanitarian law field. But, in general, the effect of such actors on international law as a whole has been conservative. In pursuing their respective agendas and mandates, they emphasised and defended certain aspects of international law against the possible overbearing or neglect of governments, acting alone or in concert, and of international organisations. In a sense, international law may be undergoing a process which resembles the constitutional history of states such as the UK and the US in the nineteenth century: by becoming more responsive to public debate and by admitting more players, those states did not see the basic structure of their legal system changed, but reinforced.

This assessment may sound both complacent and provocative. Just to avoid possible misunderstandings, it should perhaps be underlined that the generally conservative effect of the activities of 'social groups and political and judicial actors' is compatible with their frequent self-perception as agents of change on the ground. Also, a conservative effect of the activities of 'social groups and political and judicial actors' on international law is neither necessarily beneficial nor can it be taken for granted. Where the instrumental approach of many actors towards international law is not effectively counterbalanced, the legitimacy of international law as a programme and framework which is shared by all relevant actors is called into question. But the danger of a lack of counterbalance is probably not so great. After all, the experience of the past decade has been that even the 'last remaining superpower' proved unable to use international law as an instrument of change. A more relevant concern may emerge when the traditional mutual contestation between States is amplified, and not blurred, by the mutual contestation between different groups and independent institutions. This might lead to a logjam which would make it difficult to conclude new treaties and to adapt international law to changing circumstances.

The next decade will probably neither reignite the hopes of the nineties, nor witness the overbearing of a 'sole remaining superpower'. It could raise a question which a stocktaking of the past two decades would not help to resolve: how to preserve international law's relevance in a G20 world? Such a world needs to generate sufficient agreement for the conclusion of new treaties, to adapt the law to changing circumstances and preferences, and to address the question of global justice. It is doubtful whether these needs will be satisfied easily. Rising states and regions might perceive the need to assert themselves, not only vis-à-vis the United States and the West, but also vis-à-vis each other. The recent climate change negotiations symbolise writing on the wall. Much may depend on how states, institutions, and the law can cope below the formal processes of change. It is doubtful whether courts will be able, with their interpretative and *de facto* legislative powers alone, to keep international law up to date. In the course of justice alone, none of us should see salvation. It is also unlikely that states, social and political groups will be able to achieve their goals by informally superseding or undermining formal international law. Hopefully the idea of the rule of law is capable of providing a unifying and progressive concept in today's world in which the concept of democracy has lost some of its capacity to do so. International law today persists and develops between such hopes and threats. Its performance during the past twenty years can give us some confidence that its basic rules will remain resilient to pressures, but it is an open question what this is worth.

The legitimacy of international law depends on the credibility of its underlying assertion: that it is not an instrument of change for certain actors, but a programme and a framework which all relevant actors share. While the credibility of this assertion has come under pressure here and there during the past twenty years, international law's legitimacy has remained basically intact and remains an exploitable but also an exhaustible resource.

Part II:

1989–2010: Legalisation and Law-Making

6

Less is More: International Law of the 21st Century—Law without Faith

ALAIN PELLET*

TODAY'S INTERNATIONAL LAW deeply differs from what it has been until recently. And this difference is rather paradoxical in that:

- on the one hand, the need for law has never been as intense as it is in the contemporary international society; while,
- on the other hand, confidence in international law (and in some respect, the veritable mystique of international law) which had developed after World War I, has faded in favour of a much more practical or utilitarian approach.

These are the two aspects I will successively deal with in this brief contribution.

FIRST PROPOSITION: NEVER HAS THE THIRST FOR LAW BEEN MORE INSATIABLE THAN IN THE CONTEMPORARY INTERNATIONAL SOCIETY

It is commonplace to note that international law was born, much before Grotius' systematisation, with the modern state (beginning during the 12th or the 13th century), characterised by its sovereignty—that it alone enjoys at the international level. The state, as the usual form of organisation of human societies, and international law have grown hand in hand and for a good reason: international law is as necessary to the state as air is to human beings or water to fish. In a society characterised by the pure juxtaposition of entities pretending to be, at one and the same time, 'sovereign over all' (*souveraines par-dessus tout*) and equal with one another, law is the only means to ensure that each state's sovereignty is limited only by the (equal) sovereignty of other states.[1]

Indispensable as it has always been for regulating the relations in inter-state society, this traditional law was limited to a small number of international rules, applicable to a small number of subject matters: war; diplomatic relations and *jus communicationis* (including law of the sea and trade)—and this was all. Things moved only slowly until

* Professor of International Law at l'Université Paris Ouest, Nanterre-La Défense; Member and former Chairman of the ILC.

[1] This principle is reflected in Max Huber's famous dictum: 'Sovereignty in the relations between States signifies independence.' (Arbitral Award, 4 April 1928, *Island of Palmas* case, *RIAA*, vol II, 838).

the First World War when the collision of European imperialisms (a result of a distorted and absolute notion of state sovereignty) led the World to its first apocalyptic disaster and induced the people of the first post-war years to show and organise solidarity to fight against the scourge of war, or illness (just think of the 1918 'Spanish flu'—infinitely more devastating than the H1N1 influenza…). Consequently, a first normative quantitative threshold is obtained: in parallel with the proliferation of the 'offices' of the League of Nations (LoN), international law–*jus gentium* as it was still commonly called—starts its inflationist growth in grasping topics which were, until then, parts of the 'reserved domain' of the state—that is, exclusively regulated by domestic laws.[2] Labour law, intellectual cooperation, health, agriculture, public education, and even nationality (think of the famous 1930 Convention) become the object of international rules.

The Second World War gave a new impulse to this phenomenon, with, for example, the bursting out of human rights within the international legal sphere. This was in large part a reaction to the inability of the democracies which, at the eve of the war, could not have lawfully interfered (had they wanted to…) with the threat of extermination of the German Jews. The contemporary legal discourse says the opposite to what Goebbels is said to have declared following Franz Bernheim's claim to the LoN's denouncing the fate of the Jews within the Third Reich:[3] 'Gentlemen, the Third German Reich is a sovereign State and we are masters of our own home. All that has been said by this individual is not your business. We do what we deem necessary with our own socialists, our pacifists and our Jews'[4] (although this version is not an exact reflection of this dark and infamous episode).

However, during the after-war period, the increase in the scope of international law has been quantitatively limited. Indeed more and more treaties, including codification conventions, were concluded and treaty rules tended to overtake non-written rules which traditionally regulated inter-state relations: diplomatic and consular relations, law of the sea, international responsibility—just to mention the most well-known parts of the codification enterprise. The purpose was mainly to complete and refine existing customary rules.

During the last ten, maybe fifteen, but certainly not more than twenty years, we can witness a fundamentally different phenomenon. In sharp contrast to the slow process of filling up the lacunas of traditional international law, we now see an unmanageable

[2] For early criticisms of this theory, see N Politis 'Le problème des limitations de la souveraineté'(1925) 1 *Recueil des cours*, 5–117 or G Scelle 'Critique du soi-disant domaine de compétence exclusive' (1933) *RDILC* 365.

[3] For the French text of that petition, introduced by application of the German-Polish Convention of 15 May 1922 on Upper Silesia, which provided for a right of petition for minorities, see the LoN document: C.314.1933.I.B, (19 May 1933) (1933) 7 *J.O.S.d.N.* 838.

[4] See Marc Agi, *De l'idée d'universalité comme fondatrice du concept des droits de l'homme d'après la vie et l'œuvre de René Cassin,* 354 (Alp'azur, Antibes, 1980) or Mario Bettati, *Le droit d'ingérence – Mutation de l'ordre international,* 18 (Odile Jacob, 1996). See also: René Cassin 'Les droits de l'homme' (1974) IV 140 *R.C.A.D.I.* 324. The examination and suites devoted to the Bernheim petition are more 'scientifically' presented by Greg Burgess, who remains nevertheless faithful to the emblematic character of this episode, 'The Human Rights Dilemma in Anti-Nazi Protest: The Bernheim Petition, Minorities Protection, and the 1933 Sessions of the League of Nations', CERC Working Papers Series, n° 2/2002, 56 or by Jan Herman Burgers 'The Road to San Francisco: The Revival of the Human Rights Idea in the Twentieth Century' (1992) *Human Rights Quarterly* 455. The German text of Goebbels' speech, read to the journalists (and not before the LoN Assembly), was published *in Joseph Goebbels, Signale der neuen Zeit* (*Messages de l'ère nouvelle*) (Munich: Zentralverlag der NSDAP, 1934).

eruption of international law rules, a true normative big bang or tsunami. If I may indulge myself in a page of self-advertising, I finished, just one year ago, the update and revision of the big handbook in public international law that I co-author with Patrick Daillier and Mathias Forteau.[5] As we had let more than eight years pass between the 7th and 8th edition, the simple update of what wishes to be a comprehensive panorama of modern international law has been a Herculean task—with nothing in common with the first seven editions. Up to now, the successive editions could be prepared mainly on the basis of the case-law of the International Court of Justice, the work of the International Law Commission, some arbitral awards and a limited number of multilateral conventions which, from one edition to another, could be counted on one hand's fingers. Since we were meticulous, we added some important judgments of the European and American Courts of Human Rights, and, of course, the international law books published in between. The task of updating did not amount to nothing but it was manageable.

However, all at once, from the mid-1990s, the machinery has grown out of control and it has become virtually impossible for one, two or even three authors to 'swallow' and 'digest' the impressing mass of legal information—which is indispensable to introduce a full picture of the existing general international law. The new rules appear in heaps of treaties and soft-law instruments, adopted by, or within the framework of, a greater number of institutions and in domains that are ever more diversified. And these luxuriant legal norms ('more or less legal'—whether the opponents of 'relative normativity'[6] like it or not…) are implemented through varied and heterogeneous mechanisms on which information is not always easy to be found notwithstanding the internet God.

Following the work of the ILC on fragmentation initiated by Bruno Simma and subsequently addressed by Gerhardt Hafner and Martti Koskenniemi,[7] it has become fashionable to speak of the 'fragmentation' of international law. But the word does not properly describe the new state of things—at least it does not describe it completely. Indeed, there is a dispersion and a 'crumbling' of international law in that the fora where it is created and implemented have become scattered in at least two ways:

- there exists a 'vertical fragmentation' since the international legal norms are elaborated and applied not only at the universal level, but also at the regional

[5] P Daillier, M Forteau, A Pellet, *Droit international public* (Paris, LGDJ, 2008).

[6] The fame of the concept is much due to P Weil's article, 'Vers une normativité relative en droit international ?, (1982) *RGDIP*, 5, and in English: 'Towards Relative Normativity in International Law?' (1983) *AJIL* 413. See also A Pellet 'Le "bon droit" et l'ivraie – plaidoyer pour l'ivraie', *Mélanges Charles Chaumont* (Paris, Pedone, 1984) 465; Ch Leben 'Une nouvelle controverse sur le positivisme en droit international public' (1987) *Droits* 121 and more recently, two opposite perspectives by A Boyle 'Soft-Law in International Law-Making', in M Evans (ed), *International Law* (Oxford, OUP, 2003) 2, 141 and D Shelton 'International Law and "Relative Normativity"', ibid, 151.

[7] For the Report of the Study Group on the Fragmentation established by the ILC see Erik Castrén Institute of International Law and Human Rights, *Fragmentation of International Law: Difficulties Arising from the Diversification and Expansion of International Law* (Helsinki, 2007) III-306 (see also A/CN.4/L.682 (2006)). A rich literature exists on the subject: see, inter alia, P-M Dupuy 'The Danger of Fragmentation or Unification of the International Legal System and the International Court of Justice' (1999) *NYUJlIL* 791, G Hafner 'Pros and Cons Ensuing from Fragmentation in International Law' (2004) *Michigan JlIL* 849, B Simma 'Fragmentation in a Positive Light' (2004) *Michigan JlIL*, 845, A Gattini 'Un regard procédural sur la fragmentation du droit international', (2006) *RGDIP* 303, R H Vinaixa and K Wellens (ed) *L'influence des sources sur l'unité et la fragmentation du droit international : travaux du séminaire tenu à Palma, les 20–21 mai 2005* (Bruylant, Bruxelles, 2006) XXII.

level[8]—or level*s* since the continental organisations must be distinguished from the sub-regional and bilateral levels;
- there is also a 'horizontal fragmentation' in that specific branches of international law flourish, all of them aspiring to some degree of specificity and, at least, give rise to abundant normative developments which, more often than not, are accompanied by the creation of implementing mechanisms that even a 'generalist' in international law cannot set aside.[9] One cannot neglect what happens in environmental matters, human rights, international criminal law or investment law.

And, it is noticeable that in *all* these fields, not only international legal instruments (hard or soft) blossom, but also that the instruments create mechanisms, the 'jurisprudence' of which constitutes an indispensable and inseparable complement to the norms they edict. Today, one cannot decently do general international law (either as an academic or as a practitioner) without some knowledge (which, by necessity, can only be superficial) of the judgments of the regional human rights courts (which grow exponentially in number), of the criminal courts and tribunals, of the WTO Appellate Body, of the ICSID—or ICSID-like—arbitrations, etc. And I leave aside the rules applicable in the regional organisations of economic integration like the European Union, NAFTA or the Mercosur since, even though they are 'a new legal order of international law'[10]—whether the Court in Luxemburg likes it or not[11]—they are sufficiently autonomous vis-à-vis the international legal order to be apprehended separately.

Today's international law covers virtually all fields of human activity. It has become impossible reasonably to accept the very idea of a 'reserved domain' or, in the words of Article 2, paragraph 7 of the Charter of the United Nations, of 'matters which are essentially within the domestic jurisdiction of any State'. Nowadays, there simply does not exist anything of the kind.[12] There is definitely no exaggeration in speaking of the 'big bang' of international law. It is therefore paradoxical to note, at one and the same time, that there has never been such a need for legal rules at the international level, and that law is no longer envisaged as a tool for peace—or, in other words, that the World has lost confidence in international law. This latter observation is my second proposition.

SECOND PROPOSITION: LAW IS NO LONGER ENVISAGED AS A TOOL FOR PEACE—OR, IN OTHER WORDS, THE WORLD HAS LOST CONFIDENCE IN INTERNATIONAL LAW

The title of the well-known book by Clark and Sohn, *World Peace through World Law*,[13] has been the motto of the international community since the end of the First World War (even though the first edition of the book appeared only in 1958). At the end of the war the trauma was such that the world's leaders were desperately in search of the miracle

[8] See for instance J Dutheil de la Rochère 'Mondialisation et régionalisation' in Loquin (ed), *La mondialisation du droit* (Litec, 2000) 435.

[9] B Simma and D Pulkowski 'Of Planets and the Universe: Self-contained Regimes in International Law' (2006) 17 *EJIL* 529.

[10] ECJ, Judgment of 5 February 1963, *Van Gend en Loos*, Case 26/62, *EC Rep*. 1.

[11] See the Judgment of the ECJ in *Costa v ENEL*, 15 July 1964, case n° 6/64.

[12] Or the concept, as it is used today, has a completely different meaning (see R Kolb, 'Du domaine réservé – Réflexions sur la théorie de la compétence nationale' (2006) *R.G.D.I.P.* 597).

[13] G Clark and L B Sohn *World Peace through World Law* 2nd edn (Cambridge, Harvard UP, 1966) 535.

recipe for avoiding the renewal of the nightmare and putting a final end to the use of force in international relations. They thought they had found it by adopting legal rules to that end and by ensuring the application of those rules through an international organisation with global competence: the League of Nations. This was an apparently sensible reaction to the purely inter-state Westphalian world predating the 'Great War'. However, it was quickly apparent that the construction was purely abstract and unrealistic. So were the legal theories which then flourished in reaction to the cynical positivism that was the quasi-exclusive analysis of international law before 1914: the Kelsenian theory of 'pure theory of law', the jusnaturalism of Verdross, another Austrian professor, or the 'sociological objectivism' of the French professor Georges Scelle. These theories were certainly more attractive morally and politically than the 'positivist voluntarism' inherited from Vattel but they share the failure of the League of Nations after 1935: the new post World War law could bark but it could not bite.

After World War II, the reaction was the adoption of the Charter and the creation of the UN, which certainly represents progress—if only because it has avoided an apocalyptic Third World War—even though the UN largely remains a paper tiger. But the creation of the UN does not address the problem of today on which I focus. The interesting thing for us is that the 'mystique' of international law did not disappear after the failure of the League of Nations.

Indeed international law is more than discrete in the UN Charter.[14] The expression 'international law' appears only three times:

- in Article 13, which mentions 'the progressive development of international law and its codification' as one of the functions of the General Assembly;
- in Article 1, paragraph 1, according to which one of the purposes of the United Nations is '[t]o maintain international peace and security, and to that end ... to bring about by peaceful means, and in conformity with the principles of justice and international law, adjustment or settlement of international disputes or situations which might lead to a breach of the peace'. International law can appear as one (among others) of the means to maintain international peace and security, which is the aim of the new organisation;
- but at the same time, in the preamble the 'peoples of the United Nations declare themselves to be determined' 'to establish conditions under which justice and respect for the obligations arising from treaties and other sources of international law can be maintained'. This rather inverts the formula: it is not 'world peace through world law', but rather, 'world law through world peace'![15]

The least that can be said is that the 'Peoples of the United Nations' pay lip service to international law in the Charter but do not show a spectacular enthusiasm to praising it as a credible means to ensuring international peace and security or the welfare of mankind. And yet...

[14] For a systematic view on the question, see M Forteau 'Le droit international dans la Charte des Nations Unies' in Cot, Pellet, Forteau (ed), *La Charte des Nations Unies. Commentaire article par article* 3rd edn (Paris, Economica, 2005) 111.

[15] The perversion of the initial logic of the system, through its instrumentalisation, has been denounced as dangerous, see eg A Cassese, 'Return to Westphalia? Considerations on the Erosion of the Charter System', in Cassese (ed), *The Current Legal Regulation of the Use of Force* (Leiden, Martinus Nijhoff Publishers, 1986) 503.

In fact, the practice of the majority of states was far ahead of this limited expectation. International law was the object of a very intense hope and states toughly fought legal struggles. It is probably no accident that one of the first subsidiary organs created by the UN General Assembly was the International Law Commission whose first achievements were impressive, for instance the adoption of the Vienna Conventions on diplomatic and consular relations and the Vienna Convention on the Law of Treaties. Georges Abi-Saab has aptly referred to the 1960s as 'the prodigious decade'.[16] Even though recourse to the ICJ was parsimonious, the Court enjoyed unanimous respect (at least in the West) and had opportunity to adopt positions of principle on crucial issues with politically important impacts (the best example being probably that of the 1949 Advisory Opinion on *Reparation for Injuries Suffered in the Service of the United Nations*). The legal offices inside the Ministries of Foreign Affairs and international organisations rapidly developed and achieved a growing influence.[17]

During the 1960s and the 1970s, classical international law was the object of vociferous attacks by the new countries of the Third World with the support of the Soviet bloc, through their global challenge of the former colonial order and old economic international order.[18] But this, too, bore witness to the confidence they put in international law as a means for change.

But all of this is over. For the worse or the better, this mystique of international law has vanished.[19] I leave aside the cynical contempt for international law shown by the US Bush Administration, for instance its partly unsuccessful attempt to torpedo the International Criminal Court, or the 'sovereignist' approach of emerging powers such as China, India and Brazil, or the blunt disrespect for international law of Iran or Israel. I am referring to the usual behaviour of 'normal' states (even if they probably are a minority), which 'normally' abide by international law—most European countries for example (including mine usually—even if President Sarkozy has a very special idea of what international law allows regarding deprivation of nationality or the treatment of the Roma in France…).

Then, let's only focus on these countries which usually will comply with their international obligations. They have become incredibly conservative, resistant to change, not cautious but cowardly. Apart from the WTO Agreements or Rome Statute of the ICC, no 'great' multilateral conventions have been concluded over the past decades. However, many multilateral technical conventions or conventions on secondary or 'residual' issues have been agreed upon. This is not to say that these numerous instruments are negligible (I include among them the 2007 Disappearance Convention and the important Ottawa Convention on Anti-Personal Mines) but they are not part of a global enterprise of

[16] 'Cours général de droit international public' (1987) 207 *Recueil des cours* 149.

[17] See eg G Fitzmaurice, 'Legal Advisers and Foreign Affairs', (1965) *A.J.I. L*72; G Guillaume 'La direction des affaires juridiques du ministère des Affaires étrangères', in *Guy Ladreit de Lacharrière et la politique extérieure de la France* (Paris, Masson, 1990) 267; Symposium, 'The Impact of International Law on Foreign Policy Making, The Role of Legal Advisers' (1991) *E.J.I.L.*131; A Cassese, 'Role of Legal Advisers in Ensuring That Foreign Policy Conforms to International Legal Standards'(1992) 14 *Mich. J. Int'l L* 139.

[18] For an engaged Third-World vision, see for example G Abi-Saab, 'The Third World and the Future of International Legal Order' (1973) *Egyptian Review of Int'l Law* 27. As for the Soviet approach, see W E Butler (ed), *Perestroika and International Law* (Nijhoff, Dordrecht, 1990) VI-330.

[19] This is actually the credo of the critical legal studies school. See Ph Allott, *Eunomia*, 2 (Oxford UP, 2001) 487 or M Koskenniemi, *From Apologia to Utopia: The Structure of International Legal Argument* (Lasismeliton Kustannus, Helsinki, 1989). And for an outside view of the phenomenon, see J P Cot 'Tableau de la pensée juridique américaine' (2006) *RGDIP* 537.

deepening the global approach to international law. They reinforce the existing network but they do not expand it nor improve its character.

The same could be said of the recent judgments of the International Court of Justice. Some are debatable or disappointing, others are objectively good, but that is not the point. While the Court complies rather well with its dispute settlement role, the present judges in The Hague, contrary to their predecessors, do not see themselves as 'improvers' of international law. The authors of the glorious Advisory Opinions in *Count Bernadotte*[20] and *Reservations to the Genocide Convention*[21] had dared to grasp opportunities to do so. In the best of cases, as in *Romania v Ukraine*,[22] the ICJ synthetises the existing law and clarifies the contentious issue. For the rest, caution and 'just the dispute' or 'just the question' seem to be the motto.

Finally, a lack of achievement can also be observed in the ILC.[23] There is the *magnum opus* on State Responsibility but it has remained in the form of (draft) Articles of which the General Assembly has taken note. In my point of view this half way is fortunate: had a diplomatic Conference been conveyed, no doubt that all which makes it a success—the very fortunate balance between conservative rules and some prudent step forwards—would have been 'killed' by a conservative coalition. In letting the Articles live their own life there is some chance for the balance to be preserved. Apart from the Articles on State Responsibility the ILC has achieved very little. Unilateral Acts of States, the only topic which had some ambition, has been killed in its *status nascendi*;[24] the working group on Shared Natural Resources has given birth to a decent but limited draft[25] on the Law of International Aquifers; the Guide to Practice on Reservations to Treaties is a hopefully useful but very technical instrument. I am curious to see how states will welcome the ILC proposal to include an aspect of the making of customary law on its agenda.

The truth is that states—which have virtually proposed *no* topic to the ILC during the two last decades (even the draft Statute of the ICC was more or less an invention of the ILC itself)—have no project, no design, no ambition for the ILC. And I am afraid that this holds true for international law as a whole: states do not 'trust' international law; at worst they breach its rules (but this has always been the case: unbreachable rules are not legal rules); at best they consider it a useful tool for day-to-day conduct but, 'World Peace through World Law', 'Development through a New International Legal Order', clearly appear as slogans of a remote past. There are signs of new partial 'faiths', in human rights and environmental law in particular. However, confined to 'isms' ('human-rightism'; 'environmentalism'), they lose sight of the global common interest. And I am not sure that we, the supposed Vestals of the Temple, have kept the sacred fire either: either we content ourselves with a 'pragmatic', breathless approach or we wallow in sterile 'critical' approaches.

[20] ICJ, Advisory Opinion, 11 April 1949, *Reparation for Injuries Suffered in the Service of the United Nations*, (1949) *Reports* 174.

[21] ICJ, Advisory Opinion, 28 May 1951, *Reservations to the Convention on the Prevention and Punishment of the Crime of Genocide*, (1951) *Reports* 15.

[22] ICJ, Judgment, 3 February 2009, *Maritime Delimitation in the Black Sea (Romania v. Ukraine)*.

[23] I will abstain here from continuing to harp on the change of its composition—from eminent scholars to diplomats See A Pellet 'La Commission du Droit international, pour quoi faire?', in *Boutros Boutros-Ghali Amicorum Discipulorumque Liber – Paix, développement, démocratie* (Bruylant, Bruxelles,1998) 583.

[24] The *Guiding Principles Applicable to Unilateral Declarations of States Capable of Creating Legal Obligations* were adopted in 2006 (see the ILC Report on the work of its fifty-eighth session, doc. A/61/10, 369).

[25] On the law of transboundary aquifers, the Draft Articles on which were adopted in 2008, see the ILC Report on the work of its sixtieth session, 2008, A/63/10, 27–79.

Without being a *laudator temporis acti*, I cannot help myself but to think that we have missed something…

7

The Process of Legalisation After 1989 and its Contribution to the International Rule of Law

ANDRÉ NOLLKAEMPER*

I. INTRODUCTION

ONE OF THE defining features of the development of the international legal order after 1989 is the enduring increase in the amount of legal rights and obligations that govern the relations between states, between states and international institutions and, to a lesser extent, other subjects of international law. Precise figures are only to a limited extent available. Existing databases, notably the UNTS-database,[1] are only of modest use. Nonetheless, any cursory assessment of available data suggests that there indeed has been a significant increase in such rights and obligations.

Some international-relations scholars, and lawyers writing from an international-relations perspective, have coined this trend a process of 'legalisation'.[2] While its added conceptual value is open to dispute (see further section II), the term legalisation is a relatively convenient term to capture what Goldstein, Kahler, Keohane and Slaughter, in what still is the seminal contribution on this theme, saw as a dominant trend at the turn of the century: 'In many issue-areas, the world is witnessing a move to law'.[3]

* Professor of Public International Law, Amsterdam Center for International Law, University of Amsterdam. The author acknowledges the assistance of Anna Gilsbach, Christopher Hopwood, Isabelle Swerissen and Camilla Wright in preparing this paper.

[1] United Nations Treaty Collection, 'UNTS Database', treaties.un.org/Pages/UNTSOnline.aspx?id=1, accessed 9 November 2010. The database provides information on treaties and treaty actions with respect to treaties registered with the UN, but searches involving larger numbers are notoriously complicated and the keyword selection often seems arbitrary and unreliable.

[2] See for instance the special issue of (2000) 54 *International Organisation* edited by J Goldstein, M Kahler, R O Keohane and A M Slaughter. See also C Brütsch and D Lehmkuhl (eds), *Law And Legalisation In Transnational Relations* (Routledge, London and New York, 2007); D P Jinks, 'The Legalisation of World Politics and the Future of U.S. Human Rights Policy' (2002) 46 *St Louis ULJ 357*; V Gauri and D M Brinks, 'The Elements Of Legalisation And The Triangular Shape Of Social And Economic Rights: Introduction', in V Gauri and D M Brinks (eds), *Courting Social Justice: Judicial Enforcement Of Social And Economic Rights In The Developing World* (Cambridge University Press, 2008).

[3] J Goldstein, M Kahler, R O Keohane and A M Slaughter, 'Introduction: Legalisation and World Politics' 54 (2000) *International Organisation* 385, 385.

Outside international law, the process of legalisation more often than not will have a negative connotation. Making informal relations and social norms (say: greeting one's colleagues at an international-law conference) subject to legal consequences, in principle, is not a prospect that many people would cherish.

Legalisation originating from an international-law context is generally seen in more favorable terms. The distinct character of international society makes the romantic view that informal relations are normatively superior to legalised relations less likely. Moreover, since the role of consent remains so dominant, the result is that relations will be legally regulated only with consent of those regulated. Indeed, the process of law making is so cumbersome that many would appraise legalisation in international law in positive terms. That positive assessment may in part be induced by the instrumentalist value of legalisation: it can allow the achievement of particular social objectives. But beyond such instrumentalist goals, legalisation may be seen as an important contribution to the further advance of the rule of law in international law affairs. It may replace, in particular areas, prevalence of power politics by a rule-based system. In the work of the UN on the rule of law at the international level, more international law is indeed seen as central element in the further development of the international rule of law.[4]

However, the proposition that legalisation furthers the rule of law in international affairs would be too simple. The fundamental weaknesses of the international legal order, that make the ideal of the international rule of law far removed from present-day reality, cannot be simply overcome by ever more international laws. It may be necessary to differentiate between different types of international norms. It is also questionable whether it is proper to speak of a contribution to the rule of law irrespective of the actual use and enforcement of such newly adopted rules.

In this chapter I will examine the process towards legalisation after 1989, in line with the general theme of the 2010 European Society meeting, and evaluate this trend from the perspective of its possible contribution to the rule of law. I will first explore the main trends of legalisation after 1989 (section II). In sections III and IV, I will respectively examine the possible contribution of legalisation to the rule of law at, respectively, the international and the domestic level. Section V contains brief conclusions.

II. THE CONCEPT OF LEGALISATION

Before assessing the trends towards legalisation a few words on the concept are in order. In international law the term legalisation is not commonly used. In its narrow legal meaning it refers to legalisation of foreign public documents.[5] However, the concept has drifted in from international relations literature and now appears to be increasingly used to refer to a process of increase in (the use of) law.

While legalisation in this broader sense has no widely shared meaning, from the perspective of international law we can readily agree on the core aspect of the phenomenon, that is: legalisation entails more law.[6] The term then refers to the emergence

[4] UN Doc. A/RES/55/2 (2000) 3; UN Doc. A/RES/60/1 (2005) 29; UN Doc. A/61/636 – S/2006/980 (2006) 6; UN Doc. A/63/226 (2008) 18; UN Doc. A/64/298 (2009) 19; UN Doc. A/62/121 (2007) 5.

[5] Convention Abolishing the Requirement for Legalisation for Foreign Public Documents (adopted 5 October 1961, entered into force 24 January 1965) 527 UNTS 189.

[6] J C M Schuyt, 'Bronnen van Juridisering en hun Confluentie' (1997) 72 *Nederlands Juristenblad* 925, 926.

and development of legal norms for the ordering of relations between subjects of international law. This may involve new treaties or protocols, development of existing instruments through amendment or otherwise, or it may involve the extension of existing treaties to newly ratifying states. It may not be obvious that using legalisation in this way has much conceptual value. The development of legal norms can also be referred to by terms such as law making, regulation, legislation or even codification. However, each of these terms has its own distinct meaning and limitations, and the term legalisation may be conveniently used as an umbrella term capturing diverse trends of an increasing number of international rights and obligations.

The term legalisation can be extended to refer to the subsequent process in which subjects increasingly make use of legal norms to organise their mutual relations, including the settlement of any disputes that may arise in these relations.[7] Whether or not the term should be used in this second sense is debatable. On the one hand, and contrary to the position taken by some (notably US) scholars,[8] a legal norm that in practice fails to guide behaviour is still a legal norm. In that respect, more and more legal norms create legalisation irrespective of their use. On the other hand, it may be said that an increasing use of legal norms, even irrespective of an increase in the quantity of such norms, means that the relations between relevant actors are to a greater extent governed by law in practice. In that sense one can speak of increasing legalisation as being determined by the use of law in practice.

It therefore may be proper to distinguish degrees of legalisation, depending on whether it involves only the adoption of more legal rules, and/or also entails the increase use of legal norms in practice.[9]

In literature, we also find other uses of the term legalisation. In what probably is the most widely cited account of the term, Abbott *et al* have used it to refer to a combination of three elements: obligation, precision and delegation.[10] While we can readily agree that there can be no legalisation without obligation, the other two criteria seem to be located at different levels of analysis. Precision is a useful factor to distinguish legalisation processes. A treaty consisting of only hortatory norms will less effectively regulate the relations between actors bound by such norms than a treaty containing very specific norms. It makes sense to say that in the latter case there is a qualitatively different process of legalisation than in the former case. In assessing trends of legalisation we may have to differentiate according to the character, scope and precision of legal norms.

[7] ibid.

[8] M Reisman, 'A Hard Look at Soft Law' (1988) *Proceedings of the 82nd Annual Meeting of the American Society of International Law* 373; J E Alvarez, *International Organisations as Law-makers* (Oxford University Press, 2006).

[9] See also M Finnemore and S J Toope, 'Alternatives to "Legalisation": Richer Views of Law and Politics' (2001) 55 *International Organisation*, 734, 744 (noting that '[u]nder a broader view of law, the legalisation of politics encompasses more than just the largely technical and formal criteria of obligation, precision, and delegation. It encompasses features and effects of legitimacy, including the need for congruence between law and underlying social practice.')

[10] K W Abbott et al, 'The Concept Of Legalisation' (2000) 54 *International Organisation*, 17. This definition is also used by D P Jinks, 'The Legalisation of World Politics and the Future of U.S. Human Rights Policy' (2002) 46 *St Louis ULJ* 357 and J Goldstein and L L Martin, 'Legalisation, Trade Liberalisation and Domestic Politics: A Cautionary Note' (2000) 54 *International Organisation* 603; J R Cohee, 'The WTO and Domestic Political Disquiet: Has Legalisation of the Global Trade Regime Gone Too Far?' (2008) 15 *Ind J Glob Leg'l Stud* 351.

Also delegation, including the granting of competence of international institutions to interpret, apply, and enforce the law,[11] is a criterion by which we can identify particular types of legalisation. A defining feature of the process of legalisation after 1989 is that more and more institutions have been set up charged with tasks of law making, interpretation and supervision—where a low degree of precision may be accompanied by high degree of delegation.

The approach of Abbott *et al* is problematic, however, in as far as they would suggest that precision and delegation can somehow compensate for the absence of obligation. This would make it possible to consider processes involving precision and delegation, but not involving obligation, in terms of legalisation. In this vein, it has been said that research on legalisation should not only explain when precise, binding and independent regimes facilitate international co-operation; but should also capture a broader range of law-like arrangements affecting international and transnational relations.[12] Others have written that a definition of legalisation that includes legal obligation as a defining element hinders rather than helps empirical research and that a fuller consideration of law and its role in politics might produce concepts 'that are more robust intellectually and more helpful for empirical research'.[13] While anyone will realise that there are substantial normative developments beyond the realm of law (indeed, it seems that the process of legalisation as legal phenomenon is paralleled by an increasing use of 'soft law' instruments),[14] it is conceptually not helpful to collapse the distinction between them and use the term legalisation as a term that catches all such normative developments. Indeed, for the purposes of the present inquiry, use of legal and non-legal instruments will have quite different implications for the international rule of law—which by definition rests on a formal conception of legality.[15]

III. THE TREND TOWARDS LEGALISATION

If we limit the concept of legalisation to the combined phenomenon of more legal rules and the increasing use of such rules in the actual relations between subjects of international law, it can readily be determined in the period after 1989 there was significant change. An easy, though perhaps not the scientifically most sound, illustration is the changing size and scope of textbooks: compare the sixth edition of Shaw with its 1331 pages of text[16] with the 516 pages in the first edition.[17] The increase in number of pages may in part be due to new insights or choices of the author. For instance, whereas the first edition only briefly refers to international humanitarian law, the sixth edition has an entire separate chapter on the topic; it is not obvious that there is much new law that would account for that increase. But otherwise, the extension largely reflects a trend of legalisation. A handful of pages on international environmental law turned

[11] Abbott, 'The Concept of Legalisation', 18.

[12] C Brütsch and D Lehmkuhl, 'Complex Legalisation and the Many Moves to Law', in Brütsch and Lehmkuhl, *Law as Legalisation* (2007) 9.

[13] Finnemore and Toope, 'Alternatives to "Legalisation"', 743.

[14] See D Shelton, *Commitment and Compliance: The Role of Non-Binding Norms in the International Legal System* (Oxford University Press 2003) 535.

[15] B Z Tamanaha, *On the Rule of Law: History, Politics, Theory* (Cambridge University Press, 2004) 91.

[16] M N Shaw, *International Law* 6th edn (Cambridge University Press, 2008).

[17] M N Shaw, *International Law* 1st edn (Cambridge University Press, 1977).

into a full-fledged body of law that took up an entire 50-plus-page chapter, discussing many new treaties.

Other chapters reflect not so much an increase in the number of rules of international law as an increasing practice of using international law for conducting relations between states and other subjects. For instance, the first edition contains six pages on individuals and human rights and criminal responsibility, whereas in the sixth edition we find separate chapters on both international and regional protection of human rights, and a separate chapter on individual criminal responsibility in international law (a topic that took up a bare two pages in the first edition). Also, the section on international law before domestic courts is twice as long in the sixth edition as the first, mostly with new practice.

An accurate measurement of legalisation is highly complex and perhaps senseless. To mention one problem: what is the unit to be used in counting? Treaties, articles, practice based on such treaties? We should also take into account that new rules in part may change or replace old rules, and do not so much lead to new laws as to different law. Nonetheless, a quick look at treaty numbers suggests a clear trend. That trend is particularly clear for states that were directly affected by the fall of the Iron Curtain. Consider the following figures on treaty-making practice of a random sample of such states. The numbers of Council of Europe treaties rose for Albania from 0 in 1989 to 72 in 2009; for Bulgaria from 0 to 79, for Poland from 1 to 83 and for Rumania from 0 to 99.[18] For the same states, the number of treaties registered in UNTS rose for Albania from 19 to 274, for Bulgaria from 122 to 220, for Poland from 138 to 208 and for Rumania from 99 to 259.[19]

At a global level, the movement is less spectacular, but nonetheless distinctly observable. The number of multilateral treaties registered with the UN between 1969 and 1989 stands at 371, whereas the number of treaties registered between 1989 and 2009 stands at 1286. The rise in bilateral treaties is slower, from just over 21000 between 1969–2009 to well over 26000 between 1989 and 2009.[20]

An assessment of an increase in the uses of international law is still much more complex, but the increase in numbers of international courts and their practice,[21] the rise of international institutions with a role in the interpretation and supervision of international obligations,[22] as well as the increasing practice of national courts[23] all suggest that legalisation is not limited to more laws on papers. We can also refer to the tremendous increase in binding resolutions of the Security Council (from less than 20 before 1989 to 469 after 1989, an increase of more than 2000%). All of such factors provide evidence that we have indeed witnessed an unprecedented process of legalisation.

[18] Data from Council of Europe Treaty Database, 'Statistics on signatures and ratifications', conventions.coe.int/Treaty/Commun/ChercheStats.asp?CM=17&CL=ENG, accessed 8 November 2010.

[19] Data from UNTS database, 'Participant Search', treaties.un.org/Pages/UNTSOnline.aspx?id=3, accessed 9 November 2010.

[20] Data from the United Nations Treaty Collection, 'UNTS Database'.

[21] Generally on the increase in the number of international courts and their activity: C P R Romano, 'The Proliferation of International Judicial Bodies: The Pieces of the Puzzle' (1999) 31 *NYU J Int'l L & Pol* 709; R P Alford, 'The Proliferation of International Courts and Tribunals: International Adjudication in Ascendance' (2000) 94 *Am Soc'y Int'l L Proc* 160; B Kingsbury, 'Foreword: Is the Proliferation of International Courts and Tribunals a Systemic Problem?' (1999) 31 *NYU J Int'L L & Pol* 679.

[22] See eg G Ulfstein (ed), *Making Treaties Work: Human Rights, Environment and Arms Control* (Cambridge University Press, 2007).

[23] See A Nollkaemper, *National Courts and the International Rule of Law* (Oxford University Press, 2011).

IV. CONTRIBUTION TO THE RULE OF LAW AT THE INTERNATIONAL LEVEL

Legalisation is often seen as relevant for advancing the rule-of-law agenda. Developing more treaties and securing wider participation are dominant themes in the work of the UN on the rule of law at the international level. The Secretary-General noted in his report *In larger freedom* that

> Support for the rule of law must be strengthened by universal participation in multilateral conventions. At present, many States remain outside the multilateral conventional framework, in some cases preventing important conventions from entering into force. .... I urge leaders especially to ratify and implement all treaties relating to the protection of civilians.[24]

The causal relationship between more treaty ratification and a stronger rule of law at the international level is far from clear, however. For one thing, we need to distinguish between law as instrumentalist idea versus law as a constraint on power.[25] More international laws that seek to secure particular social objectives (say, combating climate change, securing social security for migrant workers or banning cluster munitions) in itself do not strengthen the rule of law. The increase in the number of laws only tells us that states have agreed to deal with these issues by law, rather than by other instruments—that is: they have chosen for rule *by* law. Indeed, if anything, the enduring trend of legalisation makes clear that states, and international institutions, increasingly have chosen to rule by law. But rule by law is in itself not rule of law.[26]

In some respects, adoption of more treaties, even when these are adopted with an instrumentalist aim, nonetheless may strengthen the rule of law. For they strengthen the commitment of states,[27] limit pre-existing discretion in the exercise of power and replace it by control of law.[28] Moreover, interested (and injured) parties (whether states or private parties) could on the basis of a legal obligation hold the state accountable for its policies relating to, say, climate change or social security of migrant workers, rather than voicing disagreement. In that respect, new obligations, by definition, add an element of control.[29] They may ensure that public policy is not only guided by power and will of states, but guided by agreed norms that protect in part the weak from the strong. This is part of the concept of supremacy (or primacy) of international law over politics.[30]

It might be objected that the adoption of new rules is neutral for the control of power, since it only replaces one norm with another. In the concept as defined above, legalisation refers to the development of new law, or the new use of law. It thus suggests a dynamic development of expansion and intensification. It may be argued that this construction mistakes continuity for change. For it may be said that the development of new law by definition involves replacing an existing legal norm. For instance, a new set of norms that regulate, say, trade in chemicals, or the use of cluster-munition, simply alters a

[24] UN Doc. A/59/2005 (2005), para 136.

[25] T Nardin, 'Theorising the International Rule of Law' (2008) 34 *Review of International Studies*, 385, 385.

[26] S Chesterman, 'An International Rule of Law' (2008) 56 *Am J Comp L* 331, 333.

[27] Jinks, 'The Legalisation of World Politics' (2002); B A Simmons, 'The Legalisation of International Monetary Affairs' (2000) 54 *International Organisation* 573, 573.

[28] H Owada, 'Reconceptualisation of the International Rule of Law in a Globalizing World' (2008) 51 *Jap YB Int'l L* 3, 9.

[29] J Crawford, 'International Law and the Rule of Law' (2003) 24 *Adel L Rev* 3, 10.

[30] A Watts, 'The International Rule of Law' (1993) 36 *Ger YB Int'l L* 15, 22; Owada, 'Reconceptualisation' (2008) 11.

pre-existing background norm that permitted that particular activity.[31] In this respect, legalisation does not so much provide new law, as it provides different law. However, from the perspective of the rule of law, there are qualitative and quantitative differences between a simple liberty that allows them to use cluster munitions, or to trade chemicals, on the one hand, and treaties that limit such use and that require them to adjust domestic legislation, on the other. The second category has a qualitatively different impact on the rule of law.

The effect of legalisation (even if it results from an instrumentalist agenda) on the rule of law can be illustrated by elements of the rule of law at the international level identified by Sir Arthur Watts, in what probably remains the best analysis of the rule of law at the international level. One of these elements is the completeness of the law.[32] The idea of the rule of law is premised on the existence of a body of law. But obviously there are qualitative differences between a situation in which a very limited number of rules exist, on the one hand, and a situation with a very extensive body of rules, covering many or most areas in which public power is exercised, on the other. In the latter case, courts to which jurisdiction has been allocated will have more laws on the basis of which they can decide cases. Completeness is in large part a function of general principles,[33] but will also be a function of more extensive treaties in different areas of international affairs; in this respect ongoing legalisation supports the development of a rule of law.

Another element of the rule of law which is supported by the trend of legalisation is certainty.[34] The rule of law requires that the body of law has reached a state of development in which the law can be certain and predictable.[35] General principles and customary international law are not necessarily incompatible with the rule of law, but a qualitative distinction can be drawn from the perspective of certainty and predictability between, for instance, a customary rule prohibiting transboundary harm and a treaty prohibiting emissions of certain chemicals that have transboundary effects.

While in this respect and some other respects the mere phenomenon of legalisation may have certain supportive effects on the international rule of law, a number of qualifications are in order. First, a positive relation between legalisation in the sense of more treaties and more decisions of international institutions and the rule of law presumes that treaties actually constrain (powerful) states.[36] But that presumption is not necessarily valid—treaties may in fact confirm and justify rather than control power,[37] and the actual effect of treaties (or decisions of international organizations) depends on a case-by-case analysis.

Second, in addition to such elements as completeness and certainty, the ideal of an international rule of law also presumes universality, that is: rules must apply also to all members of the community.[38] Here the pattern post-1989 is mixed. On the one hand, it is true that part of the process of legalisation involves more multilateral treaties of,

[31] D Kennedy, *The Dark Sides of Virtue: Reassessing International Humanitarianism* (Princeton University Press, Princeton 2005) 349.

[32] Watts. 'The International Rule of Law', 26.

[33] ibid, 27.

[34] ibid, 28.

[35] ibid, 28; Owada, 'Reconceptualisation', 10.

[36] Watts, 'The International Rule of Law', 23.

[37] See eg R Brewster, 'Rule-Based Dispute Resolution in International Trade Law' (2006) 92 *Va L Rev* 251 (explaining the preference of states for rules-based systems for dispute settlement in terms of power relations).

[38] Watts, 'The International Rule of Law', 27; Crawford, 'International Law', 11; Nardin, 'Theorising', 399.

potentially, world-wide application.[39] On the other hand, it should be observed that there are significant differences between regions. The numbers of new treaties in Europe are, unsurprisingly, significantly higher than in Asia, the Americas and Africa. Consider the following figures: for Europe the number of regional treaties classified as such by the UNTS database stands at 424, 214 of which were concluded after 1989. For other regions these figures differ significantly: for Asia 43 out of 88 date from after 1989; and for Africa 104 out of 243. Compared to Europe, in particular, the Asia-Pacific region suggests patterns of low legalisation. Kahler noted in this respect that 'regional islands of high legalisation, such as Europe, coexist with other regions that have largely rejected legalised institutions. Variation occurs across issue-areas as well as time.'[40]

Third, as indicated above, a positive relation between more treaties and the rule of law presumes that treaties are reflected and applied in practice. Just as new treaties that are unmatched by practical effect may be unworthy to be qualified in terms of legalisation, they do not offer much for the international rule of law. Completeness and certainty are not in themselves sufficient to establish the rule of law—the law also has to be effectively applied.[41] Despite progress in such areas as dispute settlement and international supervisory procedures, a major difference continues to exist between national and international law—where effective consequences of non-application are often lacking.[42] The principle of voluntary jurisdiction of international courts remains a fundamental weakness of the international rule of law[43] that may undo, or at least limit, much of the potential impact of the process of legalisation on the international rule of law. It is therefore on good grounds that the UN, and states commenting on the UN process, have attributed much weight to strengthening the role of the International Court of Justice and, more generally, processes of dispute settlement.[44]

Fourth, and most importantly, to assess the impact of legalisation on the rule of law we have to recognize the structural dimensions of the rule of law. More law, even when complied with and even when accompanied by procedures to secure compliance, does not necessarily further the rule of law if the structural elements of the international legal order do not support such a rule of law.[45] The weakness of the rule of law at the international level does not so much consist of a shortage of international laws, but results from the structure of the international legal order, based on sovereign equality, and a lack of effective means to protect the weak from the powerful. It is this structural dimension that seemed to inspire the reference to the rule of law in the Friendly Relations Declaration.[46] The dominant solution of the international legal order is the prohibition of the use of force—if there was no prohibition on the use of force, compliance in many other areas may not have been sufficient to call the system a rule-of-law system. This overriding importance of the prohibition on the use of force, and the prohibition of intervention,

[39] As indicated above, the number of multilateral treaties registered with the UN between 1969 and 1989 stands at 371, whereas the number of treaties registered between 1989 and 2009 stands at 1286.

[40] M Kahler, 'Legalisation as strategy: The Asia-Pacific case' (2000) 54 *International Organisation* 549.

[41] Watts, 'The International Rule of Law', 35.

[42] Owada, 'Reconceptualisation', 10 (noting that 'it should [...] be frankly acknowledged that these substantive restrictions on States are not fully matched by a comparable institutional framework for enabling the rule of law to prevail and to achieve its desired ends in international society').

[43] Chesterman, 'An International Rule of Law', 357; Owada, 'Reconceptualisation', 14.

[44] UN Doc. A/59/2005 (2005) para 139.

[45] Watts 'The International Rule of Law', 16.

[46] UN Doc. A/RES/2625 (1970); Watts, 'The International Rule of Law', 25.

are exceptions to the otherwise formal (that is: non-substantive) concept of rule of law.[47] It is for these reasons on good grounds that many states have, in their submissions to the UN process relating to the rule of law at the international level, emphasised the need to strengthen and better comply with the principle of non-intervention and non-use of force.[48] Also the Security Council itself tends to see rule of law at the international level in direct relationship to protection of peace and security.[49]

While the principles relating to the use of force are not at all static, as illustrated by debates on legality of use of drones,[50] anticipatory self-defence[51] and the military dimensions of the responsibility to protect,[52] these developments are much slower and of quite a different character than the rapid process of legalisation identified above. Strengthening of the rule of law in this area is more a matter of enforcement and application of existing structural principles than an enduring development of new law.

There are other areas of international law which contribute to the international rule of law at a more structural level. The codification and partial clarification of the law of international responsibility is one example.[53] The development of this body of law has been modest, and certainly does not show the speedy process of legalisation identified in section 2. Yet its contribution to the international rule of law is disproportionally more significant—the responsibility for wrongdoing is a key element of the international rule of law.[54] Also here, progress is more a matter of more use and implementation of international responsibility than development of more rules and principles.[55]

V. CONTRIBUTION TO THE RULE OF LAW AT NATIONAL LEVEL

Quite a separate effect of the process of legalisation is the strengthening of the rule of law at the national level. Several institutions have since long adopted the aim to strengthen the rule of law at the national level—a movement that can be compared to and sometimes is part of attempts to impose or at least support a preferred model of democracy[56] and 'good governance'.[57] The rule of law specifically has been targeted, for instance by Millennium summit,[58] the EU[59] the OAS[60] and the African Union.[61]

[47] Watts, 'The International Rule of Law' 24; UN Doc. A/RES/64/116 (2010); UN Doc. A/RES/63/128 (2009); UN Doc. A/RES/62/70 (2008); UN Doc. A/RES/61/39 (2006).

[48] UN Doc. A/62/121 (2007), Egypt: paras 3,6; Germany: para 3; Kuweit: para 3; UN Doc. A/C.6/64/SR.8 (2009), paras 12, 18, 33, 44 and 91; UN Doc. A/C.6/64/SR.9 (2009) para 82.

[49] eg on 22 June 2006, the Security Council met to discuss 'Strengthening international law: rule of law and maintenance of international peace and security', and, in a presidential statement, reiterated the need for the Secretariat to provide proposals. See UN Doc. S/PRST/2006/28 (2006).

[50] C Jenks, 'Law from Above: Unmanned Aerial Systems, Use of Force, and the Law of Armed Conflict' (2009) 85 *North Dakota L Rev* 649.

[51] L Van den Hole, 'Anticipatory Self-Defence under International Law' (2003) 19 *Am U Int'l L Rev* 69; A N Guiora, 'Anticipatory Self-Defence and International Law – A Re-Evaluation' (2008) 13 *Journal of Conflict and Security Law* 3.

[52] G Evans, 'From Humanitarian Intervention to the Responsibility to Protect' (2006) 24 *Wis Int'l L J* 703; A L Bannon, 'The Responsibility to Protect: The U.N. World Summit and the Question of Unilateralism' (2006) 115 *Yale L J* 1157.

[53] J Crawford, *The International Law Commission's Articles on State Responsibility: Introduction, Text, and Commentaries* (Cambridge University Press, 2002).

[54] I Brownlie, *The Rule of Law in International Affairs: International Law at the Fiftieth Anniversary of the United Nations* (Martinus Nijhoff Publishers, 1998) 79.

[55] Watts, 'The International Rule of Law', 45.

[56] See J d'Aspremont, 'Democracy Building Instruments', (2008–2009) 9 *Chi Int'l L* 1, 7–13 ('International

One of the defining aspects of legalisation after 1989 is that many of the new international laws are of a regulatory nature and are addressing issues that also are subject of national law. Indeed, legalisation is in part the product of the same processes that drive legalisation at domestic level. For instance, environmental treaties in part reflect the same agenda as domestic environmental legislation. In many areas there is thus a strong connection between international and national legalisation. We can explain legalisation through the prospective consequences of international law for domestic political outcomes.

The link between international legalisation and national law is confirmed by empirical data. The issue areas that show significant increase are precisely those where a large proportion of the treaties are of a regulatory nature. For instance, the UNTS database shows for the subject area 'war' an increase of 22 out of 193 after 1989—a mere 11 per cent. In contrast, the percentages are much higher for issues where treaties have a more regulatory character: Investment: 1067 out of 1473 after 1989 (72%); environment: 645 out of 919 after 1989 (70%); terrorism 54 out of 62 after 1989 (87%); criminal law: 661 out of 952 after 1989 (69%). For human rights the increase is less substantial, 62 out of 214 after 1989 (38%)—probably because we have reached the point where adding yet another treaty serves few purposes.[62]

Comparable to the situation at the international level, the phenomenon of legalisation as such, in principle, is neutral in terms of its effects on the rule of law. New treaties often require adjustment of national law, but a change of national law in itself does not cause a change in the rule-of-law qualities of national law. Also in this context an essential distinction needs to be drawn between the instrumental aims of international law and their effects on the rule of law. It might even be said that more and more international laws upset the rule of law domestically as they may require changes in the laws domestically—but that argument would incorrectly assume that the rule of law would prefer stability over change. Change in law, whether emerging from international or national political processes can be perfectly compatible with the rule of law, as long as it follows the ordinary procedures for such change. But the point remains that such change, also if it comes from international law, in itself does not strengthen or otherwise change the rule-of-law quality of national law.

administrations of territories promote democracy'); G H Fox, Humanitarian Occupation (Cambridge University Press, 2008) 156 ('Growing bureaucracies at the UN and regional organizations are now devoted to democracy promotion').

[57] For a discussion of these trends, see H P Aust and G Nolte, 'International Law and the Rule of Law at the National Level', in R Peerenboom, M Zürn and A Nollkaemper (eds) (2012, forthcoming).

[58] UN Doc. A/60/L.1 (2005) para 134.

[59] Article 6 of the Treaty on the European Union: 'The Union is founded on the principles of liberty, democracy, respect for human rights and fundamental freedoms, and the rule of law, principles which are common to the Member States.' see also Article 9 ('essential elements') of the Partnership Agreement Between the Members of the African, Caribbean and Pacific Group of States, of the one Part, and the European Community and its Member States, of the Other Part ('Cotonou Agreement') (Official Journal L317/3 of 15 December 2000), as revised in 2005 (Official Journal L209/27 of 11 August 2005).

[60] OAS, Declaration of San Salvador on Citizen Security in the Americas, OAS Doc. AG/DEC. 66 (XLI-O/11) (adopted 7 June 2011); OAS, Declaration of Lima on Peace, Security and Cooperation in the Americas, OAS Doc. AG/DEC. 63 (XL-010) (adopted 8 June 2010); Article 3 of the Inter-American Democratic Charter (adopted 11 September 2011).

[61] AU, Declaration on the theme of the summit: 'Towards greater Unity and Integration through Shared Values', Assembly/AU/Decl. (XVI) (adopted 31 January 2011); Article 4 of the Constitutive Act of the African Union (adopted 11 June 2000).

[62] United Nations Treaty Collection, 'UNTS Database'.

It is in fact only a small part of international law that aims at rule-of-law qualities. Treaties in such areas as human rights, but also development and security, expressly refer to and support the rule of law. The fact that these different types of treaties refer to the rule of law reflects the fact that the rule of law at the domestic level can fulfill multiple purposes, including protecting individual rights, creating conditions for economic stability and growth, and security.[63]

Beyond the aim of particular treaties to contribute to the rule of law domestically, some of the requirements of the rule of law may themselves constitute particular rules of law.[64] That holds in particular for human rights, including such requirements as legality and independence of courts. There is little doubt that in this respect human rights constitute the cornerstone of the rule of law, at the national level, that international law supports.[65] In the *Golder* case, the European Court of Human Rights underlined the central role of the rule of law in the Convention.[66] It stated that the profound belief in the rule of law was one reason why states decided to 'take the first steps for the collective enforcement of certain of the Rights stated in the universal Declaration'. Also the Southern African Development Community (SADC) Tribunal recognised the rule-of-law implications of human rights.[67]

Strengthening these rule-of-law impacts of human rights has little to do with the trend towards legalisation as a phenomenon entailing more international law (discussed above). Rather, it is a matter of better recognition and application of existing human rights provisions. It is remarkable that apart from human rights law, the general concern of the international community with the significance of the domestic rule of law, for instance as a means to make failed states more effective, has only to a very limited extent been made part of positive international law. In this respect, there is room and indeed need for further legal appraisal of the impact of rule of law promotion on general international law and for legal development.[68]

As for the strengthening of the rule of law at the international level, the strengthening of the rule of law at the national level depends more on the actual use and application of international law at the domestic level than on the increase in rights and obligations. In this context, it is relevant to observe that the move towards treaty making in former iron-curtain states is matched with an opening of constitutions that make many international treaties directly applicable in national law, mostly giving a prioritised treatment to human rights.[69]

[63] Chesterman, 'An International Rule of Law', 343.

[64] Watts, 'The International Rule of Law', 22.

[65] Brownlie, *The Rule of Law,* 65.

[66] Convention on the Protection of Human Rights and Fundamental Freedoms (adopted 4 November 1950, entered into force 3 September 1953), ETS No. 5.

[67] SADC Tribunal, *Mike Campbell (Pvt) Ltd and Others* v. *Republic of Zimbabwe*, Decision of 18 November 2008, 48 ILM 534, 540 (holding that 'the concept of the rule of law embraces at least two fundamental rights, namely, the right of access to the courts and the right to a fair hearing before an individual is deprived of a right, interest or legitimate expectation. [...] Article 4 (c) obliges Member States of SADC to respect principles of 'human rights, democracy and the rule of law [....]').

[68] See R Peerenboom, M Zürn and A Nollkaemper, 'Conclusion: From Rule of Law Promotion to Rule of Law Dynamics' in ibid, *Dynamics of the Rule of Law in an Era of International and Transnational Governance* (2012, forthcoming).

[69] E Stein, 'International Law in Internal Law: Towards Internationalisation of Central-Eastern Constitutions' (1994) 88 *AJIL* 427; Owada, 'Reconceptualisation' (2008) 18 (on prescription of rule of law domestically).

While the large category of regulatory treaties in itself is in principle neutral in terms of its rule-of-law quality, in one respect it has effects that may undermine rather than support the rule of law. Legalisation to some extent reduces the role of politics, negotiation and even democracy. This has been a common theme in the discussions of legalisation of the trade regime.[70] The problem became in particularly significant given the impact on national level—the impact of legalisation on national law is directly connected with the rule of law at the international level. The limited legitimacy of international institutions as well as the impact of legalisation on the domestic separation of powers and democratic processes may offset some of the gains that legalisation may bring in terms of rule of law at the international level. Precisely in areas where international law prescribes domestic laws and performs tasks of adjudication, assessment, or review of domestic decision making, compliance with the rule of law at the international level becomes critical. In this respect, much may be gained from development of principles or legality in international institutions[71] as well as a system of control of decisions of political organs.[72] The deepening of the process of legalisation in terms of its reach into domestic legal orders, indeed will depend on that legalisation itself being embedded in a proper international rule of law.

VI. CONCLUSION

The trend towards legalisation after 1989 seems undeniable. Its impact for the quest for the rule of law at the international level appears to be rather modest, however. In large part, legalisation seems the result of an instrumentalist project by which international law is used to achieve particular social objectives. In a way, the growth of this body of law presumes a functioning rule of law system, but in itself does not really produce it. It does, however, make a further contribution to the completeness, predictability and universality of international law—which all are essential features of the international rule of law. It can also be added that in many areas, perhaps most notably human rights, criminal law and investment law, we have seen a major increase in the use of international law, in particular in international courts and tribunals.

The changes at the more structural level of the international rule of law, revolving around sovereignty, non-intervention, use of force, and also secondary principles of responsibility and dispute settlement, are much slower, and seem to be governed by altogether different dynamics than the process of legalisation that characterises the period after 1989.

In addition to the impact on the rule of law at the international level, legalisation may contribute to the rule of law at domestic level. The domestic level remains critical since the performance of international obligations in many respects presumes a strong rule-of-law quality at the national level, and in that respect the relation between international law and national law in itself is a structural element of the international rule of law.

[70] J R Cohee, 'The WTO and Domestic Political Disquiet: Has Legalisation of the Global Trade Regime Gone Too Far?' (2008) 15 *Ind J of Glob Leg'l Stud* 351 (discussing the critique that 'while a strong rule of law ensures that nations abide by their commitments to the WTO, legalisation has too often resulted in undemocratic developments, with judges and lawyers filling gaps left (sometimes intentionally) by negotiators').

[71] Brownlie, *The Rule of Law*, 216.

[72] J Crawford, 'International Law and the Rule of Law' (2004) 24 *Adelaide Law Review* 2.

Its vulnerability is in a way the mirror image or the structural weakness of the rule of law at the international level, arising out of sovereign equality of states. The process of legalisation in terms of the many new treaties adopted after 1989 hardly seem to have had any influence on that structural aspect. More important is the parallel process (that also may be captured by the term legalisation) of opening of national constitutions and willingness of national courts to adjudicate international claims.

The quest for the rule of law, both at the national and the international level remains, perhaps by definition, unfinished. Apart from the continuing structural weakness arising from the sovereign equality of states, that affect both the rule of law at the international and at national level, the increasing regulatory nature of international law and its effects domestically call for further strengthening of the rule-of-law quality internationally, notably in international institutions. In this respect, the development of more and more international laws that back up and steer domestic law has set in motion a self-perpetuating process of legalisation. In this respect, the process of legalisation in the period 1989–2009 is unlikely to have been the final stage, but rather has been a sign of things to come.

8

Typologie des Résolutions de l'ONU Créatrices de Droit International Général

ANNE-THIDA NORODOM*

I. INTRODUCTION

ROSALYN HIGGINS a défendu l'idée selon laquelle tout débat mené au sein des Nations Unies appartient pour partie au processus de création du droit international[1]. Cette analyse ne peut être que confirmée lorsqu'il s'agit, comme ici, de démontrer qu'il existe différents processus institutionnalisés de création de normes de droit international général par les résolutions de l'ONU ; il est toutefois nécessaire d'y apporter quelques précisions. Il faut dans un premier temps souligner la différence entre, d'une part, les Nations Unies en tant qu'institution et, d'autre part, les résolutions de l'ONU, c'est-à-dire le droit produit par cette organisation en raison de sa personnalité juridique. En nous concentrant sur les actes unilatéraux de l'ONU, nous écartons dès lors d'autres moyens pour l'ONU de participer à la formation du droit international. Sont ainsi exclues de notre étude les conventions internationales initiées par les organes des Nations Unies et les travaux de la Commission du droit international, qui bien qu'instaurée par une résolution de l'Assemblée générale, relève davantage de la dimension institutionnelle que strictement normative de l'ONU.

L'objet de cette étude ne concerne donc que les résolutions, soit le droit dérivé de l'ONU fondé sur l'acte primaire et constitutif de l'Organisation[2]. Même si le sujet a déjà été amplement traité, l'évolution du droit dérivé des Nations Unies justifie qu'on s'y intéresse de nouveau. Dans les années 70, période faste de l'Assemblée générale du fait du blocage du fonctionnement du Conseil de sécurité, des études ont été menées concernant les effets juridiques des résolutions de l'Assemblée[3]. Les conclusions étaient alors

* Professeur de droit public, Université de Rouen.

[1] Higgins (R.), 'The Development of International Law by the Political Organs of the United Nations', *ASIL Proceedings*, 1965, vol 59, 116, 121.

[2] G Bastid-Burdeau, 'Quelques remarques sur la notion de droit dérivé en droit international' 161 in N Angelet, O Corten, E David, P Klein (eds), *Droit du pouvoir. Pouvoir du droit*, Mélanges offerts à Jean Salmon, Bruxelles, Bruylant, 2007, LI-1627, 164.

[3] On peut citer par exemple G Arangio-Ruiz, 'The Normative Role of the General Assembly of the United Nations and the Declaration of Principles of Friendly Relations', *R.C.A.D.I.*, 1972/III, vol 137, 419; O Asamoah, *The Legal Significance of the Declaration of the General Assembly of the United Nations*, The Hague, M Nijhoff, 1996, XVIII; J Castaneda, 'Valeur juridique des résolutions des Nations Unies',

partagées : certains suggéraient un effet obligatoire de ces résolutions[4], adoptant dès lors une interprétation contraire au sens des dispositions de la Charte ; d'autres préférant une lecture plus orthodoxe et considérant ces actes comme de simples déclarations d'intention politique[5] voire parfois comme une étape dans la codification du droit international[6]. Les échecs de l'Assemblée générale pour mener à bien certains projets de formation du droit international, à l'image du droit du développement et du nouvel ordre économique international, mettront fin à ces débats et aboutiront généralement à la conclusion d'une absence d'effet juridique obligatoire des résolutions de l'ONU sans pour autant leur nier tout effet, mais en restant toutefois dans l'incapacité de pouvoir rigoureusement le qualifier. La conclusion manquait donc de clarté. Une seconde vague de réflexion a surgi dans les années 90 au moment de la prolifération normative du Conseil de sécurité[7], tendance qui fut confirmée et renforcée à la suite des attentats du 11 septembre 2001[8]. Entre la fin des années 80 et aujourd'hui, le doublement voire le triplement du nombre des résolutions adoptées par le Conseil chaque année[9] a nécessairement amené les auteurs à chercher quelle pouvait être la portée juridique de ces résolutions. Le débat était toutefois différent de celui mené concernant l'Assemblée générale puisque la Charte, dans ce cas précis, attribuait effectivement un effet obligatoire aux seules décisions du Conseil de sécurité ; encore fallait-il pouvoir identifier ces décisions.

La perspective choisie dans cet article est différente de celle adoptée dans les précédentes études même si elle les recoupe nécessairement. Soixante-cinq ans après l'adoption de la Charte des Nations Unies, vingt-ans après le début de l'explosion de la puissance

R.C.A.D.I., 1971, vol 129, 205 ; ME Ellis, 'The New International Economic Order and General Assembly Resolutions: The Debate Over the Legal Effects of General Assembly Resolutions Revisited', *Calif.West.Int. LawJ.*, 1985, vol. 15, 647; CC Joyner, 'U.N. General Assembly Resolutions and International Law: Rethinking the Contemporary Dynamics of Norm-creation', *Calif.West.Int.LawJ.*, 1981, vol. 11, 445; B Sloan, *United Nations General Assembly Resolutions in our Changing World*, *op cit*; 'General Assembly Resolutions Revisited (Forty Years Later)', *B.Yb.I.L.*, 1987, vol. 43, 39; de Visscher (P.), 'Observations sur les résolutions déclaratives de droit adoptées au sein de l'Assemblée générale de l'Organisation des Nations Unies', 173, *in Festschrift für Rudolf Bindschedler*, Bern, Stämpfli, 1980, XII-638.

[4] G Arangio-Ruiz, *The UN Declaration on Friendly Relations and the System of the Sources of International Law*, The Netherlands, Sijthoff and Nordhoff, 1979, 341, 299.

[5] M Lachs, 'The International Law of Outer Space', *R.C.A.D.I.*, 1964-III, t. 113, 7.

[6] K Bailey, 'Making International Law in the United Nations', *ASIL Proceedings*, 1967, 233, 235; Bastid (S.), 'Observations sur une "étape" dans le développement progressif et la codification des principes du droit international', 132-145, in Faculté de droit de l'université de Genève/IUHEI, *Recueil d'études de droit international en hommage à Paul Guggenheim*, Genève, Tribune, 1968, XXI-901.

[7] Voir notamment K Herndl, 'Reflections on the Role, Functions and Procedures of the Security Council of the United Nations', *R.C.A.D.I.*, vol. 206, 1987, 289; P Klein et A Schaus, 'Deux poids, deux mesures? : l'inégalité dans l'application du pouvoir de décision du Conseil de sécurité', 59, in Centre de droit international U.L.B., *La guerre du Golfe et le droit international: entre les lignes*, Bruxelles, Servais-Creadif, 1991, 214; S Sur, *Security Council Resolution 687 of 3 April 1991 in the Gulf Affair, Problems of Restoring and Safeguarding Peace*, New York, United Nations, VI-90; R-J Dupuy (ed), *Le développement du rôle du Conseil de sécurité*, colloque, La Haye, 21-23 juillet 1992, Dordrecht, M. Nijhoff, 1993, XVIII-495.

[8] T Christakis & J Tercinet, 'Le pouvoir normatif du Conseil de sécurité: le Conseil de sécurité peut-il légiférer ?', *R.B.D.I.*, 2004, vol. 37, 528; M Fremuth and J Griebel, 'On the Security Council as a Legislator: a Blessing or a Curse for the International Community?', *N.J.I.L.*, 2007, vol. 76, 339; LM Hinojosa Martinez, 'The Legislative Role of the Security Council in its Fight Against Terrorism: Legal, Political and Practical Limits', *I.C.L.Q.*, 2008, vol. 57, 333; A Orakhelashvili, 'The Acts of the Security Council: Meaning and Standards of Review', *Max Planck Yb.U.N.L.*, 2007, vol. 11, 143; CH Powell, 'The Legal Authority of the United Nations Security Council', 157 in JG Benjamin and L Liora (eds), *Security and Human Rights*, Oxford, Hart Publishing, 2007, XXXIII-391.

[9] On note par exemple qu'en 1989, le Conseil de sécurité avait adopté vingt résolutions, alors qu'en 2008 il atteint soixante-quatre résolutions et en 2009, quarante-sept résolutions.

normative du Conseil de sécurité, le recul paraît aujourd'hui suffisant pour évaluer le travail accompli par les organes de l'ONU et comprendre dans quelle mesure la capacité normative de cette organisation internationale à compétence générale et universelle a pu influencer, modifier voire former de nouvelles normes de droit international général.

Se pose alors la question de l'interaction entre ces deux ensembles normatifs que sont l'ordre juridique des Nations Unies et l'ordre juridique international. Deux principes peuvent s'opposer à la création par le droit des Nations Unies de normes de droit international général. Premièrement, l'ordre juridique des Nations Unies est délimité parce que dérivé du traité constitutif établi par les Etats membres originaires et circonscrit au respect du *principe de spécialité* auquel est soumis toute organisation internationale. Pourtant il s'agit d'une organisation internationale à compétence générale, ce qui pourrait laisser entendre que le droit des Nations Unies soit assimilé au droit international dans son ensemble. Cette idée ne peut pourtant être qu'infirmée : si le droit des Nations Unies est bien du droit international, il n'est pas tout le droit international, étant nécessairement limité, en tant que droit d'une organisation internationale, par le principe de spécialité. Celui-ci s'applique certainement d'une manière particulière s'agissant de l'ONU, mais il s'applique néanmoins et explique par exemple que le droit des Nations Unies ne régisse pas ou peu le droit international économique ou le droit des investissements, relevant davantage de la compétence de l'OMC ou de celle du FMI. Seconde objection à l'interaction entre droit des Nations Unies et droit international général : le droit d'une organisation internationale ne peut créer du droit international général dans la mesure où, fondé sur un traité, il est soumis au *principe de l'effet relatif*. Ce débat relève pour l'essentiel de l'interprétation des articles 2, paragraphe 1, alinéa h de la Convention de Vienne sur le droit des traités et 2, paragraphe 6 de la Charte et ne concerne pas directement la question posée ici de l'établissement d'une typologie des résolutions créatrices de droit international[10]. Nous comprenons donc ici le droit international général comme désignant les règles ayant des effets de droit uniquement à l'égard de l'ensemble des Etats[11]. L'objet de l'étude est donc d'apprécier les catégories de résolutions de l'ONU susceptibles de former de nouvelles normes de droit international applicables à l'ensemble des Etats. Pour ce faire, il convient d'identifier ces résolutions (I) avant de pouvoir par la suite les classer selon leurs effets sur la formation du droit international général (II).

[10] La question du dépassement de l'effet relatif de la Charte relève aujourd'hui d'un débat avant tout théorique : l'ONU tend vers l'universalité et la question de l'effet relatif ne peut se poser, pour l'instant, pour des sujets autres que les Etats. Le droit international général ne s'impose ni aux ONG, ni aux individus, ni aux firmes multinationales, il en est de même pour le droit des Nations Unies, même si l'ONU accorde une place de plus en plus importante à la société civile internationale. *Contra* v. M Forteau, 'Le dépassement de l'effet relatif de la Charte', 121, in R Chemain et A Pellet, *La Charte des Nations Unies, constitution mondiale ?*, Paris, Pedone, 2006, 237, 130.

[11] En ce sens, le droit international désigne 'des règles qui ont capacité, de par leur abstraction, par leur détachement de toute situation déterminée, voire de tout instrument juridique spécifique, à régir la communauté internationale dans son ensemble. Mais cette universalité demeure une hypothèse, sous réserve de plus ample examen qui peut laisser place à des dérogations spécifiques en fonction de situations particulières' : J Combacau et S Sur, *Droit international public*, 8ème éd, Paris, Montchrestien, 2008, XXVI-818, 46.

II. L'IDENTIFICATION DES RÉSOLUTIONS CRÉATRICES DE DROIT INTERNATIONAL GÉNÉRAL

L'identification des résolutions susceptibles de créer du droit international général constitue la première difficulté de ce sujet. Rappelons d'ailleurs que la Charte des Nations Unies n'emploie pas le terme de « résolution », auquel elle préfère celui de « décision » ou de « recommandation ». A la lecture des dispositions de la Charte il semble difficile d'établir précisément les effets juridiques de chacune de ces catégories, à l'exception des décisions du Conseil de sécurité, énoncées à l'article 25, qui se voient explicitement attribuer un effet juridique obligatoire confirmé par l'article 48 énonçant les modalités d'exécution des décisions du Conseil. L'effet juridique obligatoire des résolutions ne fait pas non plus de doute lorsque les résolutions sont amenées à régir le fonctionnement interne de l'Organisation, à l'instar des décisions de l'Assemblée générale relatives aux questions importantes (art. 18 al. 2) ou des décisions du Conseil économique et social (art. 67). Cependant, on le sait, la Charte n'offre aucune définition de la « décision ».

S'agissant des résolutions du Conseil de sécurité, la mention du chapitre VII de la Charte au sein de la résolution permettrait d'affirmer le caractère obligatoire de celle-ci, privilégiant une interprétation téléologique du texte : l'utilisation des mesures coercitives du chapitre VII ne peut effectivement se fonder que sur une résolution obligatoire et donc une décision du Conseil, selon les termes de l'article 25. Cependant, à la lecture de certaines résolutions du Conseil de sécurité mentionnant pourtant le Chapitre VII, il est possible de douter du caractère décisoire de certaines dispositions. Faut-il donc considérer la résolution dans son ensemble (la simple mention du Chapitre VII emportant alors le caractère obligatoire de toute la résolution) ou alors interpréter la résolution disposition par disposition en vérifiant systématiquement la présence ou l'absence d'un vocabulaire coercitif ? Nous défendons cette seconde méthode d'interprétation dans la mesure où la rareté de l'utilisation des termes coercitifs dans les résolutions du Conseil de sécurité atteste de leur importance et de leurs effets particuliers, en l'occurrence obligatoires, lorsqu'ils sont délibérément choisis par les Etats membres du Conseil. Une lecture disposition par disposition des décisions s'impose selon nous, au détriment d'une lecture globale des résolutions des organes de l'ONU[12]. Sous cette réserve, il paraît utile d'affiner la classification des résolutions selon leurs éventuels effets juridiques pour le droit des Nations Unies et pour le droit international dans son ensemble.

La classification des résolutions est nécessaire afin d'établir une vue d'ensemble du droit dérivé de l'ONU et de pouvoir tirer des conclusions sur les effets potentiels de ces résolutions au moment de leur rédaction et de leur adoption. La distinction classique établie entre décision et recommandation est utile mais insuffisante pour atteindre cet objectif : d'abord parce que, comme nous l'avons vu, elle n'est pas assez fine pour décrire les effets des résolutions en fonction de leurs dispositions précises ; ensuite parce qu'ainsi que l'a énoncé la Cour internationale de justice, la qualification par un organe d'une de ses résolutions n'est pas probante[13]. Seule une lecture précise de ses dispositions permettra d'évaluer l'ensemble des effets de la résolution concernée. Survient alors une

[12] Cette interprétation est confirmée par la Cour internationale de justice : *Conséquences juridiques pour les Etats de la présence continue de l'Afrique du Sud en Namibie (Sud Ouest Africain) nonobstant la résolution 276 (1970) du Conseil de sécurité*, avis consultatif, C.I.J. *Recueil* 1971, para 114.

[13] *Compétence de l'Assemblée générale pour l'admission aux Nations Unies*, avis consultatif, C.I.J. *Recueil* 1950, 7 ; *Sud ouest africain*, deuxième phase, arrêt, C.I.J. *Recueil* 1966, 50, para 98.

seconde difficulté : les résolutions, constituant des actes unilatéraux d'organes politiques délibérants, sont souvent le fruit de compromis politiques. Tout en prenant en compte cette dimension politique[14], il est nécessaire d'isoler la partie juridique de la résolution si l'on veut pouvoir identifier les résolutions créatrices de droit international général. Ainsi, au-delà de la distinction entre décision et recommandation, il convient de dégager les dispositions de portée normative de celles qui ne le sont pas.

Au regard de ces deux prémisses, il a fallu élaborer une méthode pour non seulement identifier les résolutions créatrices de droit international général mais surtout classer ces résolutions selon la manière dont elles influençaient le développement du droit international. Nous avons utilisé une méthode inductive en cherchant à savoir, dans un premier temps, pour chaque branche du droit international, si des résolutions de l'ONU constituaient la source des instruments juridiques existants. Les résolutions ayant effectivement influencé la formation du droit international ont été regroupées, dans un second temps, en fonction de la nature de leurs effets sur le droit international. Les catégories de résolutions ainsi établies ont permis de définir les critères d'identification communs nécessaires pour que le droit dérivé des Nations Unies puisse former de nouvelles normes de droit international général :

- **Le caractère normatif des dispositions.** Toutes les résolutions ne sont pas susceptibles d'influencer la formation du droit international général : il faut distinguer ce qui est normatif de ce qui ne l'est pas. L'identification d'un énoncé normatif est donc indispensable à la classification des résolutions afin d'écarter les simples dispositions politiques. Cependant, une disposition normative pourrait voir ses effets se limiter à la sphère du droit interne de l'Organisation sans avoir des effets dans le droit externe à savoir le droit international général. Une seconde distinction s'impose donc.
- **Droit interne ou droit externe.** Il ne suffit pas de différencier le droit interne du droit externe de l'ONU pour identifier les résolutions dont la portée normative ne se limiterait pas à l'ordre juridique de l'Organisation. En effet, certaines résolutions dites externes ne sont finalement destinées qu'à avoir des effets entre les membres de l'Organisation et non sur le droit international général en raison notamment de leur absence d'effet juridique obligatoire. Nous différencions alors l'effet *normatif* indispensable à l'identification d'une résolution susceptible de créer du droit, de l'effet *juridique* qui qualifie l'influence normative du droit des Nations Unies en dehors de son système juridique pour permettre le développement du droit international général. Les résolutions de l'ONU doivent dès lors posséder un effet normatif et externe pour être susceptible de former de nouvelles normes de droit international général. Cependant, cette qualification est encore insuffisamment précise pour répertorier tous les effets des résolutions et leurs mécanismes d'influence sur le droit international : à l'intérieur des catégories générales précédemment énoncées, une subdivision peut être établie entre les résolutions thématiques et les résolutions circonstancielles.

[14] Michel Virally rappelait ainsi la dimension intrinsèquement politique du droit des organisations internationales: 'l'étude des organisations internationales exige, à la fois, une exacte appréciation des réalités politiques, la connaissance des lois qui gouvernent la dynamique des institutions et la compréhension des mécanismes juridiques nécessaires à leur fonctionnement': *L'O.N.U. d'hier à demain*, Paris, Seuil, 1961, 189, 21. La Cour l'a quant à elle clairement affirmé s'agissant des Nations Unies: '(…) les Nations Unies sont une organisation politique, ayant une mission politique d'un caractère très important et à domaine très large » et qui « agit par des moyens politiques vis-à-vis de ses membres': *Réparation des dommages subis au service des Nations Unies*, avis consultatif, C.I.J. *Recueil* 1949, 179.

- **Une résolution thématique ou circonstancielle.** L'objet de l'ONU étant le maintien de la paix, une grande part des résolutions est destinée à résoudre un conflit armé. Les résolutions qu'on qualifiera de circonstancielles sont ainsi rattachées à un conflit particulier et sont sans aucun doute les plus répandues dans la pratique des organes de l'ONU. Depuis les années 90 s'est toutefois développée une pratique d'un nouveau genre avec l'adoption de résolutions thématiques, non rattachées à un conflit particulier, qui visent soit à synthétiser le contenu de résolutions circonstancielles antérieures sur un thème particulier (ex : les civils au cours des conflits armés, le VIH et les opérations internationales de maintien de la paix) ou une région particulière (ex : l'Afrique), soit plus rarement à énoncer des normes de portée générale en relation avec le thème énoncé dans le titre de la résolution (ex : la lutte contre le terrorisme). Cette précision apportée dans la classification des résolutions est importante pour identifier plus clairement le contenu de la résolution et consécutivement le processus d'influence de ces résolutions sur la formation du droit international. Toutefois, les trois critères précédemment énoncés (le caractère normatif, externe et thématique ou circonstanciel) peuvent encore être précisés afin d'affiner la typologie des résolutions créatrices de droit international général. Les processus de formation de la norme de droit international général ne seront en effet pas les mêmes selon l'organe auteur de la résolution dans la mesure où, en vertu de la Charte des Nations Unies, l'Assemblée générale et le Conseil de sécurité ne possèdent pas la même compétence normative et ne peuvent dès lors influencer la formation du droit international de manière totalement identique.
- **Le critère organique.** Les mécanismes d'influence des résolutions de l'ONU transcendent la distinction entre les résolutions de l'Assemblée générale et celles du Conseil de sécurité puisque les deux organes sont compétents de manière égale pour adopter des recommandations et des décisions, normative ou non, de droit interne ou de droit externe. Le critère organique n'est pas le plus intéressant pour identifier les effets des résolutions sur la formation du droit international général, toutefois, la mission de ces deux organes attribuée par l'acte constitutif de l'Organisation influence nécessairement le contenu des résolutions. Selon l'article 18 de la Charte, les décisions de l'Assemblée générale ne relèvent que du droit interne de l'ONU et ne peuvent créer du droit international général ; elles seront par conséquent exclues de cette étude, contrairement aux recommandations normatives externes de l'Assemblée générale qui peuvent indirectement favoriser la formation du droit international général comme nous le verrons par la suite. Quant au Conseil de sécurité, la question se pose différemment. Il convient d'isoler l'ensemble de ses résolutions de droit externe, seules susceptibles de créer du droit international général, et de différencier parmi elles les recommandations des décisions dans la mesure où le mécanisme d'influence sur la formation du droit ne sera pas le même. Apparaît dès lors le critère final pour apprécier et différencier les mécanismes d'influence du droit dérivé des Nations Unies sur la formation du droit international : l'identification de l'effet juridique obligatoire de la disposition contenue dans la résolution d'un des organes de l'ONU.
- **L'effet juridique obligatoire de la disposition.** La distinction entre recommandation et décision est insuffisamment précise pour catégoriser l'ensemble des résolutions de l'ONU et rendre compte de leur diversité. Elle apparaît pourtant nécessaire mais uniquement au terme de l'identification des précédents critères de classification des résolutions. Il n'est utile d'apprécier le caractère obligatoire de la résolution

que si précédemment on est assuré de son caractère normatif et externe. Le critère organique, à la lecture de la Charte des Nations Unies, permettra d'apporter des indices sur la portée obligatoire de la résolution. C'est finalement cet effet juridique obligatoire qui autorisera l'identification non pas des résolutions susceptibles de former du droit international général mais des mécanismes de formation de ce droit par l'entremise des résolutions de l'ONU.

A la lumière de ces différents critères, chacune des résolutions du Conseil de sécurité a été analysée ; permettant ainsi d'avoir une vision d'ensemble des résolutions de cet organe afin d'infirmer ou de confirmer l'hypothèse de départ selon laquelle les résolutions de l'ONU peuvent créer du droit international général. Il n'a pu être fait de même pour les résolutions de l'Assemblée générale plus nombreuses et dont le contenu est très hétérogène. Nous avons choisi de nous concentrer sur les déclarations adoptées par l'Assemblée générale en présupposant leur caractère normatif et externe. On considère alors que toutes les recommandations normatives et externes de l'Assemblée générale suivent le même processus que les recommandations de même nature du Conseil de sécurité pour créer des nouvelles normes de droit international général. Deux mécanismes institutionnalisés de formation du droit international par les résolutions de l'ONU sont alors identifiables. On différencie d'une part le processus *graduel* de formation du droit international général par les recommandations normatives et externes de l'Assemblée générale et du Conseil de sécurité et d'autre part le processus *direct* de formation du droit international général par les décisions normatives et externes du Conseil de sécurité, les résolutions de ce second type étant exclues de la compétence de l'Assemblée générale.

III. LA DIFFÉRENCIATION DES PROCESSUS INSTITUTIONNALISÉS DE FORMATION DU DROIT INTERNATIONAL GÉNÉRAL

L'établissement d'une typologie n'est utile que si elle aboutit à tirer des conclusions permettant de s'écarter d'une analyse purement descriptive. L'identification des résolutions créatrices de droit international général offre une classification plus fine des actes unilatéraux des organes de l'ONU selon leurs caractéristiques et leurs effets. L'objet de cette étude étant d'apprécier l'influence des résolutions sur la formation du droit international général, l'élaboration d'une typologie permet de comprendre que toutes les résolutions ne produisent pas du droit international selon les mêmes processus. Il s'agit ici de démontrer que l'ONU a permis d'instaurer de nouveaux processus de création du droit en dehors des mécanismes classiques que sont par exemple les conventions internationales ou la coutume. L'ONU a ainsi institutionnalisé les processus de formation du droit international existant en les rendant plus systématiques sans pour autant s'émanciper de la logique consensualiste du droit international. Le consentement de l'Etat reste requis pour former une nouvelle règle de droit, la personnalité juridique objective de l'ONU n'a pas modifié cet état de droit. On note ainsi deux degrés d'institutionnalisation en fonction du mode de formation du droit international par les résolutions de l'ONU : une institutionnalisation *simple* lorsque les recommandations normatives et externes de l'Assemblée générale et du Conseil de sécurité participent à la formation graduelle du droit international général et une institutionnalisation *complexe* lorsque les décisions normatives et externes du Conseil de sécurité participent à la formation directe du droit international général.

A. Le Processus Graduel de Formation du Droit International Général par les Recommandations Normatives et Externes de l'ONU

Les résolutions de l'ONU, de l'Assemblée générale et du Conseil de sécurité pour l'essentiel, s'apparentent à une pratique collective des Etats membres, rassemblés au sein d'un organe, ces derniers peuvent donc exprimer leur point de vue par l'adoption de ces actes unilatéraux et la nature de leur vote. Ce mode de formation de nouvelles règles de droit international doit être distingué des modes existants, coutumier ou conventionnel.

Se pose dès lors la question de la transparence de la personnalité juridique de l'organisation internationale. En d'autres termes, le vote de l'Etat vaut-il consentement de ce dernier ? Il paraît difficile de répondre par l'affirmative et ce pour deux raisons. Tout d'abord, si l'on considère que les votes des Etats lors de l'adoption de ces résolutions engagent ces derniers, l'Organisation est de ce fait privée de toute personnalité juridique puisque l'adoption de la résolution est attribuée à chaque Etat membre et non à l'organe qui les rassemble. Or la capacité normative d'une organisation internationale dépend de sa personnalité juridique, celle-ci ne pouvant être niée. Seconde raison d'ordre essentiellement pratique, en ce qui concerne les recommandations, les Etats peuvent accepter de voter en faveur de ce type de résolution en raison justement de leur caractère non obligatoire. La précision apportée par certains Etats selon laquelle leur vote ne les engagerait pas, ne doit pas être interprétée comme une confirmation *a contrario* de l'engagement de l'Etat au moment d'un vote favorable[15]. Au contraire, elle ne fait que confirmer une réalité déjà connue selon laquelle l'Etat n'entend pas s'engager par ce vote[16]. Même si certains auteurs refusent d'y voir une absence totale d'engagement de la part de l'Etat considérant qu'il ne peut finalement y avoir d'acte gratuit de l'Etat[17], il reste difficile de considérer le vote comme un consentement lorsqu'il s'agit de l'adoption d'une recommandation. Toute autre interprétation conduirait à freiner l'adoption de résolutions normatives et externes susceptibles un jour de devenir de nouvelles normes de droit international positif.

Les organes de l'ONU peuvent adopter des recommandations normatives et de droit externe mais ces caractéristiques ne sont pas suffisantes pour les considérer comme des substituts aux conférences diplomatiques donnant lieu à la conclusion de conventions internationales. Il s'agit d'une pratique collective *institutionnalisée* des Etats proche de la pratique généralisée des Etats, requise comme élément d'extériorisation de la coutume, sans pour autant pouvoir lui être entièrement assimilée. L'institutionnalisation est

[15] Pour une interprétation du vote en tant qu'explicite acceptation du contenu de la résolution comme droit, v. K Bailey, 'Making International Law in the United Nations', *op cit,* 235: l'auteur précise néanmoins qu'en sus du vote à l'unanimité une pratique conforme est nécessaire. Il est alors difficile de percevoir si le caractère obligatoire de la résolution est attribuable au vote, à la pratique des Etats ou à l'association des deux. Dans l'hypothèse décrite par l'auteur, le contenu de la résolution devient obligatoire en vertu d'un processus qui se veut proche de celui permettant l'élaboration de la coutume.

[16] *Certaines dépenses des Nations Unies (article 17, paragraphe 2 de la Charte),* avis du 20 juillet 1962, C.I.J. *Recueil* 1962, op. indiv. du juge Spender, 192.

[17] E David, 'La portée juridique des actes institutionnels', 223, in Institute of Public International Law and International Relations of Thessaloniki, *Thesaurus Acroasium*, vol. 19, Thessaloniki, 1992, XVI-617, 250.

caractéristique de la formation du droit international dans le cadre des organisations internationales : la fréquence des sessions, leur périodicité, leur fonctionnement justifient la qualification d'un nouveau processus de formation du droit international que l'on qualifiera de graduel.

L'originalité de ces résolutions se manifeste par un effet juridique variable qui justifie le caractère graduel du processus de formation. Ces recommandations, normatives et externes, ne peuvent créer directement du droit international général c'est-à-dire qu'elles ne peuvent être intégrées au corpus du droit international positif puisque le consentement des Etats n'a été à aucun moment exprimé. Si la dimension institutionnelle de ce processus facilite la mise en œuvre d'une pratique cohérente et généralisée des Etats, elle ne suffit pas à s'émanciper de leur volonté. Le caractère institutionnel de l'Organisation a ainsi une incidence sur la « formalisation de la pratique, sans commune mesure avec celle qui la caractérise dans l'ordre relationnel »[18]. Il y a donc possibilité de cumul de la pratique des Etats et celle des organes mais également dédoublement fonctionnel des Etats entre la sphère relationnelle et la sphère institutionnelle.

Ces recommandations de l'ONU peuvent finalement avoir des effets créateurs de droit international, à condition que les Etats aient manifesté leur consentement explicite à être liés postérieurement à l'adoption de la résolution. Le caractère normatif et externe de ces recommandations ne suffit pas à faire de cet acte unilatéral une source formelle du droit international. Les résolutions participent à la formation de nouvelles normes, mais sans pouvoir échapper au « fondement du droit international qui est la volonté des Etats »[19] ; c'est la raison pour laquelle on ne peut parler dans cette hypothèse que d'institutionnalisation simple de la formation du droit international.

Le débat sur l'effet des recommandations est dès lors renouvelé : les recommandations normatives et externes de tous les organes délibérants de l'ONU, et non pas uniquement de l'Assemblée générale, contribuent à accélérer le processus de formation de la norme coutumière, mais ne s'identifient pas totalement à lui. S'il est vrai que c'est toujours l'analyse du comportement de l'Etat qui permettra d'évaluer l'effet de la résolution et non l'inverse[20], la dimension institutionnelle de l'ONU et la spécificité de la pratique de ses organes délibérants font des résolutions normatives externes un processus long, graduel mais particulier de formation du droit international général. La majorité des résolutions de l'ONU relèvent de ce schéma de structuration du droit international, alors que d'autres, dont le nombre est plus limité, créent du droit international général plus directement.

B. Le Processus Direct de Formation du Droit International Général par les Décisions Normatives et Externes du Conseil de Sécurité

Seules les décisions normatives et externes du Conseil de sécurité sont concernées par le processus direct de formation du droit international général. En effet, les décisions

[18] G Cahin, *La coutume internationale et les organisations internationales,* Paris, Pedone, 2001, 782, 252.

[19] B Stern, 'Le droit international du développement, un droit de finalité ?', 43, in M Flory, A Mahiou et JR Henry (dir), *La formation des normes en droit international du développement*, Paris/Alger, Editions du CNRS/Office des publications universitaires, 1984, 393 , 47.

[20] Christophe Schreuer énonçait déjà en 1977: 'it is not the recommendation which serves as the standard for the conduct of States, but the conduct which serves as the standard for the evaluation of the recommendation': 'Recommendations and the Traditional Sources of International Law', *GYbIL*, 1977, vol. 20, 103, 108.

de l'Assemblée générale ou même du Conseil économique et social peuvent certes être normatives mais relèvent du droit interne et sont dès lors exclues de la catégorie visée puisqu'elles ne peuvent influencer le droit international général. Ce processus de formation du droit international général est qualifié de direct dans la mesure où, contrairement au processus précédemment exposé, il ne nécessite pas la réitération du consentement des Etats pour que les normes du droit des Nations Unies deviennent du droit international général.

Pour ce faire, le caractère décisoire de ces résolutions est nécessaire mais non suffisant. Les décisions institutionnelles de l'Assemblée générale relèvent par exemple à la fois du droit des organisations internationales et du droit interne de l'ONU. Elles constituent du droit mais ont un objet particulier et interne qui représente un obstacle majeur à leur possible influence sur la formation du droit international général. Les effets de ces résolutions sont limités, dans leur champ d'application personnel et matériel, à l'ordre juridique des Nations Unies. Il s'agit donc d'un simple pouvoir normatif obligatoire de l'Assemblée, circonscrit au fonctionnement institutionnel de l'Organisation. Il en est de même des décisions thématiques internes du Conseil de sécurité : bien qu'obligatoires et de portée générale pour l'ensemble des Etats membres de l'ONU, ces résolutions régissent le fonctionnement et la coordination des organes subsidiaires. Sans être nécessairement fondées sur le Chapitre VII de la Charte, l'utilisation d'un vocabulaire coercitif peut suffire à leur conférer un caractère obligatoire. On trouve, par exemple, ces résolutions dans les domaines tels que le désarmement, la tutelle ou la consolidation de la paix. S'agissant de droit interne, ces décisions enrichissent surtout le droit des Nations Unies et non le droit international général. Elles peuvent parfois contribuer à l'évolution du droit des organisations internationales mais du fait du mimétisme des autres organisations internationales : il s'agit alors davantage d'une coïncidence que d'un véritable mécanisme d'influence du droit des Nations Unies sur le droit international. De manière générale, la nature purement interne du contenu de la décision fait obstacle à l'influence du droit de l'Organisation sur le droit international général, malgré leur caractère général et obligatoire.

Sont dès lors concernées par ce processus direct de formation du droit international général deux catégories de résolutions : les décisions circonstancielles exécutives et les décisions thématiques externes du Conseil de sécurité.

Les décisions circonstancielles exécutives créent directement des normes de droit international général et leur formation est nécessaire à la résolution d'un conflit. L'effectivité de la norme s'avère donc limitée dans le temps. On peut citer deux exemples de ce type de résolutions : le Conseil de sécurité a contribué à modifier les règles de compétence judiciaire en matière pénale par rapport à la compétence de la Cour pénale internationale établie dans le Statut de Rome[21] et il a obligé des Etats à réglementer les activités du commerce de diamants[22]. Ces résolutions précisent la nature de la fonction

[21] Résolution du Conseil de sécurité 1497 (2003), 1 août 2003, S/RES/1497 (2003), para 7. La résolution 1497 (2003) empêche le Conseil de sécurité de déférer une situation au procureur, selon les termes de l'article 13 du Statut de Rome. De plus, même si la situation remplit les conditions visées à l'article 12, paragraphe 2 du Statut relatif à la compétence personnelle de la Cour pénale internationale, le procureur est tenu de surseoir à enquêter et à poursuivre à la demande du Conseil de sécurité fondée sur une résolution adoptée en vertu du chapitre VII de la Charte, en application de l'article 16 du Statut. Pour une analyse détaillée de cette disposition, v. Catherine Denis, *Le pouvoir normatif du Conseil de sécurité*, Bruxelles, Bruylant, 2004, XVI-408, 87.

[22] Résolution du Conseil de sécurité 1306 (2000), 5 juillet 2000 : oblige les Etats parties au conflit à prendre les mesures nécessaires pour interdire l'importation directe et indirecte sur leur territoire de tous les diamants bruts

créatrice de droit du Conseil de sécurité. Cette fonction est exercée le plus souvent dans l'urgence, de manière particulière, dans la mesure où elle est rattachée à la résolution d'un conflit ; elle est en outre temporaire et conditionnée par le rétablissement de la paix et de la sécurité internationales. On a pu contester le caractère normatif de ces résolutions du fait de leur absence d'effet définitif. Toutefois une norme définitive peut être modifiée et la succession des résolutions ne suffit pas à démontrer leur absence de caractère définitif ; il permet d'expliquer l'évolution du contenu des résolutions et leur adaptation rapide aux besoins de la situation dans le cadre d'un ensemble juridique cohérent. Dans cette hypothèse, le Conseil de sécurité crée des normes de droit international général mais ce pouvoir normatif s'exerce dans le cadre limité de ses compétences normatives d'urgence.

Une autre catégorie de résolutions créatrices de droit international général, selon le processus direct, est constituée des décisions thématiques externes du Conseil de sécurité. Ces résolutions ont un effet obligatoire, leur contenu n'est pas limité à un conflit particulier mais est d'ordre général, contrairement aux résolutions circonstancielles, et leur objet ne vise pas simplement à réglementer le fonctionnement institutionnel de l'Organisation et des organes subsidiaires du Conseil de sécurité. Il s'agit pour l'essentiel des décisions thématiques relatives à la lutte contre le terrorisme[23] et aux armes de destruction massive[24], qui énoncent des obligations précises allant au-delà de la simple obligation de vigilance et disposent d'un champ d'application personnel plus étendu que celui des conventions applicables en la matière. Ces obligations ne peuvent en effet s'appliquer à des entités autres que les Etats membres de l'ONU mais s'imposent à ces derniers sans que leur consentement ait à être exprimé ou renouvelé.

Le Conseil de sécurité, dans le cadre restreint des décisions thématiques externes et plus accessoirement des décisions circonstancielles exécutives, est donc susceptible de créer directement de nouvelles normes de droit international général pour l'ensemble des Etats membres de l'ONU, soit aujourd'hui la presque totalité des Etats existants. Ce faisant il a instauré, depuis le début des années 90 et de façon plus soutenue depuis 2001, un mécanisme institutionnalisé de création du droit international général. Le Conseil de sécurité ne se contente pas dans ce cas de mettre au service des Etats ses moyens opérationnels et techniques pour faciliter la formation de nouvelles normes, il agit de façon plus élaborée selon un processus de formation du droit qui lui est propre. Les particularismes de l'ordre juridique international, à savoir le statut des Etats comme sujets de droit primaires et l'absence de structure supra-étatique, empêchent toute assimilation du pouvoir normatif du Conseil de sécurité à un pouvoir législatif centralisé. La spécificité du processus de formation de nouvelles normes de droit international général par le Conseil de sécurité est pourtant réelle, c'est la raison pour laquelle on parlera ici d'institutionnalisation complexe.

en provenance de la Sierra Leone. Mais surtout le Conseil de sécurité décide que 'ces mesures ne s'appliqueront pas aux diamants bruts contrôlés par le Gouvernement sierra-léonais au moyen du régime de certificat d'origine lorsque le Comité aura fait savoir au Conseil, compte tenu d'avis d'experts, obtenus par le Secrétaire général à la demande du Comité, qu'un régime efficace est pleinement opérationnel'. Ce faisant le Conseil de sécurité impose à l'Etat sierra-léonais par une mesure individualisée et circonstancielle, un comportement et des obligations qui consistent à mettre en place un système de certification de ses diamants.

[23] V. notamment la résolution du Conseil de sécurité 1373 (2001), 28 septembre 2001.

[24] V. notamment les résolutions du Conseil de sécurité 1540 (2004), 28 avril 2004, et 1810 (2008), 25 avril 2008.

IV. CONCLUSION

L'ONU permet finalement l'institutionnalisation des processus de formation du droit international en leur offrant un caractère permanent et régulier : institutionnalisation simple lorsqu'il s'agit des recommandations normatives et externes des organes délibérants de l'ONU, institutionnalisation complexe lorsqu'on évoque les décisions normatives externes du Conseil de sécurité. La formation du droit international par le droit dérivé des Nations Unies doit par conséquent s'émanciper du débat sur la portée de la *soft law* qui conduit le plus souvent à des conclusions stériles dans la mesure où il est inutile de chercher à attribuer une valeur juridique obligatoire à un acte dont la portée n'est explicitement pas de créer directement du droit. Les processus institutionnalisés de formation du droit international ne s'émancipent pas quant à eux de la logique consensualiste du droit international.

La grille de lecture des résolutions de l'ONU proposée ici se heurte toutefois aux limites de toute classification en tentant de systématiser les effets d'instruments essentiellement politiques, soumis aux aléas du pragmatisme étatique et des relations internationales. Il est certain qu'il s'agit d'une vue simplifiée d'une réalité plus complexe mais l'objectif est d'offrir d'une part aux Etats une meilleure vision de l'influence des résolutions qu'ils adoptent et d'autre part aux éventuels destinataires de ces résolutions une plus grande sécurité juridique.

La question qui survient alors est de savoir si la classification des résolutions de l'ONU selon leurs effets et les mécanismes de formation du droit international général qui en découlent peuvent être transposés à d'autres organisations internationales. Cette typologie est-elle la même pour des organisations plus techniques telles que l'OACI, ou dont la composition n'est pas uniquement interétatique comme l'OIT, ou encore dont le principe de spécialité est plus strictement appliqué à l'image de l'OMS ou de l'OMC ? La compétence normative d'une organisation internationale influence son mode de gouvernance[25]. Par conséquent, dans quelle mesure le mode de gouvernance de l'ONU est-il transposable aux autres organisations internationales ? L'élaboration de typologies semblables pour les résolutions adoptées dans le cadre d'autres organisations internationales favoriserait une meilleure coopération entre ces organisations et faciliterait peut-être l'émergence d'un nouveau modèle de gouvernance mondiale.

[25] V. Cassese (S.), 'The Globalization of Law', *NYUJ Int'l Law and Politics*, 2005, vol. 37, 973, spec 986–90; J Cohen et CF Sabel, 'Global Democracy ?', *NYUJ Int'L Law and Politics*, 2005, vol 37, 763; Slaughter, 'The Accountability of Government Networks', *Indiana J of Global Legal Studies*, 2001, vol 8, 347.

9

Law-making by Scholarship? The Dark Side of 21st Century International Legal 'Methodology'

JÖRG KAMMERHOFER*

I. INTRODUCTION

MANY, IF NOT most, of the approaches to international legal scholarship that are currently *en vogue* live off the claim that international society has changed fundamentally since the political upheaval of 1989. On an intellectual historian's view, the post-Cold-War developments in legal scholarship have brought about a weakening of more strictly legal(ist) readings of law and a strengthening of substantialist, political readings. In espousing the claim of change in the law in its various manifestations, the proponents of these methodologies subconsciously actualise a much more radical claim: legal scholarship is seen as in some sense *making* international law. It will be argued in this paper that at the basis of this claim to law-making by scholarship lies a fundamental, deep-seated and fatal methodological confusion. Despite—or perhaps because of—how far we have come in thinking about theory and method, the dangers of admixing methods willy-nilly in order to support a preferred outcome (the much praised 'holism' and 'instrumentalism') are not always perceived by colleagues. A performance appraisal of international law must include a hard critical look at whether the way legal scholarship goes about its business can be successful in finding the law. Hence, in this contribution, a particular aspect of this methodological confusion will be criticised from the standpoint of a normativist-positivist approach that focuses on the law in force, rather than on the value-preferences of a scholarly elite.

In such new research areas as 'international constitutionalism'—but not only there—we find established a mix of international relations (a look at the 'international practice' of institutions, for example), of legal and of moralist methodologies (eg, the 'cosmopolitan paradigm' as the ideal-type of constitution). All this may be considered necessary to improve the condition of the world by fellow international lawyers but it is to be doubted whether such an approach is consistent with the ethos of scholarship—and whether such approaches can lead to greater knowledge about the law or the world.

* Senior Research Fellow at the Hans Kelsen Research Group, University of Freiburg.

The 'brave new world' of the post-Cold-War years and the new-found confidence of international lawyers in the power of their words have a dark side.

This paper will develop its argument in three steps. First, two recent approaches (and one that remains popular) will briefly be introduced as a 'phenomenology of methodological confusion' (Section II). Second, we will take the recently re-invigorated Article 31(3)(c) of the Vienna Convention on the Law of Treaties 1969 (VCLT)—used to great effect by sections of scholarship as an expression of the principle of 'systemic integration'—as a case study (Section III). Systemic integration in the form developed by scholarship is no less than law-making by those not empowered by the law to make the law. This *modus operandi* will be contrasted with an ethos of scholarship as trying to find—not to change—our object of cognition and to present an alternative vision of what international legal scholarship can validly be about (Section IV). If legal scholars persist on using legal analysis and (personal) politico-moral values in happy admixture to achieve the result they would prefer to see, what chance do we have of finding out what international law actually requires?

II. A PHENOMENOLOGY OF METHODOLOGICAL CONFUSION

Current approaches to international legal scholarship can be characterised in part by the temptation that factors beyond the sum total of positive international law exert on many scholars or, rather, by the extent to which these factors influence their analysis of the law. Moral, political or simply practical considerations enter the argument of many writers on international law to a considerable degree. While the present paper will not attach moral censure to this feature, it must be pointed out that it does unquestionably have a rather important consequence: the admixture of methods vastly decreases the likelihood of correctly cognising the law. In the brief cross-section that follows, just a few of the more popular approaches are characterised by their specific methodological traits; the three approaches are also among those which the present author has earlier had the opportunity to criticise in more detail.[1]

A. Orthodox Generalists

This is the *ancien regime* of the international law world and its members make up the core membership of the International Court of Justice and the International Law Commission (ILC). While they are generally regarded as 'positivists' or traditionalists, this does not mean, however, that they adhere to a 'strict' or 'legalist' conception of their subject. If it serves their particular purpose they may diverge from such an interpretation, construct politically or morally convenient arguments and abandon the old orthodoxy in favour of a new one. A case in point is the post-2001 change in the orthodox doctrine on self-defence law: as paradoxical as it may seem, orthodoxy in this case means movement. The '*Nicaragua* consensus' (ie that the judgment on the merits

[1] This section is based on two earlier papers: J Kammerhofer, 'Orthodox Generalists and Political Activists in International Legal Scholarship' in M Happold (ed), *International Law in a Multipolar World* (Abingdon, Routledge, 2011); J Kammerhofer, 'Constitutionalism and the Myth of Practical Reason. Kelsenian Responses to Methodological Problems' (2010) 23 *Leiden Journal of International Law* 723.

in *Nicaragua*[2] reflects the 'correct' reading of Article 51 UN Charter) is no longer considered orthodox by the most powerful traditionalist (generalist) scholars. Those who have not changed their conception of self-defence since 2001 and still cling to the restrictive reading of the right of self-defence are now considered unorthodox.

Orthodox generalists mainly wish to find amicable, practicable, or desirable solutions to disputes in accordance with their personal cosmopolitan internationalist politics. They have developed a unique 'methodology' for dealing with the increasing politicisation and moralisation of international legal practice and scholarship: they 'fudge' the law when the strict application of law would not lead to the desired outcome. In our case, narrow readings of self-defence would restrict states' freedom of action and need to be brought in line with the new realities of international life.[3] A typical element of the orthodox generalist approach is that legal scholarship tends to become an apology for (widespread) state behaviour. The fundamental re-interpretation of Article 51 thus functions as the instrumentalisation of a hermeneutic technique for political purposes (see Section III). The law is re-read in light of the behaviour of the subjects of law—their behaviour is re-read in a favourable light. Another characteristic element is orthodoxy's unquestioned acceptance of generally accepted doctrines of legal scholarship. The role of practice in the interpretation of treaties is not as straightforward as its unquestioned acceptance by orthodox scholars would have it. Not questioning a problematic notion just because it is generally accepted could be called methodologically unsound. One may raise the question whether the word 'methodology' accurately describes such a pragmatic approach.

B. Political Activists

This type of scholar tends to incorporate support for particular political causes (such as human rights, the environment, poverty or minorities) in scholarly writings. Again, one can ascertain a divergence of scholarship as it is practised and an ethos of scholarship which is defined as the apolitical analysis of the law. While in scholarly literature the most political elements of such activism are subliminated rather than openly expressed, it is nonetheless present and influences the opinions expressed therein. Louis Sohn, for example, argues that 'international law on the subject of human rights is made by *the people that care*',[4] ie, that law is made by a specific sub-set of scholars. Thus, he argues that scholars in effect should do or are doing the job allocated to politicians as policy-makers.[5] As with orthodox generalists, one can observe a moralist-political instrumentalisation of the role of legal scholars. Some human rights scholars—those with an activist bent—decide against the law and positivism and for an approach that they believe will further the cause of human rights. The following statement is representative of that approach:

[2] *Military and Paramilitary Activities in and against Nicaragua (Nicaragua v United States of America)*, Merits, Judgment of 27 June 1986, ICJ Reports (1986) 14.

[3] PH Kooijmans, 'The Legality of the Use of Force in the Recent Case Law of the International Court of Justice' in S Yee and J-Y Morin (eds), *Multiculturalism and International Law. Essays in Honour of Edward McWhinney* (Leiden, Nijhoff, 2009) 455.

[4] LB Sohn, 'Sources of International Law' (1995) 25 *Georgia Journal of International and Comparative Law* 399, 399 (emphasis added).

[5] See also B Stevens, 'Litigating Customary International Human Rights Norms' (1995) 25 *Georgia Journal of International and Comparative Law* 191, 200; RB Lillich, 'The Growing Importance of Customary International Human Rights Law' (1995) 25 *Georgia Journal of International and Comparative Law* 1, 28.

'Clearly, doctrinal rigour is not of the utmost importance ... treaty practice, custom and general principles are liberally combined so as to achieve the desired result: increased promotion and protection of human rights'.[6]

Taking domestic law as contrasting example: who would argue that the law is different just because one's cause is worthy and just (rather than because the law itself differentiates)? Would anyone claim that the number of parliamentarians required to pass a proposed constitutional amendment is lower if it concerns a new human right, rather than a morally neutral provision? Why should the situation be different in international law? In effect, activist scholars also fudge the law to further goals which are not expressed as positive international law; they put their own politico-moral views above a legal reading of the positive law in force and supplant scholarly analysis by their special interest.

C. International Constitutionalists

Another, newer, approach wishes to emphasise the constitutional elements in international law. It is followed by a sizeable number of European and particularly by German scholars.[7] For many, constitutionalist scholarship entails a 'value-added' or substantialised concept of constitution—the need to find a 'deeper' meaning behind the patchwork of international legal regulation. Constitutionalism is also based on methodological confusion which significantly lessens the benefits of the constitutionalist project for the analysis of international law. International constitutionalism starts out as empirical approach: it is 'taxonomic, rather than normative';[8] it is 'an analytical tool and not a normative argument'.[9] Yet it does transcend empirical science. The idea of a 'cosmopolitan paradigm' as developed by Mathias Kumm, for example, breaks the barrier between empirical and normative modes of analysis, because cosmopolitanism is an ideology, not a framework for empirical analysis. Consequently, 'the world-constitutionalism argument cannot derive its force entirely from its explanatory value. ... the concept cannot be understood appropriately if it is regarded as purely "analytical" or "descriptive" tool'.[10] However, this methodological plurality is subliminal as well.[11]

At times it seems like constitutionalists employ a defence-in-depth vis-à-vis predictable criticism from the positivist side, which allows them to withdraw to the

[6] J Wouters and C Ryngaert, 'Impact on the Process of the Formation of Customary International Law' in MT Kamminga and M Scheinin (eds), *The Impact of Human Rights Law on General International Law* (Oxford, OUP, 2009) 111, 127.

[7] See, eg JL Dunoff and JP Trachtman (eds), *Ruling the World? Constitutionalism, International Law and Global Governance* (Cambridge, CUP, 2009); J Klabbers, A Peters and G Ulfstein, *The Constitutionalization of International Law* (Oxford, OUP, 2009); Bardo Fassbender, *The United Nations Charter as the Constitution of the International Community* (Leiden, Nijhoff, 2009).

[8] JL Dunoff and JP Trachtman, 'A Functional Approach to International Constitutionalization' in JL Dunoff and JP Trachtman (eds) *Ruling the World? Constitutionalism, International Law and Global Governance* (Cambridge, CUP, 2009) 3, 4.

[9] ibid, 26.

[10] O Diggelmann and T Altwicker, 'Is there Something Like a Constitution of International Law?—A Critical Analysis of the Debate on World Constitutionalism' (2008) 68 *Zeitschrift für ausländisches öffentliches Recht und Völkerrecht* 623, 631.

[11] S Gardbaum, 'Human Rights and International Constitutionalism' in JL Dunoff and JP Trachtman (eds), *Ruling the World? Constitutionalism, International Law and Global Governance* (Cambridge, CUP, 2009) 233, 234.

next level when challenged.[12] The first defence is that constitutionalism is merely an empirical analysis of the totality of valid positive law. If attacked on the grounds that constitutionalist writings frequently contain overly optimistic description of certain elements that allegedly are part of international law's constitution (such as of the 'legislative powers' of the Security Council),[13] the second defence contends that the constitutional view is merely an extrapolation of trends towards constitutional*isation* already perceptible in positive law.[14] Yet many of these trends are unlikely to come to pass and the analysis of *de lege ferenda* developments is tainted by perceptions of a preferred outcome and is unrealistic in its projections. The third line of defence is that this trend *should* be realised and that it is the expression of some absolute value—we need to work for a better world and international law has to have a constitution.[15] In effect, constitutionalisers magic law from taxonomy and thus espouse a form of natural legal scholarship.

III. THE DOCTRINE OF SYSTEMIC INTEGRATION AS METHODOLOGICAL QUAGMIRE

But all this is merely a short—and perhaps overly polemical—description of some fashionable approaches. From one point of view, the specific approach chosen does not matter terribly much, for most post-1989 approaches to international legal scholarship do not have an ethos of scholarship that requires them to leave law-making to those whom the law authorises to make law. Far more important than a correct taxonomy of theoretical approaches is the consequences a theory has on the doctrine of international law—for it needs to be stressed that theoretical decisions *do* have practical results. In the following, we shall look at the freshly revived Article 31(3)(c) VCLT around which recent writings[16] and Section F of the ILC Report on Fragmentation (2006)[17]—with the

[12] Diggelmann, *Constitution*, 640.

[13] Fassbender, *United Nations*, 96: 'Today, the constitutionality of such legislative acts of the Council is generally accepted'. This hardly seems an accurate portrayal of the (very contentious) debate amongst international lawyers on this point.

[14] Fassbender, *United Nations*, 158.

[15] B-O Bryde, 'Konstitutionalisierung des Völkerechts und Internationalisierung des Verfassungsrechts' (2003) 42 *Der Staat* 61, 62; JA Frowein, 'Konstitutionalisierung des Völkerrechts' in *Völkerrecht und Internationales Privatrecht in einem sich globalisierenden internationalen System. Auswirkungen der Entstaatlichung transnationaler Rechtsbeziehungen* (2000) 427, 430.

[16] F Baetens, 'Muddling the Waters of Treaty Interpretation? Relevant Rules of International Law in the *MOX Plant* OSPAR Arbitration and *EC–Biotech* Case' (2008) 77 *Nordic Journal of International Law* 197; D French, 'Treaty Interpretation and the Incorporation of Extraneous Rules'(2006) 55 *ICLQ* 281; J Kurtz, 'Adjudging the Exceptional at International Investment Law: Security, Public Order and Financial Crisis' (2010) 59 *ICLQ* 325, 362; B MacGrady, 'Fragmentation of International Law or "Systemic Integration" of Treaty Regimes: *EC–Biotech Products* and the Proper Interpretation of Article 31(3)(c) of the Vienna Convention on the Law of Treaties' (2008) 42 *Journal of World Trade* 589; N Matz-Lück, 'Harmonization, Systemic Integration, and "Mutual Supportiveness" as Conflict-Solution Techniques' (2008) 17 *Finnish Yearbook of International Law 2006* 39; C McLachlan, 'The Principle of Systemic Integration and Article 31(3)(c) of the Vienna Convention'(2005) 54 *ICLQ* 279; C McLachlan, 'Investment Treaties and General International Law'(2008) 57 *ICLQ* 361; P Sands, 'Treaty, Custom and the Cross-Fertilization of International Law' (1998) 1 *Yale Human Rights & Development Law Journal* 85.

[17] M Koskenniemi, 'Fragmentation of International Law: Difficulties Arising from the Diversification and Expansion of International Law. Report of the Study Group of the International Law Commission' in International Law Commission, *Documents of its Fifty-Eighth Session*, A/CN.4/L.682 (2006) 206–243 (paras 410–480).

help of international tribunals[18] and the ICJ in *Oil Platforms* (2003)[19]—have created the doctrine of systemic or systematic integration.[20] This new doctrinal construct has widened the reach of Article 31(3)(c) VCLT to the point where it can be used by scholars to impose 'one right solution' to situations of inter-regime norm conflict in international law or to fill *lacunae* in one regime by means of importing norms from another regime. Recently, for example, the concept has been part of Jürgen Kurtz's effort to reconcile the possible conflict before international investment tribunals of the customary exception of necessity in the law on state responsibility and BIT-specific treaty exceptions on necessity.[21] For our purposes, the use of the doctrine of 'systemic integration' is ideal, because it clearly demonstrates how scholarship arrogates itself the competence to *make* law—subliminated and hidden under the claim merely to interpret it in a fashion that is particularly suited to the fragmented nature of international law and that manages to 'solve' the problems arising from this phenomenon.

(1) But how does scholarship use the doctrine of systemic integration to make law? The argument is that the systematic nature of international law (as expressed in Article 31(3)(c) VCLT)[22] has consequences. Systemic interpretation allows rules 'to appear as parts of some coherent and meaningful whole'.[23]

> The foundation of [the principle of systemic integration] is that treaties are themselves creatures of international law. ... [T]hey are predicated for their existence and operation on being part of the international law system. As such they must be 'applied and interpreted against the background of the general principles of international law' ... [The principle] flows ... inevitably from the nature of a treaty as an agreement 'governed by international law' ...[24]

Some elements of legal scholarship argue that 'the normative environment' must be taken into account in the process of interpretation[25] for international law to be a meaningful whole and to be a purposeful instrument. This is a substantialist view of perceiving law as a system[26] rather than a motley collection of rules. However, the specific legal effects that follow from the use of the systemic integration argument for the sum-total of positive international law are seldom addressed in writings.

(2) Before we proceed to a critique of the doctrine's theoretical foundations, a specific example may be useful to illustrate the method of those who espouse the doctrine. For convenience,[27] we will use Jürgen Kurtz's excellent paper in the *International and*

[18] eg *Dispute Concerning Access to Information Under Article 9 of the OSPAR Convention, Final Award (Ireland v United Kingdom)*, Permanent Court of Arbitration, Award of 2 July 2003; *Golder v United Kingdom*, Judgment of 21 February 1975, ECHR Series A no 18 (1975); *Loizidou v Turkey*, Merits, Judgment of 18 December 1996, ECHR (1996-VI) 2216; *Al-Adsani v United Kingdom*, Judgment of 21 November 2001, ECHR (2001-XI) 79; *United States—Import Prohibition of Certain Shrimp and Shrimp Products*, WTO, Appellate Body Report of 12 October 1998, WT/DS58/AB/R; *EC—Measures Affecting the Approval and Marketing of Biotech Products*, WTO, Panel Report of 7 February 2006, WT/DS291–293/R.

[19] *Oil Platforms (Islamic Republic of Iran v United States of America)*, Merits, Judgment of 6 November 2003, ICJ Reports (2003) 161, 181–2 (paras 40–1).

[20] This section builds on an earlier paper: J Kammerhofer, 'Systemic Integration, Legal Theory and the ILC' (2010) 19 *Finnish Yearbook of International Law 2008* 157.

[21] Kurtz, Adjudging.

[22] Koskenniemi, *Fragmentation*, 23 (para 33).

[23] ibid, 208 (para 414).

[24] McLachlan, Systemic Integration, 280.

[25] Koskenniemi, *Fragmentation*, 211 (para 419).

[26] Baetens, Muddling, 197.

[27] The choice of that paper was arbitrary among those applying the doctrine of systemic integration and in no shape does it reflect on the scholarly merits of its author.

Comparative Law Quarterly on the necessity defence before investment tribunals.[28] In trying to reconcile the operation of two possibly applicable exceptions to the substantive duties of the host state of an international investment—necessity under customary international law and necessity clauses under BITs[29]—before investment tribunals, Kurtz prefers a method which has the doctrine of systemic integration at its heart. For him, the drafters of BITs 'incorporated select customary norms and also constructed new treaty norms with a different tenor and direction from the protections at customary international law'.[30] This leads to the obligation of a tribunal faced with the dual claim of necessity 'to give effect to *both* the treaty exception and the customary defence'[31] which means that both exceptions are equal 'primary legal standards' and that '*only* if breach is determined by the composite application of these rules'[32] would the defence of necessity be successful before an investment tribunal.

It is easy to see how the customary norm is thus *sub silentio* integrated in treaties. In tune with the other proponents of the doctrine of systemic integration, Kurtz seeks to portray this inclusion as a specific form of contextual interpretation of the BIT within the purview of Article 31(3)(c) VCLT. 'Thus understood, article 31(3)(c) enables a tribunal to interpret and apply a treaty instrument in relationship to its normative environment, "other" international law'.[33] Not only does he seek to include the customary norm into the BIT, but the reach of the exception of measures necessary for 'essential security interests' in Article XI US–Argentina BIT (and similar exceptions elsewhere) may be enriched by sources that can only marginally be described as 'legal'.

> There are more targeted external sources that can be used to shed light on this question. In particular, the work of the UN Commission on Human Security ... [which] argues that traditional notions of State security must be augmented by ... 'human security'. ... This analytical framework suggests that outbreaks of financial crises might engage security concerns (defined to encompass human security objectives), thereby triggering the operation of the BIT exception.[34]

The end-result—applying Kurtz's method to the Argentine financial crisis and its aftermath in (ICSID) arbitration—cannot be surprising:

> Where the very ability of a State to meet these continuing and elementary needs of citizens is endangered through financial crises, human rights law offers a critical anchor to justify a claim to engagement of 'essential security interests'.[35]

However, all this cannot hide the awkward question that one must confront after the comfortable feeling of having 'solved' a question merely by interpretation has worn off: where in international investment law does one find all the rules Kurtz envisages? Alternatively, where do BITs incorporate such rules? Is that really a question

[28] Kurtz, Adjudging.
[29] Arguably, the customary defence of 'necessity' is codified in: General Assembly, *Articles on Responsibility of States for Internationally Wrongful Acts*, A/RES/56/83, Annex, 12 December 2001 (Article 25). The example of a BIT used by Kurtz is Article XI Treaty between the United States of America and the Argentine Republic concerning the reciprocal encouragement and protection of investment, 14 November 1991.
[30] Kurtz, Adjudging, 357.
[31] ibid, 358.
[32] ibid, 356.
[33] ibid, 362.
[34] ibid, 362.
[35] ibid, 364.

of interpretation or rather one of the conflict of norms, a much less flexible issue?[36] Perhaps the friendliest interpretation of the paper is that it is directed towards giving advice to tribunals regarding the practicalities of deciding within their (wide) margin of appreciation. Still, the spectre of norm-conflict continues to loom on the horizon, for the view of a problem from an arbitral tribunal's point of view may be an important *practical issue*, but is not a scholarly analysis required to penetrate beyond the pragmatic towards an analysis of the law in force, even if that does not 'solve' the problem? Do we need law at all for a purely pragmatic decision?

(3) The theoretical critique of the doctrine of systemic integration can perhaps best be approached from a 'legal common sense' perspective. This involves a focus on the positive international law in force and contrasts this analysis (ie finding the law) to the doctrine and the claimed consequences. The difference between the two—namely that positive law does not support much of what the doctrine claims—will form the core of the critique. In this format we are restricted to highlighting one problem of the doctrine of systemic integration, namely that interpretation cannot do what the proponents ascribe to it; and that in ascribing to systemic interpretation these powers, scholars seek to *make* law.

On a *legal* view, systemic integration cannot be a function of interpretation properly speaking. Interpretation is the cognition of legal norms and norms need to be cognised for them to be understood by humans. Humans start a process of interpretation immediately upon looking at a legal text, irrespective of whether the text seems clear or not. Systemic integration is typically explained as a cognitive tool to interpret one norm 'in the light' of others. 'This is all that Article 31(3)(c) requires; the integration into the process of legal reasoning … of a sense of coherence and meaningfulness'.[37] Interpretation properly speaking, however, cannot influence norms. Because interpretation is merely a hermeneutic process or technique, it exists anterior to norms and cannot be regulated itself. In cognising a norm, human beings can take into account any number of factors, including other norms. Norms are no more than a frame of possible meanings, for all texts are subject to the vagueness that is inherent in language;[38] also, a norm may deliberately leave a choice for the tribunal, as is typically the case for penal norms and their sentencing guidelines.[39]

> In all these cases the law to be applied only provides a frame, within which there is more than one possibility of application. Any act that stays within this margin and gives the frame a possible sense is legal. … If 'interpretation' is to be understood as epistemic ascertainment of the meaning of the object to be interpreted, the result of a legal interpretation can only be the ascertainment of a frame (which is the law to be interpreted) and thus the cognisance of multiple possibilities [of meaning], which are possible within the frame.[40]

[36] On the present author's view on the complexities of norm-conflict in international law, see: J Kammerhofer, *Uncertainty in International Law. A Kelsenian Perspective* (Abingdon, Routledge, 2010) 139.

[37] Koskenniemi, *Fragmentation*, 211 (para 419).

[38] H Kelsen, *Reine Rechtslehre* 2nd edn (Vienna, Deuticke, 1960) 348. Customary norms—while themselves not verbal or verbalised norms—are vague as well, because their content is a transferral of a behavioural pattern into a norm.

[39] ibid, 347.

[40] 'Das anzuwendende Recht bildet in allen diesen Fällen nur einen Rahmen, innerhalb dessen mehrere Möglichkeiten der Anwendung gegeben sind, wobei jeder Akt rechtmäßig ist, der sich innerhalb dieses Rahmens hält, den Rahmen in irgendeinem möglichen Sinn ausfüllt. … Versteht man unter "Interpretation" die erkenntnismäßige Feststellung des Sinnes des zu interpretierenden Objektes, so kann das Ergebnis einer

Therefore, interpretation *properly understood* is the cognition of the frame rather than of 'one correct meaning'. In the hermeneutic process of interpretation no decision can be made between multiple choices in cognising the norm, because *all* possible meanings are equally possible. If it were truly a matter of interpretation, systemic integration would have to change the norm to be interpreted prior to interpretation or it would have to choose between multiple possible meanings based on external sources that do not—on a legal view—make up the norm (even if they happen to be other parts of international law). In both cases, the interpreter would go beyond cognition towards application or change.

In other words, if we take the proponents of systemic integration at their word when they wish to describe it (in light of Article 31(3)(c) VCLT) as interpretation, the doctrine cannot produce the intended result. Interpretation cannot solve the underlying conflict of norms between, for example, two slightly (?) different necessity exceptions in international treaty law and customary international law. Consistent with their view of the function of interpretation, a large part of international legal scholarship argues that norm-conflicts are a result of and can be avoided by interpretation,[41] for conflicts can, on their view, be established only through interpretation. However, norms are merely a frame of possible meanings and may have a multitude of possible meanings. Hence, the norm cannot be any one of its meanings and the frames (the norms) themselves conflict, not the norms' meanings—norms conflict prior to interpretation. Norms cannot be changed by interpretation and interpretation cannot resolve norm-conflict. 'Because interpretation of legal norms is legal cognition and because cognition of law can neither create nor invalidate legal norms, interpretation cannot solve conflicts of norms'.[42] In response it can be argued that in a post-Kantian world, cognition 'creates' the norm *for the observer*. On the plane of the ideal, however, the norm is valid irrespective of cognition. Because norms themselves are not changed by interpretation, they are also not changed by interpreting them while 'taking into account' other norms. Interpretation has to stop where the norm fails to be more precise,[43] because the norm is the limit of legal cognition.[44]

(4) Taking up the problem faced by international investment tribunals when they have to decide how to deal with rival necessity exceptions again, the proponents may

Rechtsinterpretation nur die Feststellung eines Rahmens sein, den das zu interpretierende Recht darstellt, und damit die Erkenntnis mehrerer Möglichkeiten, die innerhalb dieses Rahmens gegeben sind'. Kelsen, *Reine Rechslehre,* 2nd ed, 348 (all translations are by the present author).

[41] CW Jenks, 'The Conflict of Law-Making Treaties' (1954) 30 *BYIL 1953* 401, 428; J Pauwelyn, *Conflict of Norms in International Law. How WTO Law Relates to Other Rules of International Law* (Cambridge, CUP, 2003) 244–74; E Vranes, 'Lex superior, lex specialis, lex posterior—Zur Rechtsnatur der "Konfliktlösungsregeln"' (2005) 65 *Zeitschrift für ausländisches öffentliches Recht und Völkerrecht* 391, 398.

[42] 'Da Interpretation von Rechtsnormen Rechts*erkenntnis* ist, Erkenntnis des Rechts aber eben so wenig wie Rechtsnormen erzeugen, d.h. in Geltung setzen, die Geltung von Rechtsnormen aufheben kann, kann Interpretation die Lösung eines Normenkonflikts nicht leisten'. H Kelsen, *Allgemeine Theorie der Normen* (Vienna, Manz, 1979) 179.

[43] AJ Merkl, 'Zum Interpretationsproblem' (1916) 42 *Zeitschrift für das Privat- und Öffentliche Recht der Gegenwart* 535 reprinted in H Klecatsky, R Marcić and H Schambeck (eds), *Die Wiener rechtstheoretische Schule. Ausgewählte Schriften von Hans Kelsen, Adolf Julius Merkl, Alfred Verdross* (Vienna, Europa, 1968) 1059, 1063; G Winkler, *Rechtstheorie und Erkenntnislehre. Kritische Anmerkungen zum Dilemma von Sein und Sollen in der Reinen Rechtslehre aus geistesgeschichtlicher und erkenntnistheoretischer Sicht* (Vienna, Springer, 1990) 218.

[44] R Walter, 'Das Auslegungsproblem im Lichte der Reinen Rechtslehre' in G Kohlmann (ed), *Festschrift für Ulrich Klug zum 70. Geburtstag* (Cologne, Deubner, 1983) 187, 191; H Mayer, 'Die Interpretationstheorie der Reinen Rechtslehre' in R Walter (ed), *Schwerpunkte der Reinen Rechtslehre* (Vienna, Manz, 1992) 61, 62.

construct a counter argument that these tribunals do have to and in fact do decide and solve the problem. Their solution is binding on the parties and tribunals frequently take account of each other's awards in taking their own decisions, which may over time form at least a *jurisprudence constante*, if not a customary or even common law.[45] Is that not evidence enough that systemic integration is a valid doctrine of international law? It is true that the situation is categorically different with tribunal judgments or other organs of international law authorised to apply a norm and in issuing a judgment creating a lower-level norm. These are two different functions: the cognition of law versus law-making according to the rules on law-creation in the hierarchy of norms.

> In the application of law by a legal organ, the cognitive interpretation of the law to be applied is combined with an act of will by which the law-applying organ chooses between the possibilities shown by cognitive interpretation. ... This act of will differentiates the legal interpretation by the law-applying organ from any other interpretation, especially by ... legal scholarship.[46]

An arbitral award of an ICSID tribunal is, however, not a logical deduction from the law that is applied, but an act of will that creates new law. For example, the awards in the *Lauder* and *CME* cases[47] are as little a logical deduction from the US–Czech Republic and Netherlands–Czech Republic BITs as a criminal judgment is a deduction from the penal code. The essential element turning a judgment into a positive norm is that it claims to be obeyed, eg 'the accused ought to spend six months in prison'. This is a *decision*, not a deduction. It is an act of norm-creation in which the tribunal chooses one of the possible meanings of the higher-level norm and this decision is (in the original sense of the word) arbitrary—the meaning decided upon does not suddenly become the only possible meaning or the only content of the norm for all eternity. For example, if all investment tribunals were suddenly to exclude 'regulatory measures' from the scope of indirect expropriation in International Investment Agreements (IIA), the norms in the IIAs themselves would not be changed. What cannot be disputed, however, is that such a move would have immense practical impact. Again, however, the treaty law—and even, arguably, customary law—would not change because investment jurisprudence had found a *jurisprudence constante*.

(5) On a legal analysis, therefore, the doctrine of systemic integration cannot do what its proponents want it to do: either one interprets and is free to ignore surrounding norms or an organ applies the law—but not in a process of interpretation. In this sense, this strain of scholarship takes away the competence of the organs to decide and turns 'political' decisions over to scholarship on the basis of the erroneous view that scholarship is somehow better equipped to make this choice than those whom the law authorises to make them. Political decision—the originary decision—should remain where it belongs, ie with those the law authorises to make them, like treaty and customary law-makers or tribunals making individual norms. It should not and, legally speaking, cannot be

[45] Zachary Douglas's recent book attempts to construct precisely such a 'common law' of investment: Z Douglas, *The International Law of Investment Claims* (Cambridge, CUP, 2009).

[46] 'In der Anwendung des Rechtes durch ein Rechtsorgan verbindet sich die erkenntnismäßige Interpretation des anzuwendenden Rechtes mit einem Willensakt, in dem das rechtsanwendende Organ eine Wahl trifft zwischen den durch die erkenntnismäßige Interpretation aufgezeigten Möglichkeiten. ... Durch diesen Willensakt unterscheidet sich die Rechtsinterpretation durch das Rechtsorgan von jeder anderen Interpretation, insbesondere ... durch die Rechtswissenschaft'. Kelsen, *Reine Rechslehre,* 2nd ed., 351.

[47] *Ronald S Lauder v Czech Republic*, UNCITRAL, Final Award of 3 September 2001, 9 ICSID Rep 62; *CME Czech Republic B.V. v Czech Republic*, UNCITRAL, Partial Award of 13 September 2001, 9 ICSID Rep 113.

appropriated by scholarship following its own political agenda. Systemic integration is thus unmasked as yet another—methodologically unsound—tool appropriating law-making status to an intellectual elite, rather than having us live with the imperfect state of international law.

IV. CONCLUSION: BACK TO A LEGAL COMMON SENSE

It may be easier, more accepted and more *en vogue* to argue that scholarship 'makes' law rather than sticks to the law, but the way we are going about it means overstepping our boundaries as legal scholars. The example of the doctrine of systemic integration has shown what these tactics, what law-making by scholarship can lead to, for it is submitted here that we are tripping over our own feet in the process and obscuring our view of the law. In addition, the increased instrumentalisation of legal scholarship based on values external to the law means that we should not be surprised to be accused of pursuing an internationalist political agenda. Two practical consequences may arise from the claim that scholarship 'makes' law.

First, we may no longer be able to cognise the law. That is not a very popular or accepted argument in the post-realist and post-modernist environment. Critical Legal Scholars will say, 'there is no law to cognise any more—our debates are the law'; indeed, Martti Koskenniemi has recently defined the body of law at issue here thus: 'International law is an argumentative practice'.[48] Equally, Legal Realists can claim with some force: 'we *make* the law in propounding it in textbooks or articles and getting the arguments accepted by the courts and states'. While both arguments may not be the case, it is powerful stuff in the senior common room—it is more doubtful if it will persuade in the council chamber. The second, far more worrying consequence is that we may eventually end up not being trusted (or needed) by our customer base. If decision makers realise or suspect (even if wrongly) that we are pursuing our own agenda, our opinions will no longer have the nimbus of scholarship. In effect, we will be reduced to second-rate amateur politicians.

The alternative is clear: we must return to, or, rather, explore a concept of legal scholarship that focuses on the analysis of the law in force, rather than of the law we wish to see. This is merely (as mentioned above) a form of 'legal common sense', for it can be only common sense to want to know what is the law on any given subject without falsifying the outcome by intermingling it with politico-moralist wishful thinking. We expect to talk about the law when we set out to talk about the law, rather than indulging in anthropological analysis on the meta level of the nature of the 'argumentative practice'[49] surrounding the norms themselves.

On the one hand, such a view would be in a natural opposition to natural law approaches, because natural law theories presuppose the possibility of absolute values, hierarchically higher than all positive law. Such absolute values cannot exist,[50] because all

[48] M Koskenniemi, 'Methodology of International Law', in R Wolfrum (ed), *Max Planck Encyclopedia of Public International Law* (Oxford, OUP, 2008) para 1, online edition at www.mpepil.com.

[49] ibid, para 1.

[50] M Jestaedt, 'Der Rechts- und Demokratietheoretiker Hans Kelsen—Eine Einführung' in M Jestaedt and O Lepsius (eds), *Hans Kelsen. Verteidigung der Demokratie. Abhandlungen zur Demokratietheorie* (2006) vii, xvi–xvii; H Kelsen, *Reine Rechtslehre. Einleitung in die rechtswissenschaftliche Problematik* (Vienna, Deuticke, 1934) 21; H Kelsen, *General Theory of Law and State* (Cambridge, Harvard University Press, 1945) 393; H

values are relative: the Ought that makes up all norms is only a claim to be observed; that claim is equal to all other 'Oughts'. The noblest ideal is only one claim amongst others. On the other hand, somewhat surprisingly, a faithful analysis of positive law is also not in complete accordance with traditional positivism as understood in international legal scholarship. The absolutisation of the notion of state—that states necessarily have certain rights, that sovereignty is a pre-legal precondition of international law—is too reminiscent of natural law to be accepted by those sticking to the law in force.

Realistically speaking, this approach is not likely to become popular any time soon, for it remains too tempting to give in and exercise the 'power' of legal scholarship in shaping the legal world. Indeed, it may also seem heartless to abstain from changing the world for the better when we are just discovering the power our words can have on those in power. However, if we want to be called scholars properly speaking, we will have to find the self-discipline and restraint to analyse the law in force and leave the rest for others.

Kelsen, 'Die Grundlagen der Naturrechtslehre' (1963) 13 *Österreichische Zeitschrift für öffentliches Recht* 1 reprinted in H Klecatsky, R Marcić and H Schambeck (eds), *Die Wiener rechtstheoretische Schule. Ausgewählte Schriften von Hans Kelsen, Adolf Julius Merkl, Alfred Verdross* (1968) 869.

10

Judicial Law-making in International Criminal Law: The Legitimacy Conundrum

MARJAN AJEVSKI*

I. INTRODUCTION

IN AN ESSAY devoted to the sources of international criminal law, the *Oxford Companion to International Criminal Justice* has a very enigmatic sentence. It says that '[u]nlike other international tribunals, the ad hoc tribunals[1] do apply the principle of *stare decisis*'.[2] The explanation that follows this enigmatic sentence is one that we have heard echoed in the past and has, by now, acquired an almost a mantra-like status. The explanation is that, in other international judicial systems, even though judicial decisions have been assigned a subsidiary status in international law, they play an 'important role in determining precisely what the law is'.[3] According to this narrative, international judicial decisions are followed because they express the legal principles that govern that specific legal issue. They discover and verify the existence of the unwritten law that is the hallmark of the international system. In short, judicial decisions identify the law, but they never 'are the law'.[4]

A more sophisticated version of this narrative is presented in the seminal work of Judge Shahabuddeen, *Precedent in the World Court*.[5] Taking us through the way that the International Court of Justice (ICJ) uses its prior cases and the cases of the Permanent Court of International Justice (PCIJ), which resembles pretty much a precedent based

* SJD Candidate in Comparative Constitutional Law, Legal Studies Department, Central European University (Hungary).

[1] The phrase '*ad hoc* tribunals' refer to the International Criminal Tribunal for Yugoslavia (ICTY) and the International Criminal Tribunal for Rwanda (ICTR).

[2] Dapo Akande, 'Sources of International Criminal Law' in Antonio Cassese (ed in chief), *The Oxford Companion to International Criminal Justice* (OUP, Oxford, 2009) 53; but see also Guido Acquaviva and Fausto Pocar, 'Stare Decisis' in Rüdiger Wolfrum (general ed) *The Max Planck Encyclopaedia of Public International Law* (Max Planck Institute for Comparative Public Law and International Law, November 2007).

[3] See *The Oxford Companion to International Criminal Justice*, ibid, 53.

[4] ibid, explaining in short the difference in the way that other international law courts see their own use of previous case and the way that the *ad hoc* tribunals have created a precedent-based system. But see also Malcolm N Shaw, *International Law* 6th edn (Cambridge University Press, Cambridge, 2008) 103 and 128 regarding municipal courts and international law.

[5] Mohamed Shahabuddeen, *Precedent in the World Court: Hersch Lauterpacht Memorial Lectures* (Cambridge University Press, Cambridge, 1996).

system, Judge Shahabuddeen, nevertheless, concludes that the ICJ does not follow any doctrine of *stare decisis*, even though it ascribes a precedential value to its own case-law. In that sense, the decisions of the ICJ have the status of non-binding precedent, one that can certainly create law *over time,* one that is unquestionably authoritative and has a normative pull but it is not, on its own, binding as such.[6]

This assessment of the place of judicial decisions in international law is as close as most scholars and judges are willing to go in extending the sources of international law as stated in Article 38(1) of the ICJ Statute.[7] Moreover, as everybody in international law is painfully aware, the Article 38 sources are in no hierarchical order: treaties, customs, general principles as the sources of law, while 'judicial decisions and the teachings of [...] [scholars are] subsidiary means for the determination of rules of law'.[8]

And yet, in a very young but dynamic branch of international law, two courts have decided to follow the doctrine of *stare decisis* as a rule in their deliberations.[9] One of the questions that arises here is: why? Why did the International Criminal Tribunal for Yugoslavia (ICTY) and the International Criminal Tribunal for Rwanda (ICTR) decide to adopt a doctrine of *stare decisis*, a doctrine that is inherent with the notion that judicial decisions are binding precedent and that previous decisions will be followed provided that there are no cogent reasons for departing from such precedent? In this chapter, I will explore the reasons for this adoption and especially the role the issue of legitimacy has played in the adoption of the doctrine of *stare decisis*.

I start my analysis with the presupposition that judges, and judicial decisions, for all intents and purposes, create law. They create law in the very real sense that Judge Shahabuddeen described, through changing and shaping the law. Courts make law for a very simple reason; a legal system has to offer two, sometimes competing, parameters: legal certainty and responsiveness to societal change.[10] As such, courts have to establish legal certainty by having a consistent system of substantive outcomes through their decisions, ie arrive at the same conclusion for the same sets of facts, and at the same time be open to the changing societal circumstances that would make their jurisprudence out of date. Consequently, courts have to shape and change the law since the environment that they are operating in also changes.[11] In short and in a very realist sense,[12] judges and courts are law-makers. It is in the restraint and legitimisation of this judicial normative pull where a lot of the confusion as to whether international judgments are law lies.

My argument will proceed in four parts. In Part I, I will explain the master narrative of the international system and the concept of the legitimacy in international law-making

[6] See more generally Chapters 7 and 8, 'The Possibility of Judge-made International Law and Stare Decisis' in ibid, 67.

[7] For instance see Shaw, *International Law*; Malcolm D Evans (ed), *International Law* 2nd edn (OUP, Oxford, 2006); Vaughan Lowe, *International Law* (OUP, Oxford, 2007); Alan Boyle and Christine Chinkin, *The Making of International Law; Foundations of Public International Law Series* (OUP, Oxford, 2007); Rebecca M M Wallace, *International Law* 4th edn (Sweet & Maxwell, London, 2002).

[8] Article 38 (1)(d) of the ICJ Statute.

[9] *Prosecutor v Zlatko Aleksovski* (Appeal Judgment) IT-95-14/1-A, 24 March 2000 (hereafter the *Aleksovski* Appeals Chamber judgment).

[10] See for a discussion on this issue the *Aleksovski* AC judgment, paras 92–97.

[11] For instance see Winfried Brugger, 'Legal Interpretation, Schools of Jurisprudence, and Anthropology: Some Remarks from a German Point of View' (1994) 42 *Am J Comp L* 395.

[12] For a good overview of the points of view of the Realists movement in the United States see Brian Z Tamanaha, *Beyond the Realist-Formalist Divide: The Role of Politics in Judging* (Princeton University Press, Princeton and Oxford, 2010) 67.

that it entails. In Part II, I will explain the master narrative in the French legal system and its concept of the legitimacy in law-making. I chose France because it has a typical continental-law concept of the sources of law where judicial decisions and scholarly doctrine are not law but authorities.[13] Judicial decisions have a normative pull and are followed in an almost precedent like fashion but they are not law as such.[14] Furthermore, France is also one of the more fervent upholders of the sources of law versus authorities' distinction.[15] In short, the stand on the doctrine of sources in France is very similar to the doctrine of sources in international law but with very different results. In Part III, I will present the distorted international law master narrative of the international criminal law regime as seen by the ICTY and the ICTR through their jurisprudence. In Part IV, I will offer some explanations as to the reasons why the ICTY and the ICTR have chosen to have a system of *stare decisis* and relate this to the changing master narrative of international law and challenge the idea of a non-binding precedent and especially the idea of judicial decisions as subsidiary sources.

II. PART I—THE INTERNATIONAL LAW MASTER NARRATIVE: THE SOURCES OF LAW AND THE STATUS OF JUDICIAL DECISIONS IN INTERNATIONAL LAW

A. The Concept of Master Narratives and Legitimacy

Before I start my analysis, I introduce the idea of master narratives. A master narrative is, in short, a story.[16] It is a story about the system itself; 'a governing underlying narrative that each legal system tells itself—more and less openly—about why it is constructed the way it is, why it operates as it does, and why this makes good sense'.[17] A master narrative is the underlying premise that any legal system is based upon. It deals with the basic legal formants[18] of a system, their position relative to each other in a specific hierarchy, the interactions between those legal formants and the reasons for them. It establishes 'the basic internal logic of [the] system as mainstream legal actors understand it'.[19]

A master narrative is extremely important for purposes of legitimisation. In a sense, a source of law or a law-making exercise is legitimate because it conforms with, fits-in, and complies with, this master narrative. The narrative does not have to be a long and complex story. Quite the contrary, it is usually short, simple and condensed.[20] Nevertheless, this narrative 'founds or establishes the legitimacy of that system for those who operate within it'.[21] In that sense, legitimacy, since it is based on a master narrative,

[13] Mary Ann Glendon, Michael Wallace Gordon and Christopher Osakwe, *Comparative Legal Traditions: Texts Materials and Cases on the Civil and Common Law Traditions, with Special Reference to French, German, English and European Law* 2nd edn (West Publishing Co, St Paul, Minn, 1994) 192.

[14] ibid, 207–09.

[15] See especially the discussion on prospective overruling presented in Chapter 5 in Mitchel De S-O-L'E Lasser, *Judicial Transformations: The Rights Revolution in the Courts of Europe* (OUP, Oxford, 2009) 121–134.

[16] Mitchel De S-O-L'E Lasser, 'Transforming Deliberations' in Nick Huls, Maurice Adams and Jacco Bomhoff (eds) *The Legitimacy of Highest Courts' Rulings: Judicial Deliberations and Beyond* (T M C Asser Press, The Hague, 2009) 37.

[17] ibid.

[18] On the idea of legal formants see Rudolfo Sacco, 'Legal Formants: A Dynamic Approach to Comparative Law (Instalment I of II)', (1991) 39 *Am J Comp L* 1.

[19] Mitchel De S-O-L'E Lasser, *Transforming Deliberations*, 37.

[20] ibid.

[21] ibid.

is always self-referencing. A legitimate action is what the system says it is.[22] Therefore, what is the master narrative for the international system? What role does this narrative give to judges and courts? What makes judicial decisions legitimate in international law?

B. The International Law Master Narrative and the Doctrine of Sources

Every student of international law is familiar with this short master narrative. The international system is a 'horizontal [one], consisting of over 190 independent states all equal in legal theory [...] and recognising no one in authority over them'.[23] The states are the ones that 'create the law and obey and disobey it'.[24] International law, as contrasted to national law, is a reversal of its basic foundational principle, that of sovereignty.[25] While sovereignty on a domestic level means that the sovereign, in whatever form it takes (parliament, monarch, etc.) 'can do no wrong',[26] in the international system, all sovereigns, as an oversimplification, have to comply with international law. International law, on the other hand, is a system of norms that 'seeks to secure the conditions that allow sovereign States to co-exist, and to enable each state to choose what kind of society will exist within its borders'.[27]

When it comes to law and law-making, Article 38 of the ICJ is the authority on the subject of sources of international law. Judicial decisions, although important and present an authority, do not make law nor are they precedent.[28] One author, Malcolm N Shaw, likens international courts, and especially the ICJ, to English courts, who, while determining the law through interpretation also create it.[29] It is at the story of international courts where the narrative on sources and international law-making gets a little blurry.

For instance, at the time of the drafting of Article 38 or its equivalent in the PCIJ's Statute, some members of the Advisory Committee of Jurists have said that 'judicial decisions state, but do not create, law'.[30] Baron Descamps put it even more plainly when he said that '[d]octrine and jurisprudence no doubt do not create law; but they assist in determining rules which exist. A judge should make use of both jurisprudence and doctrine, but they should serve only as elucidation'.[31] One of the more noted guides to how international courts use cases in their reasoning is the seminal work of Judge Shahabuddeen, *Precedent in the World Court*. In Judge Shahabuddeen's opinion, judicial decisions, *over time*, can make law. They create international law through helping in its development, which inadvertently leads to some law-making. Nevertheless, the fundamental principle that must be followed is that international courts must decide in accordance with international law as defined in treaties, custom or general principles.[32]

[22] ibid, 38.
[23] Shaw, *International Law*, 6.
[24] ibid.
[25] Vaughan Lowe, *International Law*, 6.
[26] ibid, 6.
[27] ibid, 7.
[28] Shaw, *International Law,* 67 but see especially 109.
[29] ibid,110.
[30] Lord Phillmore's remarks to the Advisory Committee of Jurists quoted in Shahabuddeen, *Precedent in the World Court*, 49.
[31] Baron Descamps as quoted in Boyle and Chinkin, *The Making of International Law*, 267.
[32] Shahabuddeen, *Precedent in the World Court*, 69.

Regardless of what different authors make on the point of whether international decisions, even incidentally, make law, the overwhelming consensus is that, in the international legal system, there is no place for a system of *stare decisis*. Some courts may use cases from other jurisdictions as part of their reasoning in their law-discovery process, but they do not follow them out of some idea of binding precedent in international law. They follow them out of the conviction that the decisions have 'got it right' when it comes to the legal principle involved. The use of internal case-law is in the format of non-binding precedents, following the courts' own case-law when appropriate and distinguishing them when not.[33]

International courts have echoed this master narrative in their decisions as well. The ICJ for example has said that

> It is clear that the Court cannot legislate [...] Rather its task is to engage in its normal judicial function of ascertaining the existence or otherwise of legal principles and rules applicable to the threat or use of nuclear weapons. The contention that the giving of an answer to the question posed would require the Court to legislate is based on a supposition that the present *corpus juris* is devoid of relevant rules in this matter. The Court could not accede to this argument; it states the existing law and does not legislate. This is so even if, in stating and applying the law, the Court necessarily has to specify its scope and sometimes note its general trend.[34]

Furthermore, international judgments have a limited legal effect and are only binding for the parties in the dispute and for the specific issue that was resolved. Early on, the PCIJ has noted the limited effect that international judgments have in international law by saying that 'Article 59 of the Statute, [...] does not exclude purely declaratory judgments. The object of this article is simply to prevent legal principles accepted by the court in a particular case from being binding upon other States or in other disputes'.[35]

Other courts have echoed this master narrative and have accepted their law-discovering role in international law. Even international criminal tribunals have stated this general preposition. The ICTY has said that

> Being international in nature and applying international law *principaliter*, the Tribunal cannot but rely upon the well-established sources of international law and, within this framework, upon judicial decisions. What value should be given to such decisions? The Trial Chamber holds the view that they should only be used as a "subsidiary means for the determination of rules of law" [...] Hence, generally speaking, [...] the International Tribunal cannot uphold the doctrine of binding precedent (*stare decisis*) adhered to in common law countries. [...] Clearly, judicial precedent is not a distinct source of law in international criminal adjudication. The Tribunal is not bound by precedents established by other international criminal courts such as the Nuremberg or Tokyo Tribunals, let alone by cases brought before national courts adjudicating international crimes. Similarly, the Tribunal cannot rely on a set of cases, let alone on a single precedent, as sufficient to establish a principle of law: the authority of precedents (*auctoritas rerum similiter judicatarum*) can only consist in evincing the possible existence of an international rule. More specifically, precedents may constitute evidence of a customary rule in that they are indicative of the existence of *opinio iuris sive necessitatis* and international practice on a certain matter, or else

[33] ibid, Ch 8, 97; but see also generally Boyle and Chinkin, *The Making of International Law*; Shaw, *International Law*; Vaughan Lowe, *International Law*; Ian Brownlie, *Principles of International Law* 6th edn (OUP, Oxford, 2003); Wallace, *International Law*.

[34] *Legality of the Threat or Use of Nuclear Weapons, Advisory Opinion, ICJ Reports 1996*, 226, para 18.

[35] *Case Concerning Certain German Interests in Upper Silesia, (Germany v Poland)* PCIJ Rep Series A No. 7. 19.

> they may be indicative of the emergence of a general principle of international law. Alternatively, precedents may bear persuasive authority concerning the existence of a rule or principle, ie they may persuade the Tribunal that the decision taken on a prior occasion propounded the correct interpretation of existing law. Plainly, in this case prior judicial decisions may persuade the court that they took the correct approach, but they do not compel this conclusion by the sheer force of their precedential weight. Thus, it can be said that the Justinian maxim whereby courts must adjudicate on the strength of the law, not of cases (*non exemplis, sed legibus iudicandum est*) also applies to the Tribunal as to other international criminal courts.[36]

To conclude, in the master narrative of international law, courts and their decisions have a subsidiary role to play. They discover the law but do not make it. Even if they do occasionally venture into a law-making function, it is limited and incidental and only noting the general trend of development of the law. In any case, there is no binding system of precedent in international law since there is no system of *stare decisis*, even within a specific judicial system. International judicial decisions are, like the writings of scholars, an *authority* and not a source of law. I will now turn to examine what role this doctrine of sources of law plays in other national systems, namely the French, in the light of judicial legitimacy.

III. PART II—THE CONTINENTAL LAW MASTER NARRATIVE: THE FRENCH EXAMPLE OF REPUBLICAN LEGITIMACY

The doctrine of sources set in Article 38 of the ICJ Statute is, at least as far as judgments and scholars are concerned, a reflection of the continental law doctrine of sources. On the continent it is said that judicial decisions (jurisprudence) and the writings of scholars are, since the time of Gény, *authorities*.[37] It is because of this that I now turn to France to see what role the doctrine of sources plays in the legitimisation of the normative power of judicial decisions. I chose France because it is on the more extreme end in the stringent application of this doctrine. Consequently, it will allow me to show the function that this doctrine of sources plays in a continental law system and the systematic requirements to meet its desired goal of restraining judicial normative pull.

On one hand, common law systems have resolved the issue of judicial law-making, for historical reasons, by allowing the full force of law to judicial decisions. Nonetheless, in order to restrain the normative power of judges, who are elected in a more political fashion and are organised in a judicial organisation of coordinate authority,[38] common law systems use a different technique of judicial legitimisation through a public argumentative model.[39] Through requiring judicial candour[40] ie a thorough explanation

[36] *Prosecutor v Zoran Kupreckic et al*, (Trial Chamber Judgment) IT-95-16-T, 14 January 2000, para 540 (hereafter *Kupreckic* TC judgment); but also see *Prosecutor v Zlatko Aleksovski*, (Appeals Chamber Judgment) IT-95-14/1-A, 24 March 2000, paras 92–115 (hereafter *Aleksovski* AC judgment).

[37] Mitchel De S.-O.-L'E. Lasser, *Judicial Deliberations: A Comparative Analysis of Judicial Transparency and Legitimacy* (Oxford, OUP, 2004) 173; but see also Glendon and others, *Comparative Legal Traditions*, 207; Daniel Terris, Cesare P R Romano & Leigh Swigart, *The International Judge: An Introduction to the Men and Women who Decide the World's Cases* (Oxford, OUP, 2007) Appendix C, 248.

[38] Mirjan R Damaska, *The Faces of Justice and State Authority: A Comparative Approach to the Legal Process* (New Haven and London, Yale University Press, 1986) 23.

[39] Lasser, *Judicial Deliberations*, 338.

[40] Scott Altman, 'Beyond Candor', (1990) 89 *Mich. L. Rev.* 296; Gail Heriot, 'Way Beyond Candour', (1991) 89 *Mich L Rev* 1945; Scott C Idleman, 'A Prudential Theory of Judicial Candour', (1995) 73 *Tex L Rev* 1307.

of the cognitive steps taken during deliberations of the individual judge, the judges themselves, as individuals, have to explain the reason why they arrived at a certain solution.[41]

To understand why, in France and for the most part of the continent, judicial decisions do not have the force of law outside of the parties to the dispute, we have to go back to the time of the French Revolution. One of the results of the French Revolution was the complete mistrust in judges and courts of the *Ancien Régime*. The other important results, at least for this paper, were the supremacy of the legislature over other state branches with its monopoly of law creation, and the establishment of the concept of Republican Institutionalism as a model of management of governmental affairs.[42] In France, like in most of the continent, judicial decisions do not make law, they, together with scholars, are assigned to the realm of *authorities*. It is important for us to understand how remarkably intricate the process of legitimisation of judicial decisions in France is in order to see that legitimacy and legitimisation is a multi-layered and contextual issue. In short,

> The French system functions on the basis of an institutional and republican conception of judicial control and legitimacy. This system aims to select, educate, and train a small corps of elite, representative, and state-sanctioned jurists to manage their judicial decision-making in an enlightened and coherent fashion. The French pursue this goal by: (1) entrusting the judiciary with the task of handling legal controversies in such a way as to promote the general interest and the public good; and (2) constraining judges by placing them, throughout their careers, in a reliably meritocratic and hierarchical institutional framework. Accordingly, the traditional French system grants its judges a privileged and sequestered deliberative space in which to engage in particularly frank, communal, and highly substantive debates that, by virtue of their very seclusion, are intentionally denied the force and status of law.[43]

The French judicial discourse operates on two different plains, one is on the official plane where judges decide cases through issuing short, terse and authoritative judicial decisions giving the appearance that there is a straight path between the text of *la loi* enacted by parliament and the specific judicial outcome.[44] The holding flows directly from *la loi* to the recipient of justice through the judge serving in the true Montesquieuian idea of the judge as the mouthpiece of the law.[45]

The second plane is the hidden internal discourse which is frank, open to societal changes and mindful of the existing jurisprudential line of legal solutions. It is in this secluded discourse that French judges follow their previous decisions, take care of legal certainty while also adapting, modifying and changing the law. In a sense, it is this secluded, internal deliberation that has normative weight. Moreover, it is this secluded internal deliberation that has, in the perception of the Realist tradition, the law-shaping power that must be constrained.[46]

[41] Mitchel De S-O-L'E Lasser, 'The European Pasteurization of French Law', (2005) 90 *Cornell L Rev* 995, 1002–1003; for the working of a judicial mind see also Albie Sachs, *The Strange Alchemy of Life and Law* (Oxford, OUP, 2009) 47.

[42] Lasser, *Judicial Deliberations*; Lasser, 'The European Pasteurization of French Law', 1001–1015 and see also Mitchel De S-O-L'E Lasser, 'Judicial (Self-) Portraits: Judicial Discourse in the French Legal System' (1995) 104 *Yale L J* 1325.

[43] Lasser, 'The European Pasteurization of French Law', 1002 (footnotes omitted).

[44] In a sense, judicial decisions in both the US and France operate as if they were linguistic tropes of general statutes and laws: generally see Mitchel De S.-O.-L'E. Lasser, '"Lit. Theory" Put to the Test: A Comparative Literary Analysis of American Judicial Tests and French Judicial Discourse' (1998) 111 *Harvard L. Review* 689.

[45] Lasser, 'Judicial (Self-) Portraits', 1342.

[46] Lasser, *Judicial Deliberations*, 31.

The constraint of the normative power of the internal judicial dialogue is made on two fronts, one on information transmission about the law and two, on an institutional basis. The short, syllogistic judicial decisions—the French public judicial discourse—is, not surprisingly, terse on information regarding the legal basis and legal reasoning of the decision. Consequently, the only legal basis for the decision is the quoted number of the Article in the specific *loi*.[47] In order for any actor to follow the current state of the law, she has to turn to another legal actor in the system, the French academic.

French academics spend a considerable amount of their time publishing case notes in specialised journals dedicated to the jurisprudential outputs of the different French highest courts. In these case notes they contextualise the decision of the highest French courts, place it in the line of previous jurisprudence, enunciate the legal principles that it is based on and criticise the legal outcome for its consistency with the legal system and the prevailing doctrine on the issue, its adherence to previous precedent and its synchronisation with the prevailing social conditions.[48] In a sense, judges do not control the way their jurisprudence is perceived in the legal system. Consequently, there is a dialogic relationship between judges and academics both holding one piece of the puzzle of the normative meaning of the law.[49] A further consequence to this normative power of both academics and judges is their assignment to *authorities* rather than formal sources of law. They share the same step on the normative ladder.[50]

A further restraint on the normative pull of judicial decisions is the institutional constraints that are built in the French state system. Both French academics and judges are formed in the process of the same free, open, and meritocratic educational system that installs French republican values in its participants.[51] Furthermore, the bureaucratic authority model[52] of the French judiciary further constrains judges in their decision-making process.[53] On the one hand, all judges have to be mindful of the fact that climbing the judicial ladder requires good reports from one's superiors, who would not look kindly to an overly zealous young judge experimenting with the law. On the other hand, only in the simplest cases do French judges decide on their own. Collegial deliberations are the rule in France, not the exception. Coupled with the unsigned collegial decision at which no dissents are allowed, this closes the door to any single or even a group of 'rogue' judges to wielding too much normative power.[54] In the French system, but around the continent as well, normative power should firmly be in the hands of the legislative branches, not the judiciary. It is now time to turn to international criminal lawyers and see how they have dealt with the problem of legitimisation of judicial decisions and whether they have stuck to the international law master narrative.

[47] Generally see Lasser, '"Lit. Theory" Put to the Test'.
[48] See Lasser, 'Judicial (Self-) Portraits'; Lasser, *Judicial Deliberations*, 307.
[49] ibid.
[50] ibid, 311; Glendon and others, *Comparative Legal Traditions*, 192–210.
[51] Lasser, 'The European Pasteurization of French Law', 1012.
[52] Damaska, *The Faces of Justice and State Authority*, 18.
[53] Lasser, 'The European Pasteurization of French Law', 1012.
[54] ibid.

IV. PART III- INTERNATIONAL CRIMINAL LAW AND STARE DECISIS: A JUDICIAL CONSTRUCT

If there is anything on which international scholars and international courts agree, it is on the issue of the lack of a *stare decisis* system in international law. Or at least that was the case until a decade ago. As I have said, scholars in the Max Plank Encyclopaedia of Public International Law and the *Oxford Companion to International Criminal Justice* have pointed out that a system of *stare decisis* is in operation at the ICTY and ICTR.[55] The basis for this claim is both the way that the *ad hoc* tribunals use their own case-law and several explicit pronouncements that the *ad hoc* tribunals have made in different judgments. Let me start from the way that the ICTY and ICTR use their own case-law.

If one starts to read a judgment of the ICTY or ICTR, especially a trial chamber judgment handed down after 2003, and looks at the part of the judgment that usually goes under the heading 'as to the law' one cannot but notice the extensive use of previous case-law. A typical footnote section in one page would look like this:

> 727 *Kvocka* Trial Judgement, para 149.
> 728 *Krnojelac* Trial Judgement, para 182.
> 729 *Kvocka* Trial Judgement, para 143.
> 730 *Krnojelac* Trial Judgement, para 182.
> 731 *Celebici* Trial Judgement, para 495.
> 732 *Kunarac* Appeals Judgement, para 153.
> 733 *Kunarac* Appeals Judgement, para 153.
> 734 *Kunarac* Appeals Judgement, para 155, *Kvocka* Trial Judgement, para 153; *Krnojelac* Trial Judgement, para 184.
> 735 *See* for example *Celebici* Trial Judgement, para 494 and *Kvocka* Trial Judgement, paras 137-141.
> 736 *Kunarac* Appeals Judgement, para 148; *Kvocka* Appeals Judgement, para 284.[56]

When it comes to discussing general requirements under the law of the statutes, the ICTY and the ICTR quote extensively from their previous judgments. They use tests that previous Trial Chambers (TC) and Appeals Chamber (AC) have constructed in their judgments, almost disregarding the presence of the text of the statute or the various conventions.

However, it is not only that they follow the previous solutions of the appeals or trial chambers in a precedent-based fashion because the previous chambers have 'got it right'. Quite the contrary, this adherence to former rulings is based on a judicially constructed formal rule of binding precedent. In the *Aleksovski* AC judgment, the ICTY created a formal system of *stare decisis* while answering the question posed initially by the prosecutor as to whether international decisions have a precedential value.[57] The ruling that the Appeals Chamber came up with, even though probably not fully realising the fact at the time, was earth-shattering. It said that

> 107. The Appeals Chamber, therefore, concludes that a proper construction of the Statute, taking due account of its text and purpose, yields the conclusion that in the interests of certainty

[55] See footnote 2 and accompanying text.
[56] *Prosecutor v Fatmir Limaj and others*, (Trial Chamber Judgment) IT-03-66-T, 30 November 2005, footnotes on page 84 of the judgment.
[57] *Aleksovski* AC judgment, paras 87–91.

and predictability, the Appeals Chamber should follow its previous decisions, but should be free to depart from them for cogent reasons in the interests of justice.
108. Instances of situations where cogent reasons in the interests of justice require a departure from a previous decision include cases where the previous decision has been decided on the basis of a wrong legal principle or cases where a previous decision has been given *per incuriam*, that is a judicial decision that has been 'wrongly decided, usually because the judge or judges were ill-informed about the applicable law'.[58]

The consequence of this is that now the TCs of the ICTY and the ICTR are bound by the judgments of the AC and that the AC itself is the only one that can depart from a previously decided precedent and only with cogent reasons. With this judgment the AC ushered in a new type of language in the discourse of international law, that of overruling, of properly and improperly decided previous precedents and the need to depart from a previous line of precedents. An example of this is the discussion in the Decision by the AC in the *Zigic* case where it decided to depart, ie overrule, from a previous judgment citing 'cogent reasons'[59] (without explaining the cogent reasons) for the departure. Judge Shahabuddeen, in his attached declaration, even goes on to say that 'not every disagreement (however strongly felt) with previous case-law requires a departure',[60] thereby strengthening the notion of a precedent-based requirement in the *ad hoc* tribunals system. The question now arises, why did the judges of the *ad hoc* tribunals create a system of *stare decisis* within their jurisdiction? And even more importantly, how did they manage to do it so seamlessly, even though the implications for the doctrine of sources are earth-shattering?

V. PART IV—STARE DECISIS IN INTERNATIONAL LAW: SYSTEMATIC REQUIREMENTS

One cannot construct a system of *stare decisis*, regardless of how much one desires such a system, without several necessary institutional or systemic requirements. In fact, a system of *stare decisis*, no matter how much we would like to believe to the contrary, did not operate in the UK or in the USA before the mid-nineteenth century.[61] Rather, a system based on the notions of natural law was in operation in most common law countries.[62] It was with the onset of positivism, the development of reliable case reporting systems and the existence of a hierarchical judicial system with a supreme court on the top of a pyramid that ushered in the era of *stare decisis*.[63] A doctrine similar to the one we have now in international law, that is to say one of judicial decisions as evidence of the law and not law as such, was in operation in the UK and USA before the 1800s.[64] Yet, with the onset of an improved case-reporting system and the existence of a hierarchical court

[58] ibid, paras 107–108 (footnote omitted).
[59] *Prosecutor v Zoran Zigic*, (Appeals Chamber Decision on Zoran Zigic's Motion for Reconsideration of Appeals Chamber Judgment) IT-98-30/1-A Delivered on 28 February 2005, decided on 26 June 2006 (hereafter *Zigic* AC decision).
[60] ibid, para 2 of Judge Shahabudeen's statement attached to the decision.
[61] Frederick G Kempin, Jr, 'Precedent and Stare Decisis: The Critical Years, 1800 to 1850', (1959) 3 *American Journal of Legal History* 28.
[62] ibid, 30.
[63] ibid, 31.
[64] ibid, 29.

system coupled with the decline of natural law theory, a system of binding precedent emerged. However, it is important to note that a system of *stare decisis* is not a pre-ordained result once the systematic requirements are in place.[65] *Stare decisis* is but one way of using past experience and it is highly contingent on the master narrative of the system in question. It always involves a choice, mostly on the part of the judiciary.

Something similar may be in operation at the level of the *ad hoc* tribunals. For almost a century now, we have had a reporting system for international judicial decisions, either in the Cambridge edited *International Law Reports*,[66] the *Oxford Reports on International Law*,[67] *The Oxford Companion to International Criminal Justice*,[68] the *Max Plank Encyclopaedia on International Public Law*,[69] or in the *American Journal of International Law* which regularly publish case notes of different jurisdictions connected to international law.[70] Furthermore, almost all international courts now publish their judgments, either in paper publication in a journal form or more recently, electronically on the internet. This publication of judgments and accompanying materials has led to the decline of the role of scholars in international law as purely scholars and not judges or legal advisers in contentious cases.

There is also no need to stress the hierarchical nature of international criminal courts. It is obvious even on a superficial glance that they are organised with several trial chambers and an appeals chamber on the top. Furthermore, the *ad hoc* tribunals have a common appeals chamber. This hierarchical system is unusual in other international courts and specific to the more recently created international dispute resolution mechanisms.

It is at this point where the issue of legitimacy gets its full swing. The sources-of-law doctrine has its function. Like in continental law systems, the sources of law in international law have the function of protecting legislative supremacy, specifically, the centrality of states in the horizontal system of sovereign and equal states. Law in this sense, following the international law master narrative, can originate only in states themselves. Consequently, treaties and customs are the direct results of the actions of states and their explicit will, while the general principles of law are elucidated from states' own national systems. On the other hand, judicial decisions and the opinion of scholars are not law because they do not emanate from the direct will or actions of states. Therefore, judges and scholars can only state what the law is but not make it.

This is where the shift occurs. Courts do make law—plain and simple. They have a strong normative pull, especially in a system of law that is largely unwritten.[71] Therefore, their law-making endeavours have to be curtailed. In France, that has been achieved through an intricate system of bifurcation of public and private discourse for judges and republican institutionalism which forms judges in the mould of French republicanism coupled with collegial and unsigned deliberations.[72]

[65] ibid, 29.

[66] For more on the reports see www.justis.com/data-coverage/international-law-reports.aspx or (last visited December 8, 2010).

[67] For more see www.oup.com/online/us/law/oril/ (last visited December 8, 2010).

[68] Cassese, *The Oxford Companion to International Criminal Justice.*

[69] For more on the online encyclopaedia see www.mpepil.com/ (last visited December 8, 2010).

[70] For more on the International Legal Materials see www.asil.org/ilm/ilmindx.htm (last visited December 8, 2010).

[71] See the discussion presented with footnotes 2–5 and 23–36.

[72] See discussion presented footnotes 37–42.

At the international level, this system of constraint on judges is lacking. Not only are judges elected to international tribunals in a highly political way[73] there are also very few mechanisms that would ensure professional quality whilst on the bench. Very few institutional constraints exist in terms of the election, training and deliberations of international judges.[74] There is no unified education system that would mould judges in a specific ethos since there is no specific ethos to begin with. Quite the contrary, the international system, if not value neutral, is value plural.[75] Consequently, the international system has had to develop some informal mechanisms for constraining judges.

There are, furthermore, other elements that are lacking from the international system that would not help in the legitimisation of judicial decisions. For one, there are no world academics, no rush to publish case notes, no need to fit a decision of a court into prevailing legal doctrine about a certain legal institute or to criticise it for its specific result. If in the time of Hugo Grotius the legal scholar shaped the law, this is no longer the case. One does not need any longer to know the opinion of scholars to know the situation of the law in a given international field. If there is a court, like international criminal courts, that deals with the specific field then one can find the shape of the law more in judicial decisions than in the writing of scholars. If one picks up a modern textbook on international criminal law, one would not be surprised to see a mountain of case law in the footnotes.[76] This is not so for an international criminal law textbook prior to 1990.[77]

Consequently, if judges wish to legitimise their judicial decisions they have to adopt a different method, one familiar to Common Law courts, namely the method of public argumentation.[78] For an international judicial decision to be legitimate, it has to allow for the reader, any reader, to know the judges' reasons for that specific outcome. Furthermore, judges are personally responsible for the decisions that they have arrived at.[79] This is accomplished by issuing signed judgments with the possibility for separate and dissenting opinions, which present an opportunity for de-masking conflicting interests of conflicting legal theories within the same judicial text.[80] Judges also give extensive reasons for separate issues that are put forward by any of the parties; they review the evidence extensively and give reasons why each piece of evidence was found convincing or not. It is of no surprise that a single international criminal law judgment runs in the hundreds of pages accompanied with extensive footnotes and annexes.

It is because of this method of legitimisation that the establishment a system of *stare decisis* proceeded so smoothly. If the international system lacked a hierarchical judicial system, international criminal law did not. The already existing legitimisation method made this transformation so smooth. The legitimisation method strengthened the judges'

[73] Terris, Romano & Swigart, *The International Judge*, 15.

[74] ibid, 21.

[75] Consequently the widespread formal or informal requirement of regional representation of judges, see ibid, 23.

[76] See for instance *The Oxford Companion*; Antonio Cassese, *International Criminal Law* 2nd ed (Oxford, OUP, 2008); Alexander Zahar & Göran Sluiter, *International Criminal Law: A Critical Introduction* (Oxford, OUP, 2008).

[77] M Cherif Bassiouni (ed), *International Criminal Law, Volume I—Crimes* (New York, Transnational Publishers, 1986).

[78] See footnotes 39 and 40 and the accompanying text.

[79] Generally see Lasser, *Judicial Deliberations* and Lasser, 'The European Pasteurization of French Law'.

[80] ibid.

hand and allowed them to construct a system of *stare decisis*, which strengthened the system of precedent by making it formally binding, which strengthened the use of the legitimisation method, which entrenched the system of binding precedent. As with the other two systematic requirements, hierarchy and accurate and available transmission of case information, the legitimisation method allowed for a smooth transformation from a system of informal judicial precedent to a formal system of *stare decisis*. However, if this specific method of legitimisation of judicial decisions was not already present at the time of the *Aleksovski* decision in both international law and, consequently in international criminal law, the judges at the ICTY and ICTR would have had to change much more than to turn the switch of non-binding, authoritative precedent, to a formally binding precedent system of *stare decisis*.

11

Revisiting Monism's Ethical Dimension

GEORGE RODRIGO BANDEIRA GALINDO*

I. INTRODUCTION

SPEAKING ABOUT MONISM and dualism has become a taboo, nearly a sinful act, in international legal scholarship. For several decades, jurists from around the globe have stressed how futile and useless the theoretical debate about the relationship between international and municipal law is. Expressions such as *discussion d'école* or 'dialogue of the deaf' and others have been repetitively used to describe it.[1] However, the specter of these theories still haunts international lawyers. In the twenty-first century, several articles and books covering topics related to the relationship between international and municipal orders have referenced the debate. Even if most scholars continue to criticise monism and dualism, they are unable to disentangle themselves from the vocabulary developed by the theories' supporters in the beginning of the twentieth century. Transformation, incorporation, reception, system, conflict, and basic norm are just a few examples of terms used today in a way not far different from the theories' 'founding fathers'.

That relationship of love and hate, dependence and criticism, is, in my view, a reflection of two different, but closely related, phenomena. First, it reveals the discomfort many international lawyers experience in terms of dealing with putting the discipline's past in its proper context. The turn to pragmatism that was in vogue after the end of World War II (and still is in many intellectual circles)[2] fundamentally meant trying to break with international law's past and to look ahead to a promising world governed by rules. In this world, theory would be supplanted by empiricism and history by tradition. Second, it shows the resistance of many to the realisation that, during the interwar years, monism and dualism were embedded with deep ethical considerations about how the world should be organised.[3] Authors such as Hans Kelsen wished to place international lawyers

* Adjunct Professor of International Law, University of Brasilia (Brazil). I wish to thank Ingo Venzke and Martti Koskenniemi for reading and commenting on a first draft of this article.

[1] See, among many, the classical studies of Pierre Lardy, *La force obligatoire du droit international en droit interne* (Paris, LGDJ, 1966) 15 and Sir Gerald Fitzmaurice, 'The General Principles of International Law Considered from the Standpoint of the Rule of Law' (1957 II) 92 *Recueil des Cours*, 70.

[2] See, for instance, David Kennedy, 'A New Stream of International Legal Scholarship' (1988) 7 *Wisconsin International Law Journal* 1.

[3] One of the few exceptions in recent scholarship is Janne Nijman and André Nollkaemper, 'Introduction' in Janne Nijman and André Nollkaemper (eds) *New Perspectives on the Divide between National and*

in their proper political ideologies. That is something many try to avoid today. Lawyers are not allowed to be activists or revolutionaries.

In the next pages, I will examine the ethical foundations of some of the most prominent supporters of monism during the interwar period. My central thesis is that we cannot understand what monism really is or what it intends to do without connecting the project of unity of international law and municipal law to deep ethical convictions.

In every single approach in international law, moral choices need to be made. However, by ethics, I mean much more. As Nardin argues:

> The institution of morality is particularly concerned with duties that arise from the rules or precepts that constitute it, whereas the ethical realm also includes a concern with ideals and ends that go beyond these duties, and especially with the outcomes of action.[4]

My focus on monism does not mean that dualism has no ethical dimension at all. On the contrary, the roots of dualism can be found in what is called the *tradition of international law*. A tradition that emphasises sovereignty and the idea that international law is a law of coordination.[5] However, such ethical dimension is essentially allergic to changes and it relies on the current situation of international legal norms and institutions.[6] This seems to explain why dualism sounds much more descriptive than normative.

This article is divided into two parts. In the first part, I will focus on some of the criticisms of monism and, consequently, on the idea of the unity of law, highlighting that that critique was more directed toward monism's 'lack of reality' than toward its ethical foundations as projects of change. In the second part, I will prove that underneath three different (and influential) versions of monism in the interwar period lay deep ethical concerns focused on the possibilities for change in international law. At the end, concluding remarks will be presented.

II. THE OLD (AND NEW) ATTACK ON MONISM

Alexander Somek, summarising the debate between monists and dualists, underlines an important aspect that grounds most of the criticism made with respect to the former: reality. He states, with some irony: 'Dualism, it seems, is the most straightforward manner of conceptualising public international law. Indeed, dualism seems to be very much alive, while monism is dead'.[7]

International Law (Oxford, Oxford University Press, 2007) 1, 6. However, they suggest that the debate must be overcome because it was developed in a different historical context.

[4] Terry Nardin, 'Ethical Traditions in International Affairs' in Terry Nardin and David R Mapel (eds) *Traditions of International Ethics* (Cambridge, Cambridge University Press, 1992) 1, 3.

[5] See, especially, Murray Forsyth, 'The Tradition of International Law' in Nardin and Mapel, *Traditions*, 23. This tradition was later influenced by Hegel's strong nationalist conception of the State. See, eg, J G Starke, 'Monism and Dualism in the Theory of International Law' (1936) 17 *British Yearbook of International Law* 66, 68.

[6] A good example of such approach is Jean Cohen's conception of 'constitutional pluralism'. Although recognising the need for change in international law, Cohen's thick support for sovereignty poses a tremendous obstacle to the emergence of different approaches in international legal thinking. See Jean L Cohen, 'Sovereignty in the Context of Globalization: A Constitutionalist Pluralist Perspective' in Samantha Besson and John Tasioulas (eds), *The Philosophy of International Law* (Oxford, Oxford University Press, 2010) 261.

[7] Alexander Somek, 'Kelsen Lives' (2007) 18 *European Journal of International Law* 409, 421.

In his Hague Academy lectures, given in 1923, Triepel restated many of the points he had previously made in his *Völkerrecht und Landesrecht*, published in 1899. But he also had the opportunity to respond to the criticism made about dualist theory a few years earlier by Kelsen. He started his refutation of Kelsen's monism by saying that it did not 'pay attention to the realities'. Russian and English laws do not belong to the same legal system nor were Dutch or Chinese bills dependent upon one sole basic norm.[8] This counterargument defines one of the most recurrent attacks on monism throughout the years.

Self-declared dualists barely exist. But some recent and growing literature on the relationship between international and municipal law, sometimes called pluralist literature, persists in attacking ideas that conceive of the interaction between international and municipal law in terms of unity. Their main argument is about reality. Two examples will suffice.

Neil Walker uses the term 'disorder of orders' to characterise the state of the relationship between different normative orders, be they national, international, transnational, supranational, or any other. Now, 'each of these units must negotiate their boundary relations inter se as well as with the states themselves'. And this negotiation contains no single meta principle of authority—sovereignty or supremacy of international law—to guide the relations among orders; conversely, a number of meta principles compete with each other for supremacy.[9]

Another influential variation of pluralism is Teubner and Fischer-Lescano's idea of regime-collisions. For them, global law is invariably fragmented. Different regimes emerge with no hierarchy uniting them. In such a scenario, '[r]ather than secure the unity of international law, future endeavors need to be restricted to achieve weak compatibility between the fragments'. Since differentiation seems to expand unpredictably, law's role is 'at the very best, [to] offer a kind of damage limitation'.[10]

These arguments are grounded in the idea that reality undermines any possibility of a unifying conception encompassing the different legal orders. They become more powerful when confronted with recent judgments, such as *Kadi*,[11] by the European Court of Justice, and *Medellín*,[12] by the US Supreme Court, that supported a profound dualistic conception of the relations between the international and domestic orders. The former judgment's support for dualism is even more impressive because of the alleged European Union tradition of respect for international law and the inclination, in many of the constitutions of its members, toward monism.

Even international lawyers belonging to traditions of thought close to monism have shown some resistance to accepting the supremacy *tout court* of international law over do-

[8] Heinrich Triepel, 'Les Rapports entre le droit interne et le droit international' (1923-I) 1 *Recueil des Cours* 77, 86.

[9] Neil Walker, 'Beyond Boundary Disputes and Basic Grids: Mapping the Global Disorder of Normative Orders' (2008) 6 *International Journal of Constitutional Law* 373, 387.

[10] Andreas Fischer-Lescano and Gunther Teubner, 'Regime-Collisions: The Vain Search for Legal Unity in the Fragmentation of Global Law' (2004) 25 *Michigan Journal of International Law* 999, 1045.

[11] European Court of Justice, Joined Cases C-402/05 and C-415/05 P *Yassin Abdullah Kadi, Al Barakaat International Foundation v Council of the European Union, Commission of the European Communities* [2008] ECR I-6351. The court stated that 'an international agreement cannot affect the allocation of powers fixed by the Treaties or, consequently, the autonomy of the Community legal system', para 282. For an excellent critical account of the judgment, see Gráinne de Búrca, 'The European Court of Justice and the International Legal Order After *Kadi*' (2010) 51 *Harvard International Law Journal* 1.

[12] *Medellín v Texas*, 552 US 491 (2008).

mestic law. For example, Anne Peters argues, after commenting on recent international and domestic judicial practice rejecting the supremacy of international law that 'there is no legal rule to decide which norm should prevail' nor a 'legal rule to resolve the competing claims to authority raised by the international and the domestic constitutional actors'. She then advocates a turn from form to substance, stating that more important norms, such as fundamental rights, should prevail over less important ones.[13] In a similar vein, André Nollkaemper recently stated, after reviewing judicial practice, that the respect for fundamental rights must be prioritised in issues relating to international and municipal law, since 'blind obedience to the supremacy of international law is not the same thing as the rule of law'.[14]

Related to the contestation that monism lacks reality, an immense debate has continued to rage over the unity and fragmentation of international law that involves not only scholars but also practitioners.[15] Such an argument also raises some deep theoretical questions about coherence and order in international law. Although the debate only obliquely touches on the relationship between international and municipal law, clearly, it also affects that relationship.[16] If coherence cannot be found in the core of international law, it can barely serve to unify international law, municipal law, and a number of other legal orders that have emerged or gained prominence in recent years. Given that picture, certainly, dualism is alive today, as is its criticism of monism.

Clearly, the idea of the unity of law needs to be subjected to scrutiny. In a world where difference is cultivated in the name of freedom and equality, monism may sound imperialistic and oppressive. However, from my point of view, the great legacy of monism is not its internal logic or its precise depiction of developments in international law. What lies behind monism is not the idea of unity or coherence, but a conception about how to change the world in a time of peril, such as the interwar years. In the next section, I will deal briefly with three monistic theories founded on strong ethical convictions.

III. MONISM AND ETHICS

A. Hans Kelsen: International Law as *Civitas Maxima*

The prevailing view among legal philosophers is that one of the main aims of Kelsen's Pure Theory of Law was to decouple moral and ethical considerations from the scientific study of law. Kelsen himself made this statement clear several times.

[13] Anne Peters, 'Supremacy Lost: International Law Meets Domestic Constitutional Law' (2009) 3 *Vienna Online Journal on International Constitutional Law* 170, 196, available at www.internationalconstitutionallaw.net/download/e76a6cefb44dfa2e40d73e6db88c5f2a/Peters.pdf.

[14] André Nollkaemper, 'Rethinking the Supremacy of International Law' (2010) 65 *Zeitschrift für öffentliches Recht* 65, 83.

[15] The literature on fragmentation is enormous. A starting point must be the International Law Commission's study on the issue: International Law Commission, *Fragmentation of international law: difficulties arising from the diversification and expansion of international law* (Report of the Study Group of the International Law Commission, finalized by Martti Koskenniemi (2006) UN Doc A/CN.4/L.682). The study of P M Dupuy became classical in the defense of the unity of international law: Pierre-Marie Dupuy, 'L'unité de l'ordre juridique international' (2002) 297 *Recueil des Cours* 9. For a summary of a number of criticisms against the idea of unity, see Mario Prost, *Unitas multiplex: Les unités du droit international et la politique de la fragmentation* (McGill University—Doctoral Thesis in Civil Law) (2008).

[16] This is shown in many articles that appeared in Janne Nijman and André Nollkaemper (eds), *New Perspectives on the Divide between National and International Law* (Oxford, Oxford University Press, 2007).

However, some commentators have stressed how ethical principles played an important role in Kelsen's Pure Theory of Law.[17] But those aspects of Kelsen's ideas are evident only in his writings of the 1920s. When Pure Theory of Law was under growing attack, Kelsen tried to refine it, purging exogenous considerations (eg, political or ethical) from its core. But this did not prevent him from returning to ethical considerations, even indirectly, in some of his later writings.

One of the keys to understanding Kelsen's postulation of the supremacy of international law over municipal law is his adoption of the doctrine of *civitas maxima*, as professed by Christian Wolff. He developed this idea in a lengthy way in *Das Problem der Souveränität und die Theorie des Völkerrechts*.[18] In Kelsen's view, the legal hypothesis that international law is a universal legal order encompassing state legal orders and superior to them could be identified with Wolff's proposition of a superior universal community. Such a universal community, for Kelsen, was the personification of the international legal order.

In his defense of international law as *civitas maxima*, Kelsen recognised that the idea had its roots in natural law and saw no incompatibility between *civitas maxima* and the equality between states, a typical ethical concept. However, his main focus at that time was to accommodate the idea within the broad picture of the Pure Theory of Law and launch a strong attack against the concept of sovereignty.

Civitas maxima would appear again in his most important study on the relationship between international and municipal law, his Hague Academy lectures, entitled *Les rapports de système entre le droit interne et le droit international public*. Here, he provides a systematic view of monism and dualism, which would appear, although in a slightly modified way, in his subsequent writings.

One of the main differences between *Les rapports de système* and later works is that in the former Kelsen makes explicit where the foundations of his conception of the supremacy of international law can be found: in the idea of *civitas maxima*. The state, *strictu sensu*, is the World State that will emerge, since there is no difference in kind between international and municipal law, but only a difference in terms of degree, the state being more evolved. Referring to the 'juridical unity of humanity' and its 'temporary' division in states, Kelsen stressed that *civitas maxima* is 'the political core [noyau] of the hypothesis of the primacy of international law'. For objectivist legal theory, he added, the 'notion of law is identical to that of international law'; at the same time, and for this very reason, it is a 'moral notion'. For him, international law *is* already a *civitas maxima*.[19]

The ethical dimension in Kelsen's defense of the supremacy of international law is still more evident when he proposes the elimination of the notion of sovereignty. Noticing that it is 'the revolution in social conscience' that really matters, the elimination of the notion of sovereignty must be defended not only 'for the love of a juridical construction'

[17] See the reading of Massimo La Torre and Cristina García Pascual, 'La utopia realista de Hans Kelsen' in Hans Kelsen, *La Paz por medio del Derecho*, 2nd edn (Madrid, Trotta, 2008) 9, 23. More explicitly, see Agustin E Ferraro, 'Kelsen's Highest Moral Ideal' (2002) 3 *German Law Journal*, available at www.germanlawjournal.com/index.php?pageID=11&artID=200. Ferraro advances such interpretation more thoroughly in Agustin E Ferraro, 'Kelsen y la ética universalista' (1998) 21-II *Doxa* 129.

[18] See the Italian translation: Hans Kelsen, *Il problema della sovranità e la teoria del diritto internazionale* (Milano, Giuffrè, 1989) 355.

[19] Hans Kelsen, 'Les rapports de système entre le droit interne et le droit international public' (1926-IV) 14 *Recueil des Cours* 227, 325.

but also because it is an obstacle to transforming the international community into a *civitas maxima*. Here, he emphasises that social change and legal theories come together and that the 'moral superiority' of legal objectivism is founded in a concern for the organisation of the world by means of international law.[20]

The expression *civitas maxima* disappeared from Kelsen's later major works. Some commentators say that this happened because he realised how ambiguous and idealistic it sounded.[21] World War II and his condition of *émigré* in the United States, it seems, compelled Kelsen to make his ideas about a *civitas maxima* more flexible and practical. If in *Les rapports de système*, he criticised the skepticism of the *civitas maxima* as an attempt to 'measure a theory' by 'political ends',[22] he needed to consider political reality in his theory in order to be taken seriously in a world suffering because of the tragedy of war. In *Peace Through Law*, Kelsen intends to do so.

The sometimes neglected preface of the book reveals how the political reality affected the author and how international law should be an instrument of a broad ethical purpose: the building of peaceful relations among nations. He argues that war is 'mass murder, the greatest disgrace of our culture, and that to secure world peace is our foremost political task, a task much more important than the decision between democracy and autocracy, or capitalism and socialism'.[23] It is interesting to contrast this statement to another made in the last paragraph of his Hague Academy lectures: '[t]he organisation of the World into a universal State ought to be the ultimate end, still far indeed, of every political effort'.[24] The statements are really close in meaning, except for the substitution of the World State, the *civitas maxima*, for peace.

Nevertheless, this move did not mean the abandonment of the idea of the World State. The main premise of Kelsen's book seems to be that since a World State is not possible under the then political situation, peace could be achieved only through the development and the sophistication of international legal mechanisms already existent at that time. For him, a durable peace 'can be sought only within the framework of international law—that it is to say, by an organisation which, in the degree of its centralisation, does not exceed that of the usual type of international communities'.[25] But that is a second-best option, since '[t]here can be no doubt that the ideal solution of the problem of world organisation as the problem of world peace is the establishment of a World Federal State'.[26]

The book rarely touches upon the issue of the relationship between international and municipal law. However, it represents a significant transition in Kelsen's international legal thinking. From then on, he would continue to defend the supremacy of international law, but avoid mentioning notions such as *civitas maxima*, World State, or the 'moral superiority' of monism with the prevalence of international law. This is exemplified by the publication, in 1945, of his *General Theory of Law and State*. In this book, Kelsen approached the prevalence of national or international law still as an ethical and political problem involving two cognitive theories: objectivism (associated with pacifism and

[20] ibid, 326.

[21] Charles Leben, 'Hans Kelsen and the Advancement of International Law' (1998) 9 *European Journal of International Law* 287, 295.

[22] Kelsen, 'Les rapports', 319.

[23] Hans Kelsen, *Peace through Law* (Chapel Hill, University of North Carolina Press, 1944) viii.

[24] Kelsen, 'Les rapports', 326.

[25] ibid, 12.

[26] ibid, 5.

the prevalence of international law) and subjectivism (related to imperialism and the prevalence of national law).[27] If it is true that, even in his writings of the 1920s, Kelsen associated the prevalence of international law with the objectivist cognitive theory, in his *General Theory of Law and State*, he tried to purge the idealism he could be accused of by defending the existence or the emergence of a *civitas maxima*.

Despite his attempt to 'refine' the Pure Theory of Law, purging from it ethical considerations, clearly, he did not succeed. As is well known, Kelsen said that both kinds of monism—with the prevalence of international law on one side and the prevalence of municipal law on the other—were admitted by his theory. Opting for one monism was an ethical or political choice, supposedly outside the realm of Law. However, the free choice was only apparent, since advocating for the prevalence of municipal law is useless in conceiving the idea of international law as such. One of Kelsen's main efforts was to prove that international law really existed. To do that, he had no option: he needed to choose the prevalence of international law.[28]

Hence, it is possible to say that the supremacy of international law, as supported by Kelsen, was merely a consequence of a deep ethical conviction on the unity of law (and humankind) in a single state (*civitas maxima*). Even after his attempt to make this point less evident in his theory, it remained one of its basic foundations.

B. Hersch Lauterpacht: International Law as Transition to a World State

Different from Kelsen, Hersch Lauterpacht was proud of conceiving his system of law as a derivation of ethical concerns. He considered himself a monist, but in a different way from his former teacher at the University of Vienna. In any case, his monism is also grounded in a deep ethical conception.

In a study dated 1932 and later incorporated in perhaps his most influential book, *The Function of Law in the International Community*, Lauterpacht clearly showed that posture. By using the domestic analogy to analyse the nature of international law, he contended that authors should not characterise international law as a law of a primitive society. In his view, this perspective inhibited change and progress in international law and also sanctioned 'its imperfections'.[29] Instead of looking to the past, international lawyers must look, he adds, to the future and predict what international law will become: a World State. If they do this, they will realise that international law is only 'incomplete and in a state of transition'.[30]

The idea of the transition of international law to a World state exerted a great influence on Lauterpacht's most systematic study on monism and dualism: his course at The Hague Academy of International Law, in 1937. Lauterpacht's monism was, in his own words, 'qualified by dualism'. Like other international lawyers of that time, he regarded international law as 'the superior and comprehensive legal order of which the systems of national jurisprudence are in a real sense delegated

[27] Hans Kelsen, *General Theory of Law and State* (Cambridge, Harvard University Press, 1945) 386.

[28] For this very good point, see Agustin E Ferraro, 'Kelsen y la ética universalista' (1998) 21-II *Doxa* 129.

[29] Hersch Lauterpacht, 'The Nature of International Law and General Jurisprudence' in Elihu Lauterpacht (ed) *International Law: Being the Collected Papers of Hersch Lauterpacht. Vol. 2: The Law of Peace* (Cambridge, Cambridge University Press, 1975) 3, 20.

[30] ibid, 19.

systems of law'.[31] At the same time, he tried to distance himself from other monists, admitting that his monism was not always consistent, since it was deduced 'from the actual practice of states and judicial tribunals'[32] and contradictions exist in practice (leading to the separation and not to the unity of legal systems). He summarises, in a very clear way, stating that '[j]ust as international law is at present an imperfect law in a stage of transition to true law, so its monistic structure is not absolute and thoroughgoing'.[33] This imperfection was shown, for example, in the need for treaties to be transformed in English municipal law and the lack of supremacy of international law in several domestic laws.[34]

But those contradictions seen in practice did not shake the supremacy of international law, from Lauterpacht's perspective. He visualised a future in which states would not enact any legislation (including constitutional legislation) contrary to international legal rules. This would happen 'when history has once more entered upon a stage of consciously strengthening international law'.[35] Lauterpacht overtly admitted history has a *telos*: the transition of international law into a true law, with the law of the state's being a model for this purpose. As a result, dualism's interference in the supremacy of international law is only provisional, existing only in the confines of domestic law; for international law, municipal law remains subordinated.

Lauterpacht's later works would deal only sporadically with the debate between monists and dualists. One possible explanation for this disengagement with the theories is that his *oeuvre* shows a turn from the theoretical liberal effort of conceiving international law as the image of the liberal State to a legal pragmatism far from theory and doctrine, something that would be vehemently celebrated by post-World-War-Two international lawyers.[36] But this turn to pragmatism did not happen abruptly.

For instance, in his most lengthy study on the relationship between international and municipal law, *Is International Law Part of the Law of England?*, originally published in 1939, Lauterpacht tried to avoid engaging in the debate on the theories. His intention was to prove empirically, rather than theoretically, that the rule of international law's being part of the law of the land helped to affirm the supremacy of international law over municipal law. But he still committed himself to monism while considering that 'the universal law of the *civitas maxima* [international law] is part and parcel of the law administered by the courts'.[37]

The defense of a World State and the proposition that international law is a transition stage to that state would reappear in a very dense study, written during World War II, but only circulated to a small audience, *The Reality of the Law of Nations*. When questioned about the purpose of the Law of Nations, he stated that there were five, the last being:

[31] Hersch Lauterpacht, 'General Rules of the Law of Peace' in Elihu Lauterpacht (ed) *International Law: Being the Collected Papers of Hersch Lauterpacht. Vol. 1: General Works* (Cambridge, Cambridge University Press, 1970) 179, 213.

[32] ibid, 214.

[33] ibid, 214.

[34] ibid, 225.

[35] ibid, 229.

[36] For this interpretation, see Martti Koskenniemi, 'Lauterpacht: The Victorian Tradition in International Law' (1997) 8 *European Journal of International Law* 215, 261.

[37] Lauterpacht, 'Is International Law Part of the Law of England?' in Elihu Lauterpacht (ed) *International Law. Vol 2*, 537, 549.

> [T]he creation of the conditions and institutions calculated to bring about the transition to the realisable and certainly not infinite ideal of the Federation of the World conceived as a commonwealth of autonomous States exercising full internal independence, rendered both just and secure by the power of the impersonal sovereignty of the *civitas maxima*.[38]

At the same time, he showed a significant lack of hope in international legal science, for it was not capable of 'hasten[ing] the development' of international law. Instead, international practice should be the main aim of international lawyers for change to happen.[39]

In a similar vein, in a very influential article, *The Grotian Tradition in International Law*, published in 1946, Lauterpacht ascribes to Grotius (or the Grotian tradition) a concern for the unity of law—its being international the most important part—and the idea that the development of international law would render it 'a true system of law both in its legal and in its ethical content'.[40]

Finally, in a manuscript only published after his death—a revised edition of *Oppenheim's International Law*—Lauterpacht not only refused to deal in a more thorough way with the theories but also disqualified them as 'unreal' and with 'no practical consequences'. He makes a clear division between the practical and doctrinal aspects of the issue of 'international law and the law of the State' and stresses that his concerns lay in the former.[41] This position may sound strange for someone so involved with theory in previous works. Still even from a 'practical' point of view, he continues to profess a monism with the prevalence of international law in the following pages of the chapter. In any case, this is the point where his turn to pragmatism regarding the relationship between international and municipal law seems to be complete, although monism is still behind many of his arguments.

C. Georges Scelle: World Federal State

Starting from different premises than those of Kelsen and Lauterpacht, Georges Scelle came to similar conclusions on the relationship between international and municipal law. For him, monism and, consequently, the supremacy of international law could both be found empirically because solidarity was the key to understanding any kind of legal system, be it primitive (international law) or well developed (state law). For him, ethics plays a role in conceiving the relationship between international and domestic law because it conditions the development of legal structures and propels the emergence of a world federation.

[38] Lauterpacht, 'The Reality of the Law of Nations' in Elihu Lauterpacht (ed) *International Law. Vol. 2*, 22, 47.

[39] ibid, 44.

[40] Hersch Lauterpacht, 'The Grotian Tradition in International Law' (1946) 23 *British Yearbook of International Law* 1, 18.

[41] Lauterpacht, 'International Law—The General part' in Elihu Lauterpacht (ed) *International Law. Vol. 1*, 1, 151. In the editor's note to the piece, Sir Elihu Lauterpacht mentions that in the original table of contents of the chapter there was a section entitled 'The So-Called Monistic and Dualistic Doctrine'. However, no manuscript or typescript copy was found. Owing to his turn to pragmatism, we might conjecture whether Lauterpacht really wished to include this section on the chapter—maybe he changed his mind.

Scelle's theory of federalism at the international level occupies a central role in many of his writings before World War II. Here, I will briefly focus on two of his most representative and influential written works.

In his *Précis de Droit des Gens*, Scelle develops a whole theory to explain why solidarity stimulates the development of both domestic and international law. At the very foundation of his thinking lies the idea that social fact creates solidarity, in other words, links between human beings.[42] This is something no one can avoid. However, solidarity may threaten the organisation of society if it has no constraints. Law comes from the need to establish those constraints. In this sense, it is natural, or biological. In his own words, law is 'a social imperative reflecting a necessity born from the natural solidarity'.[43] Hence, he concludes that law has only one source: solidarity.[44]

Given the fact that solidarity is not restricted to a single nation as it is impossible for a society to remain isolated, Scelle believes that notions such as sovereignty cannot persist, for they create the idea of a legal subject with unrestrained competences. Similarly to Kelsen, he states that if sovereignty exists, it can be found only within the 'global human society'.[45]

Using the domestic analogy, Scelle advocated that in political societies, including domestic and international law, three functions exist: legislative, judicial, and executive. Once again, like Kelsen (and Lauterpacht), Scelle insisted that such functions can sometimes be seen in a confused way due to the degree of evolution of each political society. This gave him the background to explain why those functions were not so well separated in international law as they were in domestic law.[46]

The concept of legal personality, in Scelle's theory, has a strong connection with the relationship between international and municipal law.[47] If solidarity permeates the frontiers among states, the true subjects of international law are the same in international and municipal law: the individuals. 'An international society is a collectivity of individuals, legal subjects, which already belong to national societies'. In other words, individuals belong, at the same time, to national societies, but also to a broader society, the 'human society'.[48] This led Scelle to maintain that municipal law and international law are only two categories of a broader inter-social universal law. The relationship among different societies was what he called 'pure or inorganic legal federalism', something that normally evolved slowly. In such a scheme, the law existent within a nation state should be adapted to be in conformity with the law that exists among the different societies. In other words, municipal law is, for Scelle, necessarily subordinated to international law. The monistic unity of law and the superiority of international law to municipal law were, thus, guaranteed in Scelle's theory.

[42] Georges Scelle, *Précis de droit des gens: Principes et systématique. Tome I* (Paris, Sirey, 1932) 2. It is well known that Scelle's theory of international law paid a huge tribute to León Duguit's ideas, as he admits in one of his most important articles. See Georges Scelle, 'La doctrine de L. Duguit et les fondements du droit des gens' (1932) 1-2 *Archives de Philosophie du droit et de Sociologie Juridique* 83. The influence of sociological jurisprudence in Scelle's works is intelligently discussed in Janne Elisabeth Nijman, *The Concept of International Legal Personality: An Inquiry into the History and Theory of International Law* (The Hague, TMC Asser Press, 2004) 192.

[43] Scelle, *Précis I*, 3.

[44] ibid, 6.

[45] ibid, 14.

[46] ibid, 18.

[47] Some authors argue that the distinctiveness of Scelle's monism lay in its connection with the issue of international legal personality. See Nijman, *The Concept*, 222.

[48] Scelle, *Précis I*, 28.

However, Scelle's monism was not primarily based upon logic, but on social facts. Scelle qualified his monism differently from the version supported by Kelsen. Indeed, he criticises the latter for not paying due attention to realities—a critique already posed by dualists. He opposed the strict distinction between is (*sein*) and ought (*sollen*), proposed by Kelsen, because a legal norm is a 'conscious deduction from the laws of the phenomenal world'.[49]

One year after the publication of his *Précis*, Scelle was invited to lecture at The Hague Academy of International Law. His course, entitled *Règles Générales du Droit de la Paix*, is, in many aspects, a summary of the ideas contained in *Précis*, although, sometimes, in a clearer way. However, that piece seems to contain a strident urgency in the development of international law into world federalism. More than once, Scelle highlights the year 1933 as a historical moment in which sovereignty and national interest were prioritised over international law.[50]

Scelle perseveres on the idea that States are only national divisions of the global international society, in the same way that States are divisions of a federation. But there is no such a thing as a society of States. Even at the international level, society is composed of individuals, 'and nothing more than individuals'.[51] Furthermore, there is no difference in kind between national societies and the international society. Every group within a nation state is, at the same time, within the international sphere. For him, the international phenomenon is not a 'degradation' of the state phenomenon, but an 'integration' of it, since it leads to a social shape that is above the states and 'ends in a Federal State'.[52] This is what he called social monism, which led to legal monism.[53]

International legal rules, in Scelle's view, prevail over domestic rules. Such supremacy comes from the fact that the international legal system is an inter-social legal system that is superposed to State legal orders. Hence, that inter-social legal order (international law) governs or automatically conditions the underlying legal orders (municipal laws).[54] But for him, monism has less to do with the subordination of domestic laws to international law than with 'absorption' of State laws into international law. According to him, '[m]onism is more fusion than hierarchy'.[55] The domestic analogy runs deep in Scelle's conception of monism. For him, the historical process of absorption of States into a federal structure, in which a gradual centralisation occurs, leaving to States several issues to regulate, can also be used to explain the relationship among different social orders, be they international or national.[56]

Scelle's federalism is also influenced by a conception of progress. For him, in every single inter-social phenomenon appears, at the same time, what he called pure federalism or legal federalism, that is, the relationship among different legal orders that already exists. But such federalism will be transformed into an institutional or constructive legal federalism in the future,[57] leading to world federal structures.

[49] ibid, 40.
[50] Georges Scelle, 'Règles générales du droit de la paix' (1933-IV) 46 *Recueil des Cours* 331, 332.
[51] ibid, 343.
[52] ibid, 345.
[53] ibid, 346.
[54] ibid, 350.
[55] ibid, 353.
[56] ibid, 352.
[57] ibid, 355.

In the end of his Hague Academy lectures, Scelle gives an explicit account of how ethics played an important role in his ideas. He argues that notions such as justice and morals were not at the foundations of law; they were one of the factors that conditioned its very existence, in the sense of being psychological conditions to social biology, something that was regulated by law.[58] Putting ethics at the foundations of law would certainly distance his theory from social facts.

For Scelle, due to the idea of solidarity, the unity of international and municipal law was not something someone could choose; it sits in a dimension that is previous to the act of choosing: it is necessary and even inevitable.[59] Nevertheless, the building of an institutional or constructive federalism demanded from international lawyers care and a high sense of morality. Only making such an ethical choice would enable them to tie the emergence of one law to the regulation of a global society.

After the end of World War II, Scelle's writings would become increasingly distant from theory and significantly more pragmatic. However, his ideas about federalism and the relationship between international and domestic law would remain basically untouched.[60]

IV. CONCLUSION

New versions of dualism are popular because of dualism's explanatory force and supposed closeness to reality. Clearly, international law cannot fall into the realm of idealism. This would be irresponsible in the face of so many problems that afflict the globe today. On the other hand, the act of describing and providing answers to a given world, with no perspectives of change, is too reductionist to the role of lawyers as political participants. Many scholars seem to have lost that critical sense that, throughout history, has helped to forge notions such as freedom and equality. The reactions of many to the European Court of Justice judgment in *Kadi*, for example, were to adapt their theories or to attack old concepts in international law in the name of a reality that is not yet fixed. If the content of fundamental rights are well defined in Europe (something not at all evident!), there are many struggles to define them on a global scale. In case of conflict, should international law succumb only to European fundamental rights? These and other questions could be posed. The main point is that international lawyers cannot be hostages of a given reality. Paradoxically, while defending a plurality of (legal) orders, many dualist arguments became fixed about the idea of how to order the relationship among orders. What is right or just became, in the minds of many dualists, something to be found only within the boundaries of a given order.

The monist message that persists is not that international law is coherent, united, or well ordered; it is that a different world is possible. It is possible in the shape of a *civitas maxima*, a federation, or any other institutional design. Kelsen, Lauterpacht, and Scelle's theories seem, at present, to be relics from the time when everything could be achieved

[58] ibid, 692.

[59] R J Dupuy argues that, for Scelle, the primacy of a given norm exists in order to 'give satisfaction to a social need felt by a vaster society'. At the same time, he recognises that, for Scelle, law is a conjunction of ethics and power. René-Jean Dupuy, 'Images de Georges Scelle' (1990) 1 *European Journal of International Law* 235, 237.

[60] For a brief biography of Scelle and a list of his publications, see Antonio Tanca, 'Georges Scelle (1878–1961). Biographical note with bibliography' (1990) 1 *European Journal of International Law* 240.

by the power of reason and progress would one day come, no matter what. But they also experienced a great deal of discomfort in terms of the organisation of the world. They imagined and protested because the suffering of the war was too painful. It does not matter whether they were right. All that matters is that they said in their writings that something was not right about the world.

When Kelsen, Lauterpacht, and Scelle spoke about monism, they were also speaking about a constitutional mindset. For them, international law was primarily a project of change, and it seems clear that they, in different ways, believed that

> spiritual perfection prepares a constitutionalist mindset from which to judge the world in a manner that aims for universality, impartiality, and all the virtues of the 'inner morality of law': honesty, fairness, concern for others, the prohibition of deceit, injury, and coercion.[61]

As stated before, the most important legacy of monism lies not in the idea of coherence, hierarchy, or even supremacy of international law, but in its treatment of the world as an open reality for different projects. Instead of overcoming the debate between monism and dualism, international lawyers should carefully examine it. Forgetting cannot be allowed if we care about the present and the future. Yes, monism must be alive!

[61] Martti Koskenniemi, 'Constitutionalism as Mindset: Reflections on Kantian Themes about International Law and Globalization' (2007) 8 *Theoretical Inquiries in Law* 9, 33.

12

Domestic Courts as the 'Natural Judge' of International Law: A Change in Physiognomy

ANTONIOS TZANAKOPOULOS*

I. INTRODUCTION

INTERNATIONAL LAW IS a decentralised legal system: very few institutions have been established to control law creation, law interpretation, law application and law enforcement. The institutions that do exist are found mainly in sectoral regimes. In view of what is perceived as an 'inherent weakness' of international law, namely the lack of central (and thus robust) law application and law enforcement machinery, a claim was made early on and repeated occasionally, that domestic courts could (and should) step in and fill the void by 'doubling' as international (judicial) organs, when called upon to adjudicate claims under international law.[1] For many decades this remained a largely unrealised possibility. A number of 'avoidance techniques' were devised by domestic courts to evade international law questions,[2] which they viewed as more properly within the ambit of the executive; the executive is, in the final analysis, the actor charged in most (if not all) domestic legal systems with the conduct of foreign affairs.[3]

* Lecturer in International Law, University of Glasgow [antonios.tzanakopoulos@glasgow.ac.uk]. This is a first take on what is hoped to evolve into a full-length article. Comments are welcome and may be directed to the address above. Many thanks are due to Professors Christian Tams and George Pavlakos, as well as to the participants in Agora 12 of the 4th ESIL Biennial Conference. The usual disclaimer applies.

[1] See eg Y Shany, 'No Longer a Weak Department of Power? Reflections on the Emergence of a New International Judiciary' (2009) 20 *EJIL* 73, 74–5; M Shah Alam, 'Enforcement of International Human Rights Law by Domestic Courts: A Theoretical and Practical Study' (2006) 53 *NILR* 399, 400; RA Falk, *The Role of Domestic Courts in the International Legal Order* (Syracuse, NY, Syracuse UP, 1964) xi. This is along the lines of Scelle's theory of dédoublement fonctionnel (on which more later on): *Précis de droit des gens* (vol II, Paris, Sirey, 1934) 10–12; see also generally Y Shany, 'National Courts as International Actors: Jurisdictional Implications' (2008–2009; available at www.ssrn.com) 13 ff.

[2] See generally E Benvenisti, 'Judicial Misgivings Regarding the Application of International Law: An Analysis of Attitudes of National Courts' (1993) 4 *EJIL* 159; on the same or similar devices being used by courts to avoid review of acts of international organisations see for a summary A Reinisch, *International Organizations before National Courts* (Cambridge, CUP, 2000) 391.

[3] Cf draft article 9(3) as proposed by Special Rapporteur GG Fitzmaurice in his First Report on the Law of Treaties (1956) II *YILC* 104, 109 and commentary at 118–19 for an example of the primary role reserved to the executive branch.

However, domestic courts are increasingly engaging with the interpretation and application of international law, according less deference to the executive in relevant matters. A number of scholars have pointed this out, most usually justifying it as a necessary consequence of the increased interdependence of states, and of the extension of the scope of international law, most crucially with respect to the granting of rights to individuals.[4] Empirical evidence may lend some support to this assumption: *Oxford Reports on International Law in Domestic Courts*, for example, was live in 2010 with over 700 cases, another 900 awaiting publication, from almost 100 jurisdictions, starting with cases decided since 2000 only.[5] Even though much more thorough empirical research would be required in order to prove conclusively that domestic courts are now increasingly engaging with international law, this is the assumption on which the following rests.

The aim of this chapter is to consider whether domestic courts can indeed be said to constitute the 'natural judges' of international law (section II). If so, and if domestic courts are indeed taking up their role as natural judges of international law in practice (section III), then this will have significant repercussions on the physiognomy of international law (section IV). In that, the chapter assumes a by-and-large well-functioning, independent, and impartial domestic judiciary, operating within a legal order which establishes the separation of powers, introduces checks and balances in their exercise, and ensures respect for judicial decisions.

II. THE 'NATURAL JUDGE' OF INTERNATIONAL LAW

In the endeavour to determine whether domestic courts are meant to be the 'natural judge' of international law, the first task is to define this notion of 'natural judge'. The term is not employed here in the sense of 'legal' or 'lawful' judge as this is known in some civil law jurisdictions, ie the judge provided for by law.[6] This latter principle aims to curb removal of cases from one particular jurisdiction (within one state) to another (within the same state), eg the *ad hoc* removal of cases from the ordinary courts to another court, tribunal, or committee that did not originally have jurisdiction to deal with the particular dispute.

The term is rather employed in what could be called its Benthamite sense of the 'immediate' or 'ordinary judge', ie the judge that will necessarily have first contact with a case and who can be removed only through a centrally instituted judge.[7] If international law does not centrally institute any judge, it remains to be seen whether it is domestic courts that should be deemed the 'natural', 'immediate', or 'ordinary' judges of international law.

[4] See eg E Benvenisti and GW Downs, 'National Courts, Domestic Democracy, and the Evolution of International Law (2009) 20 *EJIL* 59, 62; Shany, 'International Actors', 1; as well as the presentation by C Espósito, 'Rising Expectations on the Role of National Judges in the Promotion of Global Justice: An Appraisal' in Forum 5 of the 4th ESIL Biennial Conference (3 September 2010).

[5] Hereinafter: ILDC; available at www.oxfordlawreports.com.

[6] See eg Article 8 of the Greek Constitution; Article 101(1) of the German Grundgesetz; cf Article 25(1) of the Italian Constitution.

[7] See J Bentham, 'Draught of a Code for the Organization of the Judicial Establishment in France' in *The Works of Jeremy Bentham* (vol 4, Edinburgh, William Tait, 1843) Title V § 1 Articles I–III. The term seems to have been employed in this sense by the Swiss Federal Tribunal in *Librairie Hachette v Société Coopérative* (1967) reported in 72 ILR 78, 80–1.

A. Interpretation and Application of International Law

International law does not centrally institute any judge. In the decentralised international legal system, the *prima facie* arbiter of legality of its own and anyone else's conduct is the state itself. Both arbitral tribunals,[8] and the ICJ[9] have recognised this power of auto-interpretation of states, which has been characterised as 'one of the most general principles of international law'.[10]

The power of states to determine for themselves their legal situation is a necessary corollary of the lack of compulsory, centralised law determination in the international legal system. This power can only be *completely* abolished through the introduction of third party disinterested determination of the merits of disputes.[11] The addressees of most legal rules are the states. They necessarily interpret the rules themselves in the first instance,[12] they determine the existence of a breach and decide on potential responses.

The power of auto-determination comes at a price: states exercise it at their own risk. States put forward suggestions as to the interpretation of a legal rule and its application in a specific case—but their suggestions are only that, suggestions; they are not determinative of the actual position under international law. Only an organ empowered by law authentically to interpret and apply the law can finally determine the position under the law. In the decentralised system of general international law, this organ will usually be a virtual, composite organ, made up of—at least two—states.[13] Yet in the absence of a decision of this virtual organ (for lack of agreement, for example) and in the absence of a centrally instituted disinterested third party to resolve the dispute, then the first instance, where the power of auto-interpretation and auto-determination is exercised by states at their own risk, becomes *de facto* also the last.

[8] See *Air Services* (1978) 18 RIAA 417, 443 [81]: 'each State establishes for itself its legal situation vis-à-vis other States'; *Lac Lanoux* (1957) 12 RIAA 281, 310 [16]: 'il appartient à chaque État d'apprécier, raisonnablement et de bonne foi, les situations et les règles qui le mettent en cause'. See also H Kelsen, *Reine Rechtslehre* 2nd edn (Vienna, Franz Deuticke, 1960) 324.

[9] See eg *Hostages* [1980] ICJ Rep 3, 28 [53]; *Reservations* [1951] ICJ Rep 15, 26; *Nicaragua* [1986] ICJ Rep 14, 134 [268].

[10] *Lac Lanoux*, 1957, 310 [16].

[11] Cf H Lauterpacht, *The Development of International Law by the International Court* (London, Stevens and Sons, 1958) 159; JL Brierly, 'Sanctions' (1932) 17 *Transactions of the Grotius Society* 67, 70–1. See also P Malanczuk, 'Zur Repressalie im Entwurf der International Law Commission zur Staatenverantwortlichkeit' (1985) 45 *ZaöRV* 293, 296. Cf the WTO AB in *Canada—Continued Suspension* [2008] WT/DS321/AB/R [371]. In the law of treaties, it has been noted that the only alternative to an agreement of the parties (as to the existence of invalidity of a treaty or to the bringing about its termination or suspension) is the 'sentence d'un juge international': F Capotorti, 'L'extinction et la suspension des traités' (1971) 134 *RdC* 417, 564; cf A Tzanakopoulos, 'Article 67' in O Corten and P Klein (eds), *The Vienna Conventions on the Law of Treaties* (Oxford, OUP, 2011) 1546, 1551–5.

[12] Cf G Abi-Saab, '"Interprétation" et "Auto-Interprétation"—Quelques réflexions sur leur rôle dans la formation et la résolution du différend international' in U Beyerlin (ed), *Recht zwischen Umbruch und Bewahrung—Festschrift für Rudolf Bernhardt* (Berlin, Springer, 1995) 9, 14–15; generally J Pauwelyn, *Conflict of Norms in Public International Law* (Cambridge, CUP, 2003) 93: 'norms of international law are seldom "finished products", simply requiring implementation'.

[13] At the very least, the concurring will of another state is required for a bilateral obligation to be created. In this sense, the organ of the international community competent to create, determine, and apply law is a *composite* organ, made up—on occasion—of at least two states (or their competent representatives), but a *unitary* organ still: H Kelsen, *Allgemeine Staatslehre* (Berlin, Springer, 1925) 174–5. This is in line with the 'established principle' enunciated by the PCIJ that a rule can be authoritatively interpreted only by the one who can amend or repeal it: *Jaworzina* [1923] PCIJ Ser B No 8 at 37.

Still this is a far cry from bringing in domestic courts as the natural judges of international law: it rather shows the state to be the natural or immediate judge. The state is, from the perspective of international law, a unitary entity. Courts are organs of the state, and may as such partake in the exercise of the power of auto-interpretation. But most domestic legal orders will reserve this power to the executive, which is given wide discretion in conducting the state's foreign affairs, deciding against which foreign state to bring a claim and against which foreign state to respond.

B. The 'Directionality' of International Obligations

The brief exposition above obviously does not render a complete picture. One must also take into account the 'directionality' of the international obligations assumed by states, as this has consequences for the position of domestic courts. What is meant by 'directionality' is whether a given international obligation addresses the state with respect to its actions towards other states, ie whether it prescribes or proscribes certain conduct exclusively on the international level, or whether it addresses the state with respect to taking certain conduct or guaranteeing certain results within its domestic jurisdiction. In the former instance the international obligation is 'extrovert' or 'outward-looking': it addresses the state in its conduct on the international level towards other states. In the latter it is 'introvert' or 'inward-looking', it mandates conduct within the domestic jurisdiction. The prohibition of the use of force and the prohibition of intervention are obvious examples of outward-looking obligations, while obligations under human rights law, or under the law of immunity, are inward-looking obligations.

The characterisation either way does not necessarily affect the synallagmatic (ie based on the notion of reciprocity) or non-synallagmatic character of the obligation: an outward-looking obligation will usually be synallagmatic, but an inward-looking one could just as easily be either. Human rights obligations are non-synallagmatic for example, whereas obligations under BITs, or WTO obligations, or those under the law of immunity, are synallagmatic. This character of the obligation is still important. It aims to clarify that though inward-looking, an obligation may still retain a horizontal, in parallel to its vertical character: ie it may at the same time create rights for individuals *and* regulate relations between states.[14]

Most international obligations at the beginning of the twentieth century, and up to and including the UN Charter, were primarily outward-looking. One can think of the laws of war and neutrality, the law of the sea, or the prohibition of force and intervention. Few rules directly penetrated the protective veil of domestic jurisdiction, primarily those referring to the treatment of aliens and the law of immunity. However, many obligations assumed since then have tended to be inward-looking: this includes a vast array of human rights obligations both under customary law and under relevant treaties,[15] and a great number of other obligations which require state action within the

[14] Cf for the terminology D Schloss, 'Treaty Enforcement in Domestic Courts: A Comparative Analysis' in idem (ed) *The Role of Domestic Courts in Treaty Enforcement—A Comparative Study* (Cambridge, CUP, 2009) 1, 6. An example of an inward-looking, synallagmatic obligation that has been found by the ICJ to create an individual right is that of consular notification under Article 36(1) VCCR: see *LaGrand* [2001] ICJ Rep 466, 494 [77]; *Avena* [2004] ICJ Rep 12, 35–6 [40].

[15] See C Tomuschat, *Human Rights—Between Idealism and Realism* 2nd edn (Oxford, OUP, 2008) 110–12.

domestic jurisdiction: obligations under the law of international trade, obligations under international environmental law, obligations for the prosecution and punishment of international crimes, the elimination of international terrorism or the non-proliferation of weapons of mass destruction (including those imposed by the Security Council by means of Chapter VII resolutions) and others.

The distinction between these two types of obligations, based on their 'directionality', is important. Outward-looking obligations, intended to be fulfilled at the international level in the conduct towards other states, will rarely give rise to a claim before the domestic courts of a state.[16] They are intended to limit the state in the conduct of its international relations, but it will be difficult for claimants to either establish the requisite standing (showing sufficient 'legal interest') or to convince the court to intervene in what has traditionally been seen as the prerogative of the executive. Outward-looking international obligations are not typically translated into claimable rights in the domestic legal order.

Inward-looking obligations, on the other hand, obligations undertaken by the state with respect to its conduct within its domestic jurisdiction, are aimed either at limiting the power of the state to take measures that are to be implemented internally, or at obliging it to take such measures. The structure of an obligation as inward-looking can be seen as compensating for the lack of overarching institutional structure in international law: these obligations are incumbent upon all organs of the state, whether executive, legislative, or judicial. Looked at from within the state, however, and particularly from the perspective of individuals, state obligations limiting discretion or imposing conduct are primarily placed on the state's executive branch, which usually has both the legislative and executive initiative. Domestic courts have a reactive role in this connection: they are called upon to check that the executive is acting in compliance with the law.[17] That law includes international law, when international law places limitations or commands specific conduct.[18] Individuals may further derive rights from the international obligations assumed by the state. From their perspective then, whether the right that has been violated by executive action stems from international or domestic law is in the first instance irrelevant. From the perspective of domestic courts, in turn, entertaining the claim should be nothing unusual: it is their proper role to police the actions of political branches for compliance with the law.

It is then ordinary for individuals to bring claims against the state before domestic courts, when they perceive that their rights have been violated, or that the government has acted illegally within the domestic jurisdiction. Given that a vast array of international obligations nowadays are of the 'inward-looking' type, and given, further, that these obligations cover almost all aspects of contemporary life, many of them will fall to be considered by domestic courts.

C. The Obligations of Domestic Courts under International Law

The state is the natural judge of international law; and of all state organs, it is domestic courts that will usually be called upon to check the conformity of state conduct with

[16] Though they may be raised as a defence, as in *R v Jones (Margaret) and others* [2006] UKHL 16.

[17] To quote Lord Bingham, 'The Rule of Law' (2007) 66 *CLJ* 67, 78: 'The historic role of the courts has ... been to check excesses of the executive power ...'.

[18] Cf ibid 81–2; further idem, *The Rule of Law* (London, Allen Lane, 2010) 110 ff.

international law. Domestic courts are then *de facto* the immediate judges of international law. But are they also *de jure*?

An easy objection would be that international law itself is extremely dualist when it comes to its relationship with national legal orders: decisions of domestic courts are, like all of domestic law, mere facts on the international level.[19] Until however these facts fall to be decided as to their legality by a competent organ (as described above) they remain the final position on the application of a particular international rule by a given state.

Furthermore, even if it treats domestic court decisions as facts, international law indeed obliges domestic courts to entertain arguments under international law and apply international law to resolve disputes. As organs of the state, domestic courts must also fulfil the state's international obligations, while their non-compliance with an international rule will engage the state's international responsibility. Domestic courts will also be, usually, the last line of defence, the last opportunity for the state to comply with an international obligation.

This is evident in 'an important principle of customary international law',[20] namely the one requiring the exhaustion of local remedies before bringing international claims: when an inward-looking rule has been violated,[21] and when the claim is one to which the rule of exhaustion of local remedies applies,[22] the primary role in adjudicating a potential claim will rest with domestic courts. For the local remedies rule to be complied with, it is enough that the 'essence of the claim' has been brought before a domestic court 'without success'.[23] This makes the claim admissible on the international level, but does not mean that a violation has taken place: if the domestic court addresses the essence of the claim by applying in substance (and correctly) international law, then there will have been no violation.[24] This shows that the international legal order affords the state one last chance to avoid a breach, by directing the domestic court to apply—in substance—international law. In fact it demonstrates that states themselves, in having established the local remedies rule, have sought to reserve for their courts the final chance (for the unitary state) to comply with international law.[25] In that, the international legal order expressly acknowledges the domestic court as the ordinary judge of international law with respect to claims to which the local remedies rule applies.

[19] *Certain German Interests in Polish Upper Silesia* (Merits) [1926] PCIJ Ser A No 7 at 19. However, domestic court decisions can be argued to constitute, in appropriate circumstances, a secondary source of international law under Article 38(1)(d) ICJ Statute. Also, domestic court decisions constitute final authority for the application of an international rule that involves a *renvoi* to domestic law, such as Article 5(1) ECHR. Cf also *Barcelona Traction* [1970] ICJ Rep 3, 33–4 [38].

[20] *ELSI* [1989] ICJ Rep 15, 42 [50].

[21] The relationship between inward-looking rules and the local remedies rule is evident in that the rule does not apply in cases where the breach took place outside the jurisdiction of the state: cf NJ Udombana, 'So Far, so Fair: The Local Remedies Rule in the Jurisprudence of the African Commission on Human and Peoples' Rights' (2003) 97 *AJIL* 1, 6 with further references.

[22] The claims to which the local remedies rules apply are not necessarily limited to the sphere of diplomatic protection: cf ILC Commentary to Article 44(b) ASR at [4].

[23] *ELSI* (n 20) 46 [59]. Cf *Avena* (n 14) 35–6 [40].

[24] Cf *Norwegian Loans* [1957] ICJ Rep 9, 40–1 (sep op Lauterpacht).

[25] But see AA Cancado-Trindade, *The Application of the Rule of Exhaustion of Local Remedies in International Law* (Cambridge, CUP, 1983) 287, who argues that the rule has a 'negative' character in cases of diplomatic protection and a 'positive' one in the field of human rights. In the former instance it applies as a bar to the admissibility of the claim, in the latter as an inherent part of the system of protection.

The inverse proposition also exists, and further demonstrates that states themselves see their domestic court as the final opportunity to avoid a violation: US courts for example acknowledge a legal interest of the state to intervene in judicial proceedings between private parties, and even to appeal the decision of a lower court, where that decision would result in a breach of US international obligations.[26] This also shows that, even in situations where the local remedies rule does not apply, the court still remains obligated under international law to apply the substance of international rules in a case before it, otherwise it will put the state in breach.

D. Interim Conclusion

The international legal order then does not solely allow domestic courts to be the immediate or natural judge of international law; in fact it obligates them to be so if a question of international law falls to be decided by them. With many international rules today being inward-looking, they may be raised in domestic litigation not only by individuals, but also by the state itself. As such, the potential role of domestic courts as the immediate or ordinary judges of international law has increased over the last decades. The question is whether the courts have realised this potential.

III. DOMESTIC COURTS AND INTERNATIONAL LAW: BEYOND FORMALISM

The assumption in this paper is that domestic courts are increasingly 'warming up' to applying international law, even though they still exercise significant restraint in a number of circumstances. More importantly, the methods in which they apply international law are quite diverse and still to a large extent fluid, and are said to depend on the domestic legal order's provisions about its relationship with the international legal order.

A. Monism, Dualism and Consistent Interpretation

It can be argued that whether and to what extent a domestic court will allow itself to apply international law depends on whether domestic law adopts a monist or a dualist approach to the international legal order. In the former case the legal order is understood as unitary, and in some cases even as endorsing international law's claim to supremacy; thus the domestic court is (or should be) under a mandate to apply international law and perhaps to give precedence to it. In the latter case, the two legal orders are clearly separated, and the domestic court applies only domestic law, including foreign and international law that its domestic law directs it to apply.

In reality this distinction is more theoretical than real.[27] In fact it can be argued that there is not a single monist state in the world. Even those that consider themselves to be

[26] See eg *Tachiona v US* 386 F 3d 205 (2d Cir 2004); ILDC 1090 (US 2004).

[27] A reason is, for example, that the increasing permeability of the domestic legal orders to international regulatory effects has blurred the (supposedly clear) boundary between the domestic and the international legal order: Benvenisti and Downs, 'National Courts', 62; cf E Benvenisti, 'Reclaiming Democracy: The Strategic Uses of Foreign and International Law by National Courts' (2008) 102 *AJIL* 241, 245.

monist apply international law, even as supreme law, because they are directed by their constitution to do so.[28] And conversely, ardent dualist states accept a monist relationship between the domestic legal order and customary international law.[29] Furthermore, states will usually adopt domestic implementing acts to comply with inward-looking obligations, thus to an extent obliterating the need for considering the more remote source of the regulation, ie international law.[30] In any case, there is one method of applying international law by a domestic court that is completely independent of any theoretical anxieties about the adoption of a monist or dualist approach,[31] and even largely independent from provisions in domestic law. This is the method of consistent interpretation.

Domestic courts of many states apply international law primarily through consistent interpretation of their domestic law in cases before them, irrespective of whether the state is to be designated (or is self-designated) as monist or dualist.[32] In fact even the domestic courts of some of the most strictly dualist states have made international law applicable in their domestic legal orders by adopting a strong presumption of conformity of domestic law with international obligations of the state.[33] This requires that the court engage in consistent interpretation of all domestic law, so as to apply it without causing conflict with the state's international obligations.

The lengths to which the court will go in order to reconcile domestic law with international obligations vary. It has been argued for example that New Zealand's accession to the Optional Protocol to the ICCPR led its courts to establish an especially strong presumption of conformity that extends far beyond Covenant rights—while the accession of the UK to the ECHR had no similar effects on English law; rather it was through the HRA 1998 that a strong rule of consistent interpretation was established and this rule remained limited to Convention rights.[34] Still the HRA presumption has a parallel in the presumption that parliament did not intend to give the executive any authority to digress from constitutionally protected rights in the absence of explicit language or necessary implication.[35] It could be argued that this put parts of international law on par with UK constitutional law as far as domestic courts are concerned—in traditionally one of the world's most staunchly dualist states. Further, it should be pointed out that the

[28] Cf G Gaja, 'Dualism—a Review' in J Nijman and A Nollkaemper (eds), *New Perspectives on the Divide between National and International Law* (Oxford, OUP, 2007) 52–3; Shah Alam, 'Enforcement', 404. Cf P Capps 'The Court as Gatekeeper: Customary International Law in English Courts' (2007) 70 *MLR* 458, 463.

[29] See I Brownlie, *Principles of Public International Law* 7th edn (Oxford, OUP, 2008) 41 with further references; but see further Capps, 'Court as Gatekeeper', 458 ff.

[30] An example is the implementation of Security Council binding resolutions in domestic legal orders: see generally V Gowlland-Debbas 'Implementing Sanctions Resolutions in Domestic Law' in eadem (ed), *National Implementation of United Nations Sanctions—A Comparative Study* (The Hague, Martinus Nijhoff, 2004) 33 ff.

[31] In fact, as observed by Schloss, 'Treaty Enforcement', 8, there is little correlation between the monism-dualism dichotomy and the actual practice of domestic courts.

[32] G Betlem and A Nollkaemper, 'Giving Effect to Public International Law and European Community Law before Domestic Courts: A Comparative Analysis of the Practice of Consistent Interpretation' (2003) 14 *EJIL* 569, 571 and 574–5 with further references; Benvenisti, 'Reclaiming Democracy' 252. See also the comment by Judge Paulus in the discussion following the presentation by Espósito (mentioned at n 4), that the role of national judges is to 'fit' international requirements into their domestic legal order.

[33] Examples include the UK, Australia, Canada, India, New Zealand, Israel, and others.

[34] See P Sales & J Clement, 'International Law in Domestic Courts: the Developing Framework' (2008) 124 *LQR* 388, 393–4.

[35] See eg *R v Secretary of State ex p Pierson* [1998] AC 539, 573G and 575D (Lord Browne-Wilkinson); cf *R v Home Secretary ex p Simms* [2000] 2 AC 115, 131F (Lord Hoffman).

general trend of increased engagement with international law by domestic courts has not left English courts unimpressed.[36]

Be that as it may, the approach of the domestic courts of New Zealand demonstrates the power of domestic courts in transforming the domestic understanding of the relationship between international and domestic law, and of their own mandate to apply international law, through the adoption of a robust principle of consistent interpretation. This principle demonstrates a 'deep commitment' to apply international law.[37]

The adoption of a strong presumption of conformity and the concomitant principle of consistent interpretation furnishes the domestic court with a very elegant possibility to take up its role as the natural judge of international law. Claims at the international level become subsidiary, if they are available at all. This means that the international law question can effectively be raised and answered at the domestic level. When the outcome is deemed unsatisfactory, international procedures will be called upon to review the 'facts' (including potential decisions of the domestic court) and determine whether a breach of an international obligation has taken place. The process then at the international stage is merely subsidiary or supervisory; intervention will be limited to when the domestic process fails to address the issues appropriately and conform to the international obligation.[38] The situation that emerges is not unlike the one that exists in certain regional or sectoral regimes. In these, even though international courts or tribunals have been granted quasi-compulsory jurisdiction to deal with disputes,[39] they are in most cases in a subsidiary position to domestic courts,[40] who are the natural and ordinary judges of claims under the regime.

Application of international law by domestic courts through consistent interpretation does not only establish the domestic courts' position as the ordinary or natural judge of international law. It also has the potential to appease fears of usurpation of the powers of the (democratically legitimised) legislature to the extent that it does not allow for *contra legem* interpretation of domestic law.[41] The limits here are particularly fluid:

[36] In many cases during the 2000s, as for example *Kuwait Airways Corp v Iraqi Airways Co (Nos 4 and 5)* [2002] UKHL 19; *R (Campaign for Nuclear Disarmament) v Prime Minister* [2002] EWHC 2777 (Admin); *R (Abbasi and another) v Secretary of State for Foreign and Commonwealth Affairs* [2002] EWCA Civ 1598; *R v Jones* (n 16), English courts have allowed extensive international legal argument, when some years before the objection of non-justiciability would have prevailed without much discussion: see D Williams, 'Courts and Globalization' (2004) 11 *Indiana Journal of Global Legal Studies* 57, 62 and cf Capps, 'Court as Gatekeeper', 470 and fn 56; cf generally K Reece Thomas, 'The Changing Status of International Law in English Domestic Law' (2006) 53 *NILR* 371, 371 ff.

[37] Shany, 'International Actors', 10.

[38] Cf ibid 20–1.

[39] Quasi-compulsory because it is still dependent on state consent, but this is provided at the outset: it is part of a package deal, a condition for joining the relevant regional or sectoral regime. Such courts and tribunals are, for example, the ECtHR, the WTO Panels and AB, and also the EU courts (on the latter point cf C Leben, 'Hans Kelsen and the Advancement of International Law' (1998) 9 *EJIL* 287, 296–8; cf also Betlem and Nollkaemper, 'Consistent Interpretation', 582–4, who argue that the doctrines of direct and 'indirect' effect (as they call the principle of consistent interpretation) yield almost the same results and thus there is no fundamental divide between the application of international and EC law by Dutch courts: the difference is one of degree rather than one of kind).

[40] With the exception, eg, of the obligation of domestic courts to request interpretation by preliminary reference to the ECJ. As to the ECHR see M Villiger, 'The Principle of Subsidiarity in the European Convention on Human Rights' in MG Kohen (ed), *Promoting Justice, Human Rights and Conflict Resolution through International Law*—Liber Amicorum *Lucius Caflisch* (Leiden, Martinus Nijhoff, 2007) 623–37.

[41] Cf Betlem and Nollkaemper, 'Consistent Interpretation', 576–7; Benvenisti, 'Reclaiming Democracy', 241 with further references.

when is it that interpretation becomes amendment?[42] Different courts will draw their own line at different places.[43] But it is worth pointing out that the principle of consistent interpretation best reconciles the obligation of domestic courts to apply international law with their obligation to respect the separation of powers, blurry and fluid as this separation is itself.

B. The 'Dark Side' of the Rule of (International) Law

'Effectively enforced, law does not simply constrain power. It is also a source of power.'[44] Indeed domestic courts, in assuming their positions as the natural judges of international law, enhance its enforcement; in particular, by forsaking deference to the executive and applying international law, they use it as a sword against the executive, rather than the traditional shield that it used to be:[45] they use it to constrain the power of the executive.

But in international law it is the executive that mainly influences the development, and has the initiative for the assumption of international obligations and the adoption of international rules. If international law is the sword, rather than the shield, surely the sword cuts both ways. Executives have not missed the opportunity to use the sword themselves.

An excellent example is furnished by action taken within the framework of the UN Security Council as part of the response to the 'threat to the peace' that constitutes international terrorism. States, in particular those that have a leading role in the Council, faced with resistance from their domestic courts when trying to adopt wide-ranging restrictive measures against terrorists, used the powers granted to the Council under Chapter VII of the Charter. Under cover of Article 103, which guarantees precedence to obligations under the Charter, including those imposed by binding resolutions, they created and developed a sanctions regime that targeted individuals 'associated with' Al Qaida and the Taliban.[46]

The regime imposes an international obligation on UN member states to take wide-ranging restrictive measures against individuals designated by the Security Council (through a Sanctions Committee) without at any point giving them a meaningful and effective way of challenging their designation.[47] This is in violation of the well-established right to a fair trial, including the right of access to a court and the right to an effective remedy.[48] But domestic courts were, at first sight, powerless to react: the obligation, implemented by domestic acts, came straight from the Security Council. No treaty could be invoked in response: Article 103 precluded this.

[42] Cf Betlem and Nollkaemper, 'Consistent Interpretation', 584.

[43] See succinctly Lord Bingham, 'Rule of Law', 71 with further references.

[44] M Kumm, 'International Law in National Courts: The International Rule of Law and the Limits of the Internationalist Model' (2003–2004) 44 *Virginia Journal of International Law* 19, 27.

[45] Benvenisti, 'Reclaiming Democracy', 243.

[46] SCR 1267 (1999) ff; see most recently SCR 1822 (2008) and 1904 (2009).

[47] See in detail A Tzanakopoulos, 'Domestic Court Reactions to UN Security Council Sanctions' in A Reinisch (ed), *Challenging Acts of International Organizations before National Courts* (Oxford, OUP, 2010) 54, 54 ff.

[48] See ibid and A Tzanakopoulos, 'United Nations Sanctions in Domestic Courts: From Interpretation to Defiance in *Abdelrazik v Canada*' (2010) 8 *Journal of International Criminal Justice* 249, 249 ff.

Faced with such a situation, some influential domestic courts took what many international lawyers saw as a regressive step: instead of going further up and trying to argue *ius cogens* against the Security Council decision, thus taking further early jurisprudence by the EU Court of First Instance and the Swiss Federal Tribunal in *Kadi*[49] and *Nada*[50] respectively, they took flight in what was seen as blatant dualism. They sharply distinguished the domestic from the international legal order, and since the acts complained of before them were not the Council decisions, but rather their domestic implementing acts, they struck them down by relying on domestic constitutional law. Prime examples in this trend are the EU ECJ's *Kadi*[51] and the UK Supreme Court's decision of 27 January 2010.[52]

In fact, however, close reading of both of the aforementioned cases reveals that the courts made a very conscious and very strained effort to avoid international law, precisely to avoid the effect of Article 103 of the UN Charter. If this is not clear enough when the ECJ claims that the Community may comply with the obligation under the resolution in any number of ways and only the particular one that it selected is contrary to fundamental rights guaranteed by primary Community law (as if the Community could somehow else comply with the obligation to blacklist Kadi except by blacklisting him), it becomes abundantly clear when the Lords respond to a defence raised by the UK Government. Arguing on the basis of *Al-Jedda*,[53] the Government contended that Article 103 overrides rights under the ECHR, and the claimants should fail. The Court curtly responded that claimants in the particular case did not raise any arguments under the ECHR but only under domestic constitutional law, and thus there was no opportunity to invoke Article 103 or *Al-Jedda*.[54]

Is this revelation of the 'dark side' of international law the turning point that will send domestic courts, only recently having started to really embrace international law, back into the more familiar territory of not meddling in it?

IV. THE PHYSIOGNOMY OF INTERNATIONAL LAW: PRINCIPLED DECENTRALISATION

Despite the assumption that domestic courts may finally be assuming their rightful positions as the natural judges of international law, perhaps the allegedly radically dualist decisions by the ECJ and the UK Supreme Court demonstrate a regression, a sharp distinction between the international and the domestic legal order, akin to that evident

[49] Case T-315/01 *Kadi v Council and Commission* [2005] ECR II-3649.

[50] *Nada v SECO* (14 November 2007) 1A.45/2007; ILDC 461 (CH 2007).

[51] Joined Cases C-402/05 P and C-415/05 P *Kadi* and *Al Barakaat v Council and Commission* [2008] ECR I-6351. The CFI, renamed 'General Court of the EU' after the entry into force of the Lisbon Treaty, grudgingly applied the ECJ *Kadi* reasoning in *Kadi II*, Case T-85/09 *Kadi v European Commission* (30 September 2010); see for brief comment A Tzanakopoulos, '*Kadi II:* The 1267 Sanctions Regime (Back) Before the General Court of the EU' [2010] EJIL:Talk! (16 Nov), available at www.ejiltalk.org. The EU courts are considered as being 'domestic courts' to the extent that—as they argue—they belong to an *ordre juridique propre*, a separate (and arguably self-contained) legal order. In this sense they are not much different from domestic courts, which mostly also see themselves as belonging to a separate legal order, the domestic or municipal one.

[52] *HM Treasury v Mohammed Jabar Ahmed and others (FC); HM Treasury v Mohammed al-Ghabra (FC); R (Hani El Sayed Sabaei Youssef) v HM Treasury* [2010] UKSC 2 (hereinafter: *A et al*).

[53] *R (Al-Jedda) v Secretary of State for Defense* [2007] UKHL 58.

[54] *A et al* (n 52) at [75] (Lord Hope, with whom Lord Walker and Lady Hale agree); [174] (Lord Rodger).

in the much criticised decisions of the US courts in *Sanchez-Llamas*[55] and *Medellín*.[56] Or perhaps a crucial distinction can—and in fact should—be drawn.

If domestic courts are (supposed to be) the natural judges of international law, then the ECJ and UK Supreme Court decisions can be seen in a completely different light, which radically separates them from those of the US courts mentioned above. The former decisions rely indeed on domestic constitutional law to defeat an international obligation. But they do so quite clearly to avoid a provision under international law that the executive(s) can be seen as abusing: the provision of Article 103 of the UN Charter, granting the executives (in their own view) the power to supplant any international obligation when acting under Chapter VII.

Most importantly, however, they decide on the basis of domestic provisions that are *in substance* mirrored in international law: they uphold well-established aspects of the right to a fair trial, enshrined both in international treaties (Article 14 ICCPR, Article 6 ECHR) and guaranteed under customary international law.[57] Much like the District Court of Jerusalem argued in *Eichmann* that Eichmann's crimes were not just crimes under Israeli law,[58] the Canadian Federal Court claimed, in upholding the constitutional rights of a Canadian citizen subject to the 1267 regime, that these rights were not just rights under the relevant Canadian Charter, but also under international law.[59] This is in sharp contrast to the US courts' defence of a domestic provision of mere procedural nature (the procedural default rule); or to the move in Oklahoma to amend the State Constitution in order to prohibit state courts from 'considering international law or Sharia law' or indeed 'the legal precepts of other nations or cultures', without however explaining why such a move was necessary.[60]

This has significant implications: much less than belie the domestic courts' position as the natural judges of international law, it highlights two aspects of that position that may have far-reaching repercussions on the physiognomy of future international law in general.

The first one relates to the role of domestic courts in developing international law through practice. Domestic courts are state organs and thus they engage in state practice. Their decisions partake in the development of international law. More importantly, however, they are also judicial decisions. As Fitzmaurice stated in *Barcelona Traction* 'judicial pronouncements *of one kind or another* constitute the principal method by which the law can find some concrete measure of clarification and development'.[61] It is conceded that he was talking about the value of *obiter dicta* by an international court,

[55] *Sanchez-Llamas v Oregon* 548 US 331; ILDC 697 (US 2006).

[56] *Medellín v Texas* 552 US 491 (2008); ILDC 947 (US 2008).

[57] See for example explicitly the Portuguese Constitutional Court, which in *A v B* (15 June 1999) Case 0345/99; ILDC 1529 (PT 2009) clearly establishes the parallels between Articles 6 ECHR, 14 ICCPR, and 10 UDHR, and Article 20(4) of the Portuguese Constitution (at H2). See also the position of the HRC with respect to the ICCPR: as Tomuschat, *Human Rights*, 117–20 with further references, notes, the HRC has adopted the 'substantive criterion' of ICCPR effectiveness within a domestic legal order, rather than rely on formal considerations of whether the Covenant is incorporated into domestic law or is directly invocable before domestic courts (at 117). Arguably, the HRC has even opined that protection afforded on the basis of a domestic instrument of constitutional rank is even more effective than protection on the basis of the Covenant itself (at 118).

[58] 36 ILR 18 at [12] (emphasis added).

[59] Case T-727-08 *Abdelrazik v Canada* (4 June 2009) 2009 FC 580; ILDC 1332 (CA 2009).

[60] See for comment J Ku, 'Oklahoma's Unnecessary Law to Ban Citation of Sharia and International Law' [2010] Opinio Juris (15 June), available at opiniojuris.org.

[61] *Barcelona Traction* (n 19) 64 [2] [emphasis added].

while domestic court decisions are mere facts from the perspective of international law. But to put it as succinctly as Nollkaemper, 'a court is a court'.[62] The core function associated with the international judicial role is that of 'settlement of disputes by an independent and impartial body of judges through a legal procedure *resulting in* the application of international legal standards'.[63] That is precisely what the decisions of domestic courts above (the ECJ and the UK Supreme Court) resulted in, even if they did not explicitly rely on international law. Their pronouncements were definitely judicial pronouncements 'of one kind or another', and they 'resulted in' the application of standards that exist in the international legal order. In that, domestic court pronouncements are also a principal method for the clarification and development of international law.

It could then be argued that the decisions of the ECJ and the UK Supreme Court on the 1267 regime, when seen against the background of other decisions, such as those of the Irish High Court in *Bosphorus*,[64] the Canadian Federal Court in *Abdelrazik*,[65] the English High Court in *Othman*,[66] and others, may actually go a long way into either consolidating certain human rights as part of *ius cogens*, or alternatively clarifying the normative hierarchy in international law, by showing Article 103 of the UN Charter to be a rule of occasional priority rather than one of normative hierarchy, certain human rights ranking above it, even if they have not yet reached the level of *ius cogens*.[67] The potential for law development that resisting courts could have in this respect should not be underestimated.[68] It is particularly strong in the face of no organised opposition on the international or transnational level.[69]

Similarly it could be argued that domestic courts may eventually take the front seat at clarifying any effects that *ius cogens* may have with respect to sovereign immunity. In *Arrest Warrant* the ICJ looked at their jurisprudence and concluded that there was no clearly established practice[70] (as even the PCIJ had done in *Lotus*[71] on another matter). If a general practice indeed emerges, then this will have primarily emerged through the jurisprudence of domestic courts, which will have effected a change in international law. Even the judgments of the Greek Supreme Courts (Areios Pagos and Special Supreme Court) in *Distomo*[72] and of the Italian Corte di cassazione in *Ferrini*[73] can be seen as having at least initiated developments in this respect, which culminated in a case pending before the ICJ.[74]

But this is not the only effect that the position of domestic courts as natural judges of international law has. Another important effect is that they effectively force the state into compliance with their view of what international law commands. This constitutes

[62] A Nollkaemper, 'The Role of Domestic Courts in the Case Law of the International Court of Justice' (2006) 5 *Chinese Journal of International Law* 301, 308.

[63] Shany, 'International Actors', 13 [emphasis added].

[64] *Bosphorus v Minister for Transport* [1994] 2 ILRM 551.

[65] (n 59).

[66] *R (Othman) v Secretary of State for Work and Pensions* [2001] EWHC Admin 1022.

[67] See for the argument A Tzanakopoulos, 'Collective Security and Human Rights' in E de Wet and J Vidmar (eds), *Judicial Practice on Hierarchy in International Law: A Place for Human Rights?* (forthcoming 2012; available at www.ssrn.com).

[68] Cf Benvenisti, 'Reclaiming Democracy', 268; Benvenisti and Downs, 'National Courts', 65 ff.

[69] Cf Benvenisti and Downs, 'National Courts', 69.

[70] [2002] ICJ Rep 3.

[71] [1927] PCIJ Ser A No 10.

[72] ILDC 287 (GR 2000) and ILDC 87 (GR 2002) respectively.

[73] ILDC 19 (IT 2004).

[74] See ICJ Press Release No 2008/44 (23 December 2008).

a significant change in the physiognomy of international law, which is no longer applied and enforced exclusively by executives. The application and enforcement take place—if still in a decentralised manner—at least in accord with the decision of a learned judicial body, that has applied legal method in the determination of the content of the relevant rules.

Where the domestic court forces the executive to violate international law (as for example in the cases decided by the ECJ and the UK Supreme Court on the 1267 regime, which arguably result in clear violation of the relevant resolutions and Article 25 of the UN Charter), even then it can be argued that this enforced breach pushes the executive to translate the court's decision into a possible defence under international law. This defence cannot be that 'the domestic court so decided', nor can it be based on a wholesale adoption of the domestic court's reasoning, which in the instance ostensibly rests on domestic law. Domestic law cannot justify the breach of an international obligation.[75] Rather, the defence will have to rest on a translation of the domestic court's decision into international legal terms, which is relatively simple when the decision rests on a domestic argument that is similar in substance to what could be argued under international law. The ensuing dispute on the international level would allow for further clarification of the position under international law. Again, the state's position will not have been based on any shady or 'discretionary' consideration, but will have been forced upon it by the reasoned decision of a court.

V. CONCLUSION

The assumption of domestic courts of their proper role as the natural or ordinary judges of international law is not a panacea. It will not be fully realised easily, nor is it an unequivocally positive development, as it may lead to conflicting practice and a cacophony in the interpretation and application of international rules (in their substance). To the extent it will be realised, it will not necessarily cure what some see as the chronic illness of under-institutionalisation and under-enforcement that any decentralised legal system is sure to suffer. What it *will* do is perhaps pave the way for a more reasoned application of international law, whether through the clarification and development of its rules or through forcing the executive to take positions sanctioned by international law, both domestically and, potentially, internationally. This already will constitute a major change in the physiognomy of international law, reducing the uncertainty that comes with its decentralised character and moving it towards a more coherent legal system. Otherwise, it will bring to the fore the conflicting approaches of states to particular international rules, which—in the final analysis—is the necessary first step towards recasting or further developing these rules.

[75] Articles 27 VCLT; 3 ASR.

Part III:

1989–2010: International Law and the State

13

Statehood after 1989: 'Effectivités' between Legality and Virtuality

ANNE PETERS*

I. INTRODUCTION

THE PERIOD SINCE 1989 has seen statehood at both its peak and its low point. On the one hand, a quasi-colonial (Soviet) empire dissolved, and numerous new states emerged both in the territory of the former Soviet Union and elsewhere. Moreover, aspiration to statehood is unbroken. Secessionist movements all over the world seek to become independent states, and some precarious political territorial entities reclaim the status of a state. However, the foundations of these claims are uncertain. Is Kosovo a state? And if yes, why is Abkhazia not a state? What about Somaliland, Taiwan, or Palestine?

On the other hand, statehood is at its low point. The globalisation of markets and the emergence (or simply our taking note) of global problems (ranging from global warming to migration and diseases to finances) have, especially in the 1990s, led to the perception of a weakening or even decline of the nation state.

The concomitant international legal discourses have been those on secession and ethno-nationalism on the one hand, and those on the transformations or even disaggregation of states, on the waning of sovereignty (as the *differentia specifica* of states), and on transnational networks and multilevel governance, on the other hand. How do these discourses relate?

II. STATEHOOD AS EFFECTIVENESS

In order to understand better these seemingly irreconcilable trends and discourses, we must first ask what 'state' in the sense of international law means. James Crawford has summarised statehood in one word: 'effectiveness'.[1] The argument of this chapter is that 'effectiveness' is and should be a necessary, but not a sufficient criterion for statehood.

* Professor of international and constitutional law at the University of Basel, Switzerland.

[1] James Crawford, *The Creation of States in International Law*, 2nd edn (Oxford, Clarendon Press, 2006) 37. See also Charles de Visscher, *Les effectivités du droit international public* (Paris, ed A Pedone, 1967) 34: '[L]'Etat est envisagé par le droit international comme une effectivité menée à terme'.

In addition, legality, and maybe even legitimacy also determine statehood. Moreover, the standard of effectiveness is a relative one. In the era of globalisation, no state, facing interdependence and powerful business and financial actors, is fully effective.

The idea of statehood as effectiveness reflects a facticist approach to statehood. From that perspective, the state is a primary fact, un '*fait primaire*', as Georges Abi-Saab put it.[2] Seen that way, a state is an extra-legal, or meta-juridical, factual arrangement. And these facts are mainly the result of geography, of history, of politics, of military strength, of fortune. This also means that the formation (or creation, or emergence) of a state, and its disappearance, are extra-legal events.[3]

From this point of view, the standard for assessing whether a political entity is a state or not, is not 'legal or illegal' and even less 'legitimate or illegitimate'. According to Dionisio Anzilotti, writing in 1928, 'there are no legitimate and illegitimate states. The legitimacy of the state resides in its existence'.[4] Therefore, the yardstick for measuring whether an entity has reached the status of statehood, is—from that facticist perspective—'success or failure'. Recognition as a state may be awarded when the point of no return has been reached ('ultimate success theory').[5] The consequence of this approach is also that secession is neither prohibited nor allowed by international law. Secession happens in an international legal vacuum. 'Lawfulness' is no category for evaluating secession.

The merit of this facticist view of statehood is that it avoids over-regulation and the hubris of lawyers. It acknowledges that not all situations are suited for being resolved by law. A 19th century German constitutional scholar put it as follows: '*Das Recht hört hier auf*' ('law ends here').[6]

However, the facticist approach to statehood deserves criticism and needs refinement. Focusing only on the 'is' glorifies the *fait accompli*.[7] The purely facticist view implies an abdication of international law, and leaves an international legal vacuum. Ultimately, the result of this facticist approach is that the 'law' of the more powerful governs and determines whether there is a state or not.

It is important to realise that statehood, as other legal institutions such as property, needs a factual basis, but that lawyers ascribe a legal significance to these facts. The facts are, and must—for a legal treatment—be 'conceptualised'.[8] Another German constitutional lawyer, Georg Jellinek, acknowledged this by saying that the state has 'two sides', a 'sociological' and a 'legal' side.[9] The post-1989 concept of 'failed state' mainly

[2] Georges Abi-Saab, 'Cours général de droit international public' (1987-VII) 207 *Recueil de Cours* 9, 68.

[3] See Opinion No 1 of the Badinter Commission of 29 November 1991: 'the existence or disappearance of a state is a question of fact'. (repr. in *EJIL* 3 (1992) 182).

[4] Dionisio Anzilotti, *Corso di Diritto Internazionale*, vol I (Roma, Athenaeum, 1928) 154–55 (transl. by the author). De Visscher, *Les effectivités* (1967) 36: 'C'est au fait de l'Etat, effectivité menée à terme et tenue pour stabilisée, que le droit international s'attache sans mettre en question les facteurs qui ont amené sa formation'.

[5] See US S.Ct., *William v Bruffy*, 96 US 176 (1877) 186, on the quality of the southern 'Confederate States' that attempted to secede from the United States of America. See in detail Théodore Christakis, 'The State as "Primary Fact": Some Thoughts on the Principle of Effectiveness' in Marcelo Kohen (ed), *Secession—International Law Perspectives* (Cambridge, Cambridge University Press, 2006) 138, 147.

[6] Georg Meyer and Gerhard Anschütz, *Lehrbuch des Deutschen Staatsrechts*, 7th edn (München, Duncker & Humblot, 1914–1919) 906.

[7] Christakis, 'State as Primary Fact' 157.

[8] Alfred Verdross, 'Entstehung von Neustaaten und der Neustaaten nach dem Weltkriege' in Karl Strupp (ed), *Wörterbuch des Völkerrechts und der Diplomatie*, vol I (Leipzig, De Gruyter, 1924) 283, 285 writes that 'der sog. "de facto" Staat kein blosses Faktum, sondern ein Tatbestand des Völkerrechts ist, an den bestimmte Rechtswirkungen geknüpft werden. Auch der "de facto-" Staat ist daher, wie jede Rechtserscheinung de jure.

[9] Georg Jellinek, *Allgemeine Staatslehre*, 3rd edn (Berlin, Verlag von O Häring, 1914) 174.

refers to this factual side of statehood.[10] And the post-1989 concept of the 'rogue' state or 'state sponsor of terrorism' refers to its legal side.[11] Because lawyers should be interested in the state as a legal person (as an international legal subject), they should mainly be interested in the legal side.

Here comes in effectiveness as a transformator. When asking for an effective government over a people and a territory, for stable boundaries, and for respect of *uti possidetis*, lawyers apply the principle of effectiveness.[12] The principle of effectiveness, used as one or *the* criterion of statehood, has a dual meaning. It means, first, real power as opposed to powerless or even virtual institutions. But effectiveness also means something else: it means extra-legal power as opposed to institutions satisfying standards of legality or even legitimacy.

III. THE FIRST ANTAGONISM: VIRTUALITY

Effectiveness in its facticist sense is 'the quality of what exists in fact, of what exists concretely and really; it is opposed to what is fictitious, imaginary, or purely nominal'.[13] Effectiveness thereby integrates power and control into the law. Effective control or simply actual power or practice figure as a condition for the existence of a rule or entitlement. This is not only the case with statehood, but also with the title of prescription, and with practice as an element of customary law. Effectiveness also governs the international recognition of a state's conferral of its nationality on persons, and effective control is crucial for attributing international responsibility to states for behaviour of non-state actors. Overall, effectiveness is a pervasive principle of international law. As a requirement of statehood, effectiveness has been defined as the existence of 'a sufficient degree of internal stability as expressed in the functioning of a government enjoying the habitual obedience of the bulk of the population'.[14]

The rationale of the principle of effectiveness in international law is two-fold. First, in the absence of a centralised international law enforcement agency, the legal subjects must enforce their rights in a decentralised fashion, for instance by sanctions. If they lack the power to do so, their rights remain hollow. In the long run, such a situation would undermine the international legal order as a whole.

[10] See on failed states below note 18. But note that the Foreign Policy failed state index lists both indices relating to the effectiveness of government, and others pertaining to the realm of legality/legitimacy, such as 'group grievances' and 'human rights'.

[11] The term 'rogue state' has never been a juridical term of US law. In contrast, the term 'state sponsor of terrorism' is being used in US laws. Its application has concrete legal consequences, notably restrictions of US foreign assistance, ban on defence exports and sales, controls over exports of dual use items, and the loss of immunity of the state when sued in US courts. In July 2010, four countries had been designated as sponsors of terrorism: Cuba, Iran, Sudan and Syria. The post-1989 categorisation of states as such and the use of the label did not, however, entail *international* legal consequences, for instance the abandonment of the principle of sovereign equality.

[12] De Visscher, *Les effectivités* on effectiveness in the concept of state at 34; Jean Touscoz, *Le principe d'effectivité dans l'ordre international* (Paris, R Pichon et R Durand-Auzias, 1964); Monique Chemillier-Gendreau, 'A propos de l'effectivité en droit international' (1975) 11 *Revue belge de droit international* 38; Heike Krieger, *Das Effektivitätsprinzip im Völkerrecht* (Berlin, Duncker & Humblot, 2000); Christakis, 'State as Primary Fact'.

[13] Touscoz, *Le principe d'effectivité* 1 (transl. by the author). See also Hiroshi Taki, 'Effectiveness', Max Planck Encyclopedia of Public International Law 2010 (www.mpepil.com): effectiveness means that 'a factual situation strongly affects legal norms'.

[14] Hersch Lauterpacht, *Recognition in International Law* (Cambridge, Cambridge University Press, 1948) 28.

Especially with regard to statehood, the requirement of effective government has a second rationale. It secures the fulfilment of international legal obligations.[15] Moreover, a minimum of effectiveness is needed in order to determine the will of the people, which is in turn a requirement of self-determination.[16] Effectiveness thereby stands in the service of legal order.[17]

Considering these rationales, the principle of effectiveness does not merely constitute a 'legal camouflage' of a given power constellation, and is not inevitably an application of the adage *ex factis jus oritur* ('might makes right'). In contrast, the principle of effectiveness itself serves a genuinely normative function. Effectiveness can be qualified as a bridge concept which brings together the factual and the legal side of statehood. But effectiveness is a matter of degree. There is no bright line between effective and ineffective (in the sense of virtual).

One group of more or less ineffective states is formed by what political scientists have called 'failed states'.[18] The failed state index dressed up by Foreign Policy is currently headed by Somalia, Chad, and Sudan.[19] The category as such, the correct parameters for it, and the appropriateness of sticking that label on certain states are controversial.[20] But it is basically accepted that some states are ineffective and virtual to a great degree. Still, they are treated as states under international law.[21]

Second, more or less all states have arguably become less effective in the face of globalisation, in the sense that their (factual) *capacity* to furnish public goods such as security and liberty has diminished. Global governance, the strengthening of transnational or even supranational regimes, large-scale privatisation and liberalisation and the rise of non-state actors have been both a cause and effect of this trend. This diagnosis is controversial. Others have claimed that globalisation has empowered, not weakened, states.[22] There is probably agreement that the states' factual performance of the traditional functions ascribed to them has been modified by globalisation. These modifications relate mainly (albeit not exclusively) to the states' effectiveness.

These two phenomena, failed states and globalisation, demonstrate that the 'full' effectiveness of a territorial-political entity functions—in real life—not as a necessary condition for statehood. It seems to be, under certain conditions, dispensable or substitutable. A very weak degree of effectiveness seems to suffice to treat an entity such

[15] Joe Verhoeven, *Droit international public* (Bruxelles, Larcier, 2000) 54.

[16] Lauterpacht, *Recognition* 55.

[17] Christian Hillgruber, *Die Aufnahme neuer Staaten in die Völkerrechtsgemeinschaft* (Frankfurt a.M., Peter Lang, 1998) 399.

[18] First to use the term were probably Gerard Helman and Steven Ratner, 'Saving Failed States' (1992–1993) 89 *Foreign Policy* 3.

[19] Failed States Index, first published by Foreign Policy in 2005, version of 2010 under www.foreignpolicy.com/articles/2010/06/21/2010_failed_states_index_interactive_map_and_rankings.

[20] Neyire Akpinarli, *The Fragility of the 'Failed State' Paradigm* (Boston, Martinus Nijhoff, 2010). Akpinarli suggests to speak of absence of effective government instead, in order to avoid the pejorative overtone of 'failure'.

[21] International law does not have any mechanism to divest ineffective states of their status, unless they are completely dismembered, as it was the case with the Soviet Union and the Federal Socialist Republic of Yugoslavia. The reasons for the lack of the concept of 'de-recognition' will be discussed below in part IV.B.

[22] Linda Weiss, 'Introduction: Bringing Domestic Institutions Back in' in *idem* (ed), *States in the Global Economy. Bringing Domestic Institutions Back In* (Cambridge, Cambridge University Press, 2003) 1. See for the financial sector Peter Haegel, 'Standard-Setting for Capital Movements: Reasserting Sovereignty over Transnational Actors?' in Anne Peters, Lucy Köchlin, Till Förster and Gretta Fenner Zinkernagel (eds), *Non-State Actors as Standard Setters* (Cambridge, Cambridge University Press, 2009) 351.

as Kosovo or Somalia as a state in the sense of international law. The gist of my chapter is that this is in principle a good thing, but should not be exaggerated.

IV. THE SECOND ANTAGONISM: LEGALITY/LEGITIMACY

Effectiveness has the second meaning of extra-legality, as opposed to legality. When we ask for effective institutions in that sense, we mean that they need not satisfy standards of legality, let alone legitimacy. This is not to say that these institutions may be illegal, but that legality is not a relevant yardstick. This was basically what Anzilotti meant.[23] However, this notion of effective statehood had already been abandoned before 1989.

A. Conditions of Legality Preventing Statehood

The legal principles of the prohibition on the use of force and of self-determination have mattered for statehood. If these principles are violated in the course of an attempt to state-building, no state can come into existence, despite being effective in the sense of functional. Put differently, these standards of legality have worked as a barrier impeding the acquisition of statehood. They are thus additional, negative criteria of statehood. The two cases which gave rise to this new rule were Southern Rhodesia and the Turkish Republic of Northern Cyprus.

i) Self-determination and Non-use of Force

In 1965, Southern Rhodesia was established in disregard of the principle of *self-determination*.[24] The foundation of that political entity, based on a racist ideology, violated the right of the (black) majority population. The entity was therefore no state in the sense of international law, although it was initially fully effective. The Security Council stated that Rhodesia's declaration of independence had 'no legal validity'.[25] The political entity was considered to be an 'outlaw' not capable of being recognised as a state.

The second relevant principle, *prohibition of the use of force*, was applied with regard to the Turkish Republic of Northern Cyprus (TRNC). Because the Turkish invasion was an unlawful use of force, the republic proclaimed in 1983 is not a state, although it has enjoyed a high degree of effectiveness (in the sense of stability) until today, and is inevitably taken into account as a political player in the negotiations on the territorial questions in Cyprus. That principle was also applied to the Baltic States, whose statehood was, despite the unlawful annexation by the USSR in 1940, never extinct, and merely restored after 1989.[26]

[23] Dionisio Anzilotti, *Corso* 154; De Visscher, *Les effectivités* 36.

[24] See on South Rhodesia JES Fawcett, 'Security Council Resolutions on Rhodesia' (1965–66) 41 *BYIL* 103, 112; Crawford, *Creation of States* 128; Hillgruber, *Aufnahme neuer Staaten* 554.

[25] SC Res 217 (1965), para 3.

[26] In 1990/91, the Baltic states did not proclaim their independence but their 're-establishment of statehood'. See eg the Act on the Re-establishment of Lithuania of 11 March 1990. Third states and the EU (then EC) partly avoided the term 'recognition'; see eg the declaration by the European Political Cooperation of 27 August 1991, in which '[t]he Community and its Member States warmly welcome the *restoration* of sovereignty and

The *doctrinal justification* for elevating these two principles to negative indices of statehood is that these principles pertain to the body of *ius cogens*. If a treaty violating these rules is void, then the creation of a political-territorial entity which violates them must be a legal nullity, too, and so its result. The product of a nullity cannot be an international legal person, and hence no state in the sense of international law: 'wrongful birth' precludes statehood.

The legal consequence is that all other states are under an obligation of non-recognition.[27] This obligation has been spelled out in Security Council resolutions, for example with regard to the TRNC,[28] and is laid down in Article 41(2) of the ILC Articles on State Responsibility. It now forms part of international customary law.[29] Non-recognition must extend to the entity itself, to its 'nationals', and to the legal acts the entity performs.

On the other hand, an effective political entity should not be placed in an international legal vacuum, because this would result in a lack of protection of the affected populations. Therefore entities short of statehood should be considered to be bound by the most basic principles of general international law (especially by the prohibition of the use of force, customary human rights and IHL).[30] In practice, however, violations of human rights by a contested entity such as the TRNC, Abkhazia, or Transnistria have been attributed to the 'mother state', that is to say Turkey, Georgia, and Moldova.[31]

In this context, it is crucial to distinguish between international legal personality and the legal capacity to perform international legal acts. International legal personality is the precondition for the capacity to act on the plane of international law, but not all international legal persons enjoy all kinds of capacities. For example, natural persons cannot conclude international treaties. So being bound by international law, in other

independence of the Baltic states' (emphasis added). See also President of the Security Council, SCOR S/PV/3007, 12 September 1991: 'The independence of the Republic of Estonia, the Republic of Latvia and the Republic of Lithuania was *regained* peacefully' (emphasis added).

[27] This obligation was first spelled out as a *political* one in the Stimson doctrine concerning Japan's unlawful annexation of Manchuria and establishment of the puppet state Manchukuo which lasted from 1932–1945. That entity was not recognised by most states, for reasons both of lacking effectiveness (dependence on Japan) and illegality (product of use of force).

[28] See UN SC Res 541 (1983), para 7; Res 550 (11 May 1984), para 3.

[29] ICJ, *Legal Consequences of the Construction of a Wall in the Occupied Palestinian Territory*, Advisory Opinion of 9 July 2004, ICJ Reports 2004, para 159.

[30] See the famous case *Kadić v Karadzic*, in which claimants sought (under the US-American Alien Tort Claims Act), civil law damages for atrocities committed by officials of the Republica Srpska. Here the US American Court of Appeals was satisfied that Srpska was, despite not being recognised, a state in the sense of international law. But the court also stated that, for holding that state's officials liable under customary human rights law (as incorporated into domestic civil law) it was immaterial 'whether statehood in all its formal aspects exists'. US Court of Appeals, Second Circuit, *Kadić v Karadzic*, 70 Fd 3d 232, 244 (2d Circ. 1995).

[31] ECHR, *Loizidou v Turkey I* (preliminary objections), admissibility decision of 23 March 1995, appl No 15318/89, Series A 310 (1995), paras 62–64; ECHR, *Loizidou v Turkey II* (merits), appl No 15318/89, judgment of 18 December 1996, Reports 1996-VI, 2234, paras 56–57; ECHR, *Cyprus v Turkey*, Great Chamber, appl No 25781/94, judgment of 10 May 2001, ECHR 2001-IV, para 77; ECHR, *Assanidze v Georgia*, appl No 71503/01 (2004) (on the autonomous republic of Adjaria). In ECHR, *Ilascu v Moldova and Russia*, appl No 48787/99, judgment of 8 July 2004, the Court attributed responsibility both to Moldova and to Russia (paras 331, 333, 391–394). Likewise, international legal responsibility for violations of international law in Namibia has been attributed to South Africa due to its physical presence in the territory, independent of the illegality of that presence (ICJ, *Legal Consequences for States of the Continued Presence of South Africa in Namibia (South West Africa) Notwithstanding Security Council Resolution 276*, Advisory Opinion of 21 June 1971, ICJ Reports 1971, 16, para 117.

words being saddled with obligations, is something different from being able to perform legal acts.

It is important to realise that territorial entities which are not states (and which are in political science called para-states,[32] quasi-states, de facto states,[33] state-like entities,[34] de facto regimes,[35] and the like) lack the general legal capacity to perform valid international legal acts (such as concluding treaties or issuing unilateral acts). An entity short of statehood does not have treaty making capacity, and concomitantly cannot be bound by purely *contractual* obligations, unless its contracting partner (implicitly) acknowledges or confers that capacity to the respective entity.[36] The latter idea begs the question whether such a bilateral conferral is legally possible or whether treaties between states and non-state territorial entities should rather qualify as agreements outside the realm of international law. But these doctrinal problems leave untouched the fact that non-state territorial entities must respect general customary international law, notably the prohibition on the use of force.

ii) Further Legal and Legitimist Conditions of Statehood?

A fundamental question is whether, beyond non-use of force and self-determination, other international legal standards or even standards of legitimacy,[37] might also come into play. Legality and legitimacy standards can overlap, because ideally international law itself embodies legitimacy, and therefore—inversely—legitimacy can also flow from observance of positive law. Applying such a standard would mean that any violation of these standards could prevent the acquisition of statehood, even if the territorial-political entity in question were effective.

a) Territorial Integrity? The principle of territorial integrity is most often cited as the main legal counter-principle to a claim to statehood. However, territorial integrity cannot deploy the same legal effect as the two other legal principles (self-determination and non-use of force) because it differs in three relevant respects.

First, in a world completely divided into states, any formation of a new state inevitably affects the territorial integrity of another state. (Consent of the affected state precludes wrongfulness, but does not eliminate the fact that integrity is lost). This is different with regard to the other principles. The formation of a new state need not inevitably involve military means. Nor does it inevitably affect the right to self-determination of another people.

[32] Kataryna Pelczyinska-Nalecz, Krysztof Strachota and Maciej Falkowski, 'Para-States in the Post-Soviet Area from 1991 to 2007' (2008) 10 *International Studies Review* 370.

[33] Scott Pegg, *International Society and the De Facto State* (Aldershot, Ashgate, 1998).

[34] This is the qualification of Abkhazia by the Independent International Fact-Finding Mission on the Conflict in Georgia, report ('Tagliavini-Report') of September 2009, Chap 3, 134 (www.ceiig.ch/Report.html).

[35] Jochen A Frowein, 'De Facto Regime', Max Planck Encyclopedia of Public International Law 2009 (www.mpepil.com).

[36] Anne Peters, 'Treaty Making Power', Max Planck Encyclopedia of Public International Law 2009 (www.mpepil.com), paras 13–14.

[37] Legitimacy is here understood as a normative concept; to be legitimate then means to be worthy of being recognised. The claim of a political entity to statehood is normatively legitimate if it satisfies—depending on the preferred yardstick—our moral judgment, conforms to positive international law, or finally when it is socially accepted and/or brings about beneficial effects in reality ('output-legitimacy'). The fact of social acceptance does not only constitute legitimacy in the sociological sense, but may also be an indicator of normative legitimacy under the premise that popular attitudes must be taken seriously.

To set up territorial integrity as a 'trump' against statehood would make the formation of new states basically impossible and thereby deprive the concept of a legal claim to statehood of all practical utility. The application of the other two legal principles leaves space for the creation of new states.

Second, self-determination and non-use of force are *ius cogens*, whereas territorial integrity is not. The nullity of a countervailing act is accepted only with respect to violations of *ius cogens*.

Third, the deeper reason why self-determination and non-use of force are peremptory norms is that these principles protect natural persons, human beings. In contrast, territorial integrity of a state protects the state as such. This objective is, in a humanised international legal order, no end in itself, but has only an instrumental value. For these three reasons, the protection of territorial integrity cannot function as an absolute legal barrier to statehood.

This insight allows us to assess better a case such as Abkhazia. The political entity is quite effective and *de facto* independent from Georgia since 1991, and also from Russia. Still it has not been generally recognised, except by Russia and three other states.[38] All relevant international organisations (UN, OSCE, EU, and Council of Europe) have condemned the secession of Abkhazia from Georgia.

The primary reason for the non-recognition as a state is not the lack of effectiveness but the lack of legality. On the one side, there was clear illegality preventing statehood: the unilateral declaration of independence was brought about by an unlawful use of force. And on the other side, a positive legal basis of statehood was missing. Even if there had been an entitlement to independent statehood, based on the right to self-determination, such an entitlement must be realised in accordance with the proper *procedures*. Use of force is no accepted means. This means that the 'positive' legality cannot erase the failure to comply with the 'negative' legality criterion, which is non-use of force. The secession cannot be justified or tolerated as a 'remedial secession' because other means (negotiations directed at establishing autonomy) had not been exhausted.

Unfortunately, a number of international institutions' texts condemning the secession of Abkhazia chiefly pointed to the violation of territorial integrity of the mother state Georgia. For the reasons explained above, this is unsatisfactory. To be legally sound, condemnations should rather be based on the unlawful use of military means by the secessionist groups.[39]

b) Democracy Another legal standard which might function as a new (negative) criterion for statehood is democracy. If such a negative criterion were accepted, a territorial entity which did not come about democratically and which does not seek to establish democratic government structures would not qualify as a state.

Indeed requirements of democracy, imposed on states, already form part of international law as it stands.[40] They are therefore both a standard of international lawfulness and of

[38] Nicaragua, Venezuela, Nauru. Moreover, Transnistria, itself not a recognised state, has recognised South Ossetia and Abkhazia, and the territories themselves have recognised each other.

[39] cf ICJ, *Accordance with International Law of the Unilateral Declaration of Independence in Respect of Kosovo*, Advisory Opinion of 22 July 2010, para 81: 'the illegality attached to these declarations of independence thus stemmed not from the unilateral character of these declarations as such, but from the fact that they were, or would have been, connected with the unlawful use of force or other egregious violations of norms of general international law, in particular those of a peremptory character (ius cogens)'.

[40] Anne Peters, 'Dual Democracy' in Jan Klabbers, Anne Peters and Geir Ulfstein, *The Constitutionalization of International Law* (Oxford, Oxford University Press, 2009) 263, 273.

legitimacy. International law seems to require *new* states, such as the successor states of the Soviet Union or of Yugoslavia, East Timor and the Democratic Republic of the Congo, to be democratic.[41] Moreover, post-conflict regime building with international support has always been democratic, also in the event of state continuity. In particular international territorial administration, such as in Bosnia-Herzegovina or in Kosovo, has been understood as necessarily leading to a democratic state and must be democratic itself.[42]

Third states and international organisations involved in the (re-)construction of a state seem to be obliged to endow that state with a democratic regime.[43] Although democratic government is no formal condition of admission to the United Nations, the internationally supervised processes of 'making' new states such as East Timor or Montenegro had guaranteed that those states were indeed democratic.

Kosovo internationally committed itself in its declaration of independence to be a democratic state.[44] All pledges in that declaration are expressly directed at all other states,[45] and thereby made the attachment of 'conditionalities' to the acts of recognition superfluous. All in all, these developments suggest the emergence of democracy as an international legal condition of statehood for new states.

This standard of democracy is, however, not, or at least not strictly, applied to existing undemocratic states. Their status is left untouched. Nobody suggests their divestiture on the ground that they violate the democratisation policies of the United Nations.[46] This difference in treatment of old and new states at first sight appears as a deplorable application of double standards. However, it is much more difficult to realise democratic reform in an established state than starting from scratch. The different international legal standards imposed on old and new states therefore seem justified by considerations of stability and respect for vested interests.

B. Legality Standards as a Positive Catalyst for Statehood

The use of standards of international legality as a positive catalyst for statehood seems to be the novel development of the post-1989 era.[47] That said, we must keep in mind that the international legal principle of self-determination for colonised peoples had

[41] For a decade or so, there seems to have existed a universal customary obligation for all states, including 'old' ones, to work progressively towards democratisation. Moreover, a prohibition of retrogression incumbs on democratic states. However, certain persistent objectors remain, especially China and states of the Middle East and South East Asia.

[42] Mariano J Aznar Gómez, *La administración internacionalizada del territorio* (Barcelona, Atelier, 2008) 192 and 198.

[43] Jean d'Asprémont, *L'Etat non démocratique en droit international* (Paris, Pedone, 2008) 75.

[44] Kosovo's Declaration of Independence of 17 February 2008, para 2.

[45] The authors of the declaration 'hereby affirm, clearly, specifically, and irrevocably, that Kosovo shall be legally bound to comply with the provisions contained in this Declaration. … We declare publicly that all states are entitled to rely upon this declaration'. (para 12). The question is, however, whether the declaration is a unilateral act capable of legally binding Kosovo on the international plane, because Kosovo's capacity to perform valid international legal acts is doubtful.

[46] For a recent study on democratisation as enhancing politics of poverty reduction see United Nations Research Institute for Social Development, *Combating Poverty and Inequality* (2010), chap 11 'Democracy and the Politics of Poverty Reduction', 283.

[47] For an examination of 'what might be called addenda to the Montevideo criteria—additional elements in what makes a state' see Thomas D Grant, *The Recognition of States: Law and Practice in Debate and Evolution* (Westport, Praeger, 1999) 83.

been used as the legal basis for, or entitlement to, decolonisation already since the 1950s. However, it is only after 1989 that this legal claim has been rewarded in state practice outside the colonial context.

i) Self-determination as an Entitlement to Remedial Secession

The breakup of the Soviet Union and of Yugoslavia can be interpreted as an application of post-colonial self-determination. In any case, virtually all former Soviet and Yugoslav republics invoked self-determination.[48]

The acceptance of secession in that situation does not necessarily mean that there is a 'right' or an 'entitlement' to secession and to statehood. Rather, it means that an eventual secession and the ensuing statehood will, under narrow conditions, not be qualified as illegal. This is the idea of remedial secession, where secession appears as an option of last resort in a situation where a people's right to internal self-determination has been persistently and massively violated and all other means have failed. Additionally, any extraordinary allowance to secede would have to be realised through the appropriate procedures, notably a free and fair referendum on independence, or backed by democratic elections, ideally under international supervision.[49]

The idea of remedial secession is most often traced back to paragraph 7 of the General Assembly's Friendly Relations Declaration *a contrario*.[50] However, that savings clause has so far not crystallised into a customary rule.[51] The Canadian Supreme Court's opinion on Québec left the question open, but leaned towards accepting remedial secession in principle.[52] A decision of the African Commission on Human and Peoples' Rights confirmed the concept, while finding the pre-conditions not fulfilled for the Katangese people in Zaire.[53] For the question of statehood this means that the international legal principle of self-determination functions, even if not as a legal title to statehood, at least as a catalyst, and in that sense positively.

ii) Legality Standards as a Substitute for Effectiveness?

The ensuing question is how the emerging and tentative standards of international legality relate to the established standard of effectiveness with regard to the qualification of an entity as a state. In the extreme, legality standards might be a substitute for effectiveness. Put differently, international legality might compensate for the lack of effectiveness.

[48] The Kosovar Declaration of Independence of 17 February 2008 did not rely on self-determination, but on the will of the people.

[49] See eg the Opinion No 4 of the Badinter Commission on Bosnia-Herzegovina which required a referendum as a precondition for recognition by the EC (repr. in ILM 31 (1992) 1501–3). In scholarship Anne Peters, *Das Gebietsreferendum im Völkerrecht* (Baden-Baden, Nomos, 1995); Antonello Tancredi, 'A Normative "Due Process" in the Creation of States through Secession' in Marcelo Kohen (ed), *Secession—International Law Perspectives* (Cambridge, Cambridge University Press, 2006) 171, 190.

[50] UN GA Res 2625 (XXV) of 24 October 1970. See also the similar wording of the Vienna Declaration and Programme of Action of 12 July 1993, A/CONF.157/23, part I.2., of the World Conference on Human Rights.

[51] Antonio Cassese, *Self-Determination of Peoples: A Legal Reappraisal* (Cambridge, Cambridge University Press, 1995) 121 and 123. But see ICJ, *Accordance with International Law*, sep op Judge Yusuf para 11.

[52] Supreme Court of Canada, *Reference Secession of Quebec*, judgment of 20 August 1998, repr. in ILM 37 (1998), 1340 ff, paras 134–5, 138, 122.

[53] African Commission on Human and Peoples' Rights, *Katangese Peoples' Congress v Zaire*, case 75/92 (1995).

Bosnia-Herzegovina has been the key case of that type. It apparently enjoyed a legitimacy bonus, and its statehood has been called a legal fiction. The legitimacy bonus also played for Kosovo, at least in the eyes of those states (over 70 as of September 2010) which have recognised Kosovo as a state although it is not, or hardly, effective. The official governmental statements on recognition rarely give a justification for that act. Many highlight that Kosovo is a *sui generis* case. One of the political (and I submit valid legal) reasons for recognition is that Kosovo's claim to statehood is being perceived as legitimate. Its statehood could be seen as the result of a rightful exercise of the international right to self-determination, and as a lawful sanction of massive human rights violations committed by Serb institutions.

iii) The Legality of Failed States: Vested Rights and Protection from Intervention

Other entities, such as Somalia, Chad, and Sudan, neither fulfil criteria of effectiveness (determined by indicators such as the existence of a public service, the existence of a security apparatus, and the degree of external intervention), nor of legitimacy (measured by indicators such as group grievances, human flight, uneven development, and economic decline). Still they are treated as states under international law, even if labelled 'failed' in policy speak.

Why are the standards of statehood so much more demanding for new claimants of statehood? If Sudan, Zimbabwe, the DR Congo, or even Afghanistan were measured with the same yardstick as Abkhazia, they would surely not qualify more as a state than the break-away region of Georgia. Still, international law does not foresee any procedure for divesting these ineffective and even often arguably illegitimate entities[54] the status of a state. In fact, Article 6 of the Montevideo Convention on the Rights and Duties of States of 1933, which is often referred to as an authoritative enumeration of the international legal criteria for statehood, explicitly proclaims: 'Recognition is unconditional and irrevocable'.[55]

The lack of an institution of divestiture or 'de-recognition' can be justified in legal terms. One is the rationale underlying the principles of legal certainty, vested interests, legitimate expectations, and *uti possidetis*.[56] The common idea behind these institutions is that stability is a value which ultimately serves human beings and therefore deserves legal protection.

Second and equally important is the insight that divesting these territories of their status as states would strip these territories of the protection by the international legal principle of non-intervention, and thus leave them (and their populations) prey to great powers' geo-strategic ambitions. With regard to the so-called failed states (just as with regard to the not-yet-states), a distinction can be made between international legal personality and the legal capacity to perform international legal acts.[57] 'Failed states' might be qualified as international legal persons that are fully protected by non-

[54] cf Jean François Bayart, Stephen Ellis and Béatrice Hibou (eds), *The Criminalization of the State in Africa* (Oxford, James Currey, 1999).

[55] Art 6 sentence 2 of the Montevideo Convention on the Rights and Duties of States of 26 December 1933.

[56] cf Barbara Delcourt, 'L'application de l'uti possidetis juris au démembrement de la Yougoslavie—règle coutumière ou impérative politique?' in Olivier Corten (ed), *Démembrement d'Etats et délimitations territoriales* (Bruxelles, Bruylant, 1999) 35.

[57] As stated above, international legal personality is the precondition for the capacity to act on the plane of international law, but not all international legal persons enjoy all kinds of capacities.

intervention, but which (temporarily) lack full capacity to perform all sorts of valid legal acts on the international legal plane.[58]

The two situations of 'new' *effectivités* without statehood, and 'old' statehood without *effectivités* demonstrate that legal principles and normative considerations play a decisive role in the legal qualification of territories. It is not 'effectiveness' that is the crucial factor for qualifying Chad as a state and Abkhazia not, but the legal principles of vested interests, legitimate expectations, and non-intervention. What probably matters most in practice is that the 'failed states', in contrast to contested entities such as Abkhazia, Somaliland, Nagorny Karabakh, and many others do not threaten the territorial integrity of any other state, whereas Abkhazia and its likes do. But this should, as explained above, be only a minor consideration.

V. CONCLUSION: THE NORMATIVISATION OF STATEHOOD AND THE DIALECTICS OF 'MIGHT' AND 'RIGHT'

The problem of the 'normativisation' of statehood as just explained might be that it carries with it an overstatement of the power of the law, which in the long run leads to the devaluation of the law. On the other hand, we need to admit, with Jean-Jacques Rousseau, that law and legitimacy are the necessary long-term basis of political power.[59]

The solution to the puzzle lies, I submit, in the pursuance of a middle ground. Effectiveness and legality are not simple opposites, because, as explained, effectiveness is itself a legal principle which performs normative functions. But to the extent that effectiveness has an a-legal quality, considerations of effectiveness and of legality form a system of communicating vessels. Put differently, there is a dialectics of 'might' and 'right'. A relative weakness of effective government can be compensated by a surplus of legality/legitimacy.

Effectiveness is a necessary, but not sufficient criterion of statehood. It must be complemented by criteria of legality and of legitimacy. Still, effectiveness remains indispensable. It must not be substituted by indices of legality or legitimacy, because such an approach would transform the international legal system into a purely virtual one which could not perform its ordering function. However, because effectiveness is a relative concept, it is difficult to call a government arrangement completely non-effective.

Kosovo and Bosnia-Herzegovina are special cases because they are under international administration. 'Effectiveness' does not mean much here. Any qualification of these two as states can rely almost only on factors of legitimacy. Although most governmental statements on the recognition of Kosovo merely pointed to the *sui generis* situation, and did not mention self-determination as an entitlement to statehood, a number of states in their written statements in the ICJ proceedings assessing the conformity of Kosovo's declaration of independence with international law relied on self-determination.[60] Kosovo's claim to statehood has mainly been accepted by the international community

[58] Daniel Thürer, 'Der Wegfall effektiver Staatsgewalt: "The Failed State"' in *idem*, Matthias Herdegen and Gerhard Hohloch, *Der Wegfall effektiver Staatsgewalt: 'The Failed State'* (Berichte der Deutschen Gesellschaft für Völkerrecht 34, Heidelberg, FC Müller, 1996) 9, 16, 32, 42.

[59] cf Jean-Jacques Rousseau, *Du contrat social* (orig. Amsterdam, Chez Mar Michel Rey, 1762), Book I, Chap 3: 'Le plus fort n'est jamais assez fort pour être toujours le maître, s'il ne transforme sa force en droit, et l'obéissance en devoir'.

[60] See, eg, the written statement by Switzerland addressed to the ICJ of 25 May 2009, paras 63–68.

(or by leading states) as seemingly the only way to end serious human rights violations, discrimination, and mass murder of large parts of the population. But maybe the credibility and consistency of international law were served better by not calling these internationally administered and non-effective territories (Bosnia-Herzegovina and Kosovo) 'states'.

The upshot is that if, and only if, the international legal rules defining states continue to embody the concept of effectiveness in the sense just described, that is as a preventer of purely nominal 'states' which would not be able to comply with international law, as a necessary but not sufficient condition of statehood, and as to some extent compensable but not substitutable by the legitimacy of a claim to statehood, international law will perform well as a factor of order in international relations. Only then it can be said that '[t]hough this be madness, yet there is method in't'.[61]

[61] William Shakespeare, *The Tragedy of Hamlet, Prince of Denmark* (1603) Act I, Scene 2 (Lord Polonius).

14

From the National Border to the National Eleven: A (Partial and Partisan) Appraisal of the State System's Performance since the End of the Cold War

BOLDIZSÁR NAGY*

I. THE ASSUMPTIONS

THE STATE SYSTEM is understood here as the system of states and the sphere of international interactions in which states play the dominant role. The object of this investigation, however, is not the system itself but its constitutive elements. The puzzle to be resolved is simple: have the definition and the function of states changed in a remarkable and presumably irreversible way in the last two decades?

The analysis will appraise the 'performance' of international law in shaping states since 1989, that is during the last two or three decades. Whatever occurred to states and the perception of the states before that time will be taken for granted, in fact that will be the basis of comparison. Naturally, there is no stable, Archimedean point in the pre-1989 period from which to measure. In those decades changes—probably no less dramatic—took place, especially seen with a contemporary eye (think of the slowly forgotten process of decolonisation). Nevertheless as an analytic tool it will be assumed that there were typical features and standard functions of states, at least in the fields to be scrutinised.

Two further premises must be highlighted. First, this review is subjective. Not only is it limited to a few 'appreciable changes' but those will be evaluated in a partisan way. The choice of the topics and their appraisal will be that of a liberal international lawyer, sympathetic to critical legal approaches. Second, several changes in the functioning of states (and their system) will not be scrutinised although they are no less important than those under the looking glass.

* The author would like to acknowledge the generous help of the Max Institut für ausländisches öffentliches Recht und Völkerrecht for the support granted to him while working on the draft of this essay and of Professors Armin von Bogdandy and István Pogany whose comments helped eliminate some of the many imperfections. Responsibility for the remaining ones naturally lies with the author.

II. STATEHOOD—ANY CHANGE?

Which entities qualify as states? What are the functions characterising them? Have the criteria of statehood changed; are there still functions which can be associated only with the state level of organisation not with sub-state or with supranational entities? Is the state still the social organisation that determines and reconstructs the boundaries of a society, of a bounded political community? Can one still be a member of a state and must one be the member of solely one state?

Many of these questions are common to political science and international law. Nevertheless the answers that are sought here will be confined to the narrative of international law.

It is appropriate to start with a text composed in 1987 and published in 2000 in the highly respected *Encyclopedia of Public International Law* written by the author of one of the leading German treatises on International Law, Karl Döhring. Contrary to what Scelle had felt in 1950 when he 'had been active in international law for more than fifty years and still did not know what a State was and he felt sure he would not find out before he died',[1] Professor Döhring states that 'International law needs a general and commonly accepted definition suited to the requirements of all inter-State relations'.[2] Then comes his suggestion: 'The State in international law is an entity having exclusive jurisdiction with regard to its territory and personal jurisdiction in view of its nationals'.[3] The definition of the state—going back to Jellinek—is based on the 'doctrine of the three elements': population—territory—government.

The elaboration of the three elements reveals the following points of interest for the coming analysis:

'Membership in the State population is determined by laws on nationality'[4] which is to say that civic nationality creates membership of the state and the community of nationals—no matter how heterogeneous this community is—forms the constitutive element of the state, the population. This implies that resident foreigners are not seen as part of the population.

The essential importance of state territory is justified by the fact that 'inside this territory the competent government is exclusively entitled to take legal and factual measures. Hence a government which tries to exercise authority beyond its territory would commit a violation of international law'.[5] It follows from this that every state is entitled to prohibit the exercise of authority by another state on its own territory. Concrete delimitation of the state's territory is an 'unavoidable requirement of international law' and states are 'strictly obliged' to mark clearly the boundaries of their territory.[6]

What we learn about the government is that its democratic character is irrelevant; its rootedness in the will of the governed is not a requirement. All that matters is that 'in exercising its power [it] must be capable of acting independently of foreign

[1] J Crawford, *The Creation of States in International Law*, 2nd edn (Oxford, Oxford University Press, 2006) 38, (indirectly) quoting the ILC Yearbook, 1950/I, 84.

[2] K Doehring, 'State' in *Encyclopaedia of Public International Law*, Vol 4 (North Holland, Elsevier, 2000) 600.

[3] ibid, 601.

[4] ibid.

[5] ibid, 602.

[6] ibid.

governments'. Effectiveness in legislation and law enforcement, coupled with sufficient power to accomplish duties under international law must characterise the government.[7]

If it was appropriate to start with Döhring's text in the authoritative Encyclopedia it is no less appropriate to have a short look into Crawford's seminal treatise on statehood, as he summarises its criteria in the second edition. Are states still the entities composed of nationals as defined by the laws on citizenship, living in a well bordered territory and governed by an effective government where foreign powers must not exercise jurisdiction? A close reading of Crawford's book suggests that his view of statehood, published in 2006, puts the emphasis elsewhere, away from the doctrine of the three elements.

There seem to be four main strands of thought: first, the importance of effectiveness and possessing defined territory, permanent population and a government is downgraded;[8] second, other factors are added, notably, independence; third, the *differentia specifica* of statehood is not seen in these but in other factors; and fourth, it is assumed that the creation of states is a legally regulated process not simply a fact, therefore entities created in a way prohibited by international law may not qualify as states no matter how effectively they may control certain territories.

After establishing that there is neither a minimal size nor a requirement of contiguity concerning the territory and stating that even substantial boundary disputes do not, of themselves, bring statehood into question, Crawford concludes: 'The only requirement is that the State must consist of a certain coherent territory effectively governed—a formula that suggests that the requirement of territory is rather a constituent of government and independence than a distinct criterion of its own'.[9]

As to the criterion of permanent population his view is that states must have a permanent population, but 'it is not a rule relating to the nationality of that population'.[10] Even new states may be entitled to withhold nationality from some of the residents of the territory.[11]

'[G]overnment is the most important single criterion of statehood as all others depend on it',[12] but in fact a right or title to exercise governmental authority is enough: (temporary) lack of effective authority does not exclude statehood. The authority may not extend to the entirety of the territory and may be limited to 'some degree of maintenance of law and order and the establishment of basic institutions'.[13] Government as a precondition for statehood is, beyond a certain point, relative: whether it is justified or not depends on facts as well as on competing claims.

This is how independence becomes paramount, the 'central criterion of statehood'.[14] Independence in essence means 'the separate existence of an entity within reasonably coherent frontiers; and its not being subject to the authority of any other State or group of States'.[15]

[7] All views on government: ibid, 603.
[8] Of the more than 700 pages constituing the book 254 are devoted to the concept of statehood, of which 173 deal with the theory in a narrow sense of which the doctrine of the three elements takes up less than 16.
[9] Crawford, *The Creation of States,* 52.
[10] ibid.
[11] ibid, 53.
[12] ibid, 56.
[13] ibid, 59.
[14] ibid, 62.
[15] ibid, 66. Internal quote omitted.

Crawford claims that the special elements distinguishing states from other persons in international law and 'constitut[ing] in legal terms the core of the concept of statehood' are five principles:

1. '[P]lenary competence to perform acts, make treaties and so on, in the international sphere…';[16]
2. Exclusive competence with respect to their internal affairs (but international law may impose constraints). However 'their jurisdiction over internal matters is prima facie both plenary and not subject to the control of other states';[17]
3 'In principle States are not subject to compulsory international process, jurisdiction, or settlement without their consent…';[18]
4. States are formally equal; they have equal status and standing;[19]
5. Derogation from the above principles will not be presumed.[20]

Essentially, in Crawford's view, '[t]o be a State is to have a range of powers and responsibilities at [the international] level'. It is some of these powers and responsibilities I am going to scrutinise to see why the relativisation of the doctrine of the three elements is justified and supported by evidence from the specific fields of migration and citizenship.

III. WHERE TERRITORY AND CONTROL ENDS—THE MOVING BORDER

Remember the Berlin Wall? It epitomised borders of the pre-1989 period: a brick wall just a few metres in height, carefully kept sand running along the eastern side to expose footsteps, electric fences further away, maybe a concrete road for the border guards' jeeps; watch towers within shooting distance. The whole of Central and Eastern Europe was surrounded by such devices, forming the Iron Curtain: a fixed hardly trespassable line, clearly demarcated in space. In fact before the Schengen system gradually became applied borders between members of the (then) European Community were equally strictly controlled, except for the few free travel areas within which movement of persons (but not of goods) was much less cumbersome. As Malcolm Anderson and Didier Bigo state: 'Borders and frontiers were seen, in political science, geography, and law as unproblematic concepts until the collapse of communism and the increased pace of European integration in the later 1980s. Frontiers were conceived as the outer limits of the power of a sovereign state upon a population in a specific space'.[21]

That perception neatly fits the classical view of the state described above. However, the way borders function today, how they signify the outer perimeter of the state has fundamentally changed—and with that the perception of statehood.

Borders have become multidimensional. Partly moved away from the legal perimeter of the state territory, borders perform their functions at times very different from the moment

[16] ibid, 40.
[17] ibid, 41.
[18] ibid.
[19] ibid.
[20] ibid.
[21] A Malcolm and D Bigo, 'What Are EU Frontiers for and What Do They Mean?' in K Groenendijk, E Guild and P Minderhoud (eds), *In Search of Europe's Borders* (The Hague, Kluwer, 2003) 7, 8.

of entry into that territory. On the other hand—and especially in the Schengen area—an inward movement is also present: states (border guards) exercise control functions deep within their own territory which in the 'classical period' were performed at the borderline or within a few kilometres distance from it. So the idea that states' territories (and therefore: states themselves) are clearly separated, that where (the jurisdiction of) one state ends the other's starts, (or there lies an internationalised territory) is no longer valid.

Many experts have noted the changed character of the border. A pioneer is Elspeth Guild, who already in 2001 made clear that 'the borders are no longer defined in terms of the territory which they "contain" but in respect of the people moving across them. The borders are no longer a physical place but a legal one'.[22] A more recent voice is that of Ayelet Shachar who, reviewing the US, Canadian and Australian practice of exercising migration control, asserted that

> what has dramatically changed in recent years is the location of 'our gates', which no longer stand at the country's territorial edges. Instead, the border itself has become a moving barrier, a legal construct that is not tightly fixed to territorial benchmarks. This *shifting border of immigration regulation,* as we might call it, is selectively utilized by national immigration regulators to regain control over their crucial realm of responsibility, to determine who to permit to enter, who to remove, and who to keep at bay.[23]

Let us review some of the salient features of the moving, multidimensional borders, or in other words the extraterritorial immigration control tools.

A. Visas

Nationals of roughly 140 countries representing the wide majority of the world's population may be stopped from entering an EU member state or the US before departure. In 2010, the European Union listed only 36 countries and two territories, the nationals of which may enter without visa.[24] In the same year, the US applied its visa waiver program to 36 countries.[25] Simply, the denial of the promise to grant entry holds them up. The border of the destination country appears in the form of a consular officer in the country of intended departure. Not only is it far away but the denial of entry may very well be the outcome of cooperation between several EU member states.[26]

Visas requirements are collective stigmas. The population of a whole country is penalised for the deeds of a few or out of sheer fear and xenophobia. Why are the borders moved to the remote and dark offices in consulates? The Commission of the European

[22] E Guild, *Moving the Borders of Europe,* Inaugural lecture delivered on the occasion of the assumption of the professorship of the CPO Wisselleerstoel at the University of Nijmegen, 30 May 2001, 68.

[23] A Schachar, 'The shifting border of Immigration Regulation' (2007) 3 *Stan J CR & CL* 165, 167.

[24] Council Regulation (EC) No 539/2001 of 15 March 2001 listing the third countries whose nationals must be in possession of visas when crossing the external borders and those whose nationals are exempt from that requirement. The list includes Andorra, the Bahamas, Barbados, Brunei, the Holy Sea, Monaco, San Marino, St Kitts and Nevis. These have relatively little weight, especially if we compare them with the excluded giants, like China, India, Indonesia, Russia, and others.

[25] travel.state.gov/visa/temp/without/without_1990.html#countries.

[26] See Article 48 of Regulation (EC) No 810/2009 of the European Parliament and of the Council of 13 July 2009 establishing a Community Code on Visas, (Visa Code), OJ L 243/1, 15.9. 2009 on the possibility of denying a visa to someone in respect of whom an alert to that effect has been placed into the Schengen Information System.

Union gave three possible lines of argument for putting a country on the 'black list'.[27] The reason may lie in the danger of illegal immigration, in the wish to prevent crime, or in the general perception of international relations.[28]

The troubles with these arguments are manifold.[29] First, they contribute to the stigmatisation of whole populations. Both the 'danger of illegal immigration' and the 'prone to crime' hypotheses—when extended to a whole nation—are prejudicial and amount to a collective punishment. Moreover little reliable statistical evidence is available, not to speak of the self-fulfilling prophesies when the threat of illegal immigration is measured by the number of denied visas.

Second, assuming that visas may play a role in interstate relations, their imposition as leverage against a state in fact harms its population, and in the context of the EU it even means that the political opponent of a single Member State automatically becomes the target of all the states participating in the system.

Third, visas are the main obstacles to the access to the territory by asylum seekers. A Central European observer cannot avoid remembering how painful it was to witness that at the beginning of the Bosnian War one after another European state restored visa obligations for the people living in Bosnia and who were seeking security abroad.

In conclusion one can state that whereas the visa system before 1989 (and after its widespread introduction following the First World War) was mainly an interstate political tool, by now it has become a complex vehicle for the remote control of migration, of moving the border to the countries of departure in order to exclude the large majority of people of the world from the freedom of travel. Moreover, in the European Union, decisions on including a country into the visa list, as well as on granting or denying an individual's application, are frequently collective decisions which therefore transform the individual state's prerogative to decide over admission to an entitlement of a great number of states.

B. Carrier Sanctions

Who will ensure that no-one will arrive on a country's territory without a proper visa? Who will guarantee that the territory remains inaccessible by a barrier performing the function of the guarded border, located hundreds if not thousands of kilometres away? Well, the carrier that would transport the passenger. Whereas in the Cold-War period carriers—mainly air carriers—were obliged only to return a person to the point of departure or to a third country if they carelessly took on board a passenger without the appropriate documentation, the situation has changed under the Schengen system and in other states that introduced carrier sanctions. Carriers may be fined up to several thousand euro[30] or USD[31] per person carried to the destination country. In order to avoid

[27] COM (2000) 027 final.

[28] ibid.

[29] For a detailed analysis see eg E Guild, 'The Border Abroad—Visas and Border Controls', in K Groenendijk, E Guild and P Minderhoud (eds), *In Search of Europe's Borders* (The Hague, Kluwer, 2003) 87, 97

[30] The Council Directive 2001/51/EC of 28 June 2001 supplementing the provisions of Article 26 of the Convention implementing the Schengen Agreement of 14 June 1985 prescribed that fines should amount to at least 3000 euros per person or at least to 500 000 euros as a lump sum penalty.

[31] The US Immigration and Nationality Act as codified under 8 USC 1323 envisages a 3000 USD fine per person.

this eventuality carriers deny boarding to persons whose documentation they believe to be inadequate.[32] In doing so, carriers perform border guards' functions, exercise authority normally belonging to the state. The private and the public collapse, the power to exclude from the territory is exercised by a private legal person and its employee.[33]

C. Interdiction

If carriers prohibit boarding then what can persons unable to cross the remote control barrier do? They try to avoid border controls; they virtually eliminate the border by ignoring it. In response, the border is reconstituted in internationalised areas or on territories of other states. The 1993 *Sale v Haitian Ctrs. Council* case[34] and the US practice endorsed in it (against the views of UNHCR), the 2001 *Tampa* incident and the ensuing Australian practice of interception in international waters and excision of territory, the European Union's and its Member States' efforts to interdict migrants (whether illegal or forced)[35] long before reaching the national territory all point to the direction of relocating border controls and thereby the function of the border.

The conundrum of interdiction at the sea, especially on the high seas—whether as rescue or simply in order to prevent the arrival of a vessel not in distress—has been the subject of much debate. This debate mainly focuses on the duty of the stakeholders not to commit acts which would amount to *refoulement*.[36] A more recent and thorough analysis of the complex problems[37] maintains that interdiction of ships not being in distress and flying a flag is a prerogative of the warships of the flag state. Government ships of other states may pay a visit only if they acquire the explicit permission of the flag state. In other words, the UNCLOS regime[38] prevails and remains unaltered by the Protocol against the smuggling of migrants by land, sea and air, supplementing the United Nations Convention against transnational organised crime (2000).[39] Guild notes that 'the fact that FRONTEX uses the term "diversion" rather than "interception" is because of the sensitivity that the latter term, unless justified in international law, may be equivalent of piracy'.[40]

[32] B Melis, *Negotiating Europe's Immigration Frontiers* (The Hague, Kluwer, 2001) 179.

[33] V Guiraudon, 'Before the EU Border: Remote Control of the "Huddled Masses"', in K Groenendijk, E Guild and P Minderhoud (eds), *In Search of Europe's Borders* 191, 203. A Shachar, 'The Shifting Border of Immigration Regulation' (2008–2009) 30 *Michigan Journal of International Law* 809, 831.

[34] 509 U.S. 155 (1993).

[35] M-T Gil-Bazo, 'The Practice of Mediterranean States in the Context of the European Union's Justice and Home Affairs External Dimension. The Safe Third Country Concept Revisited' (2006) 18 *International Journal of Refugee Law* 571, 575.

[36] A careful review, recalling the major incidents is to be found in S Trevisanut, 'The Principle of *Non-Refoulement* at Sea and the Effectiveness of Asylum Protection', in A von Bogdandy and R Wolfrum (eds), *Max Planck Yearbook of United Nations Law* Vol 12 (Leiden, Brill, 2008) 205, especially 233 analysing the situation on the high seas.

[37] See in general R Barnes, 'The International Law of the Sea and Migration Control' in B Ryan and V Mitsilegas (eds), *Extraterritorial Immigration Control Legal Challenges* (Martinus Nijhoff, Leiden, 2010).

[38] Article 110 on the right to visit. Suspicion of carrying illegal migrants is not among the entitling scenarios.

[39] 40 ILM (2001) 384, Article 8 (2): 'A State Party that has reasonable grounds to suspect that a vessel … is engaged in the smuggling of migrants by sea may so notify the flag State, request confirmation of registry and, if confirmed, request authorisation from the flag State to take appropriate measures with regard to that vessel'.

[40] E Guild, *Security and Migration in the 21st Century* (Cambridge, Polity, 2009) 187.

In respect of vessels not flying a flag and not admitting a nationality even after inquiry there is a right to visit and perhaps also to interdict and return, but, as Barnes himself states 'there is little doubt that States are bound by Article 33 [of the Geneva Convention relating to the status of refugees] obligations of *non-refoulement*, and there is evidence to suggest that this obligation is not territorially circumscribed'.[41] Fischer-Loscano, Löhr and Tohidipur reach a more resolute conclusion, establishing in their well-documented article that:

> The non-refoulement obligations prohibit European border officials from turning back, escorting back, preventing the continuation of a journey, towing back or transferring vessels to non-EU coastal regions in the case of any person in potential need of protection, as long as the administrative and judicial examination of the asylum application has not been completed on European territory. European border officials are bound by this obligation even when operating extraterritorially. In the case of measures at sea, this applies inside the 12 mile zone, as well as in the contiguous zone, on the high seas and inside the coastal waters of third countries.[42]

D. Excision of Territory

If people cannot be prevented from arriving on the territory then the territory has to be 'removed'—and the illegal migrants trying to enter the territory with it. Following the Tampa incident Australia has introduced an 'excision policy' according to which it legally removes parts of its own territory from the application of its immigration and asylum laws.[43]

First this led to the removal of asylum seekers arriving without a visa to another country (Nauru and Papua New Guinea) where their asylum claims were processed After refugee status determination Australia may or may not have 'resettled' to Australia those who were found to be in need of protection.[44] This was a costly operation[45] and in 2008 gave way to a 'domestic solution' in which people are transferred to Christmas Island and held there provided two conditions are met: they reached Australia's jurisdiction by boat and without a valid visa.[46] Unauthorised boat arrivals on the mainland or in any other non-excised part of Australia have access to the normal refugee determination system

[41] Barnes, The International Law, 134.

[42] A Fischer-Lescano, T Löhr, and T Tohidipur, 'Border Controls at Sea: Requirements under International Human Rights and Refugee Law' (2009) 21 *International Journal of Refugee Law* 256, 296.

[43] Migration Amendment (Excision from Migration Zone) Act 2001 (Cth); Migration Amendment (Excision from Migration Zone (Consequential Provisions)) Act 2001 (Cth); Migration Amendment Regulations 2005 (No 6) (Cth). For the period of 2001–2007 when processing took place in Nauru and in Papua New Guinea, see S Kneebone, 'The Pacific Plan: The Provision of "Effective Protection"?'(2006) 18 *International Journal of Refugee Law* 698. For a map of the excised territories see www.immi.gov.au/media/fact-sheets/81-excision-places-map.pdf.

[44] Kneebone notes that Australia took 58% of the resettled persons and New Zeeland 38%, the remaining going to other countries: Kneebone, The Pacific, 708.

[45] 'From its inception in September 2001 until 31 December 2007, the total number of asylum seekers processed on Nauru and Manus Island was 1367 people, and on average most were there for one year. The cost of this offshore processing amounted to $305 million; around $2500 per asylum seeker per week'—J McAdam, and T Garcia, *Submission on Refugees and Asylum Seekers to the National Human Rights Consultation Secretariat Attorney-General's Department Central Office* 34, fn 130 www.humanrightsconsultation.gov.au/www/nhrcc/submissions.nsf/list/7D3822576B6ABCF2CA2576070019EBD9/$file/Gilbert_+_Tobin_Centre_of_Public_Law_Jane_McAdam_AGWW-7SW85E.pdf.

[46] Australian Human Rights Commission, *Immigration Detention and Offshore Processing on Christmas Island*, 2009 Report, 12, www.hreoc.gov.au/human_rights/immigration/idc2009_xmas_island.html visited 29 August 2010.

according to Australian law, whereas offshore arrivals are subject to a specific procedure with very limited guarantees.[47]

By removing those who wish to cross the Australian borders and at the same time removing them from the application of the law, Australia has redefined the relationship between territory and state authority. In Shachar's words

> ...in practice excision represents the ultimate attempt to regain control over cross-border movement in the age of globalization, by exercising, wherever the regulatory state's immigration officials see fit, its authority to determine whom to include and whom to exclude – by redefining and shifting the very spatial reach of a nation's territorial and jurisdictional boundaries: moving the border of immigration regulation in response to perceived threats by unauthorized migrants and high-risk travellers.[48]

E. Conclusion on the Moving Borders

The above and the other features that have not been discussed here,[49] all point to a new understanding of the role of territory, boundary and jurisdiction of the state. Borders and border controls have become more variegated. Within the Schengen system the internal borders have become invisible and formal controls are not in practice.[50] At the same time the external borders of the EU as well as the borders of several industrialised states have become multidimensional. They no longer appear as a 'wall', a single barrier where decisions on exit and entry are taken, where jurisdiction starts and ends (and which is the line to be defended against security threats). Rather they have become a complex of measures exercised on the territory of other states or in international zones, frequently preceding in time the actual departure towards the geographical border, or even preventing that departure.

IV. THE PEOPLE OF THE STATE: MEMBERSHIP? NATIONALITY? INHABITANTS?

A set of perplexing questions arise as one moves on to the next element of statehood: population. For Professor Döhring it meant the nationals, not the residents. For Professor Crawford the permanent population embraces nationals and non-nationals alike. Exploring this difference leads to intriguing questions concerning the relationship of state-society-political community, which in turn raises the questions of civic versus ethno-cultural citizenship,[51] of assimilation versus multiculturalism or cosmopolitanism, and the role of borders functioning as bridges and separators, as defining the inside/outside dichotomy.

[47] ibid, 14; McAdam-Garcia, Submission on Refugees, 187–8.

[48] A Shachar, The Shifting Border, 832.

[49] Liaison officers and immigration officers posted abroad, digital data collection before departure (PNR, ESTA), details of the Schengen Information System and others.

[50] The UK and Ireland decided not to lift their border controls—although they participate in some aspects of the Schengen system—Bulgaria, Romania and Cyprus still have to maintain borders controls in respect of other Schengen states, and a number of non-EU states are also incorporated into the 'borderless' area (Iceland, Liechtenstein, Norway and Switzerland).

[51] Although the concepts of 'nationality' and 'citizenship' could be differentiated, the following text will not do that, because in international law and legal studies there is no consensus concerning their meaning.

A. The World of *Nottebohm*

How simple was the world of *Nottebohm*![52] Mr Frederic Nottebohm left Germany for Guatemala in 1905 and 34 years later, at the outbreak of the Second World War and thereafter he was still treated by Guatemala as an enemy national, in fact removed from the country and prohibited from returning. 'Naturalization … involves his breaking of a bond of allegiance and his establishment of a new bond of allegiance. It may have far reaching consequences and involve profound changes in the destiny of the individual who obtains it. It concerns him personally', said the Court[53] in 1955. It presumed that a national of a state ought to become wedded to the country's 'traditions, its interests, its way of life' and assume obligations—other than fiscal obligations—and exercise the rights pertaining to the status thus acquired.[54] Nationality meant a genuine and effective bond to one state and one state only. Binary codes operated: friend or foe.

Nationality was and remained a ground for stigmatisation, for treating the individual according to schemes which may not at all fit her, as illustrated by the visa obligation.

The concept of nationality is dangerous[55] as in encountering another state's jurisdiction it occasionally deprives the individual from all her idiosyncratic characteristics, it is a generalisation at the most abstract level treating in some cases more than a billion nationals of a country as if there were no relevant differences among them, as if nationality was a common denominator expressing 'traditions, (national) interests, way of life'.

But is it? Debates on the meaning and importance of nationality are rampant. As Kymlicka and Norman have noted in a review article written in 1994, citizenship has become the 'buzz word' among thinkers on all points of the political spectrum.[56] It still is, especially in light of the European Union establishing and developing its own citizenship concept.[57]

B. Contradicting Developments Concerning Nationality: Light or Thick

In the field of nationality bidirectional movements can be observed. On the one hand the link between nationality (citizenship) and the actual political community becomes weaker and weaker; while the basis of belonging to the political community is to a decreasing measure dependent on possessing the nationality of the state. This leads many observers to speak of post-national citizenship and the loss of the value of possessing citizenship in addition to long term residence rights.[58]

[52] *Nottebohm Case* (second phase), Judgment, ICJ, Reports of Judgments, Advisory Opinions and Orders 1955, 4.

[53] ibid, 24.

[54] ibid, 26.

[55] Although dangerous, it is necessary to have rights.

[56] W Kymlicka and W Norman, 'Return of the Citizen: A Survey of Recent Work on Citizenship Theory' (1994) 104 *Ethics* 352, 352 footnotes omitted.

[57] A reflection of this sustained interest is the outstanding activity and the excellent website maintained by the European University Institute's Robert Schuman Centre 'European Union Democracy Observatory on Citizenship', the EUDO. See eudo-citizenship.eu/.

[58] The works of Yasemine Soysal and of Thomas Hammar are most frequently referred to. See eg C Joppke, 'The Inevitable Lightening of Citizenship' (2010) 51 *Archive of European Sociology (Archives européennes de sociologie)* 9, 14.

On the other hand states still assume in certain contexts that the main bond between the population of a state and the state itself is nationality, therefore in their treatment of foreigners, in opening or closing their gates to them they assume the unity of the state and the community of its nationals. Naturally the most remarkable identification of state and national is the treatment of EU member state nationals in other member states. Undesired illegal immigrants from the accession countries 'posing a danger to the order and the labour market of the country' became overnight fellow EU nationals entitled at least to 6 months stay as work-seekers.[59]

A third strand of change in the role of citizenship is the increased tendency of extending or restoring nationality to persons who do not live on the territory of the (re)naturalising state.[60] That is a final blow to the idea that the state, the political community (the polity) and the residents of a territory constitute an organic triad.

The underlying reason for these changes in legal terms is the transformation of the meaning of nationality. We no longer live in the world of Nottebohm, one can no longer claim that 'dual nationality is an undesirable phenomenon detrimental both to friendly relations between nations and the well-being of individuals concerned'.[61] State-membership is less and less based on nation-membership, if the nation is understood as a 'community of language, mores, or belief'.

Next to this thinning of nationality Joppke observes the opposite tendency as well, namely how states try to re-nationalise citizenship,[62] how they try to increase again the gap between residents and citizens and how they make efforts to reintroduce elements into the naturalisation process which would assure that the foreigner who acquires citizenship at the same time becomes part of the cultural nation, which then is assumed to assist her integration into the society.[63] This process of increasing the difference in status between the resident population and the narrower group of nationals may be seen as an effort of affluent Western societies to silence populist far-right voices.[64]

C. Decoupling Nationality from the Body Politic

Moving away from the Nottebohmian world and the unity of state-territory nationals is taking another form as well. Granting or restoring nationality to a large number of people who do not reside in the territory of the state is on the increase, as Anne

[59] The French policy of returning nationals of Romania and Bulgaria having Roma origin has met with very critical reactions in the Fall of 2010. For EU Justice Commissioner Viviane Reding's views see www.bbc.co.uk/news/world-europe-11027288.

[60] A Peters, (2010) 'Extraterritorial Nationality: Between Human Rights, State Sovereignty, and Fair Principles of Jurisdiction', manuscript on file with author.

[61] N Bar-Yaacov, *Dual Nationality* (London: Stevens and Sons, 1961) 4 as quoted by D Kochenov, *Rounding up the Circle: The Mutation of Member States' Nationalities under the Pressure of EU Citizenship*, EUI Working Papers RSCAS 2010/23, 6.

[62] Joppke, The Inevitable Lightening, 14.

[63] For a poignant comment on the embarrassing and vain effort to locate fundamental national cultural identifyers see Kochenov, The Rounding, 10, fn 82.

[64] 'These campaigns are desperate, yet ultimately futile, rearguard actions against the inevitable lightening of citizenship in the West, that is, against a citizenship that is easy to access, whose rights do not go much beyond the rights that many non-citizens already enjoy, and whose identity is thin and procedural, incapable of sharply setting apart one nation-state society from other such societies' (Joppke, The Inevitable Lightening, 12).

Peters has observed.[65] Naturally the problem is exacerbated by the fact that due to the *ius sanguinis* principle—unless a limit is placed on the succession of generations—millions of foreigners may have the nationality of a country they have never set foot in.[66] That in itself challenges the identification of nationality and the body politic, or—if voting and other sensitive rights and duties are recognised to people permanently residing abroad—the link between territory and permanent population understood as the political community.

This is precisely the problem. If one accepts that citizenship should mean membership in a state understood as the formal framework of the political community, and stakeholders should be the citizens,[67] or as Ayelet Shachar argues, a *jus nexi* should govern membership in the polity,[68] then the rules entitling the expatriates to vote or entitling foreign nationals to acquire the nationality without establishing genuine links with the actual political community, point in the opposite direction.

A case in point is the 2010 amendment of the Hungarian Law on Nationality.[69] It provides that 'on application, a non-Hungarian citizen can be naturalised on preferential terms if at least one of his relatives in the ascendant line was a Hungarian citizen or he shows the likelihood of having descended from Hungary and certifies his knowledge of the Hungarian language'. With this move Hungary has embarked on a course of mixing up cultural-historic nationhood and a territorially bounded political community.[70]

There is one more development which also affronts the classical doctrine of the state's sovereign right to determine who belongs to the political community and the circle of its nationals.

D. Enter the Supranational

The European Court of Justice has delivered an important judgment on 2 March 2010 in the *Janko Rotmann* case.[71] At stake was the principle of the state's exclusive right to determine who is (and who ceases to be) its citizen. The question was whether the Union vindicated a right to interfere or at least substantively to influence the decision of member states about the extent of their political community. The court gave its vision of the 'bedrock of nationality': it is 'the special relationship of solidarity and good faith between [the state] and its nationals and also the reciprocity of rights and duties' (para 51). Primary law attaches great importance to the status of European

[65] Peters, Extraterritorial Nationality, 6, 16.

[66] CoE report Doc 8339 of 5 March 1999, *Links between Europeans living abroad and their countries of origin*, Committee on Migration, Refugees and Demography, 38.

[67] 'The basic idea is that all those and only those individuals have a claim to membership in a particular polity who can be seen as stakeholders because their individual flourishing is linked to the future of that polity', R Bauböck, 'Global Justice, Freedom of Movement and Democratic Citizenship' (2009) 50 *Archive of European Sociology (Archives européennes de sociologie)* 1, 29.

[68] 'What is required here is not mere physical presence in the territory but also the passage of time and social connectedness, the latter referring to the requisite "center of life" criteria, which itself can be interpreted in more generous or more stringent ways', Shachar, *The Birthright Lottery Citizenship and Global Inequality* (Cambridge, Mass, Harvard University Press, 2009) 179.

[69] Act No LV of 1993 as amended by Act No XLIV of 2010.

[70] It has to be noted that Hungarian nationals not having a permanent address in Hungary are—at present—excluded from voting in the national elections.

[71] *Case C-135/08 Janko Rottmann v Freistaat Bayern*, decided on 2 March 2010. Not yet reported in ECR.

citizenship, therefore the proportionality principle has to be applied and the decision-making authority—when deciding on the withdrawal of nationality granted earlier—must

> take into account the consequences that the decision entails for the person concerned and, if relevant, for the members of his family... In this respect it is necessary to establish, in particular, whether that loss is justified in relation to the gravity of the offence committed by that person, to the lapse of time between the naturalisation decision and the withdrawal decision and to whether it is possible for that person to recover his original nationality (para 59).

This means nothing less than the EU's (through its court) announcing its claim to be part of the equation entailing state, territory and citizenship.

V. CONCLUSION

The aim of this chapter has been to show that the concept 'state' has undergone remarkable and potentially irreversible changes in the last two decades. Territory no longer means a circumscribed physical space surrounded by borders. Its outer perimeter has become blurred and multidimensional: border controls are frequently exercised beyond the geographic state territory, occasionally not even by state agents.

As regards the concept of population it has been demonstrated that the Nottebohmian world in which citizenship, population and state were seen as closely linked and dual nationality as a menace, has been replaced by contradictory tendencies. On the one hand a more embracing view and practice places long-term residents (almost) on a par with nationals and thereby leads to a loss of the importance of nationality and lays the foundation for post-national citizenship or 'citizenship light'. On the other hand an opposite tendency is also to be noted: a desire to reinstate the importance of nationality. That importance is taken for granted by those whose nationality leads to being stigmatised by visa obligations, exclusion from labour markets and the like.

The emerging practice of extending nationality to those who do not even live in the territory may constitute the final blow to the perception of state as based on the nationals-territory-body politic unity.

These tendencies are novel only when compared with the pre-1989 period, the start of which can be identified with the modern, post-feudal and nationalist world of the 19th century, in matters of travel even later, namely in the post-First-World-War period of closing the borders. Both the blurred borders and the multiple layered loyalties linked to feudal hierarchies instead of a territorial power were frequent in earlier times.

We might now witness what Tom Franck has identified more than a decade ago: 'The trend toward self-identification does suggest ... that some significant and growing part of humanity is seeking community with others based on commonalities that are neither genetic nor territorial'.[72] In the year of the soccer world championship, for a few weeks this commonality seemed to be the tribalistic devotion to the victory of the national eleven. In those days the national eleven (frequently staffed by players whose family background linked them to other countries or continents) represented the state and the nation in a

[72] T M Franck, 'Clan and Superclan: Loyalty, Identity and Community in Law and Practice' (1996) 90 *American Journal of International Law* 359, 382.

transmuted sense, it acted as the target of the bond of allegiance. This shift in allegiance may have been temporary but it seems certain that in the matrix of territory, boundary, population and state remarkable changes have occurred in the past two decades.

15

A Comment on Peters and Nagy: The State in Critical Perspective

TARAK BARKAWI*

I APOLOGISE FOR not being a lawyer, which means that my fellow panellists will not receive the kind of technical feedback on their papers they would rightly expect. I hope the audience can help make up for my failings in this respect.

I will start with a cautionary tale about the intersection between political science and history. Many political scientists and scholars of international relations use the findings of historians as if they were 'data', facts, history with a capital 'H', the objective true history of what actually happened. They are sometimes more or less aware that historians disagree among themselves, and this offers the tempting possibility—as one, not very good pre-doc once told me—of finding the historian who says the 'right' things, that is, who supports the preferred theory of the social scientist.

Now I have spent a great deal of time in archives and I can report there are no simple straightforward facts there, no 'brute facts' with which the one true history can be written. Historians in fact disagree profoundly amongst themselves, and they employ and debate general analytic categories and arguments—what we social scientists would call theories; and they also differ in respect of their overall political perspective, which frames their choice of theory, subject matter, and the tale they choose to tell. The same archive can lead to two or more radically different histories. And so we have histories, not History, and so my not very good pre-doc could indeed find a history that was felicitous for his argument.

The point of the story is this: international legal analyses are underpinned by particular sociologies and histories of the international system. At the first level, there is an interface between a legal argument and some set of phenomena that are taken to be true about the world. At a second level, there is a very delimited set of sociologies and histories that you engage with. Said another way, only a very few social and political perspectives are allowed to inform the mainstream of the legal debate. You have your favourite political scientists, as it were, who are felicitous for your arguments and your politics. I want to try and identify some of the blind spots that arise, and suggest what a more critical engagement with a wider range of perspectives in the social sciences might offer.

* Senior Lecturer at the Centre of International Studies, University of Cambridge.

It is not only a wider range of social science perspectives that are at issue. In his keynote, Professor Hurrell spoke of the need to see the world from the point of view of others, of alternate non-Western histories. While he did not actually do much of this—focusing instead on the power political inadequacies of liberal accounts—he placed this need in the context of what he called the 'provincialisation of the West': the relative decline of western power and the rise of new powers. There is a great deal to this, but whereas Professor Hurrell is a sceptic of the use of imperial categories to understand the world since 1945, I am not. So for me what is at stake are not only non-western views, but alternative experiences of the West, alternative histories about the encounter of the West with other parts of the world.

What I would draw attention to are not only the inadequacies of liberalism writ large in the face of power politics, but of the participation of liberalism in those power politics, of various incarnations of the civilising mission, of 'progress', in all of the West's imperial adventures and interventions into the non-European world. This is a liberalism which sees certain bad guys but not others, and which always manages to paint the West—whose wealth and power rests on long, violent and on-going histories of control and domination—as the site of progress, justice, freedom and all that is good. Liberal categories work to highlight certain crimes and villains, but hide others. So, mass death at the hands of state authorities is an unparalleled crime, holocaust, genocide; even greater mass death as a result of the operation of grain markets and the predictable famine that results under the watchful eye of state authorities and the economy they control—as in British India—does not even register in our imaginations as a crime against humanity, in part because liberalism places the operation of markets in the private sphere, in civil society, as if these existed outside the formal responsibilities of state, outside of the order created by state power. You can see here why many Indians have a rather different history than the one of white man's burden/they brought us railways—for it was those very railways that whisked the grain away to international markets.

I invoke all of this to show in the first instance the dependence of all political and legal analyses on certain histories, not others, and to ask us to think about this interface. But secondly I do so because in Anne Peters' paper there is what I would take to be a too easy identification of that which is legitimate and good with that which is liberal and democratic, understood in contemporary western terms. The good virtual states are the objects of western intervention, Kosovo and Bosnia, the basis of what she calls at one point a 'humanised' international legal order as a final objective; the bad illegal but effective states are those that are not a product of such intervention and international administration, such as Abkhazia and Northern Cyprus. I am hardly going to defend these last two but what I want to identify here is the securing normative orientation provided by liberalism—in which the kinds of crimes committed in Kosovo and Bosnia required international intervention in the name of humanity and the establishment of virtual but legitimate states, while the kind of civil society mass death and suffering that the regular operation of markets engenders stands entirely outside our imagination of what constitutes a crime against humanity. One travels under the sign of the fully human; the other stands outside of a humanised legal order, even as a final ideal objective. I would put to you that this is a very curious humanism indeed, but it is the one made possible by liberalism.

Let me bring these broad strokes to bear more directly on the question of the state and how we might think about it. Part of Peters' argument is pinned on a certain reading of globalisation, as something that has occurred in the last few decades and as something that, on her reading—channelling her chosen political scientists—compromises the power and effectiveness of states. All states, she says, have become less effective with globalisation. This is a particular 'liberal' reading of globalisation, one that ignores a range of debate not only about the historical time frame of globalisation, but also about the place of the state. For many of us, globalisation is authored by and transformative of states. Note that for Peters, 'all' states are affected—a move which dovetails with the formal sovereign equality of states—yet this is a curious read of what globalisation does to states. Powerful liberal capitalist states in the core of the international system used a variety of devices to rewrite the relationship between public and private power, between capital, labour and the state both at home and in a variety of subordinate states around the world. Thus the heyday of 'globalisation' in the 1990s could be read as a radical international extension of state power—that of core states and the international entities with state-like powers (eg WTO, IMF) with which they enmeshed the economies and polities of the global South. What would happen to Peters' argument if she read this critical globalisation literature—and the array of facts, events, institutions, histories that it invokes—rather than the globalisation literature she chose to rely on?

Key to liberal readings of globalisation and of the state is the formal distinction between the private and the public sphere. Property, markets, capital are located in the private sphere while official state institutions are classed as 'public'. The connection between this distinction and liberal accounts of globalisation is obvious: to the extent the power of the 'private' sphere increases, that of the public sphere decreases; thus 'globalisation' weakens states. A profoundly powerful assumption here is that the state and state power are equated with formal, official, public institutions. This is a liberal sociology of the state, and it operates in some measure behind even the most realist of international lawyers—the state as an official, public institution.

When I turn to questions of armed force, I will come back to this liberal official state but let me contrast this account of the state with a different one that begins from this insight: the public/private distinction is *internal* to the state; it is the state which constitutes the public/private boundary and polices and regulates it. Thus property is not something outside the state in the private sphere, but something constituted by the state, in part through a legal regime it enforces. The 'state' comes to mean a broader regime of order and power that includes economic and political elites. On this reading, the liberal official state performs a key strategic function: it removes property, and with it economic power, from the public sphere where democracy operates. In this way, the most horrific divisions in wealth and power become completely compatible with liberal civil and political rights. It is precisely this kind of democracy—capitalist democracy, that severely limits democracy as popular rule—that Peters invokes as a legal condition for legitimate and lawful statehood. Indeed, in actual practice, mere 'elections' serve to meet this criterion in internationally administered territories.

Now I have done this in very schematic fashion, playing out a potted version of the great debate over the capitalist state, which has many incarnations in political science, sociology, international political economy and international relations. Note specifically, and firstly, that in most discourse on international law with which I am familiar—admittedly limited though that is—only one side of this debate ever seems to show up, presented *as if* this was how the world was, *as if* the social scientists had worked it out for you, *as if* the law could take for granted a particular rendering of reality. Secondly, this particular rendering of reality—an account of globalisation that leaves out state power and international hierarchy—is one that is already implicated in the very politics of globalisation. The idea that individual states cannot defend their welfare and social rights against 'the market' is part of how 1990s style globalisation was politically made, at home and abroad.

I want to draw out an implication. Power, law, and inquiry are bound up with one another. Our terms of analysis not only reflect but participate in making the world, and its hierarchies of order and power. This is clearly and obviously the case with law which must by its nature be grounded in an existing set of power relations. What I find so curious here is that liberal international lawyers would ever believe any differently. There is this illusion that liberalism, like knowledge, somehow stands outside of power, is critical of it, on the side of the weak and so on. But liberalism, capitalism, imperialism are intimately bound up with one another in the course and character of western world power. I will come at this again from another direction when I invoke another strangely obscured but fundamental element of state, coercive power, and what the implications are of the actually existing relations of armed force in world politics for understandings of the states system.

I turn now to look at how this combination of politics, legal analysis, and social inquiry operate in Nagy's paper, because I believe these relations work very differently there, leaving him with a less satisfying legal argument perhaps—in that his conclusions are open ended—but a more satisfying account of what a 'border' might be and how it participates in ordering international hierarchy.

Like Peters, Nagy's paper takes off from the idea that something has changed in the world of states, borders and territorial jurisdiction. He looks at transformations in the character of statehood and borders as seen through the EU. He draws on scholarship about frontiers which now operate in extra-territorial space, functioning as spigots which let in some flows and choke off others. Thus our imagination of frontiers as a 'border', a 'wall', is fundamentally incorrect. Moreover, wrapped up in immigration and visa regimes, these controls of flows function to mark entire populations as criminalised, polluted, suspicious, and undesirable. The legal implications and analysis flow from an alternate read of what is happening empirically, one accessed by looking at how and where border controls actually function.

But then in other ways, Nagy too gets caught up in the world of official state sovereignties and the formal equality of states, as lawyers inevitably must. He uses the EU as an example of what has changed about contemporary statehood, but one simply cannot extrapolate from the EU to the rest of the world. Moreover, it is the EU and the US and other powerful states that operate extra-territorial border controls, and it is racialised populations of lesser human beings who are subject to sharper controls, and consequently become undocumented aliens, a cheap and flexible source of labour, and a convenient site for nativist, nationalist politics of the kind we see in full flow in France, Australia, and the US. That is, Nagy's analysis makes no sense unless we work in an account of international hierarchy in which some states exert powers—official, sovereign as well as informal powers—over other territories and movements of populations. Also, although the word does not appear in his text, only an account of racial hierarchies—of gradations of white folks and brown and black folks could possibly make sense of the world he describes. Let's not beat around the bush about just who is kept out of the West and who is let in and allowed to move around. I wonder what would happen to international law if the racial apartheid that operates daily in our airports, on the high seas, on our borders wherever they function was accepted as a set of facts about the world. Let me also underline that this racial apartheid is fostered, enforced, and part and parcel of the supposedly liberal, democratic progressive West, the very one that supplies the 'normative' standards of legitimacy, of 'right', that Peters wants to invoke over mere effectiveness in the criteria of statehood.

Let me now leave behind the substance of the papers and take up what I take to be a basic contradiction between legal and empirical analyses of the states system. In doing so, I want to confront the issue of hierarchy that I have touched on in different ways. For a variety of reasons, the international law of states is committed to notions of formal sovereign equality of the legal persons that make up the states system. But the world of states is unquestionably one of powerful hierarchies, which sometimes organise themselves internationally—Bretton Woods; WTO; NATO—and which sometimes operate out of discrete centres of state power—Washington; Moscow.

It is interesting that Nagy notes that much of what he says about statehood—mobile borders, layered sovereignties, multiple loyalties—was true of the old imperial world. We sometimes get fooled into this idea that this world disappeared in the decades after 1945 with the formal sovereign independence of the colonial empires. But of course, as anyone familiar with the history of the Cold War and now of the War on Terror knows, a key modality by which powerful states exert power is to shape the internal sovereignties of subordinate states. Whether one was talking about France in Africa, or the US in Latin America and elsewhere, or the Soviet Union in Eastern Europe, subordinate states became semi-sovereign dependencies—their governments often installed and removed at will through a variety of sometimes covert and sometimes overt manoeuvres.

Quite clearly in these cases—and we are talking about much of the world for much of the last 60 years—a world of international hierarchy operates in and through, as well as underneath, a world of formally equal sovereignty. Thus, what I'm calling realist international law—states as formally equal persons—is utterly detached from the realities of power in world politics. Let me pick out just one key dimension in which this is so. When scholars of international relations use the term sovereignty they are sometimes referring to the legal world of formally equal states. But another meaning the term has for them is that of political military autonomy—the ability to independently wage war as the *sine qua non* of a 'real' state. This incidentally, is why the EU is not a state—not only because it lacks an army but because NATO and most European militaries can only operate to limited extent in the absence of the US and its command, control and intelligence capabilities.

In the world of international hierarchy that I've been describing, the militaries of subordinate states are not sovereign, but rather are 'advised and assisted' extensions of the armed forces of core states and their policies. This is demonstrated by the fact that they are chiefly concerned with 'internal security'—their violence is directed at their own populations. In US interventions in the Cold War as in the War on Terror, a chief purpose of policy is military-to-military relations which train up the security forces of subordinate states to police and terrorise their populations in ways which accord with the interests of the major powers. Again I am being schematic, but there are long and on-going histories of 'security assistance' through which the coercive apparatuses of subordinate states are articulated with international hierarchies of power. One dimension of this is the way in which the EU spends a great deal of effort training and assisting the border control agencies of its near abroad, articulating them with its racial hierarchy of population controls.

At what I would take to be the core of state power—armed force—we find not only a world of competing armed sovereignties among powerful states—the anarchical world of International Relations theory—but also a world of hierarchy and forms of military and political control for which some derivative of the word 'imperial' is not inappropriate. The 'states' of this hierarchical world are completely compatible with the world of formally equal 'effective and legitimate' sovereignties. They have the entire apparatus of formal statehood, even as they are fundamentally penetrated by more powerful states. As armed force is at the core of any definition of state, it would seem that this international constitution and use of force ought to have profound implications for international legal analysis about the contemporary status of statehood.

What I want to leave you with is a question. Peters speaks of legal and legitimate but virtual states—Kosovo, Bosnia—and effective, ie not virtual, but illegitimate states like Abkhazia or Northern Cyprus. But for me, and in respect of the relations of armed force and control I have sketched out, what is effective and what is virtual about statehood is a far more complicated matter than international law seems willing to grapple with. Where the legal fictions, political power, and empirical realities intersect is far from straightforward. A key device for simplifying this matter, and for holding on to various liberal and realist narratives about international law, is the question of which empirical analyses, which social science perspectives, you allow in; and which you keep out. And so one might do well to pay more attention to the interface between international law and political science broadly conceived.

Part IV:

1989–2010: International Law and International Institutions

16

Paradise Lost? De-formalisation, Control and Trust in International Institutions

JAN KLABBERS*

I. INTRODUCTION

ONCE UPON A time, it was perfectly possible for well-known international lawyers to write general textbooks without discussing the Security Council in any detail. Thus, Ian Brownlie's classic, in its 4th edition, mentions the Council a few times (for example when discussing admission of new UN members), but not enough to warrant its own index entry.[1] And much the same applies to Antonio Cassese's first textbook, aptly titled *International Law in a Divided World*: some mention of the Council, but no separate index entry.[2] The message then was clear: the world was divided, international law was held hostage by power politics, and indeed, the same held true with respect to international organisations.

This had not always been the case. International organisations had been greeted with great optimism when they first burst upon the scene, sometime in the late 19th and early 20th centuries. They were generally considered to engage in useful activities, all the more so because they could insist to be immune to politics. The German lawyer Friedrich Meili wrote in 1889, in a small book on several international organisations in the field of transport and communication, that international organisations could possibly be the start of a global law ('Weltrecht')[3] and, a few pages later he poetically suggested that international unions are the 'flower buds' of international law: their fate will be the fate of international law.[4]

* Jan Klabbers is Professor of International Law at the University of Helsinki, and Director of the Academy of Finland Centre of Excellence in Global Governance Research. Much of this paper was conceived when he was Inaugural Fellow at the Straus Institute for the Advanced Study of Law and Justice at New York University Law School, 2009–2010.

[1] See I Brownlie, *Principles of Public International Law*, 4th edn (Oxford, Clarendon Press, 1990). The most recent edition is the 7th, which does have a separate entry for the Security Council. See I Brownlie, *Principles of Public International Law*, 7th edn (Oxford, Oxford University Press, 2008).

[2] See A Cassese, *International law in a Divided World* (Oxford, Clarendon Press, 1986). Cassese's more recent *International Law*, 2nd edn (Oxford, Oxford University Press, 2005) has a separate Security Council entry.

[3] F Meili, *Die internationalen Unionen über das Recht der Weltverkehrsanstalten und des geistigen Eigentums* (Leipzig, Duncker & Humblot, 1889) 57.

[4] Meili, Die internationalen Unionen, 73.

In much the same vein, Edouard Descamps could conclude five years later that international organisations were here to stay and found their main raison d'être 'en dehors de la sphère brûlante de la politique où ils n'aspirent pas à pénétrer'.[5] While he warned against too much optimism, he immediately ignored his own warning, only to conclude that international organisations contribute by modest means to a great result: 'le rapprochement fraternal des peuples et la paix stable du monde.'[6] This then pointed to a paradoxical situation: precisely by presenting themselves as a-political, international organisations contribute to what is arguably the greatest political goal of all: world peace. Hence, their emergence killed two birds with a single stone.

The same sentiment would continue unabated in the writings of publicists throughout the 20th century. Paul Reinsch, the *auctor intellectualis* of functionalist theory in international institutional law, in the first decade of the 20th century wrote glowingly and full of hope about organisations: they were the harbingers 'of a law common to the entire civilised world', containing the seeds of 'world law' or 'universal civil law'.[7] Half a century later, Nagendra Singh, the future President of the ICJ, could write that international organisations contributed to the 'salvation of mankind'.[8] That's quite something: international organisations were expected to bring paradise to earth.

All those authors premised their thoughts on a clear distinction between international organisations and international politics. International organisations were technical, exercising functional jurisdiction, based on what was considered necessary for the furtherance of common goals. Their missions were a-political, and it was only on this basis that they could be considered to have any chance of success. And if they had a political goal to begin with, as some conceded, then it was the abstract and general goal of world peace, something few of course could ever disagree with. What this left unspecified, of course, were the conditions of world peace, issues of distributive justice, et cetera.

II. DESPAIR AND DISARRAY

Singh's claim about the salvation of mankind was part optimism, part despair, because by the time he wrote his words (1958) the Cold War had already crept in. The Security Council quickly found itself paralysed, even on such a seemingly innocent topic as membership,[9] and the General Assembly, while hyperactive and instrumental in developing activities such as peacekeeping or trying to rejuvenate the sources of international law, was unmasked as little more than a debating club, capable of announcing a New International Economic Order or equating Zionism and racism, but without many ripples outside the meeting

[5] See E Baron Descamps, *Les offices internationaux et leur avenir* (Brussels, Académie Royale de Belgique, 1894) 52.

[6] Descamps, Les offices internationaux, 53.

[7] PS Reinsch, 'International Administrative Law and National Sovereignty' (1909) 3 *American Journal of International Law* 1, at 1, 2 and 5, respectively. For more on Reinsch's contribution, see J Klabbers, 'Re-thinking Functionalism: Paul S Reinsch and the Making of International Institutional Law', NYU Straus Institute Working Paper (2010).

[8] See N Singh, *Termination of Membership of International Organisations* (London, Stevens and Sons, 1958) vii.

[9] For a fine study, see Th D Grant, *Admission to the United Nations: Charter Article 4 and the Rise of Universal Organization* (Leiden, Martinus Nijhoff, 2009).

halls in New York and Geneva. And other organisations awaited a similar fate: the GATT, for instance, became colloquially known as the General Agreement to Talk and Talk.[10]

Even the regional organisations could not escape entirely: the EC became subjected to 'euro-sclerosis', in the term of art of the 1970s and 1980s, having first overshadowed the Council of Europe and Benelux. Nothing much, moreover, seemed to occur in the OAS or the OAU, never mind in organisations such as NATO, which even saw a partial withdrawal from one of its bigger member states. Indeed, withdrawal from international organisations was not unheard of, and plagued organisations as diverse as UNICEF and the ILO.

So, when the Wall tumbled down, international organisations were generally in a state of disarray, a circumstance that was aggravated still by the collapse of the International Tin Council. The Tin Council's fall from grace suggested that international organisations could be mismanaged, and that it was by no means impossible that those harbingers of peace and happiness, those carriers of Descamps' 'rapprochement fraternel des peuples et la paix stable du monde', could actually do something wrong. Paradise seemed lost.

The first couple of years after the fall of the Wall saw a regeneration of hope and optimism: for a few short years, paradise seemed regained. The Security Council united for a few times, condemning the attack on a PanAm flight over Lockerbie and sending troops to liberate Kuwait. The GATT transmogrified into the WTO, while the EC transformed itself so as to become the EU. It even turned out possible to set up a new organisation in the ever-difficult field of arms control, in the form of the OPCW, based on the 1993 Chemical Weapons Convention. Admittedly, some influential ones disappeared, such as the Comecon and the Warsaw pact, but those had always been seen as fig leaves for Soviet power at any rate—consequently, they had hardly qualified as 'real' organisations.[11]

Either way, looks can be deceptive. To some extent, the regeneration after 1990 was not regeneration at all. The WTO turned out to be an institution without powers, interesting mainly as judicial authority: it is in essence little more than a non-discrimination rule with a dispute settlement body attached to it.[12] The EU may have realised its internal market, but made a move back to inter-governmentalism at any rate: the second and third pillars (as they were called at the time) departed from what had until then been proudly heralded as 'the Community method', and the introduction of subsidiarity in the Maastricht Treaty put a limit on the Community method, as did the reminder, in that same treaty, that the EU was based on the idea of conferred powers.

Within the UN, the regeneration may have been real, but was short-lived: experiences in Somalia, Rwanda and the former Yugoslavia suggested that sometimes it was easier to do nothing than actively operate so as to maintain peace and security.[13] If this was the salvation of mankind, then perhaps mankind could do without.

And elsewhere, regeneration came at a price: the price of the Rule of Law, to put it poignantly. This was most prominently the case perhaps with the re-birth of NATO

[10] UNCTAD, by the same token, is sometimes said to stand for 'Under No Circumstances Take Any Decision'.

[11] For an argument to this effect, see B Schwartz and E Leven, 'International Organizations: What Makes Them Work?' (1992) 30 *Canadian Yearbook of International Law* 165.

[12] The classic analysis along these lines is A von Bogdandy, 'Law and Politics in the WTO—Strategies to Cope with a Deficient Relationship' (2001) 5 *Max Planck Yearbook of United Nations Law* 609.

[13] For a highly plausible explanation in terms of bureaucratic culture, see M Barnett and M Finnemore, *Rules for the World: International Organizations in Global Politics* (Princeton, Princeton University Press, 2004).

following the publication of a series of strategy concepts (in 1991 and 1999) which effectively changed NATO's constitution: without amendment, without the involvement of domestic parliaments, without any of the normal constitutional guarantees one has come to expect in the western world.[14] Even the traditional justification for leaving the Rule of Law behind could not properly be invoked: NATO was re-invented not in the face of grave danger, but because the grave danger (perceived danger, at any rate) that had led to its creation no longer existed. Without an enemy, NATO needed a new lease on life, but could hardly point to increased security concerns after the Wall had come crashing down—at least not until 9/11 made this argument seem a bit more credible again.

Similarly, some of the UN's activities would be difficult to reconcile with the Rule of Law in international affairs. Libya already hinted at this when it started the Lockerbie proceedings; the ICJ unfortunately never accepted the challenge. More prominently perhaps, the Security Council's sanctions mechanisms are difficult to reconcile with due process and the like, and the administration of territory by the UN and other international organisations also gives rise to many issues of due process, transparency, and participation.[15]

Indeed, the increased profile of international organisations generated increased critiques. The most visible manifestation was the 'Battle of Seattle': thousands of people going to the streets to protest against the WTO, perhaps not all of them aware that the WTO itself is, as it proudly proclaims, 'member-driven'. This points to an important phenomenon: the more visible international organisations are, the more they come to be seen as political actors in their own right, and the more they come to be seen as political actors in their own right, the greater the call for some form of control. The earlier ideas of international organisations being beyond politics yet contributing to the eminently political goal of world peace turned out to be untenable.

III. CONTROL AND DE-FORMALISATION

This means that control has become one of the headings under which much of the international institutional law of the last two decades can be captured. The other, as already alluded to, is de-formalisation. NATO's renaissance is an example of doing things not 'by the book', but by circumventing the book. Other examples abound. Some organisations were specifically set up so as to keep them far away from the law: the OSCE is an example, as were and are G7, G8 and G20. Less visible, but equally informal, international organisations such as the Council of Baltic Sea States, the Shanghai Cooperation Organization, and Black Sea Economic Cooperation (note how the word 'organisation' is missing from its name) were all created as informal gatherings, and matured into something a bit more formal and institutionalised.[16] The EU was, rather curiously, thought not to be an international legal person for a number of years (despite

[14] A useful overview is provided by S Bölingen, *Die Transformation der NATO im Spiegel der Vertragsentwicklung: Zwischen sicherheitspolitischen Herausforderungen und völkerrechtlicher Legitimität* (Saarbrücken, VDM Verlag Dr Müller, 2007).

[15] See J Farrall, *United Nations Sanctions and the Rule of Law* (Cambridge, Cambridge University Press, 2007).

[16] See J Klabbers, *An Introduction to International Institutional Law*, 2nd edn (Cambridge, Cambridge University Press, 2009) 10.

having a foreign policy and global superpower ambitions)[17] and Anne-Marie Slaughter has drawn attention to informal decision-making in networks of civil servants.[18] Most tellingly perhaps, the protection of the environment is done by and large by informal means: MOPs or COPs make the decisions, and in case a state fails to deliver, it is gently persuaded into compliance through an informal compliance procedure.

It is true, of course, that informal entities have existed also during the Cold War. Indeed, many owed their existence to the cold war: this would apply to, say, the Wassenaar Arrangement, dealing with export controls and non-proliferation of weapons, and the OSCE started its life, as is well-known, as the CSCE. The justification at the time was that informality was the default position, when considerations of high politics would make a formal arrangement difficult to sell. What has changed since the end of the Cold War is that informality has become a matter of choice: one possible dish on the smorgasbord of options.[19]

There is, to some extent, a connection between the emergence of de-formalisation and control as the two leading issues of the last couple of decades. It is not difficult to hypothesise that whenever relevant decisions are taken out of the public view, there will arise some demand for some form of control. But there is a second connection as well, more difficult to spot but for that no less troublesome: both de-formalisation and control may come to lead to distrust of public authority.

So how does that work? The link between de-formalisation and distrust will be obvious: where public authority is exercised out of the public view and with no means of control, democratic or otherwise, there is little reason to trust the authorities. The legitimacy (to use that fashionable, if often abused, phrase)[20] of global governance is at risk, and will come to depend fully on the outcomes of policy (so-called output legitimacy).[21] But if these are problematic—think global financial crisis, think climate change—then trust will quickly erode. Thus, for the moment: de-formalisation may contribute to distrust.

But how does control lead to distrust? After all, control is supposed to enhance trust in public authority, not undermine it. Yet, control is often conceptualised in deontological form. We create rules, expect institutions to abide by these rules, and devise procedures for testing this obedience. This comes with two problems. One is that the existence of rules typically invites behaviour that is acceptable under the rules, or can be justified. It invites 'pushing the envelope'; it is no longer about doing the proper thing, or acting justly or honestly, but about acting within the limits of the rule and seeing what you can get away with. And this may not necessarily be trustworthy behaviour, if only because rules tend to be imperfect.

Second, the existence of rules invites the creation of tribunals, monitoring mechanisms, inspection panels, or compliance officers. Ironically perhaps, this creates another layer of relations of trust: we cannot trust public power, but we need to trust the judges, the

[17] On the implausibility of the position that the EU be devoid of international legal personality, see J Klabbers, 'Presumptive Personality: The European Union in International Law', in M Koskenniemi (ed), *International Law Aspects of the European Union* (The Hague, Martinus Nijhoff, 1998) 231.

[18] See AM Slaughter, *A New World Order* (Princeton, Princeton University Press, 2004).

[19] See J Klabbers, 'Institutional Ambivalence by Design: Soft Organizations in International Law' (2001) 70 *Nordic Journal of International Law* 403.

[20] Compulsory reading is M Koskenniemi, 'Legitimacy, Rights, and Ideology: Notes towards a Critique of the New Moral Internationalism' (2003) 7 *Associations* 349.

[21] On the distinction between input legitimacy and output legitimacy, see FW Scharpf, *Governing in Europe: Effective and Democratic?* (Oxford, Oxford University Press, 1999).

inspectors, the compliance officers and auditors to make the system work.[22] But who judges the judges? Who audits the auditors? Who inspects the inspectors? The philosopher Onora O'Neill, whom it is appropriate to cite here in Cambridge, has spoken of the 'culture of suspicion' that is put in place by all sorts of accountability mechanisms. She advocates that instead of fantasising about total control, the only reasonable way to prevent control from lapsing into distrust altogether is to set up what she calls 'intelligent accountability'.[23]

IV. DISTRUST AND SUSPICION

So far, it is plausible to suggest that attempts to come to control international organisations stop short of living up to 'intelligent accountability'. In the Academy and in legal practice as well, several attempts have been undertaken, and are still being undertaken, to come to some kind of control. At least four different approaches can be distinguished, accompanied by the less systematic idea of creating some form of judicial review of the acts of international organisations; a position that increased in popularity after the Lockerbie case first occupied the ICJ.[24] But this plea for review is not terribly systematic, if only because it is not always clear what exactly the applicable law would be. It is one thing to call for review of Security Council acts, but if there is no law governing the Council, then review itself is bound to remain fruitless.

All in all, most of the work on control can be classified into four different groups. The first of these is what one may call the traditional approach: in much the same way as international law has rules on the responsibility of states, so too is it possible to imagine rules on the responsibility of international organisations. And if those organisations are seen as distinct from, but based on, member states, then it follows that rules on the responsibility of those member states can also be envisaged. Several academics have gone this way in the mid- or late 1990s, and so has the *Institut de Droit International*, focusing on member state responsibility. The International Law Commission is working on responsibility of international organisations *per se*, and caught on the horns of a problematic dilemma: it needs to adapt the rules on state responsibility (since two distinct regimes on responsibility in international law is not a good idea), but cannot overcome the circumstance that organisations are, really, not exactly the same as states and cannot be treated as black boxes: their member states always shine through.[25]

Besides, it remains unclear, as a matter of principle, which wrongful acts international organisations could commit to begin with. The ICJ held in 1980 that as subjects of international law, international organisations 'are bound by any obligations incumbent upon them under general rules of international law, under their constitutions, or under international agreements to which they are parties',[26] but it remains unclear how far this goes. The notion of 'general rules of international law' may perhaps cover the entire

[22] See generally M Power, *The Audit Society: Rituals of Verification* (Oxford, Oxford University Press, 1997).

[23] See Onora O'Neill, *A Question of Trust* (Cambridge, Cambridge University Press, 2002) 45, 58.

[24] See, eg, GR Watson, 'Constitutionalism, Judicial Review, and the World Court' (1993) 34 *Harvard International Law Journal* 1.

[25] See generally CM Brölmann, *The Institutional Veil in Public International Law: International Organisations and the Law of Treaties* (Oxford, Hart, 2007).

[26] See *Interpretation of the Agreement of 25 March 1951 between the WHO and Egypt*, advisory opinion, [1980] ICJ Reports 73, para. 37.

corpus of customary international law—if so, it would no doubt also include human rights obligations, space law obligations, et cetera. But it is perhaps more plausible and coherent to hold that the notion covers merely the general rules of the international legal system: the customary rules on the making of international law and on responsibility.[27] Since organisations are parties to few treaties, and since it is not immediately self-evident that they are bound by all rules of customary international law, it might be the case that there simply is not much general international law that applies to them. The work of the International Law Association, focusing somewhat more broadly on accountability, aims to circumvent this problem by developing so-called Recommended Rules and Practices without being very specific as to the basis of obligation and deriving some of these recommended standards from the internal law of international organisations, but this too remains vulnerable: why is organisation A bound to meet with obligations B or C?

A second approach is the Global Administrative Law Approach (GAL), which wrestles with the same problem and tries to overcome it by positing the existence of a global administrative space, which would then be governed by notions borrowed from domestic administrative legal orders.[28] Some exponents see this as utterly unproblematic;[29] others aim to fit it into the framework of international law through the medium of general principles,[30] and the main proponents of GAL seem to work foremost on the basis of the default idea that there is nothing really objectionable about such things about procedural notions such as transparency, participation, or proportionality.[31] Even in the absence of a clear basis of obligation, still few would object—so the reasoning seems to go.

Third, there is the constitutionalist approach, which by and large posits that at least some organisations are based on constitutional values from which they derive their legitimacy and, accordingly, they are bound to respect those values. These may include procedural ideas but will also, typically, include substantive human rights obligations. Put to the test though, there is general consensus that very few international organisations can be said to be constitutional in this particular way. Some posit that it applies to the UN, but then have to draw the conclusion that much of the Security Council's work is unconstitutional—a conclusion understandably shied away from. Some posit that it applies to the WTO, but the leading study (by Cass)[32] makes a strong skeptical case, if only because the WTO's human rights catalogue would be highly selective: the freedom to trade, but no rights to an adequate standard of living. The last one standing then may be the EU, but that is hardly representative.

[27] After all, if states can be bound only on the basis of consent and would be allowed to object persistently, why would it be different for international organisations, if these are supposed to be independent and separate legal persons? In short, the idea that the entire corpus of customary international law would be binding on international organisations demands a theory of obligation, yet none has been put forward (unless one counts claims that some of those customary norms are morally right and therefore legally binding; if so, however, one should wonder again why the same would not apply to states and their obligations).

[28] Seminal is the special volume of *Law and Contemporary Problems*, edited by B Kingsbury *et al* under the title *The Emergence of Global Administrative Law* (2005) 68 *Law and Contemporary Problems* 1.

[29] See DC Esty, 'Good Governance at the Supranational Scale: Globalizing Administrative Law?' (2006) 115 *Yale Law Journal* 1490.

[30] See A von Bogdandy *et al* (eds), *The Exercise of Public Authority by International Institutions: Advancing International Institutional Law* (Berlin, Springer, 2010).

[31] One problem here is, incidentally, that proportionality is hardly a merely procedural idea: its precise conceptualisation may well have serious distributive consequences.

[32] See DZ Cass, *The Constitutionalization of the World Trade Organization: Legitimacy, Democracy, and Community in the International Trading System* (Oxford, Oxford University Press, 2005).

Fourth, some organisations have installed compliance officers, or created departments of internal oversight, over the last decade or so. One finds these in the financial institutions (from World Bank to, for instance, NIB), but also elsewhere: NATO has such an organ, and even the OSCE, extra-legal as it claims to be, has set up an internal oversight mechanism. Their tasks are easier in that they are merely to test whether the organisation in question lives up to its internal procedures, standards and guidelines; the question as to the basis of obligation is therefore less prominent. Even so, the underlying approach is again that standards are set against which behaviour can be tested, and that may again result in distrust. In addition, most attempts at self-regulation may invite charges of window-dressing.

V. VIRTUE AND INTEGRITY

While all those approaches have their uses in complex societies, including the international society, they miss the vital point that rules often need interpretation, that rules can be circumvented, and that rules never decide on their own application. This seems to call for ever more tribunals and auditors and watchdogs, but doing so will only result, in Onora O'Neill's phrase, in a 'culture of suspicion'. Moreover, there might be situations where legal rules can't settle the issue.

The first of these may arise when the legal situation remains unclear. A possible, if horrendous, example relates to the genocide in Rwanda. It is plausible to claim that the UN should have intervened on grounds of morality; it would be less immediately clear that the UN violated a legal rule when it did not intervene.[33]

Second, there may be situations where the law is deficient. A possible example may relate to the use of more or less forced repatriation of refugees in Cambodia in the early 1990s: the number of refugees had grown so big, and the situation had become quasi-permanent to such an extent that the UNHCR, in particular Sergio Vieira de Mello, decided to send people back even if they would not do so voluntarily, having secured an agreement with the local authorities that the refugees concerned should not be harmed. Refugee law, so Vieira de Mello must have thought, was simply not capable of meeting the exigencies of the situation.[34]

Third, there may be situations where the law points in different directions. One oft-heard example is that of the World Bank and its possible human rights obligations. Should the World Bank follow its own constituent treaty (which instructs it to base its decisions on economic grounds alone) or should it take human rights into account? It might be attractive to prefer human rights, but doing so presupposes an argument about the supremacy of human rights, even over constituent documents.[35]

Fourth, in some cases the law may leave quite a bit of discretion to decision-makers, as is (many would say) the case with the Security Council. If it is indeed the case that the Security Council can decide as it pleases while disregarding any legal rule—other

[33] On Rwanda, see eg Barnett and Finnemore, Rules for the World.

[34] For a description of what went on, see Vieira de Mello's biography by S Power, *Chasing the Flame: One Man's Fight to Save the World* (London, Penguin, 2008) eg 67. Power quotes Vieira de Mello as saying 'If we don't find a compromise… we will permanently kill asylum' (67).

[35] The World Bank's (then) position was set out by I Shihata, 'Human Rights, Development and International Financial Institutions', (1992) 8 *American University Journal of International Law and Policy* 27.

perhaps than *ius cogens* standards, although even that might still raise questions—then something else is needed to prevent the Security Council from 'going overboard' and ensure the legitimacy of its actions.

Legal rules, in short, can hardly be expected to do more work than they capable of, and in situations where legal rules are absent, or are considered insufficient, or clash, or leave discretion, the most plausible complement would be to insist on the virtues of decision-makers, both within international organisations themselves and within influential member states.[36] That sounds like a trite observation, hopelessly unworkable, but at least it taps into one familiar sentiment: friend and foe alike agree that the UN under Hammarskjöld or, more recently, under Kofi Annan, was a different body from the UN under Waldheim. Obviously, styles of leadership and the character traits of leaders do have some influence on how the organisation is run, how it is perceived and, indeed, on how it acts.

How then to give effect to virtue ethics in the context of international organisations? One way of implementing virtue ethics relates to appointments of leadership. Appointments of people in leadership positions should not only take place on the basis of seniority, geographical representation, whether they are nationals of important donor states, or as plum rewards for long careers serving a political party, and not even on ability. All these factors may come into play, but to these should be added the individual's sense of virtue. If nothing else, this will at least prevent unsavoury public spectacles about leaders being castigated for sexual harassment of employees, or pocketing large sums of money from their home governments while in the employment of international organisations. On a bigger scale, it may also help sensitise the Security Council to the idea that rights concerning access to justice remain of relevance even in the fight against global terror, or help sensitise the World Bank to the idea that economic development should not come at the expense of people to be displaced.

Another point is to insist that the organisation actually stays relatively close to its functions. The WFP was set up to provide food in emergency situations; it was not set up to fight turf battles with other organisations on who gets to be present in crisis areas, who assumes main responsibility, or who receives the biggest funding. And the same applies to the agencies with which it often competes: UNICEF and UNHCR come to mind. Public administration scholars speak, in a similar vein, of conserving the values upon which an organisation is based.[37] While sometimes castigated as inherently conservative, such an approach can also be deemed progressive by stimulating a mindset of responsibility rather than a culture of suspicion.

[36] The classic exposé is Aristotle's *Nicomachean Ethics*. I have used the edition published as Aristotle, *Ethics* (London, Penguin, 1976). More current versions include some of the work of Alasdair McIntyre, *After Virtue: A Study in Moral Theory*, 2nd edn (London, Duckworth, 1985), and Rosalind Hursthouse, *On Virtue Ethics* (Oxford, Oxford University Press, 1999). Among lawyers, there is a recent branch of scholarship focusing on the virtues of lawyers and judges, exemplified by Colin Farrelly and Lawrence B Solum (eds), *Virtue Jurisprudence* (Basingstoke, Palgrave MacMillan, 2008) and Steve Sheppard, *I Do Solemnly Swear: The Moral Obligations of Legal Officials* (Cambridge, Cambridge University Press, 2009).

[37] The seminal work is LD Terry, *Leadership of Public Bureaucracies: The Administrator as Conservator*, 2nd edn (Armonk NY, Sharpe, 2003).

VI. TO CONCLUDE

The law of international organisations sometimes carries biblical overtones, inevitably perhaps: already the League of Nations was based on a 'covenant' (a biblical term, signifying the union with God), and inspired by the devout Christian Woodrow Wilson.[38] It is probably no coincidence that Nagendra Singh used the term 'salvation' in connection with international organisations. In this spirit, we may well conclude that over the last two decades or so, the discipline has come to the realisation that part of paradise has been lost: international organisations are in need of control, and not as benign as people thought a century ago. The paradise they once seemed to promise proved to be out of reach. Whether paradise can be regained is a different matter; it would seem better though not to wait for divine intervention or install a culture of suspicion but, instead, demand that political leadership acts responsibly.

[38] See JW Schulte Nordholt, *Woodrow Wilson: Een leven voor de wereldvrede* (Amsterdam, Meulenhoff, 1990) 59, 297.

17

Panels, Médiateurs et Mécanismes Informels de Contrôle des Activités des Organisations Internationales: Entre Accountability *et* Responsibility

PIERRE KLEIN*

L'UNE DES CARACTÉRISTIQUES marquantes de la période 1989–2010 réside sans nul doute dans le développement spectaculaire du phénomène de l'organisation internationale. Ce développement s'est traduit par des manifestations aussi diverses que la réactivation du rôle des Nations Unies dans le domaine du maintien de la paix et de la sécurité internationales, la création de l'OMC en tant que cadre institutionnel pour la réglementation du commerce mondial ou la multiplication des initiatives de coopération régionales ou sous-régionales dans toutes les parties du monde[1]. Pourtant, ces développements recèlent aussi ce que l'on pourrait appeler leur « part d'ombre ». La multiplication et la diversification des activités des organisations internationales ont en effet eu pour conséquence l'accroissement des risques d'atteintes aux droits d'autres sujets de l'ordre juridique international—Etats mais, surtout, personnes privées. C'est dès lors très logiquement que, depuis quelques années, la question de la responsabilité des organisations internationales en est venue à occuper une place centrale parmi les principales questions qui retiennent l'attention des auteurs, mais aussi des acteurs du droit international. Les travaux consacrés à cette thématique par la Commission du droit international des Nations Unies depuis 2002 témoignent de façon particulièrement visible de cet intérêt.[2] Toutefois, en dépit de son ampleur, ce dernier exercice se révèle—inévitablement—limité, dans la mesure où il a pour objectif de proposer un régime général de responsabilité applicable aux organisations internationales, sans se pencher de manière plus concrète sur les possibilités réelles de mise en œuvre d'une telle

* Professor, Director of the Centre for International Law, Université Libre de Bruxelles.

[1] Ces développements ont été amplement commentés et analysés par la doctrine. Voy. e.a. pour une analyse d'ensemble de la discipline, José Alvarez, « International Organizations : Then and Now », *A.J.I.L.*, 2006, 324 et ss., ainsi que les développements exposés en ce qui concerne de très nombreuses organisations internationales, universelles comme régionales, dans la première partie de *Bowett's Law of International Institutions* (6ème éd. par Philippe Sands et Pierre Klein, Londres, Sweet & Maxwell, 2009).

[2] Voy. en particulier le projet d'articles sur la responsabilité des organisations internationales adopté en première lecture par la Commission en 2009 (*in* Rapport de la C.D.I. pour 2009, doc. A/64/10, 14 et ss.).

responsabilité.[3] De plus, le projet a pour vocation essentielle de couvrir les relations de responsabilité entre organisations internationales et Etats, ou entre organisations, et ne prétend pas s'étendre aux situations de responsabilité de cette dernière catégorie de sujet avec les personnes privées.[4]

Pourtant, l'un des problèmes les plus fréquemment mis en évidence en la matière est précisément celui de l'absence de toute possibilité de recours à l'encontre des organisations internationales lorsque leur responsabilité paraît être engagée en raison de la violation de règles relevant du droit de l'organisation ou du droit international « général ». Les difficultés sont bien connues : d'une part, l'immunité de juridiction absolue dont bénéficie la très grande majorité des organisations internationales empêche tout recours devant les juridictions nationales. D'autre part, en dépit du fait que les règles régissant le fonctionnement de la plupart des organisations imposent l'établissement de mécanismes de recours permettant l'examen de telles réclamations (quoiqu'en des termes parfois restrictifs, à l'instar de la section 29 de la Convention de 1946 sur les privilèges et immunités des Nations Unies, qui n'impose cette obligation que pour le règlement des différends de droit privé auxquels l'Organisation est partie)[5], de tels mécanismes n'ont été concrètement mis en place que dans un nombre très réduit d'organisations internationales.[6]

Néanmoins, la pratique récente de quelques organisations semble refléter une certaine évolution dans ce domaine—on pourrait même parler (de l'amorce) d'une tendance… Trois mécanismes institués dans les dernières années, en lien avec certaines activités des organisations concernées susceptibles d'avoir un impact particulièrement significatif sur des personnes privées tierces à ces organisations méritent de retenir l'attention à cet égard :

- le panel consultatif des droits de l'homme (*Human Rights Advisory Panel*) institué dans le cadre de la Mission des Nations Unies au Kosovo (MINUK) ;
- le *Human Rights Review Panel* institué dans le cadre de la mission EULEX de l'Union européenne au Kosovo ; et
- le bureau du médiateur institué par résolution 1904 (2009) du Conseil de sécurité pour les réclamations relatives à l'inscription ou au maintien sur les « listes noires » établies dans le cadre de la lutte contre le terrorisme.

Il convient sans nul doute d'y ajouter une institution qui apparaît déjà maintenant bien établie : le panel d'inspection de la Banque mondiale, créé en 1993, qui a depuis lors servi de modèle à des mécanismes similaires qui ont été mis sur pied dans la quasi-totalité des autres institutions financières internationales.

L'objectif de la présente contribution est, d'une part, de présenter succinctement ces mécanismes et d'en dégager les principaux traits communs, ainsi que, d'autre part, d'en proposer une évaluation au regard des débats sur la responsabilité (ou la responsabilisation…) des organisations internationales. Pour poser la question en

[3] Ce dernier exercice serait d'ailleurs impossible à mener dans un tel cadre, puisqu'il impliquerait forcément un examen de la situation et de la pratique de chaque organisation internationale en la matière et ne permettrait pas l'élaboration de règles ayant vocation à recevoir une application générale.

[4] Voy. en particulier les articles 32, § 2 et 49 du projet (*loc. cit.*).

[5] *R.T.N.U.*, vol. 1, 17.

[6] Voy. e.a. sur ce point Pierre KLEIN, *La responsabilité des organisations internationales dans les ordres juridiques internes et en droit des gens*, Bruxelles, Bruylant, 541 et ss.

d'autres termes, ces mécanismes constituent-ils le stade le plus abouti d'un processus visant à instaurer une « responsabilisation » (*accountability*) générale des organisations internationales, ou une simple étape intermédiaire dans la mise en place de mécanismes de mise en œuvre de leur responsabilité dans un sens plus strictement juridique du terme (*responsibility*) ?

I. LES MÉCANISMES DE RECOURS INSTITUÉS AU SEIN DE CERTAINES ORGANISATIONS INTERNATIONALES ET LEURS CARACTÉRISTIQUES ESSENTIELLES

Il ne sera question ici que des mécanismes institués depuis quelques années au sein de certaines organisations internationales et ouverts à des plaignants extérieurs, qui paraissent refléter un mouvement de « responsabilisation » de ces organisations. Ce n'est pas à dire pour autant que cette tendance à la responsabilisation ne se manifeste pas également sous d'autres formes. On peut en particulier penser à l'institution, depuis un certain nombre d'années, de mécanismes internes destinés à superviser le fonctionnement de diverses organisations internationales. Des institutions comme le Groupe d'évaluation indépendante (IEG) ou le département d'évaluation des opérations (OED) au sein de la Banque mondiale[7], le Bureau des services de contrôle interne (OIOS) au sein des Nations Unies[8] ou encore les procédures d'audit mises sur pied dans diverses organisations participent clairement de ce mouvement. Les mécanismes examinés ici se distinguent toutefois clairement de ces structures strictement internes et de nature clairement administrative, en ce qu'ils visent à permettre à des personnes tierces à une organisation internationale qui sont affectées par les activités de celle-ci de faire entendre leur voix et de demander des comptes à cette organisation par le biais de mécanismes qui sont, pour la plupart, de nature quasi- ou para-juridictionnelle.

A. Les Mécanismes Institués

Le Panel d'Inspection de la Banque Mondiale

Le panel d'inspection a été créé par une résolution du Conseil d'administration de la BIRD et de l'IDA de 1993[9], qui a fait l'objet de révisions en 1996 et 1999. Le panel est composé de trois membres désignés par les administrateurs, et est chargé de se prononcer sur les demandes d'inspection présentées par tout groupe d'au moins deux personnes « directement affectées par une action ou une omission de la Banque qui découle du non-respect par la Banque de ses politiques ou de ses procédures opérationnelles concernant la conception, l'évaluation et/ou l'exécution d'un projet financé par la Banque [...] à condition que [...] ce manquement ait eu ou risque d'avoir des effets néfastes importants » (para. 12). Si le panel estime que les conditions de recevabilité sont remplies, il présente

[7] Voy. www.worldbank.org/oed/.

[8] Voy. www.un.org/depts/oios/.

[9] Résolution n°IBRD 93-10 ; Résolution n° IDA-93-6, 22 septembre 1993. Ces textes, ainsi que celui des clarifications, sont disponibles à l'adresse suivante : web.worldbank.org/WBSITE/EXTERNAL/EXTINSPECTIONPANEL/0,,contentMDK:20173262~menuPK:64129254~pagePK:64129751~piPK:64128378~theSitePK:380794,00.html.

une recommandation aux Administrateurs quant à la question de savoir si la demande doit donner lieu à une enquête (para. 19). Si les Administrateurs en décident ainsi, l'inspection est alors menée, et le panel soumet ses conclusions aux Administrateurs « sur la question de savoir si la Banque s'est conformée à toutes ses politiques et procédures pertinentes » (para. 22). Il revient *in fine* aux Administrateurs de se prononcer sur les décisions qu'ils estiment éventuellement devoir être prises en fonction des conclusions du rapport.

Le rôle du panel a été défini comme celui d'un « fact-finding body on behalf of the board »[10].

Le panel a été saisi de 67 requêtes entre 1994 et 2010 et, jusqu'en 2009, avait procédé à une inspection dans 26 cas (les autres requêtes étant déclarées irrecevables et un petit nombre étant toujours en attente d'une décision). Il n'existe par contre pas de données chiffrées aisément accessibles sur les constats atteints par le panel (de violation ou de respect par la Banque des politiques opérationnelles et des autres instruments applicables) ni sur les suites réservées aux rapports du panel.

Ainsi qu'on l'a indiqué, le panel créé au sein de la BIRD et de l'IDA a par la suite servi de modèle pour le développement de mécanismes similaires—sous des dénominations diverses— au sein de six autres institutions financières internationales, tant sur le plan universel qu'à l'échelle régionale (Banque interaméricaine de développement, Banque asiatique de développement, Société financière internationale, Agence multilatérale de garantie des investissements, Banque européenne de reconstruction et de développement et Banque africaine de développement)[11].

Le Panel Consultatif des Droits de l'Homme de la MINUK

La question des atteintes aux droits de l'homme reprochées à la MINUK dans le cadre de l'administration provisoire du Kosovo par cette mission a suscité de nombreux débats, en raison, en particulier, de l'absence de tout mécanisme de recours contre les autorités des Nations Unies[12]. Dans un premier temps, une compétence limitée a été conférée à cet égard au médiateur pour le Kosovo[13], avant de lui être retirée[14]. C'est en vue de combler cette lacune qu'a été créé le panel consultatif des droits de l'homme par un règlement de la MINUK adopté en 2006[15]. Le panel n'est toutefois entré en fonction qu'en 2008.

[10] Clarifications de 1999, para. 12.

[11] Voy. e.a. Richard E. Bissel et Suresh Nanwani, « Multilateral Development Bank Accountability Mechanisms : Developments and Challenges », *Manchester Journal of International Economic Law*, 2009, 2 et ss.

[12] Voy. e.a. Elizabeth Abraham, « The Sins of the Saviour : Holding the United Nations Accountable to International Human Rights Standards for Executive Order Detentions in its Mission in Kosovo », *American University Law Review*, 2003, 1291 ff. ; Tobias Irmscher, « The Legal Framework for the Activities of the United Nations Interim Administration in Kosovo: The Charter, Human Rights and the Law of Occupation », *G.Y.I.L.*, 2001 ; Julia Werzer, « The UN Human Rights Obligations and Immunity : An Oxymoron Casting a Shadow on the Transitional Administrations in Kosovo and East Timor », *Nordic Journal of I.L.*, 2008, 105. Voy. aussi le rapport de Human Rights Watch, « Better Late than Never—Enhancing the Accountability of International Institutions in Kosovo », juin 2007.

[13] Regulation N° 2000/38 on the Establishment of the Ombudsperson Institution in Kosovo (UNMIK/REG/2000/38, 30 juin 2000), para. 3.1.

[14] Regulation N° 2006/6 amending UNMIK Regulation N° 2000/38 on the Establishment of the Ombudsperson Institution in Kosovo, 16 février 2006.

[15] Regulation N° 2006/12 on the Establishment of the Human Rights Advisory Panel (UNMIK/REG/2006/12, 23 mars 2006).

Cette institution a compétence pour examiner les réclamations de personnes ou de groupes de personnes prétendant être victime d'une violation des droits de la personne par la MINUK (section 1.2). Sa compétence est limitée aux réclamations portant sur des violations commises avant avril 2005 (section 2), et la date limite pour l'introduction de réclamations a été fixée au 31 mars 2010[16]. Les trois membres du panel sont nommés par le Représentant spécial du Secrétaire général pour le Kosovo, sur proposition du président de la Cour européenne des droits de l'homme (section 5.1). Si le panel estime qu'une réclamation est conforme aux conditions de recevabilité fixées par le texte, il se prononce alors sur l'existence d'une violation et, le cas échéant, adresse une recommandation au Représentant spécial. Ce dernier dispose d'un pouvoir discrétionnaire et exclusif quant aux suites qu'il estime nécessaires de donner au constat réalisé par le panel. Le caractère strictement consultatif du panel est rappelé de façon très explicite dans le règlement qui l'institue (sp. section 1.3).

En 2010, le panel avait été saisi de 516 réclamations, et avait rendu près de quatre-vingts décisions sur la recevabilité et onze rapports au fond. Dans plusieurs d'entre eux, il a conclu à la violation de normes de protection des droits de la personne par la MINUK[17].

Le Panel de Contrôle des Droits de L'homme (Human Rights Review Panel) d'Eulex au Kosovo

Le rôle de la MINUK au Kosovo a été réduit de façon progressive. Nombre de ses fonctions ont été reprises—au moins *de facto*—par les nouvelles institutions kosovares et certaines par d'autres organisations internationales. C'est en particulier le cas dans le domaine du droit et de l'administration de la justice, où c'est maintenant l'Union européenne qui joue un rôle central, via sa mission EULEX. Visiblement inspirées dans une large mesure par le panel consultatif de la MINUK, les autorités européennes ont créé en 2009 le Panel de contrôle des droits de l'homme (Human Rights Review Panel)[18]. A l'instar du panel de la MINUK, le HRRP peut être saisi de réclamations relatives à des violations des droits de la personne dans le contexte de l'exécution des missions d'EULEX[19]. Son pouvoir est strictement consultatif ; il lui revient de déterminer si une violation des droits de la personne a ou non été commise et de formuler, le cas échéant, des recommandations quant aux mesures qui devraient être prises en conséquence. Le panel est composé de trois membres, dont un juge relevant de la mission EULEX. Les deux autres membres sont nommés par le chef de la mission EULEX. Les plaintes ne sont recevables que si elles concernent des faits survenus au Kosovo après le 9 décembre 2008[20]. Elles doivent par ailleurs répondre à d'autres exigences de recevabilité, basées dans une large mesure sur les règles applicables devant les organes internationaux de protection des droits de la personne.

[16] Administrative Direction n° 2009/1 Implementing UNMIK Regulation N° 2006/12 on the Establishment of the Human Rights Advisory Panel (UNMIK/DIR/2009/1, 17 octobre 2009), section 5.

[17] Voy. les statistiques disponibles sur le site internet du Panel (www.unmikonline.org/human_rights/index.htm).

[18] EULEX, Accountability Concept Paper, 29 octobre 2009.

[19] Voy. www.hrrp.eu/.

[20] Règles de procédure du panel, adoptées lors de sa première session, 9 juin 2010, règle 25.2. (disponibles sur le site du Panel).

A l'automne 2010, le panel avait été saisi de plusieurs plaintes, et avait rendu quatre décisions d'irrecevabilité[21].

Le Bureau du Médiateur auprès du Comité des Sanctions du Conseil de Sécurité

Si le recours par le Conseil de sécurité à des sanctions « ciblées », visant des individus ou des entités spécifiques, particulièrement dans le cadre de la lutte contre le terrorisme, est initialement apparu comme un progrès significatif par rapport aux sanctions « classiques », aux effets souvent indiscriminés, les inconvénients liés à leur mise en œuvre sont toutefois apparus relativement rapidement. Plus spécifiquement, ce sont les procédures suivies par le Comité des sanctions du Conseil de sécurité contre Al Qaida et les Taliban pour l'inscription sur les listes et le retrait de celles-ci des noms des personnes visées par ces sanctions qui ont assez rapidement suscité d'importants problèmes[22]. L'absence de toute garantie pour les droits des individus et groupes concernés et le fait que cette procédure est strictement unilatérale ont fait l'objet de sévères critiques, de la part de la doctrine[23] comme de certaines juridictions nationales ou régionales. La plus connue d'entre elles est sans nul doute celle qui a été formulée par la Cour de Justice des Communautés européennes dans les affaires jointes *Kadi et Al Barakat*. La Cour y a, même si c'est de façon indirecte—puisqu'elle ne se prononçait pas sur les résolutions du Conseil de sécurité en cause elles-mêmes, mais sur les règlements adoptés pour leur donner effet dans l'ordre juridique communautaire—souligné l'incompatibilité de ces procédures avec les normes essentielles de protection des droits fondamentaux[24].

Ces diverses critiques paraissent avoir joué un rôle important dans la décision prise par le Conseil de sécurité, en décembre 2009, de créer auprès du Comité des sanctions un Bureau du Médiateur, chargé de recevoir et d'examiner les demandes visant à la radiation des noms d'individus ou de groupes des listes établies par le Comité[25]. Lorsqu'il est saisi d'une telle demande, le Médiateur doit recueillir les informations pertinentes relatives à la demande et à la situation du requérant, avant que s'ouvre une période de conciliation « au cours de laquelle le dialogue peut être engagé avec le requérant » (para. 5 de l'annexe). Au terme de cette étape, il revient au Médiateur d'établir un rapport reprenant les informations recueillies et celles relatives au déroulement de la phase de conciliation. Le Médiateur doit, sur cette base, présenter au Comité des sanctions « les principaux arguments relatifs à la demande de radiation » (*ibid.*, para. 7). C'est ce dernier organe qui se prononce *in fine* sur la demande de radiation (*ibid.*, para. 10–12). Le Médiateur informe alors le requérant de la décision d'acceptation ou de rejet de sa demande, en lui fournissant certains éléments de motivation de cette décision (para. 13).

Le premier Médiateur (une médiatrice en l'occurrence) a été désigné par le Comité des sanctions en juin 2010, et le Bureau du Médiateur a entamé ses fonctions peu après.

Les différents mécanismes qui viennent d'être succinctement présentés ont été institués—et ont rempli leurs fonctions, pour les plus anciens d'entre eux—à des fins et

[21] Voy. le site du panel (*loc. cit.*), sous « cases ».

[22] Comité créé par la résolution 1267 (1999) du 15 octobre 1999.

[23] Voy. e.a. Andrea Bianchi, « Assessing the Effectiveness of the UN Security Council's Anti-terrorism Measures : The Quest for Legitimacy and Cohesion », *E.J.I.L.*, 2006, sp. 903.

[24] Affaires jointes C-402/05 P and C-415/05 P, *Yassin Abdullah Kadi et Al Barakaat International Foundation c. Conseil de l'Union européenne et Commission des Communautés européennes*, 3 septembre 2008, sp. paras 323.

[25] Résolution 1904 (2009) du 17 décembre 2009, para. 20 et annexe II.

dans des contextes très différents. Ils n'en présentent pas moins un certain nombre de caractéristiques communes, que l'on va maintenant brièvement évoquer.

B. Les Caractéristiques Essentielles des Mécanismes de Recours Institués au Sein de Diverses Organisations Internationales

• On l'a dit, le trait commun à ces différents mécanismes qui apparaît le plus significatif est sans nul doute le fait qu'ils sont ouverts aux personnes privées tierces à l'organisation concernée, qui seraient affectées par les actions—ou omissions—de cette dernière. Dans le cas des panels, des critères de recevabilité des demandes ont chaque fois été institués, qui ne paraissent cependant pas de nature à restreindre de manière excessive l'accès des plaignants à ces mécanismes. Les deux mécanismes de création plus ancienne (le panel d'inspection de la Banque Mondiale et celui de la MINUK—encore que cette qualification soit très relative dans ce dernier cas) ont ainsi été utilisés de façon soutenue et ont été saisis d'un nombre significatif de recours, dont un nombre appréciable a été examiné au fond.

• Dans trois cas sur quatre, la création du mécanisme de recours répond clairement à des pressions et demandes extérieures (remises en cause des pratiques de la BIRD à la fin des années 1980, vives critiques adressées à la MINUK en ce qui concerne la protection des droits fondamentaux, entre autres par diverses instances internationales dont la Commission de Venise du Conseil de l'Europe[26], résistances à l'application des sanctions « ciblées » du Conseil de sécurité sur le plan national ou régional). Ces mécanismes ont donc été institués essentiellement en réaction à ces critiques et pressions extérieures. Seul le Human Rights Review Panel d'Eulex fait exception à cet égard, car sa mise sur pied apparaît plutôt s'inscrire dans une démarche « préventive » ou proactive (à la suite, très vraisemblablement d'une réflexion nourrie par le précédent de la MINUK).

• Les mécanismes sont tous composés d'experts indépendants, et certaines dispositions des règles qui les établissent visent précisément à garantir cette indépendance de manière institutionnelle. Cependant, dans tous les cas, ces experts sont nommés par l'autorité dont il s'agit de contrôler l'activité. Ceci n'a toutefois pas empêché que, dans les faits, les deux mécanismes plus anciens se soient illustrés par un fonctionnement empreint d'un haut degré de professionnalisme et de rigueur. Leur indépendance ne paraît avoir été à aucun moment effectivement mise en cause.

• La compétence *ratione materiae* de ceux de ces mécanismes qui peuvent être caractérisés comme « quasi-» ou « para-judiciaires » s'avère relativement limitée. Ainsi, la compétence du panel d'inspection est restreinte à un certain nombre de règles internes propres à la Banque mondiale (dans une large mesure les « politiques opérationnelles » régissant les opérations de cette institution dans différents domaines). De même, celle du panel consultatif de la MINUK est limitée aux droits de la personne protégés par un certain nombre d'instruments internationaux énumérés dans le règlement instituant le panel. Il n'est donc pas question, pour ces différents mécanismes, de se prononcer sur toute allégation quelconque de manquement à d'autres types d'obligations internationales (en particulier les normes internationales de protection des droits de la personne pour le panel d'inspection de la Banque mondiale).

[26] Voy. l'avis de la Commission sur les droits de l'homme au Kosovo : établissement éventuel de mécanismes de contrôle, avis n° 280/2004, doc. CDL-AD(2004)033 du 11 octobre 2004, para. 91 e.a.

• Les mécanismes analysés sont tous de nature consultative. Même si le fonctionnement de la plupart d'entre eux (les panels) présente des parentés certaines avec le fonctionnement d'organes judiciaires, leur pouvoir est dans tous les cas limité à la présentation de recommandations destinées aux organes politiques des organisations concernées. Ces derniers seuls disposent d'un pouvoir de décision—souvent assez largement discrétionnaire—quant à la mise en œuvre de ces recommandations et quant aux mesures correctives qu'il convient éventuellement d'adopter. La compétence des mécanismes de recours examinés se limite—au plus—au constat d'une éventuelle violation, sans que des conséquences particulières puissent en être tirées (en particulier en ce qui concerne la réparation éventuelle de dommages qui auraient été subis par les plaignants en raison des actions ou omissions de l'organisation concernée).

Le Bureau du Médiateur institué par la résolution 1904 (2009) se distingue encore plus nettement sur ce point, car son rôle apparaît de nature essentiellement administrative ; on pourrait le qualifier de simple mécanisme d'appui à la décision de l'organe politique auquel il est rattaché (le Comité des sanctions).

• Dans la même logique d'ensemble, il n'existe aucune voie de recours supérieur qui permettrait éventuellement de remettre en cause les conclusions atteintes par ces mécanismes dans une affaire donnée. Dans le meilleur des cas, seules existent des procédure de révision ou de ré-examen dans certaines circonstances particulières, mais qui restent aux mains du mécanisme de contrôle lui-même.

*

Ces principales caractéristiques des mécanismes en cause étant établies, il est maintenant possible de passer à une appréciation plus critique de ceux-ci.

II. UNE PROPOSITION D'ÉVALUATION DES MÉCANISMES DE RECOURS INSTITUÉS AU SEIN DE CERTAINES ORGANISATIONS INTERNATIONALES

Il apparaît clairement, à ce stade, que le bilan que l'on peut dresser de l'établissement des différents mécanismes de contrôle qui viennent d'être passés en revue ne peut être que mitigé et donner lieu à des appréciations contrastées. Comme on va le voir, cette différence de constat s'explique en réalité dans une large mesure par la conception même que l'on peut se faire de ce que doit—ou devrait—être le régime de responsabilité auquel sont soumises les organisations internationales—ou plus exactement le critère de responsabilité applicable à cette catégorie de sujets.

A. Un Bilan Mitigé—Des Évaluations Divergentes

Lorsqu'on établit un bilan de la pertinence et de l'efficacité des mécanismes étudiés dans la présente contribution, il est clairement possible, selon les perspectives, de voir un verre à moitié vide ou à moitié plein.

Il est certainement (au moins) à moitié vide au regard des exigences généralement acceptées qui sont requises de mécanismes de recours, particulièrement au regard des règles protectrices des droits de la personne (droit à un recours effectif). Car il convient assurément de garder à l'esprit que c'est bien ce qui est en cause dans toutes les situations concernées par ces mécanismes : dans tous les cas, il s'agit de violations (potentielles ou alléguées) de droits dont un certain nombre peut être qualifié de droits fondamentaux (droit à la vie, à l'intégrité physique, à la liberté de la personne, au procès équitable, à la propriété, à ne pas subir de déplacement forcé, à un environnement sain, etc.). A cet égard, aucun des mécanismes décrits plus haut ne « passe le test » : ils pèchent, entre autres, par l'absence d'indépendance dans le processus de nomination de leurs membres, l'absence d'un véritable pouvoir de décision, ou encore l'inexistence de recours à un échelon supérieur.

Comme l'a par exemple relevé Lord Hope dans une décision rendue par la Cour suprême du Royaume-Uni au début de l'année 2010 à propos de la création par le Conseil de sécurité du Bureau du médiateur du Comité des sanctions, « [w]hile these improvements are to be welcomed, the fact remains that there was not when the designations [inscriptions sur les listes] were made, and still is not, any effective judicial remedy'[27]. L'absence de toute garantie de mise en œuvre effective des recommandations adoptées par les instances examinées ici—et de perspective de réparations matérielles (en tout cas pour le panel de la Banque mondiale)— constitue également une limitation cruciale à l'efficacité de ces mécanismes.

De plus, on ne peut manquer de relever que les organisations mêmes qui ont institué ces instances (ou certains organes au sein de ces organisations) se sont parfois efforcés de limiter de manière sensible la portée de ceux-ci. Ce fut le cas de la direction de la BIRD qui, jusqu'aux clarifications de 1999, a eu recours à la technique des plans d'action ou de remédiation pour tenter d'éviter que des inspections soient effectivement réalisées par le panel dans certaines situations[28]. La réaction des autorités de la MINUK aux travaux du Human Rights Advisory Panel a elle aussi été pour le moins mitigée. Celles-ci ont ainsi limité de manière drastique la portée de l'activité du panel, en disposant, par une directive administrative de 2009, que les requêtes présentées au panel devaient être déclarées irrecevables si ces demandes étaient aussi susceptibles d'être introduites auprès de l'Organisation dans le cadre des procédures classiques visant la réparation des dommages causés aux tiers (*third-party claims*)[29]. On en revient ainsi, pour cette catégorie de plaintes—qui représente une part substantielle de celles dont a été saisi le panel—aux mécanismes strictement unilatéraux et purement administratifs qui sont applicables dans le contexte de l'ensemble des opérations de maintien de la paix pour l'examen de telles réclamations[30]. Le panel a de ce fait été contraint de déclarer irrecevables plusieurs dizaines de requêtes qu'il avait pourtant préalablement déjà jugées admissibles en application de ses règles de fonctionnement initiales[31].

[27] HM Treasury v Mohammed Jabar Ahmed and ors (FC); HM Treasury v Mohammed al-Ghabra (FC); R (on the application of Hani El Sayed Sabaei Youssef) v HM Treasury [2010] UKSC 2, 27 janvier 2010, para. 78.

[28] Voy. e.a. sur ce point Anne Lagerwall, « Le panel d'inspection peut-il réellement contrôler la conformité des actions de la Banque mondiale alors qu'il en est l'organe ? », à paraître in *Revue belge de droit international*, 2010.

[29] Administrative Direction n° 2009/1 Implementing UNMIK Regulation n° 2006/12 on the Establishment of the Human Rights Advisory Panel, UNMIK/DIR/2009/1, 17 octobre 2009, para. 2.2.

[30] Voy. sur ces mécanismes (*Claims Review Boards*) le rapport du Secrétaire général sur les procédures instituées pour la mise en œuvre de l'article VIII, Section 29, de la Convention sur les privilèges et immunités des Nations Unies, adoptée par l'Assemblée générale le 13 février 1946, doc. A/C.5/49/65, 24 avril 1995, paras. 17 et ss.

[31] Voy. e.a. la décision du panel en date du 31 mars 2010 dans l'affaire *Kadri Balaj (on behalf of Mon Balaj), Shaban Xheladini (on behalf of Arben Xheladini), Zenel Zemeli and Mustafa Nerjovaj against UNMIK* (case N° 04/07) para. 48.

Aux limitations structurelles de ces mécanismes de contrôle évoquées ci-dessus sont ainsi venus s'ajouter des obstacles dressés par les administrations mêmes dont ces procédures avaient pour but de contrôler les agissements. Pour ces différents motifs, l'on pourrait donc être tenté de livrer un bilan relativement négatif des mécanismes de contrôle institués—plus ou moins—récemment au sein de quelques organisations internationales.

Pourtant, il ne manque pas d'arguments pour voir, à l'inverse, le verre comme étant (au moins) à moitié plein. Il en est en premier lieu ainsi car la création de ces mécanismes représente indubitablement un mouvement et une évolution notables par rapport à la situation antérieure, où de telles possibilités de présenter une réclamation ou de faire valoir ses droits auprès de l'organisation à laquelle il était reproché de les ignorer étaient tout simplement inexistantes. Pour la plupart des organisations concernées[32], il s'agit d'un développement sans précédent.

C'est ce qui explique certainement les appréciations parfois très laudatives dont les plus anciens de ces mécanismes ont fait l'objet. C'est particulièrement le cas du panel d'inspection de la Banque mondiale, qui a suscité une abondante littérature. L'éloge le plus appuyé est sans nul doute celui que l'on trouve dans une publication intitulée *Accountability at the World Bank—The Inspection Panel at 15 Years* (2009), où la création du panel d'inspection de la Banque mondiale est qualifiée « d'éclat de génie » et d'« innovation unique dans la gouvernance internationale » (par son président, il est vrai…)[33]. En des termes plus modestes, les auteurs ont fréquemment mis en évidence l'apport que représentait le panel en permettant aux personnes et aux groupes affectés par les projets de la Banque de faire entendre leur voix au sein de celle-ci, et en assurant à des individus et des ONG un accès à une organisation jusque-là très fermée à de telles participations extérieures[34]. La contribution du panel à la mise en place d'une certaine « culture de responsabilité » au sein de la Banque a également été mise en évidence, de même que l'impact réel de ce mécanisme sur l'évolution des projets de cette institution susceptibles d'entraîner des effets négatifs pour les populations.

Dans le même ordre d'idées, la création du panel consultatif des droits de l'homme de la MINUK a permis de rompre avec l'image d'une administration territoriale qui se serait trouvée « au-dessus des lois » et immunisée de toute forme de contrôle effectif—et de responsabilisation—pour les conséquences de ses (in)actions. Elle permet elle aussi aux individus ou groupes qui se disent affectés par les agissements des Nations Unies au Kosovo de faire entendre leur voix et leurs griefs, et contraint l'Organisation à prendre la mesure des éventuelles conséquences négatives de ses activités sur les populations du territoire soumis à l'administration internationale.

Il apparaît donc clairement, au total, que deux types de jugements peuvent être portés sur ces mécanismes, en des sens en fin de compte assez largement opposés. Ces différences d'appréciation paraissent en réalité refléter dans une large mesure une différence de paradigme.

[32] A l'exception notable de l'Union européenne, qui possède des mécanismes de recours judiciaires ouverts aux personnes privées contre les actes des institutions ; il convient toutefois de relever que ces voies de recours n'étaient pas accessibles pour contester les actes de la mission Eulex au Kosovo.

[33] p. ix ; cette publication est disponible en ligne via le site internet du panel d'inspection, à l'adresse suivante : web.worldbank.org/WBSITE/EXTERNAL/EXTINSPECTIONPANEL/0,,contentMDK:22333794~pagePK:64129751~piPK:64128378~theSitePK:380794,00.html.

[34] Voy. e.a. Laurence Boisson de Chazournes, «Le Panel d'inspection de la Banque mondiale: à propos de la complexification de l'espace public international », *Revue générale de droit international public*, 2001, No 1, 145.

B. Une divergence d'appréciation qui s'explique largement par une différence de conception de la notion même de responsabilité

Le terme « responsabilité » n'est clairement pas dépourvu d'ambiguïtés sémantiques. Des conceptions fort différentes de ce qu'il est censé recouvrir comme situations—et comme conséquences de celles-ci—paraissent manifestement coexister, particulièrement en ce qui concerne les organisations internationales. L'unique terme que connaît la langue française reflète mal une polysémie[35] nettement plus apparente en langue anglaise, où l'on retrouve une différenciation—en particulier—entre les termes *responsibility* et *accountability*. C'est sur cette différenciation que l'on s'appuiera maintenant pour proposer une tentative d'explication de la différence de lecture qui vient d'être mise en évidence.

Le premier constat opéré dans la sous-section qui précède (celui du verre à moitié vide) s'inscrit plutôt sur une toile de fond marquée par une approche très « juridicisée », et la référence à des règles « dures », au regard desquelles les mécanismes analysés ici paraissent présenter de sérieuses insuffisances. C'est, dans une large mesure, l'approche retenue par la CDI dans son traitement de la problématique de la responsabilité des organisations internationales et traduite par le recours au vocable de « *responsibility* ».

Cette approche, on le sait, a été jugée par certains (parfois en des termes assez durs) trop théorique, abstraite, déconnectée des réalités et des conditions réelles dans lesquelles les organisations internationales contemporaines doivent accomplir leur mission[36].

La suggestion a été émise, à cet égard, que le concept d'*accountability* s'avérait plus adapté à la situation spécifique des organisations internationales que celui de responsabilité, dans le sens plus strictement juridique du terme (*responsibility*)[37]. L'*accountability*[38] serait en quelque sorte une version atténuée de la responsabilité au sens juridique classique—dans le sens proposé par les auteurs qui paraissent favoriser l'inscription de la problématique qui nous occupe ici dans ce paradigme, il s'agirait plutôt d'une obligation primaire de comportement que d'une obligation secondaire, dont relèvent les règles sur la *responsibility*, selon la typologie classique[39]. En soi, le paradigme de *l'accountability* serait plus adapté aux organisations internationales—même si les fondements précis de ce diagnostic ne paraissent pas toujours évidents à cerner. Et envisagés à cette aune, les mécanismes examinés dans la présente communication s'avéreraient largement satisfaisants, en ce qu'ils contraignent les organisations

[35] Cette polysémie se reflète bien dans les sept définitions différentes qui sont données du terme dans le *Dictionnaire de droit international public* (J. Salmon, dir.) Bruxelles/Paris, Bruylant/AUF, 2001, 994.

[36] Voy. e.a. José Alvarez, « International Organizations : Accountability or Responsibility ? », Luncheon Address, CCIL, 27 octobre 2006 ; disponible à l'adresse suivante : *www.asil.org/aboutasil/documents/CCILspeech061102.pdf*.

[37] *Ibid*., voy. aussi, de manière plus nuancée, Jan Klabbers, *An Introduction to International Institutional Law*, Cambridge, C.U.P., 2ème éd., 2009, 292.

[38] Ce terme est par ailleurs lui aussi particulièrement large, et sa polysémie est tout aussi avérée. Dans son rapport de 2004, l'International Law Association incorpore dans ce vocable trois degrés de « responsabilité »: « forms of internal and external scrutiny, irrespective of potential liability/responsibility », « tortious liability [private law] », « responsibility arising out of acts or omissions which do constitute a breach of international and/or institutional law » (« Accountability of International Organizations », Berlin Conference, 2004, 5 ; disponible à l'adresse suivante : www.ila-hq.org/en/committees/index.cfm/cid/9). On l'emploiera ici essentiellement dans le premier de ces sens.

[39] Sur l'identification du concept d'*accountability* comme renvoyant plutôt au domaine des normes primaires, voy. sp. Laurence Boisson de Chazournes, « Changing Roles of International Organizations : Global Administrative Law and the Interplay of Legitimacies », *International Organizations Law Review*, 2009, 662.

concernées à rendre des comptes sur (certaines de) leurs activités et sur la manière dont elles les mènent, sans pour autant les engager dans le « carcan » des règles classiques de la responsabilité au sens plus strictement juridique du terme. En un sens, on pourrait d'ailleurs voir dans l'instauration de ce type de mécanismes—avec les diverses limitations qui ont été évoquées ci-dessus—la preuve même que le paradigme de l'*accountability* est le seul qui soit véritablement adapté à cette catégorie particulière de sujets que sont les organisations internationales, tout autre type de procédure ou mécanisme de contrôle se révélant par essence inappropriés. Comme l'écrit par exemple à ce sujet Jan Klabbers, en conclusion de la présentation qu'il livre du panel d'inspection de la Banque mondiale,

> [...] organizations are supposed to control themselves, rather than be held accountable later by others. As such, this may signify a move away from traditional legal thought about responsibility[40].

Si cette différence de paradigme entre *accountability* et *responsibility* explique largement les différences d'appréciation que l'on peut porter sur les mécanismes en cause, il n'est pas sûr, toutefois que la conclusion selon laquelle les mécanismes de *responsibility* sont incompatibles avec l'essence même des organisations internationales s'impose de manière si évidente.

Il est manifeste que les modalités de fonctionnement des mécanismes ou institutions de contrôle étudiés ici constituent autant d'expressions des limites de ce que les organisations internationales paraissent prêtes à accepter à l'heure actuelle. Des mécanismes de contrôle, certes, mais aux pouvoirs et compétences réduits : organes consultatifs, disposant au mieux de pouvoirs de recommandation, voire simples soutiens à la décision de l'exécutif dans d'autres cas. Faut-il pour autant conclure à une impossibilité conceptuelle d'aller au-delà ? L'établissement de mécanismes contraignants, disposant de véritables pouvoirs de décision, imposant éventuellement des réparations matérielles dans certains cas est-il inconcevable sur le plan théorique ou pratique ?

Rien ne semble à vrai dire imposer pareille conclusion. A bien des égards, la phase actuelle semble plutôt correspondre à une étape dans le développement des organisations internationales, et dans le-lent-processus de « responsabilisation » dans lequel certaines d'entre elles au moins sont progressivement engagées. Les mécanismes en questions ont pour l'essentiel été institués à la suite de pressions extérieures, et de la réalisation du fait que les pouvoirs croissants exercés par les organisations concernées doivent s'accompagner de contrepoids et de contrôles. Une telle évolution paraît tout à fait susceptible de se poursuivre. D'autres pressions, d'autres réflexions et mises en cause provoqueront selon toute vraisemblance des évolutions ultérieures dont rien n'interdit de penser qu'elles déboucheront un jour sur la création de véritables mécanismes de mise en œuvre de la responsabilité des organisations, dans le plein sens du terme, sans qu'il y ait d'« impossibilité génétique » à cela, ou d'incompatibilité fondamentale avec l'essence même des organisations internationales.

[40] *Op. cit.*, 293.

18

Compliance with Decisions of International Courts as Indicative of their Effectiveness: A Goal-based Analysis

YUVAL SHANY*

INTERNATIONAL COURTS AND tribunals have become a mainstay of international relations in the 21st century. As a growing number of international disputes are referred to international adjudicatory mechanisms, and an increasing number of legal norms depend on permanent judicial bodies for their interpretation and application (ie, a rise in 'upstream' state activity leading to adjudication), more and more attention has been directed to the question of compliance with rendered international court decisions (ie, 'downstream', post-judgment, state activity).[1] The subject has been discussed in numerous new books and articles in the fields of international law and international relations,[2] and increasingly finds itself on the agenda of international organisations.[3] An illustrative example may be the Council of Europe's (CoE) practice of issuing annual reports discussing the execution of European Court of Human Rights (ECtHR) judgments from 2007 onwards.[4] Other judicial and quasi-judicial bodies have

* Hersch Lauterpacht Chair in Public International Law, Faculty of Law, Hebrew University of Jerusalem. The research for this article was undertaken with the support of a European Research Council Starting Grant for Frontier Research and with the help of Ms Sharon Avital. I also thank Joel Trachtman, Carlos Espósito, Sigall Horovitz, Gilad Noam, Rotem Giladi, Erin Gray, Sivan Shlomo, Thorbjorn Bjornsson, and Yael Vias for their useful comments and references.

[1] For a discussion of 'upstream' and 'downstream' acceptance of international judicial authority, see P Couvreur, 'The Effectiveness of the International Court of Justice in the Peaceful Settlement of International Disputes', in AS Muller et al (eds), *The International Court of Justice: Its Future Role after Fifty Years* (London, Kluwer Law International, 1996) 83, 110.

[2] See eg, S Mitchell and P Hensel, 'International Institutions and Compliance with Agreements' (2007) 51 *American Journal of Political Science* 721; C Schulte, *Compliance with Decisions of the International Court of Justice* (Oxford, OUP, 2004); Aloysius P Llamzon, 'Jurisdiction and Compliance in Recent Decisions of the International Court of Justice' (2008) 18 *EJIL* 815; C Paulson, 'Compliance with Final Judgments of the International Court of Justice since 1987' (2004) 98 *Am J Int'l L* 434; C Hillebrecht, 'Rethinking Compliance: The Challenges and Prospects of Measuring Compliance with International Human Rights Tribunals' (2009) 1 *Journal of Human Rights Practice* 362.

[3] See eg, EC Press Release, 'Financial Penalties for Member States who fail to comply with Judgments of the European Court of Justice: European Commission Clarifies Rules', 15 Dec 2005.

[4] See Council of Europe—Committee of Ministers, Supervision of the Execution of Judgments of the European Court of Human Rights: First Annual Report (2007); Council of Europe—Committee of Ministers, Supervision of the Execution of Judgments of the European Court of Human Rights: Second Annual Report

also indicated a growing interest in monitoring follow-up activities in order to encourage compliance with their decisions.[5]

It appears that the increased attention paid to compliance with international judgments—understood hereby as a causal relationship between judicial decisions and state practice, leading to a convergence of the two[6]—is built on the assumption that compliance offers us a useful perspective for evaluating the international rule of law. For example, in a 2006 speech given to the UN Security Council, International Court of Justice (ICJ) President Rosalyn Higgins linked between international law's systemic welfare and compliance with ICJ judgments, stating that strengthening international law may also mean 'ensuring compliance with decisions of international bodies'.[7] In addition, compliance with judicial decisions has been perceived as a building block of institutional legitimacy and effectiveness.[8] For example, the foreword to the first CoE Report on Execution of ECtHR Judgments states that: 'Supervision of execution is… an essential element of the credibility of the system and the efficiency of the actions of the Court'.[9]

The purpose of this paper is to revisit some of the assumptions concerning the usefulness of studying compliance with international judgments, by focusing in particular on the relationship between remedy compliance—ie, compliance with the remedial portions of international judgments, and international court effectiveness. In a nutshell, I argue that one cannot understand the relationship between remedy-compliance and effectiveness without considering the impact that courts actually have on state practice, and without assessing the ways in which remedy compliance advances the goals of international courts (mainly, through promoting primary norm compliance, dispute resolution, and regime support and legitimisation). A more comprehensive and contextual examination may show that studying remedy compliance is, at times, a useful way for understanding court effectiveness; but at other times the links between these two concepts are tenuous.

I. GIVING REMEDY COMPLIANCE A MEANING

A first, sometimes overlooked,[10] point relating to the utility of using remedy compliance as a proxy for judicial effectiveness is that remedy compliance may be strongly influenced not only by the respective power relations between the relevant international court and

(2008); Council of Europe—Committee of Ministers, Supervision of the Execution of Judgments of the European Court of Human Rights: Third Annual Report (2009).

[5] See, for example, the designation of a Special Human Rights Committee Rapporteur for Follow-Up on Communications. Rules of Procedure of the Human Rights Committee, Rule 95, UN Doc. HRI/GEN/3/Rev. 1 (2003).

[6] See Benedict Kingsbury, 'The Concept of Compliance as a Function of Competing Conceptions of International Law' (1998) 19 *Mich J Int'l L* 345, 348.

[7] Rosalyn Higgins, Speech at the United Nations Security Council's Thematic Debate on 'Strengthening International Law', 22 June 2006.

[8] For an extensive discussion of definitions of judicial effectiveness, see Yuval Shany, Assessing the Effectiveness of International Courts: 'A Goal-Based Approach', *AJIL* (forthcoming in 2012).

[9] CoE, 1st Report on ECtHR Judgment Execution, 7. See also *Baena-Ricardo et al. v Panama,* I/A CHR Ser C, No. 104) (Nov. 28, 2003)(*Competence*) para 129.

[10] See eg, EA Posner and JC Yoo, 'Judicial Independence in International Tribunals', 93 *Calif L Rev* (2005) 28 ('A tribunal is effective if states comply with its judgments'); Paulson, Compliance with Final Judgments, 2004.

losing states, but also by two additional variants: the substantive positions endorsed by the judgment in question which the remedies give expression to, and the specific type of remedies issued. It may be hypothesised, in this regard, that the less objectionable for the losing party the substantive portion of the court judgment is, and the less onerous the remedies issued, the greater the judgment's 'compliance pull' is expected to be.[11] This basic insight on compliance is supported not only in the international legal realism literature (often using game theory models to illustrate the interplay between state interests and compliance),[12] and the literature on international legitimacy (linking compliance to the perceived procedural and substantive legitimacy of the underlying norms);[13] it also finds support in some empirical work, which suggests that 'high-cost' judgments (ie, judgments the compliance with which adversely affects important state interests in a significant manner) are less complied with than 'low-cost' judgments (ie, judgments that can be complied with, without sacrificing important state interests).[14] Alternatively, it has been suggested that stronger *ex ante* enforcement mechanisms are needed to stimulate compliance with 'high cost' judgments.[15] As a result, international courts exercising discretion as to how to formulate their judgments, and what remedies to issue, may arguably impact the degree of compliance pull that their decisions would generate by aiming 'high' or 'low' (by facilitating different levels of state resistance).[16]

A key challenge confronting international courts in connection with remedy design derives from the tension between the two constitutive elements of compliance—norm-practice convergence and judicial causation or impact: the less onerous the remedies issued by the international court are, the smaller is the potential change in state practice brought about by these remedies and thus the less 'deep' (and more 'shallow') is the court's impact.[17] In Koskenniemic terms, judicial remedies may fail to impact state practice either because they are rejected by states as utopian—completely divorced from their interests, or apologetic—reflective of practices existing independently of the judgment—and therefore meaningless.[18] Put differently, high levels of correlation between state practice and court judgments may be, at times, equally indicative of judicial impact as of the lack thereof. Thus, measuring compliance only by way of examining norm-practice

[11] See eg, DP Forsythe, 'The International Court of Justice at Fifty', in AS Muller et al (eds), *The International Court of Justice: Its Future Role after Fifty Years* (London, Kluwer Law International, 1996) 385, 396. Other potential factors affecting the 'compliance pull' of remedial orders, which will not be discussed here, are the order's specificity (arguably, more specific orders lend themselves to greater compliance); see TM Franck, *The Power of Legitimacy Among Nations* (New York, Oxford University Press, 1990); and the inclusion in the judgment of 'legitimizing statements' rendering it more acceptable to the parties. See T Treves, 'Aspects of Legitimacy of Decisions of International Courts and Tribunals', in Wolfrum, Rüdiger; Röben, Volker (eds) *Legitimacy in International Law* (New York, Springer 2008) 169.

[12] See eg, EA Posner and J Goldsmith, *The Limits of International Law* (Oxford, Oxford University Press, 2005) 154; AT Guzman: A Compliance Based Theory' (2001) 90 *Cal L Rev* 1823, 1846; L Henkin, *International Law: Politics and Values* (Kluwer Law International, The Hague,1995) 50; GW Downs *et al*, 'Is the Good News About Compliance Good News About Cooperation?', (1996) 3 *International Organization* 379, 380.

[13] Franck, *Power and Legitimacy*.

[14] See eg, D Hawkins and W Jacoby, 'Partial Compliance: A Comparison of the European and Inter-American American Courts for Human Rights' (2008) 4, www.stevendroper.com/ECHR%20Hawkins%20and%20Jacoby%20APSA%202008.pdf ('We find some evidence that compliance is higher when it is easy').

[15] See eg, BA Simmons, 'Capacity, Commitment, and Compliance', (2002) 46 *Journal of Conflict Resolution* 829, 843.

[16] For a discussion of 'compliance pull', see Franck, 'The Power of Legitimacy', 23 ff.

[17] For a discussion of the parallel phenomenon of 'compliance depth', see Downs *et al*, 'Is the Good News About Compliance', 383.

[18] M Koskenniemi, *From Apology to Utopia: The Structure of International Legal Argument* (Cambridge, Cambridge University Press, 2005) 17.

convergence, without considering the nature of the judgment and remedies in question and their relationship to pre-existing practices and interests, may tell us very little about judicial impact.

Assessing judicial impact through the combined study of the aforementioned two elements—action (judgment) and reaction (state practice), may enable us to formulate, in turn, an opinion on judicial effectiveness—understood hereby as the degree in which international courts attain their goals.[19] This is possible, however, only if judicial impact is discussed in light of the goals of international courts. Such a discussion would help us contextualise remedy compliance as a potential indicator of judicial effectiveness.

My research on international judicial effectiveness posits that most international courts are created in order to advance the following four principal overarching goals (referred to in my work as 'ends' or 'ultimate ends'). Such goals provide us, *inter alia,* with a critical angle to assess judicial performance and to establish the contribution of remedy compliance towards judicial goal attainment:

a) Promoting compliance with the governing international norms (primary norm compliance)
b) Resolving and preventing international disputes and problems (dispute resolution or problem-solving)
c) Contributing to the operation of related political institutions and cooperative regimes (regime support)
d) Legitimising associated international norms and institutions (regime legitimisation)

To be sure, these ends are formulated in an open-ended manner and are non-exclusive in nature; they can also accommodate a plethora of more specific goals (such as deterrence, norm internalisation, normative development, etc), and support even more abstract ultimate ends (such as increasing legal security or political integration). Moreover, the ends listed hereby overlap with one another and are often inter-related (eg, regime legitimisation, for instance, promotes norm-compliance and *vice versa*). As a result, one specific judicial act may simultaneously advance more than one end. At the same time, some ends may be in tension with one another, and a specific judicial decision that promotes one end may adversely affect the realisation of another (for example, upholding a legal norm, which runs contrary to important state interests, may fail to resolve a political dispute and jeopardise the regime in which the court operates).[20]

A goal-oriented perspective to analysing remedy compliance can help us better evaluate the 'trade-offs' that judgment formulation and remedy design by international courts entail, and contribute to our understanding of the significance of remedy compliance. Put differently, the questions I pose are whether and to what degree compliance with judicial remedies, which derive from a specific substantive judgment, promote the attainment of the ends of the relevant court (in other words, do the judgment and remedial orders included therein invite a high or low degree of goal attainment?). In line with the methodology employed in my broader work on the effectiveness of international courts, a fuller analysis of judicial performance should also consider judicial cost effectiveness

[19] For a discussion, see Shany, 'Assessing the Effectiveness of International Courts'.

[20] See eg, JE Martus and JW Helsing, 'Conclusions: Toward a More Integrated Approach' in JE Martus and JW Helsing (eds), *Human Rights and Conflict: Exploring the Links between Rights, Law and Peacebuilding* (Washington, USIP Press Books, 2006) 511; A Valls, *Ethics in International Affairs: Theories and Cases* (Lanham, Rowman & Littlefield Publishers, 2000) 39.

(ie, whether the court could have attained its goals through less costly means) and judicial efficiency (whether the court's operations generated unintended costs or benefits).[21]

II. EXAMINING ECTHR REMEDY COMPLIANCE

A. Examining Impact

Recent developments relating to the structuring of ECtHR remedies may illustrate the importance of adopting a more comprehensive approach towards the study of remedy compliance. The ECtHR has long boasted perfect or close to perfect remedy compliance rates.[22] This record stood in marked contrast with the poorer levels of remedy compliance normally attributed to some other international courts—for instance, the Inter-American Court of Human Rights (I/A CHR),[23] and was sometimes used to support claims about the relative effectiveness of the ECtHR.[24] The recent promulgation of CoE Reports on Execution of ECtHR Judgments allows us to critically examine this seemingly impressive record of compliance.

Traditionally, the two main remedies awarded by the Court were declaratory statements that a violation of the European Convention on Human Rights (ECHR) has occurred and compensation orders referred to by the Court as 'just satisfaction'[25]—requiring the payment of monetary sums covering pecuniary and non-pecuniary damages and costs (such sums tend to be relatively modest in scope).[26] The conservative approach taken by the Court towards remedy design reflects the view that the manner in which right violations should be reversed and prevented is best left to the contracting states themselves.[27] Given their limited degree of intrusiveness and negligible financial implications, it is not surprising that states tend, by and large, to comply with compensation orders and fully pay the sums awarded to victims by the Court. (Still, CoE reports suggest that significant delays in payment of compensation sometimes occur).[28]

Although the payment of compensation to victims of human rights violations is clearly an impact generated by the ECtHR, the strong 'compliance pull' of such remedial orders appears to be best explained by reference to their limited onerousness, and not to the unique institutional pull of the Court or other Council of Europe organs. Indeed,

[21] Shany, 'Assessing the Effectiveness of International Courts'.

[22] 2007 CoE Report on Execution of ECtHR Judgments, 10.

[23] See eg, Hawkins and Jacoby, 'Partial Compliance', 25 ('full compliance has occurred in six of the 92 cases for which there are compliance reports'). See also Fernando Basch et al, 'The Effectiveness of the Inter-American System for the Protection of Human Rights: Quantitative approach on the System's operation and the compliance with its decisions', www.adc-sidh.org/images/files/adctheeffectivenessoftheinteramericansystemfortheprotectionofhumanrights.pdf (2009)

[24] See eg, J Waldock, 'The Effectiveness of the System Set Up by the European Convention on Human Rights', (1980) 1 *Human Rights Law Journal* 1.

[25] European Convention for the Protection of Human Rights and Fundamental Freedoms, 4 Nov. 1950, art 41, ETS 5 (as revised by Protocol 11) (ECHR); JC Sims, 'Compliance without Remands: The Experience under the European Convention on Human Rights, (2004) 36 *Arizona State L J* 639, 644.

[26] See eg, MW Janis *et al*, *European Human Rights Law: Texts and Materials* (2008) 99.

[27] See eg, CD Gray, *Judicial Remedies in International Law* (1990) 152; Fernanda Nicola and Ingrid Nifosi-Sutton, *Assessing Regional Cooperation: New Trends before the European Court of Human Rights and the European Court of Justice* (2007) 12.

[28] According to the 2007 CoE Report on Execution of ECtHR Judgments, payment is not processed within the prescribed timelines in 41% of the cases) (219).

once the ECtHR started indicating more intrusive remedies—including individual non-monetary remedies (such as orders to reopen faulty legal proceedings and adopt other *restitutio ad integrum* measures), and general measures, requiring states at times to adopt broad legal or policy reforms,[29] compliance rates appear to have significantly dropped.[30] Thus, there seems to be a correlation between remedy design and compliance rates, on the one hand, and between remedy design and judicial impact, on the other hand.

It is interesting to note in this context, that the meager rates of full remedy compliance generated by the I/A CHR (7% according to one study)[31] can be explained, in part, by the degree of intrusiveness of the remedies that Court issues. I/A CHR judgments often specify onerous individual and general measures, with significant financial and political implications.[32] Given the apparent different aims of ECtHR and I/A CHR remedies ('low aiming' versus 'high aiming'), it is difficult to pronounce, merely on the basis of measuring norm-practice convergence rates, whether one court generates more impact than the other.

B. Examining Effectiveness

When applying a goal-oriented approach to the issue at hand in order to assess the relationship between remedy compliance and judicial effectiveness, it becomes even clearer that the ECtHR's high remedy compliance rates may have only tenuous links to the Court's effectiveness. Arguably, the ECtHR is entrusted with two principal and related goals: securing compliance with regional human rights norms (primary norm compliance),[33] and supporting the Council of Europe's mission of achieving of greater unity among its member states (regime support).[34] In addition, the Court may be expected to legitimise the operation of regional norms and institutions (regime legitimisation) and provide specific remedies to human rights victims (dispute resolution or problem-solving).[35]

[29] See for example *Broniowski v Poland*, 2004-V Eur. Ct. H.R. 1; *Öcalan v Turkey*, 2005-IV ECHR; *Popov v Russia*, Judgment of 13 July 2006; *VgT v Switzerland* (No. 2), Judgment of 30 June 2009. See also L Wildhaber, 'The European Court of Human Rights: The Past, The Present, The Future', 22 (2007) *Am U Int'l L Rev* 521, 534.

[30] 2007 CoE Report on Execution of ECtHR Judgments, 230; CoE Report on Execution of ECtHR Judgments, 63; 2009 CoE Report on Execution of ECtHR Judgments, 63 (all three reports suggest that 46% of the 'leading cases', requiring general measures of compliance, remain pending before the CoE after 2 years from the date of judgment).

[31] Hawkins and Jacoby, 'Partial Compliance', 4.

[32] For a survey of development related to the I/A CHR's remedial practices, see TA Antkowiak, 'Remedial Approaches to Human Rights Violations: The Inter-American Court of Human Rights and Beyond', (2008) 46 *Colum J Transnat'l L* 351.

[33] ECHR, art. 19 ('To ensure the observance of the engagements undertaken by the High Contracting Parties in the Convention and the Protocols thereto, there shall be set up a European Court of Human Rights'). See also *Ireland v United Kingdom*, 25 Eur Ct HR (ser A) P 154 (1978); *Karner v Austria*, App No 40016/98, 38 Eur Ct HR 24 (2003); D Shelton, 'Form, Function, and the Powers of International Courts', (2009) 9 *Chi J Int'l L* 537, 564.

[34] ECHR, preamble ('the aim of the Council of Europe is the achievement of greater unity between its members and that one of the methods by which that aim is to be pursued is the maintenance and further realisation of human rights and fundamental freedoms').

[35] SC Greer, *The European Convention on Human Rights: Achievements, Problems and Prospects* (Cambridge, Cambridge University Press, 2006) 167.

Review of the CoE Reports on Execution suggests that the high rates of compliance with compensation orders do not necessarily translate into high rates of primary norm compliance (which would potentially also have contributed to the Court's mission of fostering the harmonisation of human rights practices across Europe). First, the frequent incidence of repetitive cases submitted to the Court[36]—that is, cases alleging state conduct already identified by the ECtHR as a violation of the Convention,[37] appears to suggest that Court judgments have a limited impact on primary norm compliance. In other words, states pay compensation and continue to violate the Convention. Second, recent changes in the ECtHR's attitude towards remedy design can be explained, in part, as an acknowledgement on its part of the limited impact its monetary awards generate—a state of affairs that has undoubtedly contributed to the Court's exploding case load.[38]

To be clear, even compliance with 'low cost' monetary remedies is not necessarily meaningless. Compliance in individual cases may serve one of the goals of international courts—to solve specific problems through legal means (what Greer refers to as 'individual justice').[39] Furthermore, even 'shallow' remedy compliance helps project an image of acceptance of the court's authority by states, contributing thereby to its perceived legitimacy (which, in turn, strengthens the 'compliance pull' of its decisions). Still, as explained before, the value of remedy-compliance may be pegged to the level of remedy onerousness; and compliance with trivial remedial measures contributes less towards legitimising a court than compliance with the more intrusive remedies it issues.

In addition, it is plausible that compliance with 'low cost' remedies would be conducive after all to the attainment of primary norm compliance: the cumulative costs associated with paying a large number of modest awards could prod states over time to change their practices (or create more effective local remedy programs).[40] In addition, one should certainly not ignore the accruing reputational harm which repetitive declarations of a violation may inflict,[41] and the process of dialogue between Strasbourg and national authorities, facilitated by repeated litigation, which could lead over time to a better internalisation of the Convention.[42] In the same vein, repeated judgments may embolden local norm entrepreneurs,[43] and mobilise civic society to push for legal reform at the domestic level.[44]

Still, it cannot be ruled out, at least in some cases, that states welcome the possibility of 'buying' the ability to continue and violate the Convention through the payment

[36] According to the 2007 CoE Report on Execution of ECtHR Judgments, 80% of the new cases submitted that year were repetitive or clone cases (that is, raising similar issues to cases already decided or pending)(at 218), as were 90% of older cases still pending in 2007 (213).

[37] See eg, 2009 CoE Report on Execution of ECtHR Judgments 40 n 31 ('Italy eg has a total of 2,471 cases, representing some 31% of the total of cases pending for execution, it has to be borne in mind that more than 2 000 of these cases relate to one single problem, the excessive length of judicial proceedings'). See also Greer, *The European Convention*, 158.

[38] ibid, 160.

[39] ibid, 167.

[40] See A Mowbray, *Cases and Materials on the European Convention on Human Rights* 2nd edn (Oxford, Oxford University Press, 2007) 428 (discussing the Italian Pinto act).

[41] See eg, Guzman, International Law, 1868.

[42] See eg, A-M Slaughter, 'A Global Community of Courts', (2003) 44 *Harv Int'l L J* 191, 216; R Goodman and D Jinks, 'How to Influence States: Socialization and International Human Rights Law', (2004) 54 *Duke L J* 621, 666.

[43] See eg, HH Koh, 'Why Do Nations Obey International Law?' (1997) 106 *Yale L J* 2599, 2649.

[44] See JL Cavallaro and EJ Schaffer, 'Less as More: Rethinking Supranational Litigation of Economic and Social Rights in the Americas', (2004) 56 *Hastings L J* 217, 281; B Simmons, *Mobilizing for Human Rights: International Law in Domestic Politics* (Mass, Harvard University Press, 2009) 126.

of nominal sums.[45] By complying with monetary orders, states reduce some of the reputational harms associated with the substantive human rights violation they have committed. Such a reputational redemption, when combined to the prestige associated with ongoing membership in the CoE, may embolden states to violate the Convention again in the future.[46] Thus, remedy compliance in itself may, or may not be, predictive of prospective primary norm compliance.[47] Only a qualitative study of the context in which remedy compliance occurs may enable us to form a more definite view of the contribution of remedy compliance to international court effectiveness.

A goal-based analysis also illustrates the difficulty of comparing between the ECtHR and I/A CHR's levels of effectiveness only on the basis of their respective remedy-compliance rates. It appears possible to argue that compliance with the I/A CHR 'high cost' general and individual remedial measures is 'deeper' than compliance with the 'low cost' remedies traditionally issued by the ECtHR. At the same time, low levels of remedy-compliance at the I/A CHR might reflect negatively on the legitimacy of that Court and the legal regime in which it operates; this unintended side effect may eventually undermine the Court's goal-attainment potential. An argument can thus be made that, in the long run, the incremental raising of the costs of remedy compliance is more likely to prove conducive for goal attainment than aiming high from the start.

Ultimately, only a careful context-rich study of remedy compliance may tell us something meaningful about its relationship to court effectiveness, cost effectiveness and efficiency. With relation to the ECtHR and I/A CHR, such a study should consider, for example, the different political and cultural environments in which the two courts operate[48]—a difference which may impact the courts' goal-attainment potential and dictate particular choices of substantive judgment formulation and remedy design.

III. COMPLIANCE WITH ICJ REMEDIAL ORDERS IN THE BOSNIAN GENOCIDE AND AVENA CASES

A. Examining impact

A second set of examples illustrating the limited utility of examining remedy compliance in a de-contextualised manner involves the reactions of Serbia and the United States to the ICJ judgments in the *Bosnian Genocide* and *Avena* cases, respectively.[49] The

[45] cf OW Holmes Jr, 'The Path of the Law' (1897) 10 *Harvard Law Review* 457 (discussing the law from the point of view of the 'bad man'). For an interesting analogy, see U Gneezy and A Rustichini 'A Fine is a Price' (2000) 29 *Journal of Legal Studies* 1 (requiring parents to pay a fine for picking-up their children late from pre-school increases, not decreases, the number of late pick-ups).

[46] cf OA Hathaway, 'Do Human Rights Treaties Make a Difference', (2002) 111 *Yale L J* 1935 (treaty ratification may lead to more treaty violations).

[47] See Greer, *The European Convention*, 174; LJ Conant, *Justice Contained: Law and Politics in the European Union* (New York, Cornell University Press, 2002) 50.

[48] See eg, Ruth Mackenzie *et al*, *Manual on International Courts and Tribunals* (Oxford, Oxford University Press, 2010) 383; D Cassel, 'Inter-American Human Rights Law: Soft and Hard', in D Shelton (Ed), *Commitment and Compliance: The Role of Non-Binding Norms in the International Legal System* (Oxford, Oxford University Press, 2004) 393, 395.

[49] *Application of the Convention on the Prevention and Punishment of the Crime of Genocide* (Bosnia and Herzegovina v Serbia and Montenegro), Judgment of 26 February 2007 (*Bosnian Genocide*); *Avena* (Mexico v US), 2004 ICJ 12.

substantive outcome of the *Bosnian Genocide* judgment can be understood as a 'splitting of the difference' between the disputant parties,[50] which left both of them feeling somewhat pleased (and disappointed) about the judgment's outcome.[51] In the same vein, the remedial portion of the judgment also signifies a split outcome: the Court rejected Bosnia's request for monetary compensation and assurances or guarantees of non-repetition, and held that the declarations it had issued concerning Serbian violations of the Genocide Convention and ICJ provisional measures constituted a sufficient remedy.[52] Still, Serbia was ordered by the Court to put on trial or extradite to the ICTY genocide suspects.[53]

It is unclear whether Serbia complied with the judgment. While one senior suspect of genocide, Karadzic, has been located and transferred to the ICTY after the issuance of the judgment, the other senior suspect of genocide, Mladic, is still at large.[54] (There are no other suspects wanted for genocide by the ICTY at large; no-one has been charged in Serbia for the Bosnian genocide).[55] However, it is important to note that Serbia did not dispute, before or after the judgment, its duty to prosecute or transfer genocide suspects to the ICTY; instead, it argued that it lacked information on the ICTY suspects' whereabouts, evidence enabling the prosecution of other suspects, etc.[56] As a result, it is hard to formulate a clear opinion as to whether the remedies prescribed by the ICJ—which confirmed by and large Serbia's independent obligations under international law—had any impact on Serbia's actual conduct; or even whether any subsequent change in Serbian policy has actually occurred (regardless of whether such a change can be attributed to the ICJ).[57]

The *Avena* judgment has been much clearer in its outcome—generating a clear winner (Mexico) and loser (the US). The Court held that the US violated the Vienna Consular Relations Convention by failing to inform criminal suspects holding a Mexican nationality of their right to consular assistance, and ordered the US 'to provide, by means of its own choosing, review and reconsideration of the convictions and sentences of the Mexican nationals'.[58] (The Court did, however, afford the US some discretion in the manner of implementing the 'review and reconsideration' process).[59]

[50] Y Shany, 'Bosnia, Serbia and the Politics of International Adjudication' (2008) 45 *Justice* 21. See, more generally, G Abi-Saab, 'Fragmentation or Unification: Some Concluding Remarks' (1999) 31 *NYU J Int'l L & Pol* 919, 930.

[51] *Nerma Jelacic,* Dismay and Jubilation Over Hague Court Judgment, *Balkan Insight, 26 Feb 07,* birn.eu.com/en/72/10/2365/?tpl=30 ('Serbia's Prime Minister Vojislav Kostunica hailed the judgment as especially important, as it freed Serbia of genocide charges'). See also ibid ('Haris Siljadzic, the Bosniak member [of the Bosnia and Herzegovina Presidency], said the judgment gave partial satisfaction in that it said Serbia had violated the UN's genocide convention by failing to prevent the crime or punish the perpetrators').

[52] *Bosnian Genocide,* at para 471 (9).

[53] ibid, at para 471(8) 'Serbia shall immediately take effective steps to ensure full compliance with its obligation under the Convention on the Prevention and Punishment of the Crime of Genocide to punish acts of genocide as defined by Article II of the Convention, or any of the other acts proscribed by Article III of the Convention, and to transfer individuals accused of genocide or any of those other acts for trial by the International Criminal Tribunal for the former Yugoslavia, and to co-operate fully with that Tribunal'.

[54] This article was submitted to publication in early 2011. On May 26th, 2011 Mladic was arrested in Serbia, and extradited to the ICTY shortly thereafter.

[55] See Council of Europe, Serbia: Compliance with obligations and commitments and implementation of the post-accession co-operation programme – Fourth Report (2008–2009), COE Doc. SG/Inf (2009) 3.

[56] Kim Sengupta, Serbs claim Mladic left country years ago, The Independent, 30.11.2007.

[57] For a general survey of methodological problems in identifying compliance, see Kingsbury, above ne 6, 346.

[58] *Avena,* 2004 ICJ at 64.

[59] For a discussion, see Yuval Shany, *Regulation Jurisdictional Relations between National and International Court* (Oxford, Oxford University Press, 2007).

The reaction of the US authorities to the judgment has been mixed. One state governor (in Oklahoma) relied explicitly on the ICJ judgment when commuting a death sentence;[60] furthermore, the President published a memorandum in which he instructed all state courts to comply with the judgment,[61] and one state court (in Arkansas) substituted a death sentence with life imprisonment following review of the proceedings against one of the Mexicans covered by *Avena*.[62] In addition, new administrative guidelines seeking to inculcate the duty to provide consular notifications were distributed among US law enforcement agencies.[63]

Still, the ICJ judgment was strongly resisted by powerful elements with the US judiciary at the state and federal level. Such elements viewed attempts to reopen criminal proceedings as an intrusion upon their authority to conduct criminal proceedings without external interference and to construe the domestic legal effects of US treaty obligations.[64] Eventually, the Supreme Court rejected the President's attempt to order state courts to give effect to *Avena* as unconstitutional,[65] and affirmed a state court decision refusing to implement that ICJ judgment.[66] Moreover, the Supreme Court rejected in another, non-death penalty case (not covered by the *res judicata* effect of *Avena*) the general legal construction of the Vienna Convention embraced by the ICJ.[67] In parallel to these manifestations of judicial resistance, the US has withdrawn after the *Avena* judgment from the Vienna Convention's Optional Protocol—thus removing future disputes over consular relations from the jurisdiction of the ICJ[68] (reducing thereby the 'compliance pull' of the relevant primary norms).[69]

[60] Sean D Murphy, *U.S Practice in International Law Volume 2: 2002–2004* (New York, Oxford University Press, 2005) 33.

[61] The President's memorandum for the Attorney General, issued on 28 February 2005, stated that the United States would 'discharge its international obligations' under *Avena* 'by having State courts give effect to the decision'.

[62] *Request for Interpretation of the Judgment of 31 March 2004 in the Case concerning Avena and Other Mexican Nationals* (Mexico v. US), Application of 5 June 2008, para 12.

[63] See US State Dept., *Consular Notification and Access: Instructions for Federal, State, and Local Law Enforcement and Other Officials Regarding Foreign Nationals in the US and the Rights of Consular Officials to Assist Them* (3rd ed, 2010).

[64] *Sanchez-Llamas v Oregon*, 548 U.S. 331, 353 (2006) ('judicial power includes the duty to say what the law is.' If treaties are to be given effect as federal law under our legal system, determining their meaning as a matter of federal law 'is emphatically the province and duty of the judicial department,' headed by the 'one supreme Court established by the Constitution'); *Ex Parte Medellin*, 280 S.W.3d 854, 862 (Texas Crim. App. Ct., 2008) (Cochran J, Concurring))('Although we accord the greatest respect to, and admiration for, the International Court of Justice (ICJ) and its judgments, we, like the Supreme Court, cannot trample on our own fundamental laws in deference to its judgment. We would give even the Devil the benefit of our American law, but if we cut down our laws to suit another sovereign that operates under a different system of justice, we could not stand upright in the lawless winds that would then blow').

[65] *Medellin v Texas*, 552 U.S. 491, 525 (2008) ('the President has an array of political and diplomatic means available to enforce international obligations, but unilaterally converting a non-self-executing treaty into a self-executing one is not among them'). The President's memorandum for the Attorney General, issued on 28 February 2005, stated that United States would 'discharge its international obligations' under *Avena* 'by having State courts give effect to the decision'.

[66] ibid, 499.

[67] *Sanchez-Llamas*, 548 U.S at 355 ('*LaGrand* and *Avena* are therefore entitled only to the "respectful consideration" due to an interpretation of an international agreement by an international court. Even according such consideration, the ICJ's interpretation cannot overcome the plain import of Article 36').

[68] Letter from Condoleezza Rice, Secretary of State, to Kofi A Annan, Secretary-General of the United Nations, 7 March 2005.

[69] See J Quigley, 'The United States' Withdrawal from International Court of Justice Jurisdiction in Consular Cases: Reasons and Consequences', (2009) 19 *Duke J Comp & Int'l L* 263, 272.

It appears that a comparison of the records of compliance with the two ICJ judgments tells us very little about relative judicial impact: the *Bosnian Genocide* judgment appears at first glance to have attracted a higher rate of norm-practice convergence than the *Avena* judgment, but it also introduced fewer remedial requirements to begin with (extraditing two suspects, as opposed to reopening some 50 death-row cases) and can therefore be deemed to represent a 'lower cost' judgment with more limited impact potential. At the same time, the *Avena* judgment did have a clear impact on the President's memorandum and on two sentence commutations, whereas the actual impacts of the ICJ judgment on Serbia's conduct are unclear. As a result, it is hard to formulate a definite opinion as to which judgment had in actuality the greater 'compliance pull'.

B. Examining Effectiveness

The very limited judicial impact, which the two case studies suggest, also complicates our ability meaningfully to establish the degree in which remedy compliance contributed to the effective functioning of the ICJ. As proposed above, such an investigation of effectiveness must consider the substantive judgment outcome and remedies issued in light of the goals of the ICJ: its responsibility for upholding international law norms and resolving inter-state disputes;[70] its support of the operation of the UN and some affiliated organisations and agencies (particularly through the exercise of its advisory competence) and its conferral of some degree of legitimacy on international law norms and institutions.[71]

Given the unclear or marginal impact of the ICJ on the practices of the two losing states, it is unlikely that primary norm compliance was significantly promoted through remedy compliance: Serbia did nudge towards fulfilling its obligation to surrender or try genocide suspects, but it is not clear if, and to what degree, this effect can be attributed to the ICJ; at the same time, the *Avena* judgment may have saved the life of two Mexican convicts, but appears to have had limited or no impact in most cases involving the obligation to review and reconsider consular notification cases. In addition, although the US appears to have revised its administrative practices relating to the issuance of consular notifications after the *Avena* proceedings, such improved primary norm compliance may have more to do with the high profile litigation in *Avena* and other consular notification cases,[72] then with any particular judicial remedy issued by the ICJ. In fact, the US administration's decision to renounce the Vienna Convention Optional Protocol suggests that resistance to certain norms embraced by the ICJ judgment remains as strong after *Avena* as before it.

Assessing the effect of remedy compliance on the attainment of the ICJ's dispute settlement goal appears to be equally challenging. There is some indication that the post-2007 measures taken by Serbia—the surrender of Karadzic and, in particular, the 2010 apology issued by the Serb Parliament for the Srebrenica massacre,[73] contributed

[70] See eg, Y Shany, 'No Longer a Weak Department of Power? Reflections on the Emergence of a New International Judiciary', (2009) 20 *EJIL* 73, 80.

[71] See eg, GZ Capaldo, *The Pillars of Global Law* (London, Ashgate, 2008) 132.

[72] *LaGrand* (Germany v US), 2001 ICJ 466; *Vienna Convention on Consular Relations* (Paraguay v US), 1998 ICJ 248 (Provisional Measures).

[73] RFE/RL, 'Serbian Parliament's Srebrenica Apology Hailed, Criticized', www.rferl.org 31.3.2010.

to improved relations between Serbia and Bosnia and Herzegovina.[74] However, as noted before, the causal relationship between the Court's judgment and Karadzic's transfer to The Hague is unclear; and the apology, although explicitly referring to the ICJ judgment, is not captured by a remedy-compliance analysis, since it does not correspond to any specific remedy ordered by the Court. In fact, the issuance of the Parliamentary apology, without there being an order requiring Serbia to do so, suggests that an excessive focus on measuring remedy compliance may overlook other important normative and political effects of international judgments.

With respect to the *Avena* judgment, it is clear that the US partial record of compliance has not settled its dispute with Mexico over the treatment of criminal suspects holding Mexican nationality. In fact, Mexico has unsuccessfully attempted to re-litigate the same case before the ICJ through a request for interpretation, calling on the Court to issue more specific remedies.[75] It remains unclear to what extent the aforementioned changes in US administrative practices concerning consular notification (which, again, are not captured by a remedy-compliance analysis since they do not respond to a specific remedy) would contribute to the prevention of future consular notification disputes between the US and Mexico (or the US and other countries).

With respect to the contribution of remedy compliance to legitimisation of relevant norms and institutions, one may assess that the open challenge posed by the US to the legal authority of the ICJ (manifested in its refusal to enforce the ICJ judgment through its legal system, and the rejection of ICJ jurisdiction in future consular relations cases) has adversely affected the legitimacy of the Court and the Vienna Convention system. At the same time, some commentators have argued that the ICJ's reputation has been harmed as a result of what they viewed as an overly timid approach the Court took in the *Bosnian Genocide* case.[76] While assessing changes in institutional legitimacy is extremely hard and perhaps unavoidably indeterminate, the existence of such difficult criteria supports the claim that assessing judicial effectiveness on the basis of remedy compliance in a manner detached from the goal-attaining attributes of the judgments in question may be a useless, if not misleading exercise.

IV. CONCLUSIONS

Increased attention has been devoted in recent years by international law scholars and practitioners to evaluating compliance with international judgments. Such works of evaluation consider compliance rates and records as a valuable proxy to international court effectiveness and, more generally, to ascertaining the international rule of law and the credibility of international institutions. In this contribution I tried to highlight some of the pitfalls of a de-contextualised study of remedy compliance.

First, I argued that compliance, if measured simply as the correlation of norms and state practice, is an unreliable indicator of effectiveness, since it may fail to capture the actual impact of judicial decisions on state practice. Hence, 'low aiming' courts (issuing

[74] Maja Zuvela, 'Bosnia, Serbia pledge to Mend Ties, Lure Investors', Reuters 25 April 2010.

[75] *Request for Interpretation (Application),* para 59. The application was rejected by the Court for lack of jurisdiction. *Request for Interpretation of the Judgment of 31 March 2004 in the Case concerning Avena and Other Mexican Nationals* (Mexico v. US), ICJ Judgment of 19 January 2009.

[76] See eg, J Alvarez, 'Burdens Of Proof—Note from the President,' (2007) 23 (2) *ASIL Newsletter* 1; M Milanović, 'State Responsibility for Genocide: A Follow-Up' (2007) 18 *Eur J Int'l L* 669.

remedies requiring limited consequences and/or minor changes in state practice) are expected to generate high levels of norm-practice correlation, but would not necessarily have a 'deep' impact on state practice. Second, an analysis of compliance with international judgments is only meaningful from an effectiveness viewpoint, if it is discussed in the context of judicial goal attainment. We should therefore explore whether the judgment, its remedial portions and state compliance therewith is conducive to attaining judicial goals such as promoting primary norm-compliance, resolving disputes, and supporting and legitimising regime operations.

The two sets of examples offered in this paper: changes in remedy design by the ECtHR and two state reactions to ICJ Judgments seem to support the general claims I made in this paper. In particular, the cases reviewed suggest that only a context-rich evaluation could render remedy compliance a meaningful indicator of effectiveness. Yet, it should be acknowledged that the complexity of the environment in which compliance occurs may render the relationship between remedy compliance and effectiveness too difficult to trace and assess.

19

The Security Council as Dispenser of (or with) International Law

STEFAN TALMON*

I. INTRODUCTION

SINCE THE EARLY 1990s, the Security Council has been fairly active and innovative in using its powers under the Charter of the United Nations. The Council has, for example, invoked its Chapter VII authorities to 'legislate' for the international community[1] and to create specific legal frameworks in order to address threats to international peace and security. While these frameworks typically incorporate specialised bodies of law as part of the legal foundation of the Council's response there are cases in which the Council has 'adapted' these bodies of law on an *ad hoc* basis in order to meet the threat. The Council has tailored existing rules of international law to work better in a specific set of circumstances.[2] What has euphemistically been referred to as an ad hoc 'adaptation' of applicable rules of international law to a specific set of circumstances in effect amounts to an 'alteration' or even 'abrogation' of binding treaty provisions or rules of customary international law with regard to a specific case or specific actors. The Security Council on a case by case basis tailors rules of international law to suit the needs of international peace and security or, adopting perhaps a more sober outlook, the political needs of individual Council members, thereby contributing to a culture of exceptionalism which may be seen as part of a wider 'sui generis culture' developing in modern day international law.

Increasingly concern has been expressed at the Council's practice of dispensing (with) international law. Such quasi-legislative measures were said to go 'beyond the powers conferred upon the Security Council.'[3] Cuba's representative in the Security Council stated:

* Professor of Public International Law, University of Oxford, and fellow of St Anne's College, Oxford.

[1] See, for example, S Talmon, 'The Security Council as World Legislature' (2005) 99 *AJIL* 175.

[2] See Remarks of John B Bellinger, III, Legal Adviser, U.S. Department of State, 'United Nations Security Council Resolutions and the Application of International Humanitarian Law, Human Rights and Refugee Law', International Conference, San Remo, Italy, 9 September 2005, www.state.gov/s/l/c8183.htm.

[3] UN News Centre, 'UN rights expert says Security Council's counter-terrorism measures lack legal basis', 26 October 2010, www.un.org.

> The Council has no power to amend the legal regime established by a treaty. Nor can the Council be given the power to extract norms from treaties that have been agreed to by sovereign States parties—and which generate rights and obligations solely for those parties—and make them binding on all States Members of the United Nations by invoking Chapter VII of the Charter.[4]

The Indonesian Foreign Minister in January 2009 expressly 'opposed any idea to create new international norms through the Security Council that contradict existing international norms and conventions.'[5]

This chapter examines the way in which the Security Council has used its Chapter VII powers to dispense with existing rules of treaty or customary international law and to replace them with special rules for 'special cases'. In particular, it asks what this practice means for the concept of the rule of law and international law as law if its binding rules are placed at the disposal of a political body like the Security Council.

II. SECURITY COUNCIL PRACTICE OF DISPENSING WITH EXISTING RULES OF INTERNATIONAL LAW

A. Treaty Law

Several years before the Security Council started making law for the international community, it engaged in the practice of dispensing with existing treaty provisions that would otherwise be applicable to a certain situation. In March 1992, the Security Council, acting under Chapter VII of the Charter, adopted resolution 748 (1992) in connection with the bombing of a US passenger plane over the Scottish town of Lockerbie. In that resolution, the Council decided, *inter alia*, that Libya must surrender two of its nationals charged with the bombing to either the United States or the United Kingdom for trial, disclose information, and allow full access to witnesses and evidence.[6] This was contrary to Article 7 of the 1971 Montreal Convention for the Suppression of Unlawful Acts against the Safety of Civil Aviation which allows each contracting state in whose territory a person suspected of an aircraft bombing is present to prosecute that person before its competent authorities.[7] The Security Council thus overruled a treaty provision in force between the three states.

The invasion and occupation of Iraq have given rise to further examples of the Security Council dispensing with certain treaty provisions. The Fourth Geneva Convention and the Hague Regulations on Land Warfare would have constrained the capacity of the occupying powers to carry out political and economic reforms in Iraq and to engage in the large-scale sale of Iraqi oil.[8] It has been suggested that, in resolution 1483 (2003),[9]

[4] UN Doc S/PV.4568 (Resumption 1), 10 July 2002, 14. For similar statements of Cuba, see also UN Docs A/57/PV.27, 14 October 2002, 14; A/58/PV.29, 13 October 2003, 9.

[5] Republic of Indonesia, Ministry of Foreign Affairs, 'Remarks [by] HE Dr N Hassan Wirajuda, Minister for Foreign Affairs, Republic of Indonesia, at the Pejambon Coffee', 22 January 2009, www.deplu.go.id.

[6] S/RES/748 (1992) of 31 March 1992, para 1. This paragraph must be read in conjunction with S/RES/731 (1992) of 21 January 1992, para 3, and the requests addressed to Libya by the USA and the UK.

[7] For the text of the Montreal Convention, see 974 UNTS 177.

[8] See, in particular, Article 64 of the Geneva Convention IV Relative to the Protection of Civilian Persons in Time of War, 12 August 1949 (75 UNTS 287) and Article 43 of the Regulations Respecting the Laws and Customs of War on Land, Annex to the Hague Convention IV Respecting the Laws and Customs of War on Land, 18 October 1907, (1908) 2 *AJIL Suppl* 90.

the Security Council lifted these constraints and created a special legal regime for the occupying powers in Iraq.[10] According to the Legal Adviser to the US State Department, John B. Bellinger III, the resolution allowed the occupying powers to use oil proceeds to fund long-term economic reconstruction projects and to undertake the political transformation of Iraq, activities 'that would at least arguably be outside the scope of authorities provided by the Hague Regulations'.[11] This view was shared by the other occupying power. In March 2004, the British Secretary of State for Foreign and Commonwealth Affairs wrote: 'The various measures of economic reform undertaken by the Coalition Provisional Authority have been undertaken within occupation law, *as supplemented by Security Council Resolution 1483 of 22 May 2003*.'[12] That the relevant treaty provisions were supplemented or, better, supplanted by resolution 1483 (2003) also becomes clear from the fact that the occupation authorities in Iraq based their executive, legislative, and judicial authority not only on the laws and usages of war but also on 'relevant UN Security Council resolutions including resolution 1483 (2003)'.[13]

In resolution 1546 (2004), the Security Council authorised the Multi-National Force (MNF) to take all necessary means to contribute to the maintenance of security and stability in Iraq, including 'internment where this is necessary for imperative reasons of security'.[14] Between 28 June 2004 and 31 December 2008, British forces in southern Iraq, which formed a contingent of the MNF, interned several people under this authority. Internment (that is to say, detention without charge or trial), on the ground that it is necessary for imperative reasons of security, violates the right to liberty guaranteed by article 5(1) of the European Convention on Human Rights (ECHR) which has been found to be applicable in principle to persons detained by British forces in Iraq.[15] The same is true of the largely coextensive right in article 9 of the International Covenant on Civil and Political Rights.[16] By authorising such detentions for imperative reasons of

[9] See S/RES/1483 (2003) of 22 May 2003, paras 4, 8(c), 8(e), 9, 13, 14.

[10] See, for example, M Zwanenburg, 'Existentialism in Iraq: Security Council Resolution 1483 and the Law of Occupation' (2004) 86/856 *Int'l Review of the Red Cross* 745, 759; M Sassòli, 'Legislation and Maintenance of Public Order and Civil Life by Occupying Powers' (2005) 4 *EJIL* 661, 680, 681; MJ Matheson, *Council Unbound: The Growth of UN Decision Making on Conflict and Postconflict Issues after the Cold War* (Washington, DC, US Institute of Peace, 2006), 118; GT Harris, 'The Era of Multilateral Occupation' (2006) 24 *Berkeley JIL* 1, 76.

[11] See Bellinger, 'United Nations Security Council Resolutions'. See also the statement of an Attorney-Adviser, Office of the Legal Adviser, US State Department: 'As a Chapter VII resolution, Resolution 1483 provided authorities that supervene any inconsistent limitations that may be contained in other bodies of international law, including occupation law.' (JL Dorosin, 'Jus in Bello: Occupation Law and the War in Iraq' (2004) 98 *ASIL Proceedings* 117, 119).

[12] 'Second Report from the Foreign Affairs Committee, Foreign Policy Aspects of the War Against Terrorism, Session 2003–2004, Response of the Secretary of State for Foreign and Commonwealth Affairs', March 2004, Cm 6162, 8 (emphasis added). See also the statement of the Parliamentary Under-Secretary, Foreign and Commonwealth Office, Bill Rammell, House of Commons, Parliamentary Debates, vol 413, col 359W: 12 November 2003.

[13] For the legislative acts of the occupying powers in Iraq, see S Talmon, *The Occupation of Iraq*, vol. 2: *The Official Documents of the Coalition Provisional Authority, the Iraqi Governing Council and Related Documents* (Oxford, Hart, 2011).

[14] S/RES/1546 (2004) of 8 June 2004, para 10, and the letters annexed to the resolution. See also S/RES/1637 (2005) of 11 November 2005, para 1; S/RES/1723 (2006) of 28 November 2006, para 1; S/RES/1790 (2007) of 18 December 2007, para 1, and the letters annexed to these resolutions.

[15] See *R (Al-Skeini and others) v Secretary of State for Defence* [2008] 1 AC 153 (HL).

[16] The International Covenant on Civil and Political Rights, 16 December 1966 (999 UNTS 171) was, in principle, also applicable to British troops in Iraq; see *Legal Consequences of the Construction of a Wall in the Occupied Palestinian Territory*, Advisory Opinion of 9 July 2004, ICJ Reports 2004, 136, para 111.

security, the Security Council 'qualified' these treaties,[17] and in fact exempted the United Kingdom from its treaty obligations with regard to the internment actions of its forces in Iraq, a view put forward by the UK Secretary of State and ultimately upheld by the highest British court in December 2007.[18]

Another example of treaty adaptation is the exemption from the jurisdiction of the International Criminal Court (ICC) of current or former officials or personnel from states contributing to peacekeeping operations which are not parties to the Rome Statute—a price the United States as a non-state party to the Statute and strident opponent of the ICC exacted for voting in favour of such operations with US involvement. According to article 12(2) of the Rome Statute, the ICC may exercise its jurisdiction *ratione personae* either if (a) the crime occurred in the territory of a state party of the Rome Statute, or (b) the person accused of the crime is a national of such a state. In resolution 1497 (2003), the Security Council limited the jurisdiction of the ICC with regard to the multinational force (and later United Nations stabilisation force) in Liberia. On 22 September 2004, Liberia became the 96th state party to the Rome Statute which means that crimes referred to in article 5 of the Rome Statute committed in the territory of Liberia after 1 December 2004 are, in principle, subject to the Court's jurisdiction.[19] In addition, the ICC may exercise jurisdiction over all nationals of a state party to the Rome Statute who are accused of committing any of the statutory crimes in Liberia. However, only seven weeks before Liberia ratified the Rome Statute, at a time when it had already indicated its intention to ratify, the Security Council decided that:

> current or former officials or personnel from a contributing State, which is not a party to the Rome Statute of the International Criminal Court, shall be subject to the *exclusive jurisdiction* of that contributing State for all alleged acts or omissions arising out of or related to the Multinational Force or United Nations stabilization force in Liberia, unless such exclusive jurisdiction has been expressly waived by that contributing State.[20]

The Security Council did not just exercise its right of temporary 'deferral of investigation or prosecution' under article 16 of the Rome Statute, but permanently removed all 'current or former officials or personnel from a contributing state which is not a party to the Rome Statute' from the jurisdiction of the Court, thereby modifying article 12(2) of the Statute.[21] As the provision on exclusive jurisdiction was phrased in general terms, it did not remove only nationals of non-states parties from the ICC's jurisdiction (as it was intended) but also nationals of states parties who were acting as officials or personnel of a non-state party and who would normally have fallen within the Court's jurisdiction under article 12(2)(b). By providing for the exclusive jurisdiction of the contributing state,

[17] *R (Al-Jedda) v Secretary of State for Defence* [2006] 3 WLR 954, 980 (CA).

[18] *R (Al-Jedda) v Secretary of State for Defence* [2008] 1 AC 332 (HL). The European Court of Human Rights in its judgment of 7 July 2011 in the case of *Al-Jedda v United Kingdom* did not call into question the power of the Security Council to override existing treaty law (para 101) but held that resolution 1546 (2003) had not unambiguously established a conflicting obligation displacing Art 5(1) ECHR (paras 102–106).

[19] See Articles 11(2) and 126(2) of the Rome Statute of the International Criminal Court, 17 July 1998 (2187 UNTS 3).

[20] See S/RES/1497 (2003) of 1 August 2003, para 7 (italics added). See also S/RES/1509 (2003) of 19 September 2003, para 1. The exemption at first covered the Multinational Force in Liberia which on 1 October 2003 was replaced by United Nations Mission in Liberia (UNMIL).

[21] The exemption from the Court's jurisdiction was, however, limited to 'acts or omissions arising out of or related to the Multinational Force or United Nations stabilization force in Liberia'.

the Security Council also removed the Court's territory based jurisdiction under article 12(2)(a) with regard to crimes committed by such officials and personnel in Liberia.[22]

In resolution 1593 (2005), the Security Council adopted the same approach when, again at the instigation of the United States,[23] it decided 'that nationals, current or former officials or personnel from a contributing State outside Sudan which is not a party to the Rome Statute shall be subject to the *exclusive jurisdiction* of that contributing State'.[24] As Sudan is not a state party to the Rome Statute, the Council only limited the ICC's nationality-based jurisdiction. Although the United States was again mainly concerned to protect its own nationals,[25] the exemption was phrased in wide enough terms to cover also nationals of states parties to the Rome Statute employed by the United States as foreign private military and security contractors, and foreign nationals enlisted in the US armed forces who would normally have come within the Court's jurisdiction under article 12(2)(b). With some 29,000 foreign citizens currently serving in the United States' armed forces alone, this is not a negligible group.[26] The case of Sudan differs from that of Liberia in that the Council, acting under Chapter VII of the UN Charter, had decided to 'refer the situation in Darfur since 1 July 2002' to the Prosecutor of the ICC,[27] thereby establishing the jurisdiction of the Court under article 13(b). By deciding, at the same time, that contributing states which are not parties to the Rome Statute shall have 'exclusive jurisdiction' over their nationals, officials, and personnel, the Security Council took away with one hand what it had given with the other, and thus limited the Court's treaty-based jurisdiction which would otherwise have existed under the Rome Statute.[28]

The fight against piracy and armed robbery at sea off the coast of Somalia has given rise to yet another example of treaty adaptation. The United Nations Convention on the Law of the Sea (UNCLOS) sets out the legal framework applicable to combating piracy. On 'the high seas, or in any other place outside the jurisdiction of any State',[29] every state may board, search and seize ships engaged in or suspected of engaging in acts of piracy and arrest persons engaged in such acts with a view to such persons being prosecuted.[30] UNCLOS does not say anything about 'armed robbery against ships', a term usually employed to describe illegal acts of violence against or aboard ships committed exclusively in a State's 'internal waters, archipelagic waters and territorial sea'.[31] As these

[22] It is true that the Security Council abrogated Article 12(2)(a) of the Rome Statute, as it were, 'pre-emptively' before it actually became applicable with regard to Liberia. However, the effect is the same, as the exemption was not subsequently revoked or cancelled. See S/RES/1561 (2004) of 17 September 2004, para 1; S/RES/1712 (2006) of 29 September 2006, para 1; S/RES/1750 (2007) of 30 March 2007, para 1; S/RES/1777 (2007) of 20 September 2007, para 1; S/RES/1836 (2008) of 29 September 2008, para 1.

[23] See UN Doc S/PV.5158, 31 March 2005, 3–4.

[24] S/RES/1593 (2005) of 31 March 2005, para 6 (italics added).

[25] See UN Doc S/PV.5158, 31 March 2005, 3 ('United States nationals'), 4 ('American citizens').

[26] See Julia Preston, 'U.S. Military Will Offer Path to Citizenship', *New York Times*, 14 February 2009, A1.

[27] See S/RES/1593 (2005) of 31 March 2005, para 1.

[28] See the statement of the representative of the Philippines: 'We may ask whether the Security Council has the prerogative to mandate the limitation of the jurisdiction of the ICC under the Rome Statute once the exercise of its jurisdiction has advanced.' (UN Doc S/PV.5158, 31 March 2005, 6). The delegate of Argentina said: 'We regret that we had to adopt a text that establishes an exception to the jurisdiction of the Court.' (ibid, 7).

[29] 'Any other place outside the jurisdiction of any State' includes the Exclusive Economic Zone.

[30] See Articles 105, 110 of the United Nations Convention on the Law of the Sea, 10 December 1982 (1833 UNTS 397). Somalia ratified UNCLOS on 24 July 1989 and the Convention entered into force on 16 November 1994.

[31] For a definition of 'armed robbery against ships', see, for example, Article 2(2) of the Code of Conduct Concerning the Repression of Piracy and Armed Robbery against Ships in the Western Indian Ocean and the Gulf of Aden, done in Djibouti, 29 January 2009 (IMO Doc C 102/14, 3 April 2009, Attachment I, Annex). For the definition of piracy, see Article 101 UNCLOS.

sea areas, which are sometimes jointly referred to as 'territorial waters', are subject to the sovereignty of the coastal state,[32] any action against armed robbers or pirates there is reserved to the coastal state's law enforcement authorities. Under UNCLOS, foreign warships are not allowed to pursue pirates from the high seas into the territorial waters of Somalia, or combat armed robbery in those waters. The complete failure of the state of Somalia and the lack of capacity of the Somali Transitional Federal Government (TFG) to patrol and secure either the international sea lanes off the country's coast or its territorial waters have led to a dramatic increase in piracy and armed robbery off the Somali coast and to a situation where there is no competent authority capable of fighting these illegal acts inside Somali territorial waters. The Security Council first addressed this situation in resolution 1816 (2008), deciding that states cooperating with the TFG and which have been notified by the TFG to the UN Secretary-General may temporarily:

> (a) Enter the territorial waters of Somalia for the purpose of repressing acts of piracy and armed robbery at sea, in a manner consistent with such action permitted on the high seas with respect to piracy under relevant international law; and
> (b) Use, within the territorial waters of Somalia, in a manner consistent with action permitted on the high seas with respect to piracy under relevant international law, all necessary means to repress acts of piracy and armed robbery.[33]

The resolution allowed states which had been cleared by the TFG[34] to enter Somali territorial waters and board, search and seize vessels engaged in or suspected of engaging in acts of piracy or armed robbery. All law enforcement in Somali territorial waters was to be carried out 'in a manner consistent with such action permitted on the high seas with respect to piracy'. The Security Council essentially decided that cooperating states could treat Somalia's territorial waters as if they were the high seas for the purpose of repressing acts of piracy and armed robbery at sea.[35] It thereby extended the UNCLOS provisions on the repression of piracy to Somali territorial waters and, by analogy, made them applicable to armed robbery there.[36] Although Indonesia insisted that the resolution should not 'lead to modifying, rewriting or redefining UNCLOS',[37] it is argued that the resolution amounted to a modification of UNCLOS as regards anti-piracy action off the coast of Somalia. The Russian representative in the Security Council referred to resolution

[32] See Article 1(1) UNCLOS.

[33] S/RES/1816 (2008) of 2 June 2008, para 7.

[34] The Security Council also expressly emphasised that the authorisation had been provided only following receipt of a letter from the TFG conveying its consent (S/RES/1816 (2008) of 2 June 2008, para 9; see also UN Doc S/2008/323, 14 May 2008; IMO Doc C 100/7/1, 6 June 2008, annex II, para 2). One may wonder why the anti-piracy action in Somali territorial waters needed to be authorised by the Council if the TFG had consented to it. There are at least two reasons for the adoption of a Chapter VII resolution. First, several States may not have recognised the TFG as the Government of Somalia due to the fact that its control over Somali territory was limited. For those States the TFG's consent was immaterial and could not justify a violation of Somalia's territorial sovereignty. Second, other States may have required Council authorisation for domestic political and constitutional reasons.

[35] JG Dalton, JA Roach and J Daley, 'Introductory Note to United Nations Security Council: Piracy and Armed Robbery at Sea—Resolutions 1816, 1846 & 1851' (2009) 48 *ILM* 129, 130. See also 'UN urged to toughen up on pirates in Gulf of Aden; International legal jurisdiction needed to bring pirates to trial', Lloyd's List, 2 October 2008, 3 ('Resolution 1816 effectively provides that the rules that apply to the high seas also apply in Somali waters').

[36] For a similar view, see T Treves, Piracy, 'Law of the Sea, and Use of Force: Developments off the Coast of Somalia' (2009) 20 *EJIL* 399, 407. *Contra* D Guilfoyle, 'Piracy off Somalia: UN Security Council Resolution 1816 and IMO Regional Counter-Piracy Efforts' (2008) 57 *ICLQ* 690, 696.

[37] See UN Doc S/PV.5902, 2 June 2008, 2. See also ibid, 3.

1816 as providing 'a legislative basis for action to ensure the security of shipping in the region',[38] and the Security Council itself makes clear that the resolution creates a different legal situation from the one that exists under UNCLOS when it affirms that:

> the authorization provided in *this resolution* applies only with respect to the situation in Somalia and *shall not affect the rights or obligations or responsibilities of member states* under international law, including any rights or obligations *under the Convention, with respect to any other situation*, and underscores in particular that it shall not be considered as establishing customary international law.[39]

While the resolution may not affect rights, obligations and responsibilities under UNCLOS 'with respect to any other situation', it does affect such rights, obligations and responsibilities under UNCLOS with respect to the situation in Somalia. The resolution in fact authorises action that is inconsistent with the treaty to which it otherwise defers.

B. Customary International Law Rules

As treaties and customary international law frequently overlap the Security Council has not only dispensed with applicable treaty law but also with rules of customary international law. Under customary international law, as reflected in articles 10 and 19(c) of the 2004 United Nations Convention on Jurisdictional Immunities of States and their Property,[40] State property used for commercial purposes does not enjoy immunity. The Security Council overruled this tenet on several occasions when it decided that Iraqi petroleum and petroleum products should be immune from legal proceedings and should not be subject to any form of attachment, and that all states should take any necessary steps under their respective domestic legal systems to assure this protection.[41]

The decision of the Security Council in resolutions 1497 (2003) and 1593 (2005) that nationals, current or former officials or personnel from a contributing state to a peacekeeping operation which is not a party to the Rome Statute should be subject to the exclusive jurisdiction of that contributing state not only modifies provisions of the Rome Statute,[42] but also impacts upon customary international law to the extent that it limits other states' jurisdiction over such persons on the basis of the passive personality and universality principles. This is why several states abstained from voting on these resolutions. Explaining his country's vote on resolution 1497 (2003), the German representative in the Security Council stated:

> Paragraph 7 [of resolution 1497 (2003)] not only limits the jurisdiction of the International Criminal Court (ICC), it goes beyond that. It limits national jurisdiction of third countries with respect to crimes committed by members of the multinational force or a United Nations stabilization force if that member is the national of a State not party to the Rome Statute of the ICC. Therefore, it is our view that the proposed paragraph would prevent prosecutors in States

[38] See UN Doc S/PV.6046, 16 December 2008, 3. See also ibid, 7 (Costa Rica stating that the Security Council's resolutions do 'not only have international legal grounding, but they are themselves international law').

[39] S/RES/1816 (2008) of 2 June 2008, para 9 (italics added). See also S/RES/1846 (2008) of 2 December 2008, para 11.

[40] The Convention is not yet in force. For the text, see A/RES/59/38 (2004) of 2 December 2004, Annex.

[41] See eg S/RES/712 (1991) of 19 September 1991, para 5; S/RES/986 (1995) of 14 April 1995, para 14; S/RES/1483 (2003) of 22 May 2003, para 22; S/RES/1546 (2004) of 8 June 2004, para 27.

[42] See the text above at notes 27–36.

> that may have to exercise jurisdiction over crimes committed against their nationals abroad from investigating and prosecuting those crimes. ... The second point is that prosecuting what we consider to be international crimes ... would not be possible. ... There is no precedent for that. There is no reason to limit the national jurisdiction of third countries. There is no justification for discriminating against peacekeepers from countries that are members of the Rome Statute of the ICC. Therefore, we feel that that paragraph is not in accordance with international and German law, and we regret not being able to accept it.[43]

The fact that the provision on exclusive jurisdiction was considered by several states as being incompatible, inconsistent or not in accordance with principles of international law shows that the Security Council in fact dispensed with existing customary international law rules.[44]

III. LEGAL BASIS AND LIMITS OF THE DISPENSATION WITH INTERNATIONAL LAW BY THE SECURITY COUNCIL

It has been said that resolutions under Chapter VII provide the Security Council with a convenient and helpful 'legislative device to deal with anomalous cases, to be able to amend the general rules to accommodate them or to provide an expressly exceptional solution'.[45] The legal basis of the Security Council's practice of adapting or dispensing with existing rules of international law can thus be found in Chapter VII and, in particular, articles 39 and 41 of the UN Charter. As the Security Council enjoys a wide margin of discretion not only with regard to the determination of what constitutes a 'threat to the peace' but also with regard to the 'measures' that are to be employed to maintain or restore international peace and security,[46] it will be difficult to establish that the *ad hoc* dispensation with rules of international law is generally outside the Council's Chapter VII powers.

When adapting existing rules of international law to a particular situation, the Council is first and foremost constrained by the Charter itself. As the International Court of Justice (ICJ) held in the *Admissions* case, 'the political character of an organ cannot release it from the observance of the treaty provisions established by the Charter when they constitute limitations on its powers or criteria for its judgment'.[47] Thus, only decisions which are *intra vires* the Charter acquire binding force in terms of article 25 which speaks of 'decisions of the Security Council *in accordance with the present Charter*'. Any dispensation with existing rules of international law is limited by the jurisdiction of the United Nations at large as well as by the attribution and division of competences within the Organisation.[48] In addition, any action of the Security Council must be in accordance with the purposes and principles of the

[43] UN Doc S/PV.4803, 1 August 2003, 4. See also the statements of the Mexican and French representatives, ibid, 2 and 7, respectively. With regard to S/RES/593 (2005), see UN Doc S/PV.5158, 31 March 2005, 6 (Denmark), 11 (Brazil).

[44] See also S/RES/1688 (2006) of 16 June 2006, para 7, where the Security Council overruled the Netherlands' jurisdiction over Charles Taylor on the basis of the passive personality and universality principles.

[45] C Warbrick, 'Kosovo: The Declaration of Independence' (2008) 57 *ICLQ* 675, 690.

[46] See, for example, N Jain, 'A Separate Law for Peacekeepers: The Clash between the Security Council and the International Criminal Court' (2005) 16 *EJIL* 239, 242.

[47] *Admission of a State to the United Nations (Charter, Art 4)*, Advisory Opinion, ICJ Reports 1948, 57, 64.

[48] See Talmon, 'Security Council as World Legislature', 179.

Charter.[49] None of these limits to the powers of the Security Council seems to create an insurmountable obstacle to the dispensation with existing rules of international law, especially if such dispensation is expressly undertaken in response to a threat to international peace and security.

While the Security Council, when acting under Chapter VII, is not bound to respect international law apart from the Charter and norms of *ius cogens*,[50] the Charter itself indicates that the Council's actions are subject to the principle of proportionality. This means that the dispensation with existing rules of international law must be *necessary* in order to maintain international peace and security; that is to say, the usual ways to modify obligations under a treaty or customary international law must be inadequate to achieve that aim. The principle of proportionality will in practice, however, have very little limiting effect on the Council's action as the UN Charter allows the Council a broad margin of appreciation when deciding on the necessity of its actions and on their scope. The dispensation with existing rules of international law would therefore violate the Charter only if the impact on the member states was manifestly out of proportion to the objective pursued, namely the maintenance of international peace and security.

Several states have taken the view that the Security Council does not have the power under Chapter VII to take binding decisions to amend international treaties.[51] For example, Pakistan's representative declared in the Security Council that: 'Pakistan strongly adheres to the position that the Security Council, despite its wide authority and responsibilities, is not empowered to unilaterally amend or abrogate international treaties and agreements freely entered into by sovereign States.'[52] Some 40 years earlier, the representative of the United States made a similar statement with regard to the 1960 Treaty of Guarantee for Cyprus, declaring that '[t]his Treaty or any international treaty cannot be abrogated, cannot be nullified, cannot be modified either in fact or in effect by the Security Council of the United Nations'.[53] While the Security Council may not be able *formally* to abrogate or amend an existing treaty, it can impose binding obligations upon the member states which, in case of conflict, will prevail over existing treaty obligations, including obligations under human rights treaties (and hence even the non-derogable rights contained therein, with the exception of those that have attained the status of *ius cogens*).[54] As explained by John B Bellinger III:

> The Council has authority under Chapter VII, when necessary for the maintenance of international peace and security, to authorise measures that may be inconsistent with otherwise

[49] See Article 24(2) of the UN Charter. See also the statement of the Mexican representative in the Security Council debate on the rule of law: 'The Council is bound by the purposes and principles set out in Articles 1 and 2' (UN Doc S/PV.5474, 22 June 2006, 29).

[50] Although this seems to become a minority view in the international legal literature, it is still maintained; see Talmon, 'Security Council as World Legislature', 184. For the same view, see H Kelsen, *The Law of the United Nations* (New York, Praeger, 1950) 294; and Case T-315/01 *Kadi v Council and Commission* [2005] ECR II-3649, paras 226.

[51] See UN Docs S/PV.4772, 12 June 2003, 10 (Iran), 13 (Brazil), 25 (Germany); A/58/PV.29, 13 October 2003, 9 (Cuba); S/PV.4568, 10 July 2002, 3 (Canada), 5–6 (New Zealand), 11 (France), 15 (Costa Rica on behalf of the 19 Member States of the Rio Group), 15 (Iran), 18 (Ireland), 22 (Brazil), 23 (Switzerland), 26 (Mexico), 30 (Venezuela); S/PV.4568 (Resumption 1), 10 July 2002, 2 (Fiji), 5 (Guinea), 8 (Malaysia), 10 (Syria), 14 (Cuba); A/57/PV.22, 4 October 2002, 6 (Liechtenstein).

[52] UN Doc S/PV.4772, 12 June 2003, 21.

[53] SCOR, 19th Year, 1096th Meeting, 19 February 1964, 13, para 74.

[54] For the same view, see C Stahn, 'The Ambiguities of Security Council Resolution 1422 (2002)' (2003) 14 *EJIL* 85, 99. *Contra* Jain, 'A Separate Law for Peacekeepers', 250.

> applicable treaties. Under Article 103 of the UN Charter, '[i]n the event of a conflict between the obligations of the members of the United Nations under the present Charter and their obligations under any other international agreement, their obligations under the present Charter prevail.'[55]

The obligation of UN member states under article 25 of the Charter to 'accept and carry out the decisions of the Security Council' is an 'obligation [...] under the present Charter' within the meaning of article 103. Member states of the United Nations are therefore bound by article 103 to give obligations arising from binding Chapter VII resolutions priority over any other (treaty) obligation. This view is shared by the ICJ which held in the *Lockerbie* case that 'obligations' imposed by the Security Council under Chapter VII take precedence over obligations under international treaties.[56]

While article 103 of the UN Charter speaks only of 'obligations under any other international agreement', it is today widely accepted that, in case of conflict, obligations imposed by a binding Security Council resolution also prevail over customary international law obligations.[57] In the *Kadi* case, the European Council and the Commission submitted that 'Article 103 of the Charter makes it possible to disregard any other provision of international law, whether customary or laid down by convention, in order to apply the resolutions of the Security Council'.[58]

IV. THE DISPENSATION WITH EXISTING RULES OF INTERNATIONAL LAW AND THE 'RULE OF LAW'

The Security Council's *ad hoc* dispensation with otherwise applicable rules of international law, that is, the creation of special legal regimes for 'special cases', raises concerns from the point of view of the rule of law. It was stated by the Republic of Cyprus in July 2009 in the context of the *Kosovo* Advisory Opinion: 'To allow for "special cases" results in an unacceptable dilution of the quality of the legality of the international legal system'.[59]

The debate on the 'rule of law' in international affairs is part of the wider endeavour of establishing limits to the potentially arbitrary exercise of absolute power by the Security Council in the area of international peace and security.[60] At the United Nations World Summit in September 2005, member states recognised the need for 'universal adherence

[55] See Bellinger, 'United Nations Security Council Resolutions'.

[56] *Questions of Interpretation and Application of the 1971 Montreal Convention arising from the Aerial Incident at Lockerbie (Libya v. UK)* [hereinafter *Lockerbie*], Order of 14 April 1992, ICJ Reports 1992, 3, 15, para. 39.

[57] See, for example, R Bernhardt, 'Article 103' in B Simma (ed), *The Charter of the United Nations* (2nd edn, Oxford, OUP, 2002) 1292, 1298. The Charter prevails in any case over previously established custom by virtue of the principle of *lex posterior derogat lex priori*. *Contra* R Liivoja, 'The Supremacy Clause of the United Nations Charter' (2008) 57 *ICLQ* 583, 602.

[58] Case T-315/01 *Kadi v Council and Commission* [2005] ECR II-3649, para 156. See also Case C-177/95 *Ebony Maritime SA and Loten Navigation Co Ltd v Prefetto della Provincia di Brindisi and other*, Opinion of AG Jacobs, 19 November 1996 [1997] ECR I-1111, 1124, para 27; *Lockerbie*, ICJ Reports 1992, 3, 18 (Declaration of Acting President Oda); *Prosecutor v Tadić*, Case No IT-94-1-A, Appeals Chamber, Judgment, 15 July 1999 (1999) 38 *ILM* 1518, para 296.

[59] *Accordance with International Law of the Unilateral Declaration of Independence by the Provisional Institutions of Self-Government of Kosovo*, Written Statement Commenting on Other Written Statements Submitted by the Republic of Cyprus, July 2009, 14, para 30.

[60] See A Watts, 'The International Rule of Law' (1993) 36 *German Yearbook of International Law* 15, 23; JM Farrall, *United Nations Sanctions and the Rule of Law* (Cambridge, CUP, 2007) 31.

to and implementation of the rule of law at both the national and international levels' and reaffirmed their commitment to 'an international order based on the rule of law'.[61] Since 2006, the UN General Assembly has adopted annual resolutions on 'The rule of law at the national and international levels' which proclaim the rule of law as one of the 'core [...] principles of the United Nations'.[62] While there is no universally agreed definition of the 'rule of law' and no readily identifiable content (even at the domestic level),[63] a number of formal principles are usually associated with the concept, such as supremacy of law, equality before the law, legal certainty (including clarity and predictability), avoidance of arbitrariness, and procedural and legal transparency.[64] The ICJ held in the *ELSI* case that 'arbitrariness is not so much something opposed to a rule of law, as something opposed to the rule of law'.[65] Two aspects of the rule of law, legal certainty and equality before the law, give rise to particular concern.

The principle of *legal certainty* is called into question by the *ad hoc* dispensation with otherwise applicable rules of international law. States no longer know in advance what rules will apply to a certain situation as the Security Council may change these rules at any time on the ground that the case in question is *sui generis*. The foreseeability and predictability of legal rules is, however, of as great importance as is their binding quality: both are necessary to assure states of the protection of their interests, notably allowing them to conduct their international affairs with a sense of certainty. In addition, the principle of legal certainty is called into question by the practice of the Security Council of not setting out clearly and expressly whether and to what extent it intends to dispense with existing rules of international law. For example, there is still widespread disagreement among commentators whether Security Council resolution 1483 actually exempted the occupying powers in Iraq from the strictures of Hague Regulations and the Fourth Geneva Convention and gave them wide-ranging powers for the political and economic restructuring of Iraq. The rule of law, however, requires that the law be clear and predictable.[66] In the interest of legal certainty, any Security Council resolution which is to dispense with otherwise applicable rules of international law must be explicit and must clearly indicate which existing rules are superseded, set out the rules that take their place, and how these modified rules relate to provisions of existing treaty or customary international law not expressly addressed in the resolution.[67]

The principle of *equality before the law* is reflected in article 2(1) of the UN Charter which provides that the 'Organization is based on the principle of the sovereign equality of all its Members'. Equality before the law requires that all states which come within the scope of a legal rule must be treated equally in the application of that rule. There must, in other words, be universality, generality, uniformity and consistency of application of

[61] A/RES/60/1 (2005) of 16 September 2005, para 134.

[62] A/RES/61/39 (2006) of 4 December 2006; A/RES/62/70 (2007) of 6 December 2007; A/RES/63/128 (2008) of 11 December 2008; A/RES/64/116 (2009) of 16 December 2009; A/RES/65/32 (2010) of 6 December 2010.

[63] See UN Doc A/C.6/63/SR.6, 29 October 2008, 5, para 18 (Kenya). See also Watts, 'The International Rule of Law', 15, 25.

[64] See 'The rule of law and transitional justice in conflict and post-conflict societies: Report of the Secretary-General', UN Doc S/2004/616, 23 August 2004, 5, para 6. See also Watts, 'The International Rule of Law', 26; Farrall, *United Nations Sanctions*, 40.

[65] *Elettronica Sicula SpA (ELSI) (USA v Italy)*, Judgment, ICJ Reports 1989, 15, 76, para 128.

[66] See T Bingham, 'The Rule of Law' (2007) 66 *Cambridge LJ* 67, 69.

[67] See Sassòli, Legislation and Maintenance of Public Order', 681, 690; JE Alvarez, 'The Security Council's War on Terrorism: Problems and Policy Options' in E de Wet and A Nollkaemper (eds), *Review of the Security Council by Member States* (Antwerp, Intersentia, 2003) 119, 135.

international law, and no discrimination between states in their subjection to rules of law which in principle apply to all.[68] The Security Council's '*ad-hoc*ism',[69] whereby it customises on an *ad hoc* basis the law that applies to a particular situation, thus poses a serious danger to the rule of law.

Equality, however, is not absolute. Derogations from legal rules are generally possible, but call for close consideration of the individual case and a clear justification. Only objective, legal or factual, differences can justify differentiation.[70] The reasoning that a particular situation constitutes a special or exceptional case is not, in itself, sufficient. As the International Court of Justice observed in the *Gulf of Maine* case: 'each specific case is, in the final analysis, different from all the others'.[71] In this sense, every case is a special case—a case *sui generis*. The law is made of abstract rules which are to be applied equally to each individual case; exceptions are usually laid down in the law itself and are not prescribed by political bodies on an *ad hoc* basis.

Any arbitrary and politically motivated approach to the dispensation with existing, and the dispensation of new rules of international law, that is, any approach that is guided by political or other interests of individual members of the Security Council, will call into question the general applicability and predictability of these rules, and may give rise to criticism on the grounds of selectivity and double standards in the application of these rules. In October 2008, the Chinese representative stated in the Sixth Committee of the General Assembly:

> International law should be applied uniformly. If, in international relations, States applied international law selectively or interpreted it unilaterally to their own advantage, or employed double standards when applying it, international law would be reduced to a tool of power politics and would not be able to play its role in maintaining international order.[72]

The same applies, of course, to the application of international law rules by the Security Council.

These 'rule of law' concerns are exacerbated if the dispensation of (with) international law rules seems merely to benefit the interests of one or more members of the Security Council. It is of interest to note, that in a majority of cases the adaptation of existing rules of international law served the interests of the United States and the United Kingdom. Such self-serving action may constitute an abuse of right on the part of the Security Council and its individual members.

V. CONCLUDING REMARKS

International law is generally pictured as a horizontal, decentralised legal order which lacks central organs for its creation, modification, interpretation and enforcement. However, as early as the 1930s, Hans Kelsen postulated in his *Pure Theory of Law* that the international legal order was geared towards centralisation.[73] He noted 'that not only

[68] Watts, 'The International Rule of Law', 31.

[69] See A Bianchi, '*Ad-hoc*ism and the Rule of Law' (2002) 13 *EJIL* 263, 270.

[70] See Bingham, 'The Rule of Law', 69, 73.

[71] *Delimitation of the Maritime Boundary in the Gulf of Maine Area, Judgment*, ICJ Reports 1984, 246, 290, para 81.

[72] UN Doc A/C.6/63/SR.6, 29 October 2008, 9, para 56.

[73] H Kelsen, *Pure Theory of Law* (translated from the second (revised and enlarged) German edition by Max Knight) (Clark, NJ, Lawbook Exchange, 2005) 328.

the creation of legal norms, but also their application, indeed all functions stipulated by a legal order, may be centralised [...] in this dynamic sense, that is, to be performed by one organ'.[74] In 1944, he wrote: 'The problem of world organization is a problem of centralization; and the whole evolution of the law from its primitive beginnings to its standard of today has been, from a technical point of view, a continuous process of centralization.'[75] It may be said that the turning point in the transition to a more centralised international legal order was the founding of the United Nations. The ultimate goal of this legal development, according to Kelsen, is 'an international legislative body competent to *adapt international law to the changing circumstances*'.[76] In this sense, the Security Council's practice of dispensing (with) international law may be seen as a further step towards the centralisation of the international legal order; a legal order built around the United Nations. Experience shows that functions and powers (to fulfil these functions) over time gradually gravitate towards a strong and determined centre. The UN Charter, and especially articles 25 and 103, provides the Security Council with the legal tools to further this process. Centralisation is not necessarily a counterpoint, or even a guarantee against the fragmentation of international law. As Security Council treaty action shows, it may itself contribute to the fragmentation of international law, not in the sense that the same rule is applied differently by different organs, but in the sense that the same central organ creates different rules for what it considers exceptional or *sui generis* situations.

[74] ibid, 317.
[75] H Kelsen, *Peace through Law* (Chapel Hill, University of North Carolina Press, 1944) 21 (emphasis added).
[76] ibid, 22.

20

Systemic Integration and International Investment Law

EDWARD GUNTRIP*

I. INTRODUCTION

SINCE 1989, THE number of international investment agreements (IIAs) in force has increased exponentially. This rapid growth has resulted in the development of international investment law (IIL) by virtue of the rising number of arbitral awards rendered by tribunals established under the dispute resolution provisions contained in the IIAs. Within this wider trend, there has been an additional movement towards the inclusion in IIAs of concepts and obligations drawn from a variety of legal areas such as international environmental law, international labour law and, more generally, international human rights law. Contemporaneously, much debate has taken place regarding the 'fragmentation' of public international law and the potential implications of the development of increasingly diverse and segregated fields of public international law. The prospect of using Article 31(3)(c) of the Vienna Convention on the Law of Treaties (VCLT)[1] has been mooted as a means of counteracting 'fragmentation'.

This chapter reviews the development of IIL during the period 1989–2010 in the context of the 'fragmentation' of public international law to argue that IIL is undergoing a process of systemic integration rather than 'fragmentation'. Initially, the paper defines 'fragmentation' and considers the extent to which the customary rules of treaty interpretation apply to 'fragments' of public international law. Examination then turns to the degree of 'fragmentation' exhibited by IIL at various stages of its development by reference to the provisions contained within bilateral investment treaties (BITs) and the extent to which Article 31(3)(c) VCLT could be used to interpret these provisions to achieve systemic integration. The impact of the introduction of amicus curiae submissions on the process of harmonisation is also discussed. Finally, consideration turns to the current status of IIL by examining how the intersection of IIL with other fields of international law has implications for both its current effectiveness and its future development.

* PhD Candidate, Brunel University.

[1] Vienna Convention on the Law of Treaties (adopted 23 May 1969, entered into force 27 January 1980) 1155 UNTS 331 ('VCLT').

II. FRAGMENTATION

Fragmentation is based on the premise that individual areas of public international law are becoming increasingly specialised and divided, that legal principles are becoming incoherent, and as a consequence, public international law is losing general applicability.[2]

One of the manifestations of the process of fragmentation is the development of specialised subsystems within the public international law framework (*leges speciales*). *Leges speciales* result from the establishment of treaty regimes that contain legal obligations which vary from the principles of general international law. When varying general international law, parties to a treaty may agree to deviate from primary rules (ie substantive obligations) or both primary and secondary rules (ie both substantive obligations and the rules that govern the operation and interpretation of the substantive obligations).[3]

The World Trade Organisation (WTO) and human rights treaties have been cited as examples of *leges speciales*. Both regimes are briefly considered below.

A. WTO

The WTO (established by the Marrakesh Agreement)[4] and the Dispute Settlement Body (DSB) and Appellate Body (AB) (established by the Dispute Settlement Understanding (DSU))[5] form part of a *lex specialis* regime that governs both primary and secondary rules of international trade through, amongst other covered agreements, the General Agreement on Tariffs and Trade (GATT).

The WTO governs 'the conduct of trade relations among its Members in matters related to the agreements and associated legal instruments included in the Annexes to this Agreement'.[6] Consequently, the primary rules that the WTO governs are limited to those contained in particular treaties which have a specialised focus.

When interpreting the covered agreements, Articles 3(2) and 19(2) DSU prevent the DSB and the AB respectively, from supplementing or diminishing the rights and obligations contained in the covered agreements. However, the further language of Article 3(2) DSU states that the DSB may clarify the terms of the covered agreements 'in accordance with customary rules of interpretation of public international law'.[7] The customary rules of

[2] B Simma, 'Universality of International Law from the Perspective of a Practitioner' (2009) 20 *EJIL* 266, 270; C McLachlan, 'The Principle of Systemic Integration and Article 31(3)(c) of the Vienna Convention' (2005) 54 *ICLQ* 279, 284. See generally ILC, *Fragmentation of International Law: Difficulties Arising from the Diversification and Expansion of International Law* (1 May – 9 June and 3 July – 11 August 2006) UN Doc A/CN.4/L.682.

[3] This classification is drawn from H Hart, *The Concept of Law*, 2nd edn (Oxford, Oxford University Press, 1994) 79. With regard to its application, see especially *Case concerning the United States Diplomatic and Consular Staff in Tehran (United States of America v. Iran) ICJ Reports 1980*, 41.

[4] Marrakesh Agreement Establishing the World Trade Organization (concluded 15 April 1994, entered into force 1 January 1995) 1867 UNTS 154 ('Marrakesh Agreement').

[5] Understanding on Rules and Procedures Governing the Settlement of Disputes, Marrakesh Agreement Establishing the World Trade Organization (concluded 15 April 1994, entered into force 1 January 1995) Annex 2, 1869 UNTS 401.

[6] Marrakesh Agreement Article II(1).

[7] ILC, *Fragmentation Report* [167]; O Casanovas, *Unity and Pluralism in Public International Law* (The Hague, Martinus Nijhoff Publishers, 2001) 233.

interpretation, as set out in Article 31 VCLT, permit reference to 'any relevant rules of international law applicable in the relations between the parties'.[8] Therefore, reference to law external to the WTO covered agreements is permitted when interpreting the provisions of the covered agreements.[9]

B. Human Rights Treaties

Human rights treaty regimes are considered to be *lex specialis* due to their primary rules being directed towards the protection of the rights of individuals. Given this aim, the obligations contained in human rights treaties are designed to protect a common interest rather than outline the reciprocal rights of states.[10] Consequently, the basis of specialist human rights treaties differs to the traditional form of bilateral relations between states due to its overarching objectives.[11]

However, the *lex specialis* nature of the primary rules has a limited impact with regard to the interpretation of human rights treaties, as evidenced by the approach taken by the European Court of Human Rights in *Bankovic*:

> [T]he Court recalls that the principles underlying the Convention cannot be interpreted and applied in a vacuum. The Court must also take into account any relevant rules of international law when examining questions concerning its jurisdiction and, consequently, determine State responsibility in conformity with the governing principles of international law, although it must remain mindful of the Convention's special character as a human rights treaty. The Convention should be interpreted as far as possible in harmony with other principles of international law of which it forms a part.[12]

C. Conclusion

From these two examples, it can be seen that *leges speciales* focus on primary rules in one specific field of law or protect one type of interest. Both utilise the customary rules of treaty interpretation to interpret *lex specialis* in the context of general international law. It is in relation to these characteristics that the development of international investment law will be measured.

[8] VCLT Article 31(3)(c).

[9] See especially WTO *United States–Import Prohibition of certain Shrimp and Shrimp Products—Report of the Appellate Body* (12 October 1998) WT/DS58/AB/R and WTO *EC Measures Concerning Meat and Meat Products (Hormones)—Report of the Appellate Body* (16 January1998) WT/DS-26/AB/R. See generally ILC, *Fragmentation Report* [168]; J Pauwelyn, 'Bridging Fragmentation and Unity: International Law as a Universe of Inter-connected Islands' (2004) 25 *Michigan Journal of International Law* 903, 913; McLachlan, 'Systemic Integration' 303; Casanovas, *Unity and Pluralism*, 233.

[10] E Vierdag, 'Some Remarks About Special Features of Human Rights Treaties' in L Barnhoorn and K Wellens (eds), *Diversity in Secondary Rules and the Unity of International Law* (The Hague, Martinus Nijhoff Publishers, 1995) 125; Casanovas, *Unity and Pluralism*, 154. See, eg *Reservations to the Convention on Genocide: Advisory Opinion ICJ Reports 1951*, 23.

[11] Vierdag, 'Human Rights Treaties' 125; Casanovas, *Unity and Pluralism* 155. See, eg *Case of Ireland v the United Kingdom* (App no 5310/71) (1978) Series A no 25, [239].

[12] *Bankovic v Belgium* (App No, 52207/99) ECtHR, Decision on Admissibility, 12 December 2001, [57].

III. DEVELOPMENT OF IIL

This section will consider three stages in the development of IIL during the period 1989–2010.

A. 1989–1993

In the late 1980s and early 1990s, IIAs in the form of bilateral investment treaties (BITs) started to increase in popularity.[13] At this time, BITs promoted investment protection and pursued market oriented economic policies as a result of the prevailing political and legal climate.

The need for investment protection was generated by debate during the mid 1970s regarding the establishment of a new international economic order (NIEO) in the United Nations General Assembly (UNGA). This was sought by the numerical majority of newly independent developing states. The drive by these developing states fundamentally to alter the global economic system (including how host states could treat foreign direct investment (FDI)) through UNGA Resolutions[14] had resulted in uncertainty regarding the content of the customary international law that applied to the protection of alien property. Consequently, the inclusion of explicit terms in BITs provided increased legal certainty for investors.[15] By the late 1980s, developing states were willing to accept investment focused terms within BITs because FDI provided capital for their development needs[16] which was not forthcoming from its traditional sources due to the combination of the prevailing debt crisis and a lack of foreign aid.[17]

Market-driven economic theories were encapsulated in BITs as part of the trend towards economic liberalism which was endorsed by both developed and developing states. Promoted by the Washington Consensus, economic liberalism encouraged markets (rather than states) to allocate resources most efficiently.[18] This was to be achieved by the free movement of goods and capital (including FDI) in the private sector which would, in turn, encourage development.[19]

The characteristics of BITs drafted during this time period are evidenced by the terms of the USA-Argentina BIT[20] which was negotiated on the basis of the 1987 USA Model BIT (the framework for multiple BITs concluded during this time period).

[13] United Nations Centre on Transnational Corporations and International Chamber of Commerce, *Bilateral Investment Treaties 1959–1991* (New York, United Nations, 1992) 3; UNCTAD, *Bilateral Investment Treaties 1959–1999* (New York, United Nations, 2000) 2.

[14] See especially UNGA Res 3201(1 May 1974) (S-VI); UNGA Res 3202 (1 May 1974) (S-VI) and UNGA Res 3281 (12 December 1974) (XXIX).

[15] J Salacuse, 'The Treatification of International Investment Law' (2007) 13 *Law and Business Review of the Americas* 155, 156.

[16] UNCTAD, *International Investment Rule-Making: Stocktaking, Challenges and the Way Forward* (New York, United Nations, 2009) 13; Salacuse, 'Treatification' 159; M Sornarajah, *The International Law on Foreign Investment* 2nd edn (Cambridge, Cambridge University Press, 2004) 25.

[17] UNCTAD, *Bilateral Investment Treaties in the Mid-1990s* (New York, United Nations,1998) 9; A Newcombe and L Paradell, *Law and Practice of Investment Treaties: Standards of Treatment* (The Netherlands, Kluwer Law International, 2009) 48.

[18] Newcombe and Paradell, *Law and Practice* 48; Salacuse, 'Treatification' 160.

[19] ibid.

[20] Available at www.unctad.org/sections/dite/iia/docs/bits/argentina_us.pdf ('US-Argentina BIT').

Investor certainty was created in the USA-Argentina BIT by referring, in several provisions, to international law standards, examples being: Article II(2)(a) (regarding fair and equitable treatment); and Article X(b) (regarding the relationship between the BIT and the investment contract). A similar approach was taken in relation to expropriation. Article IV(1) requires compliance with Article II(2) in the event of an expropriation (which refers to international law as a minimum standard). Article IV(2) permits judicial review to determine whether an expropriation has taken place and, if so, whether any compensation paid is in conformity with both the BIT and 'the principles of international law'. These provisions safeguarded against the risk of nationalisation and ran counter to the approach taken by developing states in the context of the NIEO, who relied on the exercise of their right of permanent sovereignty over natural resources to justify nationalisation.[21] When determining the measure of compensation, reference to international law invoked the customary international law standard, rather than the standard pursued by developing states, who sought to determine the amount of compensation owed in accordance with the national laws of the host state.[22]

The market-oriented focus of states is evidenced by the preamble to the USA-Argentina BIT which emphasises that the 'fair and equitable treatment of investment is desirable in order to maintain a stable framework for investment and maximum effective use of economic resources'. The substantive provisions of the USA-Argentina BIT reflect that investment is to be facilitated by the BIT but that the terms governing the investment itself are to be market driven to achieve efficient resource allocation. Consequently, priority is given to the terms of the investment contract in Article II(2)(c) (regarding fair and equitable treatment), Article V(1)(d) (regarding free transfer of payments), Article VII(1) (regarding what constitutes an investment dispute) and Article X(c) (regarding the relationship between the BIT and the investment contract).

It can be seen that the primary rules set out in the provisions of the BITs negotiated and entered into in the late 1980s and early 1990s focus on two substantive considerations—investment protection and efficient resource allocation. Therefore, from this perspective, the BIT regime could be said to be *lex specialis*.

BITs remained subject to the general international law principles of treaty interpretation, permitting limited recourse to law external to IIL in accordance with Article 31(3)(c) VCLT. However, given the narrow focus of the regime at this time, there was little incentive for tribunals to refer to this provision, instead preferring to interpret the IIL principles by reference to the express terms of the BITs.

In conclusion, the provisions of BITs contain specialised primary rules and whilst treaty interpretation permitted reference to external legal regimes, this power was rarely exercised.

B. 1994–2000

The period 1994–2000 was characterised by a rapid increase in the number of BITs being entered into between states[23] combined with environmental and labour standards

[21] eg UNGA Resolution 1803 (14 December 1962) (XVII) and UNGA Resolution 3201 (1 May 1974) (S-VI) Article 4(e).

[22] eg UNGA Resolution 1803 (14 December 1962) (XVII) Article 4.

[23] United Nations Centre on Transnational Corporations and International Chamber of Commerce, *Bilateral Investment Treaties 1959–1991* 3; UNCTAD, *Bilateral Investment Treaties 1959–1999* 2.

achieving prominence in international politics. These trends merged during the conclusion of the North American Free Trade Agreement[24] (NAFTA) which subsequently influenced the development of IIAs.

The negotiation of NAFTA, which includes Chapter 11 covering FDI, occurred between 1990 and 1993. During the negotiations, environmental and labour lobby groups exerted considerable political pressure on the US government to factor these interests into NAFTA as they believed that the conclusion of NAFTA would result in a 'race to the bottom' for environmental and labour standards.[25] Their views were acknowledged and acted upon by Congress, who in response to President Bush seeking a 'fast track negotiating authority' (the effect of which was to bypass Congress approval for NAFTA), permitted the 'fast track' on the condition that the President took into account the views of the lobby groups.[26] Parallel track negotiations were established which produced Article 1114 of NAFTA;[27] however, the election of President Clinton prior to final approval of NAFTA resulted in the parties to NAFTA renegotiating environmental and labour standards.[28] The final result was the North American Agreement on Environmental Cooperation (NAAEC)[29] and the North American Agreement on Labor Cooperation (NAALC).[30] These side agreements require parties to NAFTA to enforce their domestic environmental and labour provisions.[31] Failure to do so may result in another party to NAFTA invoking the dispute resolution provisions.[32] Consequently, the side agreements do not determine what environmental or labour standards are required. However, they do recognise that investment and the maintenance of environmental and labour standards are linked by requiring parties to enforce their domestic standards in the event that they are breached by foreign investors. The recognition of this relationship affected the nature of claims brought under NAFTA and the attitude of some NAFTA parties towards FDI.

Many of the claims initiated by investors under Chapter 11 contained environmental considerations because the respondent NAFTA party had justified its actions on environmental grounds.[33] For example, cases such as *Methanex*,[34] *Metalclad*[35] and *Ethyl*

[24] North American Free Trade Agreement, 32 ILM 289 and 605.

[25] R Housman and P Orbuch, 'Integrating Labor and Environmental Concerns into the North American Free Trade Agreement: A Look Back and a Look Ahead' (1993) 8 *American University Journal of International Law and Policy* 719, 725; R Housman, 'The Treatment of Labor and Environmental Issues in Future Western Hemisphere Trade Liberalization Efforts' (1995) 10 *Connecticut Journal of International Law* 301, 325; S Weintraub and J Gilbreath, 'The Social Side to Free Trade' in J Lemco and WB Robson (eds), *Ties Beyond Trade: Labour and Environmental Issues under the NAFTA* (Toronto, Canadian-American Committee, 1993) 57.

[26] Housman and Orbuch, 'A Look Back' 723; Housman, 'Treatment' 304.

[27] Which only addresses environmental standards.

[28] J Schott, 'Free Trade Agreements: Boon or Bane of the World Trading System?' in J Schott (ed), *Free Trade Agreements: US Strategies and Priorities* (Washington D.C., Institute for International Economics, 2004) 41; Housman, 'Treatment' 306; D Vogel, 'The Environment and International Trade' in O Graham Jnr (ed), *Environmental Politics and Policy: 1960s–1990s* (Pennsylvania, Pennsylvania State University Press, 2000) 88.

[29] North American Agreement on Environmental Cooperation, 32 ILM 1480 ('NAAEC').

[30] North American Agreement on Labor Cooperation, 32 ILM 1499 ('NAALC').

[31] NAAEC Article 5; NAALC Article 3.

[32] NAAEC Part Five; NAALC Part Five.

[33] As yet, no claims have been brought in relation to actions of a host state justified by reference to labour standards.

[34] *Methanex Corporation v United States of America*, Final Award of the Tribunal on Jurisdiction and Merits, 3 August 2005 available at www.naftaclaims.com/Disputes/USA/Methanex/Methanex_Final_Award.pdf.

[35] *Metalclad Corporation v The United Mexican States* (ARB(AF)/97/1), Final Award, 30 August 2000 available at www.naftaclaims.com/Disputes/Mexico/Metalclad/MetalcladFinalAward.pdf.

Corp[36] required that arbitral tribunals consider alleged breaches of NAFTA that were argued to be justifiable on the grounds of environmental protection and in some cases human health.

The introduction of the NAFTA side agreements also influenced the attitude of Canada and the USA regarding their approach to investment more generally. For example, the 1994 USA Model BIT added two preambular paragraphs that were not contained in the 1987 USA Model BIT relating to the promotion of 'respect for internationally recognized workers' rights' and 'health, safety and environmental measures of general application' respectively. The results of this change became further evident in the terms of the Canadian and USA BITs after 2000 (discussed below). Given the increasing popularity of BITs during this time, this change in attitude was influential for the future direction of the BIT regime.

The wider impact of NAFTA was to indicate to developed states, which traditionally had not been host states, that by entering into IIAs, they may become respondents in investment disputes and potentially subject to adverse awards. As a consequence of being subject to claims under NAFTA, and in light of decisions handed down by tribunals in other investment arbitration regimes, the attitude of developed states towards investor protection became more circumspect.[37] For example, the USA, who were previously keen proponents of investor protection and economic liberalism made modifications to the BITs entered into after this period to give effect to their change in attitude. The realisation that the US may potentially be liable for its actions resulted in a more balanced Model BIT that took into account, inter alia, the recognition of a state's right to regulate, the narrowing of host state obligations, the limited use of the most favoured nation clause and the removal of the 'umbrella clause'.[38]

The consequences of blending IIL with international environmental law and international labour law required the expansion of the remit of FDI to include considerations that were previously not contemplated by the IIL regime. This was a significant expansion of the primary rules encompassed by IIAs from the preceding five years. Whilst the conclusion of two side agreements in relation to a single IIA is insufficient to establish that the systemic integration of IIL had been achieved, it is indicative of the broadening scope of primary rules that arbitral tribunals were required to address when considering the terms of the IIA. Therefore, it is arguable that this period could be classified as the turning point for the systemic integration of IIL as its focus changed from narrow primary rules to international law more generally.

Reference to legal regimes outside of IIL, and the lessening of the stringent approach to investor protection, gave greater scope to arbitral tribunals to look beyond IIL when interpreting the provisions of an IIA. The inclusion of references to environmental and labour law provided arbitral tribunals with the possibility of utilising Article 31(3)(c) VCLT to turn to international environmental law and international labour law as

[36] *Ethyl Corporation v The Government of Canada*, Award on Jurisdiction, 24 June 1998 available at www.naftaclaims.com/Disputes/Canada/EthylCorp/EthylCorpAwardOnJurisdiction.pdf.

[37] G Gagne and J Morin, 'The Evolving American Policy on Investment Protection: Evidence From Recent FTAs and the 2004 Model BIT' (2006) 9 *Journal of International Economic Law* 357, 363; J Alvarez, 'The Evolving BIT' June 2009 Transnational Dispute Management Provisional Version, 8 available at www.law.nyu.edu/ecm_dlv3/groups/public/@nyu_law_website__faculty__faculty_profiles__jalvarez/documents/documents/ecm_pro_065335.pdf; C Lévesque, 'Influence on the Canadian FIPA Model and the US Model BIT: NAFTA Chapter 11 and Beyond' (2006) 45 *Canadian Yearbook of International Law* 249, 251.

[38] Alvarez, 'The Evolving BIT' 9.

applicable sources of law to inform their opinion regarding alleged breaches of IIAs. The inclusion of these terms in IIAs prevents arguments that arbitral tribunals are exceeding their jurisdiction when these legal regimes are referred to in the arbitral award.[39] Therefore, not only does the inclusion of environmental and labour law evidence a turning point in relation to the systemic integration of the primary rules of IIL, it also indicates a turning point in relation to the secondary rules as well.

In essence, although IIL was still *lex specialis*, the process of systemic integration had begun.

C. 2000 – present

The last decade can be characterised by the development of the relationship between environmental standards, labour standards, human rights and IIAs. This can be observed in the form of specific references to these laws in BITs, the emergence of corporate social responsibility and through the use of amicus curiae submissions from interested third parties in FDI disputes. Initially, these advancements were based upon the change of attitude by states such as the United States and Canada in light of their experience of NAFTA.

So as to create consistency between NAFTA and their BIT obligations, both the United States and Canada amended their Model BITs.[40]

The 2003 Canadian Model Foreign Investment Protection Agreement[41] (FIPA) prevents states from offering to waive, actually waiving or otherwise derogating from environmental measures to encourage FDI.[42] Article 10 of the FIPA also provides for 'General Exceptions' which permit a party to take measures (that are not arbitrary, unjustifiably discriminatory or a disguised restriction on trade or investment) to protect, inter alia, human health[43] and exhaustible natural resources.[44] Despite these inclusions, the 2003 Canadian Model FIPA does not address labour standards.

The 2004 USA Model BIT[45] refers to both environmental and labour standards. Article 12 is designed to discourage a party to the BIT from providing preferential treatment to an investor by weakening, or derogating from, environmental law as a means to induce FDI. Article 13 relates to labour standards. Article 13(1) provides that the parties are to 'strive' to ensure that they do not 'weaken or reduce adherence to internationally recognised labor rights' by waiving or derogating from domestic laws as a means of inducing FDI. Article 13(2) sets out which labour rights are considered to be internationally recognised for the purposes of Article 13(1). In addition to these substantive clauses, the preamble to the 2004 USA Model BIT refers to the parties' 'desire' to achieve the objectives of the

[39] ICSID Convention (concluded 18 March 1965, entered into force 14 October 1966) 575 UNTS 159 Article 25(1) confers jurisdiction upon a tribunal to resolve 'disputes arising directly out of investments'. If a BIT or IIA makes reference to legal regimes external to IIL in the context of FDI, it is arguable that breaches of these standards relate to the investment, and can therefore form part of the dispute.

[40] See generally M Kinnear and R Hansen, 'The Influence of Chapter 11 NAFTA in the BIT Landscape' (2005) 12 *University of California Davis Journal of International Law and Policy* 101.

[41] Available at www.international.gc.ca/trade-agreements-accords-commerciaux/assets/pdfs/2004-FIPA-model-en.pdf ('FIPA').

[42] FIPA Article 11.

[43] FIPA Article 10(1)(a).

[44] FIPA Article 10(1)(c).

[45] Available at www.state.gov/documents/organization/117601.pdf ('2004 USA Model BIT').

BIT 'in a manner consistent with the protection of health, safety and the environment, and the promotion of internationally recognized labor rights'.

Other states have followed the approach taken by Canada and the USA, however, this approach has not always met with approval, as was demonstrated by the Draft Norwegian Model BIT.[46]

The preamble to the Draft Norwegian Model BIT referred to the Parties achieving the aims of the BIT in a manner consistent with 'the protection of health, safety, and the environment, and the promotion of internationally recognized labour rights'. In addition to references to environmental and labour standards, the parties reaffirmed 'their commitment to democracy, the rule of law, human rights and fundamental freedoms in accordance with their obligations under international law, including the principles set out in the United Nations Charter and the Universal Declaration of Human Rights'. The substantive provisions of the BIT reflected the approach taken in the 2004 USA Model BIT and the 2003 Canadian Model FIPA.[47]

The response to the Draft Norwegian Model BIT was extremely negative. Businesses were not comfortable with the inclusive nature of the BIT and environmental and labour groups did not feel that it adequately protected these interests due to the lack of enforceable remedies.[48] As a result, Norway has temporarily abandoned its BIT program.[49]

Despite the negative reaction to the Draft Norwegian Model BIT, China has embraced a similar approach to the 2004 USA Model BIT and the Draft Norwegian Model BIT in its proposed Model BIT.

The proposed Chinese Model BIT[50] refers to improving investment flows 'in a manner consistent with the protection of health, safety and the environment, and the promotion of internationally recognized labour rights' whilst also 'emphasising the importance of corporate social responsibility'. These preambular statements are reinforced by substantive provisions in a similar form to the 2003 Canadian Model FIPA and the Draft Norwegian Model BIT.[51] The proposed Chinese Model BIT also contains Article 13 addressing corporate social responsibility by encouraging investors to undertake their investments in a socially responsible manner in compliance with the OECD Guidelines for Multinational Enterprises and the United Nations Global Compact.[52]

This brief overview of BIT provisions demonstrates that the terms of some BITs make express reference to environmental and labour standards as well as human rights. Even if a BIT is silent on these issues, the use of amicus curiae submissions under NAFTA, the UNCITRAL Arbitration Rules and the ICSID Arbitration Rules have permitted these issues to be raised in disputes between foreign investors and home states regarding the treatment of FDI.

[46] Available at www.regjeringen.no/upload/NHD/Vedlegg/hoeringer/Utkast%20til%20modellavtale2.doc ('Draft Norwegian Model BIT').

[47] See eg Article 11(1) Draft Norwegian Model BIT and Articles 12 and 13 2004 USA Model BIT and Article 24 Draft Norwegian Model BIT and Article 10 2003 Canadian Model FIPA.

[48] D Vis Dunbar, 'Norway Shelves its Draft Model Bilateral Investment Treaty', 8 June 2009 available at www.investmenttreatynews.org/cms/news/archive/2009/06/08/norway-shelves-its-proposed-model-bilateral-investment-treaty.aspx.

[49] Vis Dunbar, 'Norway'.

[50] Text available in Appendix V of N Gallagher and W Shan, *Chinese Investment Treaties: Policies and Practice* (Oxford, Oxford University Press, 2009) ('Proposed Chinese Model BIT').

[51] eg Proposed Chinese Model BIT Article 12(5).

[52] Both are voluntary codes of corporate practices regarding business conduct in relation to, inter alia, human rights. See generally www.oecd.org/department/0,3355,en_2649_34889_1_1_1_1_1,00.html and www.unglobalcompact.org/ respectively.

Arbitral tribunals first held that third parties were able to make written submissions in FDI disputes under Article 15(1) of the UNCITRAL Arbitration Rules in the *Methanex* decision,[53] a claim brought against the United States under NAFTA. The Free Trade Commission of NAFTA subsequently issued a statement on amicus curiae participation confirming that an arbitral tribunal retains its discretion to permit amicus curiae submissions under NAFTA.[54] In 2006, ICSID amended its Arbitration Rules to permit submissions from amici curiae provided that the submissions comply with the terms of Rule 37(2).[55] Although written submissions are permitted under NAFTA and the ICSID Arbitration Rules, both disputing parties must usually consent before amici curiae can attend oral hearings[56] and amici curiae are generally denied access to the documents that form the basis of the dispute by the arbitral tribunal.[57] It has been argued that these limitations reduce the effectiveness of this process as amici curiae are unaware of the actual arguments before the arbitral tribunal.[58]

Despite these restrictions, the ability of arbitral tribunals to exercise their discretion in order to accept amicus curiae submissions provides a further means by which organisations or individuals may refer to interests outside of IIL and bring them within the remit of FDI disputes.

When considering the developments in the field of IIL over the last decade, there has been an increased degree of harmonisation of the primary rules included in IIAs. Initiated by the inclusion of references to environmental and labour standards in the NAFTA regime, this trend has been transferred to the BITs of several states. Although attempts to broaden the scope of these interests to human rights more generally have not been successful yet, China's proposed Model BIT would indicate that some states remain keen to pursue this route.

One noticeable aspect of the primary rules is that the provisions that relate to considerations external to IIL are either contained in the preambles to BITs (and are therefore unenforceable) or require parties to 'strive' to comply. In the absence of bad faith, it would be difficult to prove a breach of such a provision. In light of the restricted enforceability of these provisions, from a primary rule perspective, progress has been made towards the systemic integration of IIL but the process is not yet complete.

Despite this, the secondary rules of treaty interpretation governing IIL may conceivably assist the process of systemic integration. The increasing number of references to other areas of international law within BITs potentially affects how BITs are interpreted

[53] *Methanex Corporation v United States of America*, Decision of the Tribunal on Petitions from Third Persons to Intervene as *Amici Curiae*, 15 January 2001 available at www.naftaclaims.com/Disputes/USA/Methanex/MethanexDecisionReAuthorityAmicus.pdf ('Methanex - Amici').

[54] Available at www.international.gc.ca/trade-agreements-accords-commerciaux/assets/pdfs/Nondisputing-en.pdf.

[55] Available at http:\\icsid.worldbank.org/ICSID/StaticFiles/basicdoc/CRR_English-final.pdf ('ICSID Arbitration Rules').

[56] eg ICSID Arbitration Rules 32(2); UNICTRAL Arbitration Rule 25(4) available at www.uncitral.org/pdf/english/texts/arbitration/arb-rules/arb-rules.pdf.

[57] See, eg *Biwater Gauff (Tanzania) Limited v. United Republic of Tanzania* (ARB/05/22), Award, 24 July 2008, available at icsid.worldbank.org/ICSID/FrontServlet?requestType=CasesRH&actionVal=showDoc&docId=DC1589_En&caseId=C67 ('Biwater Gauff (Tanzania) Limited v. United Republic of Tanzania') and *Methanex – Amici. cf Piero Foresti, Laura de Carli and others v. Republic of South Africa* (ARB(AF)/07/1) letter to non-disputing parties dated 5 October 2009 available at ita.law.uvic.ca/documents/ForestiNon-DisputingPartiesOrder.pdf.

[58] See generally T Ishikawa, 'Third Party Participation in Investment Treaty Arbitration' (2010) 59 *ICLQ* 373, 401.

and creates the possibility of harmonising IIL with other international law regimes. The incorporation of substantive provisions preventing waivers or derogations from environmental and labour standards and encouraging compliance with voluntary codes of conduct in relation to corporate social responsibility could result in traditional standards being interpreted in light of these aims. Further, preambular statements have previously been utilised by arbitral tribunals to interpret substantive provisions of BITs.[59] Consequently, references to environmental and labour standards and human rights in preambles may permit an arbitral tribunal to refer to these principles in an award when considering the object and purpose of the treaty in conjunction with Article 31(3)(c) VCLT. Although treaty interpretation has always been applicable to the IIL regime in this manner, the express reference in BITs to law external to IIL permits arbitral tribunals to interpret BITs in light of international environmental law, international labour law and international human rights law. This could counteract some of the difficulties regarding the limited enforceability of provisions relating to primary rules external to IIL. It may potentially result in arbitral awards considering legal regimes beyond IIL, albeit in a nuanced manner given the investment protection focus of IIAs, evidencing a certain degree of systemic integration.

Submissions on general policy considerations from third parties provide further means by which tribunals can take into account interests external to IIL. Permitting amici curiae to make written submissions on some of the wider issues relating to the dispute, including environmental and labour standards and human rights, evidences that IIL may not necessarily be the sole consideration of arbitral tribunals considering disputes under IIAs.

Some of the difficulties encountered when attempting to apply the secondary rules in the ways discussed above are addressed in the next section.

IV. CURRENT DIFFICULTIES AND FUTURE DEVELOPMENTS

The development of IIL between 1989 and 2010 demonstrates the emergence of a trend in IIAs to expand the primary rules from being drawn entirely from IIL to include principles from other legal regimes such as international environmental law, international labour law and human rights. In this sense, the IIL regime has changed its focus from a specialised primary rules regime to a regime more reflective of mainstream public international law—detracting from arguments that it may constitute *lex specialis*.

It is submitted that, despite the ongoing systemic integration of IIL in relation to its primary rules, the prospective use of Article 31(3)(c) VCLT as a means of interpreting IIAs does not provide a guaranteed means of achieving harmonisation despite its potential application described in the preceding section.

The inclusion of standards from legal regimes external to IIL would indicate that states entering these BITs do not intend for them to be interpreted in a manner that conflicts with environmental standards, labour standards and human rights. Therefore, the

[59] Preambular statements have informed the interpretation of the fair and equitable treatment standard in *Siemens v The Argentine Republic*, Award, 6 February 2007 [290] available at ita.law.uvic.ca/documents/Siemens-Argentina-Award.pdf; *Azurix Corp. v The Argentine Republic*, ICSID Case ARB/01/12, Final Award, 14 July 2006 [360] available at ita.law.uvic.ca/documents/AzurixAwardJuly2006.pdf; *Saluka Investments B.V. v Czech Republic*, Partial Award, 17 March 2006 [300] available at www.pca-cpa.org/upload/files/SAL-CZ%20Partial%20Award%20170306.pdf.

emergence of provisions within IIAs that refer to principles from multiple legal regimes necessitates that an arbitral tribunal balance the obligations under each regime in such a way as to give effect to the overall intentions of the parties to the IIA (as evidenced by the provisions of the IIA). Although Article 31(3)(c) VCLT might provide an avenue by which harmonisation may occur,[60] one difficulty that arises is determining what weight is to be given to the competing interests that exist in FDI disputes. For example, should the actions of a host state comply with its obligations in relation to international environmental law but be in breach of the terms of a BIT, the dispute resolution mechanism established by the BIT requires that the arbitral tribunal determines whether the host state's conduct is in breach of the BIT. Although environmental law may be referenced in the BIT, it is usually phrased as a soft law obligation to 'strive' to achieve the desired goal rather than the traditional investment protection provisions that are enforceable legal standards. Consequently, investor protection is likely to take precedence when determining the respective weight to be given to each obligation. Further, the manner in which the rules of treaty interpretation can be used to reconcile competing obligations from differing legal regimes is limited. Should a tribunal attempt to blend the investment clauses with non-investment interests, this would effectively amend the terms of the IIA which is beyond the scope of the power conferred by Article 31(3)(c) VCLT. In light of these considerations, it is suggested that if an act breaches an obligation to protect the investment under an IIA, reference to another legal regime when interpreting the provision is unlikely to result in the breach being exonerated.

The introduction over the last decade of written submissions from amici curiae has provided the means by which considerations beyond the terms of the IIA might be introduced before an arbitral tribunal. However, the arbitral tribunal retains a discretion regarding whether written submissions can be made, and based on the examples to date, amici curiae are likely to have limited access (if any access at all) to documents and may attend hearings only when all of the disputing parties consent. Therefore, this method does not provide a guaranteed means of drawing a tribunal's attention to issues beyond the IIA. In the most recent cases of *Biwater*[61] and *Glamis Gold*,[62] tribunals have recognised the utility of the submissions of the amici curiae concerned but have failed to make express reference to their arguments in their final awards.[63] Although the failure of an arbitral tribunal to refer to amicus curiae submissions is not conclusive, the acceptance of written submissions does not, of itself, necessarily result in an arbitral tribunal expressly considering the wider concerns presented to it by amici curiae when deciding the claim.[64]

[60] See generally A Van Aaken, 'Defragmentation of Public International Law through Interpretation: A Methodological Proposal' (2009) 16 *Indiana Journal of Global Legal Studies* 483; McLachlan, 'Systemic Integration'; B Simma and T Kill, 'Harmonizing Investment Protection and International Human Rights: First Steps Towards a Methodology' in C Binder et al (eds), *International Investment Law for the 21st Century Law: Essays in Honour of Christoph Schreuer* (Oxford, Oxford University Press, 2008).

[61] *Biwater Gauff (Tanzania) Limited v United Republic of Tanzania.*

[62] *Glamis Gold Ltd v United States of America*, Award, 8 June 2009 available at www.naftaclaims.com/Disputes/USA/Glamis/Glamis-USA-Award.pdf.

[63] Although the tribunal in *Glamis Gold* did accept evidence from the Quechan Indian Nation via videolink, impliedly recognising their indigenous rights, their legal submissions did not form part of the award.

[64] See generally C Knahr, 'Transparency, Third Party Participation and Access to Documents in International Investment Arbitration' (2007) 23 *Arbitration International* 327, 353; J Harrison, 'Human Rights Arguments in *Amicus Curiae* Submissions: Promoting Social Justice?' in PM Dupuy et al (eds), *Human Rights in International Investment Law and Arbitration* (Oxford,Oxford University Press, 2009) 411, 415.

In summary, whilst IIAs exhibit a growing tendency to harmonise in relation to primary rules, this may not be followed through at a secondary rule level due to, inter alia, the inherent difficulties in reconciling competing policies and the limited scope of amicus curiae submissions. Despite the wider scope of primary rules in IIAs, due to the restraints of the secondary rules, those international law regimes referred to in IIAs do not appear to have an impact on the awards made. In this sense, IIL remains 'fragmented'.

Going forward, an apparent solution to resolve these difficulties would be to include enforceable legal standards in the provisions of IIAs, addressing the international legal regimes outside of IIL, which an arbitral tribunal could apply by strictly adhering to its terms.

This prospect has been raised in relation to the redrafting of the 2004 USA Model BIT which commenced in 2009. In September 2009, the Advisory Committee on the International Economic Policy Regarding the Model Bilateral Investment Treaty presented its report to the Department of State.[65] This report contained the findings of a subcommittee comprised of academics, legal practitioners, arbitrators and industry representatives who had considered potential amendments to the 2004 USA Model BIT.[66]

The possibility of enforceable clauses relating to both the environment and labour standards was raised by some members of the subcommittee.[67] The main objections to this suggestion related to the difficulties in negotiating enforceable obligations in these fields, the limited scope for manoeuvrability and trade-offs when negotiating BITs (making it more difficult for the US to make the overall BIT acceptable to other states) and the resultant competitive disadvantage for the US.[68] These members of the subcommittee also thought that investment would result in an increase in living standards which, in turn, would result in the improvement of both environmental and labour standards making these clauses superfluous. Concerns were also raised that the creation of an environmental exception could permit states to disguise unfair, arbitrary, discriminatory and expropriatory actions by reference to environmental concerns. In the light of Norway's BIT experience, these comments demonstrate the difficulties in reconciling the potentially competing interests that are now contained in BITs and it does not appear that a simple solution will be found in the near future.

Despite this negative stance, it is worth noting that combining IIL and interests from other legal regimes in IIAs is a new phenomenon. The precise manner in which the interests can be balanced is yet to be determined and remains the subject of ongoing debate. Consequently, as both policy and practice develop, the systemic integration of IIL may reach a point that means that both the primary rules and the secondary rules that support them may permit IIL to be more representative of general public international law.

V. CONCLUSION

IIAs have progressed from addressing IIL as a discrete subsystem of public international law, focused solely on investment and economic liberalisation, to taking into account

[65] Report of the Advisory Committee on International Economic Policy Regarding the Model Bilateral Investment Treaty, presented to the Department of State, 30 September 2009, 8, 11, available at www.state.gov/e/eeb/rls/othr/2009/131098.htm ('Advisory Committee Report').

[66] Advisory Committee Report 1.

[67] Advisory Committee Report 8,11.

[68] Advisory Committee Report 9,12.

the broader impact of FDI by referring to its environmental impact, influence on labour standards and impact on human rights obligations. Whilst the inclusion of provisions relating to international legal regimes external to IIL would indicate that IIL is going through a process of systemic integration, this is only in relation to its primary rules. The restrictions imposed by the applicable secondary rules would indicate that IIL is still, to a degree, *lex specialis*. Despite the development of mechanisms such as amicus curiae submissions, and calls from some sectors for the inclusion of legally enforceable standards regarding other fields of public international law, it is unclear how the difficulties created by the secondary rules can be readily overcome to permit more comprehensive systemic integration. However, the merger of IIL with principles from other international legal regimes in IIAs is still in its infancy and new developments may permit the continued systemic integration of IIL.

21

The Limits of Depoliticisation in Contemporary Investor-State Arbitration

MARTINS PAPARINSKIS*

I. INTRODUCTION

STARTING FROM THE early 1960s, the concepts of politicisation and depoliticisation have been treated as instrumental for the regime of investor-state arbitration: first of all, as justifying its creation; secondly, as explaining its rationale. Aron Broches, the General Counsel of the World Bank with influence on the Convention on the Settlement of Investment Disputes between States and Nationals of Other States (ICSID Convention) second to none, was always explicit about the importance of depoliticisation. The 'political element' of the home state's discretion to espouse diplomatic protection formed the background to the ICSID (International Centre for the Settlement of Investment Disputes) Convention;[1] investor-state arbitration could 'help[] to remove investment disputes from the intergovernmental political sphere';[2] [t]he [proposed ICSID] would ... offer a means of settling directly, on the legal plane, investment disputes and insulate such disputes from the realm of politics and diplomacy';[3] and '[i]ntroducing the Convention mechanism ... (that) in particular seeks to depoliticize investment disputes ... into investment protection treaties may therefore be regarded as a particularly felicitous development'.[4] The contemporary state practice,[5] case law[6]

* D Phil (Oxon), Junior Research Fellow, Merton College, University of Oxford. I am very grateful to José Alvarez, Robert Howse and Benedict Kingsbury for discussing the law and politics of investment protection during my time as a Hauser Research Scholar at the New York University. The views expressed and the errors or omissions made are the responsibility of the author alone. Unless stated otherwise, the investment awards cited are available at icsid.worldbank.org/ICSID/Index.jsp, www.investmentlaims.com and ita.law.uvic.ca, ICJ judgments and opinions not yet published in the reports at www.icj-cij.org and the Model investment treaties at www.unctadxi.org/templates/DocSearch.aspx?id=780 and ita.law.uvic.ca/investmenttreaties.htm.

[1] A Broches, 'The Convention on the Settlement of Investment Disputes between States and Nationals of Other States' (1972) 136 *Recueil des Cours* 331, 344.

[2] A Broches, 'Settlement of Investment Disputes' in A Broches, *Selected Essays: World Bank, ICSID and Other Subjects of Public and Private International Law* (Dordrecht, Martinus Nijhoff Publishers, 1995) 161, 163.

[3] *Convention on the Settlement of Investment Disputes between States and Nationals of Other States: Documents Concerning the Origin and the Formulation of the Convention,* Volume II (Washington, ICSID, 1968) 242.

[4] A Broches, 'Bilateral Investment Protection Treaties and Arbitration of Investment Disputes' in A Broches, *Selected Essays: World Bank, ICSID and Other Subjects of Public and Private International Law* (Dordrecht, Martinus Nijhoff Publishers, 1995) 447, 457.

and legal writings consider it almost axiomatic that depoliticisation is the purpose of investment protection regime (even if differing about its implications and the degree of successful achievement).[7] Arbitrator Lowenfeld neatly summed up this consensus by saying that '[t]he essence of each of these arrangements [the ICSID Convention, Bilateral Investment Treaties (BITs) and the North American Free Trade Agreement (NAFTA)] is that controversies between foreign investors and host states are insulated from political and diplomatic relations between states'.[8]

The last two decades, particularly from the end of the 1990s, have shown a vast increase in investor-state treaty-based arbitrations. However, there often seems to be a mismatch between the promise of depoliticisation through investor-state arbitration, and the actual practice that brings different political perspectives back into the picture. To consider only the cases decided in 2010, arbitrators have dealt with complex and politically sensitive subject matters reflecting important regulatory choices regarding health and environment,[9] judicial administration,[10] economic emergencies,[11] natural resources[12] and provision of important services to the general public.[13] Contracting states are sometimes no longer willing to accept the views of adjudicators as accurately reflecting the content of relevant obligations, and engage in efforts of re-interpretation and law-making simultaneously with arbitrations.[14] Finally, even the absence of the

[5] DM Price, 'Some Observations on Chapter Eleven of NAFTA' (1999–2000) 23 *Hastings Intl Comp L Rev* 421, 427; DM Price, 'Chapter 11—Private Party v. Government, Investor-State Dispute Settlement: Frankenstein or Safety Valve?' (2000) 26 *Canada–US L J* 107, 112 (US); *Rumeli Telekom A.S. and Telsim Mobil Telekomikasyon Hizmetleri A.S. v Kazakhstan, ICSID Case no ARB/05/16, Award, July 29, 2008, para 287 (Kazakhstan).*

[6] *Banro American Resources, Inc. and Société Aurifère du Kivu et du Maniema S.A.R.L. v DRC*, ICSID Case No ARB/98/7, Award, September 1, 2000, paras 15–21.

[7] eg material at nn 1, 2, 4; DA Soley, 'ICSID Implementation: An Effective Alternative to International Conflict' (1985) 19 *Intl Lawyer* 521; IFI Shihata, 'Towards a Greater Depoliticization of Investment Disputes: The Roles of ICSID and MIGA' (1986) 1 *ICSID Rev—Foreign Investment L J* 1; J Paulsson, 'Arbitration without Privity' (1995) 10 *ICSID Rev—Foreign Investment L J* 232, 255; Price 'Some Observations' 427; Price 'Frankenstein' 112; A Newcombe and A Lemaire, 'Should *Amici Curiae* Participate in Investment Treaty Arbitration?' (2001) 5 *Vindobona J Intl Commercial L Arbitration* 22, 34; SD Franck, 'The Legitimacy Crisis in Investment Treaty Arbitration: Privatizing Public International Law through Inconsistent Decisions' (2005) 73 *Fordham L Rev* 1521, 1537; J Paulsson, *Denial of Justice in International Law* (Cambridge, Cambridge University Press, 2005) 233, 265; W-M Choi, 'The Present and Future of the Investor-State Dispute Settlement Paradigm' (2007) 10 *J Intl Economic L* 725, 732; G van Harten, *Investment Treaty Arbitration and Public Law* (Oxford, Oxford University Press, 2007) 173; R Dolzer and CH Schreuer, *Principles of International Investment Law* (Oxford, Oxford University Press, 2008) 20; M Paparinskis, 'Investment Arbitration and the Law of Countermeasures' (2008) 79 *British Ybk Intl L* 264, 273, 275, 341; CM Ryan, 'Meeting Expectations: Assessing the Long-Term Stability and Legitimacy of International Investment Law' (2008) 29 *U Pennsylvania J Intl L* 725, 733; SD Franck, 'Development and Outcomes in Investment Treaty Arbitration' (2009) 50 *Harvard Intl L J* 435, 437; R Teitel and R Howse, 'Cross-Judging: Tribunalization in a Fragmented but Interconnected Global Order' (2009) 41 *NYU J Intl L Politics* 959, 977. A recent argument for treating investment arbitrations as political still recognises depoliticisation as the traditional rationale, CH Brower II, 'Obstacles and Pathways to Consideration of the Public Interest in Investment Treaty Disputes' (2008–2009) 1 *Ybk Intl Investment L Policy* 347, 367.

[8] *Corn Products International, Inc. v Mexico,* ICSID AF Case no ARB/(AF)/04/1, *Decision on Responsibility, January 15, 2008, Separate Opinion of Arbitrator Lowenfeld,* para 1.

[9] *Chemtura Corporation v Canada,* UNCITRAL Case, Award, August 2, 2010.

[10] *Chevron Corporation (USA) and Texaco Petroleum Company (US) v Ecuador,* UNCITRAL Case, Partial Award on the Merits, March 30, 2010.

[11] *Enron Corporation and Ponderosa Assets, L.P. v Argentina*, ICSID Case No. ARB/01/3, Decision on the Application for Annulment, July 30, 2010.

[12] *AES Summit Generation Limited Aes-Tisza Erömü Kft v Hungary,* ICSID Case no ARB/07/22, Award, September 23, 2010.

[13] *Suez, Sociedad General de Aguas de Barcelona S.A., and Vivendi Universal S.A. v Argentina,* ICSID Case no ARB/03/19, Decision on Liability, July 30, 2010.

[14] A Roberts, 'Power and Persuasion in Investment Treaty Interpretation: The Dual Role of States' (2010) 104 *Am J Intl L* 179.

(politicising) home state from dispute settlement may often be more apparent than real: investors are sometimes owned by the home state[15] (and under some treaties can even *be* home states),[16] and the broader controversies between the home and host states can be brought back into the arbitral process for example by reference to countermeasures.[17]

The importance attributed to the ambiguous concept of depoliticisation is without obvious parallel in other areas of international law and international adjudication. Even though the finely nuanced relationship between international law and politics is undoubtedly important, it is uncommon to find language from the grand theoretical debates playing a role in actual law-making, interpretation and application. To provide some perspective, the International Court of Justice (ICJ) deals with complex legal and factual claims of *jus ad bellum*, *jus in bello* and international crimes, sometimes even contemplating the legal implications of nuclear destruction of mankind. Arguments explicitly using the language of politics sometimes advanced by parties unwilling to see the case go forward are likely to get summarily rejected.[18] There is thus no inevitability in using the language of depoliticisation to explain legal developments.

This paper aims to consider the added value that the depoliticisation vocabulary of the 1960s brings to the resolution of modern challenges. The analysis of the relationship will be conducted in four steps by suggesting taxonomy of depoliticisation. The loose concept of depoliticisation may be broken down into depoliticisation from the perspective of the home state (II), the host state (III), the investor (IV) and the process of dispute settlement itself (V), reflecting different historical pedigrees and different rationales for preferring particular procedural approaches. The focus of this analysis is not only the law and politics of investment law in general but also 'depoliticisation' and 'politicisation' as legal terms of art with particular legal significance. Taking the drafts of the ICSID Convention and recent arbitral cases at face value, 'depoliticisation' can also operate in the guise of different interpretative authorities, from object and purpose and broader context to preparatory materials and circumstances of conclusion. Different perceptions of the concept may lead to importantly different interpretative results, and therefore it is worthwhile to reconsider its meaning more closely.

It will be suggested that the vocabulary of depoliticisation, whatever its rhetorical value for law-making might have been in the 1960s, has no self-evident use for conceptualising and resolving modern challenges. At best, it is superfluous; at worst, assumptions about hidden systemic teleology may distract the law-maker or interpreter from identifying relevant issues, 'creat[ing] a *tertium quid* which stands, like a bank of fog on a still day, between the observer and the contours of the ground which calls for investigation'.[19] Some readings reflect particular historical circumstances no longer present; others allude to legal concepts more accurately expressed by legal terms of art; yet others may misleadingly imply that a particular legal rule has been developed on the issue. Charles Brower II has recently challenged the narrative of depoliticisation by arguing

[15] *Ceskoslovenska Obchodni Banka, a.s. v Slovak Republic,* ICSID Case no ARB/97/4, Decision on Objections to Jurisdiction, May 24, 1999, para 17.

[16] 2004 US Model BIT art 1.

[17] *Archer Daniels Midland Company and Tate & Lyle Ingredients Americas, Inc. v Mexico,* ICSID AF Case No ARB/(AF)/04/5, Award, November 21, 2007, paras 110–184; *Corn Products International, Inc. v Mexico,* ICSID AF Case No ARB/(AF)/04/1, *Decision on Responsibility, January 15, 2008*, paras 144–191.

[18] *Accordance with International Law of the Unilateral Declaration of Independence in Respect of Kosovo* (Advisory Opinion) [2010] ICJ Rep, para 27 with further references.

[19] I Brownlie, 'Recognition in Theory and Practice' (1982) 53 *British Ybk Intl L* 197.

that investment arbitrations should be viewed as political.[20] This paper goes further and challenges the usefulness of the very debate about investment arbitration between political and depolitical. As *per* Sir Hersch Lauterpacht, it has to be taken as a given that *every* international law dispute is political,[21] and therefore depoliticisation of disputes by means of an international legal argument is *ab initio* problematic.

II. DEPOLITICISATION AND THE HOST STATE

From the perspective of the host state receiving investors and investment, depoliticisation may mean one of a number of things. First of all, the elaboration of primary rules on the treatment of aliens and investors and the implementation of responsibility for their breach was historically linked with probably the most 'political' contention: the entitlement of host states to be treated as states at all. In his much-cited 1910 ASIL address, Elihu Root contextualised rules on the treatment of aliens in the international legal order. There were three possible situations: first of all, when 'control is inadequate for the preservation of order', direct military intervention took place; secondly, when 'methods of administration of justice' were different from those in civilised states, a 'similar in principle' solution of extraterritoriality was adopted; thirdly, when there was 'effective government', the 'established standard of civilization' had to be complied with.[22] It is complicated to imagine a more politicised model of law-making than one within which positions taken by participants regarding *ratione materiae* issues would simultaneously be used to review the *ratione personae* entitlement to be full subjects[23] of participation in the first place.[24] Of course, using compliance with investment obligations to define existence of the state is now only of historical interest.[25]

Second, depoliticisation may refer to the host states' negative experience from abusive implementation of state responsibility by forced reprisals.[26] From the Latin American perspective the procedural aspect was perceived, as Álvarez wrote in 1909, to constitute simply the 'use of force, such as the seizure of customs houses, pacific blockades, etc., in order to compel the recognition of claims'. It influenced the perception of the underlying substantive rules as an attempt by the US and European States to 'assur[e] unduly for their citizens who came to those countries a specially privileged situation'.[27] While the

[20] Brower II, 'Obstacles and Pathways', 348.

[21] H Lauterpacht, *The Function of Law in the International Community* (Oxford, Clarendon Press, 1933) 153; M Koskenniemi, 'The Function of Law in the International Community: 75 Years After' (2008) 79 *British Ybk Intl L* 353, 357.

[22] E Root, 'The Basis of Protection to Citizens Residing Abroad' (1910) 4 *ASIL Proceedings* 16, 19.

[23] AP Higgins (ed), *Hall's Treatise on International Law*, 8th edn (Oxford, Clarendon Press, 1924) 59; GW Gong, *The Standard of 'Civilization' in International Society* (Oxford, Clarendon Press, 1984) 14.

[24] A Anghie, 'Finding the Peripheries: Sovereignty and Colonialism in Nineteenth-Century International Law' (1999) 40 *Harvard J Intl L* 1, 52; G Simpson, *Great Powers and Outlaw States* (Cambridge, Cambridge University Press, 2004) 232.

[25] Recent practice regarding Kosovo is an example of an opposite scenario where participation in international financial institutions (International Monetary Foundation and World Bank) as well as investment protection regimes (ICSID) is used to buttress a contested entity's claim to Statehood, *Accordance with International Law of the Unilateral Declaration of Independence of the Provisional Institutions of Self-Government of Kosovo* (Request for an Advisory Opinion) Pleadings 1 December 2009 CR 2009/25 www.icj-cij.org/docket/files/141/15712.pdf 8, para 10 (Hyseni).

[26] Shihata, 'Depoliticization', 1.

[27] A Álvarez, 'Latin America and International Law' (1909) 3 *Am J Intl L* 269, 300.

crude and effectively self-judging form of implementation of responsibility is helpful in explaining both the historical resistance of developing states to primary rules that were not necessarily bad[28] and the focus of the ICSID Convention on procedure, this perspective does not contribute much to contemporary analysis. Forcible countermeasures are now prohibited as a matter of *jus ad bellum*.[29]

Third, suspicion about politicised reprisals sometimes extended to diplomatic protection more broadly, particularly when espoused by developed, rich and politically important states.[30] As Paulsson has noted, '[d]efendant States are irritated when another State requires them to defend the legitimacy of their acts'.[31] From the contemporary perspective, this approach to depoliticisation is partly without obvious practical relevance and partly misleading. In practical terms, the ICSID Convention explicitly suspends diplomatic protection during all ICSID arbitrations,[32] and even the ICJ has recognised that the role of diplomatic protection in general has 'somewhat faded'.[33] These policy concerns are therefore unlikely to illuminate contemporary debates.

However, it would simultaneously be misleading to conclude that investment dispute settlement has been completely depoliticised from diplomatic protection. Even in ICSID arbitrations, a claim may be espoused before (or in the absence of) the investor's claim or after the host state's non-compliance or it may be presented by another home state regarding its shareholders in the particular corporation.[34] It has been suggested elsewhere that explicit treaty suspensions or waivers apart, a breach of an investment treaty injures both the affected investor and the home state, and the latter can invoke the host state's responsibility concurrently with the investor.[35] The factual depoliticisation may therefore not necessarily reflect the legal one, and the breadth of the language may even misleadingly imply that particular rules have been developed on the issue.

Fourth, a seemingly forgotten aspect of depoliticisation relates to the acceptance of formalised dispute settlement by host states. The traditional narrative of the development of the law on the treatment of aliens would probably contrast Calvoesque (Latin American) host states (suspicious of specific primary rules, effective implementation of responsibility and formalised dispute settlement) with the home states (respectively optimistic in all regards). However, Lauterpacht tells the other side of the story, 'illustrated by instances in which judicial settlement was refused and recourse had to armed force in disputes obviously capable of judicial determination, on the ground that the controversy was political and therefore unsuitable for arbitration'.[36] In a number of situations during the 19th century, host states (Mexico, Greece, Siam and South African Republic) offered home states (France and Great Britain) to submit disputes about alleged mistreatment of aliens to arbitration. Home states rejected these offers since political disputes were not

[28] RY Jennings, 'State Contracts in International Law' (1961) 37 *British Ybk Intl L* 156, 159.

[29] ILC, 'Articles on Responsibility of States for Internationally Wrongful Acts' in *Yearbook of the International Law Commission, 2001, Volume II*, UN Doc A/CN.4/SER.A/2001/Add.1. (Part Two) 26 art 50(a).

[30] Shihata, 'Depoliticization', 2.

[31] Paulsson, 'Privity', 255.

[32] Convention on the settlement of investment disputes between States and nationals of other States, 18 March 1965, 575 UNTS 160 (entered into force 14 October 1966) art 27(1).

[33] *Ahmadou Sadio Diallo (Guinea v DRC)* (Judgment on Preliminary Objections) [2007] ICJ Rep, para 88.

[34] Paparinskis, 'Countermeasures', 309.

[35] ibid 281; against Z Douglas, 'The Hybrid Foundations of Investment Treaty Arbitration' (2003) 74 *British Ybk Intl L* 151, 190.

[36] Lauterpacht, *The Function*, 160.

suitable for adjudicative resolution, and in some cases even proceeded to engage in forced reprisals and warlike activities.[37] This aspect of depoliticisation, while of considerable historical interest, has no direct relevance for contemporary debates. Disputes regarding investment obligations of treaty or customary character are clearly capable of being dealt with by modern international adjudication by reference to applicable legal rules.

Fifth, the broader context of law-making and particular concerns about implementation of state responsibility also influenced the perception of primary rules. During the 1930s, the existing state practice and case law on the treatment of aliens was viewed with suspicion by traditional host states, and the attempts to invoke general principles of law were dismissed as externalisation of peculiar domestic conceptions of a limited number of states.[38] In the 1930 Hague Conference on the Codification of International Law, earlier rules on state responsibility and treatment of aliens were criticised as resulting from an abusive process of law-making. Debates about sources of law took five out of the total of available 12 days, and therefore contributed directly to the failure to reach a consensus on the substantive issues.[39] A similar preference for the state practice expressed in international fora rather than elucidation of adjudicators was apparent during the New International Economic Order debates in the General Assembly. In this context, depoliticisation was instead a preference of traditional home states.

III. DEPOLITICISATION AND THE HOME STATE

For the home state of the investor, depoliticisation may also mean a number of things. First of all, depoliticisation could reflect the attitude of the home state's officials that would otherwise have to make decisions about diplomatic espousal. As Daniel Price, the US negotiator of NAFTA, noted, '[b]y allowing the investor to litigate its claim directly, the investor's sovereign could distance itself from the dispute',[40] and 'the investor ... could resolve the dispute in a way that did not engage the political organs of the two governments'.[41] This kind of depoliticisation focuses on the transfer of decision-making authority from the domestic executive to an adjudicative body (not entirely unlike the effect that the Tate Letter was intended to have on the determination of state immunity by the State Department).[42] At the same time, it would be misleading to equate this kind of depoliticisation with irrelevance for the home states' officials of investment disputes with the host state. Price himself recognised that in practice investors would still first go to their own government to complain about the host state and ask for assistance.[43] Moreover, it is arguable that the home state's right of diplomatic espousal is restricted only during ICSID arbitrations, and it may otherwise still invoke responsibility in its own right or make a claim regarding abstract interpretation.[44] The home state's officials have also become involved in particular investor-state cases by making submissions to

[37] ibid 160.

[38] JF Williams, 'International Law and the Property of Aliens' (1928) 9 *British Ybk Intl L* 1, 19.

[39] S Rosenne (ed), *Conference for the Codification of International Law [1930]*, Volume IV (New York, Oceana Publications, Inc, 1975) 1442, 1583.

[40] Price, 'Some Observations', 427.

[41] Price, 'Frankenstein', 112.

[42] WW Bishop, Jr, 'New United States Policy Limiting Sovereign Immunity' (1953) 47 *Am J Intl L* 93.

[43] Price, 'Frankenstein', 112.

[44] Paparinskis, 'Countermeasures', 281, 309.

the Tribunal regarding legal issues in the case, sometimes even contrary to the position of the investor itself.[45] Just as with the practice subsequent to the Tate Letter and the Foreign Sovereign Immunities Act, the abdication of decision-making authority is rarely complete.[46]

Secondly, depoliticisation could refer to the controversial primary rules that were previously contested with traditional host states in different international fora. As Ruti Teitel and Robert Howse have suggested,

> Tribunalization was a technique for managing interstate political/ideological conflict surrounding economic activity and intervention by Northern and/or Western states in the global south and the eastern bloc. Direct access for investors to such tribunals served ... to deflate the underlying political tensions by blunting the political and ideological dimensions of the disputes.[47]

Despite its importance, this perspective is unlikely to be helpful for contemporary debates. As a starting point, one may wonder about plausible alternative explanations: could not one describe causality as going the other way, with tribunalisation being an almost accidental side-effect to treaty practice explicitly designed to affect precisely the politically contentious rules?[48] In any event, whatever reading of history is the better one, the changing framework of the debate minimises the contemporary importance of the perspective. The sharp distinction between home states and respondent states has disappeared, together with clear and pronounced legal differences on legal issues between groups of states.

Thirdly, depoliticisation could also suggest more broadly that 'controversies between foreign investors and host states are insulated from political and diplomatic relations between states'.[49] While the introduction of formalised investor-state dispute settlement mechanisms was undoubtedly important,[50] this reading of depoliticisation could be characterised as too broad. Both in factual and in legal terms, the relations between states may still play considerable role in investor-state arbitration. Retorsions have been used to persuade states to consent to investment arbitration in the first place.[51] Explicit restrictions of diplomatic espousal apply only during ICSID arbitrations, and it is arguable that states may otherwise still invoke responsibility in their own right.[52] If the purpose of the depoliticising strand of law-making was to exclude diplomatic protection from investment disputes, then it cannot be treated otherwise as unsuccessful.

Diplomatic relations between states may permeate the dispute as law-making or re-interpretative activities affecting the applicable primary or secondary rules.[53] A host state's failure to comply with the award could even lead to the application of countermeasures by the home state.[54] Conversely, if one adopts the view that an investor's claim under a particular treaty is an instance of delegated and modified diplomatic espousal, the

[45] *GAMI Investments v Mexico,* UNCITRAL Arbitration, Final Award, November 15, 2004, para 29.
[46] H Fox, *The Law of State Immunity*, 2nd edn (Oxford, Oxford University Press, 2008) Chapter 9.
[47] Teitel and Howse, 'Cross-Judging', 978; cf Soley.
[48] JE Alvarez, 'The Evolving BIT' (2009) 6 *Transnational Dispute Management* 6.
[49] *Corn Products International Lowenfeld,* para 1; *cf Choi 736.*
[50] Franck, 'Legitimacy Crisis', 1537.
[51] *Compañía del Desarrollo de Santa Elena S.A. v Republic of Costa Rica*, ICSID Case No. ARB(AF)/00/01, Final Award, February 17, 2000, paras 24–26.
[52] Paparinskis, 'Countermeasures', 281, 309.
[53] Roberts, 'Power and Persuasion'.
[54] Paparinskis, 'Countermeasures', 302, 309.

argument of countermeasures could be relied on by the host state.[55] The broad brush of depoliticisation is also unhelpful for answering particular interpretative questions. For example, is the wrongfulness of a state's breach of an investment obligation precluded when it would be precluded under a special secondary regime created for an equivalent WTO obligation? To say that investment law is insulated from other legal relationships is not particularly helpful, and the traditional legal tools of conflict identification and resolution have to be applied instead.[56] More broadly, investor-state arbitration is part of the international legal order, and can therefore never be completely isolated from the relations between the particular states expressed in normatively relevant terms.

IV. DEPOLITICISATION AND THE INVESTOR

Broches explained the traditional (unsatisfactory) position in the following terms:

> If the investor feels aggrieved by actions of the host government and has found no redress through the exercise of local remedies, he may seek the protection of his national government. ... the investor's government may in fact not be willing to take up a meritorious claim of the investor because it fears that to do so would be regarded as an unfriendly act by the host government and interfere with bilateral relations on other matters. This political element is likely to weigh particularly heavily if the merits of investor's case are not wholly clear in his government's view, thus withholding from the investor any opportunity to have his case judged by an impartial tribunal.[57]

The modern law of investor-state arbitration is very different in that it 'allows the true complainant to face the true defendant. This has the immense merit of clarity and realism; these virtues, and not eloquent pronouncements, are the prerequisites of confidence in the legal process.'[58] While the contrast is metaphorically powerful, to consider these developments in terms of depoliticisation[59] does not necessarily advance the understanding of the law-making process and its implications.

As has been suggested elsewhere, 'it was quite ironic how the argument sought to characterise the discretion within the law of diplomatic protection as political'.[60] To treat discretionary diplomatic espousal as more political than an investor's right to invoke responsibility requires a particular perspective of the issue. Regarding diplomatic protection, it is at least implied that to exercise discretion by reference to considerations other than merits of the claim is atypical in international law or at least undesirable. However, the discretionary nature of the bringing of claims goes with the grain of usual international practice. The invocation of responsibility is only an entitlement and not an obligation of the particular state[61] and may be exercised by reference to any kind of considerations. The 2006 International Law Commission's Articles on Diplomatic

[55] *Archer Daniels Midland,* paras 110–184.

[56] M Paparinskis, 'Equivalent Primary Rules and Differential Secondary Rules: Countermeasures in WTO and Investment Protection Law' in T Broude and Y Shany (eds), *Multi-Sourced Equivalent Norms in International Law* (Oxford, Hart Publishing, forthcoming 2011) 259.

[57] Broches, 'Convention on the Settlement of Investment Disputes', 344; cf. Price, 'Frankenstein', 112; Price, 'Some Observations', 427.

[58] Paulsson, 'Privity', 256.

[59] Ryan, 'Meeting Expectations', 732.

[60] Paparinskis, 'Countermeasures', fn 43.

[61] 2001 ILC Articles arts 42, 48.

Protection also recognise diplomatic protection to be a right and only recommend states to consider the possibility of espousal.[62] Consequently, to characterise discretion in invoking responsibility or starting judicial activities as political is not very useful; *mutatis mutandis*, almost all of international law would be political in this sense.[63]

In fact, to contrast a state's discretion and an investor's rights may be misleading in itself: a functionally more accurate comparison would be between respectively the discretion of a state and an investor and between the rights of a state and an investor. In both instances, the entity with rights also has discretion in the exercise of these rights. The investor's choice to launch the claim will also likely take into account other considerations apart from the merits (likelihood of backlash by the state, profitability of the particular and other investment activities, availability of sufficient financial resources for arbitration etc.). If the availability of discretion is the benchmark of the political, should not then a logical extension of the argument recognise investor-state arbitration just as political as the diplomatic espousal? The breadth of this perspective appears to undermine its analytical usefulness.

Another possible reading of depoliticisation would emphasise the innovation of investor-state arbitration.[64] This perspective may be respectfully criticised both in normative and pragmatic terms. For a sceptic, the conceptual novelty is not self-evident: the language of primary rules in question may be traced back for centuries;[65] the substantive and procedural debates often continue those in the classic law;[66] already in 1907 states negotiated with complete nonchalance treaties providing individuals with access to international courts;[67] and investor-state arbitration is simply a(nother) regime of invocation of state responsibility.[68] While the elegant technical craftsmanship of treaty drafters is admirable, the building blocks themselves are unexceptional elements of the traditional legal order. Moreover, the emphasis on uniqueness may leave the whole investor-state arbitration project open to criticisms that would have less force were it to be perceived as a mundane element of the established practice.[69]

[62] ILC, 'Draft Articles on Diplomatic Protection with Commentaries' in *Report of the International Law Commission on the Work of its 61st Session* UN Doc A/61/10 15 art 19(a).

[63] Of course, states may create particular rules of domestic or international law that remove this discretion and require them to engage in certain adjudicatory conduct solely on the basis of the merits of the case. For example, treaty rules on *aut dedere aut judicare* would require States to extradite or prosecute persons for particular crimes, untreaty.un.org/ilc/guide/7_6.htm. Conversely, Section 301 of the 1974 US Trade Act requires the US Trade Representative to follow NAFTA or WTO dispute settlement provisions when investigation reveals alleged violations, www.ita.doc.gov/td/industry/otea/301alert/index.html.

[64] Paulsson, 'Privity', 256; Z Douglas, *The International Law of Investment Claims* (Cambridge, Cambridge University Press, 2009) 6.

[65] For example, the idea of most-favoured-nation (MFN) clauses pre-dates international law and goes back for almost 1000 years, the recognisable form for more than 500 years and the MFN wording for more than 350 years, SK Hornbeck, 'The Most-Favored-Nation Clause' (1909) 3 *Am J Intl L* 395, 395; B Nolde, 'La clause de la nation la plus favorisée et les tarifs préférentiels' (1932) 39 *Recueil des Cours* 1, 29.

[66] J Crawford, 'Continuity and Discontinuity in International Dispute Settlement' in C Binder and others (eds), *International Investment Law for the 21st Century: Essays in Honour of Christoph Schreuer* (Oxford, Oxford University Press, 2009).

[67] See the discussion regarding the International Prize Court at the 1907 Hague Second Peace Conference, *Deuxième conférence internationale de la paix: La Haye 15 juin – 18 octobre 1907: Actes et documents*, Tome II (La Haye, Martinus Nijhoff, 1909) 789, 811.

[68] J Crawford, 'Treaty and Contract in Investment Arbitration' (2008) 24 *Arbitration Intl* 351, 355.

[69] B Legum, 'The Innovation of Investor-State Arbitration' (2002) 43 *Harvard J Intl L* 531.

V. DEPOLITICISATION AND THE PROCESS

Certain readings of depoliticisation are best characterised as directed at the process itself. First of all, somewhat similarly to the perspective of the investor, depoliticisation may refer to the relative formalisation of the process. It may be said that in the process of diplomatic negotiations between states, legal considerations could play some role in framing the background to the discussion but they would not be decisive. At the same time, in investor-state arbitration disputes would be settled according to the applicable rules of law.[70]

One may wonder whether it is accurate to frame the question in these terms. While investor-state arbitration is clearly more formalised than diplomatic negotiations, this comparison is made between the most formalised aspect of one regime and the least formalised aspect of another regime. It would be more accurate to compare respectively investor-state arbitration and inter-state arbitration and adjudication (both resolved according to law), and state-state negotiations and investor-state negotiations (where law informs the background but is not *per se* decisive). While historically the emergence of formalised investor-state dispute settlement was an important development, this feature is well-established in the contemporary legal landscape and probably not very helpful in comparing different regimes.

Secondly, depoliticisation may be applied to the integrity of the process. Gus van Harten has skilfully explored the looseness of the language of the political by deriving considerations of arbitral integrity and independence from the starting point of relative formalisation:

> The dependence of arbitrators on government and business belies the claim that investment treaty arbitration removes sensitive disputes from the political realm and subjects them to the rule of law. ... The problem with this claim is that adjudication is neither independent nor impartial where the adjudicator is appointed by a political or corporate entity on a case-by-case basis. ... It is precisely because they are not appointed and assured tenure by the state that arbitrators are exposed to undue political pressure. There can be no rule of law without an independent judiciary.[71]

The critique is not necessarily effective on its own since depoliticisation *qua* relative formalisation does not depend upon a particular vision of integrity within the formalised process. Still, it highlights an important meaning of 'political' in dispute settlement, probably used even by the proverbial man on the Clapham omnibus to contrast the (proper) legal decisions and the (improper) political ones. Independence and impartiality of the individual adjudicators are important aspects of procedural integrity of the arbitral process. At the same time, the scope and content of these requirements is already explained in considerable detail in international law of human rights and dispute settlement. To address the question in terms of depoliticisation does not add much to the understanding of the relevant issues and may in fact obscure the analytical focus.

Thirdly, depoliticisation may also refer to the practice of re-interpretation (and arguably law-making) that some states engage in simultaneously with adjudicative

[70] Newcombe and Lemaire, '*Amici Curiae*', 34.

[71] Van Harten, *Investment Treaty Arbitration*, 173. Despite being sceptical about van Harten's particular claims, Susan Franck appears to accept the link between formalisation and unbiased adjudication under the broader rubric of depoliticisation, Franck, 'Development and Outcomes', 437.

proceedings regarding particular rules. This type of politicisation may be seen as blurring the temporal and conceptual distinction between (political) law-making on the one hand and (depolitical) adjudicative interpretation and application of legal rules to particular cases on the other. The process of re-interpretation of a treaty by states raises concerns about a situation where one party to a dispute together with a third party can effectively change the content of the applicable rules. States can rely on different aspects of Article 31(3) of the Vienna Convention on the Law of Treaties (VCLT), requiring the interpreter to take into account in the interpretative process subsequent agreement (31(3)(a)) and subsequent practice (31(3)(b)).[72] In terms of subsequent agreement, states have agreed on the interpretation of investment protection rules both through pre-established institutions and in an *ad hoc* manner.[73] Pleadings and submissions by states have sometimes been treated as subsequent practice.[74] Sir Robert Jennings was sharply critical of the practice of re-interpretation[75] and the due process implications are certainly problematic. However, it is perhaps inevitable that within a decentralised legal order the authority of law-making, interpretation, application and litigation will be widely dispersed with a possibility of an only partial overlap.[76] This is not a concern peculiar only to investor-state dispute settlement. From the perspective of depoliticisation, to invoke the language of the political does not add much to the existing discussions about law-making, interpretation, due process, fragmentation and proliferation.

Fourthly, the inquiry of depoliticisation may finally be made in *ratione materiae* terms, questioning the propriety of subjecting disputes of such importance to (some type of) international adjudication. This perspective weaves together several strands of argument. The first argument draws upon the classic legal writings and state practice up to the first third of the last century, attempting to define political disputes not appropriate for judicial settlement *inter alia* by reference to their subject matter and symbolic importance.[77] The second and more recent position is that investment treaty arbitration (or its particular aspects) is inappropriate for resolving disputes about public law or public interest.[78] Brower II explicitly links these two schools of thought by using the classic criteria of political to support the view of investment arbitrations as political *qua* raising issues of public interest.[79] It is arguable that a nexus is at least implicit in the writings that rely on the concepts of 'public' in certain primary rules (like state immunity) to suggest a public nature for the dispute settlement process.[80] To the extent that the argument

[72] Roberts, 'Power and Persuasion'.

[73] Regarding arbitral interpretation of fair and equitable treatment in the first NAFTA cases, NAFTA FTC interpretation, *Methanex Corporation v US,* UNCITRAL Arbitration, Final Award, August 3, 2005 Part IV Chapter C, paras 21–23; regarding arbitral interpretation of MFN clauses in *Maffezini v Spain, National Grid v Argentina,* UNCITRAL Arbitration, Decision on Jurisdiction, June 20, 2006, paras 85.

[74] *Canadian Cattlemen for Free Trade v United States of America,* UNCITRAL Arbitration, Award on Jurisdiction, January 28, 2008, paras 188–189.

[75] *Methanex Corporation v United States of America,* UNCITRAL Arbitration, Second Expert Opinion of Sir Robert Jennings, September 6, 2001 5.

[76] Indeed, Sir Robert did not protest any impropriety when respondents in the *Lockerbie* case initiated an adoption of a Security Council resolution overruling the treaty obligations in questions, *Questions of Interpretation and Application of the 1971 Montreal Convention arising from the Aerial Incident at Lockerbie (Libya* v *UK)* (Preliminary Objections) [1998] ICJ Rep 9, Dissenting Opinion of Judge Sir Robert Jennings 99, particularly 107–112.

[77] See an overview of doctrine on the issue at Lauterpacht, *Function of Law,* 139.

[78] Van Harten, *Investment Treaty Arbitration.*

[79] Brower II, 'Obstacles and Pathways'.

[80] G van Harten, 'The Public-Private Distinction in the International Arbitration of Investment Claims against the State' (2007) 56 *Intl Com L Q* 371, 373.

explicitly or implicitly draws upon the classic doctrine of political disputes, it seems that Lauterpacht's classic critique is *mutatis mutandis* applicable to the modified modern argument. Lauterpacht made two arguments against the distinction: on the one hand, all legal disputes were to some extent political (even those relating to the treatment of individual aliens); on the other hand, all political disputes relating to legal issues were at the same time legal.[81] Since disputes about international obligations have to be taken to be political, the all-inclusive criterion is not a helpful analytical tool.[82]

VI. CONCLUSION

The present paper has addressed the nature of limits of depoliticisation, a term of respectable pedigree in investor-state arbitration. It has been suggested that despite its seemingly axiomatic nature, the vocabulary of depoliticisation has no self-evident use for conceptualising and resolving modern challenges. Some aspects of the concept may be explained in terms of historical law-making and perceptions of states in the 1960s. In other cases, depoliticisation is superfluous in alluding to relevant legal terms of art. At worst, assumptions about hidden systemic teleology may distract the law-maker or interpreter from identifying relevant issues or misleadingly suggest that certain policy purposes have already been achieved as a matter of law-making. For the purpose of convenience, the paper has broken down the ambiguous concept of depoliticisation of investment law, addressing it from the four perspectives of home states, host states, investors and the arbitral process itself. While examination of the different facets of depoliticisation highlights interesting aspects of investment law itself, in none of the cases does framing the argument in terms of depoliticisation seem to have clear value to a purely legal debate.

Perhaps the dominant meaning of depoliticisation, reflected in all the perspectives, is the removal from the dispute settlement process of the home state with its 'politicising' procedural and substantive entitlements. However, even this argument may confuse more than it clarifies, conflating a particular policy proposition with the existence of specific rules of international law. Despite the unquestionable practical importance of investor-state arbitration and the related suspension of diplomatic protection during ICSID arbitration, the positive international law still provides various ways for states to influence the process of investment dispute settlement. States may *de facto* participate in investment arbitration through state-owned or controlled investors. Except in cases of explicit waiver or suspension by treaty rules, it is arguable that home states are still entitled to invoke the responsibility of host states for the breach of investment protection obligations. More broadly, investor-state arbitration is part of the international legal order, and can therefore never be completely isolated from the relations between the particular states expressed in normatively relevant terms. It seems that depoliticisation is not particularly helpful when one reflects upon the challenges of 1989–2010. One cannot help but be sceptical about its predictive value and usefulness for illuminating the future analysis.

[81] Lauterpacht, *Function of Law*, 153.

[82] Incidentally, Lauterpacht's analysis also suggests that this type of depoliticisation is not necessarily progressive. In the 19th century practice, powerful home States refused to adjudicate disputes about the treatment of aliens and applied forced reprisals because their allegedly political character rendered them inappropriate for judicial settlement, Lauterpacht, *Function of Law*, 160.

Part V:

1989–2010: International Law and the Regions

22

La Coopération Régionale dans le Monde Post-soviétique: Bilans et Perspectives

LUCIE DELABIE*

LE CONFLIT RUSSO-GÉORGIEN de 2008 relatif au statut de l'Abkhazie et de l'Ossétie du Sud a révélé des tensions persistantes entre les États issus de l'ex-URSS face à la position dominante que la Russie exerce sur ses voisins. Cet évènement amène à s'interroger sur l'essor du régionalisme[1] dans cette partie du monde depuis les années 1990. Au-delà de la proximité géographique, qu'advient-il de la coopération entre les États eurasiatiques? Comment se manifestent, sur le plan institutionnel, les solidarités historiques, les intérêts politiques et les projets d'avenir qui leur sont communs?

Créée en 1991, la Communauté des États indépendants (CEI) a été le premier instrument d'une coopération régionale «dans les domaines politique, économique, culturel, de l'éducation, de la santé, de l'environnement». Souvent présentée comme une entité en voie de déliquescence, elle a joué un rôle non négligeable pour le développement d'une zone de libre échange, la mise en place d'une union douanière et monétaire et l'établissement de relations commerciales bilatérales fortes. En dépit de la faiblesse de ses actions en matière d'intégration, elle représente un forum de dialogue important entre les États eurasiatiques. C'est d'ailleurs dans ce cadre que se sont progressivement développées de nouvelles formes de coopération régionale.

Tandis que certains États—l'Arménie, la Biélorussie, le Kazakhstan, le Kirghizistan, l'Ouzbékistan, la Russie et le Tadjikistan—cherchent à renforcer leur collaboration en créant des organisations régionales à vocation économique ou politico-militaire, d'autres, souhaitant se libérer de la tutelle russe, se rapprochent fortement des pays d'Europe occidentale. Tel est le cas de la Géorgie, de la Moldavie et de l'Ukraine. Ainsi, depuis 1989, le monde post-soviétique semble s'être lui-même organisé en deux blocs concurrents.

Dans quelle mesure les activités de la CEI et l'essor de ces organisations régionales aux objectifs aussi larges qu'ambitieux marquent l'existence d'un véritable «régionalisme» dans cette partie du monde. Quelle place occupent ces entités dans l'ordre juridique international? Contribuent-elles à la promotion des principes internationaux défendus par les autres organisations régionales et universelles?

* Université Pierre Mendès France Grenoble II.

[1] Sur cette notion, voir S Sur, *Relations internationales, 5e ed.* (Paris, Montchrestien, 2009) 80.

Répondre à ces interrogations suppose de cerner les manifestations du régionalisme dans cette partie du monde (I) puis d'étudier comment s'articulent les activités de ces entités entre elles, avec les organisations régionales européennes et avec les organisations internationales universelles (II).

I. LE RÉGIONALISME EN EURASIE: ÉTAT DES LIEUX

L'effondrement des régimes communistes en Europe marque la fin des oppositions de blocs. Une coopération régionale entre les États de l'ex-URSS et leurs voisins asiatiques et européens devient possible; elle prend son essor dans le cadre de la CEI, donnant lieu à la mise en place d'organisations régionales qui lui sont directement ou indirectement associées (A). Mais ce phénomène ne masque que partiellement la volonté de la Russie d'acquérir le statut de première puissance régionale et l'apparition d'une nouvelle forme d'opposition Est/Ouest. Cette tendance se manifeste principalement par une ouverture de certains États post-soviétiques vers l'Asie et l'Europe (B).

A. Origines et Développement de la Coopération Interétatique en Eurasie

Les débuts du régionalisme se situent dans la création de la CEI (i). Souvent considérée comme un canal pour la mise en œuvre de la doctrine russe de l'étranger proche, cette entité connaît d'importantes limites structurelles et fonctionnelles qui incitent à la mise en place d'unions plus poussées par la création d'organisations régionales prolongeant la CEI ou s'y opposant (ii).

i. Les Débuts d'une Coopération au Sein de la CEI

Produit de la fin de la guerre froide, le but initial de la CEI est d'éviter de passer sans transition de l'URSS à l'existence de quinze États indépendants. Onze d'entre eux créent donc cette entité au programme ambitieux[2]. Réunissant cent trente nationalités sur un territoire de plus de vingt-deux millions de kilomètres carrés[3], la CEI est la première étape d'une coopération régionale dont l'un des principaux objectifs est de développer une collaboration sur la base du respect de la souveraineté et de l'indépendance de ces nouveaux États[4]. Pour y parvenir, la CEI est dotée d'une structure comprenant un conseil des chefs d'État (organe suprême), un conseil des chefs de gouvernement chargé de régler les questions d'ordre économique et social[5] et un conseil des ministres des affaires

[2] L'idée d'une telle collaboration est née d'un accord signé à Minsk le 8 décembre 1991 entre la Biélorussie, la Russie et l'Ukraine. Deux semaines plus tard, onze ex-républiques, à l'exception des États baltes, se réunissent et signent les accords d'Alma-Ata (Arménie, Azerbaïdjan, Biélorussie, Kazakhstan, Kirghizistan, Moldavie, Ouzbékistan, Russie, Tadjikistan, Turkménistan, Ukraine). D'abord observateur, la Géorgie en est devenue membre en 1993.

[3] R Yakemtchouk, 'La communauté des États indépendants' (1995) *Annuaire français de droit international* 251.

[4] L Entine, 'La communauté des États indépendants (CEI)—Chronique de sa création et de son évolution' (1993) *Revue belge de droit international* 614.

[5] Le Conseil des chefs d'État se réunit deux fois par an ; le conseil des chefs de gouvernement quatre fois par an. Les décisions de ces deux organes sont adoptées par consensus.

étrangères. Ses structures et son mode de fonctionnement ont été précisés dans la Charte adoptée le 22 janvier 1993[6].

Toutefois, dès cette époque, l'unité politique de la CEI se révèle difficile; seuls sept membres de la Communauté adoptent et ratifient la Charte[7]. Le Turkménistan et l'Ukraine, peu favorables au renforcement du processus d'intégration et souhaitant conserver leur indépendance par rapport à la Russie, refusent de signer le texte constitutif. Tandis que le Turkménistan, qui possède d'importantes ressources en pétrole et en gaz, veut en disposer souverainement; l'Ukraine reste une puissance militaire régionale importante et tient à être traitée comme telle par la Russie. À ce premier problème s'ajoute celui des objectifs très larges attribués à la CEI. D'après l'article 2 de la Charte est encouragée la coopération économique, politique et culturelle. Il s'agit non seulement de renforcer une collaboration dans les domaines de la paix, de la sécurité, du désarmement mais aussi de créer une union douanière et un marché commun[8].

Hormis ces vastes ambitions, c'est la nature juridique incertaine de la CEI qui en limite l'effectivité. En effet, d'après l'article premier de l'acte fondateur, la CEI n'est pas un État et ne possède pas de pouvoirs supranationaux[9]. Malgré sa charte constitutive qui apparente cette entité à une organisation intergouvernementale, elle reste pour bon nombre d'auteurs une institution *sui generis* sans antécédents dans les relations internationales[10]. Son originalité réside dans la coexistence de deux tendances antagonistes: instaurer une coopération plus large et sauvegarder la plus grande liberté possible pour les États membres. En outre, les activités et les organes de la CEI peuvent ne disposer que de la contribution d'une partie des États membres. Ces divers éléments obscurcissent les relations interétatiques intervenant au sein de la CEI dont les activités s'apparentent plutôt à une zone où le juridique se mêle étroitement au politique[11]. La Russie y joue par exemple un rôle prépondérant, concevant la CEI comme une «zone d'intérêt vital»[12], comme un moyen de manifester son influence régionale. Cette entité constitue une «*lex imperfecta*» où ce sont principalement des accords bilatéraux et multilatéraux qui forment l'ordre juridique de la Communauté[13]. La signature le 15 mai 1992 à Tachkent du Traité de sécurité collective (ou Traité de Tachkent) par sept États membres—l'Arménie, la Biélorussie, le Kazakhstan, le Kirghizistan, l'Ouzbékistan, la Russie et le Tadjikistan—fut par exemple considérée comme un événement majeur en matière de coopération militaire des États de la CEI[14]. Toutefois, faute d'un véritable

[6] La CEI est dotée d'un conseil consultatif de coordination (permanent), un conseil des ministres de la défense chargé des problèmes de la politique militaire et subordonné au conseil des chefs d'État. La Charte a aussi institutionnalisé une assemblée interparlementaire qui élabore des propositions communes dans la sphère d'intérêt des parlements nationaux. Sur ces différents organes, Yakemtchouk, 'La communauté des États indépendants' (1995) 256–257.

[7] L'Arménie, la Biélorussie, le Kazakhstan, le Kirghizistan, l'Ouzbékistan, la Russie et le Tadjikistan.

[8] Entine, 'La communauté des États indépendants' (1993) 617.

[9] M Diez De Velasco Vallejo, *Les organisations internationales* (Paris, Economica, 2002) 691.

[10] Yakemtchouk (n 3) 251. R Yakemtchouk, *La politique étrangère de la Russie* (Paris, L'Harmattan, 2008) 57.

[11] Yakemtchouk (n 3) 251.

[12] Voir Décret présidentiel, septembre 1995, [De la course stratégique de la Russie à l'égard des pays membres de la CEI]. *Diplomatitcheskiy vestnik.* Cité par E Piskunova, *Intérêts géopolitiques de la Russie et guerre civile en Géorgie* (CEPES, 2006) 65.

[13] Voir la conclusion, le 13 mars 1992, d'un accord sur le partage de la dette extérieure de l'ex-Union Soviétique. Yakemtchouk (n 3) 251.

[14] Les États signataires décident d'unir leurs efforts, sous l'égide de la Russie, dans la lutte contre le terrorisme, le trafic de drogue et le crime organisé.

système multilatéral de sécurité, ce sont surtout des accords bilatéraux qui ont été passés, notamment entre la Russie et plusieurs États de la CEI[15]. La coopération la plus poussée est dans le domaine économique[16] même si, là encore, l'entente est loin d'être parfaite entre les membres de l'Union. En effet, la CEI a rapidement été affaiblie par la mise en place de douanes entre les républiques.

Face à l'immobilisme de l'Organisation et aux difficultés économiques, certains États de l'ex-URSS décident de créer des unions plus poussées et plus dynamiques dans l'espace post-soviétique. La Biélorussie, le Kazakhstan, le Kirghizistan et l'Ukraine plaident notamment pour un rapprochement plus important que celui atteint au sein de la CEI. Après la création d'une zone de libre-échange en 1992 entre l'Arménie, la Biélorussie, la Géorgie, le Kazakhstan, le Kirghizistan, l'Ouzbékistan, la Russie et le Tadjikistan, ces États signent finalement le 24 septembre 1993, à Moscou, un accord-cadre d'union économique pour développer leur coopération économique et commerciale[17]. Près d'un an plus tard, est créé le Comité interétatique économique, première structure supranationale dans la région. En 1994, une union douanière est instaurée entre la Biélorussie et la Russie pour faciliter leurs échanges, à laquelle se joignent le Kazakhstan (1995) et le Kirghizistan (1996). Face au degré d'intégration insuffisant au sein de la CEI, les membres de l'Union douanière concluent en mars 1996 le Traité sur l'intégration approfondie dans les sphères économiques et humanitaires», créant la Communauté des États intégrés qui regroupe la Biélorussie, le Kazakhstan, le Kirghizistan, l'Ouzbékistan, la Russie et le Tadjikistan. En 1999, ces derniers signent, à l'exception de l'Ouzbékistan, le «Traité sur l'union douanière et l'espace commun»[18]. Toutefois, jusqu'en 2000, les activités de cette Union restent limitées.

Si la CEI a incontestablement contribué à la résolution de nombreux problèmes provoqués par la disparition de l'URSS[19], le bilan de ses activités reste mitigé. Pour remédier à ces faiblesses, les États de la région décident, à partir des années 2000, de renforcer leur collaboration par la création d'organisations intergouvernementales aux domaines d'action plus restreints.

ii. L'Essor d'Organisations Intergouvernementales aux Domaines d'Action Plus Restreints

Tout en s'inscrivant dans le prolongement des activités de la CEI, les États eurasiatiques développent de nouvelles relations par la création d'organisations intergouvernementales à vocation économique (a) ou politico-militaire (b).

a) La création de la Communauté économique eurasienne (ou EURASEC) L'EURASEC chargée d'effacer les échecs de la CEI, de contrecarrer les défis de la mondialisation et de reprendre le processus d'intégration au sein de la CEI, est créée le 10 octobre 2000. Les

[15] Voir l'accord de coopération militaire signé le 8 avril 1993 entre la Russie et le Kirghizistan ; l'accord d'amitié et de coopération du 30 mai 1992 entre la Russie et l'Ouzbékistan ; le traité de coopération russo-tadjike du 15 mai 1993. Le 2 septembre 1993, un accord militaire est conclu entre la Russie et le Turkménistan. En 1996, les chefs d'État adoptent une « conception » relative au règlement des conflits interétatiques. Yakemtchouk, *La politique étrangère de la Russie* (2008) 62.

[16] Yakemtchouk (n 3) 272.

[17] L'Ukraine et le Turkménistan s'y sont associés. La Moldavie s'y joindra le 15 avril 1994.

[18] G Galstyan, *Les intérêts géopolitiques russes dans la région Caspienne, rivalités anciennes, enjeux nouveaux*, (Paris, L'Harmattan, 2007) 211.

[19] Entine (n 4) 615.

deux principaux objectifs des membres de l'Organisation—la Biélorussie, le Kazakhstan, le Kirghizistan, l'Ouzbékistan, la Russie et le Tadjikistan—sont l'établissement d'une union douanière et la création d'un espace économique unique. On compte également trois «États observateurs»: l'Arménie, la Moldavie et l'Ukraine.

Pour mener à bien ces objectifs, l'EURASEC est dotée d'un conseil interétatique (organe suprême de l'Organisation), d'un conseil intergouvernemental (réuni deux fois par an), d'un comité d'intégration (organe permanent de l'EURASEC), d'une assemblée interparlementaire (organisme de coopération parlementaire) et d'un secrétariat[20]. Cette structure montre la volonté des membres de renforcer les liens de coopération dans une perspective d'intégration.

C'est dans ce nouveau cadre que s'est progressivement mis en place un espace économique unique entre la Biélorussie, le Kazakhstan, la Russie et l'Ukraine. Cela débute en 2003 avec la signature d'un accord sur la création d'un espace économique commun à ces quatre États. Depuis 2006, la formation de cet espace rassemblant la zone de libre échange et l'union douanière entre la Biélorussie, le Kazakhstan et la Russie est en voie d'achèvement. Fondée sur la conclusion de treize conventions par les chefs d'État et de gouvernement des États concernés[21], cette alliance devrait devenir de plus en plus active à mesure que les grands axes énergétiques de la région se dessinent. La manne énergétique, et en particulier gazière, des États membres de l'EURASEC apporterait notamment un poids politique supplémentaire à la Russie. Premier exportateur mondial de gaz, Moscou pourrait alors renforcer sa position stratégique via des accords avec le Kazakhstan et l'Ouzbékistan. Outre cet aspect, le 28 mai 2009, l'idée d'une union monétaire a de nouveau été défendue.

Les perspectives de cet espace douanier commun ne sont pas sans incidence sur la coopération entre l'EURASEC et d'autres organisations internationales. Le 9 juin 2009, lors de la réunion de l'EURASEC, Vladimir Poutine annonçait que la Russie recommencerait le processus d'adhésion à l'OMC et entamerait une adhésion groupée avec la Biélorussie et le Kazakhstan en tant qu'espace douanier commun. Si ce projet ne semble plus à l'ordre du jour depuis 2010, il illustre une réelle volonté de faire de l'EURASEC un acteur de poids dans la gouvernance économique internationale. Elle révèle aussi la place prédominante accordée à la Russie dans ce processus. D'ailleurs, cet État est le premier porte-parole de l'EURASEC au niveau international notamment lors des réunions du G8, du G20 et des BRIC.

Les accords passés entre les membres de l'EURASEC laissent présager d'une coopération régionale renforcée au sein de cette institution. Si l'Organisation paraît de plus en plus effective, elle reste néanmoins soumise à l'entente politique entre ses membres. Or, la décision de l'Ouzbékistan en 2008 de suspendre sa participation aux activités de l'EURASEC en raison de l'ineffectivité des actions menées par celle-ci illustre les tensions entre les États participants[22]. Une coopération politique s'instaure toutefois

[20] Le secrétaire général de l'EURASEC est Tair Mansurov (Kazakhstan).

[21] Les tarifs douaniers « externes », c'est-à-dire qui concernent les États tiers, doivent être unifiés. Les tarifs concernant l'énergie ne sont pas unifiés, car les objectifs et les intérêts nationaux divergent : certains États sont « protectionnistes », d'autres plus ouverts, car ils ont saisi l'intérêt à profiter des possibilités de développement que leur offrent une telle Union. En 2010, l'unification des tarifs « externes » de la Biélorussie, du Kazakhstan et de la Russie devait être achevée. Mais les taxes sur les hydrocarbures restent problématiques entre la Biélorussie et la Russie, ainsi que sur certaines matières premières comme le bois.

[22] www.cacianalyst.org/?q=node/5128. Cette position reflète les craintes de la mise en place d'une organisation supranationale dont les compétences pourraient porter atteinte à la souveraineté de l'État. Elle

progressivement au sein de l'Organisation du Traité de Sécurité Collective (OTSC), considérée comme le corollaire de l'EURASEC au plan politico-militaire.

b) La mise en place de l'OTSC Les premiers pas de la coopération régionale en matière politique et militaire datent de la signature du Traité de Tachkent le 15 mai 1992 par les membres de la CEI. Présenté comme le «bras armé» de la CEI en Asie centrale, le Traité est signé dès 1993 par l'Azerbaïdjan puis la Géorgie[23]; il entre en vigueur le 20 avril 1994. Mais très vite les tensions entre les États de la région sont perceptibles. En témoignent les réticences liées à la conclusion d'un nouveau traité de défense commune des frontières extérieures; tandis que le 26 mai 1995, l'Arménie, la Biélorussie, la Géorgie, le Kazakhstan, le Kirghizistan, la Russie et le Tadjikistan signent ce traité, l'Azerbaïdjan, la Moldavie, l'Ouzbékistan, le Turkménistan et l'Ukraine s'opposent à la présence de gardes russes sur leurs frontières. La crise du Kosovo renforce ces divergences. Le 2 avril 1999, est finalement proposé un protocole visant à renouveler le Traité de sécurité collective pour une nouvelle période de cinq ans. Seuls six États parties au traité signent ce texte; l'Azerbaïdjan, la Géorgie et l'Ouzbékistan s'y opposent. Néanmoins, le 7 octobre 2002, ceux des États partisans du maintien de l'OTSC décident de créer l'Organisation du Traité de Sécurité Collective pour approfondir le processus de coopération en matière politique et militaire. En signant cette Charte, ils montrent leur volonté de reprendre l'application du Traité de Tachkent et font de l'OTSC le complément politico-militaire de l'EURASEC[24].

Devenue effective le 18 septembre 2003, l'OTSC, dont le but est de «renforcer la paix, la sécurité et la stabilité internationales et régionales et de défendre collectivement l'indépendance, l'intégrité territoriale et la souveraineté des États membres»[25], bénéficie de la personnalité juridique[26]. Pour cela, la Charte de l'OTSC[27] institue plusieurs organes dont un conseil de la sécurité collective, organe suprême de l'Organisation, composé des chefs d'État. Il est chargé des questions relatives aux «principes directeurs régissant les activités de l'Organisation, prend les décisions requises pour atteindre ses buts et objectifs et assure la coordination des activités entreprises conjointement par les États membres à cette fin.»[28]. Existent également trois organes consultatifs[29] et un secrétariat général, dont le siège est à Moscou[30].

L'Organisation joue un rôle important dans le maintien de la stabilité et de la sécurité dans la région, notamment dans la Caspienne dont les cinq États riverains—l'Azerbaïdjan,

s'inscrit dans une tendance récente du gouvernement ouzbèke à privilégier une politique étrangère fondée sur des accords bilatéraux.

[23] Notamment dans le but d'obtenir l'aide russe pour maîtriser les conflits séparatistes du Haut-Karabakh d'une part, d'Abkhazie et d'Ossétie du Sud d'autre part.

[24] La plupart des membres de l'OTSC sont membres ou observateurs au sein de l'EURASEC : l'Arménie, la Biélorussie, le Kazakhstan, le Kirghizistan, la Moldavie, la Russie, le Tadjikistan et l'Ukraine.

[25] Charte de l'OTSC, untreaty.un.org, article 3.

[26] Charte de l'OTSC, article 22.

[27] Charte de l'OTSC, article 11.

[28] Charte de l'OTSC, article 13.

[29] Le premier est Conseil des ministres des affaires étrangères chargé de la coordination des activités entreprises conjointement par les États membres de l'organisation dans le domaine de la politique extérieure (Article 14 de la Charte). Le second est le Conseil des ministres de la défense, chargé de la coordination des activités des États membres dans le domaine de la politique relative aux forces armées, des infrastructures militaires et de la coopération en matière de matériel militaire (Article 15 de la Charte). Enfin, existe le Comité des secrétaires des conseils de sécurité chargé de la coordination des activités des membres en matière de sécurité nationale (Article 16 de la Charte).

[30] Charte de l'OTSC, article 17.

l'Iran, le Kazakhstan, la Russie et le Turkménistan[31]—considèrent que tous les litiges éventuels autour des ressources et de la délimitation de la Caspienne doivent être réglés au plan régional. Par ailleurs, la décision de mettre en place une force collective de réaction rapide (KSOR), prise à l'issue d'une session extraordinaire du Conseil de sécurité collective de l'OTSC du 4 février 2009, illustre l'essor de cette organisation régionale[32]. Cette force qui, selon le Président russe Medvedev, devrait à l'avenir, être «comparable aux forces de l'Organisation du Traité de l'Atlantique Nord», a pour objet le renforcement de la sécurité des pays de l'OTSC face au terrorisme, à l'extrémisme et au trafic de drogue ainsi que la prévention et l'élimination des situations d'urgence d'origine naturelle et technologique. Plusieurs éléments restreignent toutefois son effectivité. D'abord, tous les membres de l'OTSC, dont la Biélorussie, n'ont pas signé le traité instituant la KSOR le 14 juin 2009 à Moscou. L'Ouzbékistan, après avoir émis des doutes au sujet de cette nouvelle structure a finalement signé l'accord sur la Force collective le 20 octobre 2009[33]. Ensuite, la KSOR est cantonnée en Russie, aucune autre base n'est installée dans la région. Le 27 mars 2010, Nikolaï Bordiouja, secrétaire général de l'OTSC, a affirmé qu'une base dans le sud du Kirghizistan n'était pas nécessaire. Enfin, les conflits qui ont embrasé le sud du Kirghizistan en juin 2010 et suscité un afflux de réfugiés en Ouzbékistan montrent les limites d'une action collective menée au sein de l'OTSC. Les six chefs d'État de l'OTSC ont condamné la prétendue «seconde révolution des tulipes» qui a permis à Roza Otounbaïeva de s'emparer du pouvoir au Kirghizistan mais une intervention collective a été exclue. Le 14 juin 2010, les secrétaires des conseils de sécurité des membres de l'OTSC ont néanmoins approuvé des mesures pour régler la situation au Kirghizistan, parmi lesquelles l'envoi de fournitures pour aider le gouvernement kirghize à mettre un terme aux affrontements ethniques. Celles-ci ont été soumises aux représentants des États membres de l'Organisation; elles n'ont finalement pas été adoptées. S'il est impossible d'agir sans s'ingérer dans les affaires intérieures du Kirghizistan, le dialogue pourrait être instauré dans le cadre de la coopération régionale. Cette situation révèle une fois de plus que si la création de l'OTSC montre l'existence d'une coopération entre les États de la région, les tensions politiques limitent les perspectives d'un véritable processus coopératif en ce domaine. Face à la persistance de ces conflits d'intérêt, certains États de la région cherchent à nouer des relations avec les États voisins d'Asie centrale et d'Europe par l'intermédiaire de nouvelles organisations à vocation régionale.

B. Une Ouverture vers les Proches Voisins d'Asie Centrale et d'Europe

Devant les difficultés d'une véritable coopération au sein de l'EURASEC et de l'OTSC, certains États ont mis en place un nouveau forum de collaboration, le GUUAM (Georgia, Ukraine, Uzbekistan, Azerbaïdjan, Moldova), en opposition directe à la CEI et, indirectement à la Russie (i). De son côté, percevant les limites liées à la CEI, à l'EURASEC et à l'OTSC, la Russie cherche à étendre son influence en Asie en créant l'Organisation de Coopération de Shanghai (ii).

[31] L'Azerbaïdjan, l'Iran et le Turkménistan ne sont pas membres de l'OTSC. Toutefois, l'Azerbaïdjan est signataire de l'OTSC et l'Iran a fait part de son intérêt pour l'Organisation.

[32] Voir www.sfdi.org/actualites/a2009/Sentinelle%20182.htm#CSTO.

[33] Les autorités ouzbèkes souhaitaient notamment que le contingent des États membres de l'OTSC participant aux forces collectives de réaction rapide reste stationné sur leur propre territoire.

i. La Voie de l'Occidentalisation: le GUUAM

Pour lutter contre la domination russe au sein de l'OTSC et de l'EURASEC, certains États se tournent vers l'Occident. L'Ukraine[34] et la Moldavie[35] multiplient les relations avec l'Union européenne (UE) et n'hésitent pas à créer des organisations directement concurrentes. Tel est le cas du GUUAM dont les origines remontent à 1996–1997. À cette époque, l'Azerbaïdjan, la Géorgie, la Moldavie et l'Ukraine décident d'instituer un cadre informel de coopération pour tenir des consultations quadrilatérales[36]. L'Ouzbékistan rejoint le groupe en 1999. En 2002, est signée la Charte de Yalta (à l'exception de l'Ouzbékistan) qui institue l'Organisation GUUAM et la dote de la personnalité juridique internationale. Celle-ci comprend un secrétariat et un conseil, l'organe politique suprême de l'organisation[37]. Ce dernier peut créer des commissions ou des groupes de travail, permanents ou temporairesAlors que la Géorgie et l'Ukraine s'opposent de plus en plus ouvertement à la Russie, l'Ouzbékistan pratique rapidement la politique de la chaise vide et annonce son retrait du GUUAM en mai 2005. Les autorités ouzbèkes souhaitent en effet maintenir leur coopération avec la Russie qui représente un partenaire privilégié pour l'essor économique du pays. Depuis lors, le GUUAM valorise sa place singulière dans le voisinage partagé par l'UE et la Russie; l'avenir de deux régions est concerné, l'Europe Orientale post-soviétique et le Caucase du sud. Cela se manifeste dans l'évolution conceptuelle et institutionnelle du GUUAM, débutée avec la signature de la Charte de Yalta puis l'octroi, en décembre 2003, du statut d'observateur auprès de l'Assemblée générale de l'ONU. Par ailleurs, pour confirmer l'adhésion aux valeurs démocratiques, les États participants ont décidé de modifier la dénomination du GUUAM lors du sommet de Kiev du 23 mai 2006, créant l'Organisation pour la démocratie et le développement économique—GUAM, dont le succès est présenté comme la réussite des réformes politiques et économiques et l'introduction des mesures démocratiques dans la région[38]. La présence de plusieurs pays d'Europe de l'Est ainsi que d'un envoyé des États-Unis atteste de l'ouverture de l'Organisation vers l'Europe et les États-Unis.

Parallèlement à l'attrait de certains États pour l'Europe occidentale, la Russie cherche de son côté à renforcer son influence par une collaboration accrue avec les pays d'Asie centrale. La création de l'Organisation de Coopération de Shanghai (OCS) illustre cette tendance.

[34] L'Ukraine est un pays partenaire prioritaire de la politique européenne de voisinage de l'UE. L'accord de partenariat et de coopération (APC), entrée en vigueur en 1998, définit le cadre vaste et ambitieux de la coopération dans les principaux domaines de réforme. Un accord d'association doit remplacer l'accord de partenariat et renforcera d'une manière significative l'association politique et l'intégration économique entre l'Ukraine et l'UE.

[35] Comme pour les autres États de la CEI, les relations entre la Moldavie et l'Union européenne sont régies par un Accord de partenariat et de coopération signé en 1994, entré en vigueur en 1998 pour une période de dix ans reconductible.

[36] Les premières discussions entre ces États ont eu lieu lors de la Conférence sur le Traité sur les forces conventionnelles en Europe organisé à Vienne en 1996. Elles se sont poursuivies en 1997 lors du Sommet du Conseil de l'Europe.

[37] Le Conseil se réunit à plusieurs niveaux : Chefs d'État, chefs de gouvernement, au niveau ministres des affaires étrangères, coordinateurs nationaux et représentants permanents des États membres.

[38] www.guuam.org/doc/browse.html.

ii. L'Ouverture vers l'Asie: l'Organisation de Coopération de Shanghai

La création de l'Organisation de coopération de Shanghai, réunissant la Chine, le Kazakhstan, le Kirghizistan, la Russie, l'Ouzbékistan et le Tadjikistan, montre la tentation russe d'accroître son influence en Eurasie[39]. Les premières rencontres entre ces États—à l'exception de l'Ouzbékistan—datent de 1996 et interviennent d'abord dans un cadre informel. À partir de 1998 se forme l'alliance des «cinq de Shanghai». L'Ouzbékistan rejoint le groupe en juin 2001. Le 7 juillet 2002, est finalement signée la Charte de l'OCS. L'Inde, l'Iran, la Mongolie et le Pakistan y ont un statut d'observateurs.

L'un des principaux buts de l'OCS est de renforcer la confiance mutuelle et les relations de bon voisinage entre les États membres, de faciliter leur coopération dans les domaines politiques, économiques, commerciaux, scientifiques, techniques, culturels, éducatifs, ainsi qu'en matière d'énergie, de transports, de tourisme et d'environnement. Il est également question de sauvegarder la paix, la sécurité et la stabilité régionales et d'œuvrer à la création d'un nouvel ordre politique et économique international, plus juste et plus démocratique. Si les objectifs affichés sont très vastes, la principale préoccupation des membres de l'Organisation reste la stabilité frontalière, la lutte contre le trafic de drogue, la contrebande d'armes et le contrôle de la migration illégale. Ces dangers transfrontaliers exigent des actions menées dans un cadre régional. C'est à cette fin que les organes de l'OCS—et plus particulièrement le RATS, une structure antiterroriste régionale établie à Tachkent, capitale ouzbèke—interviennent.

La capacité d'action de l'OCS reste limitée car les principaux instruments de la coopération au sein de l'Organisation sont des accords entre les membres, adoptés à l'issue des sommets annuels réunissant les chefs d'État[40]. Les membres de l'OCS conservent ainsi leur autonomie pour toutes les questions non explicitement prises en compte par les traités, et, d'abord, en matière diplomatique. L'Organisation agit par ailleurs dans le respect des conventions passées entre la Russie et les anciennes républiques soviétiques et entre les États d'Asie centrale. En matière commerciale par exemple, si l'OCS fournit un cadre propice à l'approfondissement des échanges, notamment entre la Chine et les pays d'Asie centrale, le commerce et les investissements relèvent principalement d'un cadre bilatéral. Sur le plan militaire, avant même la création de l'Organisation, et alors que les réunions interétatiques étaient encore informelles, des accords de coopération militaire et de réduction d'armes dans les zones frontalières ont été signés (en 1996 et en 1997). Dans ce cadre, la coopération militaire russo-chinoise qui est au cœur du dispositif de l'OCS a été renforcée en 2002 par la signature d'un traité de bon voisinage, d'amitié et de coopération, qui prévoit notamment l'accroissement des ventes d'armes russes à la Chine et la formation d'officiers chinois dans les écoles militaires russes. Toutefois les faiblesses de l'Organisation ont été mises en exergue dans le domaine de la lutte contre le terrorisme. Dans le contexte des attentats du 11 septembre 2001, la Chine a notamment préféré fournir une assistance sécuritaire aux pays centrasiatiques dans un cadre bilatéral et non dans celui de l'OCS. Ensuite, l'effectivité du mécanisme régional (RATS, organe permanent de l'OCS) s'est trouvée limitée en raison de la réticence des États membres

[39] L'Organisation est dotée d'un secrétariat permanent qui a ouvert le 15 janvier 2004.

[40] Depuis la création de l'OCS, les chefs d'État se sont réunis à plusieurs reprises. Le dernier sommet a eu lieu le 11 juin 2010.

à échanger des informations sensibles dans le domaine du renseignement et par le manque de confiance de l'Ouzbékistan dans ce mécanisme[41].

Sur le plan géostratégique, l'OCS représente néanmoins la plus grande organisation régionale par son étendue géographique et par sa population. Plus important encore, elle réunit les deux puissances régionales—Chine et Russie—avec des États d'Asie centrale riches en réserves énergétiques. Au-delà de l'hétérogénéité de leurs positions politiques et idéologiques, ce qui unit ces deux pouvoirs régionaux est le désir commun de contrebalancer la présence américaine en Asie centrale. Le renforcement de la coopération militaire et politique entre Pékin et Moscou est plus particulièrement intervenu en réaction aux révolutions qui ont secoué la Géorgie en 2003 et l'Ukraine en 2004 avant de s'étendre en 2005 à l'Asie centrale avec la «révolution des tulipes» au Kirghizistan. D'ailleurs, lors du sommet de l'OCS à Astana en juillet 2005, les Russes et les Chinois ont exprimé leur opposition à toute ingérence dans les affaires intérieures des États souverains, dénonçant les tentatives américaines d'imposer la démocratie de l'extérieur dans cette partie du monde[42]. Toutefois, alors que la Russie conçoit l'OCS comme un instrument de régionalisation contre l'influence américaine, la Chine veut sauvegarder ses relations avec les États-Unis et cherche à faire de l'OCS une organisation essentiellement à vocation économique[43]. Selon certains analystes, l'OCS permet à la Chine d'être non seulement un «observateur extérieur» de tous les processus qui se déroulent dans la région, mais aussi de devenir un acteur capable d'exercer une influence croissante sur la formation d'un futur système de sécurité régionale en Asie centrale. En outre, les tensions entre la Chine et la Russie sont également visibles dans le domaine énergétique où la Chine est omniprésente en Asie centrale[44]. Si l'OCS ouvre de nouvelles voies de coopération entre l'Europe et l'Asie, les tensions politiques entre la Chine et la Russie restreignent l'efficacité de l'Organisation au même titre que l'OTSC et l'EURASEC.

*

L'émergence de nouvelles organisations intergouvernementales depuis la fin des années 1990 montre une réelle volonté des États post-soviétiques d'accroître leur collaboration dans les domaines économique et politique. La création d'organisations telles que l'OTSC et l'EURASEC ainsi que la conclusion d'accords juridiques dans ce cadre en sont l'illustration.

Toutefois, les limites à cette collaboration institutionnelle restent nombreuses en raison des faibles compétences normatives de ces organisations. Les mesures relatives au rapprochement des législations nationales, l'édiction de règles de comportement ou encore la conclusion de traités entre organisations régionales sont restreintes. Le droit dérivé de ces organisations est quasiment inexistant. Les principaux instruments d'action sont des conventions bilatérales ou multilatérales entre États membres. Aussi, ces institutions représentent-elles plus des forums de discussion entre États souverains

[41] J-P Cabestan, S Colin, I Facon, M Meidan, *La Chine et la Russie, entre convergences et méfiance* (Paris, UNICOMM, 2008) 123.

[42] *Ibid.*, 23.

[43] *Ibid.*, 117.

[44] Il existe notamment des conflits d'intérêts entre la Chine et la Russie concernant les projets de construction d'oléoducs et de gazoducs. Cabestan, Colin, Facon, Meidan, *La Chine et la Russie* (2008) 133.

et des outils de coordination de leur politique nationale que de véritables organisations d'intégration.

Cela tient en partie à la position dominante de la Russie qui cherche à conforter son influence sur la région et à maintenir ainsi l'apparence d'une communauté post-soviétique. La doctrine de l'étranger proche défendue par cet État depuis la chute du mur de Berlin conduit à des alliances fluctuantes, évoluant au fil des considérations géostratégiques. La position adoptée par l'Ouzbékistan illustre le propos. Alors que ce dernier décide en 1999, afin de marquer son indépendance par rapport à la Russie, de rejoindre le GUUAM, considéré comme une alliance anti-CEI, il quitte finalement cette organisation en 2005 pour adhérer à l'OTSC. Cette date coïncide précisément avec l'aide apportée par la Russie au gouvernement ouzbèke afin de rétablir l'ordre suite à la révolution d'Andjan. L'Ouzbéksitan se rapproche alors de la Russie qui lui a rendu service. La composition variable tant de la CEI que des autres organisations régionales (OTSC, EURASEC) explique l'efficacité limitée de ces institutions. Les tensions entre la Russie et les gouvernements favorables à une ouverture vers l'Occident, à l'image du conflit russo-géorgien de 2008 à propos de l'Abkhazie et de l'Ossétie du Sud[45], sont un autre facteur des faiblesses des organisations régionales.

Par delà les divergences entre États à titre individuel, on peut s'interroger sur les risques de concurrence entre les organisations régionales mises en place en Eurasie depuis la chute du mur de Berlin et d'autres organisations européennes qui leur préexistent comme l'UE ou l'Organisation du Traité de l'Atlantique Nord (OTAN).

II. RÉGIONALISME ET UNIVERSALISME: DES PERSPECTIVES INCERTAINES

Le bilan des activités des organisations de coopération incite à s'interroger sur le risque de concurrence entre les organisations régionales existantes (A) et entre ces organisations et les institutions à vocation universelle (B).

A. La Coopération Inter-régionale: Les Risques de Concurrence

La multiplication des organisations régionales en Eurasie témoigne des difficultés à assurer une collaboration stable impliquant des lignes directrices communes entre les États concernés. Les rapports délicats entretenus entre ces organisations et le chevauchement de leurs activités l'illustrent (i). Mais ce sont aussi les tensions entre les organisations régionales occidentales préexistantes telles que l'OTAN et l'UE et ces nouvelles institutions qui rendent mal aisé le développement d'un véritable régionalisme (ii).

i. Les Relations entre l'OCS, la CEI, l'OTSC et l'EURASEC

L'une des premières interrogations réside dans les rapports entretenus entre les organisations régionales établies dans le cadre de la CEI—l'EURASEC et l'OTSC—dont les membres sont pratiquement les mêmes[46]. Souvent considérées comme complémentaires

[45] Sur ce conflit, voir S Robert-Cuendet, 'Aspects historiques et juridiques de la crise géorgienne d'août 2008 : des conflits interethniques à la guerre ouverte avec la Russie', *Annuaire français du droit international* (2008) 173.

[46] (n 21).

l'une de l'autre, la première étant le volet économique de la seconde, à vocation militaire, la question d'une fusion entre ces deux entités se pose depuis quelques années. Décidée depuis 2006, celle-ci n'est pourtant pas encore effective.

On perçoit un début de collaboration entre l'EURASEC, l'OCS et l'OTSC. En octobre 2007, l'OTSC a signé un accord avec l'OCS, à Douchanbé, au Tadjikistan, afin d'élargir la coopération sur des questions telles que la sécurité, la criminalité et le trafic de drogue. Par ailleurs, les sommets de l'OCS devraient à l'avenir accueillir les chefs d'État des pays membres de l'OCS, les représentants des États ayant rang d'observateur ainsi que des délégués de la CEI, de l'EURASEC et de l'OTSC. Néanmoins, ces rapprochements restent limités en raison de la volonté respective de la Chine et de la Russie de renforcer leur influence dans la région. Tandis que la première fait de l'OCS un instrument de son pouvoir régional, la seconde favorise le phénomène d'intégration au sein de l'EURASEC et de l'OTSC comme des contrepoids utiles face à la présence chinoise[47].

Reste à déterminer les relations entre l'OTSC et le GUUAM. Celles-ci sont particulièrement tendues depuis la guerre d'Ossétie du Sud, principalement en raison des relations russo-géorgiennes. L'OTSC, dont la plupart des forces armées sont actuellement russes, a soutenu l'action militaire de la Russie en Géorgie et en Ossétie. De son côté la Géorgie, qui a quitté l'OTSC en 1999, prend une part active au GUUAM, organisation pro-occidentale dont les membres, soucieux de se rapprocher de l'UE et de l'OTAN, font face à la défiance de la Russie et donc, indirectement, de l'OTSC. Pour autant, l'inaction du GUUAM lors du conflit de 2008 entre la Géorgie et la Russie montre les limites de cette organisation.

ii. Les Liens Délicats avec les Organisations Occidentales Européennes: Organisation pour la Sécurité et la Coopération en Europe (OSCE), OTAN et UE

Les relations tendues entre les organisations eurasiatiques précédemment étudiées et l'UE sont en partie liées à la position ambiguë de la Russie—qui se veut le leader de ces organisations—vis-à-vis de l'Europe. Cette ambiguïté est confortée par les ingérences des États-Unis et de l'Europe dans les affaires intérieures des républiques de l'ex-URSS, de plus en plus dénoncées par les Russes[48]. Cette concurrence avec l'Occident sur le plan géopolitique se répercute inévitablement sur les positions adoptées par la Russie au sein de la CEI et des autres organisations régionales. Elle est renforcée par les hésitations de certains États de la région entre un rapprochement avec l'Union européenne ou un renforcement de leur collaboration au sein de la CEI. Par exemple, la Moldavie, tout en souhaitant collaborer avec l'UE[49], est tenue par ses engagements envers la CEI et envers l'union douanière dont elle fait partie, posant ainsi le délicat problème d'obligations internationales contradictoires. Enfin, l'élargissement de l'Union européenne en 2004, qui a conduit à l'émergence d'un voisinage partagé Russie et Europe occidentale, a accentué les tensions[50]. Face à cette situation, la Russie se refuse à évoquer l'idée de voisinage commun. Il y aurait pourtant tout intérêt à multiplier les actions en matière de

[47] Cabestan, Colin, Facon, Meidan (n 41) 117.

[48] I Facon, 'Russie-Union européenne : l'enjeu du voisinage commun', *Annuaire français de relations internationales* (2007) 621.

[49] (n 34), (n 35).

[50] Avec l'adhésion de la Roumanie et de la Bulgarie, l'UE accueille en sus comme voisin la Moldavie et entre en contact avec l'ensemble de la mer Noire.

coopération entre ces organisations et les institutions européennes, la Russie pouvant être à cet égard un élément de rapprochement entre l'Orient et l'Occident. Quelques voies de coopération se sont ouvertes notamment avec le renforcement de l'accord de partenariat et de coopération entre la Russie et l'UE («*four common spaces*») lors du Sommet de Saint-Pétersbourg de 2003. Plus largement, la collaboration se développe également dans le cadre du Conseil de l'Europe comme l'illustre la signature en 1999 par la Russie de la Convention cadre européenne sur la coopération entre les communautés territoriales (adoptée par les membres du Conseil de l'Europe en 1980)[51].

Sur le plan politico-militaire, on observe des tentatives de coopération entre l'OTSC, l'UE, l'OSCE et l'OTAN sous l'égide de la Russie. Cette dernière s'est dite prête à résoudre la crise concernant le Traité sur les forces armées conventionnelles en Europe et à participer à l'élaboration d'un traité sur la sécurité européenne. En outre, lors de la 595ème session plénière du Forum de l'OSCE le 18 novembre 2009, il a été rappelé que les membres de l'OTSC étaient favorables à des réunions avec l'OSCE, l'OTAN, l'UE et la CEI pour débattre des stratégies de sécurité et pour former un espace de sécurité commun[52]. Cette coopération est d'autant plus importante que les membres de l'OTSC sont aussi membres de l'OSCE[53]. Cependant, cette coopération entre la CEI, l'OTSC et l'OSCE a peu d'impact sur le terrain[54].

L'OTAN représente quant à elle un allié de l'OTSC dans la lutte contre l'extrémisme islamique. Néanmoins, la collaboration entre les deux organisations est encore limitée dans certains domaines, notamment celui de la lutte contre le trafic de stupéfiants en Afghanistan. Dans ce cadre, le ministre russe des affaires étrangères Sergueï Lavrov a rappelé le 9 juin 2010, que depuis six ans, l'OTAN et l'OTSC ne parvenaient pas à trouver un accord en ce domaine[55]. Les principaux rapports entre l'OTAN et les États de la région prennent la forme d'accords de partenariats[56].

Si les relations entre ces organisations régionales restent délicates, l'essor du régionalisme en Eurasie permet de compléter utilement les activités des organisations à vocation universelle, au premier rang desquelles l'ONU.

B. Régionalisme et Organisations Universelles: Les Voies de la Complémentarité

L'effondrement des régimes communistes en Europe semblait marquer la fin des confrontations idéologiques et de la guerre froide. Toutefois le radicalisme terroriste et les conflits d'intérêts économiques et géostratégiques sont apparus et, face à ces phénomènes contemporains, le rôle de l'ONU a pu être remis en cause. La multiplication des crises régionales entraînant le développement d'opérations plus actives, généralement menées sous l'empire du Chapitre VII de la Charte, suscite de la part de l'ONU un

[51] Yakemtchouk (n 10) 67.

[52] OSCE, 595e séance plénière du forum pour la coopération en matière de sécurité, 18 novembre 2009, document FSC.JOUR/601.

[53] L'Arménie, la Biélorussie, le Kazakhstan, le Kirghizistan, la Moldavie, la Russie, le Tadjikistan et l'Ukraine. Il en va de même de tous les membres de la CEI.

[54] Notamment le Rapport annuel de l'OSCE, 2007 à propos de l'interaction avec les organisations et institutions dans l'espace de l'OSCE, 156.

[55] fr.rian.ru/world/20100609/186864053.html.

[56] Dans le cadre du partenariat pour la paix, l'OTAN entretient des relations privilégiées avec l'Arménie, l'Azerbaïdjan et la Géorgie. La plupart des autres États de la région (Tadjikistan, Ukraine ...) ont également initié des activités communes avec l'OTAN.

nouvel intérêt pour les accords et organismes régionaux[57]; il semble que «le régionalisme nourri[sse] et conforte l'universalisme»[58]. Dans cette perspective, les engagements pris par les membres de la CEI et de l'OTSC en matière de contrôles transfrontaliers, de lutte contre la corruption, de lutte antiterroriste font de ces organisations un relais essentiel des actions onusiennes. Ces dernières apparaissent comme le complément indispensable à la politique de l'Organisation universelle pour assurer la paix internationale.

i. Les Rapports entre la CEI et les Nations Unies

La collaboration entre la CEI et le Conseil de sécurité des Nations Unies se manifeste dès les années 1990 par la mise en place d'opérations de maintien de la paix (OMP) sous l'impulsion de la CEI, qui a le statut d'observateur auprès des Nations Unies. Quatre OMP ont ainsi été établies dans le cadre de la CEI: en Ossétie du Sud, en Abkhazie (Géorgie), en Transnistrie et au Tadjikistan. Il importe toutefois de souligner que seule la Russie a financé ces opérations et que, pour trois d'entre elles (Ossétie du Sud, Abkhazie, Transnistrie) seuls des contingents russes ont été déployés. Par ailleurs, ces interventions n'ont pas été directement placées sous l'égide de l'ONU, même si des observateurs de l'Organisation ont été envoyés sur place[59]. Cependant, dans sa résolution 858 de 1993 le Conseil de sécurité a approuvé l'opération menée au cours de la même année par les troupes russes au sein des «groupes de contrôle tripartites» (géorgiens, abkhazes, russes). De même, les opérations de maintien de la paix menées par la CEI à partir de 1994 ont été avalisées par les Nations Unies. Dans nombre de ses résolutions le Conseil de sécurité s'est en effet félicité de la contribution apportée par la force de maintien de la paix de la CEI aux opérations menées par l'ONU—notamment celle de la MONUG pour le maintien d'un cessez le feu dans le conflit géorgien-abkhaze[60].

ii. Les Relations entre l'EURASEC, l'OTSC et les Nations Unies

L'EURASEC soutient les objectifs de l'ONU moyennant le renforcement de la coopération régionale dans des domaines tels que le commerce et le développement économique, la création d'une union douanière, l'énergie, les transports, l'agriculture et l'agro-industrie, la régulation des migrations, le secteur bancaire et financier, les communications, l'éducation, la santé et le secteur pharmaceutique ou encore la protection de l'environnement et la prévention des risques de catastrophes naturelles. Conformément aux dispositions de la Charte des Nations Unies, le Traité portant création de la Communauté économique eurasienne a été déposé auprès du Secrétaire général le 6 mai 2003. Ce traité réaffirme l'attachement des États membres de la Communauté aux principes énoncés dans la Charte ainsi qu'aux principes et normes universellement reconnus du droit international. Le statut d'observateur auprès de l'Assemblée générale obtenu le 9 décembre 2003 (résolution 58/84) permet de renforcer la coopération entre l'ONU et l'EURASEC et d'accroître les capacités d'assistance mutuelle pour garantir la

[57] M Kamto, 'Le rôle des accords et organismes régionaux en matière de maintien de la paix et de la sécurité internationales à la lumière de la Charte des Nations unies et de la pratique internationale' (2007) *Revue générale de droit international public* 800.

[58] Ibid, 772.

[59] Yakemtchouk (n 10) 61.

[60] V. notamment les résolutions 934, 937, 1036, 1150 du Conseil de sécurité des Nations Unies. Kamto, 'Le rôle des accords et organismes régionaux' (2007) 784.

paix et la sécurité régionales et mondiales. Le 6 décembre 2007, l'Assemblée générale a adopté la résolution 62/79, intitulée *Coopération entre l'Organisation des Nations Unies et la Communauté économique eurasienne*, dans laquelle on peut lire: «L'Assemblée générale note qu'il importe de renforcer le dialogue, la coopération et la coordination entre le système des Nations Unies et la Communauté économique eurasienne, et invite les institutions spécialisées et les autres organisations, fonds et programmes des Nations Unies ainsi que les institutions financières internationales à coopérer et à établir des contacts directs avec la Communauté économique eurasienne en vue d'exécuter conjointement des programmes visant à la réalisation de leurs objectifs».Sur le plan militaire, d'après la Charte de l'OTSC, les membres agissent en étroite collaboration avec tous les États intéressés et toutes les organisations internationales compétentes, compte tenu du rôle prépondérant de l'ONU[61]. Le 13 janvier 2010, à l'occasion de la réunion du Conseil de sécurité sur les organisations régionales[62], le secrétaire général de l'OTSC Nikolai Bordyuzha a affirmé que l'Organisation soutenait toutes les initiatives pour améliorer la sécurité, en particulier en Eurasie. Un accord de coopération avec l'ONU a été conclu à cette fin en septembre 2009, permettant une participation de l'OTSC aux opérations de maintien de la paix de l'ONU[63]. En mars 2010, le secrétaire général de l'OTSC a déclaré à cet égard que l'Organisation pourrait à terme participer sous mandat de l'ONU aux opérations de maintien de la paix dans différentes parties du monde: «il pourrait s'agir du transfert à la demande de l'ONU d'unités de notre Force collective de maintien de la paix hors de la zone d'action du Traité de sécurité collective, par exemple en Afrique. Evidemment, avec le consentement des présidents des sept pays membres»[64]. La collaboration entre les deux organisations est également visible en Afghanistan puisque les membres de l'OTSC ont fourni une aide à la force d'assistance en matière de sécurité (ISAF) dans ce pays. L'Organisation souhaite également développer la stratégie contre le terrorisme de l'ONU (2008–2013). Par ailleurs, elle travaille en étroite collaboration avec l'Office des Nations Unies contre la drogue et le crime (UNODC) et réunit dans ce cadre les agences chargées de la lutte contre le trafic de drogue au sein de ses États membres. Plus généralement, le 18 mars 2010, les secrétaires généraux de l'ONU et de l'OTSC, Ban Ki-moon et Nikolaï Bordiouja, ont signé à Moscou une déclaration de coopération entre les secrétariats des deux organisations. Ce document traite notamment de la coopération politique entre les deux organisations, de leur réaction commune aux crises, ainsi que de leur lutte conjointe contre le terrorisme, le trafic de stupéfiants, la migration clandestine et le crime organisé. La coopération OTSC-ONU devrait ainsi être bâtie sur des mesures conjointes «en cas de situations de crise dans certaines régions (du monde)». Ces quelques exemples montrent que les organisations régionales sont des relais importants pour l'application de mesures adoptées au niveau universel. Elles peuvent notamment inciter leurs membres à prendre des mesures en matière législative pour assurer une plus grande coordination entre les politiques nationales et contribuer ainsi à l'effectivité des normes adoptées au plan international.

[61] Charte de l'OTSC, article 8, alinéa 2.

[62] Réunion sur la coopération régionale à l'ONU, janvier 2010. Communiqué de presse www.un.org/News/Press/docs/2010/sc9840.doc.htm. Également la déclaration du Secrétaire général : daccess-dds-ny.un.org/doc/UNDOC/GEN/N10/208/51/PDF/N1020851.pdf?OpenElement.

[63] Sur les relations entre l'ONU et l'OTSC v. la 64e session de l'AGNU, 15 septembre 2009, point 125 (non publié).

[64] fr.rian.ru/world/20100318/186273693.html.

*

Ces développements illustrent l'essor d'une véritable coordination politique entre les États issus de l'ex Union soviétique. Le cadre juridique de cette collaboration reste néanmoins incertain, soumis à la variabilité des alliances politiques entre les États de la région et l'influence exercée par la Russie (financement des organisations, commandement militaire des opérations menées, entre autres). Ce manque de stabilité rend délicate la coordination entre les diverses organisations régionales créées depuis les années 1990 en Eurasie, que celles-ci soient ou non pro-occidentales.

23

Universalisme et Régionalisme en Matière d'Échanges Commerciaux Internationaux

ALBERTA FABBRICOTTI*

I. INTRODUCTION

LE DOMAINE DES échanges commerciaux internationaux nous offre d'incomparables occasions de discussion et d'approfondissement au sujet du rapport entre universalisme et régionalisme.

Ce qui rend le droit du commerce international particulièrement intriguant par rapport à d'autres matières du droit international c'est le phénomène de la prolifération d'accords régionaux ou restreints, ou pour mieux dire l'étendue de ce phénomène.

Le nombre des organisations économiques régionales a augmenté de manière exponentielle à partir du début des années 90, ce qui correspond à la fois aux derniers stades des négociations du Cycle d'Uruguay et à l'immédiat après Guerre Froide.

Trois événements ou résultats apparemment disjoints se sont donc vérifiés ou déclenchés dans un même laps de temps relativement bref. Celui-ci correspond en effet à la décennie qui s'est déroulée de 1986, quand les négociations d'Uruguay ont amorcé, à 1995, date de naissance de l'Organisation Mondiale du Commerce (OMC), puisque tous les trois événements se sont vérifiés au cours de cette marge réduite de temps. La décennie dont je parle, clairement délimitée par les étapes fondamentales de ce qu'on considère comme le dernier avatar de l'universalisme[1], nous témoigne déjà, d'une part, la définitive disparition du rideau de fer, consacrée en 1989, et, d'autre part, l'explosion du régionalisme dans le domaine des échanges commerciaux internationaux, symbolisée par la création de l'ALENA et du MERCOSUR au début des années quatre-vingt-dix[2]. Toutefois, rien n'empêche d'allonger la période de repère en la faisant coïncider avec

* Maître de Conférences en Droit International à l'Université La Sapienza de Rome.

[1] Cf. B. Kieffer, *L'Organisation Mondiale du Commerce et l'évolution du droit international public*, Bruxelles 2008, 122.

[2] Il serait peut-être plus correct de parler, pour ce qui fut le phénomène éclaté au début des années quatre-vingt-dix, d'une recrudescence du régionalisme. En effet, la progressive multiplication des blocs régionaux avait alarmé quelques clairvoyants spécialistes du GATT déjà au cours des années soixante et soixante-dix. Voir, par exemple, G. Patterson, 'The Most-Favoured-Nation Clause and Economic Integration', in XIII *European Yearbook* 1965, 145 ('En effet 50% des Parties Contractantes du GATT participant à l'un ou l'autre ensemble régional, dont aucun, à vrai dire, est entièrement conforme aux exigences de l'Accord', à la 158); F.A. Haight, 'Customs Unions and Free-Trade Areas under GATT: A Reappraisal', in *JWTL* 1972, 391.

celle de la célébration des vingt ans 1989–2010. L'accent se pose ainsi justement sur la prétendue cause, c'est-à-dire la fin de la Guerre Froide, plutôt que sur un de ces supposés effets, la revanche de l'universalisme par la création de l'OMC. D'ailleurs, pour ce qui est de la prolifération des groupes régionaux, celle-ci est un phénomène qui est toujours actif aujourd'hui, c'est pourquoi il semble inexorable et sans retour.

Les événements que je viens de mentionner posent, à mon avis, deux questions fondamentales.

Tout d'abord, y a-t-il un quelque lien causal entre la donnée historique et politique de la chute du Mur de Berlin, la donnée juridique de la création de l'OMC et celle, soit juridique que politique, de la prolifération d'organisations pour l'intégration commerciale régionale ?

En suite, comment peut-on expliquer la multiplication de systèmes juridiques partiels coexistant avec un régime multilatéral comme celui de l'OMC, qui aurait l'ambition de gouverner les échanges commerciaux au niveau universel ?

II. L'IMPACT DE LA CHUTE DU MUR DE BERLIN (EX ABRUPTO: LA QUESTION DE L'UNIVERSALITÉ DU SYSTÈME DE L'OMC)

Quoique les négociations du Cycle d'Uruguay aient commencé quand la dissolution du régime socialiste en Union Soviétique et ses satellites n'était qu'une utopie, l'idée dominante est que l'OMC soit un produit de la fin de la Guerre Froide. La création de l'OMC est considérée comme l'expression la plus évidente de l'avancée (triomphe même) du libéralisme dans les différentes parties du globe, après la chute du Mur de Berlin[3]. Sous le drapeau du libéralisme, l'institution de l'OMC aurait été le pendant, sur le plan économique, de ce qu'a représenté, sur le plan politique, la revitalisation – caractérisée par la prise en charge fréquente de situations tout à fait internes à l'État – de l'activité du Conseil de sécurité des Nations Unies en matière de maintien de la paix internationale.

D'ici jusqu'à arriver à la conclusion, comme le fait la plupart de la doctrine, que la fin de la Guerre Froide ait conduit à un succès écrasant de l'universalisme, le pas est bref. Bien au contraire, ma thèse est que la détente internationale qui est survenue après 1989 ait déchaîné, dans le domaine des échanges commerciaux internationaux, un processus inverse, portant à l'inexorable expansion du régionalisme. À la lumière de ces derniers vingt ans, tout ce qu'on peut faire, à mon avis, au lieu d'exalter l'avancée du binôme OMC/universalisme, c'est d'avancer l'hypothèse que l'universalisme ait même été la victime du succès de l'OMC!

L'erreur est déterminée par la fausse prémisse qu'il existe un lien fonctionnel entre l'OMC et la cause de l'universalisme. Il y a au moins deux ensembles d'arguments—toutes les deux en passant par le désaveu de la vocation universelle de l'OMC nonobstant ces 153 membres – qui invitent à reconsidérer cette conviction.

Le premier ensemble d'arguments est strictement lié à l'évaluation de l'impact de la chute du Mur de Berlin. J'en parlerai donc tout de suite.

[3] Ainsi B. Kieffer, *supra* note 1, 100. Le triomphe du libéralisme économique – en particulier dans sa variante américaine du capitalisme global – dans l'après Guerre Froide avait été annoncé par Francis Fukuyama en 1989 dans l'article, devenu célèbre, 'The End of History', in *The National Interest*, Summer 1989, 3–18. Fukuyama théorisait que, après la Guerre Froide, les Etats auraient été dépourvus de toute alternative raisonnable pour se défendre du capitalisme global.

L'idée d'"universalité' que je prendrai ici en considération est la plus élémentaire parmi les différents concepts possibles[4] : elle indique que le droit international est valide et contraignant pour touts le Etats. La 'vocation universaliste' dont on peut parler dans le cas de l'accord multilatéral de l'OMC (évidemment, faute de correspondance entre *membership* de l'organisation et totalité des Etats existants sur la planète), indique alors l'attitude ou la potentialité de cet accord d'être ou de devenir obligatoire pour tous les Etats quoique la liste des signataires soit actuellement plus limitée.

Premièrement, les règles de non-discrimination et de réciprocité sur lesquelles repose le système de l'OMC ne semblent avoir une envergure vraiment universelle[5]. Ce sont surtout des considérations de politique économique internationale, se rattachant à l'époque de la négociation du GATT, qui alimentent cette impression. Tout le monde sait que l'édifice juridique du GATT, ainsi que de la Charte de la Havane dans laquelle il trouvait place originairement, est entièrement implanté sur les théories libre-échangistes de l'Occident, et en particulier des Etats-Unis. Cet alignement n'était évidemment pas fortuit mais reproduisait la division du monde dans les deux plus importants blocs politico-militaires[6]: les Etats-membres de l'OTAN devenaient signataires du GATT tandis que les membres du Pacte de Varsovie prenaient part au Conseil d'assistance économique mutuelle (CAEM/COMECON)[7]. En définitive, l'ordre économique du deuxième après-guerre doit en très grande partie son origine à la Guerre Froide ou à ces prodromes, ce qui veut dire aussi que la Charte de la Havane, et par conséquent le GATT, avait été projetée avec le but d'endiguer la propagation du communisme dans le monde. Cette conclusion semble partagée par la majorité de la doctrine[8].

[4] Pour un tour d'horizon sur les différentes acceptions du terme 'universalité', voir B. Simma, 'Universality of International Law from the Perspective of a Practitioner', in *EJIL* 2009, 266–268.

[5] Déjà, comme on le sait, la grande majorité des membres de l'organisation sont des pays en développement (PED); en tant que tels, ces membres différencié en tant que tels, jouissent d'un traitement spécial et différencié, caractérisé par l'application du principe de la non réciprocité dans les négociations commerciales avec les pays développés et grâce à la mise en œuvre par ces derniers de systèmes généralisés de préférences. Le régime spécial en faveur des PED, qui a été introduit dans le système du GATT plusieurs années après le fonctionnement de l'Accord Général, est une exception qui confirme la règle générale de la non discrimination, se justifiant par des raisons d'égalité ou d'équité. Cette exception est aujourd'hui considérée comme faisant partie intégrante de la règle générale même, en d'autres termes comme si elle était englobée dans celle-ci, de sorte qu'elle n'entame pas, au moins en principe, la supposée universalité du système de l'OMC.

[6] Cf. J. Gowa, *Allies, Adversaries, and International Trade*, Princeton (Princeton University Press) 1994, 3.

[7] Ce partage soi-disant idéologique n'avait toutefois empêché à plusieurs pays socialistes de devenir membres du GATT 1947 ; par exemple, à part la Tchécoslovaquie et Cuba, membres fondateurs du GATT, qui ne connaissaient pas le régime d'économie planifiée en 1947, la Hongrie, la Pologne, la Roumanie et la Yougoslavie. Sur la participation des économies d'État ou planifiée au GATT, voir J. Woźnowski, 'The Socialist Countries' Membership in the GATT', in *PYIL* 1970, 199–225; J.M. Reuland, 'GATT and State-Trading Countries', in *JWTL* 1975, n. 3, 318–339; R. Baban, 'State Trading and the GATT', in *JWTL* 1977, n. 4, 334–353; K. Grzybowski, 'Socialist Countries in GATT', in *Am. J. Comp. L* 1980, 539–554; A.-M. van den Bossche, 'GATT: The Indispensable Link Between the EEC and Hungary ?', in *JWT* 1989 n. 3, 141–155.

[8] Ainsi, par exemple, J. Gowa, 'Bipolarity, Multipolarity, and Free Trade', in *American Political Science Review* 1989, 1245–1256 ; R.O.Keohane, 'Sovereignty in International Society', in D. Held et A.G. McGrew (dir.), *The Global Transformations Reader : An Introduction to the Globalization Debate*, Deuxième édition, Oxford (Blackwell) 2003 ; I.M. Destler, *American Trade Politics*, Quatrième édition, Washington (Institute for International Economics) 2005. Pour D.A. Irwin, P.C. Mavroidis et A.O. Sykes, *The Genesis of the GATT*, New York (CUP—The American Law Institute) 2008, 196, le problème avec cette explication de la genèse du GATT est que l'accord avait été envisagé bien avant le début de la Guerre Froide. Ces auteurs nous rappellent aussi que les Etats-Unis avait invité l'Union Soviétique et autres pays socialistes à participer au GATT et à l'Organisation Internationale du Commerce mais l'URSS avait décliné (Pourtant, la Conférence du Genève avait commencé un an après le fameux discours de Churchill sur le rideau de fer au mois de Mars 1946…). Ces mêmes auteurs admettent cependant la validité de cette explication pour ce qui concerne la fin de la partie ('end-game') de la Conférence de Genève.

Or, un des pivots des théories libre-échangistes est notoirement le rôle d'acteur principal joué par les entreprises privées: en absence duquel il n'y a ni vraie compétition, ni libre commerce international[9]. C'est la raison pour laquelle la clause de la nation la plus favorable dans sa version inconditionnée, qui est pierre angulaire du GATT, a toujours été inappropriée dans les échanges commerciaux parmi pays à économie libre et pays à économie planifiée[10], dans lesquels l'État se substitue à l'entrepreneur privé en toute occasion[11].

Jusqu'à la fin de la Guerre Froide, l'essentielle exclusion des économies socialistes des avantages du jeu multilatéral des échanges internationaux ne semble avoir soulevé beaucoup de préoccupations à l'Occident[12].

De façon plutôt surprenante, la question s'est présentée, pour ainsi dire rétrospectivement, après la chute du Mur de Berlin. Le hasard s'est produit, et j'arrive ici finalement au sujet de cette agora, avec l'explosion des groupes économiques régionaux en concomitance avec la conclusion de l'Uruguay Round, alors que tout pronostique aurait prévu une suprématie presque monopolistique de l'OMC. Bien sûr la *membership* de l'OMC a beaucoup augmenté par rapport à celle du GATT, mais ceci n'a empêché aux membres de l'organisation mondiale de prendre part à un ou plusieurs accords partiels. À la différence de la Chine, la Russie n'est pas encore devenue membre de l'OMC[13]. Tous deux ces pays n'ont pourtant pas manqué d'adhérer à des ententes économiques régionales.

À titre officieux et à un grand intervalle, les deux Directeurs Généraux de l'OMC Ruggiero et Lamy ont laissé entendre que la chute du Mur de Berlin aurait marqué le passage du bipolarisme à une situation multipolaire[14]. Pourtant, c'est un fait que l'économie mondiale s'était, pour ainsi dire, 'multi polarisé' bien avant la dissolution du bloc communiste capeyé par l'URSS: la croissance économique de l'Europe (en suite Communauté économique européenne, et après encore Union européenne) d'après-guerre avait évidemment provoqué bientôt la formation d'une triangulation; depuis déjà des années le Japon était devenu une grande puissance économique; d'autres pays

[9] 'The United States believes that international purchases and sales should be made by private enterprise' ; voici le deuxième des six principes fondamentaux rédigés par les États-Unis en vue de la négociation de la Charte de la Havane. Cf. C. Wilcox, *A Charter for World Trade*, New York (MacMillan) 1949, 14.

[10] Voir, par exemple, M. Domke et J.N. Hazard, 'State Trading and the Most-Favored-Nation Clause', in *AJIL* 1958, 55–68; G. de Lacharrière, 'Aspects récents de la clause de la nation la plus favorisée', in *AFDI* 1961, 107–117; R. Preiswerk, 'La réciprocité dans les négociations entre pays à systèmes sociaux ou à niveaux économiques différents', in *JDI (Clunet)* 1967, 5–40; E. Sauvignon, *La clause de la nation la plus favorisée*, Grenoble (Presses Universitaires) 1972, 151–168 ; E. A. Hewett, 'Most-Favored Nation Treatment in Trade Under Central Planning', in *Slavic Review* 1978, 25–39 ; E. Triggiani, 'Some Thoughts on Most-Favoured-Nation Treatment', in *IYIL* 1985, 135–139.

[11] L'article XVII du GATT est voué à intégrer dans le système de libre concurrence des marchés internationaux les entreprises de commerce d'État (State Trading Enterprises). Pour une analyse de la pratique OMC au sujet de cet article, voir *WTO Analytical Index. Guide to WTO Law and Practice*, First Edition, 2003, Volume 1, 302–309 et Second Edition, 2007, Volume 1, 229–233.

[12] Exceptionnellement, J. Viner, 'Conflicts of Principle in Drafting A Trade Charter', in *Foreign Affairs* 1947, 612–628.

[13] Un Groupe de Travail s'est constitué depuis 1993 au sein de l'OMC pour préparer l'accession de la Russie à l'organisation. Pendant plusieurs années cette procédure semblait tombée dans une impasse. Tout récemment les négociations ont cependant accéléré et, depuis ce qu'ont rapporté les médias, l'accession de la Russie est imminent.

[14] Le discours de Ruggiero remonte au 1997 et vient reproduit par J.H. Mathis, *Regional Trade Agreements in the GATT/WTO. Article XXIV and the Internal Trade Requirement*, The Hague (Asser Press) 2002, 132; celui de Lamy, prononcé à l'Université Bocconi de Milan en 2009, se trouve à la page web euro-med.dk/?p=12051&print=1 (dernière visite le 18 mai 2010).

asiatiques avaient commencé à s'imposer sur le panorama des relations économiques internationales. Selon les deux Directeurs Généraux, et une grande partie de la doctrine avec eux, la Guerre Froide et les sous-entendus problèmes de sécurité internationale auraient servi de ciment parmi les États membres du GATT et empêché la parcellisation des échanges commerciaux internationaux en plusieurs sphères d'influence régionales[15]. La fin de la Guerre Froide, en dissipant la contrainte à la cohésion ou au compromis à l'intérieur de l'OMC, aurait donc déchaîné des forces centrifuges (par rapport à l'OMC) et centripètes (par rapport aux différents pôles économiques existants). Le revirement régionaliste des Etats-Unis de ces derniers vingt ans s'expliquerait ainsi.

Les événements qui suivirent la chute du Mur de Berlin n'eurent apparemment aucune répercussion directe sur l'agenda du Cycle de négociations d'Uruguay qui était en train de se dérouler depuis 1986[16]. Il est bien possible que personne à l'époque ne fût conscient de ce que ce formidable bouleversement allait produire sur les équilibres politiques et économiques mondiaux. Comme l'avoue le Directeur Général Lamy, 'the reality is that the end of the Cold War caught everyone by surprise. It was the end of a bi-polar world. A new world order was being born'[17].

Tout le monde sait que l'Acte final portant à la création de l'OMC fut signé à Marrakech le 15 avril 1994 par 125 Etats et est entré en vigueur le 1er janvier 1995. La transformation du vieux GATT en une vraie organisation internationale comme l'est l'OMC fut acclamée avec enthousiasme. Cette transformation signifiait, en un mot, le renforcement du système juridique des échanges internationaux multilatéraux[18].

Cependant, plusieurs tables de négociations venaient de se conclure, déjà en parallèle avec les travaux du Cycle d'Uruguay, pour la création de formes d'intégration économique entre groupes restreints d'Etats membres de l'OMC[19]. Ce n'était qu'un début. Je l'ai anticipé dans l'introduction: après l'entrée en vigueur de l'Accord constitutif de l'OMC, on a assisté à une véritable prolifération d'accords commerciaux régionaux. On en compte 279 qui, ayant été notifiés à l'OMC, sont en vigueur à la date du 28 juin 2010[20].

[15] Ainsi, par example, aussi B. J. Cohen, 'The Revolution in Atlantic Economic Relations: A Bargain Comes Unstruck', in B. J. Cohen (dir.), *Crossing Frontiers: Explorations in International Political Economy*, Boulder (Westview) 1974, 102; C.F. Bergsten, 'The World Economy After the Cold War', in *Foreign Affairs* 1989–1991, 96–112 ; J. Gowa, *Allies, Adversaries, and International Trade* cit., 3–10; J.H. Mathis, *op. cit.*, 133–136; I.M. Destler, *op. cit.*, 61–63; D.A. Irwin, P.C. Mavroidis et A.O. Sykes, *op. cit.*, 196–197. Il faut tout de même remarquer que la plupart de ces auteurs sont des spécialistes en politique économique internationale et non pas des experts en droit international.

[16] Il me semble quand même bizarre qu'il n'y ait dans les archives du GATT un seul document rédigé pendant les négociations d'Uruguay après 1989 qui ait pour objet la dissolution de l'URSS ou l'extinction du Pacte de Varsovie et du COMECON. Les archives du GATT sont consultables à l'adresse web : gatt.stanford.edu. Sur les travaux préparatoires portant à l'institution de l'OMC voir T.P. Stewart (dir.), *The GATT Uruguay Round. A Negotiating History (1986–1992)*, 3 volumes, Kluwer, Deventer-Boston, 1993.

[17] Cf. le discours de Lamy, *supra* à la note 14.

[18] Sur cette évolution voir, entre autres, V. Pace, *L'Organisation Mondiale du Commerce et le renforcement de la réglementation juridique des échanges commerciaux internationaux*, Paris (L'Harmattan) 2000.

[19] Au cours des derniers stades des négociations d'Uruguay, en 1990–1994 par exemple, 33 accords commerciaux régionaux furent notifiés au Secrétariat du GATT.

[20] Une liste mise à jour des accords commerciaux régionaux notifiés à l'OMC est publiée à la page web rtais.wto.org/UI/PublicMaintainRTAHome.aspx.

III. LA PROLIFÉRATION DES GROUPES ÉCONOMIQUES RÉGIONAUX EN CONCOMITANCE ET APRÈS LA CRÉATION DE L'OMC (ENCORE, ENTRE PARENTHÈSES, LA QUESTION DE L'UNIVERSALITÉ DU SYSTÈME DE L'OMC)

Comme l'a observé le Rapport du Groupe d'étude de la Commission de droit international sur la *Fragmentation du droit international*, le fait que le phénomène de la prolifération de groupes économiques régionaux ait explosé en concomitance avec la forte relance d'un système commercial 'universel', marqué par la création de l'OMC, est un aspect contradictoire qui mérite d'être étudié séparément[21]. C'est précisément ce que cette contribution compte faire dans la présente section.

Il faut chercher à comprendre pourquoi, paradoxalement, au fur et à mesure que l'accord universel s'imposait comme une option *grosso modo* équivalente, du point de vue tant substantiel que procédural, aux modèles d'intégration économique régionale plus évolués, les Etats ont poursuivi davantage la conclusion d'accords commerciaux restreints.

Dans une perspective générale de politique économique—on l'a vu dans la section précédente—les prodromes de cette situation paradoxale sont à reconduire au bouleversement dans les équilibres politiques et économiques qui ont suivi la chute du Mur de Berlin.

D'un point de vue économique, on nous a expliqué entre autres que les négociations multilatérales au sein de l'OMC n'attirent plus les Etats comme dans le passé parce que, conséquemment aux huit cycles de réductions tarifaires et non tarifaires à l'époque du GATT, le marge pour libéraliser davantage les échanges commerciaux est devenu très limité et peu profitable au niveau multilatéral. Mieux alors accorder un traitement préférentiel, consistant en une réduction ultérieure ou élimination totale des tarifes et des autres obstacles au commerce, au niveau régional.

D'un point de vue sociologique, le refrain est que l'OMC n'est plus en mesure de fonctionner efficacement, prenant des décisions et modifiant ses règles, vue l'impossibilité d'obtenir le consensus de la part de sa (trop) nombreuse *membership*[22]. La participation à groupes régionaux plus restreints élimine ce problème à la racine.

Tout en admettant l'exactitude de ces explications, il est important à ce point-ci d'approfondir la dynamique 'renforcement de l'OMC / prolifération de groupes régionaux'. Ce qui reste à faire, en d'autres mots, c'est de vérifier la nature, ou si l'on veut la raison, de ce rapport, les termes duquel semblent s'évoluer en manière directement proportionnelle. Logique voudrait qu'il y ait, à l'origine, une sorte de cercle vicieux, raison pour laquelle au fur et à mesure que les règles de l'OMC se sont montrées rigoureuses et capables de s'imposer sur les Etats membres, ces derniers se sont pour ainsi dire mis à l'abri de ces impositions en signant un ou plusieurs accords préférentiels au niveau régional.

Comme on le sait, la formation d'intégrations commerciales régionales est prévue par l'article XXIV du GATT. D'après cet article, les membres de l'OMC peuvent s'associer

[21] Cf. *Fragmentation du droit international: difficultés découlant de la diversification et de l'expansion du droit international*, Rapport du Groupe d'étude de la Commission de droit international établi sous sa forme définitive par Martti Koskenniemi, Doc. A/CN.4/L.682, 13 avril 2006, para. 210.

[22] Sur ce problème, voir entre autres C.-D. Ehlermann et L. Ehring, 'Decision-Making in the World Trade Organization. Is the Consensus Practice of the World Trade Organization Adequate for Making, Revising and Implementing Rules on International Trade?', in *JIEL* 2005, 51–75.

en groupes restreints, créant des zones de libre échange ou des unions douanières avec le but principal d'accorder des préférences commerciales aux leur partenaires régionaux. Il s'agit toutefois d'une faculté soumise à des conditions (apparemment) précises[23], et notamment que la libéralisation parmi les membres du groupe régional se passe pour l'essentiel des échanges commerciaux (condition requise à l'intérieur) et que les droits de douane et les autres réglementations adoptées par les membres du groupe régional envers les produits importés de l'extérieur du groupe ne soient pas plus élevés ou restrictifs qu'avant l'association (condition requise vers l'extérieur). Je ne vais pas m'attarder sur l'article XXIV parce que j'imagine que tout le monde connaît ses dispositions. J'estime plus utile ici d'économiser le temps en faveur d'autres arguments.

Il suffit de remarquer que les conditions requises par l'article XXIV n'ont jamais été respectées. Pendant la période GATT, et encore au début de l'ère de l'OMC, les Etats membres ont eu carte blanche de la part de l'organisation quant à la mise en place et au fonctionnement d'ententes commerciales régionales.

Cependant, à la différence d'autres prévisions du GATT qui permettaient de manière permanente aux Etats membres de déroger au système des échanges commerciaux multilatéraux, l'article XXIV n'a été amendé ni précisé par suite de l'institution de l'OMC. Tandis que, par exemple, l'article XIX du GATT prévoyant des mesures urgentes en cas de crise par excès d'importations a été soi-disant 'renforcé' par l'Accord de 1994 sur les sauvegardes (interdisant entre autres tout genre d'arrangement menant à restrictions volontaires à l'exportation), et l'article XX concernant les exceptions générales a été spécifié par l'Accord sur les obstacles techniques au commerce et celui sur les mesures sanitaires et phytosanitaires, l'article XXIV a été simplement 'interprété' par un Mémorandum.

Vue la grande tolérance de l'article XXIV, l'établissement de zones de libre échange et d'unions douanières pourrait donc (continuer à) se présenter aux yeux des Etats membres de l'OMC comme la seule échappatoire qui peut être encore parcourue sans risques d'interférence de la part de l'organisation.

La prolifération de groupes régionaux étant devenue incontrôlable, un premier signale de rigueur a été lancé par l'Organe d'appel en 1999 dans l'affaire relative aux restrictions imposées par la Turquie sur l'importation de produits textiles et de vêtements[24]. Dans son Rapport, l'Organe d'appel 'invente' deux conditions supplémentaires par rapport à celles expressément prévues par le texte de l'article XXIV. Ces conditions concernent, d'une part, le moment où la mesure vient adoptée par le groupe régional et, d'autre part, le caractère de nécessité de la mesure même, en fonction de l'achèvement d'une zone de libre échange ou d'une union douanière[25]. Jusqu'à présent, les organes contentieux de l'OMC n'ont toujours pas constaté que ces nouveaux paramètres juridiques étaient réunis par une telle ou telle autre organisation régionale.

[23] Déjà en 1963 Kenneth W. Dam nous mettait en garde sur l'efficacité de ces conditions: 'Article XXIV appears, on first impression, to set forth a precise set of rules for determining the circumstances under which regional arrangements will be permitted. The apparent precision is quite illusory.' Cf. K.W. Dam, 'Regional Economic Arrangements and the GATT: the Legacy of a Misconception', in *The University of Chicago Law Review* 1963, 619.

[24] *Turquie – Restrictions à l'importation de produits textiles et de vêtements*, Doc. WT/DS34/AB/R (adopté le 19 novembre 1999).

[25] *ibid*, para 58.

Malgré l'étreinte imposée par la voie juridictionnelle, la prolifération des accords régionaux continue. Il est en effet illusoire de vouloir limiter ce phénomène à coups de prononcés d'un Groupe spécial ou de l'Organe d'appel[26].

Dans le susmentionné Rapport de l'Organe d'appel de 1999, l'article XXIV est qualifié avec l'épithète de 'moyen de défense'[27]. C'est pour mettre en évidence que cet article peut être invoqué pour contraster une constatation d'incompatibilité avec certaines autres dispositions du GATT.

Cette qualification de 'moyen de défense' nous suggère, je croix, entre quels termes se pose exactement le rapport actuel entre groupes régionaux et OMC. Elle nous souvient la magistrale classification des modèles de relations entre organisations régionales et organisations universelles élaborée par Michel Virally dans les années soixante-dix[28]. D'après cette classification, les susdites relations peuvent préalablement se distinguer du point de vue des finalités poursuivies par les organisations régionales dans leur rapport avec les organisations mondiales. La finalité d'un groupe régional peut être extravertie ou introvertie. La finalité extrovertie se réalise quand le groupe régional cherche à promouvoir ses propres intérêts dans l'instance universelle: les membres du groupe se présentent alors unis en avançant les thèses qu'ils défendent et en renforçant le poids des Etats provenant de la région. La finalité introvertie, au contraire, se vérifie quand le groupe régional cherche à protéger les intérêts des ses membres et ses membres eux-mêmes contre toute intervention de l'instance universelle, en séparant, ce faisant, ses membres des autres Etats membres de l'organisation mondiale.

Or, reliant ces analyses théoriques avec les considérations faites précédemment, il semble improbable que les groupes commerciaux régionaux aient principalement une finalité extravertie dans leur rapport avec l'OMC, parce que la composition plénière des organes de celle-ci combinée à la règle du consensus rend en principe vain ce genre de stratégie. Ces groupes ont plutôt une finalité introvertie prééminente: ils poursuivent une stratégie défensive, en empêchant que les rapports commerciaux entre les Etats participant au groupe soient soumis aux règles universelles des échanges internationaux, notamment celle de la nation la plus favorisée.

Sur la base de la distinction précédente, les modèles de relations entre organisations régionales et universelles roulent, toujours selon Virally, autour de trois idées: collaboration, concurrence et chasse gardée. Il ne m'est évidemment pas possible d'entrer ici dans les caractéristiques de chacun de ces modèles. Je dirai donc tout de suite que, à mon avis, le modèle inspirant les rapports entre organisations commerciales régionales et OMC se trouve à moitié entre celui de la concurrence et celui de la chasse gardée[29].

[26] J'ai déjà formulé cette conclusion dans mon ouvrage 'The WTO and RTAs: A Bottom-Up Interpretation of RTAs' Autonomy Over WTO Law', in M. Kolsky Lewis et S. Frankel (dir.), *International Economic Law and National Autonomy*, Cambridge (CUP) 2010, 136–139.

[27] Cf. Doc. WT/DS34/AB/R, par. 45.

[28] Cette classification est illustrée dans les suivants ouvrages de M. Virally: *L'organisation mondiale*, Paris (Armand Colin) 1972, 294–299; 'Les relations entre organisations régionales et organisations universelles', in Société Française pour le Droit International (dir.), *Régionalisme et universalisme dans le droit international contemporain*, Paris (Pedone), 1977, 147–165.

[29] Pour Virally la relation entre organisations économiques suit le modèle de la concurrence, 'bien que, jusqu'à présent, les communautés existantes aient reconnu les prérogatives du GATT. On peut imaginer qu'il en aille différemment à l'avenir, dans divers secteurs de la coopération internationale' (Cf. *L'organisation mondiale* cit., 297). L'Auteur se réfère probablement à l'ancien article 234 du Traité instituant la Communauté économique européenne selon lequel: 'Les droits et obligations résultant de conventions conclues antérieurement à l'entrée en vigueur du présent traité, entre un ou plusieurs États membres d'une part, et un ou plusieurs États tiers

Les organisations commerciales régionales ne semblent concerter ou coordonner leurs activités avec celle de l'OMC, ce qui marquerait une relation soi-disant de collaboration. Au contraire, soit elles prennent des initiatives parallèles et contradictoires, ce qui caractérise le rapport de concurrence, soit elles s'opposent à l'intervention de l'organisation universelle, jusqu'à prétendre d'interdire à cette dernière de s'occuper des affaires qui concernent les relations mutuelles entre leurs membres[30].

La stratégie défensive poursuivie par les organisations économiques régionales ne pouvait logiquement que s'accentuer lors du passage du GATT à l'OMC.

En partie, l'impulsion à la prolifération d'ententes régionales doit se ramener à la méthode de l'engagement unique adoptée à la Conférence de Marrakech. Si, d'un côté, cette méthode a uniformisé le régime juridique du commerce global, de l'autre, le compromis qui en résulte est inapproprié par rapport à la diversité des intérêts commerciaux des membres de la communauté internationale[31].

En général, et avec des répercussions de plus longue durée, le renforcement du système de l'OMC, et en particulier de son mécanisme de règlement des différends, ne pouvait qu'entraîner l'effet inverse d'intensifier les stratégies défensives de la part des groupes régionaux et *entre groupes régionaux eux-mêmes*, et de les multiplier. Ainsi, comme l'ont théorisé des illustres économistes, les groupes ou blocs régionaux prolifèrent suivant une dynamique d'entraînement[32] ou selon un effet de domino[33], ou sur la base d'autres paradigmes encore.

La fragmentation du système universel qui en résulte apparaît comme un phénomène inexorable et sans retour. Le traitement de la nation la plus favorisée n'est désormais plus la règle qui discipline les rapports commerciaux parmi les Etats membres de l'OMC, mais l'exception. De plus, la provocation a été lancée qu'il serait même plus correct de définir ce traitement comme celui de la nation la moins favorisée[34].

Les considérations qui précèdent me portent à soulever de nouveau des doutes sur le caractère universel du système de l'OMC. Je vais le faire moi aussi avec un but un peu

d'autre part, ne sont pas affectés par les dispositions du présent traité'. On ne peut ignorer que le phénomène du régionalisme économique soit devenu beaucoup plus important et complexe depuis 1972, quand Virally publia son livre.

[30] Michel Virally observe que ce comportement a l'effet d'étendre ainsi, abusivement, la notion de domaine réservé à la compétence 'nationale', telle qu'elle a été consacrée, au profit des États, par l'article 2, § 7 de la Charte des Nations Unies (Cf. *L'organisation mondiale* cit., 297). Un exemple de cette attitude se reliant au modèle de la chasse gardée est offert, il me semble, par l'article 103 de l'ALENA qui affirme: '1. Les Parties confirment les droits et obligations existants qu'elles ont les unes envers les autres aux termes de l'Accord général sur les tarifs douaniers et le commerce et d'autres accords auxquels elles sont parties. 2. En cas d'incompatibilité entre le présent accord et ces autres accords, le présent accord, sauf disposition contraire, prévaudra dans la mesure de l'incompatibilité'.

[31] Il m'est arrivé d'explorer cette perspective dans 'The Paradox of Multilateralizing Regionalism Through Flexibility', in *ASIL Proc.* 2009, volume 103, 119–121.

[32] Cf. S. J. Evenett, 'The Sequencing of Regional Integration', in *Aussenwirtschaft* 2004, 351–373; J.H. Bergstrand, A. Estevadeordal et S. J. Evenett, 'Introduction: The Sequencing of Regional Economic Integration', in *The World Economy* 2008, 1–4.

[33] Cf. R. Baldwin, *A Domino Theory of Regionalism*, NBER Working Paper 4465, 1993; 'The Causes of Regionalism', in The World Economy 1997, 865–888 ; R. Baldwin et P. Thornton (dir.), *Multilateralising Regionalism : Ideas for A WTO Action Plan on Regionalism*, London (Center for Economic Policy Research – CEPR), 2008, 9–10; R. Baldwin, S. Evenett et P. Low, 'Beyond Tariffs : Multilateralizing Non-Tariff RTA Commitments', in R. Baldwin et P. Low (dir.), Multilateralizing Regionalism : Challenges for the Global Trading System, Cambridge (CUP), 2009, 79–141.

[34] Ainsi, Report by the Consultative Board to the Director-General Supachai Panitchpakdi, *The Future of the WTO—Addressing Institutional Challenges in the New Millennium*, 2004, 19, paragraphe 60.

provocateur. Est-il concevable de continuer à affirmer que l'OMC est une organisation universelle, vu que la règle qui constitue la pierre angulaire de son système juridique ne régit qu'une partie minoritaire des rapports entre ses Etats membres? Cette question mérite d'être abordée à part.

IV. CONCLUSIONS

Dans le domaine des échanges internationaux, le rapport entre universalisme et régionalisme suit une logique singulière[35]. La prolifération de groupes économiques régionaux en concomitance et par la suite du renforcement du système commercial soi-disant 'universel', marqué par l'institution de l'OMC, est considérée comme un phénomène paradoxal.

Ce chapitre essaye d'expliquer les raisons de ce paradoxe.

En partie, l'explosion du régionalisme serait à reconduire à la chute du Mur de Berlin, qui précède chronologiquement d'à peine cinq années la signature des accords de Marrakech créant l'OMC. Le GATT, symbolisant l'ordre économique 'universel' du deuxième après-guerre, avait été édifié avec le but tacite d'endiguer la propagation du modèle politique et économique d'État se reliant à l'URSS. Pendant la période de la Guerre Froide, les parties contractantes du GATT auraient continué formellement à se référer aux règles communes de l'Accord Général pour des raisons de sécurité internationale. Ceci malgré le fait que l'économie mondiale s'était déjà multi polarisée, et que, par conséquent, les relations commerciales internationales s'étaient canalisées autour de plusieurs sphères d'influence régionales. La fin de la Guerre Froide, en dissipant la contrainte à la cohésion et au compromis parmi les États membres du GATT/OMC, aurait eu l'effet de libérer des forces centrifuges (par rapport à l'OMC) et centripètes (par rapport aux différents pôles économiques existants).

Celles-ci seraient, donc, les prémisses de la formidable expansion du régionalisme qui s'est manifestée depuis le début des années quatre-vingt-dix.

Pour ce qui concerne la période suivant la création de l'OMC, la prolifération de groupes régionaux s'explique assez aisément si l'on considère que les rapports entre OMC et organisations commerciales régionales sont empreints, pour reprendre une terminologie de Michel Virally, de deux idées, celle de la concurrence et celle de la chasse gardée, et non pas de celle de la collaboration. Les groupes régionaux poursuivent une stratégie défensive, en empêchant que les rapports commerciaux entre les Etats participants au groupe soient soumis aux règles universelles des échanges internationaux, notamment celle de la nation la plus favorisée. La sévérité accrue des règles et des procédures du système universel des échanges commerciaux découlant de l'institution de l'OMC ne pouvait alors qu'entraîner l'effet inverse d'intensifier les stratégies défensives de la part des groupes régionaux et de les multiplier.

[35] Une logique bien différente est, par exemple, à la base du rapport entre universalisme et régionalisme en matière de maintien de la paix internationale. Sur cette perspective, voir, entre autres, U. Villani, 'Les rapports entre l'ONU et les organisations régionales dans le domaine du maintien de la paix', *Recueil des Cours de l'ADI* 2001, Tome 290, 229–436.

24

Co-adaptation in the International Legal Order: The EU and the WTO

GEERT DE BAERE* AND ISABELLE VAN DAMME**

THE FALL OF the Berlin Wall symbolised the sudden end to the era of bipolarity and the start of a new multipolar reality. International law and international governance structures have needed time to adjust.[1] The constellation of events in the 1980s and 1990s gave rise to claims about the reality and promise of international law. The European Union (EU)[2] and the World Trade Organisation (WTO) have occupied an important place in the centre of this new hope for international law.[3]

By recounting the story of the EU and the WTO as a single history, this chapter explores how both institutions have evolved through co-adaptation.[4] The paper sketches their foundation as organisations with a common inspiration in 'peace through free trade'[5] but, ultimately, a different calling—an organisation based on far-reaching but

* Assistant Professor, Department of International European Law and Senior Member, Leuven Centre for Global Governance Studies, Katholieke Universiteit Leuven. The authors thank Dr Bart De Meester and Dr Kathleen Gutman for their comments on a draft of this paper.

** Referendaire in the chambers of Advocate General Sharpston, Court of Justice of the European Union; Visiting Lecturer, Université Catholique de Louvain. The views expressed in this paper do not represent the views of the institution in which she serves.

[1] See also P Lamy, 'Global Governance: Lessons from Europe', Speech at Bocconi University (9 November 2009), at www.wto.org/english/news_e/sppl_e/sppl142_e.htm.

[2] The term 'EU' is used herein to denote both the pre-Lisbon Union as an overarching structure founded on the European Communities (EC), supplemented by the policies and forms of cooperation established by the EU Treaty (essentially the common foreign and security policy and the police and judicial cooperation in criminal matters), and the post-Lisbon Union, which replaces the EC and the EU by a new EU, which exercises both the former Community and non-Community competences. Compare Art 1, third para, of the EU Treaty (TEU) in the pre- and post-Lisbon versions.

[3] For better or worse, these developments quickly became infused with constitutional discourse. See J Dunoff, 'Constitutional Conceits: The WTO's "Constitution" and the Discipline of International Law' (2006) 17 *EJIL* 650, 669.

[4] In biology, the term co-adaptation can refer to the mutual adaptation of species, genes or parts within an organism. It suggests, but is not conclusive evidence for, co-evolution: M Ridley, *Evolution*, 3rd edn (London, Wiley-Blackwell, 2004) 614.

[5] To say that Kant forms the common inspiration for both the EU and the WTO would be overegging the pudding. Nonetheless, some overlap exists between Kantian ideas and the foundational ideas of both institutions. For example, in *Perpetual Peace*, Kant writes about the idea of achieving peace through trade liberalization: I Kant, 'Perpetual Peace. A Philosophical Sketch' in HS Reiss (ed) *Kant: Political Writings* (Cambridge, Cambridge University Press, 2003) 114. These ideas are reflected in much of modern international law and in many institutions, including in the GATT/WTO and the EU: S Marks, *The Riddle of All Constitutions: International Law, Democracy and the Critique of Ideology* (Oxford, Oxford University Press, 2000) 35. See

regionally limited integration, on the one hand, and an organisation based on integration principally limited to trade with a universalistic vocation, on the other.

This chapter does not seek to argue that the WTO should become more like the EU[6] or vice versa. No bias for either organisation underlies it. Rather, it aims to explain the sociology and development of each organisation in the light of the context offered by the other organisation, without purporting to call for a more integrationist WTO or a more contractual treaty model for the EU. It offers an alternative metaphor for describing how mutual adaptation has sparked the evolution of the WTO and the EU.

In particular, the chapter discusses two examples of co-adaptation, taken from different periods in each organisation's history. The first example, which covers the period of 1948 to the late 1950s, studies the process through which Contracting Parties to the General Agreement on Tariffs and Trade 1947 (GATT 1947) came to tolerate European integration and responded to Member States' calls for a special status under or beyond the GATT 1947. The second example, commenting on the period from the Uruguay Round until the entry into force of the Lisbon Treaty, narrates how the negotiating agenda in the Uruguay Round called for a reconsideration of the allocation of competences between Member States and the EU, and contributed to the transformation of the common commercial policy (CCP) into one of the main building blocks of the EU's external relations policy. As these examples show, the matrix of interaction between the WTO and the EU is not the result of an overarching 'intelligent design',[7] but rather, at least partly, of co-adaptation.[8]

The chapter concludes with some observations on why the co-adaptation of the EU and the WTO illustrates how international law (including the law of international organisations), while providing the legal framework for the foundation of both the EU and the WTO, has itself been changed through the presence of these new actors, a process that has been particularly clear in the past 20 years since the fall of the Berlin Wall and the end of the Cold War. The development of each organisation, and their mutual influence, is explained as a sign of the inherent flexibility of international law.

The analysis presented in this chapter is not exhaustive. It forms part of ongoing research that aims to narrate a complete single history of both institutions and test the hypothesis of co-adaptation put forward here.

further, as regards the EU: G De Baere, *Constitutional Principles of EU External Relations* (Oxford, Oxford University Press, 2008) 220; and as regards the GATT: DA Irwin, PC Mavroidis and AO Sykes, *The Genesis of the GATT* (Cambridge, Cambridge University Press, 2008) 9.

[6] The authors of this chapter share the view that it would be misconceived to transfer EU constitutionalism into the WTO: see, eg, JHH Weiler, 'Cain and Abel—Convergence and Divergence in International Trade Law' in JHH Weiler (ed), *The EU, the WTO and the NAFTA. Towards a Common Law of International Trade* (Oxford, Oxford University Press, 2000) 1; P Holmes, 'The WTO and the EU: Some Constitutional Comparisons' in G de Búrca and J Scott (eds), *The EU and the WTO. Legal and Constitutional Issues* (Oxford, Hart Publishing, 2001) 59; I Van Damme, *Treaty Interpretation by the WTO Appellate Body* (Oxford, Oxford University Press, 2009) 87.

[7] See also M Dani, 'Remedying European Legal Pluralism: The *FIAMM* and *Fedon* Litigation and the Judicial Protection of International Trade Bystanders' (2010) 21 *EJIL* 336.

[8] Except for any more than a purely metaphorical analogy, the evolution of such man-made things as international organizations is of course not comparable to the evolution of natural species and phenomena.

I. CO-ADAPTATION OF THE EU AND THE WTO: TWO EXAMPLES

A. From 1948 until the Late 1950s: GATT Contracting Parties Adapting to the Early Forms of European Integration

The WTO as a political project can be understood only against its historical background. That history spans almost 70 years and shows how and why the GATT 1947 evolved towards the WTO covered agreements, a relatively sophisticated network of treaties with an organisation responsible for administering these treaties.

The history of the WTO builds on the practice of the GATT 1947 and various failed attempts to establish an international organisation with competence in, among other things, international trade. The most well-known attempt is the Havana Charter for an International Trade Organisation (ITO). The Havana Charter, negotiated under the auspices of the United Nations, was intended to complement the International Monetary Fund (IMF) and the World Bank in the triptych of the economic institutions envisaged during the Bretton Woods Conference. The envisaged ambit of the ITO was much broader than that of the current WTO, and included trade and employment. The explicit reference to peace and stability in the preamble to, and in Article 1 of, the Havana Charter disappeared in the GATT 1947 and the WTO covered agreements, though there is scope to interpret these agreements as being about more than purely economic integration.

The GATT 1947 was to be incorporated in the Havana Charter, and provide the basic principles governing multilateral trade in goods. It entered into force through a *Protocol for Provisional Application*, after the Havana Charter was signed. In so doing, the GATT Contracting Parties secured concessions while awaiting ratification, in accordance with national law, of the Havana Charter. In the early 1950s, the US Congress ultimately decided not to ratify, which signified the end of the Charter, and thus also the ITO. The result of these negotiations was a set of rules on multilateral trade in goods, administered by the Interim Commission of the International Trade Organisation (ICITO).[9]

By the time of the entry into force of the GATT 1947, the first steps towards regional economic integration in Europe had been taken through the Customs Convention between Belgium, Luxembourg[10] and the Netherlands, signed on 5 September 1944,[11] and the *Treaty Establishing the Benelux Economic Union* (Benelux Treaty), signed on 3 February 1958, which established an internal market, providing for the free movement of persons, goods, capital and services.[12] As a stepping stone for building the cooperation model under the GATT 1947 and the WTO, Article 9 of the Benelux Treaty foresaw that the high Contracting Parties would consult (and likely coordinate) before articulating a position in relations with third states or in international conferences/negotiations that may affect the aims of the Union.[13]

[9] Established in 1948, the ICITO was competent to prepare the entry into force of the ITO Charter.

[10] Together forming '*l'Union Economique belgo-luxembourgeoise*'.

[11] Convention douanière belgo-luxembourgeoise-néerlandaise (5 septembre 1944), Bulletin d'Information 31.05.1947, No. 5, 3e année, 51–52. Art 9 made clear that the Customs Convention, and the customs union created thereby, was to apply provisionally as the precursor for the '*Union Economique*'.

[12] Art 1 Benelux Treaty. The Benelux Treaty was and remains a temporary treaty. It was concluded initially for a period of fifty years (Art 99.1), thereafter it has remained operative for consecutive periods of 10 years until the necessary intent is expressed to terminate the Treaty (Art 99.2). On 17 June 2008, a renewed Benelux Treaty was signed in The Hague.

[13] Part 2 (Arts 15 to 54) Benelux Treaty.

Prior to signing the Benelux Treaty, the parties to the Customs Convention negotiated with Germany, France, and Italy the *Treaty Establishing the European Coal and Steel Community* (the ECSC Treaty), which was signed on 18 April 1951 and entered into force on 23 July 1952.[14] Different from that of the GATT 1947, the object and purpose of the ECSC Treaty included consideration of the fact 'that world peace may be safeguarded only by creative efforts equal to the dangers which menace it'. The third and fourth recitals in the preamble spoke of 'the fact that Europe can be built only by concrete actions which create a real solidarity and by the establishment of common bases for economic development' and of 'assisting through the expansion of their basic production in raising the standard of living and in furthering the works of peace'.

Through the institution of a common market,[15] with common objectives and common institutions, the ECSC would contribute to these goals.[16] The ECSC enjoyed legal personality.[17] Article 74 defined the powers of the High Authority of the ECSC in international trade relations, and stipulated that the High Authority had competence to act 'if it is established that countries not members of the Community, or enterprises situated in such countries, are engaging in dumping operations or other practices condemned by the Havana Charter'. In other words, by means of cross-reference, the Havana Charter thus was part of the definition of the legal basis pursuant to which the ECSC was competent to act in the field of commercial policy.

Around the time of the signing of the ECSC Treaty, certain GATT Contracting Parties started expressing concerns about the disparity of European tariffs. For example, a group of delegations affirmed the importance of the Organisation for European Economic Co-operation (OEEC) in achieving considerable tariff reductions in the Torquay GATT negotiating round.[18] Their main point concerned the potential contribution of those GATT negotiations, and previous ones such as the Geneva and Annecy conferences, to the creation of a European single market.[19] In response to a suggestion by the OEEC countries, and particularly the Benelux delegations, an Intersessional Working Party was established.[20]

Around the same time, the French delegation informed the Contracting Parties of the signing of the ECSC Treaty by Belgium, France, Germany, Italy, Luxemburg and the Netherlands, and requested that a new Intersessional Working Party be established[21] 'to carry out the necessary examination of the Treaty as soon as it has been ratified'.[22] The request was granted and another Intersessional Working Party was established.

Prior to the first meeting of the working party in September 1952, the Netherlands government prepared a statement whereby it set out officially the problems arising from

[14] The Treaty was concluded for a period of fifty years (Art 97) and expired on 23 July 2002.

[15] The Single European Act, signed on 17 and 28 February 1986, first introduced in the EEC Treaty the concept of the 'internal market', defined as 'an area without internal frontiers in which the free movement of goods, persons, services and capital is ensured in accordance with the provisions of the Treaties' (Art 8a of the EEC Treaty (TEEC), thereafter Art 14(2) of the EC Treaty (TEC), now Art 26(2) of the Treaty on the Functioning of the EU (TFEU)). See further K Mortelmans, 'The common market, the internal market and the single market, what's in a market?' (1998) 35 *CML Rev* 101; and C Barnard, *The Substantive Law of the EU. The Four Freedoms*, 3rd edn (Oxford, Oxford University Press, 2010) 9.

[16] Arts 1 and 2 ECSC Treaty.

[17] Art 6 ECSC Treaty.

[18] GATT/CP/103 (14 March 1951).

[19] ibid.

[20] GATT/IW.2/1 (8 June 1951).

[21] GATT/CP.6/41 (22 October 1951).

[22] GATT/CP.6/56 (26 October 1951).

the establishment of the ECSC.[23] The paper started from the assumption that hardly any problems would have arisen, had the GATT drafters provided for 'the concept of a partial, but close and extremely important form of integration between the economies of countries parties to an agreement like the Community'.[24] It emphasised that it was 'the avowed aim of the Community not to raise barriers to the trade of other Contracting Parties with the member countries of the group'.[25] The purpose of the paper was to request a waiver, pursuant to Article XXV GATT 1947, that would apply to certain GATT obligations assumed by the ECSC treaty partners in relation to specific provisions of the ECSC Treaty.

In response to the request, the Executive Secretary of the Intersessional Working Party on the ECSC produced a note on the legal questions surrounding the Community. At the outset it was clear that the ECSC Treaty did not fall within the scope of any of the exceptions under the GATT 1947. In particular, Article XXIV:4 did not apply because 'the Community is limited to one sector of economic activity'.[26] Therefore, the recommendation was made that the Contracting Parties decide pursuant to Article XXV:5(a) GATT 1947.[27]

Relying on Article 71 ECSC Treaty, the Executive Secretary concluded that the six ECSC Member States remained fully responsible under international law 'irrespective of the distribution of powers within the Community'.[28] The analysis appeared to be aimed at guaranteeing the other Contracting Parties that the creation of the ECSC did not in any manner take away their right to invoke the responsibility of the individual ECSC Member States for breach of obligations owed to other Contracting Parties. To that effect, the Executive Secretary relied also on the certainty provided by the establishment of the European Court of Justice (ECJ), and concluded: 'All those provisions tend to indicate that the Member States have at their disposal all the means of action necessary to ensure that the commitments shall be carried out'.[29] Despite this preliminary conclusion, the Executive Secretary continued with a description of the various powers transferred to the 'High Authority' under the ECSC Treaty, noting that it was not excluded that the exercise of these powers could be inconsistent with the GATT 1947, without appropriate redress available for Contracting Parties before the ECJ. To address that uncertainty, it was suggested to identify the institutions entitled to act for the Community in its external relations.[30]

In response, the six ECSC Member States suggested that a general principle on the scope of the waiver be established, and that in light thereof a few essential applications of the principle be identified.[31] They also proposed to design a procedure 'to settle particular cases which might arise in [the] future and which could not come under the general rule'.[32] This solution was presented as the most pragmatic one, especially due to the various relationships between the ECSC Treaty and the GATT 1947, and the fact that

[23] L/17 (8 September 1952).
[24] ibid.
[25] ibid.
[26] W.7/2 (24 September 1952), para 4.
[27] ibid, para 5.
[28] ibid, para 35.
[29] ibid, para 36.
[30] ibid, para 38.
[31] L/38 (2 October 1952).
[32] ibid.

'the future developments of the Community [are] so difficult to foresee'.[33] To that effect, they submitted a draft text of a waiver.

The preamble of the decision explained the guarantees and promises made to other Contracting Parties, which took note of the ECSC High Authority's undertaking to 'act in accordance with the obligations which would apply if the Community were a single contracting party consisting of the European territories of the member states, and, further, that within the limits of these same powers, it will participate together with the member state or states concerned in all consultations' pursuant to the GATT 1947.[34] The governments of the ECSC Member States also committed to submitting an annual report on the measures taken towards the implementation of the ECSC Treaty until the end of the transitional period. The waiver became effective in relation to coal, iron ore and scrap on 10 February 1952 and for steel products on 1 May 1953.

The ECSC Member States submitted their first annual report on the implementation of the ECSC on 12 September 1953.[35] Upon receipt, the GATT Contracting Parties decided to establish Working Party 9 on the ECSC.[36] The first report of the Working Party offers the impression of a constructive and open dialogue on the character of the Community and how its creation and commercial policies may affect the interests of the Contracting Parties other than the six ECSC Member States.[37] Overall, this report and other subsequent recordings of the discussions on the ECSC's annual reports demonstrate considerable tolerance of other Contracting Parties to the transition of the economies of the 6 ECSC Member States to a common market for a select group of products. Although concerns were raised about the introduction of new trade restrictions, such as the re-establishment of duties on steel products,[38] and the continued application by the Community of trade measures, such as export restrictions on scrap,[39] there was a conciliatory atmosphere surrounding the early discussions in the 1950s. Thus, at the initial stage, the Contracting Parties engaged in a dialogue with the ECSC High Authority with the aim of a better understanding of the objectives of the ECSC and its competences.

Contracting Parties other than the 6 ECSC Member States did fear European integration developing in splendid isolation. Assurances were given that, pursuant to the ECSC Treaty, the Member States were under an obligation to take into account the interests of third countries, including their supply constraints, and commitments made in relation to those countries, in developing their commercial policies.[40] Also in respect to other matters, such as future tariff policies, the Member States and the High Authority offered assurances that they would not introduce any protective or restrictive policies.[41] The Member States, represented by the Community, showed a readiness to enter into negotiations with third countries to address trade relations in respect of coal and steel.[42] Overall, with a few exceptions, the Contracting Parties failed to engage seriously in such

[33] ibid.

[34] G/35 (7 November 1952) 8.

[35] L/526 (20 September 1956).

[36] W.8/1/Add.9 (6 October 1953).

[37] G/56 (20 October 1953).

[38] See, eg, ibid, para 16.

[39] The ECSC High Authority repeatedly reminded the Contracting Parties of the fact that these export restrictions applied prior to the ECSC's establishment: see, eg, ibid, paras 14 and 11; L/240 (7 October 1954), para 7; also L/466 (1 December 1955).

[40] L/240 (7 October 1954), para 12; L/305 (13 January 1955), para 44.

[41] L/305 (13 January 1955), para 18.

[42] L/240 (7 October 1954), para 19; L/305 (13 January 1955), para 20.

negotiations and adopted a very hesitant approach to the development of the ECSC. Nevertheless, by 1956, the Community could rely on two agreements aimed at the reduction of tariffs on steel concluded with Austria and the USA, hoping both examples would 'dispel certain fears that have been expressed concerning the action taken by the Community with regard to tariffs'.[43] In its 1956 report, the Working Party took note of this positive development, and the continuous process in the tariff harmonisation.[44]

A few years after the adoption of the 1952 Waiver, Contracting Parties started expressing some concern about the lack of progress in integration efforts and the Community's harmonisation negotiations.[45] Some Contracting Parties were wary of the risk of allowing preferential agreements such as the ECSC too much time to transition towards an integrated economy (with respect to at least some products). Later discussions also showed how the Contracting Parties became increasingly aware of discrepancies between the Waiver and actual steps taken towards harmonisation.[46]

In response, the ECSC Member States acted forcefully in an attempt to cause a shift in perception of the type of organization the ECSC had become. In a joint statement, they recalled the GATT Contracting Parties' perception of the ECSC as 'an exceptional case justifying the application of Article XXV', but questioned whether this perception remained fully consistent with the reality of how the Community had developed:

> ... the evolution of international relations ought to result in supra-national communities being considered not as exceptional cases, but as a new juridical fact to be recognized by an adaptation of the provisions of the General Agreement on the basis of the principles proclaimed in paragraph 4 of Article XXIV of the [GATT].[47]

This was essentially a call upon the Contracting Parties to grant the ECSC a status not provided for in the GATT 1947, including under Article XXIV, which would address the problem that 'countries participating in a community might on this account experience some difficulty in continuing to carry out in respect of other Contracting Parties certain obligations arising out of the recent provisions of the [GATT]'.[48] Despite this strong claim for a special status, the ECSC Member States failed to add any substantive content to that status,[49] perhaps due to the ambiguity surrounding the ambition of the ECSC and its Member States to move towards further integration.

Indeed, a few months after the statement, the 6 ECSC Member States, in June 1955, agreed to establish a new type of community, with social and economic objectives, without any product restriction. On 25 March 1957, the ECSC Member States signed in Rome the *Treaty establishing the European Economic Community* (EEC Treaty)[50] and the *Treaty establishing the European Atomic Energy Community* (Euratom Treaty). The Chairman of the Interim Committee for the Common Market and Euratom duly notified both treaties to the GATT Executive Secretary,[51] followed by the submission of

[43] L/526 (20 September 1956), para 10.
[44] L/583 (10 November 1956), para 34.
[45] L/305 (13 January 1955), para 42.
[46] L/755 (28 November 1957), para 32.
[47] W.9/245 (7 March 1955).
[48] ibid.
[49] The statement was entirely ignored: see L/425 (17 October 1955); L/466 (1 December 1955).
[50] Art 8 of the Treaty on European Union of 7 February 1992 amended the EEC Treaty so as to establish the European Community (EC). The abbreviation 'EEC' is herein used only to refer to the original European Economic Community.
[51] L/626 (24 April 1957).

a memorandum setting out the main aspects and objectives of the EEC Treaty.[52] As was explained to the GATT Contracting Parties, the 6 ECSC Member States:

> ... decided to take a new step towards the construction of an integrated Europe through the development of common institutions, the progressive union of their domestic economies and the harmonization of their economic and social policies.[53]

From the viewpoint of the new EEC Member States, the EEC could no longer be categorised within the four corners of the GATT 1947, nor could its consistency with the GATT 1947 easily be determined. They considered that the relevant legal question was 'whether the establishment of the Community would not, on account of its very nature, fall beyond the field of application of the GATT rules'.[54] Indeed, as was later explained, the EEC was 'an organization which goes far beyond a mere customs union'.[55] Contrary to the ECSC, which required a waiver as to its limited scope in terms of products, the common market established by the EEC Treaty included 'all products ..., with no exceptions whatsoever'.[56] As a result, 'the steps taken do not merely affect substantially all the trade between the parties concerned, ..., but <u>all</u> the trade as between the constituent territories'.[57] In their view, the explanations given in the memorandum supported the conclusion that the EEC Treaty was consistent with the provisions of Article XXIV GATT 1947 and the objectives and other obligations assumed under the GATT 1947. Shortly after the communication informing GATT Contracting Parties of the new developments in European integration, the Contracting Parties prepared a consolidated list of diverse questions on the EEC Treaty,[58] pertaining to institutional and substantive matters. In its replies, the Community captured well the general tone underlying most questions, commenting that the 'fear that expansion in trade between Member States might be obtained at the expense of traditional currents of trade' was 'baseless'.[59] That exchange of views was followed by a more comprehensive process of consultations and exchanges on the scope of the EEC Treaty, especially in light of certain select provisions of the GATT 1994.[60] As a result, the EEC Member States considered that they had fulfilled the conditions of Article XXIV:5-9 GATT 1947 and asked for the Contracting Parties' recognition of that fact.[61] During that period, reporting and discussions on the ECSC also continued.[62] Ultimately, a conclusion on its GATT-consistency was never explicitly reached. The Treaty of Rome was considered acceptable *as a matter of fact*, and the institutional relationship between the GATT and the Community was equally developed on that pragmatic basis. For example, the establishment of the common customs tariff within the EEC required common action in the framework of the GATT and, because the Commission was entrusted by the Treaty with conducting trade negotiations, the Commission replaced

[52] L/637 (11 June 1957).
[53] ibid.
[54] ibid, para 3.
[55] L/656 (2 August 1957), 2.
[56] L/637 (11 June 1957), para 7.
[57] ibid, para 7 (emphasis in the original).
[58] L/639 (19 June 1957).
[59] L/656 (2 August 1957), 2. Replies to additional questions were submitted in L/732 (5 November 1957).
[60] See L/696 (4 October 1957).
[61] L/728 (26 October 1957); L/728/Rev.1 (23 November 1957).
[62] See, eg, L/715 (23 October 1957); L/686 (30 September 1957); L/755 (28 November 1957); L/804 (3 April 1958).

the Member States in the GATT system, a purely pragmatic arrangement typical of the then GATT.[63]

The EC never became a Contracting Party to the GATT 1947. The GATT 1947 and related agreements were open only for governments and no other legal persons. Irrespective of the fact that the EC enjoyed international legal personality,[64] its competence in the area of external trade relations needed to be exercised through the EC Member States that were GATT Contracting Parties. It is to that interplay between Member State and Community competences and their exercise that this chapter now turns, focusing on the period from the Uruguay Round till the entry into force of the Lisbon Treaty.

B. From Uruguay via Maastricht to Lisbon: The Uruguay Agenda and the Allocation of Competences between the Union and the Member States

From the outset, the EEC Treaty provided for the free movement of goods as well as services, while it took from 1947 to the 1994 Uruguay Round negotiations before services were substantially included in the GATT/WTO framework. In both cases the approach to trade in services has followed in the footsteps of the approach to trade in goods.[65] Moreover, the external aspects of trade in services within the Community have followed *pari passu* with the inclusion of services within the GATT/WTO framework and, therefore, form a particularly good example of co-adaptation.

The Punta del Este Ministerial Declaration launching the Uruguay Round did not provide a mandate to negotiate an entire overhaul of the multilateral trading system existing at the time. The mandate was relatively clear: protect the status quo under the GATT 1947 and its basic principles, while pursuing further liberalisation and expansion of world trade in a manner consistent with the need to promote growth and development. The opening paragraph of the Declaration made clear that the negotiations 'will be open to the participation of countries as indicated in Parts I and II of this Declaration'. Part I, Section F on 'Participation' opened the negotiations to different categories of States but not to legal persons other than States, and thus not to the EC. After four years of negotiations, the outcome of the market access negotiations on tariff and non-tariff measures was reported in the Uruguay Round (1990) Protocol to the General Agreement on Tariffs and Trade, reflecting the agreement of the GATT Contracting Parties and the EC.

The agenda for negotiations had identified three main topics for discussion: trade in services, trade-related aspects of intellectual property rights and trade-related investment measures. These issues sparked debate both in the ongoing Uruguay Round and in the Maastricht Intergovernmental Conference (IGC), and would become the main battlegrounds in the internal EC/EU debate on the scope of the CCP in years to come. As

[63] P Eeckhout, *External Relations of the European Union. Legal and Constitutional Foundations* (Oxford, Oxford University Press, 2004) 11.

[64] Art 210 TEEC, which became Art 281 TEC and after Lisbon, as regards the Union, Art 47 TEU.

[65] P Eeckhout, 'Constitutional Concepts for Free Trade in Services' in G de Búrca and J Scott (eds), *The EU and the WTO. Legal and Constitutional Issues* (Oxford, Hart Publishing, 2001) 212. See further in general M Krajewski, 'Of Modes and Sectors. External Relations, Internal Debates, and the Special Case of (Trade in) Services' in M Cremona (ed) *Developments in EU External Relations Law* (Oxford, Oxford University Press, 2008) 172.

the WTO Secretariat noted in 1995, '[t]he coincidence of internal reform with external negotiations enhanced the Community's participation in the Uruguay Round'.[66]

At stake in the Community debate was the extent of its flexibility to adapt to developments in international trade, particularly within the GATT. In Opinion 1/75, the ECJ had defined the CCP in a manner that was both wide and dynamic. Both these factors would be important in the adaptation of the CCP to the evolution within the WTO. When asked whether aid for exports and more particularly measures concerning credits for the financing of local costs linked to export operations were covered by the CCP, the Court had replied that 'such measures constitute an important element of commercial policy, that concept having the same content whether it is applied in the context of the international action of a state or to that of the community'.[67] International trade policy was therefore a factor for determining the scope of the CCP.[68] Moreover, the common commercial policy was described '[as] above all the outcome of a progressive development'.[69] By defining the CCP in that manner, the Court not only confirmed the essential flexibility of the policy, but also positioned itself as the ultimate arbiter of the scope of the Union's external trade policy.[70] The Court also defined the CCP as an exclusive Community policy. It based that conclusion on a number of arguments, but it did not refer to what could have been a clear argument in favour, namely Article XXIV(8)(a) GATT 1947.[71]

The dynamic nature of the CCP as essentially able to adapt to the evolution of international trade policy was further elaborated in Opinion 1/78, in which the Court adapted the CCP to the fact that international trade was increasingly based on regulation rather than pure liberalisation.[72] The Court thus proved that it had meant what it had said in Opinion 1/75 about the dynamic nature of the CCP. This was again made clear in the *Generalized Tariff Preferences* case, in which the Court referred to the GATT 1947 to justify its interpretation of the scope of the CCP.[73]

During the Maastricht IGC and against the background of the Uruguay Round negotiations, the Commission had put forward ambitious proposals for amending the Treaty in the field of the CCP. Member States, however, preferred to leave the scope of the CCP largely untouched except for services closely related to trade.[74] After the disappointment of the Maastricht Treaty within the sphere of the CCP, the Commission arguably attempted to achieve judicially what it had not been able to achieve through negotiation:[75] the extension of the CCP to encompass essentially all matters covered by the WTO covered agreements and more particularly all trade in services and all aspects of trade in intellectual property rights contained in the *TRIPS Agreement*. The Commission therefore requested an Opinion of the Court under what is now Article 218(11) TFEU on whether the Community had exclusive competence to conclude the Multilateral

[66] WT/TPR/S/3 (30 June 1995) (summary observations).

[67] Opinion 1/75 *OECD Local Cost Standard* [1975] ECR 1355.

[68] Eeckhout, *External Relations*, 13.

[69] Opinion 1/75, 1362–1363.

[70] cf P Koutrakos, *EU International Relations Law* (Oxford, Hart Publishing, 2006) 34.

[71] Eeckhout, *External Relations*, 15.

[72] Opinion 1/78 *International Agreement on Natural Rubber* [1979] ECR 2871.

[73] Case 45/86 *Commission v Council* [1987] ECR 1493, paras 16–19.

[74] M Cremona, 'EC External Economic Policy after Amsterdam: Authority and Interpretation within Interconnected Legal Orders' in JHH Weiler (ed), *The EU, the WTO and the NAFTA. Towards a Common Law of International Trade* (Oxford, Oxford University Press, 2000) 8; Eeckhout, *External Relations*, 23.

[75] Cremona, 'EC External Economic Policy after Amsterdam', 9.

Agreements on Trade in Goods, in so far as those agreements would concern ECSC and Euratom products, and on other questions relating to the exclusive competence of the Community to conclude the GATS and the *TRIPS Agreement*,[76] by virtue of Articles 113, 100a, or 235 TEC.[77]

As regards goods, a less contentious subject, the Court accepted that all WTO covered agreements governing trade in goods fell within the CCP, thereby adopting a broad conception of trade that was sufficiently dynamic to adapt to developments in international trade.[78] By contrast, more complex questions arose regarding the competence to conclude the GATS and the *TRIPS Agreement*.

The Court noted that the *WTO Agreement* and its annexes were the subject of a single process of negotiation covering both goods and services, and concluded from 'this trend in international trade' and from the open nature of the CCP that trade in services could not 'immediately, and as a matter of principle, be excluded from the scope of Article 113'. The Court relied on the GATS definition, in Article I:2, of trade in services to determine whether the overall scheme of the EC Treaty was not such as to limit the extent to which trade in services could be included within Article 113. As regards cross-border supplies (mode 1), the Court held that this situation was not unlike trade in goods because neither the supplier nor the consumer crosses borders. There was thus no particular reason why such a supply should not fall within the concept of the CCP. The Court, however, excluded from the CCP the three other GATS modes of supply, namely, consumption abroad, commercial presence, and the presence of natural persons.[79]

As regards the *TRIPS Agreement*, the Court was concerned that an exclusive competence to conclude the agreement might distort the internal institutional balance. Referring to the *TRIPS Agreement*'s primary objective to 'strengthen and harmonize the protection of intellectual property on a worldwide scale', the Court reasoned that were the Community to enjoy exclusive competence to conclude intellectual property harmonisation agreements with non-member-countries and, at the same time, to achieve harmonisation at the Community level, the Community institutions would escape the internal constraints to which they are subject in relation to procedures and to voting rules.[80]

Crucially, the Court also found that the allocation of competence could not depend on problems that may possibly occur in the administration of the agreements,[81] and rejected any reliance on the practical difficulties that might arise for the Union within the WTO framework as a ground for accepting a more encompassing interpretation of the CCP. It would adopt the same approach in Opinion 2/00[82] and in Opinion 1/08.[83]

Was this in fact, as some argued at the time,[84] an example of co-adaptation gone badly, and of the Court not grasping the essence of the WTO covered agreements? It has been

[76] Opinion 1/94 *Competence of the Community to conclude international agreements concerning services and the protection of intellectual property* [1994] ECR I-5267, para 1.

[77] Now Arts 207, 114, and 352 TFEU, respectively.

[78] Eeckhout, *External Relations*, 27.

[79] Opinion 1/94, paras 40–47.

[80] ibid, paras 58–60.

[81] ibid, paras 106–107.

[82] Opinion 2/00 *Cartagena Protocol* [2001] ECR I-9713, para 41.

[83] Opinion 1/08 *GATS Schedules* [2009] ECR I-11129, para 127.

[84] See, eg, P Pescatore, '*Opinion 1/94* on the Conclusion of the WTO Agreement: Is there an Escape from a Programmed Disaster?' (1999) 36 *CML Rev* 387.

remarked that the Court's Opinion, while correctly assessing the scope of the *TRIPS Agreement*, does not do justice to the actual scope of the GATS, which is not at all intended to be an instrument of immigration policy.[85] However, from an EU perspective, the Court was merely performing its role as a constitutional adjudicator and placing the CCP within the context of the overall system of EU external relations.[86] That shifting of power from the Court to the political institutions as regards WTO law is a constant feature, both as regards the scope of the CCP and the effect of WTO law within the Union.

These internal tensions resulting from the EU's participation in the WTO were also the subject of concerns expressed in the WTO. In the WTO's first trade policy review of the EU in 1995, the Trade Policy Review Body (TPRB) identified three main tendencies during the past two years (including the period since the entry into force of the Maastricht Treaty), namely:

> internal policy integration and harmonization across sectors and, more strongly, among Member States; a rapidly expanding and increasingly complex network of free-trade area and preferential relations; and active participation in multilateral trade liberalization.

The TPRB concluded that '[t]he co-existence of, and interaction among, these tendencies highlights the necessity for a strong, constantly active WTO framework to guide future trade policies and counterbalance the discriminatory impact of expanding preferential links'.[87]

While the ECJ had displayed judicial caution in Opinion 1/94, the drafters at the Amsterdam IGC decided not to gamble over whether on a future occasion the Court might reach a different solution based on, for example, the evolution of WTO law. They wrote the exclusion of intellectual property and certain categories of services into Article 133(5) TEC, with a possibility for the Council to integrate them into the regular CCP.[88] As a result, the competence to consider possible evolutions in WTO law shifted from the Court to the Treaty drafters and, partially, to the Council.[89] Article 133(5) TEC in its Amsterdam version indicated a degree of willingness of the Member States to respond to challenges highlighted in Opinion 1/94,[90] but also their discomfort with the precise limits of the scope of the CCP, particularly as regards agreements covering certain categories of services and intellectual property rights. Illustrative thereof were the rather Delphic amendments made by the Nice Treaty to Article 133. The amendments were again meant to take into account the evolution in international trade, in particular in the WTO, but they did so in such a convoluted manner that 'the Treaty drafters could have spared themselves the trouble',[91] and that 'Sisyphus would have done a better job'.[92]

[85] See GATS Annex on Movement of Natural Persons Supplying Services under the Agreement, para 4, footnote 1. See also Eeckhout, *External Relations*, 30.

[86] Koutrakos, *EU International Relations Law*, 47; also E Sharpston and G De Baere, 'The Court of Justice as a Constitutional Adjudicator' in A Arnull, C Barnard, M Dougan and E Spaventa (eds), *A Constitutional Order of States? Essays in EU Law in Honour of Alan Dashwood* (Oxford, Hart Publishing, 2011) 123–50.

[87] WT/TPR/S/3 (30 June 1995) (opening paragraph of summary observations).

[88] Art 133(5) TEC (Amsterdam version): 'The Council, acting unanimously on a proposal from the Commission and after consulting the European Parliament, may extend the application of paragraphs 1 to 4 to international negotiations and agreements on services and intellectual property insofar as they are not covered by these paragraphs'.

[89] Cremona, 'EC External Economic Policy after Amsterdam', 18.

[90] Koutrakos, *EU International Relations Law*, 60.

[91] Eeckhout, *External Relations*, 53.

[92] CW Herrmann, 'Common Commercial Policy after Nice: Sisyphus Would Have Done a Better Job' (2002) 39 *CML Rev* 7, cited in the Opinion of A-G Kokott in C-13/07 *Commission v Council*, removed from the register on 10 June 2010, para 1.

Indeed, the handiwork of the drafters offered the Commission an opportunity to dust off, once more, its old arguments on the dynamic nature of the CCP and the practical difficulties in having to act within the WTO on the basis of a non-exclusive Union external trade policy. The Commission therefore requested the Court for an Opinion on the conclusion of agreements concerning the modification and withdrawal of certain services commitments and the provision of compensation necessary as a result of EU enlargement. The Commission asked whether the conclusion of these agreements, pursuant to Article XXI GATS, fell within the sphere of exclusive or shared competences, and whether Articles 133(1) and (5) TEC (CCP), in conjunction with Article 300(2) TEC (procedure for concluding Community international agreements), constituted the appropriate legal basis for the act concluding those agreements.

At the heart of the dispute was whether the term 'services' in Article 133(5) TEC was to be interpreted in accordance with the strict definition of services in EU law, or whether it ought to be aligned with the GATS which, for example, does not distinguish between services and establishment, but does distinguish between different modes of services. A similar issue existed as regards the scope of 'commercial aspects of intellectual property' and specifically whether the scope of Article 133(5)(1) TEC would change if the scope of the *TRIPS Agreement* were to change.[93]

In Opinion 1/08, delivered on the day before the entry into force of the Lisbon Treaty, the Court concluded that the conclusion of these agreements fell within the shared competence of the EC and the Member States, and that the Community act concluding those agreements had to be based on Article 133(1), (5) and (6), second subparagraph, TEC and on Articles 71 TEC and 80(2) TEC, in conjunction with Articles 300(2) and (3), first subparagraph, TEC.[94] The Court pointed out that all international agreements relating to the fields mentioned in Article 133(6) TEC, ie culture, education, and social and human health services, fell within the shared competence of the Community and its Member States, and their conclusion required their joint participation, even if the agreements did not concern exclusively or predominantly the sectors in question. The Court explicitly affirmed the need to preserve for the Member States an effective external competence in these sensitive areas in accordance with Article 133(6) TEC.[95] Significantly, in its interpretation of the EC Treaty, the Court noted that 'given both its general nature and the fact that it was concluded at world level, the GATS assumes, as regards in particular the concept of "trade in services" (an expression used both by the GATS and by the first subparagraph of Article 133(5) EC), particular importance in the sphere of international action relating to trade in services'.[96]

In Opinion 1/94 and Opinion 1/08, the Court recognised the limits that the Treaty places on claims to an all-encompassing exclusive competence on the basis of the need for a unified approach towards the WTO covered agreements because of their importance to European integration.[97] Remarkably, neither Opinion 1/94, nor Opinion 2/00 or Opinion 1/08 contains a reference to the parallelism between the CCP and the external trade policy of a State, as was the case with Opinion 1/75 and the earlier case-law.

[93] Koutrakos, *EU International Relations Law*, 62, arguing for a strict reading of Art 133(5)(1) TEC.

[94] For a fuller account, see M Cremona, 'Balancing Union and Member State interests: Opinion 1/2008, choice of legal base and the common commercial policy under the Treaty of Lisbon' (2010) 35 *EL Rev* 378.

[95] Opinion 1/08, para 139.

[96] Opinion 1/08, para 121.

[97] De Baere, *Constitutional Principles*, 198.

Does that imply that the Court has abandoned the idea of a dynamic and flexible CCP, able to adapt to developments in international trade, notably within the WTO? Has the ECJ cut the wings of co-adaptation? Probably not. The CCP's dynamic development requires accommodating developments in international trade and maintaining loyalty to the EU's constitutional principles. Effectively, the ECJ has displayed judicial pragmatism, adapting principles to subsequent internal and external evolutions.[98]

The debates in the Convention for the future of Europe were not really focused on the CCP, yet the end result appears to be quite significant—perhaps precisely due to that lack of interest in the CCP. Article III-217 of the Constitution survived unscathed from the downfall of the document of which it was part and its content ended up in Article 207 TFEU. The latter considerably expands the Union's exclusive competence in the CCP and appears to be intended to cover essentially the full scope[99] of the WTO covered agreements.[100] Apart from 'trade in goods and services, and the commercial aspects of intellectual property', it now also covers 'foreign direct investment'.

In other words, the ECJ has not prevented co-adaptation, but has placed the key to that process in the hands of the political institutions. By successive and varyingly successful amendments of the Treaty, the drafters have shifted the decision back to the Court to 'ensure that in the interpretation and application of the Treaties the law is observed'.[101] That dialectical process has resulted in a constant adaptation to the evolution of the WTO, most recently in the form of Article 207 TFEU.

II. CONCLUSION

At its origin, the Benelux and the ECSC Treaties were somewhat of an experiment in international law; in particular, they tested the GATT 1947's tolerance for selected Contracting Parties' efforts towards integration of a type not made available under the GATT 1947. For example, the establishment of the ECSC required GATT Contracting Parties to agree on a waiver in order to permit the ECSC to be consistent with each of the 6 Member States' obligations under the GATT 1947. That waiver was required because the GATT 1947 did not envisage the type of institution and arrangements created by the 6 Member States. That was no longer the case as regards the EEC Treaty, which established a form of integration more adapted to that foreseen in Article XXIV GATT 1947 and hence no longer required a waiver.

GATT Contracting Parties resolved the consistency of the EEC with Article XXIV through guarantees and assurances that European integration would not adversely affect the interests of GATT Contracting Parties other than the EEC Member States. This pragmatic solution allowed avoiding a formal test of the EEC Treaty against Article XXIV.

[98] Koutrakos, *EU International Relations Law*, 55 and 59.

[99] With the notable exception of transport. Art 207(5) TFEU determines that the negotiation and conclusion of international agreements in the field of transport are to be subject to Title VI of Part Three of the TFEU (on transport) and to Art 218 TFEU.

[100] P-C Müller-Graff, 'The Common Commercial Policy enhanced by the Reform Treaty of Lisbon?' in AA Dashwood and M Maresceau (eds), *Law and Practice of EU External Relations. Salient Features of a Changing Landscape* (Cambridge, Cambridge University Press, 2008) 188; see also Eeckhout, *External Relations*, 54.

[101] Art 19(1) TEU.

The GATT and WTO systems accepted European integration as a fait accompli. From its early inception, however, the GATT system could not ignore the reality of the development of European integration. That reality was visible in different ways. For example, no trade round prior to the conclusion of the creation of the European customs union achieved significant results. As long as EEC Member States had not completed the implementation of their customs union, it was difficult, if not impossible, to determine the trade-offs for a successful multilateral trade negotiation. Also, an informal practice developed by which the EEC, acting on the mandate of the Member States, would brief annually all GATT Contracting Parties on the progress made in building an internal market.[102]

Conversely, the GATT/WTO has affected considerably the allocation of competences between the Union and the Member States, in part because the GATT/WTO was, to a large extent, the first forum in which it was no longer possible to permit Member States to have a separate external voice. Indeed, the expansion of the GATT and the creation of the WTO enabled the ECJ and the other EU institutions to turn the CCP into one of the most effective and powerful parts of EU external relations. However, the Court did not want to be drawn into judicially expanding the scope of the CCP to cover the entire field of WTO law.[103] It left such constitutional evolutions to the political institutions and, ultimately, to the Member States, who finally obliged (for the most part) in Article 207 TFEU. The WTO therefore forces the EU to reflect upon its quasi-federal structure and upon the division of competences between the EU and the Member States.

In sum, both the EU and the WTO show the flexible manner in which international law can adapt to the needs of a specific era. Conceived in the post Second World War period and born in the post Cold War period, both organisations represent the promise of international law to infuse international relations with legal norms and organise it according to the rule of law. There may not be a single model of governance based on international law,[104] nor arguably should there be. Nonetheless, as Crawford has argued, international law may be regarded as 'providing a formal structure, based on sovereignty, negotiation and consensus, in which we are building in a variety of ways'.[105] Both the WTO and the EU have 'sprouted' from that structure, have built on that structure and thereby changed it.

[102] See, eg, L/2179 (12 March 1964); L/2394 (15 March 1965).
[103] Eeckhout, *External Relations*, 55.
[104] As observed by Lamy, 'Global Governance'.
[105] J Crawford, *International Law as an Open System* (London, Cameron May, 2002) 28.

The UN, EU and [illegible] systems ... Europe ... [illegible] from its early operation; however, the [illegible] system could not ignore the reality of the [illegible]

[illegible]

Part VI:

1989–2010: International Law and the Challenges of 2010

25

Prosecuting Environmental Damage under International Criminal Law

MATTHEW GILLETT*

I. INTRODUCTION: ADDING AN EXTRA TOOL TO THE KIT

HUMAN CONFLICT HAS resulted in severe damage to the environment throughout the history of mankind. Over the last two decades, the natural environment has been seriously harmed on a number of occasions, most visibly during the Gulf War in 1991. With technological sophistication developing rapidly, mankind's potential destructiveness continues to increase and the international community is becoming aware of the fragility of the natural habitat. At the same time, the past twenty years have witnessed the remarkable rise of international criminal law. This body of law and practice presents an underexplored vehicle to address environmental damage. The following analysis seeks to highlight the potential, and some of the remaining hurdles, of using international criminal law to prevent and punish serious destruction of the environment.

It should be noted at the outset that international criminal law is not a panacea capable of eliminating the threat of environmental destruction. Indeed, international criminal law is inherently *post hoc*—for a trial to occur the damage must usually have already occurred.[1] Although deterrence is an aim of international criminal law, it goes beyond the core objective of ensuring that perpetrators of atrocities face justice. Accordingly, the aim of this paper is not to shift the focus of the struggle to protect the environment away from political and regulatory solutions. Rather, it is intended to explore ways in which international criminal law can be better used as an additional tool to protect the environment.

* Matthew Gillett is a Legal Officer in the Office of the Prosecutor of the International Criminal Tribunal for the former Yugoslavia. All views expressed herein are those of the author and do not represent those of the Office of the Prosecutor of the International Criminal Tribunal for the former Yugoslavia or the United Nations.

[1] There is a possible exception to this requirement under the mode of liability of attempt, which is included in the Rome Statute of the International Criminal Court, Article 25(3)(f). Given the gravity requirements underlying international criminal law, for example in Article 53 of the Rome Statute, it is unlikely, though not inconceivable, that an individual would be prosecuted for attempt in relation to damage to the environment.

II. TERMINOLOGY AND AMBIT OF THE STUDY

With respect to terminology, two theoretical approaches—anthropocentrism and ecocentrism, are referred to herein. Proponents of the former take an essentially utilitarian view, attributing value to the environment to the extent it serves the interests of humankind.[2] Proponents of the latter view ascribe an intrinsic value to the environment, so that any damage to it is a harm in and of itself, irrespective of whether human beings suffer as a result.[3]

Although the analysis herein focuses on international criminal law, it also uses the term 'law of armed conflict'. The law of armed conflict encompasses international humanitarian law (*jus in bello*), public international law concerning when states may engage in armed conflict (*jus ad bellum*), as well as human rights law applicable in armed conflict. The relationship between the law of armed conflict and environmental law is underexplored. Some guidance can be gleaned from the advisory opinion of the International Court of Justice ('ICJ') on the threat or use of nuclear weapons. It held that neither environmental law nor the law of armed conflict[4] overrides the other. At the same time, it held that environmental law informs the law of armed conflict, particularly in relation to the requirements of proportionality and necessity.[5] As such, the relationship does not fit the simple *lex specialis* model, but rather can be characterised as a dynamic reciprocal interaction.

International criminal law refers to the law, procedures, and institutions connected with the trials of persons accused of the most serious crimes of concern to the international community. The trials typically focus on notorious episodes of criminality, such as in Rwanda, Sierra Leone, ex-Yugoslavia, Cambodia, and East Timor. Various institutions have applied international criminal law over the last two decades, beginning with the International Criminal Tribunal for the former Yugoslavia ('ICTY') and the International Criminal Tribunal for Rwanda ('ICTR') in the early 1990s, following on with the creation of the International Criminal Court ('ICC') in 1998, and most recently featuring the establishment of the Special Tribunal for Lebanon ('STL').

A number of environmental treaties concern species of flora and fauna, the seas, and the atmosphere and require states to criminalise damage to those aspects of the environment.[6] Whilst these conventions fall outside the scope of international criminal

[2] See for example Brigadier-General Joseph G Garrett III, US Army, 'The Army and the Environment: Environmental Considerations during Army Operations' in Richard Grunawalt, John King and Ronald McClain (eds), *Protection of the Environment During Armed Conflict*, International Law Studies, Vol 69 (Naval War College Press, Newport, 1996) 42, 45.

[3] See for example Eric Jensen, 'The International Law of Environmental Warfare: Active and Passive Damage during Armed Conflict' (2005) 38 *Vand J Transnat'l L* 145.

[4] The ICJ referred specifically to *jus ad bellum* but the broader context of its decision has clear implications for *jus in bello* as well; *see* Legality of Threat or Use of Nuclear Weapons, Advisory Opinion, ICJ Reports 1996, 226 ('Advisory Opinion on Nuclear Weapons') para 34.

[5] Advisory Opinion on Nuclear Weapons, paras 30, 33. See also Office of the Prosecutor Press Release, Prosecutor's Report on the NATO Bombing Campaign; The Hague, 13 June 2000, PR/ I.S./ 510-e; Final Report to the Prosecutor by the Committee Established to Review the NATO Bombing Campaign Against the Federal Republic of Yugoslavia ('Final Report on NATO'), available at http://www.icty.org/sid/7846 (last accessed 4 October 2009), para 22. As another example, see the US Commander's Handbook on the Law of Naval Operations, cited in Rymn James Parsons, 'The Fight to Save the Planet: U.S. Armed Forces, "Greenkeeping," and Enforcement of the Law Pertaining to Environmental Protection During Armed Conflict', (1998)10 *Geo. Int'l Envtl L Rev* 441 478.

[6] See, eg, International Convention for the Regulation of Whaling 1946, 161 UNTS 72, TIAS 1849, 62 Stat (2) 1716, 4 Bevans 248, Article IX(3); Convention for the Prevention of Marine Pollution by Dumping from

law in its institutional form (the form of international criminal law examined in this paper),[7] they are also valid mechanisms for addressing serious environmental threats, meriting further development. The difference between those mechanisms and the ones examined in this paper is that whereas the former rely on domestic institutions for investigations and prosecutions, the latter complement domestic prosecutions with international or internationalised judicial bodies, such as the ICC. The mechanisms examined in this paper thus offer the potential added value of the procedures and resources of international institutions acting outside the confines of domestic criminal systems. Although this added value should not be over-exaggerated, it is significant in a number of respects. The ICC, for example, currently has 116 State Parties, which would be required to cooperate with the Court if it issued a warrant of arrest for an individual accused of crimes within the Court's jurisdiction. The added value would be particularly significant where the State, normally exercising jurisdiction, was unable or unwilling to try perpetrators of serious damage to the environment. In such circumstances, the Court would have an independent power to prosecute the perpetrators.

Given the current topography of international criminal law, the present study has a primary, though not exclusive, focus on prosecuting environmental damage through the mechanisms of the ICC. Whereas the other international tribunals and courts are limited to addressing crimes committed in specific geographic and temporal contexts, the ICC has a potentially unlimited temporal and geographic jurisdictional reach.[8] Furthermore, unlike the other courts and tribunals, the ICC is intended to be a permanent court.

III. THE PALTRY RECORD OF PROSECUTIONS UNDER INTERNATIONAL CRIMINAL LAW FOR ENVIRONMENTAL DAMAGE

The issue at the heart of this paper is how best to use international criminal law to address serious environmental damage. This paper does not analyse the anterior question of whether the prosecution of environmental damage should be undertaken at all, but instead proceeds on the basis that the stigma and financial consequences of a conviction make criminal proceedings an effective mechanism to counter and deter environmental destruction.[9]

Surveying the operation of international criminal law shows that it presents a potential, rather than a demonstrated, means of addressing environmental destruction. No individual has yet been convicted within this context of environmental crimes.[10] A small number of cases arising from World War II concerned instances of serious

Ships and Aircraft, 15 February 1972, Article 15(3), UKTS 119, 11 ILM 352; Basel Convention on the Control of Transboundary Movement of Hazardous Wastes and their Disposal, Article 9, 22 March 1989, 28 ILM 657.

[7] Contrast Stephen McCaffrey, 'Criminalisation of Environmental Protection', in Cherif Bassiouni, *International Criminal Law* (3rd edn) (Martinus Nijhoff, Leiden, 2008) Vol I, 1018 (listing eight indicia, the presence of any one of which would qualify an instrument as part of international criminal law).

[8] For example, under Article 13(b) of the Rome Statute, the United Nations Security Council may refer a situation to the Court from any area of the world.

[9] See Stephen McCaffrey, 'Criminalisation of Environmental Protection', in Cherif Bassiouni, *International Criminal Law* (3rd edn) (Martinus Nijhoff, Leiden 2008) Vol I, 1015.

[10] Tara Weinstein, 'Prosecuting Attacks that Destroy the Environment: Environmental Crimes or Humanitarian Atrocities?' (2005) 17 *Geo Int'l Envtl L Rev* 698.

environmental damage. The most notable was that of German General Lothar Rendulic before the International Military Tribunal at Nuremberg. In pursuit of his scorched earth tactics, German troops burnt and destroyed villages and surrounding facilities in the Norwegian province of Finmark when retreating from an advancing Russian army. Rendulic was ultimately acquitted of the charge of wanton destruction, as the Tribunal accepted that he genuinely (though wrongly) perceived the destruction to be militarily justified at the time.[11]

Since Nuremberg, there have been no significant prosecutions under international criminal law for serious damage to the environment. Neither the ICTY nor the ICTR has undertaken such prosecutions.[12] At the International Criminal Court, the charges against Omar Al-Bashir are founded upon the systematic pillaging of villages across a large area.[13] While such destruction is analogous to the widespread destruction discussed in the World War II scorched-earth cases, it is not a direct prosecution for environmental damage.[14]

Given the lack of prosecutions, an immediate question that arises is whether the lack of prosecutions for environmental damage constitutes an enforcement issue rather than a deficit in the existing legal provisions. The International Committee of the Red Cross ('ICRC'), in relation to the suggested creation of a fifth Geneva Convention for the protection of the environment, has taken the position that existing law is largely sufficient to protect the environment and that the issue is rather the enforcement of the law.[15] A symposium of military and academic experts addressing the protection of the

[11] *The Hostages Trial (Wilhelm List and Others)* 8 Law Reports of Trials of War Criminals 66 (1948); Ensign Florencio J Yuzon, 'Deliberate Environmental Modification Through the Use of Chemical and Biological Weapons : "Greening" the International Laws of Armed Conflict to Establish an Environmentally Protective Regime' (1996) 11 *Am U J Int'l L & Pol'y* 793, 815. Another German military officer, Alfred Jodl, was also prosecuted in part for scorched-earth practices in the north of Norway; Trials of War Criminals before the Nuernberg Military Tribunals under Control Council Law No.10, Part XXII, November 1945–October 1946, 568 (1948). In other proceedings, nine German civilian officials in occupied Poland were charged for their 'ruthless exploitation of Polish forestry,' involving the 'wholesale cutting of Polish timber to an extent far in excess of what was necessary to preserve the timber resources of the country'. The Committee of the United Nations War Crimes Commission found that a *prima facie* case of pillage under Article 53 of the Four Geneva Conventions was established and listed the German officials as accused war criminals. History of the United Nations War Crimes Commission and the Development of the Laws of War 496 (Her Majesty's Stationary Office, 1948) (discussing Case No. 7150); cited in Aaron Schwabach, 'Ecocide and Genocide in Iraq: International Law, the Marsh Arabs, and Environmental Damage in Non-International Conflict', (2004) 15 *Colo J Int'l Envtl L & Pol'y* 17.

[12] A committee from the Office of the Prosecutor of the ICTY enquired into the potential criminality of NATO actions during its bombing campaign against the Federal Republic of Yugoslavia in 1999. The Committee found that the NATO bombing campaign did cause damage to the environment, but that the damage did not reach the threshold required by Additional Protocol I. See Final Report on NATO, paras 14, 17.

[13] *Prosecutor v Omar Al Bashir,* Case No.ICC-02/05-01/09, Warrant of Arrest for Omar Hassan Ahmad Al Bashir, 12 July 2010, 5–7.

[14] Although the burning of villages in Darfur is similar in effect to the scorched earth policies inflicted on Norway by the Nazis during World War II, it should be noted that the crime of pillaging technically relates to the appropriation, rather than the destruction, of property; ICC Elements of Crimes, Article 8(2)(e)(v). Other ICC indictees facing charges of pillage and/or destruction of property include Germain 'Simba' Katanga and Mathieu Ngudjolo for crimes committed during the armed conflict in the Democratic Republic of Congo, Jean-Pierre Bemba Gombo for crimes committed in the Central African Republic, Ahmad Muhammad Harun and Ali Muhammad Ali Abd-Al-Rahman for crimes committed in Darfur, Sudan, and Joseph Kony, Vincent Otti, Okot Odhiambo and Dominic Ongwen for crimes committed in Uganda.

[15] Antoine Bouvier, 'Protection of the Environment in Time of Armed Conflict', International Review of the Red Cross no. 285, 567, available at http://www.icrc.org/Web/eng/siteeng0.nsf/html/57JMAU (last access 7 July 2010).

environment during armed conflict and other military operations endorsed the ICRC's position in this respect.[16]

In support of the ICRC position, there are indeed a number of provisions of international humanitarian law prohibiting or limiting the opportunity for environmental destruction. For example, in making military targeting decisions, commanders are required to pay attention to the environment,[17] and reprisals against the environment are prohibited, and thus would not provide any defence to the charge.[18] Moreover, the environment presumptively enjoys protection against intentional attacks on civilian objects.[19] Intentionally attacking the environment would thus violate the principle of distinction. It is also true that the lack of enforcement of environmental prohibitions, and international criminal law in general, is a serious problem.[20] However, it would be unwise to focus only on enforcement and ignore the significant problems remaining in the legal landscape relevant to environmental destruction. Indeed, it is difficult to overcome inadequacies in the law by enforcing those very same inadequate provisions.

IV. THE UNDERDEVELOPMENT OF INTERNATIONAL CRIMINAL LAW WITH RESPECT TO THE ENVIRONMENT

Numerous legal hurdles restrict the efficacy of prosecutions for environmental damage. For a start, there are few environmental provisions that entail criminal responsibility. The primary ecocentric prohibition—against causing widespread, long-term and severe damage to the environment—finds restatement in Article 8(2)(b)(iv) of the Rome Statute of the ICC, which is subject to considerable limitations.

The ICC, despite being the face of the future of international criminal justice, is hampered in its ability to prosecute environmental damage due to significant jurisdictional and operational constraints. Temporally, it cannot prosecute crimes that occurred prior to 1 July 2002. Materially, the crimes that it can prosecute are strictly enumerated and only include one provision (Article 8(2)(b)(iv)) explicitly addressing serious damage to the environment. As its name indicates, that one provision is hedged with qualifications that render it inapplicable to all but the most extreme incidents of environmental destruction. It incorporates a permissive military necessity test and requires a high showing of *mens rea*. Furthermore, the environmental damage has to be committed in an international armed conflict and connected with that armed conflict for liability to arise.[21] Moreover, as a customary rule, the prohibition on causing widespread, long-term, and severe damage to the environment is not considered by the ICRC to apply to nuclear weapons and may not even cover persistent objector states, such as the United States, with respect to conventional weapons.[22] Consequently, international criminal

[16] Parsons, The Fight to Save, 476.

[17] Advisory Opinion on Nuclear Weapons, paras 30–31.

[18] ICJ Legality of Nuclear Weapons, para 30–31.

[19] This is indicated *inter alia* by the placement of Article 55(2) in Additional Protocol 1 under the heading 'civilian objects'.

[20] Note, for example, the still outstanding ICC arrest warrants for *inter alia* Joseph Kony and other leaders of the Lord's Resistance Army in Uganda.

[21] See also Parsons, The Fight to Save, 451.

[22] Jean-Marie Henckaerts, 'Customary International Humanitarian Law: A Response to US Comments' (2007) 89 *Int'l Rev Red Cross* 482. *See also* John Bellinger and William Haynes, 'A US Government Response

law must be further developed in order to realise its potential as a tool for the effective prosecution of environmental destruction.

V. THE USE OF ANTHROPOCENTRIC PROVISIONS TO PROSECUTE ENVIRONMENTAL DAMAGE

Certain commentators have suggested that protecting the environment through international criminal law may be better achieved in the short term by utilising anthropocentric provisions rather than ecocentric provisions. These commentators do not seek to minimise or downplay the serious threat of environmental damage. Rather, they argue that using anthropocentric prohibitions, instead of direct prosecutions under ecocentric provisions, will be a more effective means of curbing serious harm to the environment in the short-term. Proceeding in this manner can be called the bypass approach as it eschews the direct route in favour of an alternative means of preventing and punishing environmental harm.

A leading proponent of this alternative approach, Tara Weinstein, argues that instead of doggedly pursuing direct prosecutions under ecocentric provisions, as an intermediate step 'the international community should focus on prosecuting environmental destruction when conducted to achieve another atrocity, such as genocide or crimes against humanity'.[23] Other authors express similar sentiments.[24] Prosecutions under these alternative provisions would provide litigated documentation of individual criminal culpability for environmental destruction, while at the same time avoiding some of the restrictions inherent in current ecocentric provisions.

A number of benefits would ensue from the bypass approach. First, it would avoid the potentially prohibitive requirement of proving the extent of the environmental damage with scientific certainty. Proving widespread, long-term, and severe damage beyond reasonable doubt would be extremely difficult. Using the prohibitions against wanton destruction (Article 8(2)(a)(iv) for international conflicts) and destruction of property of an adversary (Article 8(2)(e)(xii) applicable in non-international armed conflicts) and inhumane acts (under Article 7(1)(k)) could potentially capture environmentally deleterious conduct without requiring the demonstration of exacting scientific proof. Second, the bypass approach avoids the limitation on its application to international armed conflicts. Neither genocide nor crimes against humanity require a nexus to armed conflict. Third, other criminal provisions do not contain the permissive military expediency test of Article 8(2)(b)(iv), which obliges the prosecution to show that the accused knew or unreasonably dismissed the prospect that the destruction would be 'clearly excessive' in relation to the concrete military advantage anticipated.

The bypass approach is used in other settings.[25] One example is that of using persecution as a crime against humanity to punish the denial of fundamental rights, such as the rights

to the International Committee of the Red Cross Study Customary International Humanitarian Law' (2007) 89 *Int'l Rev Red Cross* 455.

[23] Weinstein, Prosecuting Attacks, 698.

[24] Mohammed Wattad, 'The Rome Statute & Captain Planet: What Lies Between "Crimes Against Humanity" and the "Natural Environment"' (2009) 19 *Fordham Envtl L Rev* 282 ('I argue that damaging the natural environment suits the concept of "crimes against humanity"').

[25] Weinstein, Prosecuting Attacks, 713.

to life, freedom and security of the person.[26] The crime of persecution centres primarily on discrimination against a protected group (political, racial, national, ethnic, cultural, religious, or gender).[27] The prosecution must prove the specific discriminatory intent of the perpetrators. However, the prosecution must also prove the physical component of the crime, which includes human rights violations as well as more tangible crimes, such as murder, torture, and sexual violence. Consequently, the crime of persecution provides a vehicle to punish human rights violations, so long as the prosecution can also show discriminatory intent. In this way human rights violations can be criminally punished, despite the fact that they constitute a harm distinct from, but nonetheless overlapping with, the harm of discrimination on a prohibited basis.[28]

An example of the application of the bypass approach in relation to environmental damage can be found in the charges against Omar Al-Bashir before the ICC.[29] Among the methods that the prosecution accused Al-Bashir of using in his genocidal campaign in Darfur was destroying 'food, wells and water pumping machines, shelter, crops and livestock, as well as any physical structures capable of sustaining life or commerce.'[30] This indicates that the use of environmental destruction to cause serious harm to national, religious, racial or ethnic groups of people (for example through large-scale killing, causing severe mental or physical suffering, inflicting conditions of life on a group of people calculated to bring about its physical destruction in whole or in part, or imposing measures intended to prevent births within the group)[31] may be charged and prosecuted under the rubric of genocide.[32]

In a similar vein, Weinstein suggests that charges of genocide and other crimes against humanity could be used to prosecute the devastating draining of the marshes in southern Iraq in the 1990s. The draining of this 20,000 square kilometre area at the meeting point of the Tigris and Euphrates rivers was accelerated by Saddam Hussein after the Shi'a population's failed uprising against his rule following the 1991 Gulf War. The effects on the ecosystem and the local population were severe. Ninety percent of the marshes dried out by the year 2000 and the number of Marsh Arabs living in the area dropped from over 250,000 in 1990 to 40,000 by 1993.[33] Prosecuting this environmental destruction under anthropocentric provisions would avoid the stringent requirements of proving

[26] See *Prosecutor v Nahimana et al*, Case No.ICTR-99-52-A, Appeal Judgement, 28 November 2007, para 986.

[27] Rome Statute of the ICC, Article 7(1)(h).

[28] In this way, the crime of persecution acts as a bridge between international humanitarian law and human rights law.

[29] Strictly speaking, the ICC uses the term 'document containing the charges' instead of 'indictment', but the latter is used herein for the sake of brevity.

[30] Prosecution's Application under Article 58, ICC-02/05-151-US-Exp and ICC-02/05-151-US-Exp-Anxsl-89; Corrigendum ICC-02/05-151-US-Exp-Corr and Corrigendum ICC-02/05-151-US-Exp-Corr-Anxsl & 2. A public redacted version was filed on 12 September 2008, ICC-02/05-157-AnxA ('Prosecution Application') para 174.

[31] See Rome Statute, Article 6(a), (b), (c) and (d).

[32] The Prosecution would have to prove genocidal intent in connection with these actions. In this respect, it is notable that although the Trial Chamber initially rejected the Prosecution's application for a warrant of arrest on genocide charges, it did so on an incorrect basis and subsequently accepted that Al-Bashir's genocidal intent was a reasonable inference based on the evidence; Second Warrant of Arrest against Omar Hassan Ahmad Al Bashir, ICC-02/05-01/09, 12 July 2010 2009, Pre-Trial Chamber 1; Judgement on the Appeal of the Prosecutor against the 'Decision on the Prosecution's Application for a Warrant of Arrest against Omar Hassan Ahmad Al Bashir', ICC-02/05-01/09-OA, 3 February 2010, Appeals Chamber.

[33] Weinstein, Prosecuting Attacks, 715.

widespread, long-term and severe damage to the environment. It would reduce the need for scientific certainty as to the sufficiently long-term duration of the damage. It would obviate the need to show a connection to an international armed conflict. Perhaps most importantly, it would eliminate the need to show that no reasonable decision-maker could have determined that the damage was not clearly excessive in relation to the anticipated military advantage.[34]

In light of the above considerations, the bypass approach has a number of advantages. Moreover, examples of its potential application are readily identifiable. In that respect, it is a promising means of addressing environmental damage.

VI. THE DISADVANTAGES OF USING ANTHROPOCENTRIC PROVISIONS TO PROSECUTE ENVIRONMENTAL DAMAGE

International criminal law has a strong symbolic component. Prosecuting environmental damage indirectly under anthropocentric provisions may result in convictions of limited symbolic impact vis-à-vis environmental values. The harm to the environment will not be recognised as a wrongful act per se. On the face of the judgment, the sanction imposed will be founded on the anthropocentric harm rather than the ecocentric harm resulting from the perpetrator's actions. From an environmental perspective, this could even be seen as a negative outcome, as it would reinforce the notion that environmental harm is criminal only to the extent that it harms humans and their property and that the environment does not merit the same level of protection that we extend to anthropocentric interests, or indeed any separate protection whatsoever.

The declaratory function of international criminal law as an expression of the international community's opprobrium militates in favour of prosecuting environmental damage under ecocentric provisions rather than indirectly under anthropocentric provisions. In addition to that abstract consideration, there are practical drawbacks to prosecuting environmental damage indirectly under anthropocentric provisions. Prosecutors pursuing the bypass route will be tempted away from proving the extent of the environmental damage. Such damage will be difficult to prove in precise terms with scientific accuracy, a difficulty compounded by the fact that judges in international criminal law, as in domestic law, tend to lack scientific training. This constitutes a strong systemic reinforcement for the traditional approach of introducing evidence of anthropocentric harm, such as murdered and wounded victims, rather than evidence of harm to the environment. A tendency not to introduce evidence of environmental damage will in turn reduce the likelihood of such damage being established and reflected in the judgments of the court, which may even weaken the international community's efforts to prohibit serious damage to the environment.

VII. THE NEED TO DEVELOP INTERNATIONAL CRIMINAL LAW TO ADDRESS ENVIRONMENTAL DAMAGE

While the use of ecocentric provisions and the bypass approach both bear potential, there are serious drawbacks and limitations inherent in these approaches. Consequently,

[34] ibid, 718.

broader measures must also be pursued to enhance the potential of international criminal law to address environmental destruction. One measure would be to focus on better enforcement of environmental protections, including through armed force. Parsons points out that military enforcement of environmental protections (which could be called environmental intervention) has the advantage of being immediate, direct, and compelling.[35] However, military intervention to prevent environmental destruction could well prove self-defeating. Military action almost inevitably causes environmental damage. Using military means is thus likely to perpetuate the very harm that is sought to be avoided. It is also questionable whether armed intervention on an environmentally protective rationale is mandated under *jus ad bellum*. Humanitarian intervention, which is both justified and necessary in qualifying circumstances, generates considerable debate about its legal parameters. Military intervention to protect the environment raises even more complex legal and political questions.

Of more pressing urgency is the need to develop international criminal law to include robust ecocentric provisions. Given the prevalence of environmental destruction, such provisions should not be limited to the most extreme examples of intentional environmental damage. Instead the provisions should extend the coverage of international criminal law so that it concretises the requirement to take environmental considerations into account in assessing necessity and proportionality, and criminalises the conscious failure to do so. The environmental component inherent in the obligations of necessity and proportionality has been recognized by the ICJ, as discussed above. Accordingly, there is a basis for developing international criminal law to apply to breaches of these requirements, at least in the case of manifest breaches resulting in serious harm to the environment. An example would be military operations undertaken in conscious disregard of the environmental impact thereof, which could have been avoided by the use of alternative means available to the perpetrator at the time. Incorporating such criminal prohibitions would be consistent with international environmental law principles and with international and domestic criminal law principles.

An intermediary step towards protecting the environment under international criminal law would be to extend the prohibition against causing long-term, widespread, and severe damage to the environment to apply during non-international armed conflicts. Currently, the relevant provision (Article 8(2)(b)(iv) of the Rome Statute) applies only to inter-State conflicts, which excludes coverage of the most prevalent form of conflicts in the post Cold-War world, non-international armed conflicts. The introduction of a parallel provision covering non-international armed conflicts could be carried out at the next review conference of the ICC. At the 2010 ICC Review Conference in Kampala the Court's jurisdiction was extended to cover crimes of using various prohibited weapons in non-international armed conflicts in addition to the Court's pre-existing jurisdiction over such crimes in international armed conflicts under Article 8.[36] This provides a template for incrementally enhancing the Court's ability to address serious harm to the environment. An extension of the Court's jurisdiction over environmental crimes would raise issues concerning the status under customary international law of the prohibition

[35] See for example Parsons, The Fight to Save, 495 ('Whatever cautions may be raised against the use of armed force as a mechanism for enforcement of the law pertaining to environmental protection during armed conflict, few enforcement tools are more immediate, direct and compelling than armed force.')

[36] See 'Draft resolution amending Article 8 of the Rome Statute', ICC Review Conference Document: RC/WGOA/1/Rev.2, 4 June 2010.

in the context of non-international armed conflicts.[37] In this respect, the adoption of such an amendment, signaling the willingness of over 100 states to criminalise serious damage to the environment in non-international armed conflicts, would constitute a strong indication that the prohibition had crystallised as a principle of customary international law.

As stated above, environmental damage committed outside of armed conflict is not subject to any direct criminal sanction under international criminal law.[38] The resulting question is whether crimes against the environment, should be established as a distinct, free-standing category of international criminal law. Crimes against the environment would have to be part of a widespread or systematic attack directed against the environment. The underlying acts could encompass, for example, reckless misconduct at nuclear power facilities;[39] testing biological weapons; intentional dumping of oil or chemical waste at sea; trade in endangered species, hazardous wastes or ozone-depleting substances; and intentional large-scale and illegal carbon emissions.[40] These prohibitions would remain in effect outside of armed conflict. Whilst this development remains a normative aspiration at the moment, models for such a category of crimes exist, for example the crime of ecocide, which appears in domestic penal codes ranging from Russia to Vietnam.[41] Establishing a category of crimes against the environment would be a proactive move in the struggle to protect the environment and to preserve intergenerational equity.[42]

The necessity of developing international criminal law to address serious damage to the environment is consistent with the principles set out in the Rio Declaration.[43] These guiding principles indicate that states must cooperate to take active measures to protect the environment. Preventing serious damage to the environment is necessary not only to prevent warfare and other harm to human interests but also because such environmental devastation is wrong per se. Although international criminal law is not a panacea to the problem, it is an additional mechanism available to the international community. If developed and used effectively, international criminal law could have a significant impact on the protection of the environment in times of war and peace.

[37] See Jean-Marie Henckaerts and Louise Doswald-Beck (eds) *Customary International Humanitarian Law*, (ICRC, Geneva, 2005) 151 ('State practice establishes this rule as a norm of customary international law applicable in international, and arguably also in non-international, armed conflicts.' Note that the rule formulated by the ICRC differs from that in Article 8(2)(b)(iv) of the Rome Statute as it does not contain a military necessity clause). But see John Bellinger and William Haynes, 'A US Government Response to the International Committee of the Red Cross Study Customary International Humanitarian Law' (2007) 89 *Int'l Rev Red Cross* 460.

[38] With the possible exception that it could be included within the crime of humanity of causing great suffering under Article 7(1)(k) of the Rome Statute.

[39] Timothy Schofield, 'The Environment as an Ideological Weapon: A Proposal to Criminalise Environmental Terrorism' (1998–1999) 26 *B C Envtl Aff L Rev* 622, 626.

[40] See Mark Drumbl, 'International Human Rights, International Humanitarian Law, and Environmental Security: Can the International Criminal Court Bridge the Gaps?' (2000) 6 *ILSA J Int'l & Com L* 325.

[41] See Jean-Marie Henckaerts and Louise Doswald-Beck (eds), *Customary International Humanitarian Law*, (ICRC, Geneva, 2005) Vol.II, 883.

[42] In this respect, crimes against the environment share a common rationale with crimes against future generations. As the world becomes increasingly aware of this pressing rationale, these two related forms of categorising wrongful conduct will develop and coalesce in a mutually re-enforcing manner.

[43] Principle 13 of the Rio Declaration on Environment and Development, A/CONF.151/26, 14 June 1992 requires that, 'States shall develop national law regarding liability and compensation for the victims of pollution and other environmental damage. States shall also cooperate in an expeditious and more determined manner to develop further international law regarding liability and compensation for adverse effects of environmental damage caused by activities within their jurisdiction or control to areas beyond their jurisdiction.'

26

La Convention d'Århus: 'Avancée Majeure du Droit International'?

CHRISTINE LARSSEN*

I. INTRODUCTION

LA CONVENTION D'ÅRHUS[1] du 25 juin 1998 sur l'accès à l'information, la participation du public au processus décisionnel et l'accès à la justice en matière d'environnement organise un système participatif dans lequel trois procéduraux contribueraient à garantir un droit à l'environnement. Grâce à ce système participatif en matière d'environnement, destiné à renforcer la démocratie, la convention d'Århus constituerait, selon ses Parties, 'l'initiative la plus ambitieuse jamais prise en matière de *démocratie environnementale*'[2], représentant, à ce titre, une 'avancée majeure du droit international'[3].

La convention d'Århus est née dans le contexte de démocratisation et de *greening*[4] suite à la chute du mur de Berlin fin 1989. Depuis l'adoption de la convention, son système participatif a amplement servi de modèle de démocratisation, au niveau de la région paneuropéenne comme au-delà de cette région. Actuellement, le système est en voie de s'étendre aux quatre coins de la planète, sans que sa qualité 'd'avancée majeure du droit international' ne soit interrogée.

Le thème de la Conférence nous a inspiré à relever ce défi.

La convention d'Århus représenterait donc une 'avancée majeure du droit international' en raison de sa qualité de 'démocratie environnementale'. Un système qui se veut démocratique, qui entend organiser le règne du *dêmos*, se doit d'assurer que l'ensemble du *dêmos* y soit inclus[5]. Par conséquent, afin de constituer une 'avancée majeure du droit

* Centre de Droit International, Université Libre de Bruxelles. La documentation est arrêtée au 29 sept. 2010.

[1] La ville danoise d'Århus fut anciennement écrite 'Aarhus'. Comme c'est souvent cette dernière orthographe qui est employée dans les documents relatifs à la convention, le lecteur trouvera ici les deux orthographes.

[2] Déclaration de Lucques, adoptée à la première session de la Réunion des Parties à la convention d'Århus, tenue à Lucques (Italie) 21-23 oct. 2002 (ECE/MP.PP/2/Add.1, 2 avr. 2004), par. 4 (**gras d'origine**).

[3] *Ibid.*

[4] Le terme *greening*—désignant l'ensemble des mesures (économiques, politiques, juridiques) destinées à incorporer des considérations environnementales—ne trouve pas de correspondant harmonisé en français. Comme nous ne souhaitons pas employer les expressions peu élégantes de 'verdisation', 'verdoiement', ou autre 'verdissement', nous utiliserons le terme *greening*.

[5] Soit directement, soit par représentation organisée (comme dans la démocratie représentative).

international', le système participatif de la convention devrait être configuré de manière telle que l'ensemble du *dêmos* y ait véritablement accès.

Conceptualisée sur la base de 'l'arbre participatif' en annexe, l'analyse retracera d'abord les racines porteuses du système participatif de la convention (II), fournira ensuite une vue générale de ce système et de son rayonnement international (III), pour enfin interroger qui pourra grimper 'l'arbre participatif' (IV).

II. RACINES PORTEUSES DU SYSTÈME PARTICIPATIF DE LA CONVENTION D'ÅRHUS

Le système participatif de la convention d'Århus éclot dans le cadre des travaux de démocratisation et de *greening* entrepris dans la région paneuropéenne suite à la chute du mur de Berlin fin 1989—cadre qui constituera notre contexte de référence.

Deux instances internationales de composition quasi identique[6] préparent, ensemble, le terrain pour la convention: la Commission Economique pour l'Europe des Nations Unies (CEE/ONU)—au sein de laquelle la convention est adoptée—et la Conférence sur la Sécurité et la Coopération en Europe (CSCE). Ces deux instances développent un *modus operandi* que notre contexte de référence symbolise tout particulièrement: la CSCE, instance diplomatique, gère les négociations politiques, la CEE/ONU conclut ce travail de fond et le coule en une forme juridique[7]. Il convient donc d'avoir spécialement égard aux travaux de la CSCE pour identifier les racines, quant au fond, du système participatif de la convention d'Århus.

La CSCE, œuvrant intensément pour l'instauration de *la* démocratie dans la région de l'ex-URSS, ne précise pas quelle vision de la démocratie elle considère comme équivalente à *la* démocratie. D'après l'examen des documents pertinents, *la* démocratie implique avant tout, selon la CSCE, la garantie de droits et libertés tendant à assurer la liberté individuelle, avec un accent particulier sur la liberté d'expression[8]. La liberté d'expression étant centrale au système participatif—la participation directe du public aux débats publics n'ayant de sens que si les participants peuvent s'exprimer librement—cette liberté constitue l'une des racines porteuses de 'l'arbre participatif'.

L'ampleur et la gravité de la pollution dans la région de l'ancien bloc de l'Est éclatent au grand jour avec l'effondrement de l'URSS. Une association 'secret / problèmes environnementaux', et son contraire: 'transparence / protection de l'environnement', s'en

[6] La CSCE et la CEE/ONU sont à l'origine composées principalement de pays de l'Europe de l'Ouest, des Etats-Unis et du Canada, ainsi que de l'URSS. Suite à la dissolution de l'URSS, les instances intègrent toutes deux les pays de l'ex-URSS, ainsi que les anciens 'satellites' de l'URSS (les démocraties populaires). Les seules différences dans la composition des deux instances dans notre contexte de référence sont les suivantes:

- le Saint Siège participe aux travaux de la CSCE, mais n'est pas membre de la CEE/ONU; et
- Israël, temporairement admis à la CEE/ONU le 26 juill. 1991 (cf. rés. ECOSOC 1991/72), ne participe pas aux travaux de la CSCE.

[7] En effet, en matière d'environnement: 'much of the political impetus [for the environmental law of the UNECE] has come from the Organization for Security and Cooperation in Europe (OSCE). It is this organization which has been the principal catalyst for environmental lawmaking by the [UNECE]' (P. Birnie, A. Boyle, C. Redgwell, *International Law and the Environment*, 3ème éd. (OUP, 2009) 72).

[8] Cf. document de la réunion de Copenhague de la Conférence sur la dimension humaine de la CSCE, juin 1990, par. 5.1, 9.1, 10.1 et 26; document de la réunion de Moscou de la Conférence sur la dimension humaine de la CSCE, oct. 1991, par. 26 et 28.9; rapport du séminaire d'experts de la CSCE sur les institutions démocratiques tenu à Oslo nov. 1991, 10.

trouvent consolidés. Grâce à la transparence environnementale, les autorités publiques, amenées à rendre des comptes sur leur manière de gérer l'environnement, agiraient dans un sens plus favorable à l'environnement[9]. Un public informé serait sensibilisé aux problèmes environnementaux, ce qui l'inciterait à vouloir participer activement à la protection de l'environnement, à deux niveaux: d'une part, un public informé adopterait un comportement plus respectueux de l'environnement, participant concrètement à la protection de l'environnement; d'autre part, un public informé serait susceptible de vouloir prendre une part directe à la gestion de l'environnement, participant politiquement à la protection de l'environnement.

Parallèlement aux travaux de démocratisation dans notre contexte de référence, le *greening* y prend ainsi une orientation participative: de nombreuses mesures tendant à assurer la transparence environnementale et la participation directe du public à la gestion de l'environnement, notamment de la CSCE[10], y voient le jour.

Au niveau mondial, le principe 10 de la déclaration de Rio du 14 juin 1992 sur l'environnement et le développement[11] prévoit que '[l]a meilleure façon de traiter les questions d'environnement est d'assurer la participation de tous les citoyens concernés, au niveau qui convient'. Le principe énonce ensuite un triptyque procédural en matière d'environnement, destiné à permettre au public[12] de prendre directement part à l'action publique en la matière:

- l'accès à l'information relative à l'environnement;
- la participation au processus décisionnel relatif à l'environnement; et
- l'accès à la justice en matière d'environnement.

Le triptyque procédural du principe 10 permet de conceptualiser et d'articuler les diverses mesures participatives que l'on trouve dans la région paneuropéenne au début des années 90, tout en insufflant un nouvel élan politique à ces mesures.

L'impulsion ainsi donnée par le principe 10 est tout particulièrement explorée par la CEE/ONU, notamment sous l'influence de la CSCE. D'une part, la CEE/ONU élabore, entre autres à partir des travaux de la CSCE, plusieurs projets participatifs détaillant l'ensemble du triptyque procédural[13]. Si ces projets ne sont pas officiellement adoptés, ils servent ultérieurement de sources d'inspiration pour le développement du système

[9] Cf., ex., l'al. 10 du préambule de la convention d'Århus.

[10] Notons en particulier la réunion sur la protection de l'environnement de la CSCE, tenue à Sofia (Bulgarie), 16 oct. - 3 nov. 1989, dont le rapport (p. 2) insiste aussi bien sur la transparence environnementale que sur la participation directe du public à la gestion de l'environnement. Précisons que, si la réunion de Sofia a bien lieu (quelques jours) avant la chute du mur de Berlin, le rapport de la réunion est adopté après ladite chute (le 5 nov. 1990). Pour les mesures participatives contemporaines d'autres instances (pan)européennes, consulter M. Déjeant-Pons, 'Le droit de l'homme à l'environnement en tant que droit procédural', in M. Déjeant-Pons et M. Pallemaerts, *Droits de l'homme et environnement* (Strasbourg, Conseil de l'Europe, 2002) 21.

[11] Déclaration issue de la Conférence des Nations Unies sur l'Environnement et le Développement (CNUED), tenue à Rio de Janeiro (Brésil) en juin 1992. Sur la CNUED, couramment dénommée la 'conférence de Rio', lire M. Pallemaerts, 'La conférence de Rio: grandeur ou décadence du droit international de l'environnement?' (1995) *R.B.D.I.*, 175.

[12] Ou, selon le cas, 'l'individu'. Le principe 10 comporte donc trois cercles de bénéficiaires de son triptyque procédural: les 'citoyens concernés', le 'public', et 'l'individu'. Cette fluctuation du cercle des bénéficiaires du triptyque procédural du principe 10 n'a certainement pas aidé à éviter l'indétermination du cercle des bénéficiaires du système participatif de la convention d'Århus (cf. plus loin).

[13] Ainsi, un projet de charte de la CEE/ONU, du 31 oct. 1990, sur les droits et obligations en matière d'environnement—organisant l'ensemble des thèmes régis par la convention d'Århus—cite en son Annexe, parmi les sources l'ayant inspiré, le rapport de la réunion de Sofia 1989 sur la protection de l'environnement de la CSCE.

participatif de la convention d'Århus[14]. D'autre part, la CEE/ONU inclut deux des trois branches du triptyque dans son dispositif juridique environnemental : dans la convention d'Espoo du 25 février 1991 sur l'évaluation de l'impact sur l'environnement dans un contexte transfrontière, qui contient plusieurs dispositions réglant l'accès à l'information[15] et la participation du public[16] ; dans deux conventions d'Helsinki du 17 mars 1992—la convention sur les effets transfrontières des accidents industriels et la convention sur la protection et l'utilisation des cours d'eau transfrontières et des lacs internationaux—qui comportent des dispositions tendant à informer et à impliquer directement le public dans la gestion des domaines qu'elles couvrent[17]. La convention d'Århus 'tient compte'[18] des dispositions 'pertinentes'—lire participatives—de ces trois conventions, dont deux sont explicitement développées suite aux instructions de la CSCE[19].

Nous avons ainsi identifié trois racines porteuses de 'l'arbre participatif': la liberté d'expression, la transparence et la participation du public. Et nous avons établi que les travaux de la CSCE en constituent une source fondamentale.

III. VUE GÉNÉRALE DU SYSTÈME PARTICIPATIF DE LA CONVENTION D'ÅRHUS ET DE SON RAYONNEMENT INTERNATIONAL

A. Vue Générale du Système Participatif de la Convention

La convention sur l'accès à l'information, la participation du public au processus décisionnel et l'accès à la justice en matière d'environnement est adoptée à l'issue de la 4ème conférence 'Un environnement pour l'Europe', tenue à Århus (Danemark) du 23 au 25 juin 1998. La plupart des pays membres de la CEE/ONU—à l'exception, notamment, du Canada, de la Russie, et des Etats-Unis—ainsi que la Communauté européenne, signent la convention[20]. La convention d'Århus est entrée en vigueur le 30 octobre 2001. Actuellement, la convention compte 43 Parties : la grande majorité des Etats membres de la CEE/ONU et l'Union européenne.

Dans la lignée des activités de démocratisation et de *greening* exposées à la section précédente, la convention d'Århus poursuit un double objectif: renforcer *la* démocratie et protéger un droit à l'environnement. L'objectif de renforcement de *la* démocratie est formulé dans le préambule[21], tandis que l'objectif de protection d'un droit à

[14] Ce que confirme le guide d'application de la convention d'Århus (*La convention d'Aarhus. Guide d'application* (New York et Genève, Nations unies, 2000) 4).

[15] Art. 3, §8 de la convention d'Espoo.

[16] Art. 4, §2 de la convention d'Espoo (v. ég. art. 2, §2; 2, §6; 3, §8; 6, §1er de la convention).

[17] Cf. art. 9, §§ 1er et 2 de la convention sur les effets transfrontières des accidents industriels ; art. 16, §1er de la convention sur la protection et l'utilisation des cours d'eau transfrontières et des lacs internationaux.

[18] Préambule, al. 23.

[19] Consulter le rapport de la réunion de Sofia 1989 sur la protection de l'environnement de la CSCE, 4-7 et 10-13.

[20] La liste des signataires de la convention est annexée (Annexe VII) au rapport de la conférence d'Århus (rapport de la quatrième conférence ministérielle 'Un environnement pour l'Europe', tenue à Århus (Danemark) 23-25 juin 1998, ECE/CEP/41). Quelques pays ont adhéré ou accédé à la convention par la suite (mais non pas ceux notés dans le corps du texte). La plupart des documents directement pertinents pour la convention d'Århus que nous citons peuvent être téléchargés du site web de la convention (www.unece.org/env/pp). Pour les documents qui n'y sont plus disponibles (le site web ayant fait l'objet de mises à jour), et qui ne peuvent être obtenus d'ailleurs, le lecteur pourra contacter l'auteure du chapitre (clarssen@ulb.ac.be).

[21] Al. 21.

l'environnement est énoncé dans le dispositif, l'article 1er imposant à chaque Partie de garantir les trois droits procéduraux du public en matière d'environnement conformément aux dispositions de la convention, afin de contribuer à protéger 'le droit de chacun, dans les générations présentes et futures, de vivre dans un environnement propre à assurer sa santé et son bien-être'.

Nous ne pouvons ici présenter l'ensemble des éléments du système participatif, prolixe, de la convention[22]. Mais, pour la suite de l'exposé, pointons quelques grandes lignes du système.

La convention distingue le 'public' du 'public concerné'. En vertu de l'article 2, §4 de la convention, le 'public' désigne 'une ou plusieurs personnes physiques ou morales et, conformément à la législation ou à la coutume du pays, les associations, organisations ou groupes constitués par ces personnes'. Au vu de cette définition large, nous considérons que le 'public' au sens de la convention équivaut au *dêmos* (dont il sera question à la section suivante). L'article 2, §5 de la convention définit le 'public concerné' comme 'le public qui est touché ou qui risque d'être touché par les décisions prises en matière d'environnement ou qui a un intérêt à faire valoir à l'égard du processus décisionnel'. Les ONG environnementales remplissant les conditions pouvant être requises en droit interne sont présumées être membres du 'public concerné'.

Le système participatif de la convention est composé de trois piliers: l'accès à l'information, la participation du public, et l'accès à la justice. L'accès à l'information comprend une branche 'passive' (accès sur demande) et une branche 'active' (diffusion spontanée d'informations par les autorités publiques). La participation du public au processus décisionnel est prévue à trois niveaux: dans le cadre de la prise de décisions relatives à des activités particulières pouvant avoir un effet important sur l'environnement; à l'occasion de l'élaboration des plans, programmes et politiques relatifs à l'environnement; et durant la phase d'élaboration de dispositions réglementaires et/ou [sic] d'instruments normatifs juridiquement contraignants d'application générale pouvant avoir un effet important sur l'environnement. L'accès à la justice en matière d'environnement est organisé dans trois hypothèses. Les deux premières hypothèses de recours entendent, respectivement, garantir l'effectivité des deux autres piliers (information et participation), tandis que la dernière hypothèse de recours est destinée à garantir l'effectivité du droit sectoriel de l'environnement.

B. Rayonnement International du Système Participatif de la Convention

Le système participatif de la convention d'Århus connaît un rayonnement international spectaculaire, tant dans le cadre de la CEE/ONU, qu'au-delà de ce cadre.

Comme nous l'avons vu, les éléments participatifs du dispositif juridique environnemental existant de la CEE/ONU inspirèrent le système participatif de la convention d'Århus. Par ricochet, le système participatif de la convention d'Århus déteint sur ses prédécesseurs. En raison de la parenté participative entre la convention d'Århus et

[22] Le lecteur trouvera davantage de détails sur le système participatif de la convention d'Århus dans nos contributions y relatives (pour une analyse fouillée et globale : 'Het Verdrag van Aarhus en de toepassing ervan in het Belgisch recht' (2005) *Tijdschrift voor Milieurecht*, 244 (I) et 474 (II)).

la convention d'Espoo[23], cette dernière a fait l'objet de la 'mise à jour'[24] la plus saillante[25] depuis l'adoption de la convention d'Århus: un protocole et deux amendements à la convention d'Espoo furent adoptés[26], afin de 'tirer parti des acquis et des nouvelles idées exprimées dans la Convention d'Aarhus'[27].

Estimant que 'the Aarhus Convention provides the OSCE with a unique tool to support environmental governance processes at the national level which in turn contributes to the countries' efforts in addressing environment and security challenges'[28], l'organisation succédant à la CSCE, l'Organisation pour la Sécurité et la Coopération en Europe (OSCE), promeut intensément le système participatif de la convention d'Århus dans la région paneuropéenne, notamment dans le cadre de l'*Environment and Security Initiative* (ENVSEC)[29].

L'article 19, §3 de la convention offre la possibilité à tout Etat membre de l'ONU, non membre de la CEE/ONU, d'adhérer à la convention, moyennent l'accord de la Réunion des Parties. Cette possibilité sera peut-être explorée dans le cadre de la mise en œuvre des lignes directrices du PNUE (cf. ci-après). Notons le rayonnement mondial[30] du système

[23] Parenté qui 'tient au lien fondamental entre l'évaluation de l'impact sur l'environnement (EIE) et la participation du public à la prise de décisions en matière d'environnement' (Analyse des liens existant entre la convention d'Aarhus et les autres conventions et protocoles de la CEE relatifs à l'environnement (MP. PP/2002/19, CEP/2002/14, 18 sept. 2002)—'analyse des liens'—par. 51).

[24] Analyse des liens, par. 62 et 109.

[25] En sus de la 'mise à jour' de la convention d'Espoo, mentionnons le protocole sur l'eau et la santé à la convention d'Helsinki du 17 mars 1992 sur la protection et l'utilisation des cours d'eau transfrontières et des lacs internationaux, du 17 juin 1999 (entré en vigueur le 4 août 2005).

[26] Ainsi:

– un protocole relatif à l'évaluation de l'impact sur l'environnement des décisions stratégiques est adopté, le 21 mai 2003, à la 5ème conférence ministérielle 'Un environnement pour l'Europe' (Kiev, mai 2003). Le protocole—qui organise la participation du public (concerné) à l'évaluation stratégique environnementale de plans et programmes susceptibles d'avoir des effets notables sur l'environnement, y compris sur la santé—est entré en vigueur le 11 juill. 2010;

– un premier amendement de la convention d'Espoo précise, comme la convention d'Århus (cf. plus haut), que le 'public' englobe les groupements de personnes, et prévoit, à l'instar de la convention d'Århus (cf. plus loin), qu'un Etat membre de l'ONU qui n'appartient pas à la région de la CEE/ONU peut adhérer à la convention avec l'accord de la Réunion des Parties. Cet amendement n'est pas encore en vigueur;

– un deuxième amendement de la convention d'Espoo établit une procédure d'examen du respect des dispositions similaire aux 'arrangements' prévus à l'art. 15 de la convention d'Århus. Cet amendement n'est pas non plus en vigueur.

Les textes précités sont disponibles à partir du site web de la convention d'Espoo (www.unece.org/env/eia).

[27] Analyse des liens, par. 62.

[28] Aarhus Centres. Platforms for Co-operation, Participation, Partnership, brochure de l'OSCE (www.osce.org/publications/eea/2008/06/31611_1163_en.pdf, non disponible en français) 2.

[29] ENVSEC, qui couvre l'Asie Centrale, le Caucase du Sud, l'Europe du Sud-Est et de l'Est, et les Balkans, a pour objet d'identifier les liens entre les problèmes environnementaux majeurs transfrontières et les problèmes sécuritaires potentiels. La CEE/ONU est membre d'ENVSEC (cf. www.envsec.org/about.php). Sur l'action de fond d'ENVSEC lire, en sus des informations et documents disponibles sur son site web (www.envsec.org), B. Snoy et M. Baltes, 'Environmental Security: A Key Challenge for the OSCE', *OSCE Yearbook 2007*, Institute for Peace Research and Security Policy at the University of Hamburg / IFSH, Nomos, 316 et s. L'OSCE a not. établi des 'centres Århus' dans les pays de la région couverte par ENVSEC. Comme l'explique l'OSCE sur sa page web dédiée à la convention d'Århus (www.osce.org/eea/13471.html), les 'centres Århus' 'serve as a link between the Government and non-governmental organizations (NGOs) in environmental policy-making and implementation. They also provide a platform for coalition-building and partnership among NGOs in addressing environmental issues. These Centres have been very active in promoting the Aarhus Convention principles at national and local levels'. D'après la page web citée, il y avait, au 30 janv. 2010, 30 'centres Århus' répartis en Albanie, Arménie, Azerbaïdjan, Biélorussie, Géorgie, Kazakhstan, Kirghizistan, Serbie et Tadjikistan.

[30] Nous ne pouvons, dans les limites du présent chapitre, présenter le rayonnement régional du système participatif. Lire, à ce sujet, M. Pallemaerts, 'The Århus Convention on Access to Information, Public Participation

participatif par le biais de lignes directrices promouvant, respectivement, l'application des principes de la convention d'Århus dans les instances internationales, et l'application mondiale du principe 10 de la déclaration de Rio.

Sur la base de l'article 3, §7 de la convention[31], la Réunion des Parties a adopté des lignes directrices 'sur les moyens de promouvoir l'application des principes de la convention d'Aarhus dans les instances internationales'—couramment dénommées 'lignes directrices d'Almaty'[32]. Les 'instances internationales' énumérées par les lignes directrices sont largement conçues[33]. De plus, les lignes directrices énoncent qu'elles s'appliquent à 'toutes les étapes internationales de tout processus décisionnel pertinent relatif aux questions d'environnement'[34]. Ne définissant ni la notion 'd'environnement',[35] ni la notion de processus décisionnel 'relatif' aux questions d'environnement, les lignes directrices d'Almaty illustrent à la fois les contours indéterminés du système participatif de la convention (cf. plus loin) et les velléités expansionnistes des partisans du système.[36] Constituant, selon le Secrétaire général des Nations Unies, 'la concrétisation de loin la plus remarquable du principe 10 de la Déclaration de Rio', la convention d'Århus serait 'un instrument de portée régionale [revêtant] une importance mondiale'—et pourrait, à ce titre, 'servir de modèle pour renforcer l'application du principe 10 dans d'autres régions du monde'[37]. Dans cet esprit, et comme nous le verrons, l'influence du système participatif de la convention sur les travaux du PNUE transparaît clairement des lignes directrices (dites 'directives') du PNUE 'pour l'élaboration d'une législation nationale sur l'accès à l'information, la participation du public et l'accès à la justice dans le domaine de l'environnement'[38], destinées à renforcer l'application mondiale du principe 10 de la déclaration de Rio.

Avant que le système participatif de la convention ne s'étende davantage sans interrogation, pointons—dans un esprit véritablement participatif et démocratique—de sérieuses difficultés du système.

in Decision-Making and Access to Justice in Environmental Matters: Engaging the Disenfranchised through the Institutionalization of Procedural Rights?', in J. C. Green & W. B. Chambers (eds.) *The Politics of Participation in Sustainable Development Governance*, (Tokyo & New York, United Nations University Press, 2006) 179; Governing Council of the United Nations Environment Programme, International legal instruments reflecting provisions contained in principle 10 of the Rio Declaration on environment and development, Report presented by the secretariat, (UNEP/GCSS.VII/INF/7, 5 February 2002—uniquement disponible en anglais), 12 et s.

[31] 'Chaque Partie œuvre en faveur de l'application des principes énoncés dans la présente Convention dans les processus décisionnels internationaux touchant [à] l'environnement ainsi que dans le cadre des organisations internationales lorsqu'il y est question d'environnement'.

[32] Les lignes directrices sont annexées à la décision n° II/4, Promouvoir l'application des principes de la convention d'Aarhus dans les instances internationales, adoptée à la deuxième session de la Réunion des Parties à la convention, tenue à Almaty (Kazakhstan), 25–27 mai 2005, (ECE/MP.PP/2005/2/Add.5, 20 juin 2005).

[33] Consulter par. 4 des lignes directrices.

[34] Par. 5 des lignes directrices.

[35] Notion qui n'est pas non plus définie par la convention d'Århus.

[36] Velléités abondamment exprimées par les partisans du système participatif de la convention d'Århus, dans de nombreux contextes. Concernant les velléités expansionnistes des Parties à la convention, consulter not. la déclaration de Riga, adoptée à la troisième session de la Réunion des Parties, tenue à Riga (Lettonie) 11-13 juin 2008, (ECE/MP.PP/2008/2/Add.1, 26 sept. 2008), par. 17 et 24.

[37] Guide d'application de la convention d'Århus, avant-propos de M. Kofi Annan, v.

[38] Conseil d'administration du Programme des Nations Unies pour l'environnement, Compte rendu du Conseil d'administration/Forum ministériel mondial sur l'environnement sur les travaux de sa onzième session extraordinaire, Bali (Indonésie), 24-26 février 2010 (UNEP/GCSS.XI.11, 3 mars 2010), Annexe I, Décisions adoptées par le Conseil d'administration/Forum ministériel mondial sur l'environnement à sa onzième session extraordinaire, SS.XI/5: Droit de l'environnement, A.

IV. QUI POURRA GRIMPER 'L'ARBRE PARTICIPATIF'?

Nous le savons : la convention d'Århus représenterait une 'avancée majeure du droit international' en raison de sa qualité de 'démocratie environnementale'.

Démocratie signifie le règne (*kratia*) du peuple (*dêmos*). Partant, afin que la convention constitue véritablement une 'avancée majeure du droit international', l'ensemble du *dêmos* devrait avoir accès à son système participatif.

La notion d'accès, centrale au système participatif[39], sera donc notre pierre angulaire: pour répondre à la question de la présente section, nous examinerons successivement l'accès théorique (A.) et l'accès concret (B.) du *dêmos* au système participatif de la convention d'Århus.

L'examen qui suit se concentre sur le cœur du système participatif, la participation du public au processus décisionnel, et spécialement sur l'article 6 de la convention, organisant la participation du public aux décisions relatives à des activités particulières pouvant avoir un effet important sur l'environnement. L'article 6—disposition centrale du système participatif—permet en effet tout particulièrement d'illustrer notre propos. Les considérations émises concernant l'article 6 sont, *mutatis mutandis* et *grosso modo*[40], valables pour le système dans son ensemble.

A. Accès Théorique du *Dêmos* au Système Participatif de la Convention d'Århus

Lorsqu'il s'agit de déterminer qui a le droit de participer au processus décisionnel en application de son article 6, la convention fait état du 'public'[41], consacrant donc, théoriquement, le principe de l'ouverture à quiconque de la procédure de participation considérée, sans qu'un intérêt particulier ne soit requis.

Or, l'accès théorique de l'ensemble du *dêmos* à un système qui entend renforcer la démocratie, aussi nécessaire soit-il, n'est pas suffisant: encore faut-il que le système soit configuré de manière telle que l'ensemble du *dêmos* y ait concrètement accès. L'article 6, §3 de la convention insiste bien sur l'importance d'assurer l'effectivité des droits participatifs du *dêmos* dans son ensemble:

[39] Comme en témoigne l'intitulé de la convention.

[40] Nous ne pouvons exposer ici les nuances. Signalons tout au plus que les auteurs du système participatif ont eu à l'esprit un *dêmos* bien fluctuant, la convention (préambule ou dispositif) faisant référence:

- à 'l'homme';
- à 'chacun, y compris dans les générations présentes et futures';
- aux 'citoyens';
- au 'public';
- au 'grand public';
- au 'public concerné';
- aux 'consommateurs';
- aux 'personnes';
- à 'toute personne';
- au 'public susceptible de participer';
- aux 'organes consultatifs « représentatifs »' (la convention d'Århus ne comportant aucun élément permettant de garantir la représentativité de ces organes); ou encore
- aux 'membres du public qui répondent aux critères éventuels prévus par le droit interne d'une Partie'.

Parmi ces notions, seules sont définies les notions de 'public' et de 'public concerné' (cf. plus haut).

[41] Cf. §2, d), ii) ; §3 ; §4 ; et §7 de l'art. 6.

> Pour les différentes étapes de la procédure de participation du public, il est prévu des délais raisonnables laissant assez de temps pour informer le *public* conformément au paragraphe 2 [de l'article 6] et pour que le *public* se prépare et participe effectivement aux travaux tout au long du processus décisionnel en matière d'environnement (italique ajouté)[42].

Mais la convention assure-t-elle réellement l'accès concret de l'ensemble du *dêmos* à son système?

B. Accès Concret du *Dêmos* au Système Participatif de la Convention d'Århus

Afin d'assurer l'accès concret du *dêmos* au système participatif, le *dêmos* doit être adéquatement informé au sujet des procédures participatives et avoir la capacité de les exercer.

Le *dêmos* doit évidemment, avant tout, savoir que les procédures participatives existent, quels y sont ses droits et comment les exercer. Si les Parties notent cette nécessité dans le préambule de la convention[43], il faut souligner qu'aucune disposition matérielle de la convention ne permet d'en assurer la réalisation concrète.

L'information générale du *dêmos* sur ses droits participatifs, si elle a lieu, ne suffit toutefois pas pour assurer son accès concret au système: même si le *dêmos* sait que les procédures participatives existent, quels y sont ses droits et comment les exercer, il doit encore disposer de toute information utile à propos d'une procédure participative déterminée. Ladite publicité doit d'abord avoir pour objet l'annonce de la procédure participative envisagée et comporter des informations relatives au déroulement de la procédure. Pendant la procédure, le public doit disposer de toute information utile pour pouvoir formuler ses observations en connaissance de cause. Les paragraphes 2 et 6 de l'article 6 de la convention règlent respectivement, de manière détaillée, ces deux aspects de l'information du public—mais uniquement au bénéficie du 'public *concerné*'. L'information est ainsi assurée au 'public concerné', et non pas au 'public' en général, alors que la convention prévoit la participation de tout membre du public aux procédures organisées en vertu de l'article 6 et insiste sur le fait que cette participation doit être effective. Au regard des paragraphes 2 et 6 de l'article 6, le paragraphe 3 de l'article paraît de peu de secours pour assurer l'accès concret de l'ensemble du *dêmos* au système participatif: comment le public en général peut-il effectivement exercer ses droits participatifs s'il ne dispose pas des informations procédurales et matérielles pertinentes? Certes, l'article 6, §6 précise qu'il s'applique sans préjudice des dispositions de l'article 4 de la convention, qui organise la publicité passive en matière d'environnement au profit de tout membre du public. Toutefois, il paraît peu probable qu'un membre du public, non considéré membre du 'public concerné'—et ne disposant donc pas des informations procédurales détaillées à l'article 6, §2—, sache qu'une procédure participative est envisagée, quelles sont les informations pertinentes pour le processus décisionnel, et auprès de quelle autorité ces informations sont disponibles.

Cette distinction entre 'public' et 'public concerné' a engendré une confusion quant aux bénéficiaires du système participatif. Les lignes directrices relatives à l'application

[42] Lors de la rédaction du par. 3 de l'art. 6, les auteurs de la convention ont perdu de vue que le par. 2 de l'art. 6 n'organise que l'information du 'public *concerné*' (cf ci-après, dans le corps du texte). Pour la participation effective du public en général, v. ég. l'art. 6, §4 de la convention.

[43] Préambule, al. 12.

mondiale du principe 10 de la déclaration de Rio l'illustrent de manière éclatante. Ainsi, les lignes directrices[44]:

- prévoient l'information procédurale du public concerné, afin d'assurer la participation effective du public;
- recommandent aux Etats de s'efforcer à assurer la participation proactive du public, comprenant la possibilité pour les membres du public concerné d'exprimer leurs opinions;
- prévoient l'information, quant au fond, du public concerné; et
- énoncent que les Etats devraient prendre dûment en considération les commentaires du public.

Nous le voyons : la distinction entre 'public' et 'public concerné' s'est transformée en un véritable amalgame[45].

Concernant le volet 'information', la convention n'assure donc pas l'accès concret de l'ensemble du *dêmos* à son système participatif. Au contraire, la distinction entre 'public' et 'public concerné' renforce[46] singulièrement la fluctuation des bénéficiaires du système, ce qui a provoqué une confusion, restreignant (parfois) le cercle des participants au seul 'public concerné'[47].

La convention fait-elle mieux pour assurer la capacité de l'ensemble du *dêmos* d'exercer ses droits participatifs?

Une disposition générale de la convention demande aux Parties de tâcher de faire en sorte que les fonctionnaires et les autorités aident le public et lui donnent des conseils pour lui permettre d'exercer ses droits participatifs[48].

La convention comporte également des dispositions particulières visant à aider le public à exercer ses droits d'accès à l'information[49] et d'accès à la justice[50]. Aucun support spécifique n'est prévu pour l'exercice du droit au cœur du système participatif : le droit de participation au processus décisionnel.

Aussi, lorsque l'assistance au public est prévue, la convention focalise sur l'appui aux membres du public qui ont été capables, par eux-mêmes, de prendre les premiers pas vers l'exercice de leurs droits; qui sont dans le système participatif ou qui sont en mesure de manifester leur souhait d'y être inclus. Ceci ne devrait pas nous faire oublier les membres du *dêmos* qui ne sont pas dans une telle position, par exemple faute de capacité physique ou matérielle[51].

[44] Ce qui suit provient (dans l'ordre) des directives 8 à 11. Les notions de 'public' et 'public concerné' sont définies comme dans la convention d'Århus (cf., respectivement, les notes infrapaginales figurant dans les directives 6 et 8)—ce qui confirme l'influence de la convention sur les lignes directrices (cf. plus haut).

[45] Pour davantage de développements concernant cette problématique épineuse, consulter C. Larssen, 'Les modalités et le déroulement des procédures d'enquête publique en matière d'environnement et d'urbanisme', in B. Jadot (dir.), *La participation du public au processus de décision en matière d'environnement et d'urbanisme. Actes du colloque organisé le 27 mai 2004 par le Centre d'étude du droit de l'environnement (CEDRE) des Facultés universitaires Saint-Louis* (Bruxelles, Bruylant, 2005) n° 19.

[46] Rappelons les fluctuations du *dêmos* dans le système participatif de la convention considéré dans son ensemble (cf. la note plus haut).

[47] Comme c'est le cas dans les mesures présentées par l'Union européenne comme appliquant la convention d'Århus (C. Larssen, 'Les modalités et le déroulement des procédures d'enquête publique en matière d'environnement et d'urbanisme', spéc. n° 19).

[48] Art. 3, §2 de la convention. V. ég. l'al. 8 du préambule.

[49] Art. 5, §2 de la convention.

[50] Art. 9, §5 de la convention.

[51] Songeons not. aux 'réfugiés, personnes âgées, minorités ethniques, handicapés physiques et mentaux, personnes sortant d'un établissement psychiatrique ou de prison, malades ou personnes en mauvaise santé, SDF

La convention d'Århus ne contient aucun élément tendant à inclure les membres marginalisés du *dêmos*[52].

La convention n'assure donc ni l'information de l'ensemble du *dêmos* dans le cadre d'une procédure participative organisée en vertu de l'article 6, ni la capacité physique ou matérielle de ce *dêmos* d'exercer son droit de participation au processus décisionnel.

Supposons que, malgré ces insuffisances, un membre du *dêmos*, qui n'est pas considéré membre du 'public concerné', dispose des capacités physiques et matérielles de participer à la gestion du bien commun, réussit à obtenir les informations relatives à une procédure déterminée—et découvre que, d'après les estimations, l'activité proposée aura un 'DLT de 1000'[53].

Qu'est-ce à dire? Est-ce beaucoup? Peu? Dans la moyenne? D'autres paramètres (et lesquels?) interfèrent-ils avec un 'DLT'? Dans l'affirmative, quelles en sont les significations dans le contexte donné?

L'accès intellectuel au système participatif ne découle pas, *ipso facto*, de la communication d'informations. Même avec des 'délais raisonnables', l'information ne se transforme pas, toute seule, en formation.

Afin que l'ensemble du *dêmos*—et non seulement les associations spécialisées—ait intellectuellement accès au système participatif, l'éducation, ici écologique, est nécessaire. En vertu de l'article 3, §3 de la convention:

> Chaque Partie favorise l'éducation écologique du public et sensibilise celui-ci aux problèmes environnementaux afin notamment qu'il sache comment procéder pour avoir l'accès à l'information, participer au processus décisionnel et saisir la justice en matière d'environnement[54].

Toutefois, à la différence des nombreux organes établis au niveau international pour rendre effectif l'un ou l'autre élément d'un des droits procéduraux du système participatif, aucun travail 'post-Århusien'[55] n'est effectué ou projeté à propos de cette disposition centrale.

Aussi longtemps que l'éducation (écologique) reste ainsi négligée du système participatif, les efforts pour assurer l'effectivité de tel (aspect d'un) droit participatif ne bénéficieront qu'à ceux qui disposent de la formation pour exercer leurs droits.

Il n'est pourtant pas nécessaire de se mouvoir loin du cadre strictement 'post-Århusien' pour trouver des initiatives offrant une perspective plus inclusive au système participatif.

et mal-logés, demandeurs d'asile, femmes ayant une charge de famille ou d'autres responsabilités en matière de soins, chômeurs de longue durée, travailleurs âgés, femmes de condition économique modeste, jeunes et enfants' (*L'accès aux droits sociaux en Europe*, Strasbourg, Conseil de l'Europe, oct. 2002, 54).

[52] Si les lignes directrices d'Almaty prévoient bien que '[lorsque] les membres du public ont des capacités, des ressources, des situations socioculturelles ou un poids économique ou politique différents, des mesures particulières devraient être prises pour garantir un processus équilibré et équitable. Les processus et mécanismes d'accès international devraient être conçus de façon à promouvoir la transparence, réduire l'inégalité, prévenir toute influence économique ou politique indue et faciliter la participation des groupes qui sont le plus directement concernés et qui pourraient ne pas avoir les moyens de participer sans un encouragement et un soutien' (par. 15 des lignes directrices), la *Task Force* constituée pour engager des consultations concernant les lignes directrices avec les instances internationales entrant dans leur champ d'application n'embraye pas sur ce mouvement inclusif.

[53] Exemple fictif inspiré de B. Komarov, *Le rouge et le vert. La destruction de la nature en URSS* (Paris, Editions du Seuil, 1981), 30 et s.

[54] V. ég. préambule, al. 14.

[55] Nous désignerons ainsi le processus international destiné à assurer l'application correcte et complète de la convention d'Århus.

En effet, la stratégie pour l'Education en vue du Développement Durable (EDD) de la CEE/ONU[56], déclarant que l'éducation 'est non seulement un droit de l'homme …, mais également une condition *sine qua non* du développement durable et un outil indispensable à une bonne gouvernance, à des décisions éclairées et à la promotion de la démocratie'[57], estime qu'elle pourrait appuyer la mise en œuvre de la convention d'Århus 'en encourageant la prise de décisions transparentes, sans exclusive et responsables ainsi que l'autonomie des individus'[58]. Ne coordonnant pas, sérieusement[59], ses efforts en matière d'EDD avec ses travaux 'post-Århusiens', la CEE/ONU ne fait guère preuve de la cohérence qu'elle demande à ses Etats membres[60].

Or, l'importance de l'éducation pour assurer une participation utile de l'ensemble du *dêmos* est régulièrement exprimée dans les mesures participatives paneuropéennes prises en amont de la convention d'Århus. Aussi, si le principe 10 de la déclaration de Rio ne comporte pas lui-même d'éléments concernant l'éducation du public, le chapitre 36 de l'Action 21, également adoptée à la conférence de Rio, énonce franchement que '[l'éducation est essentielle] pour assurer une participation effective du public aux prises de décisions'[61].

L'élan éducatif semble s'être étouffé quelque part entre la déclaration de Rio et la convention d'Århus: en focalisant sur le développement technique du triptyque procédural, les auteurs de la convention ont accordé peu d'attention à la nécessité d'assurer, avant tout, l'éducation des bénéficiaires du triptyque.

V. CONCLUSION

La convention d'Århus: 'avancée majeure du droit international'?

S'il est difficilement contestable qu'une participation accrue du public à la gestion d'affaires publiques soit une avancée, il importe—spécialement au vu du rayonnement considérable du système participatif de la convention—d'assurer que ce système constitue véritablement une avancée majeure.

Afin de vérifier l'affirmation selon laquelle la convention serait une 'avancée majeure du droit international', nous avons mis son système participatif à une 'épreuve démocratique'.

Et nous avons constaté deux types de problèmes. D'une part, la distinction entre 'public' et 'public concerné' (ainsi que la fluctuation générale du *dêmos* dans le système participatif de la convention) a provoqué une confusion quant aux bénéficiaires du

[56] Stratégie adoptée à l'issue de la réunion des ministères de l'environnement et de l'éducation de la région de la CEE, tenue à Vilnius (Lituanie) 17-18 mars 2005 (CEP/AC.13/2005/3/Rev.1, 23 mars 2005)—'stratégie EDD de la CEE/ONU'.

[57] Première page de la stratégie EDD de la CEE/ONU, encadré 'principes', deuxième alinéa.

[58] Par. 12 de la stratégie EDD de la CEE/ONU (v. ég. par. 68 de la stratégie).

[59] L'analyse annoncée sur le Centre d'échange d'informations de la convention d'Århus (*Aarhus Clearinghouse*)—intitulée ambitieusement 'linking the UNECE Strategy for ESD and the Aarhus Convention' (aarhusclearinghouse.unece.org/news.cfm?id=1000168)—effleure à peine la problématique et n'a pas provoqué davantage de travaux sur le sujet.

[60] 'Les pays devraient recenser les obligations qu'ils ont contractées en ce qui concerne la communication, l'éducation ainsi que la participation et la sensibilisation du public dans les accords en matière d'environnement et autres accords internationaux pertinents, afin de s'y conformer de manière cohérente dans l'éducation en vue du développement durable' (par. 44 de la Stratégie EDD de la CEE/ONU).

[61] www.un.org/esa/sustdev/documents/agenda21/french/action36.htm.

système participatif, restreignant (parfois) le cercle des participants au seul 'public concerné'. D'autre part, la convention n'assure pas l'inclusion concrète de l'ensemble du *dêmos* dans son système. Seuls les membres du *dêmos* disposant des informations et des capacités nécessaires—seuls ceux qui savent et ceux qui peuvent—seront, concrètement, aptes à grimper 'l'arbre participatif'.

Ces difficultés sapent la qualité démocratique du système participatif de la convention, et, partant, sa qualité 'd'avancée majeure du droit international'.

Les procédures participatives ne sont pas, *per se*, démocratiques. Tout dépend de qui y participe.

A moins que *la* démocratie ne signifie en réalité pas le règne du *dêmos*. Au vu des activités de démocratisation menées dans la région paneuropéenne dans le sillage de la chute du mur de Berlin, *la* démocratie impliquerait en effet plutôt la garantie de libertés individuelles, en particulier de la liberté d'expression, ainsi que de droits civils et politiques, dits droits de l'Homme de la 1ère génération.

La convention d'Århus reflète cette vision de la démocratie. Edifié notamment sur la liberté d'expression, le système participatif de la convention organise trois droits de l'Homme de la 1ère génération, destinés à contribuer à garantir un droit de l'Homme de la 3ème génération: le droit à l'environnement.

Où sont les droits de l'Homme de la 2ème génération dans la convention? Si celle-ci comporte bien quelques éléments de type '2ème génération', leur faiblesse—ainsi que le manque d'attention qu'ils reçoivent dans le processus 'post-Århusien'—contraste notablement avec le système participatif lui-même, soigneusement développé et attentivement suivi.

Pour que le système participatif renforce véritablement le règne du *dêmos*, il faudra agir à deux niveaux:

- clarifier les contours du système, en assurant que celui-ci s'applique bien, théoriquement et dans l'esprit de chacun, à l'ensemble du *dêmos*; et
- garantir l'inclusion concrète de l'ensemble du *dêmos* dans le système, en y incorporant, dûment, les droits de l'Homme de la 2ème génération.

Œuvrons dans ce double sens, afin que la convention d'Århus représente une avancée, majeure, du droit international.

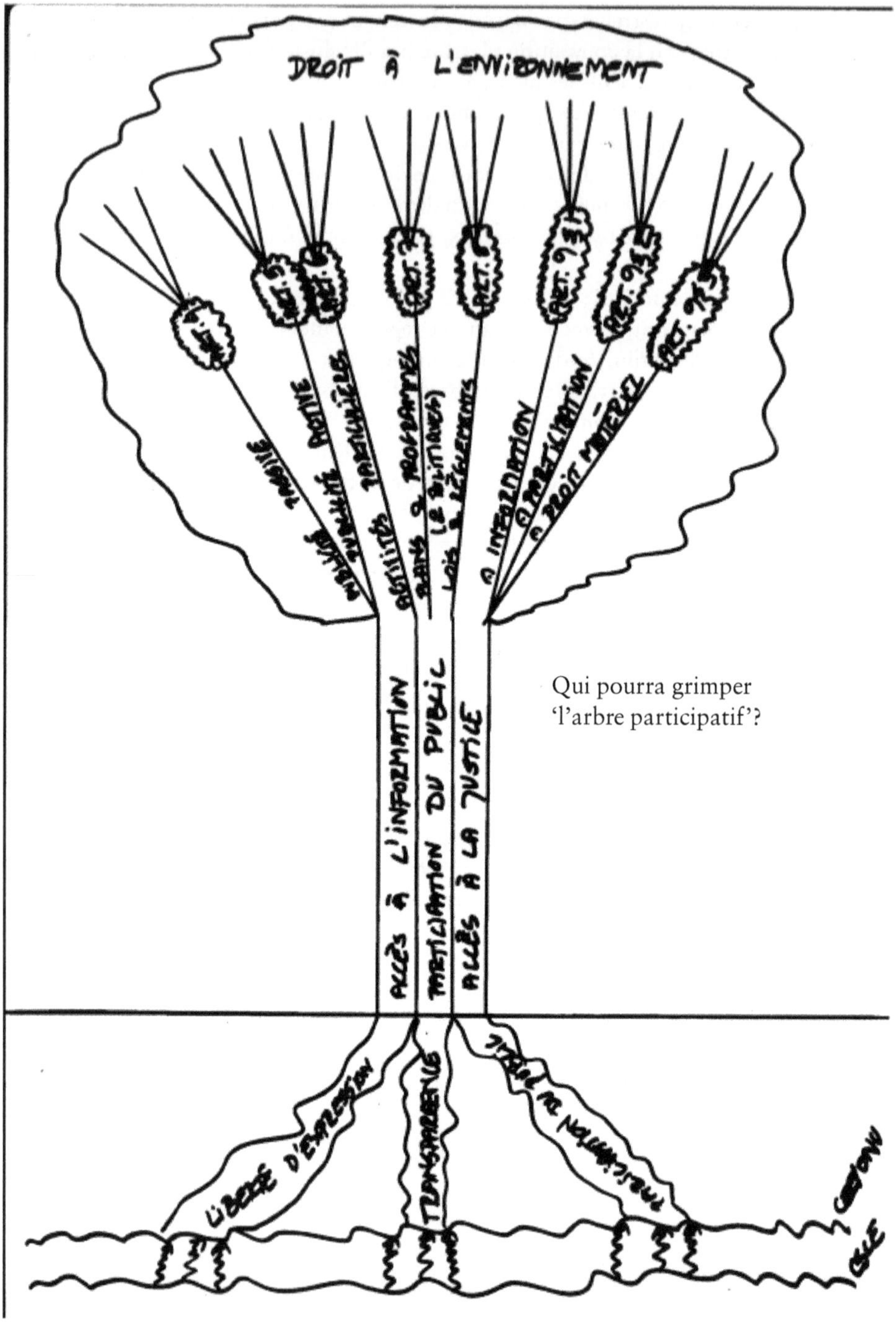

Qui pourra grimper 'l'arbre participatif'?

27

Two Decades Lost: Reinvigorating the Weak Cousin of WTO Law

MICHAEL WAIBEL*

THE PERIOD SINCE 1989, according to Philip Allott, has been the most dynamic in human history. After the fall of the Iron Curtain, it appears that international law, from international criminal law to human rights law and WTO law, evolved rapidly. But there are also dark corners in the universe of international law, which have barely been touched by international law's sunlight. One such area is international financial law.

This chapter argues that current international financial law is largely toothless and dangerously underdeveloped. The sea change in international finance since 1990 seems to have bypassed the public international law of finance and international financial lawyers. Despite dazzling growth in global capital markets, international financial law has barely changed over the last decades. Because of close interrelation between the international trade and monetary sphere, international financial law is the weak cousin of WTO law.

The chapter proceeds in three steps. First, it examines the character and evolution of international financial law. Second, it explains why international financial law is the weak cousin of WTO law. Third, it provides some reasons for the underdevelopment of international financial law. It concludes with some tentative thoughts on why the international community should worry about the weakness of international financial law in light of current and emerging challenges in international finance.

I. THE CHARACTER AND EVOLUTION OF INTERNATIONAL FINANCIAL LAW

Current international financial law is an amorphous and ill-defined field. It covers the international law of money, currency, exchange rates, international lending and financial regulation. Its substance concerns international monetary obligations, the balance of payments, exchange rate arrangements, borrowing and defaults by states and private entities, financial stability and financial regulation such as, for example, financial sanctions and capital adequacy standards.

* British Academy Postdoctoral Fellow, Lauterpacht Centre for International Law.

The actors in international finance are numerous. They range from national finance ministries and central banks, to private investors and creditors, to various international organisations such as the International Monetary Fund and multilateral development banks, to informal G groupings of states (G2, G3, G7, G8 and G20), the Financial Stability Board and the Paris Club. The Bank for International Settlements (BIS) is the oldest international financial institution dating back to 1930. When the BIS was established to administer German war reparations under the Young Plan, Professor Manley Hudson predicted that the BIS 'may come in time to exercise a large if not a dominant influence in international finance'.[1] He underscored the 'possibility of the growth of a new public international law as a result of the creation of the bank'[2]—a prospect that it may now safely be said failed to materialise.

The current international monetary order hinges, in large part, on informal monetary cooperation. This approach reminds us of the earlier model of the gold standard. The gold standard before World War I operated on the basis of an implicit commitment to international norms of good behaviour, rather than legal norms, but these conditions fractured after World War I.[3] In the first golden period of capital from the 1870s onwards, central banks cooperated effectively most of the time and responded promptly in times of crises with joint action. The commitment by the major economic powers of the day, especially Great Britain, to the gold standard appeared unlimited.[4] After World War I, domestic political opposition to the gold standard grew rapidly. The war and universal suffrage caused social and political strains in many European societies. Deep domestic conflicts about the proper balance between financial stability and employment resulted.

After World War I's massive destruction, leading international lawyers of the day such as Nicolas Politis were closely involved in the financial reconstruction of Europe. The central institutional actor in the financial reconstruction of Europe was the League's Financial Committee. Based on the largely positive experience with financial reconstruction of European states in the interwar period, the League of Nations proposed the creation of an International Loans Tribunal, though this institution never materialised.[5]

The defining moment for modern international financial law was the Bretton Woods Agreements that established the World Bank and the IMF. In 1944, the IMF Articles of Agreement marked a signature achievement. Like the United Nations Charter in the general political sphere, the IMF Articles contained a set of multilateral rules to govern state monetary conduct to break decisively with the disastrous experience of the interwar period.

The openness of the international trading and financial system are closely interwoven. International financial law is the cousin of WTO law because financial instability is poison for international trade. Future deglobalising shocks are likely to arise in the financial sphere[6] rather than in international trade. In the interwar period, the collapse

[1] MO Hudson, 'The Bank for International Settlements' (1930) 24 *AJIL* 561.

[2] ibid, 566.

[3] BA Simmons, *Who Adjusts? Domestic Sources of Foreign Economic Policy during the Interwar Years* (Princeton: Princeton University Press, 1994) 20.

[4] B Eichengreen, *Golden Fetters: The Gold Standard and the Great Depression, 1919–1939* (Oxford University Press, 1992).

[5] League of Nations, *Report on the financial reconstruction of Hungary by the commissioner-general of the League of Nations for Hungary* (Geneva, League of Nations: 1923); J A Salter, 'The Financial Reconstruction of Austria' (1923) 17 *AJIL* 116–28; League of Nations, *The Financial Reconstruction of Austria—General Survey and Principal Documents* (Geneva, League of Nations, 1926).

[6] B Eichengreen and K O'Rourke, 'A Tale of Two Depressions', www.voxeu.org, 2009; A Rose, 'The International Economic Order in the Aftermath of the 'Great Recession': A Cautious Case for Optimism,

of the gold standard and currency instability period affected trade and investment with a lag. A repeat of this experience is a possibility. Dark clouds stemming from the backlash against financial globalisation are likely to hang over the international trading system for some time.

The next section suggests that the international community has by and large failed to deliver on the early promise for international financial law.

II. THE WEAKNESS OF INTERNATIONAL FINANCIAL LAW

The verdict on international financial law since the disintegration of the Soviet Union is disappointing. Financial globalisation seems to have bypassed the public international law of finance almost entirely. By and large, international lawyers seem to be observers rather than active participants in important developments on the international financial scene, such as the formation of single currency areas, exchange rate pegs, the maintenance of international financial stability and the build-up of massive global imbalances through gradual shifts in creditor-debtor relationships.

To be sure, transnational lawyers have been essential drivers of rapid growth in global capital markets over the last two decades. They have advised on cross-border mergers, foreign investment and the purchases of securities abroad. But analyses of these developments from the public-law and macro perspective are almost non-existent. Even the International Law Association's long-standing Committee on International Monetary Law (MOCOMILA) was not untouched by these broader trends. Its biennial reports and two edited collections[7] focused mostly on current policy issues, rather than reflecting more broadly on international financial law from a public perspective. There is also little academic research on international financial law.[8]

Many developed countries today borrow as if at war.[9] Large, pent-up global imbalances in cross-border trade and borrowing raise the prospect of more widespread exchange controls. Ukraine and Iceland are two early examples of countries that introduced capital controls in economic distress. More broadly, ominous signs of financial protectionism are already visible. In the main, this retrenchment towards home markets results from the growing recognition that substantial cross-border financial activity is incompatible with the locus of regulation, supervision and the financing of bailouts almost exclusively at the national level.

The creation of the World Trade Organization has led to tremendous growth of international trade law over the last two decades. Over the last fifteen years, the WTO Dispute Settlement Body has decided a diverse and important set of cases in the field of

11 November 2009, unpublished manuscript, 6, refers to the 'quiescent 800-pound gorilla' of financial protectionism, and notes that international banking and international capital flows thus far do not seem to have been affected to any significant degree by financial protectionism.

[7] M Giovanoli (ed), *International Monetary Law: Issues for the New Millennium* (Oxford, Oxford University Press, 2000); M Giovanoli and D Devos (eds), *International Monetary and Financial Law: The Global Crisis* (Oxford, Oxford University Press, 2010).

[8] R Sarkar, *International Development Law, Human Rights, and Global Finance* (Oxford, Oxford University Press, 2009) is a rare recent exception.

[9] McKinsey Global Institute, *Debt and Deleveraging* (2010).

international trade. In international finance, by contrast, the IMF is the primary forum for inter-state cooperation and negotiation. There is no institution capable of adjudicating disputes at the international level comparable to the WTO Dispute Settlement Body. A central area where the absence of accepted methods of international dispute resolution matters is on the terms of government rescues for financial institutions.

A. Government Bailouts of Financial Institutions

The financial crisis that started in 2008 is spreading from the private to the public sector. The collateral damage from banking crises spills over to public balance sheets in the form of increasingly unsustainable debts. Over the last two years, financial institutions have written down large quantities of toxic assets and governments have provided financial assistance on an unprecedented scale. Such migration from private to public balance sheets and vice versa is a familiar story in the history of international finance.[10] As the ultimate bearers of risk, countries often take over liabilities contracted by the private sector.[11] Private boom is often followed by public bust. The most prominent channel linking sovereign and private sector balance sheets is bank insolvency.[12] Severe banking crises often become sovereign debt crises, or vice versa.[13]

In the early 1930s, a series of twin crises followed by a massive real crisis led to a worldwide depression. In *The End of Globalization*, Harold James explains this two-way interaction between sovereign and bank balance sheets in the following words: 'fiscal difficulties led to capital flight, and the withdrawal of capital weakened banks and created a potential and actual fiscal burden. Banking problems thus led to fiscal problems, because the cost of taking over bad banks strained the budget.'[14] This description is eerily familiar to observers of the crisis that broke out in 2008.

The International Monetary Fund estimates that support to financial systems totals more than $600 billion in the UK, more than $800 billion for the Eurozone and more than $1 trillion in the United States.[15] Other estimates point to even higher costs for taxpayers. Bank of England Governor Mervyn King predicted that the cost of direct or guaranteed loans and equity investment in the UK amounted to $ 1.5 trillion, the equivalent of two thirds of UK GDP.[16]

The upper bound for the cost of the US bailout exceeds $20 trillion, the equivalent of 1 ½ times US GDP, if all liabilities assumed by the government were to materialise.[17]

[10] CM Reinhart and KS Rogoff, *This Time is Different: Eight Centuries of Financial Folly* (Princeton University Press, Princeton 2009) chapter 10.

[11] DA Moss, *When All Else Fails: Government as the Ultimate Risk Manager* (Harvard University Press, Cambridge, 2002).

[12] International Monetary Fund, *Cross-Cutting Themes in Economies with Large Banking Systems*, 16 April 2010.

[13] AG Haldane, 'Banking on the state' 139 *BIS Review*, 1.

[14] H James, *The End of Globalization: Lessons from the Great Depression* (Cambridge, Harvard University Press, 2001) 31.

[15] International Monetary Fund, *World Economic Outlook*, October 2009, 29, Figure 1.8; A Ross Sorkin, *Too Big too Fail: Inside the Battle to Save Wall Street* (Allan Lane, London, 2009) 534.

[16] Speech by Mervyn King to Scottish business associations, 20 October 2009, www.bankofengland.co.uk/publications/speeches/2009/speech406.pdf.

[17] Special Inspector General for the Troubled Asset Relief Program, Quarterly Report to Congress, 21 July 2009, sigtarp.gov/reports/congress/2009/July_2009_Quaterly_Report_to_Congress.pdf.

That said, the final cost is likely to be substantially lower, but still amount to several trillion dollars. This is because the government should be able to sell some of the purchased assets for value and because some borrowers are likely to repay their loan to the government.

B. The Collapse of the Creditanstalt in 1931

The collapse of the Austrian Creditanstalt at the height of the Great Depression offers an early illustration of the ramifications of large-scale bank collapses for international financial affairs. This insolvency also played a major role in deepening the Great Depression through financial sector linkages. Redistribution from taxpayers to creditors and shareholders in major bank bailouts tends to give rise to disputes at the international level, among creditor states and between debtor and creditor states.

Austria's fiscal position after World War I had almost invariably been precarious, and led to a large stabilization loan under the auspices of the League of Nations.[18] The Creditanstalt was the result of a series of mergers of financial institutions on the brink of collapse. Its resulting behemoth was 'an integral and important part of the financial structure of the world'.[19] Its total assets exceeded one sixth of Austrian GDP and accounted for 50 percent of Austrian deposits.[20]

The threat to the stability of the Austrian banking system caused a run on the Austrian currency. The crisis soon spilled into the Germany. Creditors took the view that if Austrian banks could no longer honour their obligations, chances were that the same applied to German banks. Germany lost of half its reserves in the first three weeks of June.[21] Only the Hoover moratorium—a unilateral standstill in June 1931 on reparation payments for all European countries for one year[22]—partly stabilised the situation.

A more recent example of the shortcomings of current methods of dispute resolution in international finance is the comprehensive failure of Iceland's banking system. Iceland, the Netherlands and the UK have been locked in an intractable dispute over who is to pay for the deposits in failed Icelandic banks for almost two years, with no clear end in sight.[23] The adjudication by an independent tribunal appears unlikely. Similar disputes are also probable in other parts of the world, as government guarantees of banking systems and other emergency measures lead to disputes at inter-state level and between states and private creditors.

[18] 'League Body Meets to Assist Austria; Financial Committee Starts Work on Scheme for Relief Proposed by Dutch Banker', *New York Times*, 28 March 1921; for background see KP Berger, *Im Schatten der Diktatur: Die Finanzdiplomatie des Vertreters des Völkerbundes in Österreich, Meinoud Marinus Rost van Tonningen 1931–1936* (Böhlau, Wien 2000).

[19] Royal Institute of International Affairs, *Survey of International Affairs* (London, 1932) 63.

[20] L Ahamed, *Lords of Finance: 1929, The Great Depression and the Bankers Who Broke the World* (William Heinemann, London 2009) 404.

[21] *Lords of Finance*, 410.

[22] OD Tolischus, 'Debts and the Hoover Programme' (1932) 233 *North American Review* 389.

[23] See M Waibel, 'Iceland's Financial Crisis—*Quo Vadis* International Law', ASIL Insight, 1 March 2010, Vol 14, Issue 5.

C. The Icesave Dispute

Iceland has a population of just three hundred thousand people. In October 2008, Iceland's three major banks failed within a single week. Landsbanki, Glitnir and Kaupthing together accounted for over 90 percent of the Icelandic banking system. At the time of their collapse, their liabilities exceeded US$60 billion, more than eight times Icelandic GDP.[24] The three Icelandic banks failed when anxiety about the stability of the global financial system ran highest following the collapse of Lehman Brothers three weeks earlier. Notwithstanding the financial difficulties of its banks, Iceland so far has remained current on its sovereign debt. References to the insolvency of Iceland, as a country, gloss over this crucial fact.

The UK and the Netherlands claim that Iceland is obliged to repay them more than US$4.5 billion. The stakes in this dispute are high, particularly for Iceland. Since October 2008, Iceland, the Netherlands, and the United Kingdom have attempted to reach a settlement on the liability for retail depositors in Icesave, the failed Internet bank that had attracted a large and diverse pool of savers from across Europe. The Dutch and UK deposit insurance schemes paid out claims to the depositors at the height of the crisis without substantially consulting Iceland. They seek reimbursement from Iceland.

The dispute centres on the EC Directive on deposit-guarantee schemes, which harmonised requirements for deposit guarantees applicable to branches throughout the single market for financial services.[25] Creditors benefit from a non-discrimination guarantee under the European Economic Area (EEA) Agreement.[26] As a member of the EEA, Iceland is bound by the Directive.

There is some uncertainty whether Iceland is obliged to refund the compensation that the UK and the Netherlands paid out to depositors. The UK and the Netherlands maintain that Iceland is obligated to pay 20,887 Euros per depositor under the EEA Agreement and the Directive. A Joint Legal Opinion by four experts under the auspices of the Economic and Financial Affairs Council (ECOFIN) concluded that Iceland was obliged to ensure that its deposit-guarantee scheme was capable of indemnifying depositors.[27]

But whether this amounts to an obligation to achieve that result in all circumstances, or refers to an obligation to set up and operate an effective deposit insurance scheme with adequate capitalisation, is disputed. There are also questions as to the interpretation of these obligations in a severe banking crisis. The European Free Trade Association (EFTA) Surveillance Authority had to assess the compatibility of the Icelandic legislation with the EEA Agreement.

The British government argued that Iceland appeared ready to renege on its obligations under the Directive at the height of the credit crunch. Fearing that its depositors would not be compensated, the UK invoked provisions of the Anti-terrorism, Crime and Security Act 2001 to freeze the assets of Icelandic banks in the UK with the stated aim

[24] *Economies with Large Banking Systems*, 4.

[25] Directive 94/19/EC of the European Parliament and of the Council, 30 May 1994 on deposit-guarantee schemes, OJ L 135, 31.5. 1994, 5, as amended by Directive 2005/1/EC, OJ L79, 24.3.2005, 9.

[26] Agreement on the European Economic Area, OJ No L 1, 3.1.1994, 3. Community legislation is dynamically incorporated into the Agreement. Decision of the European Economic Joint Area Committee No. 18/94 amending Annex IX (Financial Services) to the EEA Agreement incorporated the Directive into the Agreement on the European Economic Area.

[27] Opinion on the Obligations of Iceland under the Deposit Guarantee Directive 94/19/EC, 7 November 2009.

of preventing harm to the UK economy.[28] The move caused uproar in Iceland, raised eyebrows from advocates of civil liberties and complicated the resolution of the Icesave dispute.[29]

Iceland maintains that the asset freeze played an important role in the collapse of Kaupthing. Moreover, it alleges that the other two governments failed to consult Iceland, despite a Memorandum of Understanding to the contrary.[30] Iceland takes the view that it always stood by its international obligations. It briefly considered seeking judicial review of the asset freeze in English courts or an international tribunal such as the ICJ. It ultimately decided against that course of action, and focused its energy on negotiations with the UK and the Netherlands.

After months of negotiations, the three governments in June 2009 finally agreed on two loan agreements.[31] A condition precedent for their entry into force was a state guarantee for all the guarantees of the Guarantee Fund from 2016. The guarantee shifts debt from the bank balance sheets to Iceland's sovereign balance sheet.

Faced with widespread concerns in Iceland that the loan imposes an impossible burden on future generations, the Icelandic Parliament added a series of conditions to the bill authorising the sovereign guarantee.[32] These conditions include a ceiling as a percentage of GDP on the guarantee,[33] even though the two lenders insisted on an unconditional guarantee.

The Icelandic government submitted a bill authorising such guarantee to Parliament. On 30 December 2009, the Parliament approved the guarantee, this time without conditions. Yet in early January 2010, the President of Iceland, for only the second time in Iceland's history, referred the bill to a referendum under the Icelandic Constitution.

In the run-up to the referendum, the UK and the Netherlands softened their negotiation stance,[34] but no rapid settlement could be achieved. The referendum was held on 6 March 2010. The population voted overwhelmingly to reject the law providing for the sovereign guarantee. UK and Dutch elections delayed a new round of negotiations which led to a revised set of agreements. However, 58 percent of Icelanders rejected the new agreements in April 2011. The ultimate outcome of this dispute will rest on further negotiations between the three governments concerned and possibly adjudication by an ad hoc arbitral tribunal. By global standards, this was a relatively minor crisis, but it considerably strained UK-Icelandic relations. A mechanism for settling such financial disputes at the international level could have helped the parties to converge faster on a settlement acceptable to both sides.

[28] Landsbanki Freezing Order 2008, 8 October 2008 under Sections 4 and 14 of and Schedule 3 of the Anti-terrorism, Crime and Security Act 2001; see also *De Nederlandsche Bank N.V. v. Landsbanki Islands HF*, HA-RK 08.668, District Court of Amsterdam, 13 October 2008.

[29] More than one third of Icelanders signed an online petition at InDefense, www.indefence.is.

[30] Memorandum of Understanding between the Financial Compensation Scheme and the Icelandic Deposit Insurance Fund, 31 October 2006.

[31] Loan Agreements between the Depositors' and Investors' Guarantee Fund of Iceland, Iceland and the Commissioner's of Her Majesty's Government and The State of the Netherlands, 5 June 2009, accompanied by a Settlement Agreement and Finance Agreement.

[32] Parliament approved Act 96/2009 on 28 August 2009. The Iceland President approved the law on 2 September 2009.

[33] Acceptance and Amendment Agreement, 19 October 2009.

[34] International Monetary Fund, Cross-Cutting Themes in Economies with Large Banking Systems, 16 April 2010.

The next section looks at some of the reasons why current international financial law falls short of its potential.

III. WHY INTERNATIONAL FINANCIAL LAW IS UNDERDEVELOPED

The first reason for the weakness of international financial law is that the IMF Articles of Agreement contain few legal obligations binding on its member states, such as the prohibition of restrictions on current international transactions or a prohibition on multiple currency practices.[35] Furthermore, there are few mechanisms to ensure compliance, other than peer pressure and informal cooperation. The articles were drafted at a time when private financial flows across borders were small in relation to official sector flows.

The framework provided by the IMF articles for the international monetary sphere needs to adapt to today's world in which private capital flows dwarf official ones. For a long time, relying on peer pressure by the IMF's largest shareholders on countries that needed balance of payment assistance was sufficient. But with the tectonic shifts currently underway in the global distribution of economic power, the pattern of informal monetary cooperation and IMF leverage over borrowing countries shows cracks at the seams.

Many Asian countries chose to self-insure by building up large central bank reserves, after broadly disagreeing with the IMF's approach to resolving the East Asian crisis in 1998. The European Union, when confronted with the Greek debt crisis in 2010, was also reluctant to accord the IMF the central role. The result is the European Financial Stability Fund whose aim is to guarantee financial stability in the Eurozone by providing financial assistance to Eurozone members experiencing financial distress. Over time, this new actor in international finance could assume the function of a European Monetary Fund.

IMF governance reflects the economic balance of power as it existed in 1945, with only minor adjustments thereafter, a pointed parallel to the United Nations Security Council. Substantial governance reform is essential. After 1989, the balance of power in the World Bank and the IMF barely changed to reflect the collapse of the Soviet Union and the emergence of Asia as the world's new economic powerhouse. The international community missed a great opportunity to recalibrate the mission and governance of the IMF. European countries remain vastly overrepresented in the IMF relative to their weight in the global economy, and the United States retains its de facto veto power. The EU-27's share of the voting power is 32 per cent. The US's share is 18 per cent, with a majority of 85 per cent required for decisions of the IMF Executive Board.[36] No single representative for the European Union is in sight, unlike in the WTO. There is some prospect for realignment in the near future, though it is unlikely to go far enough to substantially remedy the overrepresentation of European countries.[37]

The IMF as an institution has also been substantially weakened since 1989. It was a more respected actor in 1989 as compared to 2010. It has faced deep criticism, in

[35] Article VIII, Section 2 and Article VIII, Section 3.

[36] L Menkhoff and R Meyer, The G20 Proposal on IMF Governance: Is there Progress?, Discussion Paper No. 439, March 2010.

[37] 'EU Set for Changes to IMF Board', *Financial Times*, 2 October 2010.

particular for its role in the East Asian and Argentine crises,[38] in addition to questions about its relevance after the benign 1990s and early 2000s, at least as far as financial stability in the developed world was concerned. Many Asian countries decided to build up large reserves—a factor in the build-up of global imbalances—rather than having to rely on IMF funding ever again. Japan mooted the idea of an Asian Monetary Fund, and encountered strong resistance in the United States and elsewhere.[39] Not only in East Asia and Latin America, but also in developed economies, the IMF remains deeply unpopular across the political spectrum. As a result, the international community has in large measure been deprived of the only institution capable of being an independent arbiter in monetary matters.

The IMF's role in macroeconomic policy advice has been limited. Aside from annual Article IV surveillance over member's macroeconomic policies, the IMF's involvement in macroeconomic policy formulation in developed economies has been tightly circumscribed. By and large, the IMF only had some influence over macroeconomic policies in countries that borrowed from it. Until recently, it provided funds in substantial volume only to a few middle-income countries. It carried out the very first financial sector assessment of the United States only in 2009, *after* the crisis uncovered the fragility of the US financial system.[40]

A second reason for the underdevelopment of international financial law is that the importance of rules in this area becomes apparent only during times of deep economic strains. The few existing legal rules developed largely in response to the Great Depression and World War II. The United States as the international financial hegemon has long shown an aversion to hard legal rules in international finance. It has preferred ad hoc cooperation over binding agreements.[41]

This preference is revealed not only at the IMF, but also at other institutions such as the Paris Club for restructuring official debt. The present crisis may cause widespread disillusionment with complex and underregulated finance among policymakers and the wider public. The heavy reliance on soft law and self-regulation, nationally as well internationally, could fall out of favour. Over time, states may be more willing to legalise international financial matters. But the privatization of international financial law that occurred over the last three decades is likely to persist for some time, if only because many central actors remain convinced that such an approach, on balance, is beneficial.[42]

[38] P Blustein, *The Chastening: Inside the Crisis That Rocked the Global Financial System and Humbled the IMF* (New York: Public Affairs, 2003); J Stiglitz, *Globalization and its Discontents* (New York, WW Norton, 2003); P Blustein, *And the Money Kept Rolling In (and Out): Wall Street, the IMF, and the Bankrupting of Argentina* (New York, Public Affairs, 2005).

[39] PY Lipscy, 'Japan's Asian Monetary Fund Proposal', (2003) 3 *Stanford Journal of East Asian Affairs* 93.

[40] The IMF published the very first FSAP assessment of the United States in July 2010, United States: Publication of Financial Sector Assessment Program Documentation—Financial System Stability Assessment, IMF Country Report No. 10/247, July 2010.

[41] R Abdelal, *Capital Rules: The Construction of Global Finance* (Cambridge, MA, Harvard University Press).

[42] S Johnson and J Kwak, *13 Bankers: The Wall Street Takeover and The Next Financial Meltdown* (New York, Pantheon, 2010).

IV. CONCLUSION

Financial globalisation is no new phenomenon. The first period of global capital, ranging roughly from 1870 to 1914, resembles, and partly surpasses the second period of global capital we live in today. High capital mobility, large-scale capital flows and high degrees of capital market integration reflected in converging costs of capital are defining features of both periods.[43]

The catch, then and now: capital flows tend to be highly unstable, triggering financial crises. Such crises are an old phenomenon. The 1820s, the 1860s, the 1920s, the 1930s, the 1980s and 1990s and the 2000s have seen major waves of financial crises. Up to the 1990s, the periphery of the world economy was often hardest hit. The second half of the 19th century has been referred to as 'the period of financial debacle of government'.[44]

Continued economic openness and free capital mobility cannot be taken for granted. Historically, capital mobility is the exception, not the norm.[45] Until the 1860s, capital flows across borders faced many obstacles. The outbreak of World War I and the disastrous financial consequences of war-time financing delivered the final blow to globalisation a hundred year ago. By 1935, following the prolonged Great Depression, the world had effectively de-globalised. From 1914 to 1970, cross-border financial flows were also tightly controlled. Remnants of this approach are visible in the IMF's Articles of Agreement.

The cross-border activities of large financial institutions pose particular challenges for national treasuries. Financial institutions desire to have it both ways. The fiscal safety net underpinning many of the riskier activities of financial institutions is invariably national.[46] Financial institutions have expressed a strong desire to capture the benefits of globalisation and financial liberalisation, while relying on the tax-payer funded safety net provided by separate statehood. The tension between risk-taking by financial institutions internationally and the fiscal safety net at the national level has lead to bailout fatigue among national taxpayers.

Against the background of these challenges, the weakness of public international law of finance is particularly worrying, in particular with respect to dispute resolution mechanisms. The international community relies mainly on informal means of co-operation and regulatory networks à la Anne-Marie Slaughter in the financial sphere—the ongoing and informal exchange between officials across borders.[47] Such networks are often useful, but are likely to disappoint when they are most needed: in times of crises when policymakers face tremendous domestic pressures to re-orient their economic policies inwards and when substantial tax-payer funds are needed to maintain financial stability. Think of a Lehman Brothers-type event or the wholesale collapse of a national banking system, as Iceland experienced in October 2008.

[43] J Williamson and K O'Rourke, *Globalisation and History: The Evolution of the Nineteenth-Century Atlantic Economy* (Cambridge, MA, MIT Press, 2001) 207; H James, *Creation and Destruction of Value* (Cambridge, Harvard University Press, 2009).

[44] N Politis, *Les emprunts d'état en droit international* (Paris, Pedone-Lauriel, 1894) 3.

[45] M Waibel, 'BIT by BIT—The Silent Liberalization of the Capital Account' in C Binder, U Kriebaum, A Reinisch and S Wittich (eds), *International Investment Law for the 21st Century—Essays in Honour of Christoph Schreuer* (Oxford, Oxford University Press, 2009) 497.

[46] *Economies with Large Banking Systems*, above note 13, 22 ('the territorial nature of the risks by a large, internationally active banking sector must be internalized'); AG Haldane, *Banking on the state.*

[47] A-M Slaughter, *A New World Order* (Princeton University Press, Princeton, 2004).

The need for dispute resolution mechanisms and more developed legal rules in international finance is increasingly apparent. To deal with future upheavals in international finance, the international community needs to reinvigorate international financial law.[48] Agreement on substantive rules is needed first, coupled with an effective and independent dispute resolution mechanism to resolve disputes. Without effective and robust instruments for financial burden sharing in our world of globalised finance, international cooperation is likely to break down in the next crisis.

[48] eg the Basel Committee's Recommendations on Cross-Border Bank Resolution, March 2010 (highlighting the predominance of the territorial approach to resolving banking crises insolvencies).

28

The Poverty of Development and the Development of Poverty in International Law

SUNDHYA PAHUJA*

DOES INTERNATIONAL LAW have anything to offer to the 'poorest of the poor'? The short answer to this question is: yes, potentially. So far, however, it has offered very little. Indeed, international law is unlikely to offer very much at all if we continue to approach the question of poverty in the way we have for the past sixty years, let alone since the end of the Cold War.

A brief assessment of the current situation throws into sharp relief our collective failure over the last sixty years to improve the living conditions of most of the people in the world. Gains in poverty reduction have been what we would have to call modest, at best. According to recent World Bank statistics, almost half the world's people live below a poverty line of $2.50 per day, and many live far below that, and we could recite many more statistics about the persistence and worsening of global poverty.[1] The World Bank's own statistics about improvements on various indicators show marginal gains. If the clear decline in income poverty in China is excluded, then the percentage of people living below the poverty line in the rest of the world has barely declined over the past three decades.[2] This failure is especially marked given the fact that in the twentieth century, the world economy has grown twenty times. Over this time, not only has the world become much richer, but a huge international bureaucracy has proliferated, specifically charged with the task of alleviating poverty. William Easterley estimates that over $2.3 trillion has been spent on foreign aid alone over the last five decades.[3]

Over the same period, inequality also increased markedly. Just one indicator of that on an individualised level is that the world's richest 450 people have more wealth than the poorest 415 million combined. In regional terms, the ratio of per capita income of

* Associate Professor Melbourne Law School; Director, Law and Development Research Programme, Institute of International Law and the Humanities. My thanks to James Parker and Jeremy Baskin.

[1] World Bank Development Indicators: <data.worldbank.org/indicator>.

[2] ibid.

[3] William Easterley, *The White Man's Burden: Why the West's Efforts to Aid the Rest Have Done So Much Ill and So Little Good* (Oxford, Oxford University Press, 2007) 4.

Europe to Africa in 1960 was 30:1. In 2005, it was 40:1.[4] Along these lines, in his recent book *Farewell to Alms,* economic historian Gregory Clark suggests that in the present moment, there live on this earth both the poorest and the richest people who *have ever lived.*[5] Even if Clark is only partly right, this is a dark fact. In combination with the statistics above, it is a telling indictment of our collective failure to address the poverty related suffering of most of the people in the world.

But these failures have not cast doubt on the project of development. If anything, the development project has widened and intensified with time. One way of understanding Sant'Ana's diagnosis[6] of the next shift in development in the recent turn to indicators is as evidence of the further technocratisation and depoliticisation of the development project. Another way of understanding the turn to indicators is as a manifestation of the anxiety of results, to shore up the project in the face of its failures, and to look for new ways to measure the project to 'prove' it is working.[7]

Indeed, development is the only language in which the problem of global poverty seems to be thought or addressed in international law and institutions. In other words, *development* as both word and concept has become a *proxy* for, or synonymous with, the way we talk about questions of material well-being and global inequality. So, even the call constituting this panel moved seamlessly from the fact of material need, to the idea of development. The efforts of the world to eradicate extreme poverty and hunger, to empower women, to increase primary education, to reduce child and infant mortality, and to improve maternal health, *inter alia,* are declared to be the millennium *development* goals. Trade negotiation rounds which are meant to focus on poor countries are called the '*development* round'. The way we deal with the problem of the environment is sustainable *development.* This hold on our collective imagination remains firm even in the face of the creeping anxiety about the poor results of the development project.

The capture by development of the question of material need and the betterment of life matters because development is not just a neutral place marker. Like any term, as Schmitt reminds us, it must be understood in terms of its concrete political existence.[8] And development is not just a general encapsulation of the idea of countries improving their standard of living. It does not simply mean a general improvement of any kind in people's quality of life. In short, it is not 'just a word'.

Instead, 'development' is a specific way of knowing the world that is both discourse and institutional machinery. It also has a very particular history, and carries a great deal of conceptual baggage with it because of that. In essence, my argument is that there are four key features of development which suggest that attempts to address material suffering in the language of development are likely to fail and may even make the problem worse. These four features are: (i) the explanatory narrative about the causes of poverty;

[4] See generally, United Nations Development Policy and Analysis Division, World Economic and Social Survey 2010: Retooling Global Development, Chapter I Growth and Development Trends, 1960–2005, www.un.org/esa/policy/wess/wess2006files/chap1.pdf.

[5] Gregory Clark, *A Farewell to Alms: A Brief Economic History of the World* (Princeton, Princeton University Press, 2007) 3.

[6] Matthias Sant'Ana, 'Development in International Law: Conflict of Rhetoric and Norms, paper given at the European Society of International Law Conference, Lauterpacht Centre for International Law, Cambridge, 4 September 2010.

[7] On the turn to indicators, see Sally Merry, 'Measuring the World: Indicators, Human Rights and Global Governance' (August 24, 2009) <www.nyu.edu/ipk/files/docs/events/merry-measuring.doc>.

[8] Carl Schmitt, 'The Age of Neutralizations and Depolitizations (1929),' trans. John McCormick, (1993) 96 *Telos* 119.

(ii) the centrality of the concept of growth to development; (iii) the geographic locus of development knowledge as coming from the West for its application in the rest; and (iv) what we might call the 'religious' structure of development in which it is both process and horizon (or means and end).

Each of these four features bears a structural homology with international law in ways which reinforce the negativity of outcome they generate. Two particular consequences arise out of this. The first is that international law has no bite *between* nations vis-à-vis global poverty; and the second is that whatever potential might inhere in international law's symbolic relation to justice (and that potential might be very slight to begin with) is foreclosed when development becomes international law's horizon.

Because of this, the turns described by Sant'Ana[9] in his useful taxonomy as having taken place in development practice, discourse and doctrine in the last 20 years will not help the poor. Indeed, arguably the shifts make the problem worse, increasing the sphere of developmental intervention and intensifying its transformative violence. And although I have not the space to go into detail here, these problematic shifts include shifts toward rights based approaches and sustainable development. What the tenacity of these problems suggests is that we need to find a new normative language for political action around the question of how we share the earth which moves beyond the idioms of development and human rights. Although beyond the scope of this essay, such a language may potentially be found in the concept and traditions of the global commons.

***

Turning to the first feature of development I want to draw out here; the way the causes of poverty are understood in the institutional story as local and present causes, not global and historical causes. If we think about explanations of why some countries are poor, several causes are proffered. One story locates the causes of poverty in the political and institutional culture of poor societies—they have corrupt elites, oppressive governments, and no formal laws and institutions. In another explanation, the religious and philosophical traditions that underlie poor countries' institutions are not adapted to a modern economy, and don't reward the industriousness or co-operative talents of their members; or blame is sheeted home to the absence of infrastructure, and the limitations that offers to investors and local entrepreneurs. Another set of explanations suggest that *physical endowments* are to blame; some states have been unlucky in the geographic lottery (for example, by being landlocked). And yet others suggest that the causes of poverty lie in the history of slavery and colonial exploitation. Others focus on unfair international trade rules, and the differential impacts of the practices of some economies on others, or that certain international lending practices have created an insurmountable debt burden for some states.

If we schematise these responses, they fall into 4 categories: (i) geographic causes; (ii) historical causes; (iii) international or global causes; and (iv) national or local factors particular to the poor country in question. So, for example, the idea that poor governance and corruption explain a country's relative poverty are 'local' causes. The idea that some people are culturally not adapted to capitalism are also 'local'. The idea that colonialism created economic structures which have hindered a country's growth—such as a heavy

[9] Matthias Sant'Ana, 'Development in International Law'.

reliance on producing one or two commodities—is both international *and* historical, or the idea that global economic structures—including unfair trade rules, and agricultural subsidies in rich countries for example—prevent poor countries from trading their way out of poverty are international causes.

It is undoubtedly true that in relation to income poverty, many of these causes are operative at the same time. But the institutionalised discourse of development repeatedly locates the causes of poverty only in local and present causes, and does not—perhaps cannot—take account of international (or global) and historical causes of poverty. In other words, the institutionalised development story has a very specific explanation for what causes global poverty. The effect of understanding the *causes* of poverty in this way is to concentrate measures to address it in projects overwhelmingly directed at the transformation of the 'developing' society—and its political, legal, economic and social structures. The purpose of this transformative intervention is basically to produce what we think of as a 'modern nation state', able to compete effectively—and to trade freely—in an essentially benign international marketplace.

There have of course, been many critiques of this worldview, and from many perspectives, including from voices which speak in the idiom of development. The dependency theorists, for example, point out the way global economic structures enrich the centre at the expense of the periphery.[10] Thomas Pogge points to unfair trade rules, including agricultural subsidies as implicated in the causes of poverty.[11] Martin Wolf, from perhaps the opposite place on the political spectrum and supportive of free trade in principle, comes to the same conclusion, calling the regime of agricultural subsidies and escalating tariffs to which wealthy countries subject the exports of poor countries 'obscene'.[12] Ha Joon Chang famously indicts the ideology of free trade, demonstrating that the idea that free trade makes countries richer is both historically inaccurate and conceptually flawed.[13]

But because in the institutionalised development story, the international causes of poverty are simply not on the table, these stories can't gain any traction in juridical terms. Attempts to alleviate poverty have, for the last sixty years, not resulted in wholesale changes to the global terms of trade, nor in good faith debt forgiveness. Instead they have resulted in developing countries having to open up more and more of themselves to transformation by international agencies. So, over the same period as the ballooning debt, there has been a huge expansion in the remit of the international financial institutions.[14] The scope of the areas in which it is legal or legitimate to intervene in poor countries in the name of development has continued to widen. The conditions attached to loans used to be counted in points, now they are counted in pages. And where development institutions used to be concerned with building bridges, they are now concerned with building democracy.[15]

[10] See, for instance, Raul Prebisch, 'Five Stages in My Thinking on Development' in GM Meier and D Seers (eds), *Pioneers in Development* (Oxford, Oxford University Press, 1984) 175–191.

[11] Thomas Pogge, 'Recognized and Violated by International Law: The Human Rights of the Global Poor' (2005) 18 *Leiden Journal of International Law* 771.

[12] Martin Wolf, *Why Globalization Works* (New Haven, Yale University Press, 2005) 215.

[13] Ha-Joon Chang, *Bad Samaritans: The Myth of Free Trade and the Secret History of Capitalism* (Bloomsbury Press, 2008) See also Erik Reinert, *How Rich Countries Got Rich ... and Why Poor Countries Stay Poor* (London, Constable, 2007).

[14] Sundhya Pahuja and Ruth Buchanan, 'Legal Imperialism, Empire's Invisible Hand?' in Jodi Dean J and Paul Passavant (eds) *Empire's New Clothes* (New York, Routledge, 2004) 73.

[15] And increasingly with a gun. See Paul Collier, *The Bottom Billion: Why the Poorest Countries are Failing and What Can Be Done About It* (New York, Oxford University Press, 2008); see also William Easterly's review

International law is implicated in the institutionalised explanation of what causes poverty by its structure. It is a structure that localises responsibility through its focus on the nation-state. There is no jurisdiction within international law for calling the global, political-economic causes of poverty to account. So, even though development is understood as a global project, there is no global responsibility, only ever national responsibility. The World Bank, for example, has no jurisdiction over the rich—so even if it understands the way that agricultural subsidies, for example, hurt poor countries (which it obviously does), it is unable to do anything about them.

But the striking thing is that even though it is limited in this way, the World Bank continues both to espouse the ideology of free trade, and to support conditions imposed by the Fund which oblige poor countries to open their markets, liberalise their investment rules and so on. Recommending these policies in a perfect world is already highly contested by economists like Chang, Dani Rodrik and Erik Reinert, but enforcing them in the conditions of the global economic relations of real world has at best, to be the triumph of hope over experience—indeed, over fifty years of experience of the immiseration these policies cause.

Holding together those two contradictory possibilities—that is, the application of the theory of free trade to the poor countries with the experience of the reality of the trading order—is made possible by the way the development story explains and understands the causes of poverty, and more specifically localises the causes of poverty, vesting responsibility downwards into the nation-state, not upwards into the international community. It is also made possible by the structure of knowledge which the development story supports by its nature—knowledge *comes from* the developed world and is *applied to* the rest. The same structure of knowledge is true of human rights, dubbed the 'export theory' of human rights by Brian Simpson, extending to the singularity of its universalised model,[16] a model which following Zizek and reversing the aphorism, we might say is to, 'think local, act global'.[17] The effect of this combination is to allow the self-interest of rich countries in the form of market access and cheap primary commodities which conditionality effects, to be equated with altruism in the name of development. This recurring equation of altruism and self-interest is facilitated by the development story.[18]

International law's structural tendency to localise responsibility to the nation-state also means that when international legal solutions to global poverty are proffered, including human rights based solutions, they do not have any bite between nations, but only within them. In other words, it is difficult, if not impossible to use international law against the international. This toothlessness (as we might call it) consistently deradicalises possibilities for thinking of ways to address the question of global poverty, and removes the question of how we share the earth from the table.

So, for example, when we call for human rights, the way the structure of international law works means that those rights are directed at the nation-state within which individuals are situated. It has proven very difficult to assert human rights against former imperial

of the Collier book, William Easterly, 'Foreign Aid Goes Military!' in *The New York Review of Books* (2008). Also available online at: www.nybooks.com/articles/archives/2008/dec/04/foreign-aid-goes-military/.

[16] A W B Simpson, *Human Rights and the End of Empire: Britain and the Genesis of the European Convention* (Oxford, Oxford University Press, 2001).

[17] Slavoj Zizek, 'Knee Deep' (2004) 26 *The London Review of Books*. Available online here: <www.lrb.co.uk/v26/n17/slavoj-zizek/knee-deep>.

powers, or against rich states and their (trade) subsidies, or even against the international financial institutions. We see this difficulty play out in many examples, such as attempts to assert the right to food. Similarly calls to link labour standards to international trade would piggy back on the enforcement mechanisms of the trade regime to require poor states to respect human rights or labour standards—and incidentally privilege products from rich countries. Perhaps human rights in their most imperial guise?

This toothlessness means that calls for a more equitable global *distribution* of wealth cannot bite in legal institutional terms. The idea that we can reduce poverty without affecting the distribution or the accumulation of wealth is nonsense. But the political energy directed toward what we might call 'the global justice question' is continually captured and redirected toward the production of economic growth. A sustained analysis of historical reasons why economic growth lies at the heart of development is beyond the scope of this short chapter, however, the concept of Gross National Product (GNP or GDP) was invented in the 1950s around the same time as the concept of development.[19] It was a number that provided scientific ratification for the United States, in its position as the world's most powerful nation. It also replaced race as the measure of superiority between peoples in ways that the holocaust had made unpalatable, even to the (then still) imperial powers.[20] The end of the war, the success of independence struggles and the fatigue of Empire may have meant that former colonies were increasingly decolonising, but the universalisation of what we call international law during the imperial period meant that they could only decolonise through self-determination as nation-states (and that too within former colonial boundaries, expressed in the doctrine of *uti possedetis*).[21]

So even with the realisation of the promise of formal sovereign equality, nation-states could still be ordered in a hierarchy, but with GDP instead of race as the securing value. What kept this ladder in place was not the increasingly unpalatable idea of immutable racial difference, but a promise: that states at the bottom were included within the bosom of the international community and set on a path toward joining the ranks of the chosen few 'developed' states at the top. So, development immediately provided a way of ordering the world in which everyone was included on formally equal terms, but in which a hierarchy (and essentially the old hierarchy) was maintained. Because GDP was the new lynchpin of the global order newly structured around a *promise*, the key to that promise—economic growth—had to lie at the heart of the project. Accordingly, economic growth was—and remains—the secret beating heart of the development story.

According to the theory of economic growth, the rising tide lifts all boats. In other words, by increasing overall wealth, even if the rich got richer, some of it would eventually 'trickle down' to the poor. And the idea took hold; captured the *zeitgeist*. It was quickly embraced by people of all political and geo-political stripes. Communism, which was equally if not more 'developmental' than the First World, also embraced the need for growth as axiomatic. So even if there was fierce contestation around how growth should be achieved, growth as the objective of development was never dethroned.

[18] See also Gilbert Rist, *The History of Development: From Western Origins to Global Faith* (London: Zed Books, 1997) 90–91.

[19] Douglas Greenwald (ed), *Encyclopedia of Economics* (New York, McGraw-Hill, 1982).

[20] See Sundhya Pahuja, *Decolonizing International Law: Development, Economic Growth and the Politics of Universality* (Cambridge, Cambridge University Press, forthcoming 2011).

[21] *Uti Possedetis Jure:* 'you will have sovereignty over those territories you possess as of law'. On this point and whether it is a rule of customary international law, a general principle of law, or a 'simple practice', see Antonio Cassesse, *International Law* (Oxford, Oxford University Press, 2001) 57.

As time wore on and people began to realise the inadequacy of national income as the measure for development success, other definitions of development, and crucially, other *measures* of development, were devised, perhaps most famously the Human Development Index devised by Mahbub Ul Haq and the United Nations Development Programme in the 1990s.[22] This measure adds life expectancy and literacy to GDP to come up with a single figure indicia to denote development. Amartya Sen too, is famous for reconceptualising *development as freedom*, using what he calls the 'capabilities approach'. But even the most famous reconceptualisations, such as Sen's, still have economic growth at their heart.[23] So, the shift is not away from growth as the determinant, but *growth plus*. And international law and institutions have stayed very much within the paradigm. So for example, the Bank's most recent response to criticisms about the inadequacy of growth has been the shift to *inclusive* growth. Many NGOs try to modify the formula by demanding what they call 'pro-poor growth', and so on.

By centring the development story on *growth*, the promise to the poor is that they must invest their hopes of getting richer in increases in the overall size of the pie. This is meant to increase the size of each piece proportionately. And if this also increases the size of the rich countries' slice of the pie, or of the rich people in poor countries, well, it's just a *collateral benefit* again, of doing good for the poor. It's win-win again—self-interest and altruism happily co-existing. And of course, according to this logic, there can be no question of the pie being shared differently, or really even countenancing the idea that the pie might be of a finite size.

But arguably, the environmental facts call into question a development promise based on an infinitely expanding pie. Those facts, and the speed of the consumption of the earth's resources reveal that we can't just tweak the edges of a 'business as usual' approach. I cannot go into the environmental facts in detail here, but it is clear that those of us in rich countries consume such a large proportion of the world's resources pursuant to what some have called a 'take, make, break and discard' model that it's hard to see how we can make a good faith promise of equivalence. Given that the planet could sustain only one third of its current population if we all had the environmental footprint of an Australian, what is it exactly that we are promising?[24]

What then is happening in the world as a result of this? As the earth's limits become clearer, one option is for rich states to recognise the impossibility of the development promise, and simply to abandon it. This would mean fortifying the rich world against the clamour to 'get in', and pulling up the drawbridge. Some would say that as migration rules get tighter, and borders are policed with increasing vigilance, a version of that

[22] See hdr.undp.org/en/statistics/hdi/ at 19 November 2010.

[23] Amartya Sen, *Development as Freedom* (Oxford, Oxford University Press, 1999).

[24] The Global Footprint Network estimates we are currently using about 1.5 times the earth's carrying capacity, and on current trends we will exceed 2 planets worth by 2050. If everyone on earth was to live like an American (or an Australian) we would need approximately five planets worth of biocapacity. Put another way, at current high-income-country consumption levels the planet can sustain only around 1.8 billion people and at medium-income-country levels under 6 billion (of the almost 7 billion people now on earth). Recent scientific work by the Stockholm based Resilience Institute has attempted to identify key physical limits to the earth's carrying capacity in anything like its current form. They identify ten elements and estimate we are already close to or have exceeded four planetary boundaries (climate change, biodiversity loss, the nitrogen cycle, and the phosphorus cycle, and with ocean acidification worryingly close to the limit. See generally www.footprintnetwork.org/en/index.php/GFN/ at 19 November 2010; see also the World Wildlife Foundation's 'Living Planet Report 2010' available here: wwf.panda.org/about_our_earth/all_publications/living_planet_report/2010_lpr/ at 19 November 2010.

is already happening. But what is the international lawyer to do if she does not wish to embrace such a dystopic vision of the future? The first thing is to accept that what thinking about poverty and the environment together really means is that we need to re-think how we *share* the earth.

One possibility for such a rethinking lies in the concept of the Global Commons. There are at least two traditions of the commons, one economically centred, the other politically centred. Both traditions find expression in international law. In one tradition, the 'commons' at its broadest means 'the common wealth we share'.[25] In this politically resurgent understanding, the commons comes conceptually *before* state and international law. The application of modern (state and international) law to the commons is understood as a process of the progressive appropriation of that wealth in the name of the 'nation', through the mechanism of property rights enforced by state violence and resulting in the dispossession of the many.[26] In this story, capitalist development can be read as a series of enclosures, and the creeping commodification of an ever-expanding sphere of life, aided by modern law.

Within a different tradition, the 'commons' is represented as an area *bereft* of law. This absence of law creates a potential 'tragedy' which only law can solve. The commons here does not relate to everything shared, but only to 'rival' goods, which are both finite, and 'subtractable' in the sense that any amount used by one person is no longer available to another person. So, for example, a pond full of fish as opposed to a book full of ideas. In this strand of thought, the tragic potential for over-exploitation looms over all rival goods for which no individual or entity has direct responsibility.[27] The only way to avert the tragedy is by the *intervention* of modern law through the commodification of the resource via the creation of property rights over it, whether public or private.[28]

In the face of the earth's exhaustion, and the palpable limits of the human rights project, the possibility of a new normative ground may be promised by the notion of the commons, but only if a distinction is drawn between the economic and juristic approaches. Each conceptualisation finds expression in the rival traditions within international law. In economic approaches to the commons as a space of lawlessness, modern (international) law intervenes to avert the 'tragedy' of over consumption through the allocation of (property) rights. In contrast, in certain juristic (and political) traditions, the commons is already a law-full space and modern (international) law cuts in as imperium, appropriating what is shared, and allocating it unequally through the mechanism of private property rights. Arguably, a juristic approach to the commons could assist those seeking new normative grounds for political action in the institutional realm through an elaboration of a space that is neither utopian, nor utilitarian. The focus would lie on what we might call 'an ethics of the Global Commons' which pays specific attention to the difficulties of encapsulating legal relation 'in common', particularly relating to that which might be globally in common.

[25] Michael Hardt and Antoni Negri, *Commonwealth* (Cambridge, Harvard University Press, 2009) viii.

[26] Donald Nonini, 'Introduction: The Global Idea of the Commons' in Donald Nonini, *The Global Idea of the Commons* (New York, Berghahn Books, 2007) 1; John Pickles, 'Collectivism, Universalism, and Struggles Over Common Property Resources in the 'New' Europe' (2006) 50 *Social Analysis* 178; Emma Wittboi 'Governing Global Fisheries: Commons, Community Law and Third-Country Coastal Waters' (2008) 17 *Social & Legal Studies* 369.

[27] Garrett Hardin, 'The Tragedy of the Commons' (1968) 162 *Science* 1243.

[28] ibid.

Of course, versions of this argument have been around in some circles for a long time, but they have been relatively marginal to the development project and to international institutions so far. But in the spirit of never wasting a good crisis, it may be that the looming environmental problems and their global impacts cause us to rethink the development *promise* in a way which we haven't so far been able to. As Mao Zedong famously put it, 'There is great disorder under heaven, the situation is excellent.'

Part VII:

Appraisal

29

Pouring Away the Sweet Milk of Concord: A Call for Argument and Debate

GUGLIELMO VERDIRAME*

I WAS ASKED to report on the moments that were of particular importance and relevance to the conference theme, concentrating on: the plenary session; the agorae on international criminal law, human rights and the individual; and the forum on international law between hope and threats.

Some of the papers—the minority it has to be said—tackled the conference theme head-on; some used it as a framework; and in other cases, papers proceeded on the basis of tacit but shared assumptions about the performance of international law.

Andrew Hurrell's keynote address was clearly in the first group. He not only addressed the question of the appraisal of the performance of the system, but also raised what I might call the 'meta-question': the performance of international lawyers—as scholars and practitioners—in understanding, evaluating and criticising the system. His warning against parochialism, to which I will return, was heeded by some speakers. In his response, Sir Daniel Bethlehem invited us to consider whether the *phenomenon* of international law is not moving faster than our thinking about it, creating—I would add—the danger of institutions, principles and rules that just *happen* without concepts and ideas behind them. In one of the most important philosophical reflections on human rights to be published recently, Jim Griffin makes a similar point when he observes that there is a widening gap between philosophy and international human rights law. This is a serious intellectual danger, particularly if we bear in mind that international lawyers of previous generations, from Grotius to Hersch Lauterpacht, were thinking ahead of the *phenomenon*. Are we still capable of doing so today? Or is our ability to think ahead somewhat rusty?

Some of the sessions where the theme of the conference was not addressed head-on proceeded on the basis of what seemed to be shared assumptions about it. For example, the consensus in the international criminal law session appeared to be that, despite the great progress of the last twenty years, the system of international criminal justice has not yet fully addressed the link with the domestic level—both in terms of the capacity

* Guglielmo Verdirame is a Lecturer in International Law at the University of Cambridge and a Fellow of the Lauterpacht Centre for International Law.

of local courts to mount trials, and in terms of the dialogue between international and domestic courts on the development of substantive categories and concepts of international criminal law. In a paper that attracted much discussion in the forum on international law between hope and threat, Carlos Esposito also identified the risks and opportunities of the application of international law by national judges as a key challenge to emerge from the last twenty years, and one that is probably here to stay for the next twenty.

The human rights panel was a surprise. I have to confess that I thought Whig history would be plentiful in a panel of human rights scholars invited to assess the performance of international human rights law over the last twenty years – an expectation that did not arise from my own views, but rather from that optimistic confidence in the inevitability of progress that pervades the field of human rights. Judith Shklar famously distinguished liberalism of progress from liberalism of fear, placing contemporary liberalism squarely in the arena of progress. But I wonder whether the emotion of fear is not replacing that belief in progress which, according to Kant, even if not empirically demonstrable, is morally necessary. Fear, generally, about the fact that, as Georg Nolte put it, the 'window of opportunity' created by the end of the Cold War is over, and with it the era of self-confident liberalism. One of the defining moments in the history of the Italian left was when the Sardinian aristocrat who was then the very popular leader of the Communist Party in an interview on national television in the late 1970s dramatically, and somewhat euphemistically, announced that the 'propulsive energy of the October Revolution is probably over'. For many of our speakers the same can be said today of the propulsive energy of 1989. And, deprived of this energy, some, like Jean d'Aspremont, fear that international law may have given up on democracy to retreat to the somewhat cosier and deceptively depoliticised world of legalised human rights, with democracy now the invisible elephant in the room.

Mohammed Shahabuddin analysed the impact of the politics of identity on human rights and minority rights, noting not a few regressive tendencies in both cases. His paper, and other remarks on this question, certainly left me with the impression that what I may call the impoverishment of the individual through the reductionism of, amongst other things, the politics of identity does represent a serious intellectual challenge for the next twenty years. For a predicate of human rights as we have traditionally understood them has always been a particular notion of personhood: the idea of the self as ineffable and impregnable that runs from Augustine to Ernst Cassirer. But gone is now Bernini's Aeneas, Michelangelo's David or—to remain on familiar ground Tom Franck's empowered individual. Our unphilosophically dis-invented individual resembles, instead, an elongated Giacometti statue, with identity labels and logo stickers attached to its limbs. *Ecce Homo* for the XXI century.

The individual was at the centre of another panel, with Linos-Alexandre Sicilianos, Kaj Hober and Robert McCorquodale each noting the rise of the individual in international law, with the ultra-positivists who still resist it standing no greater chance of success than the Japanese soldiers who were still fighting the Second World War in the 1970s. I do wonder however whether the time has not come to give those ultra-positivists the honours of war and move on, on the basis that the position of the individual in international law is now settled.

In concluding, I would like to return briefly to the meta-question: how do we, international lawyers, perform when we engage the somewhat introspective task of having to appraise the performance of our subject? The striking and somewhat troubling thing is how much we agree on. It is perhaps no coincidence that the moment of greatest controversy during the conference was generated by Tarak Barkawi, an international relations scholar.

Here are some snapshots of this consensus. Weaker states are a good thing. NGOs are empowering and potentially counter-hegemonic. Sovereignty is a very bad thing, while positivism, not to mention liberalism, are so passé. And when we have to season our dislike for something (values, interests, theories, ideas or traditions) is there a better adjective than Western? Judaeo-Christian might be a close competitor.

This consensus stretches to claims that are very idiosyncratic indeed: we like individuals and want to see more of them in international law, but we don't do liberalism. We like self-determination, but we don't do state sovereignty.

Sometimes our consensus is so deep that we communicate through innuendos or silence: we talk of how international law can contribute to 'strategies of resistance', but we do not explain what or who is to be resisted and why; we want international law to be counter-hegemonic, but we gloss over the question of who the hegemons are for we all seem to know anyway. (Yet, Lavanja Rajamani's paper showed that, in the world of climate negotiations, the answer may not be as monolithic as Wilhelm Grewe would have had it.) We want international law to be transformational, but often leave the question of what it is that it should transform to a tacit understanding.

The summary of my report on the sessions I attended is thus more consensus and less controversy than one would expect, especially considering how much disagreement there would be among historians, economists and philosophers called to assess the last twenty years. In addition, there might be also the sense that—forgive the cliché—international law is turning a page. What is not clear is whether we international lawyers have (as we did at other turning points in history) a script or a series of scripts ready; that is, whether we have ideas to feed to the political processes through which international law is made so as to ensure that the next chapter of international law will not be written exclusively with the pens of power, interest or disillusionment.

30

Reflections on the Asymmetric Rule of Law in International Relations

JOCHEN VON BERNSTORFF*

IN THIS REFLECTION on the international law based institutionalisation, economic globalisation and development forums I would like briefly to address three overlapping-themes: first, the ideal of the rule of law in international relations, secondly the legitimacy question and thirdly the issue of fragmentation or defragmentation of international law.

Let me start with the topic of the rule-of-law-based institutionalisation of the international legal order. Joseph L Kunz, a disciple of Hans Kelsen and one of the brightest international lawyers of the interwar period, described the political atmosphere of the early 1920s as follows:

> Away with power politics! No more secret diplomacy, no more entangling alliances, no longer the forever discredited balance of power, no more war! Democracy and the rule of international law will change the world.... In all the dealings of the League, international law was at the heart of the discussion. Idealistic approach, optimism, emphasis on international law created the Geneva atmosphere.[1]

Twenty years later in 1939, the famous international relations scholar Edward Hallet Carr in his book, *The 20 Years Crisis*, found: 'The utopia of 1919 was hollow and without substance.... Like all utopias which are institutionalised, the post-War utopia became the tool of vested interests and was perverted into a bulwark of the status quo'.[2]

The legal climate in the post 1989 era arguably also started with a reinvigoration of the rule of law ideal in international relations. The Cold War was over. The UN Security Council authorised the military intervention against Iraq with the goal to restore the territorial integrity of Kuwait. From a Western perspective a new phase of international institutionalisation based on an allegedly emerging global consensus about the value of multilateralism, democracy, human rights and the free market economy was supposed to begin.

Twenty years later—with hindsight—it becomes clear that the assumption of such a global consensus was overly ambitious if not an illusion to begin with. Instead of an

* Professor at Tübingen University.

[1] J L Kunz, 'The Swing of the Pendulum: From Overestimation to Underestimation of International Law' (1950) 44 *AJIL* 136.

[2] E H Carr, *The Twenty Years' Crisis 1919-1939* (London, Macmillan and Co, 1940) 287.

effective UN-based multilateralism—at least the last ten years in important areas of international law were shaped by US unilateralism and coalitions of the willing operating outside international law; additionally, in the area of individualised sanctions, the Security Council itself has been criticised for failing to adhere to rule of law standards. Instead of world-wide democratisation the political elites of the new global superpower, China, have no intention to democratise their country, and Russia as well as many other countries still have a long way to go before becoming stable democracies. Holding regular elections alone does not turn autocratic institutional structures into democratic ones.

Instead of an already achieved universal consensus on the nature and the scope of human rights standards, the post-1989 era has been marked by political and theoretical divergences about the nature and role of international human rights protection. Due to the rise of religion as an ever more important political force in international relations, many political actors and groups over the last 20 years have contested traditional interpretations of the foundations and the scope of international human rights standards in sensitive areas of the human rights project.

It was the last aspect of the assumed post-1989 global political consensus—the promotion of the free market economy—which transformed international relations over the last twenty years and has been endorsed by a great majority of governments and international institutions. The institutional centre of gravity in the field of international economic policy and justice shifted from the UN General Assembly to the World Bank and to the newly established WTO. It is in the economic field that international law underwent a fundamental evolution by realising the rule of law project in international trade law and in international investment law.

While the global trade and investment regime became effectively regulated through new multilateral and bilateral legal instruments in the 1990s with strong enforcement mechanisms, other areas of international legal policy such as social development, human rights, and environmental law continue to struggle with the lack of political commitment, lack of resources and lack of formalised implementation procedures. I am not saying that there has been no progressive development in those other areas: a number of new multilateral instruments have been created, including new global human rights conventions, such as the Convention on the Rights of the Child, the Convention on the Rights of Persons with Disabilities, the Rome Statute and the Kyoto Protocol. But compared to the WTO and ICSID arbitrations these instruments rely on relatively weak enforcement mechanisms. Their impact on the daily lives of human beings around the globe has arguably been less significant than the impact of the global economic order, with both its legally institutionalised areas and those areas relying on informal and network based regulation.

The post-1989 era has created an *asymmetric rule of law* in international relations. This institutional imbalance and the fact that globally grave economic and social inequalities persist, have created various reactions in international legal and philosophical scholarship. In this context, I only want to refer to two scholarly buzzwords that have also come up in many of the discussions here at the conference: legitimacy and fragmentation.

The first one is the ever more present legitimacy debate. Does the global institutional set-up created by international law have a legitimacy problem because of inherent biases and non-transparent intergovernmental law making? If the debates in the development and globalisation fora at this conference are anything to go by, there seems to be a growing trend to question the existing legal status quo in the area of international economic law and to imagine other rules from a poverty angle. The dividing line between scholars seems to be the question whether the existing system needs to be only better implemented and interpreted to alleviate poverty—for instance by finally cutting down on agricultural subsidies in the West—or whether the system as it developed in the post-1989 era is structurally sustaining inequality and therefore needs to be reinvented. It has to be kept in mind that for governments in this context the alternative to multilateral institutionalisation is bilateralism or informal network-based (self-) regulation. While law-based multilateralism can potentially create open political fora, in which questions of global economic justice can be meaningfully debated, bilateralisation and network-based regulation tend to work in favour of the strongest actors.

Here in Cambridge, the legitimacy debate appeared in various guises. One way it has been framed is the scholarly reference to human-rights standards. As many discussions at this conference have shown, human rights for many scholars have become the substantive litmus test for legitimate international rule making and enforcement. The prime example in the area of due process-rights of affected individuals is the *Kadi* judgment of the ECJ. Additionally, the progressive doctrinal developments in the field of economic, social and cultural rights and the creation of an individual complaint mechanism for the Covenant on Economic, Social and Cultural Rights have been promoted by the ever more present networks of globally operating NGOs in this field. This can be seen as a post-1989 counter-reaction to adverse effects of economic globalisation. Since human rights as abstract entitlements can be limited and need to be concretised in institutional practice, it has become ever more important which institutional authority can claim the authority to define the duty-bearers, the scope, the limits and irreducible cores of these individual entitlements. A turn to enforceable individual rights is always also a turn away from politics to the judiciary. As a couple of interventions at this conference have highlighted, the transformative potential of the rights language in the area of social development itself has been increasingly called into doubt in the tradition of various critiques of the rights discourse.

A further observation is that the notion of national sovereignty, which since the first World War has been deconstructed by great European scholars like Kelsen and Lauterpacht in recurring waves of scholarship, is being brought back into the debate under the angle of legitimacy. Sovereignty—according to this line of argument—is supposed to protect collective decision-making in the nation state against rule making by international organisations, against informal network-based regulation of international markets ('food sovereignty') or against hegemonic interventionism by other states in the context of foreign occupation. Can the notion of sovereignty meaningfully capture certain grievances international legal scholars have with the state of institutionalisation of the international legal order, including with informal regulatory practices enabled by the corresponding gaps and silences of the law? A further version of the legitimacy debate is of course the one on accountable global governance spearheaded by the Global Administrative Law project, which attempts to look more closely into the operations of formalised and deformalised regulatory regimes from an accountability perspective.

This leads me to the last overlapping topic that often came up in this conference: the issue of fragmentation and defragmentation. The fragmentation debate can also be seen as a scholarly reaction to the problem of asymmetric rule of law in international relations. The ILC Fragmentation Report has made a claim in favour of the assumption of systemic unity of international law and Bruno Simma and Theodore Kill, in a recent article have convincingly criticised the 'disintegrative inclination' in the field of international investment law. Systemic integration through interpretation has become the glimmer of hope for the discipline as it projects its hopes on Article 31 paragraph 3 c, the provision on systemic interpretation in the Vienna Convention on the Law of Treaties.

There is however no reason for a boundless belief in de-fragmentation by the judiciary. The adjudicatory practice in special regimes so far has produced few examples that seem to justify such hopes. This has to do with applicable-law rules and the selection of judges and arbitrators. And do we really want arbitrators with a commercial law background in ICSID tribunals to define the limits of the right to water of slum dwellers in Nairobi? One thing seems clear: the asymmetric rule of law in international relations will not be reversed by the international judiciary alone.

Let me conclude by pointing out that despite these words of caution I do believe that the scholarly aspiration of systemic unity is a valuable Kelsenian legacy of international legal thought. It stands for the possibility of a deterritorialised legal discourse connecting the various functional sub-systems. Or to put it in Habermasian terms: law must always be both, a medium in the service of functional imperatives of sectoral subsystems *and* a communicative medium that remains accessible for discursive engagement and critique through the lifeworld. It is only if international law constitutes such an overarching legal discourse that fundamental experiences of injustice can be meaningfully articulated by it.

31

Quelques Réflexions en Guise de Conclusion

ANNE LAGERWALL*

LE TITRE DE la conférence suggère une question assez simple en apparence : Le droit international a-t-il bien fonctionné ces vingt dernières années ? Plus précisément, on peut se demander si le droit international fonctionne mieux aujourd'hui qu'il ne le faisait avant 1989. La réponse à ces interrogations dépend intrinsèquement de la manière dont on définit le droit international et des fonctions qu'on lui assigne. A partir de trois définitions plus ou moins classiques du droit international, je voudrais tenter une ébauche d'évaluation en m'appuyant sur tout ce que j'ai pu entendre durant ces trois derniers jours de conférence.

Si le droit international est un ensemble de règles qui vise à réguler les champs d'activité humaine de la manière la plus étendue possible, le bilan est assurément positif. Comme l'a rappelé Sir Elihu Lauterpacht tout au début de la conférence, « international law has certainly expanded in range, in substance, in depths ». La simple prolifération des règles de droit international ne nous dit toutefois pas grand chose de leur fonctionnement. Et même un juriste aussi formaliste que l'était Hans Kelsen soulignait qu'une règle de droit, pour être valide, devait être globalement respectée dans les faits. Il convient alors de se demander plutôt si le droit international est davantage respecté depuis 1989. Cette question était en filigrane des débats du forum intitulé « Conformité, jugement et dérogation ? » et si personne n'y a répondu directement, les participants ont néanmoins fourni des éléments de réflexion à ce sujet. Joel Trachtman a évoqué certains facteurs politiques à l'aide desquels il serait possible de prévoir les cas dans lesquels les Etats respectent le droit international et les cas dans lesquels ils ne le font pas. L'analyse des intérêts en balance et des coalitions possibles à l'intérieur des Etats expliquerait, dans une certaine mesure, leur attitude vis-à-vis de leurs obligations internationales. D'autres participants ont plutôt entendu mesurer le respect du droit international à l'aune du fonctionnement des tribunaux internationaux. Hugh Thirlway a estimé que la Cour internationale de justice avait fonctionné de manière satisfaisante ces vingt dernières années tout en suggérant qu'une division en deux ou trois chambres l'amènerait probablement à être plus efficace encore. Yuval Shany a, quant à lui, rappelé qu'une décision judiciaire présente un intérêt limité si elle n'est pas ensuite exécutée. Il a émis à ce sujet des propositions stimulantes.

* Professeure-assistante, Université Libre de Bruxelles.

Selon lui, plus le coût matériel et politique d'une décision est élevé pour le défendeur, plus le risque qu'il ne s'y conforme pas est grand. *A contrario*, plus le coût d'une décision est réduit pour le défendeur, plus il est probable qu'il exécute cette décision. Mais dans ce dernier cas de figure, il se demandait si on n'en venait pas finalement à permettre au défendeur de s'acquitter trop aisément de ce qu'il doit et d'acquérir par là-même une forme de droit à violer le droit international. Au-delà de ces réflexions, les débats menés dans ce forum semblaient dresser un bilan plutôt positif du fonctionnement du droit international depuis 1989. Et si on reconnaissait que certaines règles pouvaient prêter le flanc à la critique, on proposait d'en améliorer la facture. A chaque problème, sa solution. L'atmosphère générale restait en ce sens résolument optimiste.

Dans une autre perspective, on peut définir le droit international comme un outil dont on suppose qu'il permet de réaliser certains objectifs comme la paix, la justice ou l'éradication de la pauvreté, un outil qui aurait été bloqué pendant la guerre froide et puis soudainement disponible après 1989. Dans cette veine, on peut se demander si la chute du mur a offert au droit international de nouvelles perspectives l'amenant finalement à servir les causes pour lesquelles il aurait été créé. Si on adopte ce point de vue, le bilan paraît pour le moins mitigé. Certes, la troisième guerre mondiale n'a pas eu lieu. Mais des conflits ont éclaté en Yougoslavie, au Rwanda, en Afghanistan, en République démocratique du Congo, au Sierra Leone, en Angola, en Irak et encore récemment en Géorgie sans que le Conseil de sécurité des Nations Unies ne parvienne à en éviter le déclenchement ni même à en limiter la portée. Il est vrai que le Conseil de sécurité a pu adopter depuis 1989 des mesures à l'égard de certains Etats ou de certains individus, des mesures qu'il avait été incapable d'adopter auparavant. Stefan Talmon a toutefois déploré la manière dont ces mesures ont été définies et exécutées en regrettant amèrement l'absence de transparence, de prévisibilité et d'égalité dans le traitement des différentes situations dont le Conseil a été saisi ces vingt dernières années. Quant à la réalisation d'une justice internationale, on peut remarquer que plusieurs tribunaux pénaux internationaux ont vu le jour depuis la chute du mur. La Cour pénale internationale dont certains avaient rêvé dès la fin de la seconde guerre mondiale est aujourd'hui devenue une réalité. Il faut souligner que la mise sur pied de ces juridictions constitue un développement majeur dans l'ordre juridique international, un développement qui pose toutefois encore la question de savoir pour qui et pour quoi cette justice pénale internationale fonctionne. Enfin, concernant l'éradication de la pauvreté, il n'est nul besoin de préciser qu'on est très loin du compte. En somme, si le droit international est un instrument destiné à réaliser la paix et la justice ou à promouvoir la dignité humaine, son fonctionnement depuis 1989 peut sembler assez désespérant et le bilan paraît plutôt négatif.

Enfin et dernièrement, on peut encore appréhender le droit international comme un langage qui dépendrait des lieux et des moments dans lesquels il est articulé ainsi que de ceux et de celles qui l'articulent. Il s'agirait alors plutôt de savoir si on parle ce langage aujourd'hui comme on le parlait avant 1989. Cette langue est-elle morte ou au contraire, sa connaissance est-elle aujourd'hui plus répandue ? Son vocabulaire et sa grammaire ont-ils évolué depuis la chute du mur ? Ces multiples questions ne sauraient trouver de réponse univoque. Mais peut-être peut-on, à tout le moins, s'accorder sur deux points.

D'abord, le droit international est loin d'être une langue morte. Au contraire, il y a aujourd'hui davantage d'avocats, de juges, de fonctionnaires qui parlent cette langue. S'ils ne la parlent pas tous couramment, ils s'y essaient en tout cas. Plus fondamentalement, les chancelleries qui pendant la guerre froide ne s'embarrassaient pas systématiquement de justifications juridiques pour fonder leurs actions se sentent aujourd'hui visiblement contraintes de le faire. Les Etats-Unis d'Amérique et le Royaume-Uni ont recouru à la force contre l'Irak en vertu d'une autorisation accordée par le Conseil de sécurité dans la résolution 678 (1991) et ravivée dans la résolution 1441 (2003). Plus récemment, la Fédération de Russie a entrepris une attaque militaire contre la Géorgie en se prévalant de son droit à la légitime défense consacré par l'article 51 de la Charte des Nations Unies. Si ces argumentations sont peu convaincantes sur le plan juridique, il n'en demeure pas moins qu'elles font clairement référence au droit international. Or, l'utilisation de ce registre de légitimation est important parce qu'il permet précisément aux juristes d'analyser le discours juridique produit par les politiques, de le critiquer le cas échéant en évitant ainsi que les mots soient déformés et le droit international instrumentalisé à d'autres fins que celles pour lesquelles il a été créé. C'est en ce sens qu'on peut comprendre plusieurs interventions réalisées au sein de l'agora relatif aux conflits armés et au droit international humanitaire. Vaios Koutroulis a rappelé que l'égalité des belligérants est un principe qui s'applique à tout le monde, y compris les Nations Unies. Dominika Svarc a dénoncé, quant à elle, les tentatives des Etats-Unis d'Amérique d'élargir les concepts de crimes de guerre et de combattants illégaux dans le cadre de la lutte menée contre le terrorisme. Si le droit international est un langage, encore faut-il le parler correctement.

Deuxièmement, si le droit international est davantage discuté qu'avant, il n'est pas surprenant que les controverses à son sujet soient plus nombreuses, comme a pu l'illustrer le forum consacré au « système étatique ». Certes, on peut globalement se mettre d'accord sur le fait qu'en principe, un Etat rassemble une population sur un territoire situé sous l'autorité d'un gouvernement effectif et souverain. Mais que dire de chacun de ces éléments dans la réalité ? Les populations se meuvent d'un bout à l'autre de la planète depuis 1989. Les territoires fluctuent et leurs frontières sont moins physiques que juridiques, comme l'a expliqué Boldizsar Nagy. Les gouvernements sont parfois effectifs à défaut d'être souverains et parfois souverains à défaut d'être effectifs, comme l'a remarqué Anne Peters. Et plus on tente de vérifier si les éléments constitutifs de l'Etat sont réunis dans tel ou tel autre cas concret, plus on s'oppose les uns aux autres. Tarak Barkawi a suggéré que ces divergences existent peut-être parce que les réalités auxquelles on entend appliquer le droit sont construites selon des modèles idéologiquement connotés auxquels on est plus ou moins attaché si bien que lorsque les juristes examinent la même chose, ils n'identifient pas les mêmes phénomènes, malgré toute leur sincérité et leur bonne foi.

Si les juristes ne parviennent pas à se mettre d'accord lorsqu'ils parlent leur propre langue, que dire des débats qui concernent des notions empruntées aux sciences naturelles et auxquels participent des experts peu rompus à la science juridique. Les difficultés du dialogue interdisciplinaire sont apparues de manière particulièrement claire au sein de l'agora consacrée au droit de la mer. Bjørn Kunoy a bien mis en lumière l'influence qu'exerce la Commission de délimitation du plateau continental composée de géologues et d'hydrographes sur l'interprétation de la Convention de Montego Bay et les questions que cette interaction entre les scientifiques et les juristes soulève. Andrew Serdy a commenté le fonctionnement des organisations régionales de gestion de pêche et la conception de la liberté de pêche en haute mer que ce fonctionnement véhicule, en souhaitant qu'on dispose à l'avenir de l'expertise de biologistes et d'économistes de façon à assurer une bonne gestion des stocks de poissons.

De cette cacophonie, il ressort que le droit international est un langage bien vivant qui présente toujours ses spécificités par rapport à d'autres langages. Et à l'avenir, on ne peut que souhaiter que ce dialogue se développe encore et enrichisse chaque personne qui y prend part. On peut espérer que chacun puisse parler cette langue comme il ou elle l'entend avec les accents de sa ville d'origine et les expressions de sa région, tout en veillant à respecter le sens des mots et quelques règles classiques de grammaire.

32

Post-1989 as a Narrative

THOMAS SKOUTERIS*

REPORTING ON THE work of a conference whose task is to report on international law's performance during the past twenty years is, by definition, a complex exercise. For one thing, it requires a double historical representation, the telling of two histories at a time. On the one hand, it needs to narrativise the micro-level of the conference itself as a professional-social event: to place, for example, the facts in historical sequence, to describe the sociology of the group of colleagues gathered, to identify the structure and dynamics of the prevailing discourse, and so on. In parallel, the report also needs to provide the macro-level account of how international law fared during the turbulent years after the fall of the Berlin Wall: to enquire whether international law has progressed or regressed, to identify the main changes in its deep structure, doctrines, or institutions, to begin drawing conclusions about who benefits and who loses by the transformation of the field, and so on.

The complexity of this double representation may be ascribed to the large amount of information to be organised but also, and perhaps more importantly, to lessons learned from the modern science of history. During recent decades historians have amply explained how differences of opinion about the past rarely concern the reality of events, i.e. whether something 'really' happened. Disagreement rather centres on which relationships of facts make up an 'event', how historians choose which events to talk about, and how to situate traces of the past within larger stories about human progress—what historians call narrativisation.[1] The theme of this conference is a good example. Most of us recall 'witnessing' on our television screens the events of November 9, 1989, when crowds of East Germans dismantled the Berlin Wall brick by brick and crossed over to West Germany. We remember vividly that moment as bearing witness to an important incident, akin perhaps to the experience of watching live on CNN the collapse of the Twin Towers on September 11, 2001, but without being able fully to comprehend its significance. Surely, even back in 1989 the fall of the Wall logically led to the assumption that other Eastern Bloc states might undergo some transformation (in terms of economy, ideology, governance, borders,

* Associate Professor, Law Department, The American University in Cairo.

[1] See, eg, K Jenkins, *Re-thinking History* (London, Routledge,1991); H White, *The Content of the Form: Narrative Discourse and Historical Representation* (Baltimore, The John Hopkins Press,1987); A Munslow, *Deconstructing History*, 2nd edn (London, Routledge, 2006); K Jenkins et al, *At the Limits of History: Essays on Theory and Practice* (London, Routledge, 2009). For the discursive construction of international law 'events' see F Johns, R Joyce and S Pahuja (eds), *Events: The Force of International Law* (Oxford, Routledge, 2010).

etc). Few knew, however, that in 2010 international law as a whole would consider the fall of the Berlin Wall as synonymous with the End of the Cold War, as a watershed prompting a new periodisation of international law's history: 1918, 1945, and now 1989. More than a question of hindsight, the calendar event of November 9, 1989, is distinct from the narrative that is now considered an epistemological commonplace, namely the familiar post-1989 narrative of the emergence of a 'new world order', of 'globalisation', and of the 'end of history' in the wake of 1989 and lasting till our time.[2]

Witnessing an event does not tell you all that it means. Reporting on the past, constructing a historical narrative of what happened is impossible without a filter that identifies some elements as worth being included in or excluded from the story and draws relationships between them. Writing history is both about including and excluding facts and relationships, both about positive and negative appraisals of their significance within grander narratives about human, social, professional and scientific development. We consciously choose our explanations of how and why something happened and the relationships that we draw between traces of the past. It is the narrator that creates the filters and the descriptive categories for talking about the past and the criteria for its appraisal. In this context, it may appear as a truism to state that no conference report and no performance appraisal of international law can recover the past because the past did not happen in the form of a story. The past is a set of events, situations, and infinite relationships between them, only some of which we choose to talk about. Similarly, it is hard to tell the story of the 4th ESIL Biennial Conference and its performance appraisal of post-1989 international law without bringing to the fore some of the filters and the descriptive categories that carried the day during this professional gathering. Three such filters are chosen here. The first concerns the significance ascribed to the end of the Cold War as a historical event demarcating a new epoch of international law ('why 1989?'). The question to be asked here is why did the Biennial Conference, and international law as a whole, flag 1989 as the turning point of professional history, and as opposed to a different historical landmark, say the genocides in Yugoslavia and Rwanda, the Bhopal and Chernobyl environmental catastrophes, the 9/11 attacks, or any other event for that matter. What is the analytical value of this periodisation? Is there something to be gained and something to be excluded with this choice as opposed to a different one? A second filter centres on whether there is a common understanding among colleagues during the conference about the nature of '1989' as a historical event ('which 1989?'). The question here is about whether the end of the Cold War is a concrete and definable 'event' or whether it means different things to different people, leading to different kinds of consequences. The third filter concerns the yardstick for appraising of post-1989 international law ('Did we make progress post-1989?'). It searches for the criteria chosen by colleagues for their performance appraisal. Is the story of international law post-1989 a history of progress or one of regression or declension—and how do we measure progress?

Along these lines, and with a broad brush, conference presentations in the panels assigned to the present author to report on[3] seem to endorse two alternative and rather competing perspectives.

[2] For a review of such narratives see the chapter by R Lesaffer, 'The End of the Cold War: An Epochal Event in the History of International Law?' in this book.

[3] Forum 2: 'A Period of Legalisation', September 2, 2010; Agora 2: 'International Environmental Law', September 3, 2010; Agora 9: 'Development in International Law', September 4, 2010; Forum 9: 'Gaps and Silences in the Law'.

The first group of presentations deals with the first filter ('why 1989?') rather unequivocally. The end of the Cold War is pictured as a watershed: the end of ideological polarity that allegedly defines the Cold War era is claimed to have released international doctrines and institutions from the bootstraps of sterile oppositional politics. International law as a whole, the story goes, was thus able to progress by embracing more fully universal ideals such as democracy, human rights and market economy, forging greater harmony among nations and fostering an international community of states more willing and able to accept moral responsibility and global action. To enable such an unequivocal account, however, the second filter ('which 1989'?) is sometimes understated or set aside altogether. The anatomy of the end of the Cold War as a historical fact, or as a conglomerate of historical facts, is taken for granted. The discursive, ideological, or other process by which it is elevated by mainstream narratives into a pivotal 'event' is not analysed as such or questioned. Nineteen eighty nine is treated as epistemological commonplace that deserves little enquiry by the lawyer and may be used on face value or by reference to historical work done elsewhere. On the contrary, the third filter ('did we make progress post-1989?') is dealt with much more explicitly and decisively: international law has moved with steady paces post-1989 in the direction of progress, if only with a strong caveat about the need to remain alert to emerging systemic problems and new dangers (eg exceptionalism, non compliance, fragmentation, etc).

How is progress to be measured? Here authors search for continuities and patterns to be discerned in the changing structure of international law. Evidence of progress is found in the processes of increased legalisation of international relations, the proliferation of tribunals, increased accountability of individuals, increased access of individuals to international accountability mechanisms, global collective security and 'responsibility to protect' debates, the progressive endorsement of liberal democratic governance as a public policy goal. In the Legalisation panel, for example, two panellists argue that post-1989 international law became more 'legalised' on account of the fact that a tremendous increase in the number of hard and soft legal instruments has been documented, with parallel increase in the number of signatory or participating states and the enforcement of the law. These accounts carefully warn that not all of the new law is a positive development as such and that the content and quality of the substantive norms included in new instruments needs to be evaluated. In addition, new rules produce a ripple effect requiring new procedural norms for the organisation, application and enforcement of the new norms. In spite of the descriptive tone, these accounts are nevertheless laced with a positive claim according to which legalisation is ultimately a positive, progressive development that is somehow triggered or enabled by the end of the Cold War, even though the exact causal link between the two is not always explained. Similarly, in the Environmental Law panel we hear that the participatory model of non-compliance mechanisms, such as the one in the Aarhus convention, is a positive development on account of strengthening democratic accountability, albeit on the condition that access to justice and environmental consciousness are improved in tandem in order to make the institution meaningful. The Aarhus model here is seen as evidence of a welcome trend for individual access to accountability mechanisms that has found more favourable conditions to consolidate post-1989. On the 'Gaps and Silences' panel another colleague described the implementation of international electoral standards in some municipal legal orders as a positive development under some circumstances, underscoring wider endorsement and deepening of adherence to democratic governance.

Contrasting with the first group of presentations, the second set of papers takes a decidedly different tack. Instead of continuities it focuses on post-1989 'ruptures', 'discontinuities', 'gaps', and 'silences'. These presentations use examples of international law institutions, cases, doctrines, practices or experiences that, in the view of the authors, demonstrate that post-1989 international law presents a much more complex and fragmented picture than the one painted by the narratives of progress of the first group. Most importantly, that some of the dominant explications and appraisals hide from sight significant developments and consequences of the processes taking place during the last twenty years that may present an entirely different picture of what the world of international law looks like in 2010. For mainstream histories, the direction in which change occurs can be perceived as leading towards a goal that may even be unknown to the actors involved but is somehow inherent in the various stages in which history evolves (eg legalisation, democratisation, and so on). Focusing on discontinuities allows one to argue the following: a) the notion of progress and the pattern of history's evolution has inscribed in it philosophical, political and other assumptions which are difficult to sustain; b) such histories 'reduce a complex world into hierarchical blocs, following each other in a more or less monotonous parade headed by laws of interdependence, great power policies'[4] and so on; c) they fail to account for the agency of individual international lawyers in constructing these developments through historical narrative; d) they ultimately fail to account for how we got here. This second approach therefore prefers to focus on the conditions that may be dispersed in society, culture, and legal discourse that make a particular explanation about humanity or legal development seem as a compelling reality. Instead of seeing the past as made of continuities, epochs, stages of development, they look for ruptures, discontinuities and the uniqueness, rather than the teleological nature, of legal phenomena. There are many reasons why one may focus on discontinuities, such as to try to liberate the field from the grip and structural bias of hegemonic historical narratives; to write back into history what is excluded; to re-write history; to explain the discursive role of historical argument in law; to read law as a 'text'; to create imaginative space for new forms of politics; to provoke loss of faith in mainstream accounts, to reveal the structural bias of existing doctrines and institutions; and so on.

Thus with regard to the first filter ('why 1989?') these presentations argue that the importance of '1989' rests less with the real impact of these events on international law and more with how 1989 became a determinate 'event' around which an entire professional orthodoxy about the past, present, and future of international law is constructed.[5] In other words, the story of post-1989 cannot be told in any manner that is decisive or non-ideological. The story of the end of the Cold War is itself the narrative that re-organises our perception of what happened. In this vein one author explained how accounts of 1989 leave out developments in the Third World as irrelevant or marginal to the broader story of international law's evolution. He argued that a dominant theme of the 1970s and 1980s was the New International Economic Order rhetoric that was developed as a strategy of resistance by the Third World to the economic order of the time. 'End of History' arguments re-read and re-organise Third World claims in a manner that

[4] M Koskenniemi, *The Gentle Civilizer of Nations: The Rise and Fall of International Law 1870-1960* (Cambridge, Cambridge University Press, 2004) 6.

[5] See also S Newton, 'Post-war to new world order and post-socialist transition: 1989 as a pseudo-event', in F Johns, R Joyce and S Pahuja (eds), *Events: The Force of International Law* (Oxford, Routledge, 2010) 106.

disempowers them. In the 'Gaps and Silences' panel one speaker explained how the familiar argument about the positive contribution of the proliferation of international tribunals and international criminal law to international law has been experienced rather differently by those in whose name it has taken place (eg the affected communities) and, as a consequence, how some international actors may, in a way, 'appropriate' the suffering of such affected communities and turn it into a humanist project that may have little traction on the ground. Similarly, in the panel on 'Development and International Law' we heard very rich stories about how the political vocabulary and the political architecture of international economic institutions may have limited capacity to resolve problems like poverty since they may be also part of the problem rather than part of the solution, and so on.

These brief closing remarks on the 4th ESIL Biennial Conference pay tribute to the rich diversity of the high-quality papers presented. The classification of papers along two alternative modes of engagement with '1989' as an event aims to underline the intimate relationship between post-1989 appraisals and epistemic choices about how to engage the past. It proposes that the dilemmas of professional historical method define everyday legal work and require taking a stance on history. Ultimately, there is nothing methodologically neutral about our engagement with '1989' in legal work, even if this knowledge sometimes presents itself as obvious. International law histories tend to share specific, albeit often unregistered, assumptions about the past that raise, as the papers on ruptures and discontinuities argue, unsettling questions about the legitimacy of our axiomatic narratives. This conference may have well demonstrated that '1989', far from a concrete 'event' with determinate consequences for international law, may itself be a set of narratives.

33

A Call for Conceptual Clarity

AMANDA PERREAU-SAUSSINE*

I WAS ASSIGNED to four sessions, the panel on *An Era of International Law 1989–2010 in Perspective* and three agorae: one on a historical perspective on international law in our period, one on international law-making and one on international law and domestic law. I had the privilege to hear some very stimulating papers and some splendid questions. It would be invidious to single out only a few of over 16 papers in those sessions—not to mention others I heard during the conference. Instead I propose to focus on a few themes picked out from those papers and on some reflections they provoked.

Forum 1: An Era of International Law? The Years 1989–2010 in Perspective

One of the main themes that arose in the discussions as well as in the papers—including Randall Lesaffer's paper, read masterfully by Philip Allott—concerned the question of periodisation, which for Lesaffer is the occupational hazard of a historian. He said 'as a historian I face immediately criticisms of an ideological motivation routed in my own personal subjective judgements rather than in historical fact if I start to give an account of the history of international law in terms of periods'. I don't think this is just an occupational hazard of the historian; it is a judgement that the historian *has* to make if she or he is going to do good history. Good history involves careful thought. Otherwise what are you doing but offering, in the words of one of my historian colleagues 'at worst a story of a tail that wags the dog'. It is impossible to do history without making personal judgements and those judgements can be good or bad. I will return to this theme shortly.

Agora 4: 1989–2010—A Historical Perspective

In Agora 4 there was standing room only. As a student of the history of international law this was wonderful to see. Apart from anything else, those of you considering pursuing studies of the history of international law: there is a market!

One of the papers in that session I did want to pick out. Anne-Charlotte Martineau did a wonderful job of setting out the intellectual history both of the influence of the

* Amanda Perreau-Saussine is a University Lecturer in Law at the University of Cambridge and a Visiting Professor at Paris II.

Chicago Economic School on accounts of international law and of the history of the critical legal studies movement. It was a careful, detailed study and she was also not shy of making clear that she was making judgements—judgements which I personally did not share, but which were made clearly and bravely and which enabled a good thoughtful discussion to begin.

Agora 8: International Law-Making

Jörg Kammerhofer argued persuasively that we might be at risk of losing the nimbus of scholarship, if we come to see international law just as an instrumental tool for political activism or if we come to see international law as a form of global constitutionalism or if we come to see international law as generalists do, as an amicable, practical, rather intellectually irresponsible 'fudge'. Unfortunately he did not have time to defend his positive solution but he has published recently his own developing thinking on Kelsen, where he takes the opportunity to set out and defend what he understands legal common sense to be.

Agora 12: International Law in Domestic Courts

Finally, in the Agora on *International Law in Domestic Courts* one of the themes of the discussion became the relationship between the constitutional sphere and international law, in particular, whether the distinction between those two spheres is inevitably a matter for domestic courts and whether, as Antonios Tzanakopoulos suggested, that international law as developed by domestic courts might end up being a cacophony rather than a harmony. He said ultimately this is a matter of State practice and if States want a cacophony that's what it is going to be and we will have US foreign relations law as a kind of international law, and Chinese international law and Indian international law and Greek international law and British international law and maybe they are not going to be harmonious: we have just got to wait and see.

I come now to my concern and criticism. Roger O'Keefe in his wonderfully entertaining paper on gaps in the law, concluded: 'it's all about politics or something that comes before politics: us, our hearts. It's nothing to do with law'. It is this point, articulated clearly and honestly by Roger, that I find really worrying. I sensed the same point in many of the papers and many of the discussions; I think it contrasts with the movement that Andrew Hurrell outlined in his paper. He traced a relatively recent diffidence among political philosophers and scholars of international relations who, 'once upon a time' in the modern period, following people like John Rawls, had great hubris thinking that they would prescribe what justice is and leave it for international relations people and international lawyers to do the 'nuts and bolts' work of implementing this grand theory of justice. He remarked that, with the work of people like Charles Beitz and Amartya Sen political philosophers are starting to lose that hubris and are becoming a bit more humble, realising that they can learn a very great deal from engagement with concrete issues, concrete injustices, concrete debates. But, as Andrew Hurrell said at the very end of his paper, they do still have an important role to play because international relations scholars and international lawyers cannot escape the question of justice and the ancient question of the responsibilities of power.

In many of the papers I have sensed a fear and I do not quite understand what this is a fear *of*. In many of the papers and in some of the discussions people seem to be afraid of developing their thought really clearly. I don't think it was a fear of being attacked from the floor and I don't think it was a fear of loss of reputation. I think it's a deeper fear. I think it is an intellectual fear and it seems to be a fear about the pertinence or otherwise of what we are doing. One colleague suggested that what is behind this fear—which seems to me to be acting as a dangerous and unhealthy intellectual brake—is that maybe some of us are really worried that international law is not a force for good. I think if that is your worry you have a responsibility to pursue it or else change your job. Pursue it: work out what you think it is about international law specifically, in concrete cases, instead of resting in phrases that it is very easy to use to avoid thinking. In his wonderful essay of 1946, *Politics and the English Language*, George Orwell highlights how language can be used as a way of preventing thought or escaping thought. And some of the words and phrases that I've heard bandied around, like 'myth', 'story', 'social transformation', 'the many injustices', 'utopian developments', 'the complexity of international systems', 'the current structures of international law'—these phrases are being used to prevent thought; they are being used as some sort of shield. So I am with Andrew Hurrell and with Daniel Bethlehem, who helpfully highlighted for us five profoundly important challenges for the international community—where I think and hope international lawyers have an important role to play. In that vein, I call you to take responsibility. Take responsibility as international lawyers to think about how international law can and cannot contribute to those and other areas. Think concretely and build on your very real experience. Have a bit more confidence and don't be afraid to think through your own position and to argue it out more clearly. That would be my main suggestion.

Epilogue:

1989–2010: The Black Hole

34

Once Upon a Time There Was a Gap ...

ROGER O'KEEFE*

ONCE UPON A time / *Es war einmal* / *Il y avait une fois* / *C'era una volta*, way back at the end of the Cold War, the Comptroller-General for the Complete System was performing his quarterly 'stress test' on the normative integrity of the international legal system when he detected a gap. At first he did not believe it. He had been taught, and throughout his professional life had encountered nothing which caused him to doubt, that such a thing was impossible. The combination of the *Lotus* principle and the residual negative always provided an answer *in extremis*. But the gap he was dealing with here was not that sort of gap. Nor was it, as most supposed gaps are, merely a question of international law the answer to which is not to the interlocutor's liking. Here was a real gap, and an existential gap at that. The Comptroller-General for the Complete System was perplexed. I need some help with this, he thought.

Within a week, news of the gap was the subject of fevered speculation across the globe in faculties of law, ministries of foreign affairs, intergovernmental and non-governmental organisations and the boardrooms of multinational corporations. From the ends of the earth, international lawyers—academics and practitioners, positivists and naturalists, doctrinal exegetes and critical theorists—gathered to discuss the unnerving development.

The first to offer an opinion were the legal advisors to the US Department of State and the multinational corporations—respectively, one should add, although it was sometimes hard to tell the difference. To them the source and nature of the gap was obvious: it was the hole left in the international legal order by the conceptual bankruptcy of statism, a space rich in possibilities which individual and market freedoms were expanding to fill. Having no need to hear the opinions of others, and time being money, these legal advisors then went back, perhaps not quite respectively, to drafting bilateral investment treaties. The *parole* passed from the legal advisers to the various European governments, who characterised the gap as the hole left in the international legal order by the welcome collapse of anti-liberal-humanist tyranny, a space rich in possibilities for the construction of a new Europe. A spontaneous chorus of Beethoven's Ninth rang out from Lon- ... well, Paris to Berlin. (In Warsaw, Prague and Budapest they were too busy buying colour TVs, while in Sofia, Minsk and Kiev they were standing around waiting for Beethoven's rehabilitation.)

* Roger O'Keefe is a Senior Lecturer in Law and the Deputy Director of the Lauterpacht Centre for International Law at the University of Cambridge.

Next to speak were the theorists. Some of these read the gap as the silhouette of the Other. A few of the women present, whom everyone had ignored until now, discerned in the shape of the gap an unmistakable phallus. Queer theorists cheekily took to calling the gap the 'glory hole'. For his part, a kindly English gentleman, who, people whispered scarcely credibly, had worked for many years for the Foreign Office, divined in the gap the first breach in Vattelian international law opened up by a new self-constituting society of all societies. A bespectacled, boyish Finn thought the gap looked kitsch.

The international environmental lawyers showed a sense of humour by likening the gap to the plug-hole down which had disappeared the emerging right to life of whales. As the decade wore on, waggish international legal observers of western foreign policy began to liken the gap instead to the plug-hole down which had disappeared the emerging right to democratic governance. By the turn of the millennium, an Australian professor, one of several thousand present, was remarking jokingly upon the uncanny similarity between the hole and the receptacle into which the International Law Commission had deposited the concept of the criminal responsibility of states, pulling the chain afterwards.

But none of these accounts captured the true character of the gap, which, as the Comptroller-General for the Complete System had rightly apprehended, was more essential. Consternation increased. The kindly English gentleman tried to soothe raw nerves by reading to everyone from his latest novel, but this only deepened the air of anxious bewilderment. Things began to get fractious. The hole was getting a name for itself, but no-one could agree on what that name was.

The matter was eventually referred to the United Nations General Assembly, which invited the aforementioned ILC to begin work on the topic of 'Gaps and Silences in the Law'. The ILC accepted the invitation with relish—or Dijon mustard, to be precise, since it elected as Special Rapporteur for Gaps and Silences in the Law a mercurial Frenchman, who, in his eleventh report, turned to the preliminary questions of terminology and taxonomy. There were numerous types of gap, he reported, all going by a different name. Alternatively, one might say that there were numerous names for the same type of gap. This prefatory ontological question called for several reports in its own right, to which the Special Rapporteur would in time proceed; but, acutely aware as he was of the urgency of the subject, he would in his present report offer the Commission a provisional list of denominations, which should not be taken to imply any decision as to whether these denominations represented different types of gaps or different names for the one type of gap. These denominations, in no particular order, were as follows:

gap
space
hole
void
opening
discontinuity
discontiguity
lacuna
cæsura
hiatus
slit
chasm
crevasse
trou,

the last being a French word which, while often rendered into English as 'hole', carried a nuance lost in translation. In turn, the genus *trou* was divided into two species, the 'apparent *trou*' and the 'true *trou*'. Despite the best efforts of the mercurial Frenchman, however, the gap, which he provisionally believed to be a *trou*, although whether apparent or true was unclear, came universally to be referred to, in English, as 'the hole'. Even more frustratingly for the Special Rapporteur, at some stage in the course of the labours of the ILC's secretariat, the Chinese translation of '*trou*' was retranslated into French as '*espace juridique*', sowing the seeds of confusion for the next decade.

The General Assembly, despairing of seeing the completion of the ILC's study, turned instead to the International Court of Justice, seeking from it an advisory opinion on the hole. Four years later, in *Legal Consequences of the Detection of a Hole by the Preoccupied Juridical Community*, the ICJ, tentatively characterising the hole as an apparent *trou*, advised that this *trou* was a self-contained regime of no consequence to the international legal system as a whole (the choice of the last word causing problems for the interpreters when the judgment was delivered). The Court added, however, that 'in view of the present state of international law viewed as a whole … and of the elements of fact at its disposal, [it] [was] led to observe that it [could] not reach a definitive conclusion as to what would transpire in the event that the hole were a true *trou*'.

On being informed of the Court's *non liquet*, the Comptroller-General for the Complete System signed off sick.

The international criminal lawyers now sprang into action, fearing the dreaded 'impunity gap', the source of the world's ills from Srebrenica to the British pronunciation of the word 'yoghurt'. The United Nations Security Council, determining that the hole constituted a threat to international peace and security and acting under Chapter VII of the Charter, established an ad hoc International Tribunal for Criminal Holes and Yoghurt (ITCHY). The Tribunal's Pre-Pre-Trial Chamber swiftly handed down a one-word interlocutory decision on the hole. Within a fortnight, 545 articles, 37 commentaries and 14 monographs had been written and 8 new journals founded, all of them dedicated to analysing what the Tribunal had said. With some embarrassment, it was soon revealed that what had been mistaken by the stenographic intern, an over-eager American JD student, as a single-word judgment had in fact been one of the judges clearing her throat. A further 962 articles, 53 commentaries and 24 monographs hit the shelves, a blog dedicated to judicial phlegm was launched, and a Facebook tribute page in honour of the American JD student attracted over a million hits as well as a stern rebuke from the president of the Appeals Chamber.

The whole situation eventually became intolerable when a coalition of states sought to bolster the legal justification for their unilateral invasion of another state by reference to the indeterminacy of international law as manifest in the hole. In response, the UN Secretary-General established an independent expert group comprising half a dozen impartial private practitioners, whose task it was to get to the bottom of the hole, metaphorically speaking. As the practitioners' contracts with the UN stipulated payment by the word, the Organisation had enough money for only a two-page report, rendered pictorially. As it turned out, the expert group was divided over the contours of the gap. The idealists pictured the gap like this:

The realists pictured it like this:

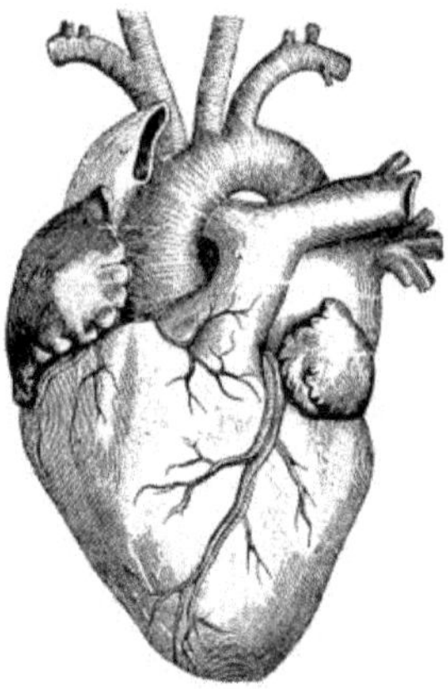

Since the practitioners would not utter a word unless they were paid for it, it was left to the assembled throng of international lawyers to interpret the diagrams for themselves.

After much debate, a consensus eventually emerged. The report indicated that at the centre of international law lies a space which the human heart is needed to fill. International law, the pictures said, has no heart of its own; rather, it is no more, but no less, than a vehicle for human values, a language of human self-ordering, a particular praxis of human willing.

In construing the report thus, some placed the emphasis—a little banally, but no less accurately for that—on how international law becomes a site for the projection of personal and institutional desires and ambitions.

Others stressed—whether any more profoundly is for the listener to judge—the incapacity of international law to secure human flourishing without first a revolution of the human heart. To this second school of thought the report seemed to say that if international law is inadequate, look for its improvement to the inadequacy of humankind: 'lie down', in the words of Yeats, 'where all the ladders start/In the foul rag-and-bone shop of the heart'.

To others still, the report expressed both of these insights. In a clandestine communication smuggled out of his prison cell on Devil's Island, Joseph Weiler reminded everyone, as 'Talmud long ago taught us', 'that even contradictory conclusions can both be the living word of God'.

The moral of the tale of the gap—or was it a hole?—is best left to the mercurial Frenchman, the ILC's Special Rapporteur on Gaps and Silences in the Law, and to his thirty-second report, which provisionally concludes that while there may or may not be gaps in international law, there are never silences. International lawyers cannot shut up. This can be a good thing, the Special Rapporteur opines, since ideas need the threshing and winnowing of informed debate. In other ways, he equally cautions, the logorrhoea of international lawyers is less salutary. Silence, the handmaiden of reflection, can be golden.

As for the Comptroller-General of the Complete System, he retired in 2010. As a token of esteem, he was named Poet in Residence at the *European Journal of International Law*, and, as the Spanish say, he lived happily and ate partridge. His old job, meanwhile, was privatised and outsourced to a normative services company in India staffed by PhDs from MIT and CalTech. But that is another story.

www.ingramcontent.com/pod-product-compliance
Ingram Content Group UK Ltd.
Pitfield, Milton Keynes, MK11 3LW, UK
UKHW051117290926
15471UKWH00010B/1732

9 781849 462020